P9-AOK-629

08/24
STRAND PRICE
$ 5.00

CALIFORNIA STUDIES IN FOOD AND CULTURE
Darra Goldstein, Editor

Cuisine and Empire

The publisher gratefully acknowledges the generous support of the Ahmanson Foundation Humanities Endowment Fund of the University of California Press Foundation.
The publisher also gratefully acknowledges the generous support of the Humanities Endowment Fund of the University of California Press Foundation.

Cuisine and Empire

Cooking in World History

———

Rachel Laudan

UNIVERSITY OF CALIFORNIA PRESS

Berkeley   Los Angeles   London

University of California Press, one of the most distinguished university presses in the United States, enriches lives around the world by advancing scholarship in the humanities, social sciences, and natural sciences. Its activities are supported by the UC Press Foundation and by philanthropic contributions from individuals and institutions. For more information, visit www.ucpress.edu.

University of California Press
Berkeley and Los Angeles, California

University of California Press, Ltd.
London, England

© 2013 by Rachel Laudan

Library of Congress Cataloging-in-Publication Data

Laudan, Rachel, 1944–
    Cuisine and empire : cooking in world history / Rachel Laudan.
        p.   cm. — (California studies in food and culture ; 43)
    Includes bibliographical references and index.
    ISBN 978-0-520-26645-2 (cloth : alk. paper)
    1. Cooking—History.   2. Food habits—History.
3. Food—Social aspects.   I. Title.   II. Series: California studies
in food and culture ; 43.
    TX645.L325   2013
    641.5—dc23   2012038609

Manufactured in the United States of America

22   21   20   19   18   17   16   15   14   13
10   9   8   7   6   5   4   3   2   1

In keeping with a commitment to support environmentally responsible and sustainable printing practices, UC Press has printed this book on Natures Natural, a fiber that contains 30% post-consumer waste and meets the minimum requirements of ANSI/NISO Z39.48–1992 (R 1997) (*Permanence of Paper*).

For my father, who farmed
For my mother, who cooked
And for Larry, who listened

CONTENTS

ILLUSTRATIONS

FIGURES

ix

MAPS

TABLES

ACKNOWLEDGMENTS

One of the secret pleasures that an author has, particularly with a book as sweeping as this, is that every page of the manuscript brings back memories. One sentence was inspired by a conversation with a friend, another by comments on a paper given at a conference, and yet another by a letter or posting on a web site. Of course this makes giving adequate acknowledgments utterly impossible. So please, my friends, realize that the brief list of names given here does not mean that you are forgotten or that our encounters did not matter. Quite the contrary. They are woven into this book, perhaps in ways that you might never have expected, but that is my responsibility, not yours.

Even so, some very special thanks are due. For early encouragement to plunge into food history, I am grateful to Elizabeth Andoh, Sonia Corcuera de Mancera, Alan Davidson, Betty Fussell, Barbara Haber, Jan Longone, Jackie Newman, Sandy Oliver, Ray Sokolov, Joyce Toomre, and Barbara Wheaton; for an early immersion in European social history, Peter Stearns; for conversations about world history, Jerry Bentley and Philip Curtin; for sending materials, Alice Arndt, Cathleen Baird, and Katy Biggs; for camaraderie and encouragement, Ken Albala, Naomi Duguid, Anne Mendelson, and Cara De Silva; for teaching me about grinding, Maria de Jésus Cabrera Parra, Margarita Muñoz Ramírez, and Alta Gracia and Lourdes Torres Sánchez; for insight into grindstones, Rafael Hernández Laguna, Manuel Olade, and the other *metateros* of Comonfort, Mexico; for answering one question after another about early Egyptian methods of making bread and beer and processing grains, Mark Nesbitt and Delwen Samuel; and for reading and commenting on early drafts, often in forms so primitive that I blush, Ruth Alegria, E. N. Anderson, Adam Balic, Cindy Bertelson, Anne Bramley, Paul Buell, Sun-ki

Chai, Kyri Claflin, Sarah Bak-Geller Corona, Kay Curtis, Diana de Treville, Julie Favella, Glenn Mack, Kelly O'Leary, Amber O'Connor, Sandy Oliver, Mary Margaret Pack, David Pearson, Charles Perry, Erica Peters, Kate Pollara, Ammini Ramachandran, William Rubel, Ruth Steinberg, Miriam de Uriarte, Merry White, and Jackie Williams. Lissa Caldwell, Barbara Santich, and a third unidentified referee sent lengthy, constructive comments. The Oxford Symposium on Food and Cookery, the Dibner Institute for the History of Science at MIT, the International Association of Culinary Professionals, the Research Chefs Association, the Culinary Historians of New York, Michigan, and Houston, the Institutos de Investigaciones Filosóficas and Antropológicas at the National Autonomous University of Mexico, the Universities of Michigan, Quilmes, Argentina, the University of California at Davis, the University of Texas at Austin, and the Vrije Universiteit, Brussels, gave me the chance to try out some of my ideas. As a freelance scholar I am deeply indebted to the Teresa Lozano Long Institute of Latin American Studies at the University of Texas at Austin, which offered me visiting research positions that made it possible to use the superb Benson Latin American Collection as well as the rest of the University of Texas library system.

Peter Dreyer took on more than would normally have been expected of a copy editor. The entire team at University of California Press, including Darra Goldstein, Sheila Levine, and Kate Marshall, could not have been more patient, professional, and supportive, while Dore Brown went not just one but many extra miles to make the book the best it could be.

Introduction

Cuisine and Empire takes seriously the fact that we are the animals that cook. Human societies, from sometime early in their history, began depending on cooked food, eating raw foods only as a supplement. Cooking—turning the raw materials of food, predominantly harvested plants and animal products, into something edible—was difficult and time-consuming and required enormous amounts of human energy. It was (and is) one of the most important of our technologies, has always provoked analysis and debate, and is interrelated with our social, political, and economic systems, with health and sickness, and with beliefs about ethics and religion. How, *Cuisine and Empire* asks, has cooking evolved over the past five thousand years?

A large part of the answer, I suggest, can be captured by tracing a sequence of half a dozen major families of cuisine.[1] These styles of cooking expanded one after the other across wide swaths of the earth's surface and are still clearly traceable in the world's culinary geography. Each had its preferred ingredients, techniques, dishes, meals, and ways of eating. Each was shaped by a culinary philosophy that defined what cooking was and how cuisine was related to society, to the natural world (including human bodies), and to the supernatural. Culinary philosophies were always subject to criticism. When those critiques reached a critical point, new cuisines were constructed from elements of the old. Sometimes a new cuisine became adopted as that of a state. Since the states that had the widest reach were empires, this is also the story of the mutual interaction of empires and cuisines, and of how the cuisines of successful states and empires were co-opted or emulated by their neighbors, accounting for their wide dispersion. In their wake followed changes in commerce and in agriculture.

Arching over the history of these cuisines is a broader story. Those that were most successful (in the sense of being consumed by the greatest number of people) three thousand years ago were those based on grains. Because storable grains allowed the accumulation of wealth, the rich and powerful were able to dine on high cuisines while everyone else ate humble cuisines. Because those who ate high cuisines had the money to set up huge kitchens and to fund culinary innovations, high cuisines are the primary focus of *Cuisine and Empire*. But this book also tells the story of the inequities and hardship caused by this culinary splintering into high and humble cuisines, and of its partial dismantling, at least in the richer parts of the world, over the past two centuries.

The analysis that shapes this book began to take shape when I lived in the Hawaiian Islands, a natural observatory for food history. Far from any other land-masses, before the arrival of humans, the islands had almost nothing edible except flightless birds, a fern, seaweed, fish, and two species of berries. The thriving culinary scene that I encountered had been created by three waves of migrants, each of which brought a culinary package to recreate its home cuisine. The first arrivals, the Hawaiians, came from Polynesia, probably in the third to fifth century C.E., and carried with them on their outrigger canoes a dozen edible plants, including their staple, taro, as well as dogs, chickens, and pigs. They used underground ovens to steam the taro, pounding it to a paste, eating it by dipping their fingers into a calabash, and accompanying it with fish or, for noble men, pork. They seasoned the meal with salt and a wide variety of seaweeds.

The next arrivals in the late eighteenth and nineteenth centuries were the "Anglos," British and Americans, who brought with them beef cattle and wheat flour. They baked wheat bread in beehive ovens and roasted beef over open fires, and later cooked with enclosed ranges or ovens. They ate from plates, using knives and forks, seasoned their dishes with salt and pepper, and served them with gravy. The third wave of migrants came from East Asia—China, Japan, Korea, and Okinawa—in the late nineteenth century to work on the plantations. They planted seeds of favored rice varieties, erected rice mills, constructed bench stoves, and cooked with woks. The East Asians steamed rice and fried or steamed fish and pork on the stovetop, ate from bowls using chopsticks, and seasoned their dishes with soy- or fish-based condiments.

Each of the three cuisines was bound together by a culinary philosophy that reflected the diners' beliefs about divinity, society, and the natural world, including their own bodies. The Hawaiians revered taro as a gift of the gods, imposed a series of strict food taboos to distinguish nobles and commoners, men and women, and used their knowledge of medicinal plants to stay healthy. Anglos, mainly Protestants, gave thanks for their daily bread, favored plain cooking that downplayed social distinctions, and thought that beef and bread were the best proteins and carbohydrates for strength and health. East Asians, mainly Buddhists, prized rice, offered food to the ancestors to strengthen family bonds, and sought to maintain their health by balancing hot and cold foods. Although in the second half of the twentieth century a fused "local food" emerged, in the home and in ethnic restaurants the Polynesian Hawaiian, Anglo, and East Asian cuisines remained distinct.

When I wrote about these different cuisines in *The Food of Paradise: Exploring Hawaii's Culinary Heritage* (1996), it struck me that this history was at odds with the slow development of peasant foods and their gradual refinement to high cuisines that I had formerly assumed to be the norm in food history. Hawaii's cuisines had not been created from the natural bounty of the islands because there was none. They had not evolved in place but had been transferred largely unchanged across thousands of miles of ocean and maintained for a century or, in the case of Hawaiian food, many centuries in the islands. I asked myself whether it was possible that the cuisines of Hawaii were not the exceptions but the rule. Might it be true that cuisines everywhere had been molded by similar long-distance transfers, subsequently rendered invisible by the construction of continuous national or regional histories? If this were the case, cuisines, culinary philosophies, and culinary transfers could provide the analytic tools for constructing a broader food history. It would have to be a world history, because if the cuisines of even tiny, remote Hawaii had been established by global movements of people, ideas, and techniques, that would have been even more true of the cuisines of less isolated parts of the world.

To embark on a world history of food seemed ambitious, but I decided I was as well prepared as the next person. I had grown up driving a tractor and feeding calves on a mixed dairy and arable farm. I'd seen what it cost my mother to prepare meals three times a day, every day, using milk from the dairy, eggs from the hens, and vegetables from the garden. I had cooked and dined with gusto on five continents. From researching the history of technology, I'd learned how to think about technological change and diffusion; from studying the history and philosophy of science, I'd got a grip on changing ideas; and from teaching social history, I'd come to understand a lot about the structure of pre-modern societies. At the University of Hawaii, where the history department is a pioneer in the burgeoning area of world history, I'd had the chance to listen to scholars such as Alfred Crosby, Philip Curtin, William McNeill, and Jerry Bentley explain how they had organized their histories of the Columbian Exchange, cross-cultural trade, war and disease, and religions—histories that broke with the traditional national boundaries. So I plunged ahead.

I knew that in constructing a grand narrative, I was bound to make factual errors and overambitious generalizations and to reveal my ignorance of key scholarship that was being published faster than I could read it. Against this, I set two considerations. First, errors are not limited to histories on the large scale. More-limited histories can just as easily go wrong due to lack of perspective, to assuming that some event or set of causes is unique, when in fact it is part of a more general pattern. Second, history is more than a pile of facts. It also seeks patterns in those facts. At different scales, different patterns emerge, as anyone who has flown over familiar territory knows. The patterns that can be detected on the ground—the grid of the streets, the signposts and traffic lights at the junctions—give way at 25,000 feet to patterns of city versus country, of the meanderings of the rivers, and of the alignments of hills and mountains. Similarly, the regional and national cuisines that we encounter every day (and that are the focus of much culinary history) cannot simply be stitched together to make a world history. The patterns such a history reveals go beyond local political and geographic boundaries. Taking heart, therefore, from Francis Bacon's aphorism that "truth emerges more readily from error than from confusion," I have tried to tell an intelligible and coherent story, trusting that readers will be generous enough to take the errors as culpable only when they make my broader theses untenable.

Those who had already written global food histories helped me sharpen my analytic categories (as well as providing a wealth of information). Reay Tannahill's pioneering *Food in History* (1973) and Linda Civitello's *Cuisine and Culture: A History of Food and People* (2004) are organized largely by states and empires; I shared the belief that states were crucial but wanted to emphasize transfers of cuisine between them. Maguelonne Toussaint-Samat's *Histoire naturelle et morale de la nourriture* (*History of Food,* 1994) follows the history of foodstuffs, and Ken Kiple's *A Moveable Feast* (2007), the career of plants; I wanted to emphasize culinary philosophy and cooking rather than the raw materials cooks worked with. In *Near a Thousand Tables* (2002) and *An Edible History of Humanity* (2009) respectively, a historian, Felipe Fernández-Armesto, and a journalist, Tom Standage, divide food history into a sequence of stages; I agree that broadly similar stages can be found in many parts of the world, but wanted to explain them as the consequence of successive waves of culinary expansion. The Australian food historian Michael Symons made cooking central in *The Pudding That Took a Thousand Cooks* (1998), a decision that I applaud; instead of presenting a series of themes, however, I wanted to write a narrative.

In addition, invaluable starting points for research were to be found in compendia such as *Food: A Culinary History from Antiquity to the Present* (1999), edited by J. L. Flandrin and Massimo Montanari; *The Cambridge World History of Food* (2000), edited by Kenneth Kiple and Kriemhild Cornée Ornelas; *The Oxford Companion to Food* (1999), edited by Alan Davidson and Tom Jaine; the *Encyclopedia of Food and Culture* (2003), edited by Solomon Katz and William Woys Weaver; and *Food: The History of Taste* (2007), edited by Paul Freedman. If they are not cited frequently in the references, it is because they have been so thoroughly absorbed into my thinking.

By focusing on cuisines (styles of cooking), my history complements and competes with those already published. Simple as the choice seems, it immediately narrowed my task. I do not discuss hunger and famine, because they are part not of culinary evolution but of agricultural, transportation, and social and political history. I treat the history of food not as progress toward some aesthetic end, such as better taste, but as a matter of the mastery and diffusion of new ways of making plants and animals edible. I do not give a prominent role to the history of farming, including such important events as the Agricultural Revolution (or the transition to farming) and the Green Revolution. If this seems strange, consider that histories of architecture, dress, or transport do not focus primarily on quarrying, lumbering, sheep herding, cotton farming, or iron mining. Stone, timber, wool, cotton, and iron are important raw materials, necessary for and imposing constraints on buildings, costume, and automobiles, but they do not drive or determine the course of their history. Similarly the history of styles of cooking deserves to be treated in its own right, not as an afterthought to agriculture.

I added a political dimension to my preliminary analysis. The most widely consumed cuisines have, since the origin of states, been those of the largest and most powerful political units. And those, in the past four thousand years, have been empires, an umbrella term I use for the different kinds of states that, by a variety of different means, have been able to project military, political, economic, and/or cultural power over significant portions of the globe. Migrants and travelers, including colonists, diplomats, soldiers, missionaries, and merchants, took their cuisines with them to the lands they settled, the embassies they ran, the garrisons they established, the missions they set up, and the enclaves from which they conducted their business. Along the roads and across the oceans, they took their know-how, their cooking equipment, and the plants and animals necessary to replicate their cuisines elsewhere. Cuisines have tended to expand and contract with empires.

It is too facile, however, to deduce that we can therefore make a simple equation of one cuisine to one empire. To begin with, migrants, merchants, and missionaries have never been limited by imperial boundaries. Furthermore, outsiders have always wanted to emulate states and empires perceived as successful. Since most people have been culinary determinists, believing literally that you are what you eat, they regularly attributed that success to the cuisine of the polity in question. As a result, the cuisines of successful empires have been co-opted by conquerors and adopted and adapted far beyond imperial boundaries. The Persians co-opted Mesopotamian cuisine, the Mongols much of Persian and Chinese cuisine; the Romans adopted Greek cuisine in the ancient world; the Japanese adapted British and American cuisine in the early twentieth century.

The result of the related processes of spreading and adopting cuisines was rarely either "fusion," in the sense of a seamless melding of the older and newer cuisines, or the creation of a totally new cuisine. Rather, cooks picked up ingredients, tools, or techniques that could be incorporated without violating their culinary philosophy. One fruit might be substituted for another, or metal saucepans might be exchanged for earthenware pots, while leaving the basic structure of the cuisine unchanged.

The creation of new cuisines followed the adoption of new culinary philosophies (and even in these cases involved reworking older cuisines). New culinary philosophies came from new ideas about politics and economics, religion, the human body, and the environment. It is impossible to tell the history of cuisine without referring to the values and ideas of Confucius, Plato and Aristotle, the Roman republicans, and Marx, for example; of Gautama Buddha, Jesus, the Church Fathers, Muhammad, Calvin, and Luther; and of the Taoists, Hippocrates, Paracelsus, and Western nutritionists. Their followers, usually minority groups for decades or centuries, began reworking existing cuisines to bring them in line with new ideas until, perhaps, they were picked up by states.

Culinary history has thus had a discernible pattern, neither mechanical nor predetermined, but not a series of random lurches either. Cuisines evolve gradually as new techniques are discovered, as new plants are incorporated, or as they are transferred by migrants. Once in a while, when new values propounded by philosophers, prophets, political theorists, or scientists are accepted by a culture or state, a new cuisine is rapidly created, sometimes in as little as a generation or two. Rejected culinary philosophies are not necessarily forgotten: they often linger in memory, to be drawn on centuries later as a critique of the reigning cuisine and as a springboard for its reform, as reformers in eighteenth-century Europe, for example, turned to the classics for models of republican cuisine. And imposed on this repeating pattern, culinary history has a direction caused by the opening of the gap between high and humble cuisines following the mastery of grain cookery and its twentieth-century closure in the richer parts of the world.

The eight chapters of *Cuisine and Empire* describe the dissemination of a sequence of cuisines across wide areas of the globe and the contribution of each to the global culinary heritage. When I use terms such as "Buddhist cuisine," it should be understood that I am referring to a whole family of cuisines linked by a common but not unvarying culinary philosophy. Within the broad family, there will be distinctions, sometimes more marked, sometimes less, between high and low cuisines. There will be variations as the cuisine spreads across space, adjusting to the other cuisines with which it comes into contact. And there will be other variations over time as culinary philosophy and techniques evolve and resources are added or lost. I trust the context will make these distinctions clear to the reader.

Chapters 1 and 2 deal with the cuisines of the ancient world. Chapter 1 shows that by 1000 B.C.E., although there must have been dozens or even hundreds of minor cuisines, most of the world's population, after having thoroughly surveyed the world's plants, had opted for one of ten major cuisines. All of these were based on roots or grains (one of them being the taro-based cuisine I encountered in

Hawaii). Of the ten, only two cuisines supported cities, states, and hierarchical societies with both high and humble cuisines. Both were based on grains. I discuss what was so special about roots and especially grains. Around the world, the grain cuisines were justified by a broadly similar ancient culinary philosophy with three main suppositions: a sacrificial bargain between gods, who gave humans grains and taught them to cook, and humans, who had to offer sacrifices (food) to the gods; a principle of hierarchy according to which different ranks of humans (and all living beings) were determined by their cuisine and deserved that cuisine; and a theory of the culinary cosmos in which cooking in the kitchen mirrored and was part of cooking as a basic cosmic process.

Chapter 2 follows how just one of the ten cuisines described in chapter 1, barley-wheat cuisine, became the basis for the major empires of Eurasia, beginning with the Achaemenid Empire of Persia and spreading westward to the Greek, Hellenistic, and Roman empires and east to the Mauryan and the Han Chinese empires. The increased efficiency and commercialization of food processing and cooking enabled empires to feed their cities and provision their armies. Philosophers and religious leaders criticized the principles of hierarchy and the sacrificial bargain.

Chapters 3 through 5 deal with traditional cuisines that were created in response to the replacement of the sacrificial bargain by universal religions offering personal salvation. Chapter 3 discusses the family of Buddhist cuisines that transformed the cooking, eating, and agriculture of the eastern half of Eurasia between 200 B.C.E. and 1000 C.E. Following the dictums of the Buddha, the culinary philosophy assigned value to avoiding meat and alcohol and embracing foods believed to enhance meditation and spiritual growth. A refined, sober Buddhist cuisine based on rice, butter, sugar, and alternatives to meat was adopted by the Mauryan Empire. Monks and missionaries spread it to the states and empires of South Asia, Southeast Asia, China, Korea, and Japan (it was the ancestor of the East Asian Buddhist cuisines I encountered in Hawaii).

In Chapter 4, I turn to Islamic cuisine. In Islamic culinary philosophy, food was one of the pleasures that prefigured life in Paradise. Reworking earlier Persian and Hellenistic cuisines in the Middle East, Islamic cuisine was based on flat wheat breads, sophisticated aromatic and spicy meat dishes, and delicate pastries and confections. At its greatest extent, Islamic cuisine, the cuisine of the most powerful empires of the middle part of Eurasia, spread from Spain to Southeast Asia and from the borders of China to the southern edge of the Sahara.

Christian cuisine, the subject of chapter 5, had origins that predated Islamic cuisine, but for a millennium and more it remained largely confined to the Byzantine Empire and the many small states of western Europe. Its philosophy stressed a sacred meal of bread and wine and alternate periods of feasting and fasting. Created by transforming Roman and Jewish cuisine, it favored raised wheat bread, meat, and wine. Its big expansion came with the Iberian empires of the sixteenth century and the transfer of a Catholic version to the Americas and trading posts around Africa and Asia. By the seventeenth century, Buddhist, Islamic, and Christian cuisines dominated the global culinary geography.

Chapters 6 to 8 trace the development of modern cuisines.[2] Modern culinary philosophy gradually abandoned the hierarchical principle for more inclusive political theories such as republicanism, liberal democracy, and socialism. It adopted the evolving nutritional theories of modern science. And it tended to view religious or ethical rules as a matter of personal choice, not state dictate. In chapter 6, I look at the prelude to modern cuisines in a former culinary backwater, northwestern Europe, thanks to challenges posed to traditional culinary philosophy by the Reformation, the scientific revolution, and the political debates of the seventeenth century. France, the Netherlands, and England all experimented with different approaches to modern cuisines, spreading them to their colonies in the Americas. What they had in common was a preference for white bread, beef, and sugar, and the incorporation of new nonalcoholic drinks.

Chapter 7 begins with middle-class Anglo cuisine (the origin of Anglo cuisine in Hawaii), based on wheat flour (chiefly in bread) and beef. Because the Anglo population grew explosively and the territory of the British Empire and the United States increased so rapidly, this was the most expansive cuisine of the nineteenth century. Industrialized food processing was essential to narrowing the gap between high and humble cuisines. As a result of the coincidence between imperial expansion and bread and beef cuisines, a global debate ensued about whether to adopt Western, particularly Anglo, bread and beef cuisine and whether to provide it for or impose it on all citizens.

Chapter 8 opens with the global spread of American bread and beef in the form of the hamburger. It describes the contest between alternative modern cuisines, particularly Western and socialist, the divergence of national cuisines with the breakup of empires, the countervailing convergence of these cuisines thanks to shared nutritional theories and institutions, particularly multinational food corporations, and the shift in distribution of high and humble cuisines from within a given state to between rich and poor nations. It discusses the food movement's critique of modern Western cuisine. In conclusion, I offer some brief comments on the global culinary geography at the end of the twentieth century and the perspectives that history can add to contemporary debates about food.

1

Mastering Grain Cookery,
20,000–300 B.C.E.

In 1000 B.C.E., when the first empires were being formed, the globe was home to fifty million or so people, about the population of present-day Italy, or slightly over twice that of Tokyo or Mexico City. Most of them were concentrated in a belt across Eurasia that swept from Europe and North Africa in the west to Korea and Southeast Asia in the east. Some still lived by hunting and gathering. Some were nomadic pastoralists who followed their flocks and herds. A tiny proportion dwelt in cities, most of which were inhabited by fewer than ten thousand souls, and even the biggest of which boasted no more than perhaps twenty-five thousand, the size of a small American college town. The overwhelming majority of people lived in hamlets and villages, growing their own food and trying to keep as much as they could out of the hands of the townsfolk. Hunters, herders, city dwellers, or peasants, each and every one of them depended on cooked food.

Cooking had begun almost two million years earlier with the appearance of *Homo erectus,* according to the Harvard anthropologist Richard Wrangham. Other anthropologists have questioned this.[1] However the matter is resolved, it is clear that humans have been cooking for a very long time. Before the first empires, indeed long before farming, they had passed a point of no return, where they could no longer thrive on raw foods. They had become the animals that cooked.

Cooking softened food so that humans no longer had to spend five hours a day chewing, as their chimpanzee relatives did. It made it more digestible, increasing the energy humans could extract from a given amount of food and diverting more of that energy to the brain. Brains grew and guts shrank. Cooking created mouthwatering new tastes and pleasing new textures, replacing the slightly metallic taste of raw meat with the succulence of a juicy charred steak, for example, and fibrous, tasteless tubers with fragrant, floury mouthfuls.

As humans became more intelligent and mastered more methods of cooking, other changes followed. It became possible to detoxify many poisonous plants and soften others that had been too hard to chew, so that humans could digest an increased number of plant species. This allowed more people to live off the resources of a given area as well as making it easier to settle new areas. Ways of treating flesh and plants so that they did not rot permitted the storage of food for the lean times of hard winters or dry seasons.

Cooking had its disadvantages. Some nutrients and minerals were lost, although on balance, cooking tended to increase the nutritional value of food. New methods of cookery introduced new dangers, such as poisonous molds and seeds with grain cookery and, more recently, botulism with canning and salmonella with prepackaged ground meat, although in general cooking made food safer. And a heavy, unremitting burden fell on those who cooked. Even so, the many advantages of cooking outweighed the disadvantages.

With cooking, plants and animals became the raw materials for food, not food itself. Given that we commonly use the word "food" to describe what farmers grow, and given that we eat nuts, fruit, some vegetables, and even fish and steak tartare without cooking, the statement that plants and animals are not food may seem counterintuitive. The fact is that most of us get only a small fraction of our calories from raw foods. Even so, that fraction is probably higher than that of our ancestors, since we are the beneficiaries of millennia of breeding that have created larger, sweeter fruits and more tender vegetables and meat. Furthermore, even what we call raw has usually been subjected to many kitchen processes. Few of us sink our teeth into raw steak unless it has been finely chopped or sliced. Raw foodists allow slicing, grinding, chopping, soaking, sprouting, freezing, and heating to 104–120 degrees Fahrenheit. In spite of modern high-quality plant foods and careful preparation, it is almost impossible to thrive on such a diet, according to evidence gathered by Richard Wrangham. In antiquity, people happily accepted that humans ate cooked food. Indeed, they saw it as what distinguished them from animals. Perhaps it is because today we place so much emphasis on "fresh" and "natural" foods—which Susanne Freidberg has shown are made possible only by changing animal life cycles, modern transport, refrigeration, and ingenious packaging—that we underestimate how much we depend on cooking. In any case, there is no escaping that with cooking, food became an artifact, like clothes and dwellings, not natural but made by humans. A sheaf of wheat is no more food than a boll of cotton is a garment.[2]

With cooking came cuisines. Techniques that proved successful with one kind of raw material were then used for others. A single raw material (such as grain) could be turned into diverse foods with different tastes and nutritional properties (gruel, bread, and beer). Instead of consuming food on the spot, humans began eating meals, since cooking required planning, storing ingredients, and time. Meals could be patterned to suit cultural preferences. Ordered styles of cooking—cuisines—became the norm. Leaving archaeologists and anthropologists to investigate the origins and early history of cooking, this book will take up the question of what these cuisines were, how they evolved, and what difference they have made in human history.

Before moving to cuisines, though, it is necessary to say a little more about what cooking is and what techniques had been mastered at the time this book begins, in 1000 B.C.E. Cooking is often identified as the use of fire. As any cook knows, however, a lot more goes on in a kitchen, such as soaking, chopping, grinding, rolling, freezing, fermenting, and marinating. The multiple kitchen operations can be classified into four groups: changing temperature (heating and cooling); encouraging biochemical activity (fermenting); changing chemical characteristics by treating with water, acids, and alkalis (leaching and marinating, for instance); and changing the size and shape of the raw materials using mechanical force (cutting, grinding, pounding, and grating, for example).

Commonly cooks use multiple operations to turn plants and animals into food. Take meat, for example. A carcass has to be skinned before meat can be cut from the bone and then into portions. These may then be eaten, or subjected to heat and then eaten, or frozen or dried or fermented so that they can be eaten at a later date. Although all these operations are part of cooking broadly understood, I often follow common parlance in describing the preliminary operations as processing and the final meal preparation as cooking. Today, in sharp contrast to the past, home cooks do very little processing, concentrating on final meal preparation.[3]

Early people employed both dry heat and wet heat. They used the sun to dehydrate fruits, vegetables, and small pieces of meat. They lit fires for grilling meat over the flames, cooking meat and roots in the hot ashes, and baking small items or doughs either directly on the embers or wrapped in clay first, or on a stone heated by the fire. Best suited to tender meats and plants, dry-heat cooking required large amounts of frequently scarce fuel. Wet heat involved steaming or boiling raw ingredients, which was possible even before pottery was available. The ingredients might be placed in tightly woven baskets, gourds, lengths of bamboo, leather bags, or even clay-lined pits that were then filled with water and brought to a boil by dropping in red-hot stones (known as pot boilers). Alternatively, leaf-wrapped meat, fish, and roots could be steamed under a covering of soil in stone-lined pits previously heated with fire. Such pit cooking, ideally suited to large pieces of fatty meat and tough roots, has been in use since the late Paleolithic. It is still widely practiced in, for example, Siberia, Peru, Mexico (pit-cooked *barbacoa*), Hawaii (imu-cooked taro and kalua pig), and the United States (pit-cooked barbecue).[4]

By breaking long complex molecules down into shorter ones, adding water molecules to starches (hydrolyzing), and unfolding long chains of proteins (denaturing), heating makes food more digestible. It also makes it safer by rendering harmless the poisons that plants manufacture as a defense against predators. It creates new tastes and flavors, particularly the appetizing aromas associated with browning, a phenomenon known as the Maillard effect after Louis-Camille Maillard, the French chemist who first described it in 1912. The converse of heating—cooling or freezing—slows spoilage.

Fermenting—employing yeasts, bacteria, or fungi to alter the chemical composition of food—has similar benefits, increasing flavor, decreasing toxicity, improving digestibility, and preserving perishable foods, as well as reducing cooking time. Humans would have encountered the new tastes and pleasing effects of fermented honey, saps, and perhaps milk early on. The history of their manipulation of such processes is lost, but they had probably learned that burying fish and meats (which is now known to create safe anaerobic conditions) prevented them from rotting and created tasty products.

Soaking and leaching soften plant foods such as beans. These two processes reduce the toxicity of acorns, a common human foodstuff. Alkaline solutions, made by adding ashes or naturally occurring alkaline minerals to water, change the texture of foods, release nutrients, precipitate starch from fibrous plants, and aid in fermentation. Acid solutions, such as fruit juices or the bile in the stomach of herbivores, "cook" fish.

The tough fibers of meat and plants could also be broken down through mechanical means. Flint or obsidian knives cut carcasses as fast as butcher's knives, a fact that always amazes my students when they try it. Stones pound and tenderize meat, shells or bones grate roots, mortars crack the hulls off grains, and grindstones reduce their kernels to flour. Breaking plants and animals down into smaller parts makes them easier to chew. It also enables the separation and removal of plant fibers that slow the passage of food through the digestive system (very important when food was more fibrous).

Then, no later than 19,000 years ago, humans took on some of the most challenging of all plant materials to cook: the tiny, hard seeds of herbaceous plants. In the 1980s, archaeologists uncovered a small village dating to 19,400 B.P. close to Lake Kinneret, better known to many as the Sea of Galilee.[5] Analyzing the food remains in hearths and trash dumps allowed them to reconstruct the cuisine. The villagers rarely ate big game, which was becoming scarce as the glaciers retreated. They had, however, thoroughly inventoried what could be turned into food. They cooked fish, twenty species of small mammals, and seventy species of birds. They also ate fruits, nuts, and beans from a hundred and forty different taxa, including acorns, almonds, pistachios, olives, raspberries, and figs. This huge selection of foodstuffs provided flavor and variety.

For most of their calories, however, the villagers depended on the tiny, often hard seeds of herbaceous plants. The archaeologists collected nineteen thousand samples, three-quarters of them only about a millimeter in length, or about the size of a mustard seed. Among them were grains of wild barley and wheat, which were to be crucial in subsequent human history. In one of the huts was a grindstone, the tool that can pulverize grains so that they don't pass whole through the digestive system.

Thus about ten thousand years before the development of farming, cooks had mastered a wide array of culinary techniques, including those for dealing with the roots and grains that were the first plants to be domesticated. With these techniques in hand, it began to make sense to labor to plant, weed, and harvest these calorie- and nutrient-rich plants. By three thousand years ago, eight to ten root and grain cuisines, depending on how they're counted, had spread far from their places of origin, although many less-widely distributed cuisines adapted to specific local circumstances coexisted with them. Soon thereafter, root cuisines were to decline in importance as grain cuisines began to support cities, states, and armies.

We know a great deal about some of the major cuisines from tools, art, and written records. Others are relatively little known, though that is shifting rapidly as new investigative techniques have been developed in the past few decades.[6] The gaps in our knowledge of the major cuisines three thousand years ago can be partially filled by examining recent research on the origin and spread of farming from the perspective of cooking. When archaeologists and anthropologists report the spread of one or another domesticated plant or animal, we can infer that culinary techniques and cuisines also spread, since without these, farm products had no use. This is not an infallible inference. There are a few cases where plants were transferred vast distances without an accompanying transfer of cuisine and technique—wheat and barley from the Fertile Crescent to China several centuries B.C.E., and maize from the Americas to the Old World in the sixteenth century, for example. In general, however, transfers of groups of plants and animals reflect transfers of cuisine that made it worth applying the considerable skill, time, and energy needed to carry plants and move animals across mountains, deserts, and oceans, acclimatize them in new locations, and raise enough of them to make a significant contribution to the pantry. Seeds, slips, roots, and cuttings took up precious space in packs carried by humans or animals or loaded in crowded vessels. They had to be protected from salt spray, frosts, and the blaze of the sun. Food and water for animals meant less for humans when supplies were often short. On arrival, plants had to be coddled until they adjusted to new soils, climates, lengths of day, and seasonal patterns. Then they had to be propagated until there was enough to feed significant numbers of people.

GLOBAL CULINARY GEOGRAPHY CA. 1000 B.C.E.

Using the sources described above, I survey the world's major cuisines, beginning with the Yellow River Valley of northern China and zigzagging around the most densely inhabited areas of the globe (map 1.1). Although our knowledge of these

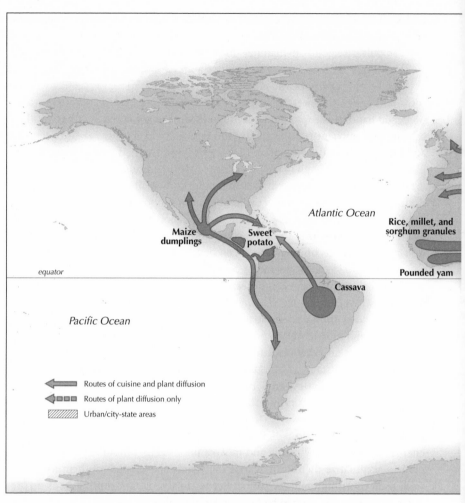

MAP 1.1. The spread of root and grain cuisines by 2000–1000 B.C.E. A large proportion of the world's population, which was concentrated in the latitudes between 40° north and the equator, depended on a handful of root or grain cuisines that had spread widely from their origins. Two of these, barley and wheat bread cuisine and millet granule cuisine, supported cities in Mesopotamia, the Nile Valley, the Indus Valley, and the Yellow River Valley. Traces of these ancient cuisines persist to this day. Solid arrows mark the probable movement of a cuisine.

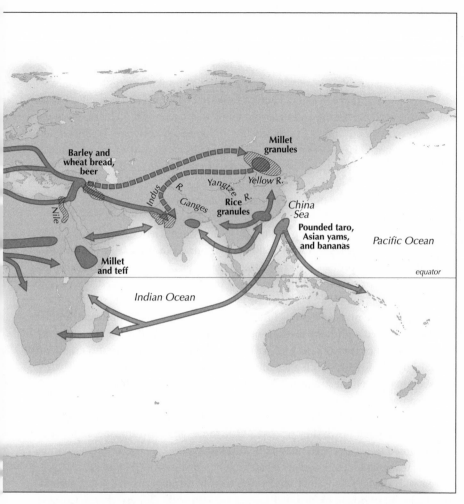

Dashed arrows indicate that the plants moved but probably not the cuisine. Sources: Bellwood, *First Farmers*, xx, 7. For China: Fuller, "Arrival of Wheat in China"; Fuller et al., "Consilience." For the Pacific: Kirch, *Feathered Gods and Fishhooks*, 61. For the Fertile Crescent and African crops and millet in China: Smith, *Emergence of Agriculture*, 68, 108, and 133. For Europe: Cunliffe, *Between the Oceans*, chap. 4. For Africa and the Indian Ocean: Fuller and Boivin, "Crops, Cattle and Commensals"; Fuller, "Globalization of Bananas."

cuisines is changing rapidly, making specific dates and routes tentative, what is unlikely to change is the conclusion that they were based overwhelmingly on roots and grains and that they had spread very widely indeed. To anticipate, certain other broad generalizations will emerge. Cities, states, and armies appeared only in regions of grain cuisines. When they did, grain cuisine splintered into subcuisines for powerful and poor, town and country, settled populations and nomads. A feast following a sacrifice to the gods was the emblematic meal everywhere, the meal that represented and united the society, as Thanksgiving now does in the United States. It is not clear whether these global parallels reflect widespread contact between societies, the logic of emerging social organization, or a combination of the two.

Steamed broomcorn millet (*Panicum miliaceum*) and foxtail millet (*Setaria italica*), tiny round grains from disparate botanical genera, were the basis of the first cuisine we encounter in the Yellow River Valley in ancient China.[7] There peasants lived in small villages, their dwellings half buried in the ground and roofed with thick thatch to protect against the freezing winters, and the interiors crammed with grain and preserved vegetables. Small patches of millet dotted the valley's fertile yellow soil, which was brought by floods and winds from the steppe.

To prepare the millet, peasants lifted heavy pestles high above mortars and let them fall repeatedly until the inedible outer hulls were cracked (fig. 1.1). Beginning around the first century B.C.E., they used foot-trodden pestles to pound grain in a mortar buried in the ground, a less demanding method. When all the hulls were cracked, they tossed the grains in a basket, winnowing away the lighter hulls. Then they steamed the grains until they were light and fluffy in three-legged pots set over small fires, a method that conserved scarce fuel. Before dipping their fingers into the communal bowl, they offered a little to the gods and the ancestors. They accompanied the millet with bites of pickled vegetables, cabbage of various kinds, mallow, water-shield (an aquatic plant), or bamboo shoots, seasoned and preserved with costly salt. Sometimes, when they had trapped small wild animals, they had a bit of boiled or steamed meat, seasoned with Chinese chives, Chinese dates, or sour apricots.

To supplement the millets, peasants turned to hemp seed, soybeans—which when steamed were dull, mealy, and gas-inducing—and rice, although it could not be counted on to ripen this far north. When their stocks dwindled before the harvest, they reluctantly resorted to wheat and barley, lumped together as *mai*, foreign grains, which travelers had brought from the Fertile Crescent in the Middle East, by around 2500 B.C.E.[8] Steamed whole like millet, these larger, harder grains stayed tough and chewy and were eaten only in the hungry time before the millet harvest.

In small fortified cities aligned to the points of the compass, rulers like King T'ang, who founded the Shang dynasty around 1600 B.C.E., according to traditional Chinese historiography, dined with their warriors on a much more lavish

FIGURE 1.1. Pounding the hulls off millet and rice was a laborious task. In this illustration, one man lifts a pestle by hand (lower right), while another uses a foot-operated device (upper right). From Song, *T'ien kung k'ai wu: Chinese Technology in the Seventeenth Century,* 92. Courtesy Pennsylvania State University Press.

FIGURE 1.2. In this depiction of a sacrifice, officiants in the Yellow River Valley of China prepare vessels of cooked meats and *chiu* (rice wine) to offer to the gods and ancestors, several centuries B.C.E. The officiants, wearing what appear to be elaborate headdresses, stand or kneel on a raised, covered platform. They and others on either side of the platform carry or work with exquisite cast-bronze vessels, the kingdom's most valuable treasures, handed down from generation to generation. From a rubbing of an engraved bronze sacrificial vessel in the Shanghai Museum reproduced in Weber, "Chinese Pictorial Bronzes of the Late Chou Period," fig. 25d. Courtesy *Artibus Asiae.*

version of millet cuisine. When the king's men seized their grain, the peasants protested: "Large rats! Large rats! Don't eat our millet!"[9] The king promised them that the sacrifices he made to the gods and ancestors would ensure them many children, bountiful harvests of millet, and victory in battle over rival monarchs and the Yi, Man, Jung, and Ti barbarians, who were said to eat neither grain nor food cooked with fire.

An engraved bronze bowl from about a thousand years later shows a sacrifice (fig. 1.2). Written sources enable us to fill in more details of what the sacrifice was likely to have been like. Vessels were arrayed on sacrificial platforms in auspicious groups of threes, fives, and sixes. There were special vessels for each kind of dish: steamed millet, representing the yin, or earthy and female aspects of the cosmos; meaty stews, for the yang, or heavenly and male aspects; and five kinds of rice wine (*chiu*), one with particles on top, one with them on the bottom, one cloudy, one sweet and cloudy, and one reddish brown.[10]

While musicians and dancers performed, chanting hymns to bring the cosmos into harmony, the king cast bones inscribed with the requests to the gods and ancestors into the fire. The pattern of cracks on the bones was thought to reveal their answer. Oxen, sheep, pigs, and dogs were sacrificed to the supreme god of the heavens, to the ancestors, to the gods of the four points of the compass, and to all the other deities. Portions of the sacrificial meat were distributed to high ranking nobles, who in turn handed them to their subjects as a way of creating loyalty.[11]

The sacrificial feast prepared in the king's kitchen would have been very different from the peasants' humble fare. The royal kitchens were staffed by a hierarchy of cooks organized by the head cook, a senior court official. The legendary I Yin, said to have turned up at King T'ang's court with his tripods for steaming and his stands for cooking meat strapped to his back, went on to become prime minister.

The junior cooks prepared the basics of the cuisine. They dried, salted, and pickled meat; preserved vegetables; sprouted and dried grains, and extracted the sweet malt syrup with water; and made rice wine (*chiu*) and vinegar (processes described in more detail in chapter 2). Sacrificial feasts demanded special dishes of meat from sacrificed cattle, pigs, sheep, goats, and dogs, carefully tempered with spices and condiments to suppress the meaty smell and balance the dishes. These could be very elaborate. In one example, the *Book of Ceremonies,* a Confucian treatise on sacrifice compiled between about 1000 and 500 B.C.E., directed cooks to:

> Take a suckling pig or young ewe, cut it open, clean it out, and fill its belly with dates [the "Chinese date" or jujube (*Zizyphus jujuba*)]. Plait miscanthus reed as a wrapping for it, seal it with clay and bake it. When the clay is all dry, break it off. Rub it with wet hands and remove the thin membrane. Take rice flour, blend it and soak it to make a thin gruel, which is added to the suckling pig. Fry it in grease. The grease must cover it completely. Into a large pot of boiling water insert a small cauldron of the seasoned meat strips. Make sure the boiling water does not cover the tripod. For three days and three nights do not stop the fire. Last, season it with vinegar and meat pickles.[12]

For the feast, servants set out mats of aromatic reeds, small stools to support the diners' elbows, and dishes of bronze, wood, bamboo, and pottery. Meat on the bone and grain went on the left of each setting, sliced meat, drinks, and syrups on the right, and around them minced and roast meats, onions, and drinks were arranged in a symmetrical pattern.[13] After making an offering to the ancestors, the king and the nobles knelt to eat, each man's seniority and valor in battle determining where he knelt and what pieces of meat he was entitled to. The warriors took morsels of the drier dishes with their fingers: meats marinated in vinegar, fried, and served over millet or rice; jerky spiced with brown pepper; and jerky seasoned with cinnamon, ginger, and salt. They scooped up *keng,* a stew soured with vinegar or sour apricots (*Prunus mume,* the "plums" of plum sauce). They nibbled on small cubes of raw beef, cured in *chiu,* and served with pickles, vinegar, or the juice of sour apricots; on meatballs of rice and pork, mutton, or beef; and on the much-sought-after roasted, fat-wrapped dog's liver. They partook liberally of *chiu.* Not even high-ranking warrior-nobles regularly indulged in such quantities of meat, but it was so important symbolically that they were referred to as meat eaters.[14]

Moving several hundred miles south to the Yangtze River, we come to the tropical monsoon region, which stretches from the South China Sea to the forest-covered archipelagoes of Southeast Asia and the shores of the Indian Ocean. We know much less about the two cuisines of this region, one based on roots, the other on rice, than we do about the cuisine of the Yellow River Valley, so what follows is tentative. To begin with the root cuisine, taro (*Colocasia esculenta*), yam (the starchy root of a vine of the Dioscoreaceae family, much tougher than the sweet potato), and the cooking banana (the starchy, high-yielding fruit of *Musa* spp., as well as its root), were boiled or steamed, and most likely pounded to pastes that could be scooped up with the fingers. People on the oceanic side of New Guinea loaded outriggers with the basics of this culinary package and sailed east into the Pacific. To sustain themselves at sea, they stowed lightweight, long-lasting dried or fermented fish, breadfruit (*Artocarpus altilis*), and bananas for food. They filled gourds and bamboo sections with water, and in addition drank the water inside coconuts.[15] They packed slips, cuttings, young plants, and taro and yams in moist moss, then wrapped them in a covering such as ti leaves or bark cloth, tucked them into palm-leaf casings, and hung them out of reach of salt spray. Breeding pairs of pigs, chickens, and dogs, which, if worst came to worst, could be eaten on the way, were carried on board. Between 1400 and 900 B.C.E., they settled many of the South Pacific islands; by between 500 and 1000 C.E., they had added Hawaii and New Zealand. Since most of these islands had few edible animals or plants, and above all no calorific starchy plants, the voyagers would have died had they not carried their own culinary package. In Hawaii, for example, they survived on flightless birds (now extinct) until the plants and animals they carried were established. Since theirs was a volcanic island without clay for pots, Hawaiians pit-baked taro and breadfruit and pounded them to a paste. They seasoned this with raw or cooked fish, grated coconut or coconut cream, roasted and ground candlenuts (*Aleurites moluccana*), seaweeds, or just a dip of seawater. For feasts, from which women were excluded, they pit-baked pig, dog, or large fish. Probably by the first millennium B.C.E., other voyagers had sailed west to Madagascar with yams, bananas, and stowaways such as rats and mice. Whether the evidence supports the claim that they were established in West Africa as well by 1000 B.C.E. is still being debated.[16] Australia, settled by 50,000 B.C.E. by humans and their dogs, remained isolated from these later voyages.

Asian rice cuisines in the monsoon area were also connected over large distances, rice (*Oryza sativa*) from the Lower Yangtze Valley having hybridized with rice from the Ganges Delta by 1000 B.C.E.[17] Cooks pounded or soaked and boiled the whole grain until the hull split, winnowed it, and then boiled or steamed the granules until tender. Alternatively, moistened grains could be pounded to flakes and dried to create an instant food for travelers.[18] Likely accompaniments in the Indian Ocean region were stews of water buffalo, pork, dog, chicken, or fish, perhaps soured with tamarind pod pulp or made creamy with milk extracted from grated coconut flesh. Sugar palm sap was made into a refreshing and, after a day, slightly intoxicating drink, or evaporated to form a sticky, brown aromatic sugar. Sugarcane, a perennial grass, was sweet to chew but too difficult to process to be a major part of the diet. It's possible that betel, the nut of a palm, was already being wrapped in the leaf of a vine from the same family as black pepper and chewed as a mouth freshener, as it is today.

Moving northwest, we come to the central area of barley-wheat cuisines, whose easternmost edge abutted the Yellow River. Originating in places such as the village on Lake Kinneret in the Fertile Crescent, the quarter-moon-shaped area extending from the eastern coast of the Mediterranean up through the eastern part of Turkey and down the valley of the Tigris and the Euphrates, this family of cuisines had spread west across the Mediterranean and Europe, south to North Africa, and east to Iraq, Iran, and northwest India. In most of the barley-wheat region, yogurt and butter were also made from the milk of cattle or sheep and goats.

Barley, preferred to wheat, was not usually boiled or steamed, as it was in the Yellow River Valley, but was made into a flavorful, grayish flatbread; a porridge or pottage of cracked grains flavored with herbs, vegetables, or meat; or a thick, flat beer. For bread, cooks pounded the inedible hulls of barley and wheat in pestles and mortars until they cracked, winnowed them away, then knelt to grind the grains on a stone (fig. 1.3). They mixed the meal (whole ground grain) with water and baked the dough.

In the Indus Valley, the Nile Valley, and Mesopotamia, the land between the Tigris and the Euphrates, barley-wheat cuisine supported small cities by 3000 B.C.E., as millet cuisine supported them in the Yellow River Valley.[19] The cuisine of Mesopotamia is the best known of the barley-wheat cuisines, already thousands of years old in 1000 B.C.E. It was prepared in cities and villages on the flat plain, hot and parched much of the year, partly marshy and covered with reeds, the home of fish and waterfowl, featureless except for the channels bringing water to irrigate the fields and the date palms lining the pathways between the fields. The abundance of rich soil and water for growing barley and wheat outweighed the lack of timber, building stone, and other resources.

The poor, including foot soldiers, prisoners, construction workers, and servants, survived almost exclusively on barley dishes, receiving roughly made conical pottery bowls containing about two liters (a little over eight cups) of barley grains, porridge, or bread daily. They ate these with a little salt and dried fish. Their diet was so meager that a popular saying went: "When a poor man has died, do not try to revive him. When he had bread, he had no salt; when he had salt, he had no bread."[20]

The ruling classes, living in cities dominated by temples in the form of square stepped pyramids, enjoyed a rich, complex cuisine. Again the exemplary meal was a feast following a sacrifice. A particularly important sacrifice was offered at the New Year, to ensure that Dumuzi, god of vegetation and fertility, sheep and sheepfolds, and the underworld, would return to the earth's surface and reunite with his spouse, Inanna, Queen of Heaven, goddess of love and war. Then the rains would come and the cycle of life would begin anew. A Sumerian vase from ca. 3000 B.C.E. (fig. 1.4) shows cereals on the bottom, then a procession of sheep and goats, and finally naked men carrying baskets of fruits and grains to Inanna, backed by two bundles of reeds, her signs of status.

One version of the *Epic of Gilgamesh*, revised and modified over thousands of years of Mesopotamian history, describes the sacrifice that Gilgamesh offered to Inanna in thanks for helping him survive the great flood. "Seven and again seven

MOYABENG A LA MEULE

UNE STATUETTE ÉGYPTIENNE DU MUSÉE DU LOUVRE

FIGURE 1.3. A woman named Moyabeng kneeling over a grindstone in southern Africa in the late nineteenth century (above) is using her full weight to shear the grain just as an Egyptian grinder in ancient Egypt would have done millennia earlier (below). Drawings from Frédéric Christol, *Au sud de l'Afrique* (Paris: Berger-Levrault, 1897), 85. Courtesy New York Public Library (1579505).

cauldrons [he] set up on their stands, [he] heaped up wood and cane and cedar and myrtle." The worshippers prayed that the vindictive, unpredictable, and demanding goddess would be satisfied with the offering. Honey was poured into a carnelian vase, butter pressed into one of lapis lazuli. The priest sacrificed an animal and poured a libation of beer. The aromas rose into the sky, and "when the gods smelled the sweet savour, they gathered like flies over the sacrifice."[21] The

FIGURE 1.4. Alabaster vase from Uruk in ancient Sumer, ca. 3000 B.C.E. At the top, an official makes offerings at the temple of the goddess Inanna. Below him, naked men bring baskets of fruit and grains; below them are sacrificial sheep and goats, and at the bottom, the reeds and cultivated grains of the region. Courtesy Hirmer Fotoarchiv GbR.

participants picked up straws of solid gold and silver and sipped from the vat. Musicians strummed their harps. The diners plucked the fragrant meats and sighed with satisfaction over the rich dishes.

For the sacred meal following a sacrifice, or for the meals offered to the gods three times a day, it was important that the instructions be followed exactly, so scribes

FIGURE 1.5. Some of the first known written recipes—twenty-one for meat stews and four for vegetable stews—inscribed ca. 1750 B.C.E. on a 6½″ × 4½″ Babylonian clay tablet. Two other tablets record further recipes, including one for a bird pie. Courtesy Yale Babylonian Collection (YBC 4644).

carefully wrote down the ingredients and the order of procedures (though not cooking times or measurements) on clay tablets. One of these tablets contains recipes for stews (fig. 1.5), another for a bird pie. After placing cooked birds on a pastry-covered platter, "You scatter over it the pluck [heart and liver] and the cut up gizzards that were being cooked in the pot, as well as the (little) *sebetu* [untranslatable] rolls that were baked in the oven. You set aside the fatty broth in which the meat was cooked in the pot. You cover the serving dish with its (pastry) 'lid' and bring it to the table."[22]

A sacrificial feast included sauces, sweets, and appetizers, hallmarks of high cuisine. Fried grasshoppers or locusts made tasty appetizers. Pickles and condiments concocted from seeds, sesame oil, vegetables, fruits, garlic, turnip, onion, nuts, and olives titillated the palate. Sauces were prepared from an onion-and-garlic flavoring base combined with a rich fatty broth thickened with breadcrumbs, the ancestors of sauces still served in the Middle East and even of present-day English bread sauce. Pomegranates, grapes, dates, and confections of milk, cheese, honey, and pistachios provided a sweet touch.

Professional cooks labored in kitchens that were as large as three thousand square feet, much of the space devoted to making grain-based dishes, bread, and beer. From the coarse groats and fine flour produced by the grinders—perhaps prisoners and convicts—cooks prepared porridge, flatbreads, and slightly leavened breads, the latter in three hundred named varieties. Dough was shaped into the forms of hearts, hands, and women's breasts, seasoned with spices, and filled with fruit, with the texture often softened by oil, milk, ale, or sweeteners. A flour-oil pastry was enlivened with dates, nuts, or spices such as cumin and coriander. Stuffed pastries were pressed into an oiled pottery mold with a design on the bottom before baking. Flatbreads were baked on the inside walls of large ceramic pots (tannurs). There is some evidence that bulgur, an easy-to-cook food (familiar today from tabbouleh salads) was made by drying parboiled wheat.

Ale was brewed following sacred ritual recorded in hymns to the goddess of beer, Ninkasi, "the lady who fills the mouth." The directions for sprouting, drying, and grinding barley to make malt, the basis for beer, have inspired anthropologists and brewers to cooperate to replicate them. Songs and hymns make clear that beer, often flavored with herbs and spices, was not only imbued with the sacred but unsurprisingly was also a source of great pleasure. It was an important food in Mesopotamia and even more so in Egypt.[23]

Dates were turned into wine or, like grapes and figs, dried in the sun so that they could be stored. Sesame seeds were pressed to yield oil, which, like butter and precious honey, was packed in jars. Fruits were preserved in honey, and fish in oil, while beef, gazelle, and other fish were salted. To make a rich sauce (*siqqu*) akin to contemporary Southeast Asian fish sauces, fish and grasshoppers were fermented with salt in pots.

To feed the cities, barley was shipped along rivers and canals. Onions of various kinds, garlic, herbs such as rue, and fruits such as apples, pears, figs, pomegranates, and grapes came from the gardens of the wealthy. The animals were driven to the city, where they were slaughtered, the lambs and the kids going to the temples and noble houses, the male sheep and goats to the officials, royalty, and nobles, the tough ox and ewe meat to the army, and the carcasses of donkeys to the dogs, perhaps royal hunting dogs.[24] Saltwater fish, turtles, and shellfish came from the salt marshes and the Persian Gulf. Dried fish, probably a specialized and regulated industry, came from the Persian Gulf and from as far away as

Mohenjo-Daro on the Indus and the Arabian Sea. Salt, excavated from the mountains or evaporated from briny springs and brackish river water, was shipped to distribution centers and packed onto asses, probably in standard-sized, solid-footed goblets.[25]

Barley was wealth. It paid for the meat and cheeses. It paid for the lapis lazuli and carnelian dishes for the sacrifice, the gold and silver for jewelry, the boatloads of copper that came down the Euphrates or from Dilmun on the Persian Gulf, the metals from Oman and the Sinai, the granite and marble from Turkey and Persia, and the lumber from Lebanon used to build the temples.[26]

Nomads around the fringes of the irrigated and cultivated areas included the Hebrews, whose daily fare largely comprised barley pottages flavored with greens and herbs and flatbreads of barley and wheat, which they farmed in oases during the growing season or acquired by bartering their barren ewes and young rams. They made yogurt and fresh cheese from the milk of their flocks, which they ate accompanied by olive or sesame oil, honey, and grape must and date sweeteners (both of which were also called honey). To conserve their flocks, the source of their wealth, they enjoyed meat only on special occasions following the sacrifice of the "fruit of the ground" (barley and wheat) and the "firstlings of the flock" (lambs and kids) to Jehovah.[27]

To the east of Mesopotamia, barley-wheat cuisine had been long established in the Indus Valley. Those who prepared it also had broomcorn millet, transferred from northern China in the second millennium B.C.E., probably along with marijuana, peach and apricot trees, and Chinese-style harvesting knives. From Africa south of the Sahara they had adopted sorghum (*Sorghum bicolor,* a millet-like grain), pearl millet (*Pennisetum glaucum*), finger millet (*Eleusine coracana*), cowpeas (*Vigna unguiculata*), and hyacinth beans (*Lablab purpureus*).[28] Villagers sacrificed to their gods. A prayer from the Yajur Veda, probably composed around 800 B.C.E., asks for both luxury and everyday foodstuffs. "May for me prosper, through the sacrifice, milk, sap [probably palm sap for wine], ghee [clarified butter], honey, eating and drinking at the common table, ploughing, rains, conquest, victory, wealth, riches. May for me prosper, through the sacrifice, low-grade food *[sic],* freedom from hunger, rice, barley, sesame, kidney beans, vetches, wheat, lentils, millet, panicum grains and wild rice."[29]

Moving west to the Mediterranean, Phoenicians (from present-day Lebanon) and Greeks spread barley-wheat cuisine along the coast of North Africa and the northern coast of the Mediterranean, respectively. Because their homelands did not support the rich stands of barley found in the irrigated river valleys, the Phoenicians made and traded luxury goods and the Greeks sold oil and wine for additional grains.[30]

The Greeks described barley as the gift of the goddess Demeter. Cooks soaked the grain, dried it, then roasted it in a shallow pan over the fire before grinding it to meal. This could be eaten as it was by travelers, mixed with water to make a

gruel or porridge, or mixed with water, milk, oil, or honey to make small flat bannocks (*maza*), the bread of the Greeks. Accompanying the barley dishes were
beans or lentils, greens or root vegetables, eggs, cheese, fish, and occasionally mutton, goat, or pork. In hard times, they could fall back on acorns and wild plants
such as mallow (in the Malvaceae family), asphodel, and vetches, normally the
food of nomads, not settled peoples. They drank wine, the gift of Dionysus, mixed
with water, not beer like the Mesopotamians and Egyptians.

The *Iliad* gives a vivid description of a warrior's feast. Achilles, the epic's hero,
ordered a great bowl to be filled with wine, mixed with less water than usual. Well-
fattened sheep, pigs, and goats were sacrificed and chopped into pieces. The fire
blazed and died down to a glowing bed of embers. Then the meat was threaded on
skewers, sprinkled with holy salt, and grilled on supports above the embers. The
warriors dined on the brown aromatic meat and barley bread served in fine baskets.[31]

Farther afield, in the forests north of the Alps, the Celts depended on barley and
wheat breads with fermented milk products for their daily fare and favored pork,
pigs being their symbol of fertility. After winning in battle, they sacrificed horses,
pigs, and cattle to the gods. For the feast that followed, pork was roasted on a spit
suspended over the andirons or firedogs or boiled in an iron cauldron. There
might also be horsemeat, beef, mutton, salt pork, baked salt fish, and slightly leavened bread. They feasted seated in a circle on the ground, perhaps on skins or a
bed of hay, in front of low tables. The king and queen took the leg of pork, the
charioteer the head, and everyone else a piece according to his or her rank.[32]

Turning back to the south, we leave the barley-wheat cuisines to examine
three overlapping cuisines in Africa south of the Sahara for which we have less
evidence.[33] In the grasslands of the Sudan and the Ethiopian highlands, people
depended on grains—millets again, though of different botanical classifications
than those of China. They pounded finger millet (*Eleusine coracana*) and teff
(*Eragrostis tef*) and cooked the meal with water to prepare gruel. The cattle that
they herded were a mix of Indian zebu cattle from India (*Bos indicus*) and native
species that tolerated drought and resisted tsetse flies, further evidence of contacts between the two regions.

To the west, in the savannah along the southern border of the Sahara, cooks
pounded, winnowed, and boiled African rice (*Oryza glaberrima*), sorghum (*Sorghum bicolor*), and pearl millet (*Pennisetum glaucum*). They also prepared a variety of squashes, sesame seeds and leaves, and Bambara groundnuts (legumes that,
like peanuts, ripen underground).

In the tropical forest zone between the savannah and the West African coast
there was a roots cuisine of boiled and pounded yams (genus *Dioscorea*). Perhaps
then as now, the resulting paste (most commonly called *fufu* today) was rolled into
spheres a little smaller than golf balls to pop into the mouth. Oil from the red fruits

of the African oil palm (*Elaeis guineensis*) helped the paste go down. Accompaniments included cowpeas (*Vigna unguiculata,* a subspecies of which is known as black-eyed peas) as well as okra and other greens. Oil palm sap spontaneously fermented to kicky palm wine within one or two days. Over subsequent centuries, migrants from the eastern grassland and the tropical forests merged the millet-beef cuisine with the yam-banana cuisine in East and Central Africa.

Crossing the Atlantic, we find three more cuisines. In the tropical lowlands, people depended on cooked cassava (also known as manioc, *Manihot esculenta*) and perhaps sweet potatoes (*Ipomea batatas,* often called yams in the United States). One variety of cassava could be simply peeled, boiled, and eaten, but it did not last in the ground; another variety lasted longer but was bitter and poisonous and required elaborate processing to make it edible. When Europeans arrived in the Caribbean, they were amazed at the work it took women to prepare the long-keeping cassava (fig. 1.6).[34]

In the Andean region, a different cuisine was based on potatoes, quinoa, beans, and amaranth. Potatoes could be freeze-dried, thawed, trampled with the feet to get rid of the skins, soaked for one to three weeks in cold running streams, and dried in the sun for five to ten days to make a light, easy-to-transport product (*chuño*). Alternatively, they were boiled, peeled, cut into chunks, and dried in the sun (*papas secas*). Cooks prepared soups and stews of processed potatoes, porridges of quinoa, quick foods of toasted quinoa, and dishes of llama, alpaca, and guinea pig meat.[35]

Maize (corn, *Zea mays*) was the basis of the most important and expansive cuisines in the Americas. The big-kernelled maize familiar to us today, capable of producing hundreds of seeds for every one sown, made its appearance around 1500 B.C.E. It was bred from a wild ancestor (*teosinte*) found in central Mexico around 7000 B.C.E., which had cobs no bigger than a finger. Maize and the grindstones to prepare it spread to the steamy forests along the Gulf Coast of Mexico, wedged between the mountains and the ocean. In the villages of the Olmec culture, women ground the maize and then boiled it with water to make a gruel (*atole*) or wrapped it in leaves for steamed dumplings (*tamales*). The tamales and gruel were accompanied by deer, dog, opossum, peccary, and raccoon meat, as well as wild birds, fish, turtles, snakes, mollusks, and shellfish. Beans, squash, tomatoes, and chiles were planted in small clearings in the forest that were surrounded by cacao bushes and towering avocado trees. Olmec priests sacrificed to the gods on stone platforms two-thirds of a mile on a side that rose a hundred and fifty feet above the swampy land. Sculptured heads of kings as much as nine feet high stood guard, ears of maize hanging from their skull coverings.[36]

By 3000 B.C.E., maize cuisines were being prepared in tropical Ecuadorian villages, and by no later than 1000 B.C.E., in the Caribbean. They displaced potatoes

FIGURE 1.6. Engraving (with legend in Italian) depicting Caribbean women carrying out the laborious, multistage process of turning poisonous cassava tubers into flatbread. After washing the roots and peeling them, sometimes with their teeth, the women grated them on an oblong board covered with stone chips stuck on with vegetable pitch. Then they squeezed out the poisonous juices between weighted boards and sieved the detoxified pulp to turn it into meal, which was dried in the sun. The meal was mixed with water and then baked on a clay griddle into a kind of bread. Courtesy New York Public Library. http://digitalgallery.nypl.org/nypldigital/id?1248957.

to secondary status in what is now Peru. Maize reached the southwest of what is now the United States in the first millennium C.E. and the northeastern United States and southeastern Canada in the second millennium.[37]

GRAINS, CITIES, STATES, AND ARMIES

Before investigating why roots, and particularly grains, became such popular choices as culinary staples, let me clarify that I use the terms "grain" and "root" in a culinary, not a botanical, sense. Just as the ancient Chinese lumped together cereals, soy, hemp, and other plants under the single term *ku,* and the ancient Indian philosophical works, the Upanishads, described sesame, kidney beans, lentils and horsegram, barley, wheat, rice, and a couple of millets as the food grains, I include seeds of various families of annual herbaceous plants, including grasses (Gramineae), beans and peas (Leguminae), mustards and cabbages (Brassicaceae), and so on, which required similar processing and were frequently mixed together.[38] Roots are all underground food storage chambers for plants, including corms and tubers, such as cassava (*Manihot esculenta*), taro (*Colocasia esculenta*), yam (Dioscoreaceae family), sweet potatoes (*Ipomea batatas*), and potatoes (*Solanum tuberosum*), along with less important species such as papyrus (*Cyperus*) in Africa, camas (*Camassia*) in North America, and oca (*Oxalis tuberosa*) in the Andes. I will say more about grains than about roots because they were to be much more important in the history of cuisines.

Roots and grains have many advantages. They are rich in calories and nutrients because they provide sustenance for the next generation of plants. They often grow abundantly in the wild. They also can be easily harvested, as American botanist Jack Harlan demonstrated in the 1970s by reaping four pounds of einkorn wheat (an archaic variety that still grows wild in parts of Turkey) in just an hour with a flint sickle. Roots could often be harvested year-round or left in the ground without rotting, and grains could be stored in granaries to provide food in the difficult seasons of cold, drought, or heavy rain, depending on the region.

Few other candidates for plant food measured up. Although some fruits, particularly bananas and breadfruit, also provided substantial calories, most were small, sour or bitter, seasonal, and hard to stockpile. Nuts, such as acorns, chestnuts, pine nuts, coconuts, and hazelnuts, are rich in calories but many are so oily that they cause diarrhea when eaten in large quantities. Because nut-bearing trees often take years to fruit, migrants who needed to reproduce cuisines quickly in a new place would have been less likely to move nuts than to move roots and grains. Leaves and shoots, low in calories, often bitter, and difficult to store, were used mainly as medicines.[39] Most societies, therefore, came to depend on two or three favorite roots or grains to provide most of their calories, that is, as their staples. Other foodstuffs, such as meat, fruits, and vegetables, provided flavor, variety, and nutritional balance. The staples that humans had picked out centuries before

1000 B.C.E. still provide most of the world's human food calories. Only sugarcane, in the form of sugar, was to join them as a major food resource.

Dependence on roots and grains came at a cost. Both are indigestible raw. Besides being tough, roots often produce poisons to protect themselves. Several abundant sources of carbohydrates, including taro, many yams, and some kinds of cassava, need detoxifying. Although few need to be processed as elaborately as cassava, many require quite a bit of effort. Certain peas and beans also contain poisons, but except for lupines, they could be detoxified simply by heating. With grains, care had to be taken to remove poisonous weed seeds such as darnel, also known as the tares of the Bible (*Lolium termulientum*), which causes a feeling of drunkenness and can lead to death. Molds that could cause hallucinations and death also had to be avoided.[40]

The chief problem with grains, however, is that they protect themselves with layers of inedible, fibrous, throat-catching coverings—an outer husk, sometimes an inner husk, and the seed coat itself—most of which have to be removed. Before grinding wheat into flour, for example, a series of laborious preliminaries had to be carried out. The archaeologist Gordon Hillman recorded the following steps still undertaken by peasants to prepare an ancient Turkish variety of wheat: (1) Thresh the wheat by beating, trampling, or sledging. (2) Rake to remove straw. (3) Winnow to get rid of lighter fragments of straw (perhaps repeating steps 2 and 3). (4) Sieve the little spikes with the grains attached to get rid of more bits of straw and weed heads. (5) Separate out and store some wheat to sow next year. (6) Store the rest. (7) When ready to continue, parch the spikelets to make the husks brittle. (8) Pound the spikelets to break the husk and release the wheat berry. (9) Winnow to get rid of husks (chaff). (10) Sieve the wheat to get rid of unbroken spikelets and weeds. Save for chickens or to use in famines. (11) Pass the wheat through a finer sieve to get rid of small impurities. (12) Dunk the wheat in water to get rid of diseased grains, poisonous darnel, and wild oats, and dry. (13) Store semi-clean wheat.[41]

If they are to be turned into bread, grains have to be ground. When I was a little girl, my father decided to make some flour from the wheat we had grown on the farm. He tried pounding it with a pestle and mortar but all he got was broken grains, not flour. He put it through the hand mincer screwed to the edge of the table with the same result. Finally, he attacked it with a hammer on the flagstone floor. After he gave up, defeated, my mother cleared up the mess. It was sobering to realize that if the commercial millers had vanished, we could have starved even with barns full of sacks of wheat.

To turn wheat into flour, you have to shear, not pound, the hard grains, which requires a grindstone, as the people of Lake Kinneret had discovered. A friend in Mexico, where hand grinding still goes on, showed me how it works. She knelt at the upper end of a grindstone, called a metate—a saddle-shaped platform on three inverted pyramidal legs, hewn from a single piece of volcanic rock (fig. 1.7). She mounded a handful of barley, took the *mano,* a stone shaped like a squared-off

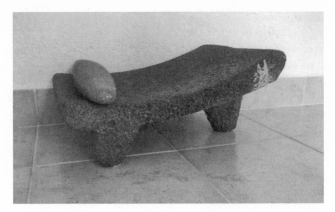

FIGURE 1.7. My metate. The angles of its surfaces have been carefully shaped to work with the oval stone *mano* and the grinder's body as a superbly efficient machine for reducing maize or other grains to flour. Photograph by the author.

rolling pin, in both hands with her thumbs facing back to nudge the grain into place, and, using the whole weight of her upper body, sheared the mano over the grain. After half a dozen motions, she had broken the grains, which now clustered at the bottom end of the metate. Carefully scraping them up with her fingertips, she moved them back to the top, and started shearing again, this time producing white streaks of flour. By the time she had sheared the grain from top to bottom five or six times, she had produced a handful of flour.

Grinding may look easy, and it is, for the first ten minutes. To grind a quantity of grain, though, as I found out when I tried, takes skill, control, physical strength, and time. I was quickly panting, sweaty, and dizzy, my hair in my eyes, and the mano slipping at awkward angles. Grinding is hard on the knees, hips, back, shoulders, and elbows, causing arthritis and bone damage. Grinding is lonely, too exhausting to allow for chatter. Kneeling to grind with the breasts swinging can be seen as submissive, demeaning, and sexually provocative, as lascivious eighteenth- and nineteenth-century illustrations of Mexican women grinding make clear. The heavy labor was relegated to women, convicts, and slaves, called "grinding slaves" in the technical language of seventh-century English court documents.[42] Even today Mexican women in remote villages grind five hours daily to prepare enough maize for a family of five or six. For generation upon generation of grinders in the bread-eating parts of the world, the author of Genesis (3:19) had it nailed. "In the sweat of thy face shalt thou eat bread, till thou return unto the ground; for out of it wast thou taken: for dust thou art, and unto dust shalt thou return."

Grains were worth the grinding and pounding in part because they yielded such fine products. Grindstones, like pestles and mortars, were the highest technology of the time, the product of centuries or millennia of experimentation with different materials and shapes. People using grinders and pounders can vary their pressure and speed to produce a variety of high-quality outputs, superior to those processed by rotary grindstones. Often it is assumed that flour was gritty and coarse. Having experimented with different grains on the grindstone, I have concluded that this is not so. A well-seasoned stone does not throw off perceptible grit. The grains can be reduced to a fine flour. With a cloth sieve, it is perfectly possible to separate the white flour from the bran to make white bread. Contemporary Mexicans who can afford it are willing to pay double for tortillas made from dough ground on the metate rather than by machine. Similarly, hand-hulled rice was insisted on by the Thai royal family even after the introduction of steam-driven rice mills in the late nineteenth century. Austrian peasants continued to pound millet by hand in the early twentieth century, because the resulting hulled grain stayed fresh, did not require long cooking, and had an appealing floury texture and sweet taste.[43]

More important still, no other raw material could be turned into so many different and delicious ingredients, dishes, and drinks as grains, which yielded toasted grains and grain powders, boiled grains, breads and pasta, sweeteners such as malt sugar, oils such as sesame, and, last but not least, alcohol. Roots could be turned into floury pastes by baking or boiling and they could be fermented, but the variety of dishes they yielded was not nearly as great.

Toasting grains made them easier to grind, lent a pleasing flavor, and made an instant food. Until the 1960s, Canary Islanders depended on what they call *gofio*— ground toasted wheat, barley, rye, chickpeas, broad beans, peas, or lupine beans (severally or combined), and, in times of scarcity, dried bracken, fern roots, and seeds of a coastal grass—for three meals a day. It remains popular even now.[44] The powder is mixed with water or milk for a gruel, with less water to make balls, and with hot water and meat, fish, or vegetables to make a thick, hot soup. The ancient Greeks probably prepared their barley meal by grinding toasted grains. Tibetans make a similar product with wheat, millet, barley, or maize (*yoe*);[45] Mexicans, with maize (*pinole*).

Steamed or boiled grain dishes were not easily portable so were eaten where they were cooked.[46] Soft grains, such as millet and rice, made appealing dishes when simply cooked with water; harder grains were usually cracked or ground first. In either case, combined with dried beans, vegetables, and perhaps meat, they were dished up in one of the most widespread and fuel-efficient dishes of premodern times, the pottage, such as the one for which Esau sold his birthright. They were also prepared as thin gruels and semi-solid porridges. The ancient Romans built their empire on barley porridge. The Chinese enjoy rice porridge (*congee*), the

Indians rice and lentil porridge (*kichree*). Polenta (millet and later maize porridge) has sustained generations of Italian peasants. Similarly, grits and mushes were staples of the American colonies. Turkish families commemorate Noah's rescue from the flood with a porridge of mixed grains, fruit, and nuts (*ashure*). Left to sour or ferment slightly, boiled grain dishes became tangy, a flavor much appreciated in eastern Europe, for example.

Bread—baked flour and water paste—was more portable, but it needed more fuel. Early bread was nothing like our puffy square loaf. Because so much of the bran had to be sifted out to make white flour, white bread was reserved for the very rich until the nineteenth century (and later in many places). Most bread was dark and flat, made of one or more of the hard grains, such as barley, wheat, oats, and later rye, often with some mixture of beans and the starchier nuts, such as chestnuts or acorns. In the Americas, maize was the main grain for flatbreads (tortillas). The simplest breads were ashcakes, doughs of meal and water baked in the ashes and then dusted off. Thinner dough could be cooked directly on the embers or on hot griddles or bake stones.[47] Pots in which fires were lit for cooking were old when the *Epic of Gilgamesh* was written; flatbreads were baked on their walls. A pot with a lid of clay created a small, simple bread oven—the Roman *testa*.[48] Bricks or clay built up in a dome over a flat surface made a beehive oven. Breads could be eaten with the fingers, used as a plate, or, like the tortilla of Mexico or the flatbread of the Middle East, wrapped around foods. They could scoop up or sop up liquids, the source of our word "soup." Pasta (boiled or steamed flour and water paste) appeared first in China (see chapter 2), then in the medieval Islamic world (chapter 4), before spreading more widely.

Oil could be obtained from a wide variety of seeds, including sesame and cabbage, by heating, pressing, or employing a combination of the two. A sweetener, malt syrup, could be made by sprouting grain, drying it, and extracting the sugar with water. Alcohol could be produced from grain if the starch was first changed into sugar. In the Americas, women chewed grain, the enzymes in their saliva effecting the transformation. In China, and perhaps in India, ground, partially cooked wheat (or sometimes millet) was allowed to go moldy, making a "ferment."[49] In Egypt, grains were sprouted, dried, and ground to make malt. The next step in all cases was to add this starter to more grain, usually cooked, allowing microbiological processes to convert the sugar to alcohol.[50] The botanist Jonathan Sauer and the anthropologist Robert Braidwood suggested in the 1950s that people turned to farming to have a regular source of grain to make beer, an idea revived in the 1980s by Solomon Katz and Mary Voight.[51] That most societies greatly esteemed beer and other alcoholic beverages with their heady effects and rich tastes is clear (fig. 1.8), although it's less obvious that this was the motivation for farming. After all, people had been experimenting with cooking grains for thousands of years before farming and had discovered that no other potential food-

FIGURE 1.8. A scorpion-man is followed by a goat carrying drinks, probably beer, taken from a large vessel. This is one of several shell-inlay panels showing animals acting like humans at an underworld banquet on the front of a magnificent bull-headed lyre in a royal tomb dating back to 2500 B.C.E. Feasting and harmonious music were part of sacred ceremonies. Courtesy University of Pennsylvania Museum of Archaeology and Anthropology (15207).

stuffs yielded such a diversity of satisfying products. It seems more likely that it was their flexibility that made grains worth farming.

Finally, and most important, although not all grain cuisines supported cities in 1000 B.C.E., it was only grain cuisines that did so, a generalization that would hold true until the end of the nineteenth century. This phenomenon, I suggest, has to do with the difficulty of provisioning large conglomerations of people, notably the cities and armies, which in the ancient world often rivaled cities in size. To sustain an individual on a staple diet of roots required consuming a large weight daily, up to sixteen pounds, one estimate suggests, though it seems improbably high.[52] Whatever the exact figure, grains had a much better nutrient-to-weight ratio: only about two pounds of grain, on average, were needed to provide 2,500 to 3,000 calories per person per day.[53] When everything had to be carried on the backs of men or animals, in lumbering oxcarts with a maximum speed of three miles an hour, or by sea, this difference between moist, heavy roots (as much as 80 percent water) and dry, relatively light grains (10 percent water) was crucial. Grains stored well too, keeping at least a year and often longer, unlike wet roots, which began to rot once out of the ground. Not until the cheap, fast steamships and railroad transport of the nineteenth century could roots compete with grains as provisions for cities.

That is not to say feeding cities or armies even with grains was easy. A pack-horse could carry two hundred to two hundred and fifty pounds of grain, enough for ten people for ten days. The problem was that a horse ate ten pounds of grain (and ten of grass) every day, so unless grain could be obtained along the route, it consumed rations equivalent to those of five men every day, and within three weeks had eaten its entire load. Water transport was more efficient. A merchant ship in the ancient Mediterranean could carry as much as four hundred tons. It cost no more to ship grain from one end of the Mediterranean to the other than to cart it seventy-five miles overland.[54] Hence grains were rarely moved more than about five miles by land, since land transport cost seven times as much as river transport and twenty-five to thirty times as much as going by sea. Cities, not sur-prisingly, were usually located on navigable rivers or good harbors.

To run a city-state or provision an army, rulers had to make sure that grains were extracted from those who worked the land, then transported to the cities and put in storage. Sometimes they demanded grain as tribute; sometimes they operated what were in effect agribusinesses farmed by slaves, serfs, or other barely free labor to produce grain; and later they exacted taxes to be paid in grain. Grains, more impor-tant, if less glamorous, than the precious metals, exotic wild animals, and beautiful slave girls that they also collected, were processed and redistributed to the ruler's household and bodyguard as pay in kind. Kings, emperors, landlords, and the great religious houses continued to collect grain long after money was invented.

As states grew into empires, root cuisines, whether in Southeast Asia and the Pacific Islands, the tropical forests of Africa, or the hot lowlands of Mesoamerica, for all their long history, became less important on the world stage (though not, of course, to those who continued to depend on them). Mostly consumed in tropical areas, root cuisines did not enter the culinary debates that swirled around the grain cuisines. The rest of this book, consequently, will be largely concerned with grain cuisines.

Grains, though, are of no use without the pestle and mortar or the grindstone. I keep my metate in a corner of the kitchen and enjoy experimenting with grinding meat, fruit, nuts, spices, and grains. I admire the spare artistry of this tool, as strik-ing as any piece of modern sculpture. It's good to be reminded that cities and states, courts and armies, writing and figuring, temples and cathedrals, all depended on those who stood to pound and knelt to grind.

HIGH AND HUMBLE, CITY AND COUNTRY, CIVILIZED AND NOMADIC CUISINES

With the rise of cities and states, distinctions in rank and status became accentu-ated. Where formerly these distinctions had found culinary expression mainly in the size of the helping and, in the case of meat, the prestige of the cut, now cuisines split into high and humble. They drew on the same staples, at least initially, but had different proportions of staple and relish, and different dishes, cooks, kitchens, and ways of transmitting culinary knowledge from one generation to the next. Rulers, priests, nobles, and warriors, as in the Yellow River Valley and Mesopotamia for example, dined on high cuisines. Their subjects survived on humble cuisines. In a further distinction, those who ate grains contrasted their civilized state with the barbarism of surrounding nomads, who, they asserted, did not eat grains. The humble cuisines of poor city dwellers also became differentiated from the humble cuisines of those who lived in the country. These distinctions were to shape culinary history until the modern period.

High cuisines were heavy in meats, sweets, fats, and intoxicants, which together provided noble diners with perhaps 60 to 70 percent of their calories. Muscle meat; tastier bits of offal from large domesticated animals, such as cattle, sheep, goats, and pigs; barnyard fowl; and animals caught in the hunt, particularly deer, antelope, and gazelles, were favored. Highly processed ingredients—the whitest hand-hulled grains or flour, oil or butter, sweeteners, and alcohol—were used partly because they were so costly. Salt—lauded as essential to the civilized life according to the Roman encyclopedist Pliny, the noblest of foodstuffs according to the historian and biographer Plutarch, and the "general of foods" according to Emperor Wang Mang, all writing in the first century C.E.—was used abundantly.[55] Exotic ingredients, paraded at ceremonies, mapped the huge extent of the king's territory for onlookers, reminding them that he commanded space, work, and transport. Appetizers, sweet dishes, and sauces, the latter described by the food writer Harold McGee as "distillations of desire," designed to titillate jaded appetites, employing expensive ingredients, and time-consuming and tricky to prepare, signaled a high cuisine.[56] No time or expense was spared in preparing the dishes: fires roared, big ovens gobbled up fuel, junior cooks chopped, stuffed, rolled, and decorated what was to appear before their monarch.

High cuisines were the cuisines of the palace and, on a less extravagant scale, noble houses, which received, processed, cooked, and redistributed to the court and army farm products taken as tribute or tax. Until a couple of hundred years ago, palace kitchen complexes were huge, staffed by hundreds or even thousands of bureaucrats, cooks of different ranks and specialties, bakers, and scullery workers. It is not unreasonable to think of these kitchens as the first big manufacturing enterprises, carrying out the food processing that today is done in factories as well as preparing meals. One section prepared high cuisines for the king and his immediate entourage, another made less prestigious dishes for the nobles, and yet another assembled humble fare for the manual workers in the palace. In creating the aura of power, the magnificence of high cuisine was as important as palaces and pyramids, purple linen and colorful silk. As late as the nineteenth century, a

British royal dinner was the favorite display at Madame Tussaud's wax museum in London. Ordinary people filed past, fingering the extravagant clothes of the wax royals and gazing at the rich dishes.[57]

The palace kitchens were a crucial arm of government, providing pay in kind for the palace workers and bureaucrats, turning out lavish meals that demonstrated the king's power to command resources, maintaining the health of the king, and, since he often travelled with his crack troops, provisioning his army. The scope of the responsibility explains why cooks (or executive chefs cum quartermasters) such as I Yin in China or Guillaume Tirel in France, who was promoted by Charles V of France to Sergeant-at-Arms and Clerk of the Kitchen, a position normally reserved for an aristocrat, ranked so high. It makes sense of why François Vatel committed suicide when a dinner he was preparing for several hundred in honor of Louis XIV fell through for lack of supplies.[58] Cooks were male professionals who worked with the royal gardeners, huntsmen, and other food providers, as well as the steward and the physician. The steward (or vizier or chamberlain), a high-ranking noble, together with the master cook, kept careful track of the foodstuffs entering and leaving the kitchens, and worked on the protocol for important feasts. The physicians collaborated with the master cook to design dishes intended to make the monarch strong, intelligent, and courageous. Together, they monitored the time it took foods to pass through the body, the changes in the coating on the monarch's tongue, the color of his urine, the consistency of his feces, and the balance of his bodily fluids. To prevent or cure illness, cooks, like pharmacists, mixed and perfected substances, the pantry and the pharmacopoeia overlapping. The Chinese word *fang*, like the English word "receipt," meant both recipe and prescription.

Diners ate in dedicated spaces such as banqueting halls, using special paraphernalia such as silver straws in Sumer, painted wine vessels in Greece, and lacquered chopsticks in China. Priests prayed, dancers and entertainers performed, and musicians (literally) set the tone for the meal, invoking cosmic harmony. Elaborate codes of etiquette specified who might dine with whom, who might watch, the clothes they should wear, what they should talk about or whether they should be silent, the order in which dishes should be eaten, and how food should be conveyed to the mouth. Rulers ate alone or with high-ranking family members or officials, their seating reflecting their rank. In India, the king dined alone, seated on a chair in front of a table laden with dishes, with an orchestra playing appropriate harmonies and female attendants in a pavilion near the kitchen working whisks and fans to keep him comfortable. In China, the emperor ate meals staged to exhibit his cosmic role, never touching foreign foods (at least in formal meals), and never eating with visiting foreigners.

Finally, high cuisines were recorded in a written literature, which included hymns and prayers that laid out the steps for sacrifice or brewing of alcohol, recipe

books specifying ingredients and techniques, manuals on kingship or estate management, records of foods entering the royal kitchen, and pharmacopeias and
works on dietetics.

Humble rural cuisines were the lot of the peasantry, a term I use simply to refer
to those who worked the land for their own subsistence and had to pay tribute and
taxes in kind, rather than to sell to the market. Making up 80 or 90 percent of the
population, they ate cuisines that were in every way the inverse of high cuisines.
The cooks were women, who labored for hours pounding and grinding roots or
grains, often out-of-doors. They stored grains and preserved foods for the lean
season in their homes, spaces they often shared with their animals.

Fuel, water, and salt were costly and limited what could be done in the kitchen.
Before beginning to cook, women had to gather scraps of brush, seaweed, dung,
furze—anything that would burn. Steaming and boiling, which use the least fuel,
were the commonest ways of cooking. A hot meal was often prepared only once a
day, other meals being cold. Water for cooking, drinking, and washing, enough for
one to five gallons a day per person (contemporary Americans use about seventy-
two gallons a day), had to be carried from a river or well; three gallons weighed
about twenty-four pounds.[59] Salt was a luxury, reserved for making salty preserves
that accompanied salt-free porridge or bread.

The average country dweller in classical antiquity obtained 70 to 75 percent or
more of his or her calories from roots or grains, the percentage rising and falling
depending on factors such as population density, war, epidemics, and the state of
farming. There is considerable evidence that following the Black Death in the mid-
fourteenth century, for example, the survivors ate better as a result of the drop in
population. Conversely, the rapid growth in population worldwide in the nineteenth and twentieth centuries meant that in the 1980s, grains still provided most
Egyptians and Indians with up to 70 percent of their calories and most Chinese with
up to 90 percent, and they still feed many of the two billion hungry in the world.[60]
To liven up these starches, or "make the rice go down," as the Chinese put it, the
poor added onions, a few boiled greens, a scrap of cheap meat, dried fish, or small
birds or animals caught with traps. Above all, dried beans symbolized the cuisine of
the poor—cheap proteins that produced gas but filled the belly a long time since
they were slow to digest. They drank gruels, water (though this was often polluted
in villages and cities), weak beer, or watery wine. Meals were eaten without ceremony using the fingers or a spoon to scoop from a common bowl. The cuisine was
memorialized, not in a written literature, but in proverbs and folk songs.

Humble cuisines could be very tasty. The staple in particular was judged by the
highest of standards. After all, if your diet consists largely of bread or rice or some
other staple, you learn to be very discerning. The accompanying relish was a mas-
terly combination of readily available, often vegetable ingredients. Igbos in Nigeria
carefully distinguished yams, to return to a root cuisine, by their age, by the skill

with which they had been pounded, and by the savor of the condiments of palm oil and chile, as I learned when I lived in the Niger Delta in the 1960s. In Mexico in the 1990s, I tasted country people's tortillas so thin and fragrant and salsas so satisfying that it became hard to put up with the cardboard tortillas common in the cities, where people with a more varied diet treated them as mere filler. Fresh herbs in the summer, fresh vegetables in the fall, fresh meat at slaughtering before Christmas, and roots and dried beans in the winter varied the otherwise dull-sounding pottage of grains, roots, greens, and a bit of meat variously known in European countries as *pot au feu, potage, bollito misto, cocido, puchero,* or *escudella.* That said, few of us accustomed to variety in the contemporary supermarket and to a choice of different meals or even different cuisines every day would be satisfied to eat the same meal day after day, as did even the more prosperous, such as the grandmother of Marimar Torres, of the important Catalan wine-making family, who "when she was young . . . had *escudella i carn d'olla* five or six times a week."[61]

Humble cuisines were always insecure, at the mercy of weather, soil, and predators beyond the peasants' control. Although famine was relatively rare, food shortage, particularly just before the harvest, was a constant. Ensuring enough to eat was a major preoccupation. As the Japanese adage advised: "All that matters is a full stomach,"[62] or as a Mexican peasant responded when I asked him why certain food stands drew so many people, "because their food fills you up." Country people were burdened with heavy taxes and rents, which they paid in kind (that is, food), or labored under indenture or slavery. Growing grains requires planning, discipline, and frugality. Humble folk tightened their belts in the hungry days of late spring and early summer, when supplies were running low. They vigilantly battled mold, rats, and mice that could destroy as much as half the grain in the granary. They set aside grain to plant the next year plus a reserve stock, preferably enough for two or three years, in case the harvest failed or warriors trampled the fields.[63] If food became really short, they worked their way down a list of less and less acceptable alternatives: wild foods and animal fodder; seed corn and breeding stock; and bark and dirt. There is evidence that, when all else failed, those suffering from famine reluctantly resorted to the flesh of those who had already succumbed.[64] Unless they lived close to the sea or a river that made it possible to move grain cheaply, villagers and poor townsfolk suffered the tyranny of the local.

All too often those who ate humble cuisines were shorter, less energetic, and less clever than those who ate high cuisines. Malnutrition in pregnant and nursing mothers and young children, lack of iodine in remote mountainous areas, and lack of iron are just some of the possible causes of mental slowness or retardation, not limited to the rural poor but more likely among them. The Italian historian Piero Camporesi commented, "One of the side effects of famine which has not been paid its necessary due was a surprising fall in the level of mental health, already organically precarious and tottering, since even in times of 'normality' halfwits, idiots and cretins constituted a dense and omnipresent human fauna (every village or hamlet, even the tiniest, had its fool). The poor sustenance aggravated a biological deficiency, and psychological equilibrium, already profoundly compromised . . . visibly deteriorated."[65] Two of the soberest and most careful of historians studying food, Peter Garnsey, who works on food in antiquity, and Steven Kaplan, the expert on bread in eighteenth-century France, quote him in agreement.[66] Kaplan points out that bread, supposedly given by God and guaranteed by the king, all too often turned into the bread of nightmares, adulterated with molds and weed seeds, drugging the poor.

The humble cuisines of poor townsfolk, who made up 90 percent of the population of ancient cities, differed from those of the country. They were usually ampler and more varied, leaving aside the truly miserable cuisine of the bottom 10 percent or so. "The city dwellers," remarked the great Roman doctor Galen in the second century c.e., "collected and stored enough grain for all the coming year immediately after the harvest. They carried off all the wheat, the barley, the beans and the lentils and left what remained to the country folk."[67] This "'surplus' should not be envisaged as something left over or going spare: whatever the state and/or landlords could extract from the peasants in the form of taxes and/or rent is defined as surplus as long as the transfer did not kill off the peasants altogether," echoes the historian Patricia Crone.[68] "The chicken is the country's but the city eats it," said the peasants.[69] Cities, they complained, were giant maws, gobbling up the food, only to excrete it into stinking sewers, clogged drains, and polluted rivers. On the other hand, city dwellers were more prone to food poisoning and waterborne parasites than their country cousins. When cities were besieged, hunger and starvation stared their inhabitants in the face.

Few city dwellers ate the home-cooked food of the rural poor. Many townsfolk were young single men, living either in cramped quarters without cooking facilities or in the households of their masters or employers. Fires were a constant hazard. Because fuel and water were expensive, street food and takeout food flourished, just as they do in the huge cities of the modern world. Other workers received meals as all or part of their wages. The elite, fearful that hungry mobs would riot, made sure that they were provided with food. Cities, although home to only a tiny proportion of the population—the million people living in Rome at the height of the empire were probably only 2 percent of the total population of the empire—stretched the food economy to the limit.

Servants and slaves bridged the gulf between high and humble cuisines. In the kitchens of the palaces and noble houses, they learned to prepare meals they could only dream of eating in their villages and doubtless gossiped about these to their families. Sometimes they prepared one of their simpler dishes for a lord jaded by rich food. So the humble knew all too well how the wealthy ate, although it was a cuisine that they could neither replicate nor aspire to.

Pastoralists followed their flocks on the lands unsuitable for farming, trading animals or animal products such as cheese or protection rights for grains. Their cuisine resembled that of the peasants, with the addition of more milk and cheese. Although today nomads do not loom large in the culinary world, from the time of the earliest states until the fourteenth century, there was constant interchange between the cuisines of the nomads and those of the settled. Nomad sons were sent to imperial capitals, and daughters married into imperial elites as strategies to buy peace. As a result, high cuisines were regularly reworked to nomad taste. In the words of Owen Lattimore, a pioneering scholar of Central Asia, "It is the poor nomad who is the pure nomad."[70]

ANCIENT CULINARY PHILOSOPHY

If, as anthropologists suggest, cooking set in train the physiological changes that enabled large brains and complex thought, in turn thinking humans developed complex theories of food, cooking, and cuisine. These topics run through the earliest epics, prayer books, philosophies, pharmacopeias, legal documents, and political manuals that followed the development of writing around 3000 B.C.E. during the centuries when complex states and empires were taking shape. They crop up in the Middle East in the *Epic of Gilgamesh,* the account books of Mesopotamian cities, the Zend Avesta of the Zoroastrians, and Leviticus, and in the Mediterranean in the *Iliad,* the *Odyssey,* the Hippocratic texts, the Galenic corpus, the *Materia medica* of Dioscorides, and the works of Plato, Aristotle, and the Stoics. They are found in China in the works attributed to Confucius, the Taoists, historians, poets, and the authors of the *Yellow Emperor's Inner Canon* and the *Herbal of the Divine Husbandman,* and in India in the Vedas, the medical and pharmacological works of the ancient Indian physicians Caraka and Suśruta, the *Mahabharata* epic, and the *Arthashastra* (Science of Politics) manual.[71] These texts were composed by the few who had mastered writing, but it seems likely that they drew on, systematized, and extended ideas common in their societies.

Moreover, these works reveal many widely shared attitudes, for all the differences within and between societies. Given the common culinary problems these societies faced and the long history of contacts between different societies, perhaps this is not surprising. The world, the authors of these works believed, was a contained, ordered, animate cosmos, not a vast undifferentiated universe. Minerals, vegetables, animals, humans from commoner to king, and spirits were ranked in a hierarchy. The cosmos had been created in the not-so-distant past and would end some day. It was enclosed by the arc of the heavens with the rising of the sun in the east and its setting in the west. Cooking drove changes in the cosmos, which humans imitated and improved on when they cultivated fields and cooked in their kitchens.

This vision of the world underlay ancient culinary philosophy, which was based on three principles: the principle of hierarchy, which posited that every rank of living being had appropriate foods and ways of consuming them; the sacrificial bargain, which specified that humans should offer foods to the gods and consume the leftovers as the emblematic meal in return for the gods' original provision of food; and the theory of the culinary cosmos, which asserted that cooking was a basic cosmic process and that foods were part of an elaborate system of correspondences with ages, seasons, compass directions, colors, bodily parts, and other features of the world.

To begin with the principle of hierarchy, each rank of living being, including minerals, which were then thought to be alive, drew on appropriate nutrients and ways of eating. Minerals and plants were nourished by water and earth. Animals ate raw meat or vegetables, alone and standing. Humans ate cooked meat or grains, reclining, sitting, or kneeling with their fellows. Cattle ate grass, while bread was for humans, said the author of Psalm 104. Eating raw plants as beasts did was tantamount to starvation for the villagers of Aphrodito in Upper Egypt.[72] Gods, who held the highest rank of all, fed on aromas that resulted from cooking—fragrant nectar or ambrosia or the odors of cooked meat and wine or beer.

Within this general hierarchy was a hierarchy of humans that justified the culinary divisions described in the preceding section. Noble, peasant, and poor city dweller all looked in horror on the nomads who traveled with their flocks across lands unsuitable for cultivation. Their fear and disdain stemmed from the fact that the nomads, using their horses and camels for mobile warfare, conquered the settled regions time and again, envious of their wealth, including their cuisine. The settled peoples of the Mediterranean, Middle East, and China described them as barely human, eating neither cooked grain nor cooked flesh. "He does not know grain, he roots for truffles like a pig. . . . He is an eater of raw meat," the farmer parents of a beautiful young girl say when she announces that she intends to marry a shepherd in a well-known Mesopotamian story.[73] The Scythians, who lived in the region that is now Ukraine, were ignorant of the civilized arts of cultivation and cooking—followers of herds, not tillers of the land (the moral equivalent of war for the lower strata of society, according to the Greeks). And the Chinese, as mentioned earlier, characterized the nomads on their borders as not using fire or grain.[74]

By contrast, the settled described themselves as fully human and civilized, living in societies with cities and eating cooked grains and meat. Barley meal and wheat flour were the "marrow of men," according to Homer.[75] In the Balkans, Italy, Turkey, China, Japan, and elsewhere the word for grain and for a meal were one and the same (in Hebrew *lehem*; in Greek *sitos*).[76] Grain's life cycle paralleled that of humans, with ceremonies performed at planting and harvest as humans performed rites of passage at birth and death.[77] Although grains defined the civilized, those lower in the hierarchy ate the less prestigious grains and the darkest bread.

The further up the hierarchy one went, the more prestigious the grain and the whiter the bread or rice.

At the pinnacle of the human hierarchy was the monarch, the pivot of the cosmos, poised between the natural and the supernatural. His palace and his city were at its geographic center. He himself was the agent of change and the carrier of destiny, and thus he had to eat the most strengthening meat and the finest grain dishes, since the health of the state depended on the health of the king. Since rank and cuisine were believed to be causally connected, it followed that eating the cuisine of a person of lower rank or of animals would turn the diner into a lesser person, or even a beast. All ancient kitchens and ancient feasts were organized so that those of like rank had like food. The king, who had no peers, often ate alone or with his immediate family. The humble resisted eating raw foods that would reduce them to animality.

Since diet largely determined moral and intellectual standing, it followed that the humble were thought to have little chance to be virtuous. For that, the cuisine of the higher ranks was a requisite. Eating refined, well-cooked food was thought to make one strong, vigorous, beautiful, and intelligent, and thus virtuous.[78] "A healthy mind in a healthy body," a catchphrase drawn from the Roman poet Juvenal, who in turn probably took it from the Greek, expressed general opinion. Food made men "better or more dissolute, more unrestrained or more reserved, bolder or more timid, more barbarous or more civilized, or more given to disputes and fighting," said Galen. It could "enhance the virtues of the logical soul, [making it] more intelligent, more studious, more prudent, and acquiring a better memory."[79] The Indian Vedas delivered the same message: "One should worship [food] for it enables a man to use all his faculties. . . . Through food comes the end of all ignorance and bondage."[80]

Just as food and cooking defined social status, they also served as symbols of social and political relations. Salt, for example, symbolized permanence and incorruptibility, and hence sealed agreements and ensured loyalty. To "eat the salt [of a person]" was the phrase for a covenant or reconciliation in Sumeria. "A covenant of salt" described God's gift of kingship over Israel to David and his sons forever. "We eat the salt of the palace" was the loyalty oath of the officials of the Persian emperors in the fifth century B.C.E. Nearly two thousand years later, when the soldiers of the Mughal emperor Jahangir realized that they were about to be defeated in Assam, they prepared to face death with the words "As we have taken the salt of Jahangir, we consider martyrdom to be our blessings for both the worlds."[81]

The cooking pot, in which diverse elements were brought into harmony, symbolized culture and the state.[82] When the Greeks founded a new colony, they carried a cauldron and a spark of fire from the mother city. Confucians argued that the king had to create harmony as the cook created harmony in the cauldron: "You have the water and fire, vinegar, pickle, salt, and plums, with which to cook fish and meat. It is made to boil by the firewood, and then the cook mixes the ingredi-

ents, harmoniously equalizing the several flavors, so as to supply whatever is defi-
cient and carry off whatever is in excess. Then the master eats it, and his mind is
made equable."[83] Centuries later, the janissaries, the Ottoman sultan's household
troops, overturned the cauldron in which their rations were cooked as a sign of
revolt (chapter 4).

The king's duty to his subjects was to ensure good harvests by sacrificing to the
gods.[84] The portion of those harvests that he extracted was then passed on to his
followers in acts of benevolence. Besides being expressions of the king's power to
command the resources of the state, the massive feasts of the ancient (and later)
kingdoms and accompanying gift giving of the leftovers were ways to buy loyalty.
In a world before a market economy, benevolence bound together ruler and ruled.
"The power to feed fed power," as the historian Amy Singer neatly expresses the
idea.[85] In China, if the sacrifice failed because the king and his officials were corrupt or out of harmony with the heavens, the peasants felt entitled to revolt while
they had the strength.[86]

The sacrificial bargain between the gods and humans paralleled the king's
beneficence to his subjects and their debt to him. The gods, the ancestors, and the
spirits were everywhere.[87] The gods had created the cosmos and humans, and had
given people the grain that made them civilized. Shen Nong (the divine husbandman) and Lord Millet in China, Dewi Sri in Bali, the rice goddess Pra Mae Posop
in Thailand, and Demeter in Greece were benign deities. Babylonians said Ea "will
bring to you a harvest of wealth, / in the morning he will let loaves of bread shower
down, / and in the evening a rain of wheat!"[88]

In return, the gods demanded that humans feed them in the sacrificial ceremony. Lord Millet, legendary founder of the Chou Dynasty, had taught the Chinese how to sacrifice, according to the Book of Songs, exclaiming, "What smell is
this, so strong and good?" when the odors of steaming millet and roasting lamb
drifted up from the sacrificial vessels. In the *Theogony,* a poem about the birth of
the gods composed by Hesiod in the eighth century B.C.E., Zeus, the greatest of the
gods in the Greek pantheon, signals to humans that they should burn "white bones
for the Immortals on altars smoking with incense."[89] In the sacrifice, humans
offered food, expecting in return good harvests, success in war, and plentiful children. Repeated time and again, sacrifice sustained and re-created the universe and
maintained cosmic harmony. Hesiod's *Theogony* is taken up with sacrifice; so too
are the Hebrew Book of Leviticus, the Indian Vedas, and the Confucian *Book of
Rites.* They explain the origins of sacrifice, give rules about how it should be performed, and record the hymns to be sung and the prayers to be said, much of
which was secret knowledge available only to the priesthood, whose training consisted in learning the sacred formulae by heart.

The sacrificial offerings (the food for the gods) with rare exceptions were from
domesticated and processed plants (grains and grain dishes, relishes, alcohol) and

the meat of domesticated animals. Barley meal was offered in Mesopotamia and Greece, wheat in Rome, millet in China, glutinous rice in Japan, and maize in Mesoamerica. "With all thine offerings thou shalt offer salt," said Leviticus.[90] Magico-medical substances, salts thrown on the flames caused them to change color, while in India, clarified butter (ghee) made them flare. Wine, mead, ale, and *chiu* were poured out in libations.

In India, fifty species of animals were considered suitable for sacrifice and thus for eating, including horses, cattle, sheep, goats, pigs, monkeys, elephants, alligators, and tortoises (a reminder of how circumscribed our culinary tastes now are). In Indo-Iranian languages, one word serves for domesticated animal, cattle, and sacrificial animal.[91] In the Middle East, cattle, sheep, and goats were sacrificed; in Greece, oxen, sheep, and goats; in Egypt, bulls or (in Thebes) rams; in northern Europe, horses, cattle, sheep, goats, and pigs; and in China, pigs, dogs, sheep, and goats. In practical terms, sacrifice and feast resolved the problem of disposing of the meat of large animals, since it was consumed at once.

Humans, the most valuable animals, were the ultimate sacrifice, as the book of Genesis reminds us. God commanded Abraham to take his only son, Isaac, to an appointed place, to build an altar, pile up the wood, bind his son, and place him on the altar on the wood. He was to slay him with his knife, presumably by cutting his throat and letting the blood drain out, and then to burn the body as an offering, the aromas rising up to God. At the last moment, God allowed Abraham to sacrifice a ram caught in a nearby thicket.[92] Although God released Abraham from this duty, there is evidence that sacrificing humans was common practice and continued relatively late in human history. Around 500 B.C.E., Gelon, ruler of Sicily, made it a condition of a treaty he signed with the Carthaginians that they give up the practice.[93] It was practiced in Peru among the Chimú people. In Aztec Tenochtitlan, the priests sliced out the hearts of sacrificial victims with obsidian knives.

"War and sacrifice" were "the great affairs of the state," the author of the *Tso-chuan (Tradition of Tso)* explained sometime between the fourth and second centuries B.C.E. "At sacrifices one presides over cooked meat, and in war one receives raw meat: these are the great ceremonies of the spirits."[94] Even wealthy Rome often slaughtered prisoners of war rather than keeping them alive. Smaller and less affluent states, facing constant food scarcity, found prisoners a burden and sacrifice a way out.

Whatever the animal sacrificed, hot, red lifeblood was spilt. "The life of every creature is the blood of it," Leviticus (17:14) says. Blood congealed into flesh, according to the Chinese, the Hebrews, and the Greeks. It was what food finally turned into in animals, said Aristotle. Consequently few societies were neutral about blood as food: some valued it highly; others prohibited it. In the first group were nomads who harvested blood from their animals, Christians who drained the blood of carcasses and used it to make sausages or thicken sauces, and the Chinese. Even today many Hong Kong Chinese mothers feed their children blood soup to sharpen their minds before examinations. In the second group were Jews and Muslims, who slaughtered animals so as to drain all blood from the body.[95]

The sacrifice was followed by the sacrificial feast—humans eating the gods' leftovers, which were charged with divine power. This might mean eating the flesh of sacrificed humans, a practice motivated not by hunger but by the logic of sharing the gods' leftovers. At least some northern Europeans ate the brains of the sacrificed in the third millennium B.C.E. The Cocoma people of Brazil, when admonished by the Jesuits for eating their dead and drinking an alcohol laced with ground bones, reportedly said that it "was better to be inside a friend than to be swallowed by the cold earth."[96] The Aztecs ate slivers of flesh from those who had been sacrificed on the pyramids. More commonly, however, the feast featured roast meat from sacrificed animals.

Sacrifice and feast might involve a huge multistate gathering or just a few family members. The officiant might be a priest, a ruler, or the head of the family. The meal might be open to the community or reserved for a select group; it might be a solemn ingestion or a riotous feast washed down with alcohol. Sacrifices could be extravagant or humble, offered by priests or kings or just ordinary people, a quick act before a meal or at a small shrine in the fields or an elaborate state ceremony. In Greece, sacrifices marked the beginning of the assembly, the appointment of magistrates, the commission of works, the start of a military campaign, the night before battle, the opening of the Olympics, the signing of a treaty, and the setting up of a new colony, using a spit, a pot, and a flame carried from the mother city, as well as birth, marriage, and death. Some people tempered awe with skepticism, formal phrases with casual conversation, high solemnity with partying and jollity. Mocking the whole affair, and thus clearly anticipating that the audience would laugh, one of the characters in a Greek comedy from the end of the fourth century B.C.E. expostulates, "The ways these vandals sacrifice! They bring couches, wine-jars—not for the gods, for themselves. . . . They offer the gods the tail-end and the gall-bladder, the bits you can't eat, and gobble the rest themselves."[97] Many, though, perhaps most, viewed the sacrificial bargain as an understandable and practical way of working with the supernatural.

The theory of the culinary cosmos was the third plank of ancient culinary philosophy. More inclusive than the humoral system, according to which bodily fluids determined temperament and health, it treated cooking as a basic cosmic process that cooks imitated in the kitchen. Cooking could be defined as the "mixing and perfecting of substances," according to the Vedic physicians.[98] The Chinese described kitchen operations as "to cut and cook."[99] Cooking eliminated the dross and revealed the true nature or essence of whatever was cooked.[100] Cooked was better than raw and thoroughly cooked was better than lightly cooked. Under-cooked or inappropriately mixed food was the major cause of illness, either because it passed through the body too fast to be digested and assimilated or because it lingered too long and putrefied. In China, water, like any other food-stuff, had to be cooked (heated) to make it more healthful, although it is not clear when this practice started.[101]

The fiery rays of the sun and the watery rays of the moon drove and sustained the cosmos, just as fire and water were the chief agents for transforming foods in the kitchen. Fire was a thing, not the motion of particles, as we now believe. It was something you could see and touch, that left a painful burn, and that danced when fed with fuel and died when neglected. The fiery rays falling on the earth caused plants and animals to grow, or congealed to form coal and oil, which then melted rock that flowed out as lava when the earth exhaled.[102] The author of the Hippocratic *On the Regimen* explained that heat or fire was "the foundation of all the functions in the body in the same way that it germinates the seed in the earth, that it governs and regulates the Universe at large; it is the cause of all consumption and growth, visible and invisible: soul, reason, growth, movement, diminution, per-mutation, sleep, consciousness of all and everything, and never ceases to act."[103] Watery rays from the cool, pale moon fell as rain and then were taken up by plants as life-giving juices or sap, or disappeared into cavities in the earth, where they might congeal into metals. When water was exhaled from the earth, it appeared as mist, dew, or the rivers that sustained life.

The cycle of life from birth to death, or from generation to corruption, in Aris-totle's terms, was, like the cosmos, driven by fire and water (fig. 1.9). Seeds were cooked into crystals (believed until the nineteenth century to be alive) or into tender, juicy young plants. When shoots poked out of the soil, cooking continued until they ripened to fruits or grains. In hot and dry conditions, they were cooked to aromatics, according to the Greeks. In well-balanced climates such as the Med-iterranean, grapes and cereals resulted. Raw plants, by contrast, were dangerously cold and wet.[104] When the sun went low in the sky, the plants died, their foliage blackening, withering, and rotting. New humans were cooked in the womb, a hot, steamy cauldron where male seeds mixed with female juices. If the cooking was not completed, humans were raw, half-baked, or crude; if it was especially rapid, they were pre-cooked, or precocious. In California, Native Americans placed ado-lescent girls in underground ovens to help the process of maturation along.[105]

Humans intervened in these cosmic culinary cycles at two points. The first was by cultivating plants, a way of cooking them. Domesticating plants was understood as cooking their juices until the fibers softened, just as if they had been boiled. Cultivated plants and cultured humans were both the result of cooking. The second took place in the kitchen. Cooks took the "fruits of the earth," as agricultural products were often called, mixed them to balance their qualities, and cooked

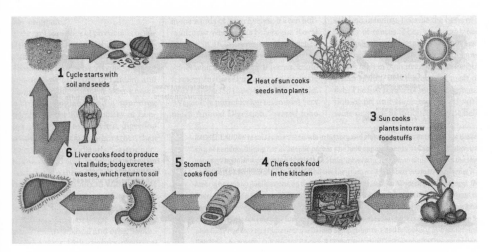

FIGURE 1.9. From classical antiquity to the seventeenth century, fire and cooking were thought to drive the cosmic culinary cycle. Similar schemes were found in other parts of the world. Courtesy Patricia Wynne.

them over kitchen fires. Further cooked or fermented in vats, grapes turned into liquid fire.

Cooked foods, when consumed, passed to the hot, steamy cauldron of the belly, where cooking (digesting) continued. (If the idea that fire can exist in the belly sounds hopelessly naive and unrealistic, the truth—that our stomachs contain corrosive hydrochloric acid—would have seemed equally far-fetched to ancient peoples.) Food was separated into blood and feces, after first being changed to a whitish liquid (*chyle*). The blood fueled the body's fires and replenished its semen, the fluid containing the seeds of new human life; the feces (ashes or cinders) were excreted. That, at least, was the Greek theory. Indian and Chinese theories were much the same. Indian physicians postulated fires that sequentially digested food, sloughing off gross matter and liberating finer body or spirit: blood and feces; flesh and thick urine; fat and sweat; bone, marrow, and semen. For Chinese Taoists, a "Triple Burner" in the stomach and intestines cooked food into sweat, saliva, gastric juices, and finally blood.

What we call fermenting was a puzzle. Was this what happened when cooking tipped into rotting, putrefaction, and corruption? Was it, with its bubbling, linked to the fizzing when salts were mixed with acids, as some classical philosophers believed? Or did those bubbles place it with liquids boiling in a cauldron, making it just another form of cooking, as the Taoists may have believed? Pregnant Chinese women were excluded from kitchens when fermenting was taking place for fear that the seed cooking in the womb would interfere with the ferment cooking in the jar.[106] Until the sixteenth century, the theory that fermenting was cooking was the majority opinion. It was to be another three centuries before the scientists began to understand the phenomenon.

Food, like everything in the cosmos, was made of three to five basic elements or principles—such as fire, water, wood, iron, and air—which, unlike elements as we understand them, could be combined in any proportions.[107] In Greek and Indian theory, one of these elements predominated in each of the fluids that circulated through the cosmos and through human bodies as the humors. Different places in the cosmos had different balances of fluids. The Indus Valley was a place of hot, dry fluids, said the ancient Indians, the Ganges of hot, moist ones. The pasty color and phlegmatic temperament of the Celts resulted from the cold, wet fluids of the north, said Galen, following Hippocrates, and the swarthy color and bilious temperament of Africans from the hot, dry fluids of the south. The Greeks and Romans congratulated themselves that the balance of fluids in their own lands best conduced to physical, moral, and intellectual health.

In the body, said the Indian doctors, wind (*vata*) corresponded to air or wind or breath and was associated with breathing and the beating of the heart. Bile (*pitta*) corresponded to fire and was associated with digestion of both food and ideas. Phlegm (*kapha*) corresponded to water and was associated with the smooth working of the body. The Indian tradition distinguished three extremes of temperament: hot and fiery (*rajasic*), calm and peaceful (*sattvic*), and dull and slothful (*tamasic*). (In the Hippocratic tradition, the predominant humor, be it blood, phlegm, yellow bile, or black bile, determined whether a person's temperament was sanguine, choleric, phlegmatic, or melancholic.) An individual's temperament could be changed by eating foods that corrected imbalance. Meat and alcohol, for example were widely regarded as heating, chicken and rice as neutral and well balanced, and vegetables as cooling. Indian physicians classified cinnamon, powdered ginger, nutmeg, and vegetable oils as heating, and fennel, green cardamom, cloves, and ghee as cooling, and cooks used them with that in mind.

Every individual was locked into a place, not only in the social hierarchy, but in the cosmos, and in a series of correspondences that linked the fluids, the temperament, colors, bodily organs, seasons, and age of the individual (tables 1.1, 1.2, 1.3, 1.4, 1.5).[108] The healthiest place to be was where you were born, where your humors and the fluids circulating through the universe were in harmony. To move away was to expose yourself to great danger. In the ancient world, the widely held humoral theory and theory of correspondences ensured that most individuals were culinary determinists, believing that what you ate made you what you were in strength, temperament, intelligence, and social rank.

Food, from another perspective, was anything that the body could turn into tissues and fluids or, using the technical term of the medieval Arab physician Avicenna, assimilate (making unlike like). Poisons, by contrast, assimilated flesh and

TABLE 1.1 Cosmological Correspondences in the Classical World

Elements	Air	Fire	Earth	Water
Qualities	Hot, moist	Hot, dry	Cold, dry	Cold, moist
Seasons	Spring	Summer	Autumn	Winter
Humors	Blood	Yellow bile	Black bile	Phlegm
Temperaments	Sanguine	Choleric	Melancholic	Phlegmatic
Stage of life	Infancy	Youth	Adulthood	Old age

TABLE 1.2 Cosmological Correspondences in India

Temperament	Characteristics	Colors	Bodily equivalents	Foods
Active *(rajas)*	Hot, active, passionate	Red	Blood	Meat, alcohol
Balanced *(sattva)*	Cool, light, pure, virtuous	White, yellow, green	Semen, milk	Butter, sugar, white rice
Inert *(tamas)*	Heavy, dull, stupid, dark, evil	Black, purple	Fat	Stale foods

TABLE 1.3 Cosmological Correspondences in Persia

Humor	Nature	Color	Taste	Bodily location	Social class	Activity
Blood	Warm, moist	Red	Sweet	Liver	Priests	Teaching
Phlegm	Cold, moist	White	Salt	Lung	Warriors	Fighting
Red bile	Warm, dry	Red-yellow	Bitter	Gall bladder	Pastoralists, farmers	Producing and serving food
Black bile	Cold, dry	Dark	Sour	Spleen	Artisans	Menial work

TABLE 1.4 Cosmological Correspondences in China

Phases	Wood	Fire	Earth	Metal	Water
Seasons	Spring	Summer	—	Autumn	Winter
Direction	East	South	Center	West	North
Taste	Sour	Bitter	Sweet	Pungent	Salty
Smell	Goaty	Burning	Fragrant	Rank	Rotten
Color	Blue-green	Red	Yellow	White	Black
Climate	Windy	Hot	Damp	Dry	Cold

TABLE 1.5 Cosmological Correspondences in Mesoamerica

Soul	In the head	In the heart	In the liver
Family	Father/masculine	Children	Mother/feminine
Qualities	Warm, dry	—	Cold, wet
Color	Red	—	White
Direction	East	—	West
Cosmos	Upper heaven	Lower heaven	Underworld

blood to themselves, causing pain and often death. The more similar food was to human flesh and blood, the more easily it was assimilated, and the more nutritious it was. Cooked foods were the easiest, cultivated (partially cooked) foods the next, raw (crude) wild foods the hardest. Sick bodies, out of balance, needed correction, one of the rare occasions that justified eating raw foods. Egyptian villagers saw raw foods as medicines, raw radishes being an antidote to poisoning, cabbage a prophylactic against drunkenness.[109] Food and medicine formed a continuum everywhere in the ancient world.

Oil, water, salt, air, spices, aromatics, and colored foods each had special significance. Oil, in the classical world and probably elsewhere, was believed to be congealed fire (as ice was congealed water), and contained the spark of life. Water, like fire, was at once an agent and an element. It was the ultimate ingredient, thought the Taoists, tasteless itself, but capable of combining other flavors into a harmonious blend.[110] Air was brain food, according to Galen, charging the blood with vital spirits and keeping it cool. It was persistently rumored that air alone sustained saints and holy men and women. Pure, sweet air was therapeutic, while foul airs were poisonous, so cities were sited away from marshes and miasmas and the houses of the wealthy were built out of range of noxious fumes. Eat breath, not grains, said the Taoists.[111] *Ch'i*, a yet more tenuous fluid, whose character was made up of components that read as "vapors arising from rice or millet (food)," suffused the universe. Linked with semen, this was the essence, energy, or strength, derived from food, that allowed the body to grow, develop, and act. Food with air as the predominant element, said Indian physicians, energized and mobilized.

Salts (understood as crystals that dissolved in water) were a panacea, particularly effective against worms, which plagued city dwellers. They prevented food and bodies from rotting or corrupting, thus halting the culinary cycle. A little brought out the flavor of bland food, without being noticeable as salt. The Egyptian *natron* (a word related to words for god and for incense), a naturally occurring mix of sodium chloride, carbonate, bicarbonate, and sulfate that could be found in dry riverbeds in the desert, preserved foods, kept boiled vegetables green and alive looking, turned sand heated in a furnace into blue-green glass, sweetened the air in temples, and preserved the disemboweled corpses of pharaohs.[112]

Spices, aromatics, and colored substances defied cold, dark, dank death. Aromatics, such as cloves, cinnamon, myrrh, camphor, and sandalwood, wafted the sweet odors of life. Green foods suggested life, red ones, blood and alcohol, white ones, milk and semen, yellow ones, the power of the sun. Gold and silver, beaten to ethereal thinness and draped over dishes, amber, jade, and pearls ground to powders and added to wine, and jade carved into drinking cups captured or reflected the life-giving essences of the sun and the moon.

In the ancient world, the rules that governed cooking and eating could be simplified to three: that you should eat according to your rank in society and place in the cosmos; that you should eat food cooked as thoroughly as possible; and that you should participate in the exemplary meal, the feast that followed the sacrifice to the gods. Did everyone obey these rules? Of course not, no more than we today follow all the rules laid down by well-meaning nutritionists. The ruling classes ate raw fruit, enjoying the frisson. The humble were delighted if they could get the powerful's leftovers. And the sacrifice could be treated with less than reverence. Does that mean the rules did not matter? Again, of course not. They laid out what was acceptable behavior and its boundaries. Diners might cross these, but they did so knowingly and at their own risk.

REFLECTIONS ON ANCIENT CUISINES

However much we may admire the artistry of ancient high cuisine, the skill and dedication of the cooks, the technical advances in food processing and kitchen technique, it's hard not to be horrified by the inequitable social system that produced a gulf between high and humble cuisines and reinforced it with rules. The issue is not specific to high cuisine, but is raised by art, music, literature, architecture, and fine clothing, the patrimony of the human race, though the inequities seem particularly poignant in the case of cuisine. Weren't those who consumed high cuisines ashamed?

It was a question that lurked behind discussions of food and politics for centuries to come, prompting the critics to create countercuisines. Ancient culinary philosophy was constantly questioned and threatened. Many saw the overweening appetite of the hierarchical state as destroying the earlier, more virtuous life of those who worked the land. As rulers arrogated to themselves the right to perform the most powerful and expensive sacrifices, sending food up in smoke, Greek philosophers, Taoists, Jews, and Christians came to reject the official state cuisine. In particular, they tended to refuse to eat the meat that had been offered in sacrifice, the meal that bound state, people, and the gods together. They created new culinary rules that, as we shall see in chapters 3, 4, and 5, were to underpin new kinds of cuisines, which I call theocratic or traditional cuisines.

However, for millennia many thought there was no escape from the sharp social distinctions signaled by high and humble cuisines. "Poverty . . . is a most necessary and indispensable ingredient in society, without which nations and communities could not exist in a state of civilisation," the Scottish merchant and statistician Patrick Colquhoun, turned London magistrate, said in 1806, ironically in an argument for raising people from destitution and misery to mere poverty. "It is the lot of man—it is the source of wealth, since without poverty there would be no labour, and without labour there could be no riches, no refinement, no comfort, and no benefit to those who may be possessed of wealth."[113] And weren't the poor resentful that they could not eat rich meats, sauces, and sweets and dubious about the rule that each rank in society needed a distinct diet? Many of the folk sayings I have quoted suggest so.

The division of cuisines into high and humble continued until the late nineteenth century, when economies of scale in food processing, combined with rising incomes, cheaper transport, and changes in farming in the richer parts of the world, made modern cuisines available to their population. Most people in these countries now eat middling cuisine, not as elaborate as earlier high cuisines but sharing many of its features. Middling cuisine is high in meats, fats, and sweets and exotic ingredients from around the globe, and low in carbohydrate staples. Often it is prepared by professional cooks in processing plants or restaurants, not by the woman of the house. It is eaten in special areas with special utensils and off special plates. And it is recorded and debated in an enormous culinary literature—cookbooks, restaurant reviews, newspaper food pages, and culinary magazines, as well as the general press.

Were there no middling cuisines in the past that bridged the gap between high and humble? The answer is, largely, no. In big cities such as Rome, Baghdad, Cairo, Alexandria, Hangzhou, and Edo the gentry, richer merchants, and professionals could become wealthy enough to be called a bourgeoisie. In seventeenth-century Europe, say, they made up about 4 to 5 percent of the population. They and medium landowners could afford to emulate high cuisines. The merchants in particular had little status, however. "The offspring of a toad is a toad and the offspring of a merchant is a merchant," was the saying in Japan, and parallel expressions were found elsewhere. In short, those who could afford middling cuisines were a small minority and one without much clout. They did not create a large market for processed foods, operating more like scaled-down versions of the court than today's urban middle classes.

The humble, constantly at risk of real hunger, had every reason not to experiment with innovative cooking techniques. When your stock of grain is diminishing daily, when you know you must preserve enough to sow the next year's crop, you are not apt to waste precious reserves on experiments that might fail. You might try, or be forced to try, new plants. The natural response was to pound or grind them in the tried and true way. When the Chinese poor adopted a high-yielding rice in the Middle Ages or Italians and Romanians adopted maize following the discovery of the Americas, more people stayed alive, but styles of cooking remained the same.

High cuisines were knitted together in a far-flung network from very early times; humble cuisines were frequently isolated from the contacts that led to innovation, condemned to the parochialism of the local. High cuisines were the engine of culinary change, generating most of the techniques now taken for granted: baking white bread, polishing rice until it is white, refining sugar, creating soy and béchamel, preparing chocolate candy, pies, and cakes. Ships set sail, factories were erected, and capital was accumulated to buy luxuries such as spices, tea, porcelain, and silver. As the German sociologist Werner Sombart noted almost a century ago, luxury, not necessity, has been an engine of change. So of all the widespread cuisines surveyed at the beginning of this chapter, most culinary change occurred in grain cuisines, and within grain cuisines in high cuisines.

The Barley-Wheat Sacrificial Cuisines of the Ancient Empires, 500 B.C.E.–400 C.E.

The millennium between 500 B.C.E. and 400 C.E. saw the continued creation across Eurasia of large empires. All were now based on barley and wheat, grains that were relatively easy to transport and store and that came as close as any foodstuff to providing a nutritionally complete diet. New varieties of wheat appeared, high in gluten and easier to process because the hull was not bound so tightly to the grain. New and appealing wheat products were developed. By the end of the period wheat had overtaken barley and millet as the source of calories—the human fuel—of the ruling classes of the Eurasian empires. It had become the most prestigious grain, a position it was to maintain (along with rice, which was soon to surge in importance) until the present.

To be a king of kings, to create and maintain an empire, a ruler had to extract enough barley and wheat to feed a large army and the functionaries and workers in the palace-city, without leaving those who farmed the land destitute. He had to be able to deliver this food to the court and to the army.[1] The foodstuffs had to be processed into storable supplies of food and cooked for large numbers of people. The more efficiently the food was processed, the more effective the storage, and the more palatable and nutritious the dishes, the more munificent the emperor could be, which resulted in more alert and energetic people to fight in the army, run the bureaucracy, build the palaces and temples, and make the clothes, jewelry, and gorgeous adornments of the court. This millennium thus saw more surplus grain extracted from humble, rural people, new and longer grain routes, more efficient food processing, and more elaborate cooking.

Beliefs in the hierarchical principle, the sacrificial bargain, and the culinary cosmos of ancient culinary philosophy were the default position of imperial elites.

The cuisines of conquered peoples, both the former ruling families and the religious minorities, had to be fitted into these categories. Members of the emperor's family were appointed to regional governorships, spreading his cuisine throughout the empire. Many also intermarried with members of the conquered royal families, leading to integration of imperial cuisines. Military personnel were frequently settled in new territories or given land grants, again spreading the imperial cuisine. Government officials, military men, and camp followers joined merchants and migrants as agents in the dispersion and consolidation of high cuisines.

The tendency toward homogenizing monarchical cuisines across empires was counteracted by two factors. First, the place of the monarch at the peak of the human hierarchy was frequently questioned by individuals and states, who then tried out alternatives. Second, minority religious groups challenged the practices of sacrifice and the sacrificial feast, suggesting alternative ways of thinking about the gods, alternatives that were gradually to lead to the creation of new cuisines (chapters 3, 4, and 5). Thus the millennium saw the canvassing of a large succession of alternatives to ancient culinary philosophy and a proliferation of cuisines.

The Persian Achaemenid Empire (550–330 B.C.E.), larger by far than any previous empire, was the bridge between the cuisine created over thousands of years in Mesopotamia and subsequent Eurasian empires. Because it was so powerful, its cuisine became a touchstone, sparking a debate about imperial high cuisine that resurfaced at intervals up until the nineteenth century. The Greeks, who had been invaded by the Achaemenids, were divided. In one camp were those who wanted to emulate Achaemenid cuisine. In another were the Spartans and Socrates, who, for all their differences, were united in rejecting the refined Achaemenid cuisine. Both Alexander the Great's Macedonians, who conquered the Achaemenids and founded the Hellenistic empires, and the rulers of the Mauryan Empire in northern India looked to the Persians for models of empire and cuisine.

The Roman and Han empires, which became the largest and most important ancient empires, were also divided regarding imperial cuisine. For centuries, the Romans depended on a plain republican diet. With the gradual shift from republic to empire, many adopted and adapted the Hellenistic high cuisine created under Alexander and his successors. In the Han Empire, centered in the Yellow River Valley, Confucians advocated a plain cuisine, while large landowners turned to Taoism to underpin a refined, luxurious high cuisine. Only in the Americas, which lacked barley and wheat, did a different grain—maize—provide the staple food for large, sophisticated states.

FROM MESOPOTAMIAN CUISINE
TO PERSIAN ACHAEMENID IMPERIAL CUISINE

In 645 B.C.E., Ashurbanipal, the last king of the Assyrian Empire, gave a feast in his capital, Nineveh, where he reportedly entertained seventy thousand guests over a

FIGURE 2.1. This reproduction of a panel known as the "Garden Party" relief, from the North Palace in Nineveh, Iraq, about 645 B.C.E., forms the centerpiece of a series celebrating King Ashurbanipal's triumphs in war and sport. Ashurbanipal reclines on a high couch drinking wine from a shallow cup, with his queen seated at his feet. In the shade of vines, the symbol of fecundity, the pair are fanned by attendants. Not shown here are the harpist providing harmonies and, directly in Ashurbanipal's line of vision, the severed head of the defeated Teumman, king of Elam in western Persia. From a print by the nineteenth-century French artist Charles Goutz-willer. Courtesy New York Public Library, http://digitalgallery.nypl.org/nypldigital/id?1619810.

ten-day period (fig. 2.1).[2] Accounts emphasize alcohol and meat, including sacrificed domestic animals and wild game killed in the hunt. A thousand cattle, a thousand calves, ten thousand sheep, and fifteen thousand lambs were sacrificed. Five hundred each of stags and gazelles, ducks, geese, and doves, as well as tens of thousands of smaller birds were killed in the hunt. Ten thousand fish were rushed to Nineveh from the rivers and ocean. Ten thousand eggs were collected. Ten thousand loaves of bread were baked. Ten thousand jars of beer were brewed, and ten thousand skins filled with wine were delivered. All those in the ancient world who heard about this extravagant feast would have understood that the dishes prepared from this list of provisions would not have simply been eaten on the spot by the king and his guests. Exhibiting munificence by distributing leftovers was an important part of the ceremony.

For five hundred years, the formerly nomadic Persians on the high plains east of Mesopotamia had been paying tribute, at least nominally, to the rich states of Babylonia and Assyria and observing the lavish feasting. In the sixth century B.C.E., Cyrus the Persian led his army down to flat, barley-rich Mesopotamia and conquered the land where Gilgamesh had wandered and Ur had seen the first recipes.[3] Between about 550 and 540 B.C.E., he went on to take all the land from the borders of India in the east to Egypt and much of what is today Turkey in the west. He called himself "King of Kings," ruling over seventy different peoples, each with their own language, king, and gods.

The Achaemenid Empire Cyrus established (named after Achaemenes, the legendary founder of the dynasty) was the largest the world had yet seen. It inaugurated a thousand years of predominantly Persian rule in the region, the Achaemenids succeeded by the Seleucids, the Parthians, and the Sassanids. Following the conquest, the business of ruling a large empire began. Many aspects—establishing legitimacy, dealing with the conquered and minority peoples, improving the food supply with agricultural, research, and infrastructure innovations, provisioning the capital and armies, and dramatizing benevolence by way of the king's feast— were connected with cuisine.

The conquering Persians, whose traditional cuisine had consisted of barley gruels and bannocks, lentils and vetches, fresh and dried ewe-milk yogurt and fresh cheese, roasted or boiled beef, lamb, and goat, greens and herbs, and dried fruits and nuts, had probably already adopted the high cuisine of Mesopotamia developed over thousands of years.[4] They sacrificed to the gods and Darius I, Cyrus's successor, aligned himself with the ritual of sacrifice in the newly evolving Zoroastrian religion. He claimed he had been chosen by Ahura Mazda, the supreme Zoroastrian god, to rescue the earth from evil and from the foods associated with it. According to Zoroastrian myth, Ahura Mazda created the sky, then the earth, then humans, and finally happiness for humans: truth, peace, and abundant food. The earth was blessed with clear fresh water, flourishing green plants, beneficent animals, and sweet fruits unprotected by skins, shells, or thorns, on which humans, unburdened with physical bodies, dined without needing to kill. Then evil entered the cosmos, turning it into a battleground: sun fought against night, summer against winter, good against bad, truth against falsehood, the garden against the desert, a sunny disposition against dark despair, and life against death. Fruits became armored with thorns, skins, and shells and tasted acid and bitter. Humans became weighed down with flesh and blood and had to eat leaves, roots, and grains and to kill animals for their meat. When they died, their bodies decayed, the putrefying flesh crawling with maggots and the air filled with a foul stench. On September 29, 522 B.C.E., the supreme god ordered Darius to lead his troops into war to return the world to virtue, at least according to an inscription that Darius himself ordered.[5] This myth of an earlier, lost age in which humans could live on fruits and vegetables parallels those found in the Old Testament and classical works.

Part of returning the world to virtue was to eat good foods that had been touched by the purifying holy fire, the symbol of righteousness—those that had been cooked, in short. The Persian root word for cooking (*pac*) means for make edible by fire. Milk, the food of purity and innocence, came ready-cooked by fire in the mother's body. So did honey, cooked by bees, the one insect good for humans. Other foodstuffs had to be heated. Chickens (which the Persians perhaps introduced from India and ultimately Southeast Asia) were seen as good because the rooster's crow heralded the return of light. Eggs were good because the concentric shell, white, and yolk echoed the cosmic spheres. Green herbs were reminders of Paradise. Eating sparingly of cooked foods, bread, meat, and wine, digesting and assimilating them without problem, turning them into blood and spirit, created good men whose bodies wafted a sweet scent. Raw foods, untouched by purifying fire, were bad. Worms, grubs, maggots, and lizards were also embodiments of evil. Bad men were those who gorged themselves, were slaves to the demon of uncontrolled appetite, ate raw foods and insects, and stank and shat to excess. The locusts that the people of Ur had enjoyed vanished from the menu.

Established religions with different gods were allowed to continue their practices, including their culinary practices. The temple of Inanna in Uruk, for example, continued to sacrifice three to four thousand lambs a year to the goddess. Two bureaus, their staff supported by temple rations, administered the herding of tens of thousands of sheep and goats for the purpose.[6]

The Jews, who fifty years before Cyrus's conquests had seen Jerusalem captured and Solomon's Temple destroyed by the Babylonians in 586 B.C.E., were offered the choice of staying in Mesopotamia, where they had been taken as captives, or returning to Jerusalem to rebuild the temple. Jewish culinary rules were laid out in Leviticus and other books of the Old Testament. Blood, animals with cloven hooves unless they chewed their cud, pork, animals with both fins and scales who lived in the water, and (echoing Persian practice) insects were all forbidden as foods. So was cooking meat in milk and dining with non-Jews. Temple priests followed rules of purification before sacrifice, slaughtered animals so that the lifeblood drained out, and refrained from offering impure fermented (corrupted) foods.

In the mid-twentieth century, scholars offered opposing interpretations of Jewish food rules, particularly the ban on pork. Marvin Harris argued that they were health measures to prevent infection by trichinosis, a parasitic disease caused by eating raw or lightly cooked pork or game infected with the larvae of the roundworm *Trichinella spiralis,* which can produce symptoms from diarrhea to death. Mary Douglas and Jean Soler contended that they were designed to create a distinct Jewish identity.[7] The latter interpretation squares better with the simultaneous proliferation of culinary rules in the Persian Empire and Indian states. With limited culinary resources, identity is most easily established by banning certain foodstuffs, cooking methods, and ways of dining. Pigs, being difficult to herd, were not popular with peoples of nomadic origin, so the force of the rule probably only became fully felt centuries later when Jews became a minority in pork-eating Roman or Christian lands.

Provisioning the cities and armies of the empire was a constant preoccupation, requiring several strategies, including increasing the supply of edible plants and improving farming. To these ends, the Persians created gardens. Planted with shade trees and other plants, laid out in pleasing geometrical patterns and filled with decorative, exotic, or huntable animals, these were in part models of the virtuous world, the paradise, that they wanted to restore in their dry, dusty lands.[8] In part, they were places to hunt to practice skills needed in warfare. And in part, they were research stations where useful or beautiful plants from all parts of the empire could be acclimatized and ennobled (a process akin to cooking in the culinary cosmogony). Darius ordered the governors of Asia Minor, and doubtless those of all the satrapies into which his empire was divided, to naturalize Mesopotamian and Persian plants, particularly high-quality grapevines. Gardens, orchards, and even fields were irrigated by miles of underground irrigation channels (qanats), the water raised by norias, bucket-rimmed wheels moved by the force of water or by donkeys that trudged in circles.

Staging posts along the new roads for government mail, couriers, administrators, and armies held stockpiles of requisitioned food. Traveling merchants carried aromatics from Arabia, spices from India, and oil and wine from Greece. The imperial cavalcade of Darius, King of Kings, his crack bodyguard and star troops, the ten thousand so-called Immortals in their gloriously colored robes, with spears tipped with silver or gold pomegranates, moved from city to city.[9] Mules pulled four-wheeled carts laden with silver vessels containing the drinking water for the king and his eldest son, water taken from the seventy bubbling pools in the Choaspes River and boiled. (Centuries later, Cicero was to point to this to show how overpampered appetites endangered the state.) Among the camp followers were close to four hundred kitchen staff: two hundred and seventy-seven cooks, twenty-nine scullery boys, thirteen dairy workers, and seventy wine filterers. In all probability, a horde of servants, secretaries, seers, physicians, poets, surveyors, soothsayers, traders, musicians, courtesans, women, and children would have followed Darius. At nightfall, huge tents were set up, the beginning of a tradition of mobile courts that was to continue until the nineteenth century in India.

Four separate capitals, with Persepolis at the apex, were constructed. Their climates were suitable for different seasons, allowing the emperor to move about comfortably to inspect his territory, dazzle his subjects, and collect their tribute. Since these landlocked capitals could gather only limited amounts of barley and wheat, it probably also made sense to move the entourage to a new capital when food from the last harvest ran out.

Tribute and taxes were collected from across the empire. A relief carved on the stairs leading to Darius's audience hall in Persepolis shows his subjects bringing beautifully worked silver vessels, cattle, camels, and donkeys. Not shown were offerings of the finest bread wheat from Anatolia, the most delicious wine from the Damascus region, the tastiest rock salt from Arabia, the scented thorn oil from the Persian Gulf region, and the limpid water from the river Choaspes. In addition, fruits, vegetables, poultry, fish, oil, wine, and beer flowed in. "The tax-payers should keep only as much of their cultivated produce as suffices for their subsistence and the cultivation of their lands," a later Persian emperor decreed in the third century B.C.E., an order that was to be repeated by rulers around the world and down the centuries.[10] In 500 B.C.E., the imperial court collected 800,000 liters of grains, enough to feed fifteen hundred people, presumably the bureaucracy and central bodyguard, for a year.[11] Grain from the emperor's landholdings probably made up the difference needed for his ten thousand troops. Parnaka, Darius's uncle and chief administrative officer for the region around Persepolis, kept careful records on tablets of the provisions that entered and of how they were distributed.

A Greek, Polyaenus, reported that a bronze pillar was inscribed with the rations for the dinner and supper for Cyrus, as well as with his laws.[12] Although the quantities are hard to interpret, this and other sources make it possible to reconstruct the types of foods served in Achaemenid palaces, including

Wheat flour and barley flour of various grades (probably for serving to guests of different ranks)

Oxen, horses, rams, geese, doves, and small birds, presumably slaughtered

Fresh, fermented, and sweetened milk

Seasonings and condiments of garlic and onions, silphium juice (a culinary and medicinal herb shortly to become extinct), apple juice, pomegranate juice, cumin, dill, celery seed, and mustard seed, and turnip pickles and capers (perhaps for sour sauces)

Ghee and oils made of sesame, terebinth (probably of the pistachio family), acanthus, and almond

Date and grape wine

Fruitcake made with sweet resin (perhaps one of the flourless "cakes" of fruits and nuts still found across the Mediterranean)

Firewood

In short, the imperial kitchens were taking their tribute and adding value to it by processing the grains into flour, the seeds into oils, the milk into yogurt, the fruits into juices for souring. With coinage only just then coming into use, what other option was there? Payment largely in kind, that is, foodstuffs or cooked food, was common until very recently and is still an important form of payment in much of the world.

The Achaemenids continued the tradition of hosting lavish dinners. Guests arrived and were seated according to a protocol that established rank, reflected in the careful placement of tables and couches, the dishes they were offered, and the frequent hand washing and drying, with constantly replenished clean napkins. Probably the emperor sacrificed to Ahura Mazda, while sacred fires burned and magi took the sacred and mysterious *haoma*, prayed, and chanted from the Zend Avesta. "I desire to approach the Myazda-offering with my praise, as it is consumed, and likewise Ameretat (as the guardian of plants and wood) and Haurvatat (who guards the water), with the (fresh) meat for the propitiation of Ahura Mazda." The fat from the sacrificed animal sizzled in the sacred fire, emitting a delicious aroma and sending smoke up to the god.[13]

Meanwhile, the cooks, each with his own specialty, labored in the kitchens. "It is all one man can do to stew meats and another to roast them, one man to boil fish and another to bake them, for another to make bread and not every sort at that, but where it suffices if he makes one kind that has a high reputation," reported Xenophon, who had seen or at least heard about these vast kitchens when serving as a Greek mercenary in the Persian army.[14] Any cook who invented a new delicacy received a reward.

Even on ordinary days, the cooks prepared the thousand animals reportedly sacrificed for the king's table: horses, camels, oxen, asses, ostriches from Arabia, geese, and cocks. For the annual dinner, lamb, kid, beef, gazelle, and horse were baked whole, an extravagant use of fuel in a fuel-short land. It is reasonable to assume that sauces that went back to Sumerian times were prepared. A Greek writer referred to the sauce *kandalous* of western Anatolia (then called Lydia), made of "boiled meat, breadcrumbs, [fresh] Phrygian cheese, dill or anise [*anethon*], and fatty meat stock," recognizably of the same genre as the sauces described on Babylonian tablets.[15] Guests drank palm or grape wine neat from elaborate chased silver horns and jars. After the meats and sauces, they were offered fruits, nuts, and confections made from sesame oil, honey, barley meal, and fresh cheese. Diners would have understood all these foods in terms of the culinary cosmogony and correspondences (table 1.3). The grilled locusts or grasshoppers so relished in earlier centuries did not appear: they had been reclassified as "bad" foods.

The guests were given food, silver and gold drinking horns, and tableware according to rank and favor, tangible reminders of the emperor's munificence. In return, his subjects offered loyalty and agreed to be "the king's eyes and ears," sending him intelligence about anything untoward going on in his realms. Xenophon, from a society that was debating whether the hierarchy of benevolence was appropriate for its own city-states, was contemptuous. Gifts to humans produced loyalty "just as it does in dogs."[16]

GREEK CUISINES AS RESPONSES
TO ACHAEMENID CUISINE

The Greeks knew a good bit about the high cuisine of their Persian neighbor. Some had traded with the Persians, establishing colonies in their territory, others had been mercenaries in the Persian army, and one, Xenophon, had written about the experience.[17] The Greek part of western Turkey had been taken by the Persians, and the Greek mainland had been invaded time and again, with Athens sacked in 480 B.C.E. After fighting that had dragged on intermittently for nearly a hundred years, the Greeks finally defeated the Persians in 450 B.C.E.

In the different city-states, along with lively debates about political life, the Greeks argued the merits of the Persian culinary politics with its lavish feasting and gift-giving to buy loyalty. Many thought Achaemenid cuisine exemplified the gargantuan desires of a despotic state, desires that led to an insatiable search for new resources and wars of aggression such as those suffered by the Greeks. By contrast, the Greeks described themselves as an abstemious people who dined mainly on vegetables, or, as they put it, leaf-chewers who had "nothing more than little tables."[18]

The key political-religious-culinary ceremony in the Greek states, as in other ancient states, was the sacrifice and the following feast. One of the most important occurred during the Olympic games, held from the eighth century B.C.E. on, but at their most flourishing in the fourth and fifth centuries B.C.E.[19] Every four years, forty thousand men from the different city-states gathered in the fertile, well-wooded valley of Olympia, shaded by mountain peaks, to watch chariot races, boxing, wrestling, javelin throwing, and foot races in the hippodrome and stadium.

Mid-morning on the third day of the games, priests began the sacrifice in the temple of Zeus, topped by a forty-foot ivory and gold statue of Zeus created by the famous sculptor Phidias. On the altar, ash from years of sacrifice, held together with water from the nearby River Alpheus, towered twenty feet into the air. One by one, a hundred oxen, draped with garlands, raised especially for the event and without marks of the plow, were led to the altar. The priest washed his hands in clear water in special metal vessels, poured out libations of wine, and sprinkled the animals with cold water or with grain to make them shake their heads as if consenting to their death. The onlookers raised their right arms to the altar. Then the priest stunned the lead ox with a blow to the base of the neck, thrust in the knife, and let the blood spill into a bowl held by a second priest. The killing would have gone on all day, even if each act took only five minutes.

Assistants dragged each felled ox to one side to be skinned and butchered. For the assembled crowd, cooks began grilling strips of beef, boiling bones in cauldrons, baking barley bannocks, and stacking up amphorae of wine. For the sacrifice, fat and leg and thigh bones rich in life-giving marrow were thrown on a fire of fragrant poplar branches, and the entrails were grilled. Symbolizing union, two or three priests bit together into each length of intestines. The bones whitened and crumbled; the fragrant smoke rose to the god.

As the sky darkened, the feast began. Each participant was served meat sprinkled with holy salt, barley bannocks, and watered wine. "The whole company raised a great cheer, while the lovely light of the fair-faced moon lit up the evening. Then in joyful celebration the whole Altis [sacred grove] rang with the banquet song." A hundred oxen divided among forty thousand diners did not go very far as a feast, each participant receiving only a taste.

Symbolically, however, the meat was crucial. Few dared express doubts about the important civic act of eating meat.[20] When they did, the reasons had nothing to do with cruelty to animals. Empedocles (and perhaps Pythagoras) worried that if souls transmigrated, you might be eating fellow humans. Plato and other members of the Academy argued that animals as rational beings deserved better than to be eaten. The Pythagoreans, famed (perhaps wrongly) as early vegetarians, were reported to prudently eat meat from time to time. The "leaf-chewing" Greeks' objection to Persian Achaemenid cuisine was not that it included meat but that apparently gargantuan quantities were served.

So the question facing the Greeks was what to do about meals other than the sacrificial feast. The Spartans proposed the most radical alternatives to luxurious Persian cuisine, though it is hard to separate fact from fiction in accounts of the diet.[21] It is known that young boys were taken away from their families at seven, to be raised as tough soldiers. They ate communally. Black broth, possibly thickened with blood, was their most famous dish, reviled from then to now by non-Spartans. Sources suggest that the boys were discouraged from eating to excess, scarcely peculiar to Spartan society, and that they may have been trained to endure hunger, also not peculiar to the Spartans. Whatever the truth of the matter, "Spartan" cuisine was emulated or disparaged in later centuries depending on the perspective of the individual or society. Black broth was praised by the Roman republican Cato the Elder, scorned by the biographer of Roman emperors, Plutarch, and imitated by French republicans following the Revolution. In the same tradition, nineteenth-century British boarding schools dedicated to training the rulers of empire taught their pupils to endure hardship, including eating a "spartan" cuisine that was deliberately unappealing.

Other Greeks were tempted by luxurious Persian cuisine. When they defeated the Persians, the city-states were prospering, colonies were established around the Black Sea and the northern Mediterranean, and trade was expanding. Although not an empire of the Persian kind, the Greeks were to be reckoned with. The city-

FIGURE 2.2. Bas-relief on a Greek sarcophagus showing spirits making olive oil. A spirit in the center collects fallen olives. Another spirit, on the right, pushes on a bar that rotates two vertical millstones around a bowl of lava rock, crushing the olives it contains. On the left, a spirit hangs on a beam to press the oil out of the olives into jars beneath. Drawing from C. Daremberg and E. Saglio, *Dictionnaire des antiquités grecques et romaines* (Paris: Hachette, 1904–7), 4: 167, fig. 5391.

states could not, however, rely on the rich harvests of barley that sustained the empires of the Middle East. Greece's soil was thin, its rainfall erratic, and much of its terrain impossible to irrigate. Country people kept a three-year supply of grain to protect against harvest failure and a four-year supply of oil, dispersed their plots of land, and tried to cheat tax collectors by leaving weed seeds in the grain or hiding water jars in their carts to increase the weight.[22] Most of the time there was barely enough or not enough to support the cities, which had to import grain from areas such as Egypt, Italy, and the Black Sea region.

On the two-thirds of the land unsuitable for grain, the Greeks grew two crops— olives and grapes—that they were able to process into highly desirable and exportable foodstuffs: olive oil and wine. Oil was used to fry, to bind toasted barley meal, to marinate, to make sauces into which to dip bread; it was also in demand as a salve, a cosmetic, and a lubricant.[23] People had been working for millennia to discover how to maximize their profit from olive trees, one of the most unpromising of the many unpromising plants from which humans have learned to produce food—a small straggly tree that takes years to mature enough to produce tiny, bitter fruits every other year that cultivation has never succeeded in making good to eat fresh. By the third millennium B.C.E., improved varieties were being cultivated in Syria, Palestine, and Crete.

The Greeks invested in heavy machinery to extract oil from olives, as shown in the charming carving of little spirits making oil in figure 2.2. On the right, one is crushing olive oil in the *mola olearia*, two cylindrical stones rotating on a horizontal axle, a method still in use at the end of the twentieth century. The olives were then pressed to extract a mixture of oil and water, the lighter oil was allowed to float to the top, and then it was siphoned off into pottery jars with pointed bottoms (*amphorae*) for shipment to buyers. Greeks had eager customers all around the Mediterranean and in Persia.

Wine, too, could be exported because it kept reasonably well, unlike beer, which, although it could be made year-round, had to be drunk within a day or so, and hence was consumed locally.[24] The Greeks improved the cultivation of vines. When the grapes were ready, they were placed in a large container and trodden by men hanging on to handles or overhead branches for balance. The juice flowed into a vat below and then was decanted into jars up to ten feet high with mouths as much as three feet wide. Some juice (must) was used in cooking and some was boiled down to make a treacly sweetener. Most was fermented to wine and stored in five- to twenty-gallon jars lined with pitch or resin or in sheep- or goatskins. When the new wine was ready, women and men sang and danced in honor of Dionysus. Considered both a medicine and a poison, wine was said to make men forget their grief, to bring them sleep, and to help those over thirty years old combat the desiccation of old age. "There is no other medicine for misery," said the playwright Euripides.

The export wine trade was a highly regulated business. The Greek states set standard sizes for the jars and had them sealed under the watchful eye of a magistrate. Then the amphorae were shipped around the Mediterranean, into what is now France, where the wine was eagerly purchased by the Celts, and across the Black Sea to the Ukraine, where Scythian warriors toasted with it in their feasts.

As Greek city populations swelled, shiploads of colonists, with seeds of barley and wheat, slips of vines, a flame from the mother city, and a cauldron, symbol of the state, sailed to the shores of the Black Sea, Sicily, southern Italy, southern France, and southern Spain.[25] On landing, they sacrificed to the gods and then built replicas of their home cities, complete with temples and public squares and narrow streets between the houses. The colonies flourished, some supporting vineyards up to fifty acres in size, others on the coast running processing plants to turn fish into fish sauce (*garum*).

In prosperous Sicily and Athens, diners began experimenting with high cuisine. Sicily, with its rich volcanic soil, produced bumper crops of barley and wheat, some of which was shipped back to the homeland. Syracuse became famed for its gastronomy, with fine fish dishes, abundant meat, and excellent wines.[26] The earliest Greek cookbooks, now lost, were written there; we know of them from Athenaeus's *Deipnosophistae* (Philosophers at Dinner), a long discussion of dining and related matters drawing on 800 authors composed around 300 c.e. Among the sources he cites is *The Life of Luxury,* a poem written around 350 b.c.e. by Archestratus, a Sicilian Greek, describing how to find the best fish and how to prepare it.

Mainland Greece, particularly Athens, experienced a cultural flowering following the defeat of the Persians. New buildings were going up, such as the Parthenon overlooking the city, theaters were staging great dramas and side-splitting comedies, and philosophers were reflecting on fundamental problems with their coteries of followers. Private banquets followed by a drinking party, called a

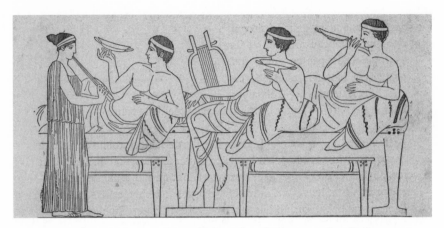

FIGURE 2.3. Three Greek men recline on high couches, drinking wine from shallow cups patterned after those of the Persians (compare the cup in fig 2.1), while being entertained by a woman musician. From René Ménard, *La vie privée des anciens: Dessins d'après les monuments antiques par Cl. Sauvageot* (Paris: Morel, 1880–83). New York Public Library, http://digitalgallery.nypl.org/nypldigital/id?1619873.

symposium (meaning drinking together), appeared as an alternative to the sacrificial feast.[27] Merchants and even successful artisans, as well as rich landowning aristocrats, now commanded enough wealth to host these all-male events. Respectable women, children, laborers, the poor, and slaves (except as servers) had no place at the gatherings.

The host would hire cooks with experience in the Persian cuisine of Asia Minor. Among the dishes they prepared were Persian-derived sauces such as *karyke*. Athenaeus cites recipes from no less than eighteen cookbooks for this sauce based on honey and must or vinegar, thickened with crumbs and flavored with herbs. Persian-style couches, each with a table in front of it, were set up in the front room of the house (fig. 2.3). Unlike the Persians, the Greeks served equal portions to all diners.[28]

The first course might be barley bannocks (*maza*) or wheat rolls, eel casserole, honey-glazed shrimp, squid sprinkled with sea salt, or tiny birds wrapped in pastry. A favored main dish was fish, preferably tuna, one of the earliest if not the earliest appearances of large fish as a luxury item.[29] It was pricey, having to be caught in the deep waters of the dangerous Mediterranean. Unlike meat, it was not sacrificed because it was believed to be bloodless, so it did not have to be whacked into equal chunks for politico-religious reasons, leaving cooks free to select the tasty shoulder (the area where the fin is attached) and belly (fig. 2.4). It encouraged a certain frisson, so digestible as to be almost dangerous because it

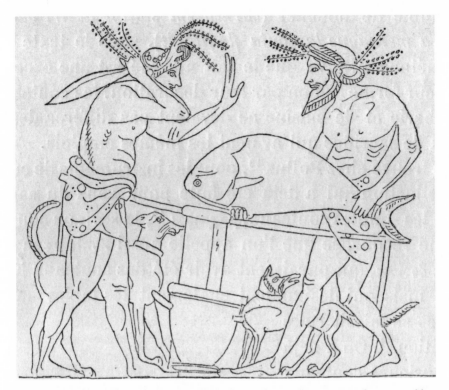

FIGURE 2.4. A man holds a tuna, a favorite food at meals preceding symposia because, unlike meat, it was not associated with sacrifices and feasts. A second man raises his knife to cut the fish, while two dogs hope for scraps. Drawing of a vase in the Berlin Museum in C. Daremberg and E. Saglio, *Dictionnaire des antiquités grecques et romaines* (Paris: Hachette, 1904–7), 1, part 2, 1586, fig. 2123.

putrefied so readily, according to humoral theory. For dessert, diners nibbled on delicacies such as sweet pastry shells, crispy flapjacks, toasted sesame cakes in honey sauce, cheesecake of milk and honey, deep-fried fresh cheese, and sesame tidbits rolled in sesame seeds. Dishes would have been carefully prepared to balance the humors (table 1.1).

Then the host poured a libation of wine for the gods and a hymn was sung. For the guests, he mixed wine and water in a beautifully decorated vessel, either three parts water to one part wine, or three parts water to two parts wine, making it about the strength of today's beer. Taken neat, as the Persians took it, it might madden or even kill young men by fueling their already dangerously bright internal fires. The slaves poured wine into the shallow cups of the waiting company. Now the men, free of the strict rules of sacrifice, debated affairs of state, discussed philosophy, observed how up-and-coming young men conducted themselves, played party games, got drunk, and bedded young slave boys and courtesans. Everyone drank at the same rate, nibbling on fresh young chickpeas in a safflower dip, eggs, almonds so young the skin was still soft, and walnuts. Beautiful slave boys poured more wine. For all its Persian influences, Greek high cuisine was prepared primarily from local foods, included only small portions of meat and few spices, and featured watered wine. It was served in equal portions to free citizens.

Even so, this new high cuisine struck many Greeks as effeminate and gluttonous. Comedians poked fun at self-important cooks who boasted that their work was based in the science of the schools of Sikon and Sophon and depended on knowledge of literature, philosophy, astrology, architecture, strategy, medicine, Democritus, and Epicurus.[30] Gluttony should be avoided, said Plato in the *Timaeus,* particularly by those who wished to be philosophers; otherwise, they would be "incapable of philosophy and music, deaf to the voice of our divinest part." Human guts, he suggested, wound and coiled to slow the passage of food so that humans would not be at the mercy of their appetites.[31]

Plato attacked high cuisine in more detail in the *Republic,* probably written about 370 B.C.E.[32] He did not need to identify it as Persian. Evoking a virtuous past as a template for the cuisine of an ideal city, he described how the citizens would "prepare their respective flours from barley and from wheat, baking bread from the wheat and kneading fine cakes from the barley, all to be placed on rushes or clean fresh leaves. They . . . [would] feast, they and their children, drinking their wine, garlanded, singing hymns to the gods, and living pleasantly together."

One of his companions, Glaucon, protested. Bread and wine, eaten on the ground rather than on raised couches, were for pigs, not Greek citizens. "If you were providing for a city of pigs, Socrates, isn't that just what you would feed them on? . . . If they are not going to be uncomfortable, I think they should recline on couches and dine off tables and eat the relish and desserts that they now have."

Socrates conceded that "they will have relish—salt, of course, and olives and cheese, and . . . they will boil up bulbs and other vegetables, as they do now in the country. And perhaps we will serve them desserts, figs and chickpeas and beans, and they will parch myrtle-berries and acorns in the ashes, and will drink moderately with their meals. And with a peaceful and healthy life of this kind, they will no doubt reach old age and pass on a similar style of life to their offspring." Glaucon was not reassured. Acorns were for the rural poor, not for the city dwellers. "There must be couches and tables, too, and all the other paraphernalia, and relish and myrrh and incense and party girls and cakes, and each of these in great variety."

Socrates responded that his was the true and healthy city, lean and fit. Many would find it inadequate, he conceded, so he would have to consider the bloated, luxurious city the "city with inflammation." Luxurious food and drink stimulated the appetite, making individuals and cities alike ravenous, causing avarice, leading to armies and to despotism, in short, to states such as Persia. His objection was not that the Persian state was unfair, unjust, or unequal: it was that it was expansionist and war-mongering.

Plato's criticism was directed at the Persians. In the rough frontier territory north of Greece, however, Philip II of Macedonia was restoring order, strengthening his army, and planning military campaigns. In 343 B.C.E., he hired Plato's pupil, Aristotle, to tutor his son Alexander. By the time of his assassination in 336 B.C.E., he had taken Greece and had set his sights on the Persian Empire.

FROM MACEDONIAN, GREEK, AND ACHAEMENID CUISINE TO HELLENISTIC CUISINE

Alexander inherited his father's ambition, aspiring to become an even greater monarch than the Persian Achaemenid rulers. From Aristotle he had learned that magnificence was a virtue in a monarch. Prodigal spending was "becoming to those who have suitable means to start with, acquired from their ancestors or connexions, and to people of high birth and reputation . . . for all these things bring them greatness and prestige."[33] One of the consequences of Alexander's expansionist, war-mongering career would be a new Hellenistic cuisine that combined Greek, Persian, and Macedonian elements. Macedonian dining resembled that of Homer's heroes, Celtic chiefs, or, in its extravagance, the Persians, more than the imagined cuisine of Socrates's frugal citizens or the high cuisine of Athens's symposiasts.[34] Diners feasted on baked whole game animals or pigs stuffed with wombs and small birds and held drinking competitions with neat wine.

Alexander led his army through Asia Minor, down through the Levant to Jerusalem, on to Egypt, where he founded the city of Alexandria, and to Babylonia in Mesopotamia. Because of his careful planning and provisioning, he managed to feed an army that at its largest consisted of sixty-five thousand troops (more than double the population of most cities in antiquity), six thousand cavalry horses, and another thirteen thousand horses to carry the baggage. The army needed a hundred and thirty tons of grain a day, while the maximum yield of wheat per square mile was a hundred and sixty tons, so every day the yield of nearly a square mile had to be requisitioned or collected, stockpiled, distributed, ground and cooked.[35]

Alexander engaged the reigning Persian emperor, Darius III, in a series of battles. After routing the emperor in one engagement, he entered Darius's royal tent. He surveyed the pure gold service, sniffed the precious incense and spices, eyed the sofas and tables prepared for Darius's dinner, and is reported to have sighed, "This, it would seem, is to be a King."[36] Near Babylon, Alexander defeated Darius in

331 B.C.E. at the battle of Gaugamela. He went on to ride in triumph through Persepolis, the magnificent capital of Darius I. Taking the royal treasures as loot, Alexander left Persepolis as it burned to the ground, leaving only its pillars standing.

Although Greek commentators suggest that Alexander sniffed at the extravagance of the rations for the Persian monarchs' dinners, in fact his dining had more
in common with Persian magnificence than with the more restrained dining of the
Greeks. The hundred-couch tent that he took on his campaigns was twice the size
of the largest of Greek feasting rooms, but even that could not accommodate the
six thousand officers he was said to have invited to dinner on one occasion. Some
had to be seated on stools. Macedonian-style drinking competitions followed the
feasts. Alexander took the cooks, pastry chefs, wine experts, musicians, and scent
makers of the Persian imperial kitchen as part of his loot.[37] He also pushed for connections with the Persians, himself marrying a Persian woman, and marrying his
men to others. In the cities of his empire, which mapped closely on to the Achaemenid Empire he had defeated, Persian flatbreads, mutton, sauces, spices, and
fruits combined with Greek fish, olive oil, garum, wine, and Macedonian hospitality to create Hellenistic cuisine.

Alexander and his retinue thus aided and in some cases probably instigated
transfers of plants between the Mediterranean and the Middle East and beyond.
Already chicken had moved west and vines east. Theophrastus, another of Aristotle's pupils, carefully recorded new plants in his *History of Plants*. Coriander and
opium were taken west to Mesopotamia and perhaps farther to Central Asia. Cit-
rons, a kind of citrus that likely came from southern China or Southeast Asia,
lemons from the Near East, cherries from Anatolia, Armenian and Persian
peaches, and Persian pistachios, rice, used as a medicine, and alfalfa for feeding
horses came west.[38]

In 323 B.C.E., at the age of thirty-three, Alexander died in Babylon after campaigning through northern India and Afghanistan. His conquests quickly divided
into three Hellenistic empires. One was centered on Greece. Another was based in
Egypt, whose capital, Alexandria, was becoming a center of Greek language and
culture. The third stretched from Turkey through the Near East to Iraq, Iran,
Afghanistan, and northern India. Hellenistic cuisine was to be adapted by the
Roman Empire and transformed by the Byzantine Empire. It was also to merge
with succeeding Persian cuisines.

FROM ACHAEMENID CUISINE TO INDIAN
MAURYAN CUISINE

In 321 B.C.E., two years after Alexander's death, Chandragupta Maurya founded the
Mauryan Empire in India, shifting the center of Indian society eastward from the
Indus to the Ganges. The capital, Pataliputra (modern Patna), located at the con-

fluence of the Ganges and Gandhaka rivers, was about nine miles in length and one and half miles in width, surrounded by wooden walls punctuated with sixty-four entry gates. The Mauryan emperors emulated the Persian Empire, modeling their writing system on Aramaic and adopting a similar road system, information services, plans for the capital, art, and architecture. In the circumstances, their high cuisine is also likely to have followed the Persian example.

The Aryans, the dominant people in the empire, came from the same ethnic roots as the Persians and had migrated to the hot, dry Indus Valley sometime after 1500 B.C.E. They depended for centuries on barley and wheat as the staples of their cuisine.[39] Meat was eaten following the sacrifice. Although not written down until much later, the oral order of service, the Rig Veda, was probably codified between 1700 and 800 B.C.E. Probably it resembled the Achaemenid sacrifice. The tools of the sacrifice were readied: tongs and pokers to build the fire, knives to butcher the carcasses, pots to boil the meat, ovens (probably) to roast the meat, baskets to hold ingredients, strainers to filter the sacred drinks, grindstones, ladles, spoons, stirrers, scrapers, and serving dishes for offering foods to the gods.[40] The sacred fire, Agni, was offered golden clarified butter (ghee). Rare mountain plants for the sacred drink, *soma* (the same as the Persian *haoma*), were ground on stones or in an ox-driven pestle and mortar (*ghani*), the stone pushing against stone reportedly sounding like the bellowing of bulls.[41] The amber juice was strained through wool into wooden tubs, then mixed with yogurt, ghee, milk, water, honey, or grains.

Many animals were sacrificed and eaten, including the horse, various kinds of deer and antelope, buffalo, sheep, pig, chicken, peacock, hare, hedgehog, porcupine, and tortoise. Each god had a preference: Agni liked bulls and barren cows; Vishnu favored a dwarf ox; Indra preferred a drooping-horned bull.[42] Hymn no. 162 of the Rig Veda listed the instructions: the animal was to be washed, soothed (since it was supposed to go willingly), anointed with sacred ghee, and strangled with a cord. Part was thrown into the purifying flames, the fire flaring, the smoke billowing, the aromas rising to feed the gods, while the ashes—the excrement—fell to the ground. The priests consumed the sacred drink, the spirit of the life-sustaining plant entering their bodies and souls, and communing with the god Soma, they saw visions. A feast followed.

Otherwise, meat was rarely served except to the king and his entourage at court, when the king went to war, and when the king was sick.[43] For court meals, the meat was tempered with spices and condiments to correct its hot, dry nature and accompanied by the sauces of high cuisine (table 1.2).[44] Buffalo calf spit-roasted over charcoal and basted with ghee was served with sour tamarind and pomegranate sauces. Haunch of venison was simmered with sour mango and pungent and aromatic spices. Buffalo calf steaks were fried in ghee and seasoned with sour fruits, rock salt, and fragrant leaves. Meat was ground, formed into patties, balls, or sausage shapes, and fried, or it was sliced, dried to jerky, and then toasted. Shoulders and rounds were dressed with ghee, sprinkled with black pepper and sea salt (probably imported from southern India), and served with radishes, pomegranates, lemons, fragrant herbs, asafetida, and ginger. Barley bannocks, boiled rice, a variety of beans (*dhal*), and vegetables rounded out the meal. Confections of ghee and sugar provided a sweet note.

When the king showed signs of ill health, meat was indicated to enhance his manliness. The semi-mythical doctors Suśruta and Caraka prescribed a concentrated broth: "Sparrows in a partridge broth, partridges in a cock broth, cocks in a peacock broth, or even a peacock in a goose broth," with ghee, acid fruits, or sweeteners.[45]

Although it was not put in final form until the second century C.E., the *Arthashastra,* a manual of statecraft written by the steward Kautilya perhaps as early as the fourth century B.C.E., probably accurately represents the role alcohol played in Mauryan court life. The manual records that intoxicating drinks were made from a staggering range of ingredients: fresh juice, boiled juice, sugar, mixtures of sugar and honey, rice gruel, and yogurt. Many were aromatized with flowers and spices. Barley or rice alcohol was made from a ferment of rice and beans in a process perhaps similar to Chinese fermentation.[46]

While the Mauryan court feasted, a growing number of ascetics rejected the elaborate state ritual of the sacrifice, the priests' demand for payment, and the hierarchical social order. They wandered from city to city, begging bowls in hand, seeking enlightenment. They became such a notable feature of the society that Megasthenes, ambassador to India from one of the Hellenistic kingdoms in the third century B.C.E., reported on them in his dispatches. They were soon to transform Mauryan high cuisine and set in train changes in cuisine across India, Southeast Asia, and East Asia (chapter 3).

ROMAN REPUBLICAN CUISINE AS AN ALTERNATIVE TO MONARCHICAL HIGH CUISINE

Far to the west, the Roman Republic, another state that depended on barley and wheat, was expanding.[47] Governed by elected officials from 509 B.C.E., when the Roman monarchy was overturned, to 44 B.C.E., Romans repudiated both the monarchical, hierarchical principle and the theory of the culinary cosmos so central to mainstream ancient culinary philosophy, though the sacrifice remained firmly in place. Their republican philosophy owed more to that of Sparta and Stoicism, a school of philosophy founded by Xeno in the second century B.C.E.

Republicans believed that the state's success or failure depended on the civic virtue of all citizens—courage, simplicity, dignity, duty, honesty, civility, reason, and temperance, including in eating—not just on the personal virtue of a monarch, such as Cyrus or Alexander. To be clear, republicanism was a far cry from democracy: the citizens in question remained a minority of the population, made up of wealthy men who formed a small ruling elite. They advocated a plain, restrained cuisine and opposed gluttony, the result of an unbridled or unnatural appetite, stimulated by the sauces and sweets of high cuisine, and rampant sexuality, thought to be closely related, both of them vices that would endanger the philosophic life and the politician's dignity, commitment to duty, and ability to command obedience. Gluttony and rampant sexuality encouraged highly undesirable luxury, a term that comes from the Latin word for the floppy, overabundant growth of plants given too much water and fertilizer. Just as soft, floppy plants were useless, so flabby soldiers and citizens (one and the same in the republic) could not be made fit for military service.[48]

Military service was crucial to war, which was the business of Rome. Each successive victory brought more wealth in the form of silver, gold, and, even more important, wheat, which had now overtaken barley in the hierarchy of grains. Roman legions first conquered the rest of the Italian peninsula. Then, after fighting that continued intermittently from 264 to 146 B.C.E., they took the wealthy city of Carthage, founded by the Phoenicians, and gained access to the rich grain lands of North Africa. In the early years of the republic, the infantry was made up of Romans who farmed in the winter and campaigned in the summer. Up to seven out of every ten free men were conscripted. They served for sixteen years, becoming disciplined, hardened soldiers capable of forced marches of twenty miles a day along the military roads.[49] The officers, probably volunteers, were land-owning aristocrats.

For republican officers, glowing good health was a virtue, achievable only by temperance and moderation, particularly in food and sex. Food, said Cicero, was fuel for the body, not something to fuss about, and that was that.[50] He turned to Darius to tell a morality tale about appetite being the best sauce. When defeated "in his flight from the enemy [Darius] had drunk some water which was muddy and tainted with dead bodies. He declared that he had never drunk anything more pleasant; the fact was, that he had never drunk before when he was thirsty."[51] To republicans, the humoral theory (table 1.1) encouraged an unhealthy preoccupation with appetite. Strong foods, hard to prepare, hard to digest, but capable of keeping a man going a long time, were best, according to Celsus, author of an encyclopedia, *Of Medicine*, about 25 C.E.[52] Strong foods included bread, lentils, fava beans, and field peas, the meat of domesticated animals, large birds, "sea monsters" such as whales, as well as honey and cheese. Soft, weak foods such as vegetables, orchard fruit, olives, snails, and shellfish were not fit for republicans and soldiers. The luxurious cuisine of the Greek colony in Syracuse made the inhabitants poor soldiers, concluded Cato the Elder.[53] The Carthaginians, tough men who lived on wheat, were worthier opponents.

Republican culinary philosophy evolved in tandem with Roman provisioning practices. Victory in battle depended on well-fed foot soldiers, officers, and animals. "Whoever does not provide for provisions and other necessities is conquered without fighting," said Vegetius, who wrote about military affairs centuries later, in the fourth century c.e. "The main and principal point in war is to secure plenty of provisions for oneself and to destroy the enemy by famine. Famine is more terrible than the sword."[54] "Roman military success," says the historian Jonathan Roth, "often depended more on bread than iron."[55]

Military cuisine made Roman warfare more orderly and predictably successful. Although soldiers sometimes lived off the land, harvesting the grain of their enemies, pillaging granaries and leaving the owners to starve, they frequently depended on advance deposits of wheat, supplied by shipowners who imported it from North Africa, Greece, and other parts of the empire. Barley bannocks or porridge were now issued to troops only as a punishment. Normally they had bread made from the newly available bread wheat variety (*Triticum aestivum*), the most prestigious grain and also plain, hard, and healthful, in line with republican culinary philosophy. As if to prevent any suspicion that this was traditional high cuisine, Roman infantrymen, not women or slaves, had to grind their own wheat and bake their own bread. The huge baggage trains and legions of camp followers common in Persian armies and to a lesser extent in Alexander's were not allowed.

A Roman soldier's standard daily ration supplied roughly 3,250 calories: two pounds of wheat (about 2,000 calories), six ounces of meat (640 calories), 1½ ounces of lentils (170 calories), one ounce of cheese (90 calories), and 1½ ounces of olive oil (350 calories), plus six ounces of vinegar and 1½ ounces of salt.[56] He also received half a gallon of water and firewood. In addition, an army mule needed five to eight pounds of barley or oats a day, plus thirteen pounds of hay, if it could not graze, and five gallons of water. In summer, the troops trudged along the roads with their food in their packs and mules carrying their goatskin tents and sixty-pound grindstones for the grain.

On making camp, one of the soldiers assembled the grindstone, placing first a skin or cloth on the ground to catch the flour, then the squat lower grooved cylindrical stone, then the top stone, which rotated over the lower one. He squatted like a woman or slave over the grindstone. With one hand he rotated the upper stone using a peg near the circumference as a handle; with the other he poured handfuls of grain into a hole in the upper stone. The grain dribbled onto the lower stone and was sheared by the movement of the upper. The flour moved toward the circumference along grooves cut in the lower stone. He could grind enough meal for an eight-man squad in about an hour and a half with this rotary grinder, compared to at least four or five hours had he used a simple grindstone.[57]

Every morning and evening, Roman infantrymen prepared meals like those they would have eaten at home on the farm. They boiled wheat to make wheat porridge or wheat pottage (wheat cooked with dried peas, beans, or lentils, a bit of oil, salt, and a little salt pork), which they dipped into with wooden spoons. Or they mixed whole-wheat flour, water, and salt and baked coarse whole-wheat bread, probably in the ashes of the campfire, to eat with a bit of cheese. In the morning, these foot soldiers ate standing up like animals outside their goatskin tents; in the evening, they ate seated on the ground in the tents like children or slaves. They drank water cut with wine or vinegar *(posca)*. Sacrifices on festival days, before they went into battle, and to celebrate victory added a treat of boiled or roast beef. On the move or near the enemy, biscuit—twice-cooked bread that lasted a long time—made an instant meal.

Adopting the rotary grindstone involved a series of trade-offs. It ground faster. The weight of the upper stone, not the weight of the grinder, did the shearing, making the work less exhausting. On the other hand, the rotary grindstone was heavier, more expensive, and more difficult to make than a simple grindstone. Nor could it produce the fine gradations of flour that the simple grindstone could deliver. Cost, weight, and quality mattered less than speed and efficiency on campaign. The army disseminated this new, clumsy, expensive but efficient technology across the empire. It stimulated the opening of stone quarries and the training of skilled stonemasons. If every squad of eight men required a mill, and if at its height, the army comprised half a million men, then some sixty thousand grindstones were lugged over the Roman roads.

A millennium and a half was to pass before any other European army was as well fed. Roman officers and infantry learned how to cook and to calculate rations. The oldest surviving Latin prose work, *On Agriculture* (ca. 200 B.C.E.), by Cato the Elder, contains notes on estate management and basic cooking and is full of the reasoning of an army officer provisioning his troops.[58] Cato, for example, calculated the rations of slaves on his estate as carefully as he would have done those of soldiers, allocating quantities of barley and wheat according to how hard the work they had to do was. He admired Spartan black broth. Instead of resorting to physicians, he relied on vegetables to regulate the system. He recommended cabbage: the leaves could be eaten as a vegetable, the seeds, of some varieties at least, could be ground to a hot mustard powder, and the sprouts could be cooked with cumin, vintage wine, and oil and seasoned with a selection of pepper, lovage, mint, rue, coriander, or garum. It helped digestion, made it easier to urinate and to sleep, cured colic, healed wounds, and burst boils. A little cabbage before a banquet (a bit of advice that reveals a human side to Cato the Elder), would allow you to eat and drink as much as you liked. And he gave precise instructions for baking the flat cakes of flour, eggs, cheese and honey to be used in the sacrifice. On the estate, meals might include wheat bread with a fresh cheese flavored with garlic, smoked Lucanian pork sausage (sausage named for Lucania, the region in the instep of boot-shaped Italy now called Basilicata), lentils, and cheesecake.

In 167 B.C.E., the Romans defeated Alexander's successor, Perseus, king of Macedonia. Romans watched for three days as the spoils of war were paraded through the streets: prisoners in chains; armor, statues, and paintings; and the utensils of fine dining, including silver drinking horns, dishes, cups, and consecrated bowls. A hundred stall-fed oxen, their horns gilded and their necks garlanded, were readied for sacrifice, and the crowd anticipated the feast to follow. Later, Rome acquired the Levant and Egypt, including the flourishing city of Alexandria. In 44 B.C.E., Julius Caesar was declared perpetual dictator, one of several events that brought the five-hundred-year history of the republic to an end.

The victory parade following the defeat of Macedonia was as important a turning point in Rome's culinary history as it was in its political history, as an imperial cuisine began to replace frugal, temperate republican cuisine. For a couple hundred years, some of Rome's leading citizens fought against the trend, repeating the argument for republican cuisine. They charged that the appetizers, sauces, and sweet things of imperial high cuisine, far from balancing the humors and preventing ill health, as the doctors claimed, caused disease. They overstimulated the appetite, leading to gluttony—the habit of eating even when hunger had been satisfied. In the first century C.E., the Roman statesman and philosopher Seneca refused mushrooms and oysters.[59] Better to be content with simple, lightly cooked, strong foods. "We have water, we have porridge, let us compete in happiness with Jupiter himself."[60] "Hunger is the best sauce," said Cicero, orator and champion of the republic, in the first century B.C.E., citing a saying attributed to Socrates.[61] He meant it literally. Citizens did not eat sauces. If it sounds familiar, it's because it echoed down the centuries, becoming a proverb in most European languages. Hunger is the best cook, goes a Polish saying. "There's no sauce in the world like hunger," said Cervantes. "Hunger is the best pickle," was Benjamin Franklin's version.

Professional cooks who prepared these appetite-stimulating delicacies were accused of spreading ill health and disease. "Are you astounded at the innumerable diseases? Count the cooks."[62] They were as unwelcome in a republic as the physicians who fussed over the unhealthy, letting blood to reduce inflamed puffy bodies. Livy, the great Roman historian, bitterly regretted that when the Romans defeated Perseus, "banquets began to be prepared with greater care and expense. The cook, whom ancients regarded and treated as the lowest form of slave, was rising in value, and what had been a servile task began to be considered as a fine art."[63]

Luxurious cuisine was as perilous to the state as to the individual. Pliny the Elder warned in the first century C.E. that Rome was frittering away its bullion on gastronomic frivolities.[64] When Romans "began to seek dishes not for the sake of removing, but of rousing, the appetite," the republic began to decline, according to Seneca.[65] Reacting to the same set of events, around 38 B.C.E., Virgil published his *Eclogues,* poems that celebrated a simple pastoral life and established Arcadia, loosely based on a pastoral region of Greece, as an ideal alternative to life in large imperial cities.

Republican cuisine opened up a space between high and humble cuisines. Unlike the latter, it did not depend on lesser grains or roots. Unlike the former, it did not favor appetizers, sauces, and sweet dishes that were thought to keep diners eating even when they were satiated. Like high cuisines, it was prepared by professional cooks, served in areas dedicated to dining with specialized utensils, and had a culinary literature that focused on basic processing rather than final meal preparation. Finally, cooking was understood differently. Whereas in high cuisine cooking was thought to refine food (as fire refined metal ores), revealing its true nature or essence, in republican cuisine, cooking was thought to obscure or change the true nature of the food. Republican culinary philosophy was picked up by the Church Fathers, the theologians who established Christian culinary philosophy in the second to fourth centuries C.E. It was revived in eighteenth-century Europe and colonial America and shaped culinary thinking throughout the Anglo world in the nineteenth century.

FROM REPUBLICAN TO IMPERIAL, HELLENISTIC-INSPIRED ROMAN CUISINE

In Rome, though, imperial cuisine prevailed. Sacrifices and sacrificial feasts continued to be the central civic act of the empire. Alongside them, private dining was on the increase. Roman emperors now offered lavish meals with ingredients from across their domains and leftovers for the guests.[66] Augustus, the first emperor, who was deified after his death, hosted one meal in which he played Apollo and his guests the other gods. The order in which his guests entered, where they were seated, and what food they were served proclaimed their place in the hierarchy. Foods brought from all parts of the empire and from earth, sea, and sky expressed his dominion over the human and natural worlds. His followers' role, now familiar, was to pledge loyalty, express the wish that the emperor should rule for years, and acclaim his legitimacy and power, accompanied by song and chant.

Roman high cuisine, however, never offered the extravagant multiday feasts of Achaemenid high cuisine. Apollo was the Greek god associated with the golden mean and temperance. Augustus advertised his personal temperance while fulfilling his imperial obligations. The biographer of the emperor Vitellius, who once filled a huge silver dish with the empire's most exotic foods—livers of char (a troutlike fish), pheasant and peacock brains, flamingo tongues, and the entrails of lampreys—used the event as a morality tale about the perils of gluttony. In Petronius's *Satyricon,* the feast of Trimalchio, an upstart millionaire, includes foods representing the signs of the zodiac, a pig spilling sausages from its belly, and a pastry figure of Priapus, his belly bulging with grapes and other fruits—it was a biting satire.

The military aristocracy, enriched by war and the income from their large estates, found that high, but not overly extravagant, dining with friends and clients consolidated bonds and confirmed rank. In Rome, about thirty thousand out of a million inhabitants had the resources to indulge in high cuisine on special occasions. The empire's other cities had somewhere between five and eighteen million inhabitants altogether, so perhaps 300,000 men throughout the empire could enjoy fine dining.[67]

Roman high cuisine was indebted to Hellenistic cuisine, with its Greek, Macedonian, and Persian roots. Society physician Galen updated Hippocrates' humoral theory of nutrition and health (table 1.1). He hailed from Pergamon, in what is now Turkey, trained in Alexandria, and was physician to two emperors in the first century C.E.[68] He warned his patients not to abstain from sex, countering the Stoics' insistence that it was for procreation alone. Instead, he said, they needed to ejaculate regularly and watch their diets. He quantified the warmth and coolness of foods into three degrees: pepper, for example, was warm in the third degree, rice and chicken were warm and moist in the first degree, and cucumber was dangerously cold in the third degree. The human body was only slightly warm, less than the first degree. When Marcus Aurelius worried that the seafood he had consumed was turning into cold, wet phlegm in his stomach, lowering his temperature, making him feverish, and turning his feces green with bile, Galen prescribed heating pepper and thin, dry Sabine wine.[69]

Greek slave cooks were hired to prepare sophisticated sauces and desserts, working with their assistants at a fire set on a bench.[70] Greek bakers made raised wheat bread, said to have been developed in Alexandria, and made possible by a new variety of wheat, *Triticum aestivum,* the gluten proteins of which trapped air. Romans began drinking wine daily and reclining on benches, like the Persians and Greeks, to dine. Spices, including black pepper, ginger, turmeric, and cinnamon, were more widely used than formerly. Athenaeus, an Egyptian Greek living in Rome at the end of the second century C.E., collected excerpts from eight hundred Greek gastronomic writers in the *Philosophers at Table* (*Deipnosophistae*).

Roman cuisine, for all its indebtedness, was no mere copy of Hellenistic cuisine. Raised white wheat bread, baked at home under a domed pot, was now the everyday grain dish in wealthy houses. Since as much as 50 percent of the grain by weight had to be sifted away to make white bread, it was something only the rich could afford. Pork, meat that had scarcely featured in Achaemenid or Greek high cuisine, was enormously popular. "The race of pigs is expressly given by nature to set forth a banquet," went a saying.[71] Pork was eaten cured and fresh (including soft, unctuous sow's womb) and made into sausages, including Lucanian sausage. Salt fish, particularly cubed salt tuna, reasonably cheap and plentiful, appeared alongside the fresh fish of Greek high cuisine, believed to be more dangerous because it rapidly putrefied. To ensure a supply of fish, connoisseurs constructed fresh- and salt-water ponds, not entirely successfully.[72] The flavorings garum and the pasty residue (*allec*) left after making it, usually mixed with wine and water, were used more frequently than in Hellenistic cuisine.[73] Sauces too were innovative, breaking with the bread-thickened brothy sauces of Persia.

Host and guests gathered for the evening dinner (*cena*) in the finest room of the house, its floors and walls often beautifully decorated with mosaics or paintings, and adorned with furniture, vessels, and implements.[74] They lay diagonally, three to a couch, on couches arranged in a ⊃-shape. Holding their plate in their left hand, they delicately picked up food with the right. Those who dined together were theoretically equals, though hosts often gave the lesser guests smaller portions, less choice pieces, and less desirable places at the table, or simply ignored them.

The dinner included appetizers, sauced dishes, and desserts, all spurned by republicans. For appetizers, diners might have lettuce (perhaps served with an oil-and-vinegar dressing), sliced leeks (boiled, sliced in rounds, and dressed with oil, garum, and wine), tuna garnished with eggs on rue leaves, eggs baked in the embers, fresh cheese with herbs, and olives with honeyed wine (*muslum*).

For the main course, slaves brought in dishes such as red mullet roasted and served with a pine nut sauce; mussels cooked with wine, garum, and herbs; sow's udder, boiled until soft and then grilled and served with sauce; chicken with a stuffing of ground pork, boiled wheat, herbs, and eggs; and crane with turnips in an herb-flavored vinegar sauce. Exotic fare, such as a pea dish, a chicken stew, and baked lamb with a sweet-and-sour sauce, attributed to Persia, added a cosmopolitan touch.

Sauces, now much more complex than earlier Persian sauces, tempered the meat or fish, adding heat to cold, wet foods or a cooling complement to hot, dry foods. Absolutely central to Roman imperial cuisine, four of the five hundred recipes in the cookbook known by the name of Apicius (derived from a couple of ninth-century manuscripts, probably themselves based on a fourth- or fifth-century compilation) deal with sauces in one way or another, and two hundred are sauce recipes.[75] Typically, sauces were made by pulverizing hard spices, usually pepper or cumin, but also anise, caraway, celery seed, cinnamon, coriander, cardamom, cassia, dill, mustard, poppy, and sesame, in a mortar. Nuts, such as almonds, filberts, and pine nuts, or fruits, such as dates, raisins, and plums, were added and the mass was worked to a paste. To this mixture, fresh herbs such as basil, bay, capers, garlic, fennel, ginger, juniper, lovage, mint, onion, parsley, rosemary, rue, saffron, savory, shallot, thyme, or turmeric were added, followed by garum and perhaps wine, must, honey, olive oil, or milk. The mixture was warmed to blend the tastes and sometimes thickened with wheat starch, eggs, rice, or crumbled pastry.

Dessert consisted of ripe fruit, such as figs, grapes, apples, pears, and plums; milk puddings; egg and fruit dishes; and pastries with cheese and honey, such as fried dough drenched in syrup or honey. One recipe was for a precursor of many of today's fried doughs. "Take durum wheat flour and cook it in hot water so that it forms a very hard paste, then spread it out on a plate. When cold cut it up in lozenges, and fry in the best oil. Lift out, pour honey over, sprinkle with pepper and serve."[76] Wine mixed with water and drunk from glass, silver, or fine pottery vessels accompanied the meal.[77] Such meals, naturally, did not occur every day. They were the exemplary meals, the special occasion meals. On a regular basis a Roman would have had a light breakfast and an evening meal much simpler than this elaborate dinner.

The empire, a universal monarchy encompassing the whole world, according to the Stoics, reached its greatest extent between 100 B.C.E. and 100 C.E., stretching from Spain in the west to Mesopotamia in the east, from Scotland in the north to the fringes of the Sahara in the south.[78] Like the Persians, the Romans tolerated people of different ethnicities and different religions provided they accepted the sacrifice, the language, the customs, and the tastes of Rome, including Roman cuisine. Naturally there were regional variations. The eastern, Greek-speaking portion of the empire was never enthusiastic about pork, for example.[79] In general, citizens in the empire (a category that gradually expanded beyond Romans but was always a select minority of males) were united by dining. As graffiti at Pompeii neatly summed it up, "He with whom I do not dine is a barbarian to me."[80]

North of the Alps, in a belt from Spain in the west to the Rhine and the Danube in the east, lived the Celts. To the Romans, who liked a landscape of cities surrounded by cultivated fields, the clearings the Celts carved out of dark forests for their settlements and fields seemed strange, threatening, and lacking in the foods that made life civilized. "The inhabitants . . . lead the most miserable existence of all mankind, for they cultivate no olives and they drink no wine," said the Turkish-born governor of a province on the Danube.[81] About the best they could say of the Celts was that they were clean, if voracious. Over time the wealthier Celts adopted the Latin language and Roman cuisine, including the round raised loaf, wine, Lucanian sausages, beans (peas, lentils, chickpeas, black-eyed peas), hard cheese, and pureed sauces. They imported wine in quantity, probably at least two and a half million gallons a year in the third century (compare this with the largest wine trade in the Middle Ages, which was twenty million gallons a year from France to Britain and the Low Countries).[82] From the third century C.E. on, romanized Celts became emperors, a contrast with the Persian Empire, where non-Persians never became emperors. Their fondness for roast and boiled pork, both fresh and salt, reinforced the existing Roman preference.[83]

Kitchen utensils and plants were also disseminated across the empire. In third-century York in northern Britain, for example, African troops introduced bowls with convex bases that could be used over a brazier. In other areas, tripods typical of the south of France could be found, as could griddles and mortars.[84] Olives and vines were planted wherever they would grow. In villas in Roman Britain, rabbits from Spain, chicken, pheasant, peacock, and guinea fowl were prized. Herbs such as coriander, dill, fennel, mint, thyme, garlic, leek, onion, shallot, parsley, rosemary, rue, sage, savory, and sweet marjoram and garden vegetables such as cabbage, lettuce, endive, carrots, parsnips, turnips, radishes, skirrets, and white mustard (for the seeds) were planted in gardens.[85] Improved varieties of apples, cherries, peaches, apricots, and figs were planted in orchards. In the reverse direction, European beets, turnips, asparagus, pears, and walnuts were established in Egypt.

The urban poor across the empire did quite well, the Romans being as proficient at provisioning large cities as they were at provisioning armies. From a population of about a hundred thousand in the third century B.C.E., Rome grew to one million in 55 B.C.E. and one and a half million a century later. Athens and Corinth in Greece, Ephesus and Pergamum in Turkey, Antioch in the Levant, and Alexandria in Egypt also had large populations. The poor, 90 percent of nearly every city's population, lived in crowded tenements. With no place to store or cook food, they grabbed fast food to eat on the street or take home. A bit of warm bread from the bakery and a sausage from an eatery or takeout shop provided a quick hot meal. If they did have pottage or porridge, they probably helped themselves from a common bowl with their fingers.[86]

State sacrifices and feasts funded by affluent Romans to establish their standing in society broke the daily routine and gave ordinary people the sense that they were part of a great city and a greater empire. The riches garnered in war or business went up in flames as animals were sacrificed and feasts prepared. As city populations increased, particularly in Rome, food shortages occurred. Rather than risk insurrection, aristocrats turned to benevolence. They handed out grains at the end of the second century B.C.E., then oil and pork, then salt and wines from the large vineyards of northern Italy in the third century C.E.[87]

In normal times, the urban poor bought or were given rations by their employers or owners of bread, wine, oil, cheese, garum, and honey.[88] Of these, the most important was bread made of wheat, not barley. "In the old days," said Galen, "people used to prepare barley-meal, but now its weakness in terms of food value is recognized. It gives little nourishment to the body. Ordinary people and those who do not take regular exercise find it quite sufficient, but for those who do take exercise in any way at all it is found wanting."[89] The humble ate bakery bread, not home-baked bread. In Rome, three hundred state-regulated, commercial, integrated mills and bakeries, one for every three thousand people, were in operation by 25 C.E. Since every inhabitant needed between one and two pounds of bread daily, depending on what else they had to eat, five hundred tons of flour had to be ground, kneaded, and baked daily. Large beehive ovens and flour and firewood bought in bulk created economies of scale: commercial bakeries' costs were much lower than those of home bakers (fig. 2.5).[90]

Many bakeries were run by the descendants of freed slaves, who sometimes became quite wealthy. Some invested in donkey mills, which cost 1,500 denarii, six times as much as a rotary mill, at a time when a pair of army boots cost 22 denarii, a farm laborer might make 2 denarii a day over and above what he received in kind,

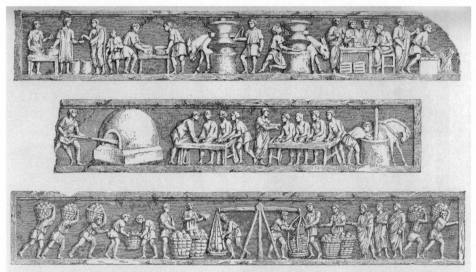

119. Reliefs vom Grabmale des Engros-Brotlieferanten Eurysaces in Rom: Mahlen, Kneten, Backen; Ablieferung des Brotes an Beamte.

FIGURE 2.5. Drawing of reliefs on the tomb of the freed slave and successful baker Eurysaces near the Porta Maggiore in Rome, showing how a Roman bakery worked. Top, right to left, workers receive a delivery of grain, which is carefully recorded by officials seated at a table. The grain is ground in donkey mills, where workers collect the flour as it flows out from between the millstones. Once milled, the wholemeal flour is sifted through circular sieves to remove the coarse bran. A supervisor checks for quality. Middle, right to left, a worker seems to be making use of a horse to move the paddle that kneads the dough. Employees or slaves shape the dough into standard-sized loaves at two long tables, and then the baker slides the loaves into the oven. Bottom, left to right, workers strain to carry baskets of bread to a weighing station, where the total is recorded. State officials in their robes check the output before the workers deliver the bread to customers. From Hans Lamer, *Römische Kultur im Bilde* (Leipzig: Quelle & Meyer, 1910), fig. 119.

and a pound loaf of bread cost about 2 denarii.[91] (When the emperor Caligula seized the animals from the bakeries of Rome in 40 C.E. to transport his palace furniture to Gaul, the mills could not be run, and famine threatened, so essential had animal-driven milling become to the food supply of Rome.) Depending on local conditions, bakers probably chose to raise the bread by allowing lactobacilli to produce a sourdough. Or they used barm, the yeasty sediment from brewing (though whether it was the same yeast as the *Saccharomyces cerevisiae* used today is not clear).

A fresco preserved at Pompeii shows a baker selling the standard-sized round Roman loaf (fig. 2.6). Here, for the first time, is bread that we can recognize, that we would probably not find strange if we were to taste it, and that would have a familiar crumb. Bakers produced several grades of bread: white for the wealthy,

FIGURE 2.6. A photograph of a round, slashed Roman loaf from
Pompeii preserved in the lava that flowed when Vesuvius erupted in
79 C.E. Courtesy New York Public Library http://digitalgallery.nypl.org
/nypldigital/id?1619829.

whole grain for the bulk of the population, coarse branny bread for the very poor.
The rural poor baked whole-grain breads in good times, or breads mixed with or
entirely made of peas, beans, chestnuts, or acorns in bad times.

Wine was made on large estates, particularly in northern and western Italy.
Surplus wine was sold to the Celts in Gaul (present-day France). A contemporary
writer describing Celtic enthusiasm for wine commented, perhaps not meaning it
literally, "They will give you a slave for an amphora of wine thus exchanging the
cupbearer for the cup."[92] In northern Europe, lightweight unbreakable barrels
replaced pottery jars for shipping, as the bas-relief from Augsburg in Germany
depicted in figure 2.7 probably shows.

Factories to make fish sauces and pastes, known since at least the fifth century
B.C.E. in the eastern Mediterranean, were set up in Italy, Libya, Spain, and Turkey—wherever there was a good supply of fish, a nearby salt works, and hot sun.[93]
The fish was packed in large vessels with herbs and salt and then left in the sun
until the fish self-digested (autolyzed), separating into liquid garum and pasty
allec, the former being decanted into amphorae for shipping. Different grades for
customers from the emperor to slaves were distinguished. Jewish customers were
guaranteed a product not tainted with mollusks, shellfish, or eels.

Hard cheese was made by pressing fresh cheese with salt.[94] Because it was drier
and more acidic than fresh cheeses, it kept well, and because it was less than

FIGURE 2.7. In northern Europe, the Celts introduced lightweight barrels to store and ship wine in place of the amphorae of the Mediterranean. This bas-relief (now destroyed) on a tomb in Augsburg, Germany, is usually interpreted as showing a cellar filled with barrels. From C. Daremberg and E. Saglio, *Dictionnaire des antiquités grecques et romaines* (Paris: Hachette, 1904–7), 5: 917, fig. 2139.

one-tenth the volume of the milk from which it was made, it was easy to carry, making it for centuries a basic supply for soldiers and travelers. It was exported all over the Mediterranean by the beginning of the fourth century. Honey was also produced commercially.[95]

The port of Ostia, just a few miles from Rome, bustled. Grain was unloaded from ships that had made the twelve-hundred-mile voyage from Alexandria, a cheaper method of transportation than hauling it fifteen miles from the hinterland. Prior to delivery to millers, it was stored in rows of pottery jars buried up to their necks in the ground.[96] Rotund or elongated amphorae filled with olive oil, conical ones with wine, pointed ones with garum, tall thin ones with olives, and small pointed ones with dates were also unloaded.[97] Wine was loaded onto ships to be sold around the Mediterranean or as far as India, where it was traded for pepper.

In the third and fourth centuries C.E., Constantinople, now the economic center of the empire, replaced Rome as the capital, shifting the culinary focus eastward to the Greek-speaking region.[98] In the fourth century C.E., Germanic peoples from across the Rhine invaded the western empire. By the mid-fifth century, Rome had shrunk to one-third of a million people and by the mid-sixth to a mere sixty thousand.[99] In what had been the western empire, Roman imperial cuisine, with its spicy sauces, its soft meats, its flavors of garum and honey, gradually declined as the food-processing plants and trade networks that had sustained it fell into disuse. Traces did remain, as they were to do after the fall of later empires. The spiced Lucanian sausage is still made under cognate names in the Levant, across North Africa, and in Greece, the Balkans, Switzerland, France, Spain, and (thanks to the later Spanish empire) Latin America.[100] More important, raised wheaten bread remained part of the culinary repertoire of Europe.

Meanwhile, as the ascetics in the Mauryan Empire were challenging imperial cuisine, Jews and Christians were doing the same in the Roman Empire. The Jews refused to sacrifice, the central political act of the empire. The Christians who had converted had once sacrificed but now refused to do so. In the early fourth century, Christianity was to become the official religion of the eastern empire, and the high and humble cuisines would be reformulated to fit Christian culinary philosophy (chapter 5).

FROM MILLET CUISINE TO HAN IMPERIAL CUISINE

After a long period of warfare and chaos in northern China, the emperor Wu (156–87 B.C.E.), like Darius I some four hundred years earlier, announced that it was his responsibility to restore order and harmonize the earth and the heavens.[101] For the next four hundred years, with only occasional periods of disorder, the Han dynasty ruled more than fifty million people scattered from Mongolia and Korea in the north to Vietnam in the south, from the China Sea in the east to the borders of the Central Asian steppe in the west. The Han Empire had many parallels with the Roman Empire, including its cuisine. Like Roman imperial cuisine, Han imperial cuisine employed wheat. In China, however, wheat-flour dough was not baked to make bread but in most cases was shaped and steamed to make a series of products collectively known as *bing,* which can be translated as "pasta". Like Roman imperial cuisine, Han cuisine explored a range of flavors. In place of fish sauce, the Chinese continued to innovate with a series of ferments. Besides parallels in food technology, there were parallel debates about culinary philosophy, particularly about the place of luxury in the state.

In a revived Confucianism, the emperor was conceived as the pivot of the universe, responsible for the sacrifice that maintained harmony in a cosmos whose primordial energy (*qi*) was differentiated into yin and yang. History moved in cycles. Individuals had a duty to cultivate the virtues, and society was bound together by a series of unequal relationships—ruled and ruler, son and father, wife and husband, and so on—in which the junior partner owed respect to the senior and the senior had to respond with benevolence to the junior. Although provisioning was an essential part of Confucian theory, the food provided had to be decent and sufficient, not luxurious. In a tale that resounded through Chinese history, Confucius praised his disciple Yan Hui. "How admirable he is! Living ... on a bowlful of grain and a ladleful of water is a hardship most men would find intolerable, but Hui does not allow this to affect his joy."[102] The sacrifice, part of good state governance, continued to hold society and cosmos together. Just as not everyone accepted republican culinary philosophy in Rome, so too many Chinese looked to other culinary philosophies, such as those of the Taoists.

The capital, Chang'an (just a few miles from present-day Xi'an), on the Yellow River, the traditional home of the Han Chinese, was a busy city of 250,000 people. Laid out on cosmic principles with wide streets, it centered on a three-mile-square palace area, home to the imperial court. The Bureau of Imperial Provisioning, with a staff of about two thousand, oversaw the kitchens, staged banquets, and supervised the *chiu* (rice wine) breweries, granaries, and storehouses, as well as farmers, fuel suppliers, herdsmen, and hunters. It also dealt with the culinary side of the sacrifice, which was lavish, as befitted the emperor's command of the known world's resources, and archaic to reflect the continuity of the sacred and imperial tradition.[103]

The Yellow River basin, flat, well-watered, and capable of producing the materials for a diverse diet, was the homeland. From there imperial armies, up to a million men strong, the rank and file made up of conscripted peasants, advanced on neighboring territories, each identified with a distinct cuisine. To the north was high, cold Manchuria, the land of milk. To the east was Korea, the land of salt and fish. The south, below the Yangtze River, was the land of soft, weak soil, abundant, luxurious growth, and sour and smelly foods. An embassy to the Mekong Delta and Cambodia in 228 resulted in two treatises: one on the trees, plants, fruits, and bamboos of the Red River in Vietnam, and the other a comprehensive survey of Sichuan. To the west was a land of rich soil and excellent diet. In the north and east, the Han established military colonies, deporting hundreds of thousands of people to settle them.[104] Presumably, like the Roman garrisons on the frontiers of their empire, they introduced their familiar plants and their processing and cooking equipment.

In the west, the Chinese advance was blocked by the steppe nomads who controlled the Central Asian trade routes. Powerful as the army was, it could not provision troops that could penetrate more than about two hundred miles beyond the Great Wall, built to mark the vague boundary between steppe and farmland. Thus began centuries of diplomacy and culinary exchange between the nomads and the Chinese. The Chinese would invite a nomad envoy—a ruler or a member of his family—to Chang'an, officially to pay homage to the emperor.[105] He would bring gifts (tribute), be allowed to trade for a few days, promising he would not attack, and would leave an important member of his court, perhaps the crown prince, as a hostage. In return, the Chinese would offer the delegation lavish banquets, and when they departed, would load them with gifts, such as royal daughters as brides, magnificent silks, and grains. Nomads became familiar with Chinese cuisine, while the Chinese received, through a series of nomad intermediaries, information about and components of Persian, Indian, and even Mediterranean cuisines. Along the long relay chain across the steppe came grapevines, the know-how to make grape wine, alfalfa for feeding cavalry horses, and, in all likelihood, rotary grindstones.[106]

Army provisioning and great estates shaped Han cuisine as it did Roman. A small wealthy ruling class supported by peasant taxes had been replaced by one of affluent large landowners, who employed peasants to run their agribusinesses. The Cho family in Sichuan, for example, had lands in cereals, ponds for farming freshwater fish, parks for game, various commercial ventures, and ironworks tended by eight hundred slaves.[107]

The occult, proto-scientific cosmic theory of the Taoists, handed down from Taoist master to pupil in isolated monasteries, appealed to families like the Chos, who were looking for guidance about the cosmos and their personal health. From the third century B.C.E. on, the Taoists had abstained from grains, and thus society. They yearned to draw closer to the spirit world, to meditate, to sup on the sweet dew of heaven, the *ch'i*, or the ether, and thus, perhaps, achieve eternal life.[108] Taoists believed in the five elements, or phases, and preached the necessity of being in harmony with the universe (table 1.4). They viewed the stomach as the seat of intuitive wisdom, the mind of thinking and judging, and the heart of willing and loving. Many of their ideas found their way into the main pharmacopeia, *The Herbal of the Divine Husbandman*.[109] Food and medicines merged into one another, the word *fang* standing for both recipe and prescription.

Taoist culinary philosophy attracted those in the Chinese elite who combined a love of spontaneity, nature, landscape painting, and calligraphy with contempt for the sacrificial rites and indifference to politics. They hoped to prolong youthfulness and life, and prepared carefully for life after death, spending fortunes on burial suits made of slabs of jade to prevent the spirit from escaping, and feasts to enjoy in the tomb, since if the deceased was not well fed, the spirit might leave the body, roaming the land as an angry, hungry ghost. Lady Dai, an aristocrat who died about 150 B.C.E., was buried with fifty-one pots laden with vegetables, rice, and cereals and another forty-eight bamboo baskets of fruit and cooked meats, labeled with strips of bamboo. Other tombs included models of wells and granaries, whole farmyards, or kitchen scenes such as the one shown in figure 2.8. This second-century scene was incised on a polished stone slab about five feet high by two and quarter feet wide that stood in the tomb of a landowner or government official in Shandong Province.[110]

An estate management and food-processing manual, *Essential Skills for the Daily Life of the People*, written around 540 C.E. by Jia Sixie, a government official, perhaps a governor from the northern state of Shandong, is a mine of information about food production and processing.[111] He describes how to till the soil, grow grains, rear cattle and sheep, maintain poultry yards, pig pens, and fish ponds, and process food, including salt making, flour milling, and malting. Starches, sweeteners, and oils were prepared on a large scale.[112] Starch for thickening sauces was made by pounding broomcorn (*Panicum miliaceum*) or foxtail millet (*Setaria*

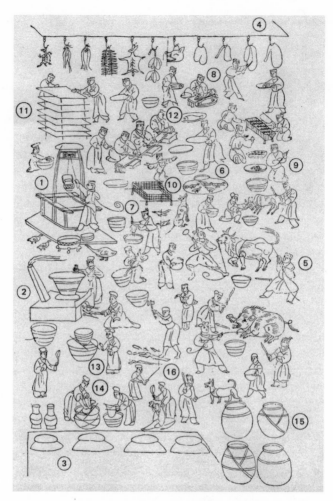

FIGURE 2.8. This scene incised on a stone slab from a second-century Liangtai tomb in Zhucheng, Shandong Province, China, shows a busy kitchen. At the top, a rack holds turtle, a deer, fish, a pig's head, and large joints of meat safely out of reach of the dogs hanging around the kitchen. Below, a stacked set of dining trays is readied, one man prepares fish, three cut meat, and a small team spears chunks of meat and cooks them over a hibachi-style grill. On the right-hand side, a sheep, an ox, a pig, a dog, and a basket of chickens are readied for slaughter, eyed by a greedy dog. Water is drawn from a well, and the fire under a steamer is stoked. Other attendants pour ferment through a pottery sieve or cloth bag to clear *chiu* for drinking. A foreman chastises a drunk. At the bottom, four large jars hold ferments, while others hold rice wine or water. So much *chiu* and meat suggests that a feast is being prepared. From *Wen wu tian di* (Cultural Relics World) 10 (1981), fig. 7.

italica), soaking it in water, and collecting and drying the granules that settled out. Malt sugar, the main sweetener, was made by sprouting grains, drying them, grinding them, and extracting the sweetener with water. Jia Sixie knew sugarcane only as an exotic plant from the far south. Oils were produced by heating sesame, hemp, perilla, colza, and other seeds, then pressing out the oil with a wedge press. The use of oil seeds may indicate a decline in the number of domestic animals, since the Chinese preferred lard, mutton fat, and beef fat for cooking.

Foods that could be preserved while retaining some of their original characteristics ("hidden" foods) included vegetables buried in earth for the winter, grapes kept in covered cisterns, dried vegetables, meat, or fish soaked in aromatic brine and hung under the rafters to dry (*fu*), cooked rice and fish with herbs and spices (*zha;* perhaps the distant origin of sushi), and vegetables such as mallow and cabbage preserved in pots with salt, brine, or rice mush (*zu;* perhaps the origin of sauerkraut). Vinegar, according to the pharmacopeias, banished ill humors from the body, harmonized the actions of the visceral organs, and led to robust good health.

In addition, the Chinese made a great variety of "halted," or completely transformed, foods, including condiments based on soybeans, grains, meat, fish, or shellfish.[113] By the time of the Han Dynasty, the techniques for making them were systematized, many having a long history. They were distinct from those of the western half of Eurasia. The Chinese began by incubating cooked grains with a complex microbial culture that we now know included fungal enzymes, spores, and yeasts in the presence of water. The resulting "ferment" was the starter for brewing or turning grains into condiments.

At the time, the process was described in Taoist terms. The first day of the seventh lunar month in late summer was the time to prepare ferments for the year's supply of rice wine. A hundred and twenty liters of wheat were divided into three portions, one of which was steamed, one dry-roasted, and one left raw. After being finely ground on the grindstone, they were mixed together. Before sunrise, a boy dressed in black was sent to draw eight hundred liters of water from the well while facing to the west, the place of death. No one was allowed to touch the water. Facing the west, workers turned the grain with the water to make a firm paste. In a thatched hut with a hard-packed dirt floor divided by paths into four squares, young boys, also facing west, shaped the paste into cakes about three inches in diameter and one inch thick. They also shaped five "kings" of the ferment. The cakes were placed along the paths and the kings were arranged in the center and the east, west, north, and south corners. Then a family member repeated sacrificial prayers three times, the onlookers knelt twice, and gifts of dried meat, wine, and pasta were placed in the moistened hands of the kings. The wooden door was closed and sealed with mud. After a week it was reopened; the cakes were turned, and then shut up again, a process repeated twice. Then the ferment cakes were sealed in an earthen jar for a week, before being hung in the sun to dry on a string passed through holes made in the middle.

The precise measurements and careful rules, even if couched in mystical rather than scientific terms, were ways of controlling the tricky and potentially dangerous process of ferment making. They hint that the Chinese thought that the wheat died as it turned into ferment, being reborn when the ferment was used.

Wheat, which a thousand years earlier the Chinese had disdained as a second-rate grain, had now joined millet as a grain of choice. The rotary grindstone reached China from the west soon after it was invented around the third century B.C.E., according to most scholars. Although they could have ground wheat earlier on the simple grindstone, grinding was now more efficient.[114] The resulting wheat flour, when mixed with water, made a dough that was malleable and moldable as a result of the protein, or gluten, that formed long plastic and elastic threads. The Chinese rolled the dough into sheets, formed it into noodles by slicing, pressing through holes, or pulling, formed it into wrappers, or shaped it into buns, before steaming and serving with meaty broths, yogurt, and sesame paste. They even learned how to make noodles from flours of grains that lacked gluten, such as millet or rice, by pouring the dough through a sieve into boiling water that set the mixture. In the sixth century, Jia Sixie gave fifteen different recipes for *bing,* a category that was now centuries old.[115]

In the third century C.E., Shu Hsi, one of China's leading scholars, had written a rhapsody praising wheat noodles and dumplings, different ones for each season.[116] Spring was the time for stuffed buns (*man-t'ou*), summer for a thin pancake, fall for leavened dough, winter for a bowl of steaming noodles. A sumptuous stuffed dumpling, a ball of kneaded dough filled with mutton or pork chopped as "fine as fly heads," said Shu Hsi, was good for every season. Prepared with costly meat, ginger, onions, spices, and black beans (presumably fermented) to neutralize the meaty smell, the filling was wrapped in exquisitely thin dough and steamed.

> And then
> With the fire blazing the broth bubbles;
> Strong fumes rise as steam.
> Straightening his jacket, straightening his skirt,
> The cook grasps and presses, beats and pounds.
> With flour webbed to his finger tips,
> His hands whirl and twirl, crossing back and forth.
> Flurrying and fluttering, fast and furious,
> The balls scatter like stars, pelt like hail.
> There is no meat stuck to the steamer,
> There is no loose flour on the dumplings.

Diners knelt at low tables, using chopsticks to take the new delicacy from fashionable, exorbitantly expensive lacquered dishes (fig. 2.9).

Humble cuisine included no such luxuries as wheat pasta but continued to be dominated by millet or roots. From about the fifth century B.C.E. on, Chinese states-

FIGURE 2.9. Engravings on the rear wall of the shrine of the Han general Chu Wei (d. ca. 50 C.E.) show ceremonial dining. The diners—men in the lower scene, women in the upper—are seated on screened platforms enclosed by looped curtains facing long, low tables with curved legs. Attendants or onlookers peer over the screens. In the background of the lower image, servants carry platters of food; in the foreground, others kneel, ladling from a large round tureen into bowls and from cylindrical vessels into two-handled cups. From Wilma Fairbank, *Adventures in Retrieval: Han Murals and Shang Bronze Molds* (Cambridge, Mass.: Harvard University Press, 1972).

men and political advisors were agreed that the state had to intervene to stabilize prices, protecting consumers from high prices and producers from low ones. Public order, indeed public morality, was dependent on having adequate food. Texts from earlier centuries collected in the Han era made clear the connection between politics and grain. "When the granaries are full, [the people] will know propriety and moderation," but "[i]f the people lack sufficiency, [the prince's] orders will be scorned. If the people suffer hardships, his orders will not be carried out."[117]

In the first century B.C.E., the food supply became more precarious. A peasant song complained that the poor had nothing but steamed millet or soybeans, with yam for a sauce when irrigation works broke down in part of the Yangtze River basin.[118] Peasants, whose payments in kind or in coin sustained the state, found themselves in a worsening situation, many going into debt and losing their plots to large landowners. The administration lost revenue, and in 117 B.C.E., it resorted to establishing iron and salt monopolies. To manage and provision its huge armies, the empire increased the bureaucracy, which extracted taxes from the peasants in the form of millet, hay and straw, and draft animals. Peasants worked longer hours and plowed more ground. Officials took head counts of the villagers, making it harder to evade paying up. The old system of a relatively small imperial establishment and a large number of independent peasants was vanishing.

Various forms of poor relief were tried. The rich, or merchants acting on their behalf, sought out distant supplies of grain, built canals and port facilities, and experimented with handouts of free or subsidized grain.[119] Peasant societies received gifts of *chiu* and oxen from the state to sacrifice to the god of the soil.[120] Most important, the state established granaries (known as ever-normal granaries) to sell grain at fixed prices in time of famine, consistent with Confucian ideology. The *Book of Rites* stipulated that nine years' grain reserves were ideal (though nearly impossible to accomplish); less than six and the situation became tense, and less than three and the government would fall.[121]

In the face of growing peasant hunger, intellectuals condemned luxury. Mencius, a follower of Confucius, saw it as the root cause of peasant poverty. The Taoist Mo-Tzu said that luxury flew in the face of austerity, frugality, and social equality.[122] Others argued that it encouraged dissipation, arrogance, and lack of virtue. Wealthy merchant families bore the brunt of the attack because they bought the land of impoverished peasants but did not grow grain on it, and they were despised because unlike gentry, farmers, and artisans, they appeared not to produce anything of value. By the second century C.E., Taoism had become an organized religion, with a doctrine, ethical codes of behavior, and an ordained priesthood dedicated to overturning traditional Chinese religious practices. Taoist opposition was symbolized by abstention from the five grains. Since grains bound society together—peasant to family, family to village, family to ruler, and family to ancestors—to abstain from grain was to reject society. Taoist charitable institutions dispensed food to the poor. As the Han Dynasty collapsed, social disorder and floods along the lower Yellow River led to starvation and disease. The Taoists emerged as messianic leaders, threatening to topple the remnants of central power.

MAIZE CUISINES OF MESOAMERICA

Moving forward in time in order to have a New World comparison, by the sixth century C.E., Teotihuacan, on the high plateau of Mexico, a few miles to the north of present-day Mexico City, was the greatest city of the Americas and probably the sixth largest in the world. Dominated by the Pyramids of the Sun and the Moon, which towered over two four-mile-long avenues, the city sprawled over nine square miles and was home to one to two hundred thousand people.

Maize was as essential to the societies of the Americas as barley and wheat were to the states of Eurasia.[123] In the high Andes, it was supplemented by quinoa and a variety of roots, including potatoes. In the hot Mayan lowlands, it was supplemented by cassava (*Manihot esculenta*), a taro-like tuber (*Xanthosoma*), and sweet potatoes. The written records of these cuisines are either just being deciphered (Mayan) or date only from the time of the Spanish Conquest. I am going to assume that the cuisine of Teotihuacan was, at least in outline, similar to the better-known cuisine of its successor city, Tenochtitlan, which the Spanish conquered in 1521.

Cooking maize was women's work, and it was much harder than the men's job of cultivating it. Women shucked it, then knelt to grind it on a quern, called a metate in Mexico, the symbol of womanhood, the spot where a baby girl's umbilical cord was buried. Mixed with water, sometimes spiced with chiles or with aguamiel, syrup made by boiling down the sap of agave plants, the ground maize made a morning or evening gruel. Wrapped in a maize husk in central Mexico or a banana leaf in the hot lowlands, portions of ground maize, perhaps enclosing a savory or sweet morsel, were steamed to make dumplings (tamales). The technique was found across the Americas.[124]

If ground dry, though, maize cannot be made into flatbreads. The dough simply crumbles and falls apart. Fortunately, no later than 300 B.C.E., it was discovered that cooking maize with ash or naturally occurring alkaline salts alters its properties. The tough outer skin softens and can be rubbed away. The maize, ground wet, forms a plastic mass that can be patted out into breads (tortillas) that, when baked on a clay griddle (*comal*), are tender and aromatic as well as flexible enough to roll around foods, acting as a plate and a spoon. The process also improves the nutritional quality of the maize, though this could not have been the original reason for adopting this laborious, complex process.[125] Nixtamalization, as it is called, was as crucial for Mesoamerican grain cookery as leavening was for western Eurasian grain cookery or pasta making was for Chinese grain cookery. For about the past two thousand years, these tortillas have been the everyday food of the Mesoamericans, though the technique did not spread to South America.

To maize tamales or tortillas were added stews of domestic turkeys and dogs, and deer, rabbits, ducks, small birds, iguanas, fish, frogs, and insects caught in the wild. Sauces were made with basalt pestles and mortars that were used to shear fresh green or dried and rehydrated red chiles, resulting in a vegetable puree that was thickened with tomatillos (*Physalis philadelphica*) or squash

FIGURE 2.10. A roll-out photograph of a Mayan vase shows a Mayan ruler seated on a throne speaking to a kneeling attendant. On the floor is a three-legged offering bowl containing tamales. On the throne is a bowl, probably containing a foamy chocolate beverage. Courtesy Justin Kerr Maya Vase Data Base (6418).

seeds. Beans, simply simmered in water, provided a tasty side dish. For the nobles, there were gourd bowls of foaming chocolate, seasoned with annatto and chile (fig. 2.10).

"Maize, our body," said the early Mexicans. According to the related Mayan creation myth, the gods had formed them from maize dough after failing with mud and with wood.[126] Around maize, a whole culinary cosmology was constructed. The world's center was green, the color of life in the arid highlands of Mesoamerica. The west, where the sun sank into the womb of the earth, corresponded to woman, and the east, where it rose again the next morning, was male and red. Maize needed both the dark, cold womb and the light and heat of the male principle. Every night, the earth, the nurturing womb of life-sustaining maize, swallowed the sun. Every day, or so it was hoped, it would reappear.

Humans had to behave so as to maintain the cosmic equilibrium, avoiding excess, gluttony, drunkenness, and unwonted sex, whether with one's spouse at a proscribed time, outside marriage, or with someone of the same sex. Old women who had fulfilled their duty to the state and the gods could get drunk with impunity. For others, doing so was punishable by death.

Teotihuacan, it was believed, was the birthplace of the present world, which had already been created and destroyed four times. The gods had met there to decide which of them was to sacrifice himself so as to become the new sun, the fifth sun to give light to the world. When the self-sacrifice of the weakest failed to set the heavens in motion again, the gods joined in a mutual sacrifice for humankind.

Even the humblest householder, acknowledging a debt to the gods, offered a sprinkle of pulque, a pinch of food, or a few drops of blood when making a fire with a few twigs and arranging the three hearthstones that supported the cooking utensils. Inhabited by the fire god Huehueteotl, the hearth was the most sacred spot in the house.

The daily offerings to the gods were mere acknowledgments of this looming debt. From time to time, the priests told them, the gods had to be fed with the blood and hearts of humans, as men had fed on the gods to have crops, water, and freedom from disease. Sometimes the people of Teotihuacan sacrificed one of their own. Often those sacrificed were captives taken in battle. The sacrificial victims performed in staged, ceremonial gladiatorial fights. When the victim was wounded and bloody, the priests took his body and arched it back. Then they sliced out his heart using a sharp obsidian knife. They burnt it in homage to the gods. If the victim was a captive, they gave the captor a bowl of blood to daub on the mouths of the images of the god in the city's temples. Then the captor flayed the body, distributed the limbs, turned the flayed skin inside out, draped it over his body, and returned home dressed as the victim, anticipating his own death. He watched as his family took solemn bites of the stew of maize without chile topped by delicate slices of the dead warrior's flesh, a sacred meal. Dying in battle and dying in sacrifice to the gods were described as good deaths. After four years, the souls of the dead returned as the butterflies that migrated in their gorgeous black and gold finery or as the hummingbirds that flitted through the trees. They returned to a gentle land of honey, milk, and chocolate.

Although Teotihuacan fell around 900 C.E., its cuisine had been adopted by the Aztecs. It was this cuisine that the Spaniards encountered when they climbed up to the plateau of Mexico in the sixteenth century.

GLOBAL CULINARY GEOGRAPHY IN 200 C.E.

By 200 C.E., a chain of interlinked cuisines stretched from the Roman Empire in the west through the empires of Persia and northern India and across the steppes to the Han Empire in northern China (map 2.1). In all of them, wheat was the favored grain for high cuisine, displacing barley and millet, now thought to be fit only for humble cuisines and for animals. Assuming a world population of about 200 million, the Han and Roman empires were probably home to around 40 percent of it,

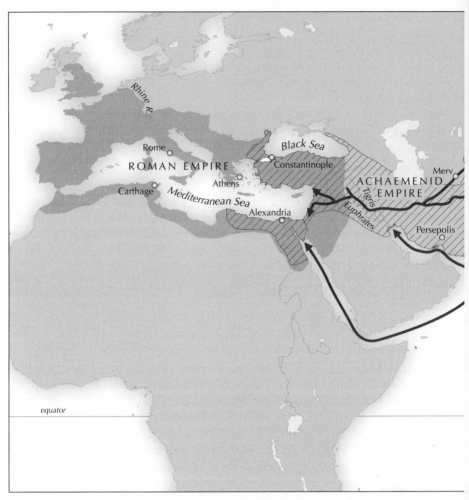

MAP 2.1. Ancient imperial cuisines, 600 B.C.E.–200 C.E. Persian Achaemenid cuisine, which built on the long culinary tradition of Babylonia, was a reference point for subsequent Greek, Hellenistic, Mauryan (Indian), and Roman cuisines, all of which depended on breads and pottages of barley and wheat, with wheat gradually replacing barley. The steamed wheat dough (pasta) of the Han Chinese high cuisine elevated wheat, which had been brought along the Silk Roads, from a low-status foreign grain to a high-status grain.

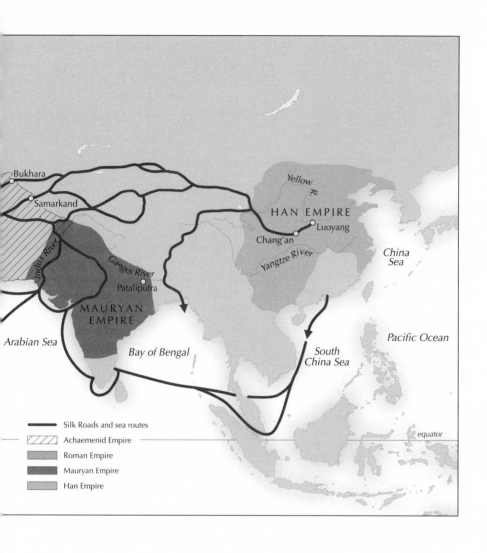

Bukhara

Samarkand

Indus River

Ganges River

Pataliputra

MAURYAN
EMPIRE

Arabian Sea

Bay of Bengal

Yellow
R.

HAN EMPIRE

Chang'an

Luoyang

Yangtze River

*China
Sea*

Pacific Ocean

South
China Sea

equator

Silk Roads and sea routes
Achaemenid Empire
Roman Empire
Mauryan Empire
Han Empire

20 percent each. If the other empires are included, then wheat eaters were ruling over half the world's population. The other major cuisines examined in Chapter 1 paled in comparison. Yet in spite of being based on the same staple, wheat cuisines had become more, not less, varied from one region to another, depending on the specific ways the grain was processed and cooked, and on the accompanying dishes. And although the ancient culinary philosophy was widely shared, critics had produced a number of alternative cuisines that better satisfied their goals.

Provisioning armies and cities with many thousands of foot soldiers or inhabitants had been mastered by developing more powerful, more efficient, and larger-scale methods of food processing and ways of providing meals for those with limited cooking facilities. Mechanical, chemical, and biochemical techniques were all improved. Animal and water power, rotary grindstones, hammer mills, and winnowing fans (in China) increased the efficiency of grain processing. In the Roman Empire, one grinder working for five hours could supply twenty people, four times as many as a grinder using a saddle quern in Ur, Nineveh, or Thebes, suggesting that the percentage of the working population that had to grind fell from 20 percent to 5 percent. In the Roman Empire, the baking of leavened wheaten bread had been perfected. In the Middle East and India, wheat flour continued to be baked into flat or lightly raised breads. In China, it was steamed or boiled to make wheat pasta (dumplings and noodles). Many soldiers and city dwellers had access to wheat products. There was to be little change in grain processing until the Industrial Revolution, and little change in the final cooking of grains until the twentieth century.

To supplement the staple, oil seeds and olives were crushed in a variety of mills and mortars and pressed in a variety of presses. Sweeteners continued to be produced by many different methods—sprouting grains (malt sugar in China), boiling down sap (palm sugar in India), boiling down fruit juices (grape and other fruit juices in the Middle East), and taking honeycombs from hives (honey in the Roman Empire). Alcoholic and lactic fermentations in the western half of Eurasia and mold ferments in the eastern half were used to make staple dishes (raised bread) and alcoholic drinks (wine, beer, and *chiu*), as well as to preserve foods (cheese and sausage in the Roman Empire, milk in the Middle East) and create condiments (fermented beans in China). Autolysis (self-digestion) produced garum in the Mediterranean and probably fish sauce in Southeast Asia.

Rural humble cuisines continued to be based on grains lower in the hierarchy, such as millet and barley, prepared as gruels, porridges, and pottages. Country people may have used a greater variety of raw materials than city dwellers, supplementing their diet with wild plants, small animals, and lake or river fish.

High cuisines had stimulated new techniques in cooking, particularly in meat dishes, appetizers, sauces, and sweet dishes. Meat was softened by fine chopping as well as long exposure to heat. Complex sauces were flavored with fermented condiments and spices and thickened with starch, ground nuts, or eggs in the Roman Empire, and with fermented condiments and spices in China. Deep-fried doughs, nuts in honey brittle, starch-thickened puddings, sweetened toasted meals, and (in the Mediterranean) sweetened cheesecakes were found across the western half of Eurasia. Professional cooks, either full-time employees or hands hired for the occasion, worked at bench stoves using complex sets of tools—pestles and mortars for sauce making in Rome, sharp knives for slicing and chopping meats in China. In Rome, diners reclined to eat, using their fingers and fine pottery or metal dishes. In China, they knelt to eat, using chopsticks to take delicacies from lacquerware.

Big landowners dominated farming, big merchants commerce. Long-distance ocean or river trade in both luxury goods (spices) and everyday foodstuffs (grains, oils, condiments) increased. Plants were transferred across the length and breadth of empires, and also between empires.

From the second and third centuries on, populations declined in the Roman and Han empires as a result of a series of plagues and infectious diseases. Long-distance travel dwindled, and eventually both empires fell to nomad attacks. The groundwork for the next big changes in cuisine had been laid. Across Eurasia, ascetics, philosophers, and religious reformers were arguing that sacrifice demeaned human relations with the sacred and failed to lead to inner spiritual transformation. Universal religions, such as Buddhism, Islam, Christianity, Jainism, Manichaeism, Judaism, Zoroastrianism, and Hinduism, had their origins in this ferment of ideas. In India and across the eastern half of Eurasia, Buddhism was transforming cuisines and bringing rice to prominence as a staple.

3

Buddhism Transforms the Cuisines of South and East Asia, 260 B.C.E.–800 C.E.

THEOCRATIC CUISINES: FROM SACRIFICE TO THE RULES OF UNIVERSAL RELIGIONS

Beginning in the third century B.C.E., questioning of the practices of sacrificial religion and the sacrificial feast began to have an effect. One empire after another abandoned state sacrifices and adopted a universal religion (or a religion of salvation) that offered a path to salvation or enlightenment.[1] Among the most prominent of the religions of salvation, which often evolved from earlier sacrificial ones, were Zoroastrianism, Judaism, Buddhism, Jainism, Hinduism, Manichaeism, Christianity, and Islam. Boundaries between the religions were frequently fluid, with crossovers between Hinduism and Buddhism in India, Islamic Sufism and Hinduism in Southeast Asia, and Taoism and Buddhism in China. Every universal religion had different branches, with differing beliefs and practices.

The transitions to new religions were rarely quick, and traces of sacrificial cuisines lingered. Romans continued to sacrifice until the fourth century C.E., northern Europeans did so, sometimes clandestinely, up through the tenth century, and the Chinese made offerings to the gods throughout imperial history. Jews cook lamb at Passover in remembrance of the sacrifice on the eve of the exodus from Egypt, Chinese take roast pigs to their ancestors' graves at Ching Ming, Muslims sacrifice a lamb or goat and distribute its remains at the Festival and Feast of Sacrifice—Eid al-Adha—and in the mass or Eucharist, Christians symbolically (or in some interpretations, literally) eat the body and drink the blood of Christ.

Nonetheless, a new period in culinary history was under way, one of traditional or theocratic cuisines in which states attempted, frequently with great success, to determine the religion and with it the cuisine of their subjects. When a religion was adopted by a state, it gained political as well as spiritual power, as rulers offered land, tax breaks, and other favors to chosen spiritual leaders. Thus temples and monasteries joined palaces as major centers of culinary innovation. Despite their shared interests, political and spiritual leaders competed for power, money, and influence. When the Buddhist monasteries were dissolved in medieval China, and when Christian monasteries were disestablished in Tudor England, tensions flared up, provoking rapid culinary change.

Two different exemplary meals replaced the sacrificial feast. In the courts and palaces, a feast or banquet with sauced meat dishes and alcoholic beverages was designed to showcase the power of the monarch and his nobles and to increase their physical strength. In the temples and monasteries an ascetic collation (a light meal consisting of a number of items), with carefully prepared, often meatless dishes was designed to demonstrate the residents' self-discipline and enhance their intelligence and spirituality. For all its restraint, this meal belonged to the realm of high cuisine, depending on luxury ingredients such as sugar, white bread, wine, tea, and coffee or chocolate, prepared in professional kitchens, and eaten in specialized settings. Although the religious might fast on the poorest of foods or take whatever appeared in their begging bowls, in the major institutions of the new religions, they also constructed new sacred high cuisines.

The most widely dispersed families of religious cuisine were, in succession, Buddhist, Islamic, and Christian. Religious cuisines that were not taken up by states (Judaism, Manichaeism), that lost state support (Zoroastrianism), or that were minority cuisines within other theocracies (Christians in medieval Islam, for example) typically modified the majority cuisine with their own rules and preferences.

The earliest Buddhist cuisine emphasized steamed or boiled rice, sugar, and ghee and shunned meat and alcohol. It began in India as the cuisine of the Mauryan Empire in 260 B.C.E. and expanded between the first and fifth centuries C.E., when India was as pivotal to the wider Asian sphere as Greece and Rome were to the Mediterranean, North Africa, and Europe.[2] Versions of the cuisine were adopted by the Kushan Empire, straddling northern India and Central Asia, by the states of Southeast Asia (along with Hindu cuisines), and, by the fifth century C.E., by different kingdoms in China, and then by surrounding states, including Korea and Japan. The eleventh century C.E. saw this expansion slow or reverse; notwithstanding, Buddhist culinary philosophy still shapes cuisines in China, Japan, Tibet, Southeast Asia, and Sri Lanka.

Islamic cuisine, which was ambivalent about wine and favored lightly raised wheaten breads, aromatic meaty stews, and sugar, took shape in the ninth century C.E., when the Baghdad caliphs modified Persian cuisine in line with Muslim culinary philosophy. Islamic cuisine spread to the sultanates in India, states in southern Spain, North Africa, and the southern fringes of the Sahara, and along the Silk Roads to the borders of China. After a brief retreat during Mongol expansion in the thirteenth century, it flowered again in the fifteenth and sixteenth centuries in the Indian Mughal Empire, the Persian Safavid Empire, the Turkish Ottoman Empire, and the kingdoms of Southeast Asia. By the seventeenth century, its greatest expansion was over, but Islamic culinary philosophy still structures cuisines in Southeast Asia, the Indian subcontinent, Central Asia, the Middle East, and North Africa and the Sahel.

Christian cuisine, with its raised wheat breads, wine, and feasting and fasting, began as a reworking of Roman and Jewish cuisines in the second and third centuries C.E. One version became the cuisine of the eastern part of the Roman Empire in the fourth century and then of the succeeding Byzantine Empire. Another, Catholic cuisine, gradually spread across the many small states of northern Europe, then exploded in the sixteenth century with the Portuguese and Spanish empires in the Atlantic Islands, the Caribbean, most of the Americas, trading posts in Africa and Asia, and the Philippines. The Protestant Reformation had complex effects, examined in chapter 6.

Buddhist, Islamic, and Christian cuisines continued to follow two of the three major principles of ancient culinary philosophy: the theory of the culinary cosmos and the principle of hierarchy. The theory of the culinary cosmos underpinned the rules "eat only cooked food" and (if wealthy enough) "eat a cuisine that balances the temperament." Cooking was a form of alchemy, the most sophisticated understanding of changes in matter then available. Cooking and alchemy used the same tools and equipment. Both sought to find the real nature or essence of a natural substance by applying the purifying power of fire. Just as a crude ore had to be refined in the fire to release the pure shining metal, so raw wheat or sugarcane had to be similarly refined to extract the pure white flour (originally "flower") or the gleaming sugar. Culinary processes such as sugar refining and bread baking were thus potent metaphors for spiritual progress. Unlike our contemporary understanding of natural food as having received only minimal processing, this earlier understanding was that processing and cooking were essential to reveal what was natural.

The hierarchical principle, which had justified the distinction between high cuisines for the court and humble cuisines for the urban and rural poor, was extended to warrant a parallel sacred ranking of ascetic collations for the religious and intellectual elite (monks, for example) and coarser cuisines for the unenlightened. In other words, the old rule "If you are a king, eat like a king, and if you are a peasant, eat like a peasant" was modified to include "if you are a holy man, eat like a holy man."

The third principle of ancient culinary philosophy, the sacrificial bargain, was replaced with the new rules of the universal religions. Similar in form, though not in content, across religions, these rules identified preferred ingredients and dishes, often ones believed to enhance contemplation, such as meat substitutes (fish, tofu, gluten), sweetened soft fruit and nut drinks, or stimulating drinks such as tea, coffee, and chocolate. They specified how to process and cook foods, including guidelines for slaughtering, and laid down rules about how cooks should purify themselves, whether fermented foods were acceptable, and which foods could and could not be combined. A third cluster of rules specified mealtimes, days of fasting and feasting, and who could dine with whom.

The rules, stricter for religious elites than for ordinary believers, were formulated and reformulated over centuries because the founders of the religions, although they relied on culinary metaphors to explain beliefs and doctrines, rarely laid down clear or consistent regulations for cooking and eating. Christians, for example, were not required to fast until the fourth or fifth century C.E. Then they were instructed to fast on about half the days of the year. Today, in the Roman Catholic Church, fasting has been reduced to a minimum.

Pilgrims traveled to the holy sites of the faith, often over considerable distances. Hindus made their way to temples such as Tirupati in southeastern India, Muslims to Mecca, Catholics to Santiago de Compostela in northern Spain. At their destination, they found sacred foods, often sweets, which they could take home.

Even more important in the dissemination of the new cuisines were monasteries, shorthand for permanent religious houses. Like courts, they were places were all ranks of society met, from clerics—usually drawn from the aristocratic or merchant classes—to their servants and slaves. Like court kitchens, monastery kitchens were huge and complex, turning out different meals for different ranks: noble and aristocratic visitors; passing merchants, monks, and nuns; the poor and indigent; the sick; and students studying in the monastery school. Like courts, monasteries received much of their income in kind from their landholdings. Like courts, they invested in food-processing equipment such as gristmills, oil presses, and sugar mills, processing and adding value to foodstuffs. These they sold or offered as gifts, thereby creating loyalty. Like courts, monasteries were part of networks that crossed state boundaries, in this case by the movement of religious orders and missionaries rather than marriage. Like courts, monasteries had formal dining protocol laid out in rule books that governed community life.

Unlike courts, however, monasteries had a corporate structure. This enabled them to avoid the inheritance disputes that plagued aristocracies and monarchies, and gave the monasteries actual (as opposed to imagined) continuity over hundreds of years. They were thus able to preserve the wealth they acquired from donations of land, tax relief, and gifts from private individuals. Monasteries created urbane outposts in far-flung areas—oases on the Silk Roads, hilly regions in remote southern China, the wooded frontier of Bengal, forests in northern and eastern Europe, and the interior of the Americas—where they disseminated new ways of food processing and cooking. Finally, religious houses provided the first opportunity for women to oversee large kitchens.

As theocratic cuisines spread, so did their preferred raw materials: plants and sometimes animals. Particularly important were the transfers of southeastern and

Chinese plants to Buddhist India, Indian plants to Buddhist China, Chinese plants to Korea and Japan, Indian plants to Islamic lands, and European plants to the Americas (through the Columbian Exchange). Royal and monastic gardens and large estates transplanted, ennobled, and grew sugarcane, rice, grapevines, tea, coffee, and other crops essential to the new cuisines.

Whereas culinary diffusion prior to world religions had primarily meant emulating or rejecting neighboring high cuisines, with world religions the relation between successive cuisines became more complex. "Fusion," the term so often used, does not do justice to the variety of interactions. One cuisine could be layered over another, as happened with the Spanish conquests in the Americas, the conquerors eating Catholic cuisine, the indigenous retaining their own cuisine. Specific dishes, techniques, plants, and animals might be adopted, as Europeans, for example, adopted distilling, confectionary, and citrus from Islam. Yet because culinary ideas and practices were identified with specific religions, every adoption involved adaptation and reworking. Bread, for example, did not take the same form or have the same significance in Islamic and Christian cuisines.

A second development paralleling the establishment of theocratic cuisine was the continued growth of gastronomy, the art of eating for its own sake rather than to display political or spiritual power. As the number of military officers, landowners, clergy, and even merchants in the cities of China, the Middle East, and Europe grew, they showed their interest in fine dining, depending on the region, by having recipes recorded in cookbooks, reading gastronomic literature, patronizing restaurants, and competing in culinary contests.

ASHOKA'S EDICT: BUDDHISM TRANSFORMS THE CUISINE OF INDIA, 250 B.C.E.–1200 C.E.

In the mid-third century B.C.E., a hundred years after Alexander's conquest of India, when the Roman Republic was still young, Hellenistic states stretched across the Middle East, and the Han Empire had yet to be founded, the emperor Ashoka ruled one of the world's richest and most populous polities. The Mauryan Empire stretched hundreds of miles from the Himalayas in the north across most of the subcontinent. In his capital on the Ganges River—Pataliputra—Ashoka presided over the sacrifices to the gods and the meaty feasts that followed. Along the roads went ascetics, dressed in rags with begging bowls in hand; many were disciples of the founders of Jainism and Hinduism and of Gautama Buddha, who had inspired a following two centuries earlier that formed the nucleus of early Buddhism.[3]

In about 264 B.C.E., edicts ordered by Ashoka began appearing across his vast lands. Some were inscribed on stone slabs, others on fifty-foot pillars of sandstone, polished to a fine gloss, crowned by statues of bulls, horses, or lions facing the four points of the compass. Depending on the region, they were in Maghadi, the official court language, Sanskrit, the priestly language, or, in Afghanistan, where Greeks, Persians, and steppe peoples mingled, Aramaic and Greek. "No living being may be slaughtered for sacrifice," said the first edict, translated in many different ways. "No festive gatherings may be held. Formerly slaughter in the king's kitchen was great; now it has almost been stopped." Thus Ashoka endorsed Buddhism, which in the following millennium was to expand and transform cuisines across the eastern half of Asia (map 3.1).

The central premise of Buddhism was that the root cause of human suffering was the illusion of a fixed world and an individual self. This illusion condemned humans to endless cycles of rebirths, as human emotions such as lust, anger, and pride drove them to commit evil actions that caused suffering to others. Buddhism called on its followers to renounce this illusory world, dedicating themselves to lives of spiritual purification and good works. Ashoka, by his own account revolted by his slaughter of thousands in the war against Kalinga, a state in east-central India, banned the sacrifice that for thousands of years had linked humans, the state, and the gods. He encouraged an emerging Buddhist cuisine, probably similar to the other emerging cuisines of Jains and reform-minded Hindus, that was based on cooked rice granules, dhal (Indian pulses), ghee (clarified butter), sugar confections, and sweetened fruit drinks.

Little is known about what happened following the edicts, but it is hard not to imagine that the ban must have appalled the priests, who lived off the fees they charged for sacrificing, and the warrior-courtiers, who distinguished themselves from commoners by eating more sacrificial meat. Ashoka's main support probably came from the merchants, manufacturers, and bankers who created much of the empire's wealth. Ranking only one step above serfs and well below aristocrats, warriors, and priests, they resented the fees the priests collected, their exemption from taxes, their carping about loans and interest on which commerce depended, and their expensive sacrifices. In succeeding centuries, India's flourishing economy depended on the alliance between Buddhists and merchants.

No edict could abolish with one blow a custom as deeply embedded as sacrifice. The court continued to sacrifice a few animals every day. Court cuisine probably went on using at least some meat, alcohol, spices, onions, and garlic and demonstrating splendor, not asceticism. Villagers, particularly in remote areas where imperial control scarcely existed, still asked priests to officiate at birth, wedding, and funeral services and to bless their humble offerings. The assassin of the last Mauryan emperor in 180 B.C.E. is reported to have reinstated the sacrifice.[4] Nonetheless, sacrifice was on the decline.

The support of the state, it may be assumed, was crucial to the creation of a high, ascetic Buddhist cuisine intended to enhance spiritual power, in contrast to high court cuisine that bestowed physical and military power. Not surprisingly, evidence for early Buddhist cuisine is scarce and conflicting. If the better-known

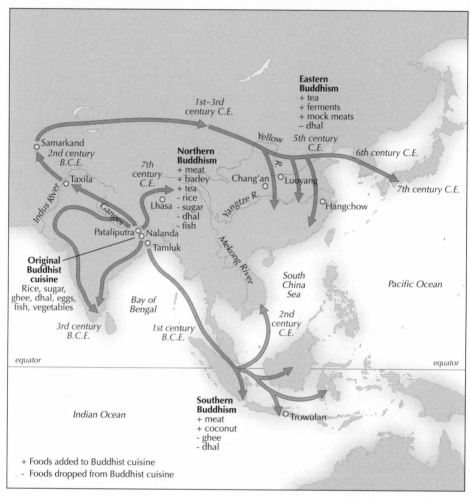

Eastern
Buddhism
+ tea
+ ferments
+ mock meats
− dhal

1st–3rd
century C.E.

5th century
C.E.

6th century C.E.

7th century C.E.

Yellow

Samarkand
2nd century
B.C.E.

Taxila

Northern
Buddhism
+ meat
+ barley
+ tea
− rice
− sugar
− dhal
− fish

7th
century
C.E.

Chang'an

Luoyang

R.

Indus River

Ganges

Lhasa

Hangchow

Pataliputra

Nalanda

Yangtze R.

Tamluk

Mekong River

Original
Buddhist
cuisine
Rice, sugar,
ghee, dhal, eggs,
fish, vegetables

South
China
Sea

Pacific Ocean

Bay of
Bengal

2nd
century
C.E.

3rd century
B.C.E.

1st century
B.C.E.

equator

equator

Indian Ocean

Southern
Buddhism
+ meat
+ coconut
− ghee
− dhal

Trowulan

+ Foods added to Buddhist cuisine
− Foods dropped from Buddhist cuisine

MAP 3.1. The expansion of Buddhist cuisine across Asia, 300 B.C.E.–1000 C.E. From its origin in the Ganges River Valley, Buddhist cuisine was spread across East and Southeast Asia by missionaries, pilgrims, and merchants. Steamed-rice cuisine became the staple of eastern empires. Beginning in 500 C.E., Buddhist cuisine was displaced in much of India by Hindu and, later, Islamic cuisines, although it still shapes the cuisines of Sri Lanka, Southeast Asia, China, Japan, and Tibet. Sources: Hinnells, *Handbook of Living Religions*, 280; Bentley, *Old World Encounters*, 70–71.

and later case of Christianity is any guide, there were debates about what the cuisine should be, divergences of practice between spiritual leaders and laypeople, and, of course, shifts across time. Two general points are clear. First, from early on there was a high ascetic cuisine that used the most desirable grains and expensive ghee and sugar, ingredients as far beyond the reach of the humble as the meat and alcohol of courtly high cuisine, though whether they were served to Buddhist monks or to their patrons is not clear. Second, Buddhist cuisine downplayed meat and alcohol, favoring alternative proteins and drinks, as well as rice, butter, and sugar. It relied less on biochemical methods of food processing than on mechanical and thermal methods, such as churning, grinding, and the application of heat.

Not only is Gautama Buddha reported to have repeatedly denounced animal sacrifice, but two of his five moral precepts—don't consume intoxicants and don't kill—also address the issue, forbidding alcohol and the soma of the sacrifice and making meat eating, necessarily preceded by killing, problematic.[5] In search of enlightenment, monks turned to fasting, extended meditation, and spiritual exercises instead of soma and alcohol. They could consume flesh, as long as they abided by the rule that they did not kill. In a list of permissible foods, the *Vinaya*, probably composed in the fourth century B.C.E. but put in written form much later, meat was included along with fish, rice, flour foods, and barley meal. Monks were expected to eat whatever was put in their begging bowls, including meat (though those who gobbled it were mocked as "false ascetics").[6] The Buddha, one story asserts, died from eating pork. Slowly, though, meat eating became less common. By the fifth century C.E., Indians (including Hindus) largely rejected the killing of cattle. By the seventh century C.E., Chinese visitors commented that Indians hardly ate meat.

Rice, wheat and barley, lentils and beans (dhal), fish and eggs, and ghee, sesame oil, honey, molasses, and sugar, said to form the basis of the Buddha's diet, became central to Buddhist ascetic cuisine. Recent scholarship suggests that Buddhists elaborated and systematized the sketchy theory of the culinary cosmos in the works of the semi-mythical physicians Caraka and Suśruta, probably giving them their present form in the late third century C.E.[7] Rice, sugar, and butter (from the fields and water buffalo of the hot, humid Ganges Valley), said the physicians, made for a calm, contemplative sattvic (pure) temperament corresponding to gold and white in the system of correspondences (table 1.2).

Hulled and polished white rice, according to the ancient physicians, fed the brain, encouraged contemplation, and was more auspicious than the heavy, gray brown peasant porridges and flatbreads made from millet, wheat, and barley in the Indus Valley. Strong spices had to be eschewed. Asafetida resin was used instead of onions and garlic, which made the breath stink. Lentils and beans, such as the golden-pink disks of masoor dhal (*Lens culinaris*) or greenish mung dhal (*Vigna radiata*), were substituted for meat. Vegetables included cabbages, cucumbers, bottle gourds, bitter gourds, eggplants, and the digestives radish and ginger.

The crisp, lacy root of the lotus, symbol of purity because the white flower rose above the mud, was used in cooking.

Ghee and sugar were alchemical-medical-culinary substances. Both were made by applying purifying fire to highly corruptible materials—milk and sugarcane juice—turning them into auspicious, incorruptible golden treasures that lasted even in the tropical heat. A passage in the *Saddharmasmrtyupasthana Sutra* (translated into Chinese early in the sixth century) states that just as cane juice was refined and purified into sugar, so monks during mediation were refined by the "fire of wisdom."[8] Cool, sweet, and unctuous foodstuffs such as sugar and ghee—savory, nutritious, agreeable, and well balanced—were associated with semen and the mind and enhanced the pleasures of exercising intelligence and sobriety. Sugar soothed hacking coughs, calmed itchy anuses, and disguised the taste of bitter medicinal herbs and tonics made with the emblic myrobalans (a large family of sour fruits still employed in Indian medicine). Both sugar and ghee might be eaten by the spoonful or used in cooking to add their flavor and power to entire dishes.

To make ghee, cows, buffalos, sheep, or goats were milked a couple of times a day. The milk from the teats, in modern orthodox Brahmin thought, and probably in ancient Buddhist thought, had already been cooked by the heat of the animal's body.[9] Churning a pot of milk using ropes wrapped around a paddle, a technique still practiced in Indian villages, was familiar to every Indian. Once milk had been churned to butter, the butter was heated over a low fire until the remaining water evaporated, leaving ghee, a pure golden ointment.[10]

With the new religions, churning became imbued with symbolic significance. From the eighth century on it became depicted time and again across southern Asia in the branch of Hinduism that worshipped Vishnu as the supreme deity. When the lesser gods appealed to Vishnu for help against encroaching demons, he ordered them to churn the primordial ocean of milk, which they did using a serpent as the rope (fig. 3.1). From the ocean emerged the sacred cow, the tree of paradise, and finally the nectar of immortality.

To extract juice from sugarcane, no easy task, the Indians adapted the ox-powered mortar and pestle (*ghani*) already used to grind oil seeds. They chopped the cane into short lengths and placed it in the waist-high mortar. Then, as figure 3.2 shows, they attached the ox to the pestle mechanism to extract the juice. It seems probable that this juice was regarded as already having been cooked by the heat of the sun, as milk had been cooked by the heat of the cow.

Pans of cane juice and crushed cane were then heated over a fire, an expensive process but one that extracted 85 percent of the juice from the cane. The more juice extracted, the more impurities there were, and to separate these out, handfuls of slaked lime (calcium hydroxide) were thrown in. What resulted was a fudge-like, semisolid crystallized sugar (*gur*) in a thick syrupy molasses. By draining and further refining this substance, Indian sugar makers obtained four products:

FIGURE 3.1. Figures churn an ocean of milk by pulling back and forth on a serpent wound around a mountain to release the nectar of immortality, a symbolic representation of the actual process women used to make butter by pulling back and forth on a rope wound around a churning staff. From Edward Moore, *The Hindu Pantheon* (London: J. Johnson, 1810), pl. 49. Courtesy New York Public Library, http://digitalgallery.nypl.org/nypldigital/id?psnypl_ort_082.

FIGURE 3.2. To grind oil seeds or sugarcane in a large mortar, releasing their oil or juice, a man drives a blindfolded ox harnessed to a large pestle in circles. When the process was complete, he pulled a plug in the bottom of the mortar to allow the liquid to flow into a vessel. Drawing by John Lockwood Kipling in *Beast and Man in India: A Popular Sketch of Indian Animals in Their Relation with the People* (London: Macmillan, 1904), 143.

thickened cane juice (*phanita*), brown sugar (*jaggery*), rock sugar (*khand*, whence our word "candy"), and crystal sugar (*shakara*).[11]

Monasteries, which were well established by Ashoka's time, brought the ascetic cuisine to a standard of excellence. Land grants and tax breaks, as well as land donated by the pious or by monks and nuns from wealthy families, made these communities wealthy. Situated on the fringes of major cities, astride the important trade and pilgrimage routes, they included pillared prayer halls, meditation cells, dome-shaped stupas that housed relics of the Buddha, and large, well-equipped kitchens. Monks abandoned their rags and began dressing in formal robes. Spiritual leaders organized the Buddha's teachings and the stories of his life. They drew up codes for the monastic life, including rules for cooking and dining. One sign of high rank was the right to be seated in a chair.[12]

Sources referring to the general state of Indian cuisine at the time allow us to attempt to reconstruct Buddhist meals. Buddhists had one main meal, taken before noon. Sweet dishes, some of them pre-Buddhist, others added by Buddhists, were auspicious, perhaps served as part of the main meal, perhaps taken as light snacks or offered to visitors. Traditional sweets included a confection of sesame seeds and brown sugar, or *jaggery;* halvahs made of flour (barley, wheat, or rice) fried in ghee with brown sugar and flavored with cardamom, pepper, or ginger; yogurt with crystal sugar (*shakara*), herbs, and spices; rice pudding; a fudge of boiled-down milk shaped like a peacock egg; flatbread stuffed with sweet bean paste and baked on an inverted pot; and a fried wheat-flour pastry coated with fine sugar. Among the new sweets were a cake of rice or wheat flour mixed with honey and cooked in ghee, and one of rice flour combined with molasses and ghee.

Savory dishes were mainly composed of grains, dhal, and vegetables, probably including white rice boiled in water or milk, perhaps sprinkled with sesame seeds; roasted barley flour mixed with yogurt; dhal soup; deep-fried patties of ground beans (*vadas*); patties of ground vegetables (*kofta*); thin, soupy sauces, perhaps gruels of barley or rice, sometimes soured with pomegranate juice and flavored with long pepper; beans and vegetables lightly dressed with ghee or vegetable oil, particularly sesame oil; white-fleshed river or ocean fish; and eggs. Ghee was the favored condiment. Yogurt could be used as a sauce. Toasted disks of ground dhal (papadums) added a crunchy contrast.[13]

After midday, no solid food was allowed. As specified in the *Vinaya,* the list of permissible foods, monks, particularly if they were weak or sick, could drink soup, nibble on sweet cakes, take milk, yogurt, cream or honey, or eat chewable foods such as roots, stems, leaves, flowers, and seeds. They could sip light medicinal drinks, such as yogurt mixed with water (*lassi*), thought to be purer than water; herbal infusions; fruit waters made with the juice of mango, Java plum (*Syzgium cumini*), banana, grape, coconut, phalsa (*Grewia subinaequalis*); and edible water lily roots, probably ground; diluted honey; and unfermented sugarcane juice. The last the monastic rules defined as the nectar of the gods.

Monastery kitchens prepared refreshments and meals for many groups other than monks. Patrons were offered sophisticated delicacies. In the seventh century, and probably much earlier, Buddhists offered visitors ascetic collations of "ghee, honey, sugar and other eatables."[14] Passing merchants and monks were fed and housed, pilgrims received foods appropriate to their spiritual journey, the sick in the infirmaries were served restoratives, and servants and lay workers were handed rations.

From the fifth to the twelfth centuries C.E., universities formed around the monasteries in Nalanda in northeast India and in Taxila, north of present-day Islamabad. The latter was the jumping-off point for Buddhists traveling to Central Asia and China. The monastery-university complexes attracted thousands of students, some from as far away as China, who preserved, studied, and annotated Buddhist scriptures and mastered the nutritional theory of Caraka and Suśruta.

Monasteries invested in animals and machines, including buffalo to work the fields, haul the cane, and power the ghanis, contributing to India's transformation from peasant subsistence to bustling commercial and manufacturing society.

Monks, often from merchant families, adeptly combined religion and business. Sugar and ghee, with their long shelf life and high value-to-weight ratio, were traded over long distances.

Plants were imported, improved by breeding, and distributed. Ashoka ordered shady groves of banyans (the tree under which the Buddha received enlightenment) and mangoes (which the Buddha had caused to sprout miraculously) to be planted along imperial roadsides. Mangoes, grapes, jackfruit, and palms were carved on the facades of the famous Buddhist stupas at Bharhut and Sanchi in central India. Several rice varieties, two wheat varieties, twelve sugarcane varieties, and three new legumes were brought into cultivation. Millets (probably via Central Asia), yams, loquats, and litchis (though these do not seem to have gained great success) were brought from China. Breadfruit, bilimbi (*Averrhoa bilimbi*), citruses, star fruit, durian, sugar palm, coconut, sago palm, and betel came from Southeast Asia.[15]

In the fifth century C.E., the Gupta emperors of northern India shifted state support from Buddhism to Hinduism, and Buddhism began losing ground in India. Hindu cuisine, with its rice, dhal, and sweets of boiled-down milk or ground lentils enriched with ghee and cardamom, overlapped with Buddhist cuisine. Hindus offered sugar and ghee to the gods. "*Jaggery* [coarse brown sugar], *payasam* [sweet rice pudding], ghee, *appam* [a rice pancake], *modakam* [a stuffed confection], curds [yogurt], *dal* [dhal], all these are to be offered as Food for the Gods," Krishna instructs in the *Bhagavata Purana*, the set of legends that marked the rise of his worship in the ninth century.[16] Honey, sugar, ghee, and rice appeared in the ceremonies that marked the passages of life. Women in the fifth month of pregnancy were given the "five ambrosias"—sugar, honey, milk, ghee, and yogurt. The newborn's lips were moistened with honey, ghee, water, and yogurt. The bridegroom was offered honey, rice, and herbs during his wedding.

In the twelfth and thirteenth centuries, Muslim invaders destroyed the remaining Buddhist monasteries and confiscated their lands. Ashoka's edicts were forgotten, his inscribed rocks and pillars covered by tangles of vines, becoming undecipherable monuments from an unknown past. India had become a land of Islamic and Hindu cuisines. The *Book of Splendors* (*Manasollasa*), composed in the twelfth century, gives an idea of the high cuisine. Nobles began their meals with mangoes and ginger and lemon pickles. They enjoyed meat, including pork, venison, rabbit, birds, and tortoises. Their vegetable dishes included eggplants, pumpkins, gourds, and plantains flavored with cumin, fenugreek, mustard seeds, sesame seeds, and black pepper. Sweets were taken in the middle of the meal. As usual, such meals contrasted with the more sober ascetic cuisine served on religious occasions (fig. 3.3).

In the fourteenth to sixteenth centuries, a high Hindu cuisine flourished in the kingdom of Vijayanagara in southern India. At the temples of Tirupati, supported by the Vijayanagara kings, the gods were fed one to six times a day with simple meals of cooked rice, green gram, yogurt, ghee, and vegetables. As monks and royalty forged

FIGURE 3.3. In this solemn ceremony recorded in the nineteenth century by a Portuguese traveler, tonsured individuals, probably Brahmins, are seated in an open-air pavilion with lights from fine fixtures flickering overhead. On the right, a turbaned man makes an offering to a seated Brahmin. From A. Lopes Mendes, *A India portugueza* (Lisbon: Imprensa nacional, 1886), opp. p. 43.

an alliance, the meals became more elaborate. Donations were used to prepare food. The priest offered it to the god, raised it to his mouth, and consumed it on behalf of the god. Morning meals consisted of four kinds of vegetable curry, four kinds of coconut-based vegetable curry, four kinds of yogurt-based vegetable dishes, rice, and a variety of drinks, including milk, buttermilk, and a fruit drink. About three-quarters of the meal was reserved for the temple staff. The remaining quarter went to the donor (whose donation was carefully inscribed in stone if it was large) to share with his household, to offer to another household or temple, or to pass on to middlemen to sell to pilgrims. The seasoned rice, fried sweet cakes, roasted and sweetened lentils, fruits soaked in milk, or milk sweets, seasoned and semisolid, could easily be parceled out into leaf cups; rich in butter and sweeteners, they lasted for the journey home.

While Hindu cuisine dominated in India, Buddhist cuisine was by now established well beyond its place of origin.

MONKS AND MISSIONARIES: BUDDHIST CUISINE EXPANDS SOUTH, EAST, AND NORTH, 250 B.C.E.–1200 C.E.

About 250 B.C.E., in the third of three Buddhist councils, reportedly convened by Ashoka himself in Pataliputra, Buddhists decided to spread their message. Instead of paying respect to local deities, as earlier travelers had done, monks and merchants set out to convert others far beyond the religion's homeland. It was a momentous change in the history of religion and in the spread of religious cuisines.

Buddhists expanded from India in three waves. The following section focuses on the second. Beginning in the third century B.C.E. and continuing to the thirteenth century C.E., the first wave (known as southern or Theravada Buddhism), often accompanied by or integrated with Hinduism, went to South and Southeast Asia, particularly Sri Lanka, Burma, Cambodia, Thailand, and southwestern China. In the fifth century C.E., Tamralipti (modern Tamluk) in western Bengal, the largest trading port on the east coast of India, had over twenty Buddhist monasteries.[17] Indian merchants dealt in cloves, nutmeg, and mace from Southeast Asia, pepper from south India, and cinnamon from Sri Lanka, establishing diaspora communities in the powerful trading states of the Malay Peninsula and Vietnam, especially the Mekong River Delta. They and monks took with them the Buddha's teaching and the Buddhist culinary package: the monastic rules, the dietary manuals of Caraka and Suśruta, and a preference for rice, ghee, sugar, and certain vegetables.[18]

The ruling classes in these Southeast Asian states looked to wealthy, powerful north India as a model, adopting its religions, music, and ceremonies, the humoral theory of nutrition, perhaps ways of processing sugar, and the elaborate dishes of Indian courts and temples. The Hindu-Buddhist Majapahit Empire, centered in Java, flourished in the fourteenth and fifteenth centuries with tributaries from present-day Indonesia, Thailand, Malaysia, and the Philippines. The hundred-square-kilometer site of monumental red brick buildings near the village of Trowulan in East Java is presumed to have been its capital. Figure 3.4, a relief on the base of a column on that site, shows a woman cooking in a kitchen.

The third and last wave of Buddhist expansion went to Tibet and the Himalayas in the seventh century C.E. There, in the chill of the high mountains and plateaus, Buddhists had no hope of growing rice, sugar, and many of the vegetables they favored. Nor did they abandon meat. In fact, they had a special curved knife for slaughtering. Five hundred years later, their meat eating contributed to the Mongol decision to adopt the Tibetan branch of Buddhism in their Chinese empire (chapter 4).

FIGURE 3.4. A woman crouches in front of pots nestled in holes on a
bench stove, the stove of choice throughout the Buddhist-Hindu
world. A relief from the base of a pillar found at Trowulan, probable
capital of the Hindu-Buddhist Majapahit Empire, based in Java.
Gelatin silver print by Claire Holt. Courtesy New York Public Library,
http://digitalgallery.nypl.org/nypldigital/id? 1124877.

MONKS AND MONASTERIES: BUDDHISM
TRANSFORMS THE CUISINE OF CHINA,
200 C.E.–850 C.E.

The second wave of Buddhist expansion is, however, our focus. In the first century
B.C.E. Buddhism widened its appeal to become a religion that offered hope for
all, not just monks and ascetics. Many Buddhists began to worship their founder

as a god. They also turned to saints (bodhisattvas) who had delayed their entry to nirvana to help their fellow men. According to the early medieval Buddhist text *Compendium of Training*, by the Buddhist scholar Santideva, the task of a bodhisattva was to help humans escape from the cycle of life and death by purification, the metaphorical "cooking of bodies."[19] The devout created murals, paintings, and statues of the Buddha and the bodhisattvas. The statues were anointed and fed with honey, sugar, ghee, and oils.[20]

Buddhist merchants and missionaries set off across Asia from northern India. They turned the Kushan Empire, which stretched across what is now northern Afghanistan and southern Uzbekistan between the first and third centuries C.E., into a Buddhist state. From there some made their way from oasis to oasis to China, crossing vast distances and challenging terrain.[21]

Han China could hardly have been a less likely place for Buddhism to take root. Shaped by Confucian values and firmly focused on this world, the Chinese were opposed to monkish celibacy, which negated family piety. Their high cuisine was dominated by wheat noodles, lamb and mutton, and fermented condiments. It was eaten with chopsticks, not fingers. Red dishes were seen as auspicious, not incitements to violence. Sacrifice was the basic duty to the state. The foods favored in Buddhism, such as rice or sugar, did not flourish in the Yellow River Valley. Buddhists, perhaps deliberately, allowed themselves to be confused with Taoists, who also practiced meditation and worshipped statues. The same landowners and literati who followed Taoism were probably attracted by Buddhists' contempt for the sacrificial rites and indifference to political life.[22]

With the fall of the Han Empire at the end of the second century C.E., Buddhists, whose monasteries helped the poor and ensured a certain stability during the ensuing civil wars, seized the opportunity to move from a minority religious group to a faith supported by political leaders. Until the mid-sixth century, Turkic emperors sympathetic to Buddhism as an alternative to Confucianism ran northern China. Rulers in the southern kingdoms used Buddhism to distinguish themselves from the native populations.

The height of Buddhist power came between the fifth and eighth centuries C.E.[23] In the fifth century, the emperor Wu, who ruled the southern Yangtze region, banned the state sacrifice of animals, decreeing that monks must abstain from meat.[24] Other rulers allowed the ordination of monks, endowed monasteries (thus gaining Buddhist merit), incorporated Buddhist practices into state rituals, and extended exemptions from certain taxes.

From the third century C.E. on, Chinese Buddhist monks had undertaken the arduous and costly journey across deserts, mountains, and tropical forests to study in India, the birthplace of Buddhism. The most famous of these was Xuan-zang, who set off in 629 C.E., picked up supplies, letters of introduction, and gifts to distribute from the ruler of Turfan, a Buddhist principality on the Silk Roads, and spent twelve years visiting holy sites and studying at Nalanda. He returned to China with relics, images, and hundreds of Buddhist Sanskrit texts, which he translated into Chinese so that the Chinese might have access to the founding writings of Buddhism.[25] A tale known as the *Monkey King*, a redaction of *Journey to the West*, his chronicle of his travels, was recounted by storytellers and performed by actors in later centuries, spreading word of his life widely among the population.

The monks who visited India were surprised to discover how different the cuisine was from their own. I-ching, who visited in the late seventh century, contrasted Indian meals, where "all vegetables are to be well cooked and to be eaten after mixing with the asafetida, clarified butter, oil, or any spice," with those of China, where "people of the present time eat fish and vegetables mostly uncooked."[26] Xuan-zang, who went half a century earlier, discovered that the Indians did not eat much meat. "Fish, mutton, gazelle and deer they eat generally fresh, sometimes salted; they are forbidden to eat the flesh of the ox, the ass, the elephant, the horse, the pig, the dog, the fox, the wolf, the lion, the monkey, and all the hairy kind." Unlike the Chinese, they ate from communal vessels, mixed foods together, and used their fingers instead of spoons and chopsticks. He was struck by "milk, butter, cream, soft sugar, sugar-candy, the oil of the mustard-seed, and all sorts of cakes made of grain used as food."[27]

The better understanding of Buddhism acquired by these monks was ultimately responsible for the introduction to China of Indian dietary theory, monastic rules, ways of processing butter and refining sugar, certain fruits and vegetables, possibly a shift to more thoroughly cooked food, and dining seated on chairs. Dhal, however never made it. And Chinese Buddhist monks were to contribute two major innovations to Buddhist cuisine: tea as a beverage and mock meats such as tofu and gluten. These changes enriched the Chinese culinary tradition, adding to but not displacing traditional Chinese techniques of steaming grains, making pasta from flour, and using ferments to make alcoholic drinks and condiments. It was a one-way transfer. There is no sign that Chinese techniques were transferred to India in this period.

Monasteries were founded in Luoyang, the capital city of the Northern Wei Dynasty (386–534 C.E.), by then the most vibrant Buddhist center in the world and the center for the translation of Buddhist texts into Chinese. When the empire shifted westward, the cosmopolitan new capital, Chang'an, had Persian, Arab, Jewish, Indian, Japanese, and Korean communities among its two million people. The ninety to a hundred Buddhist monasteries far outnumbered the Muslim, Jewish, Nestorian (Syrian) Christian, and Manichean places of worship.[28] Their great estates were economic and social powerhouses. They ran their basic agricultural and food-processing operations according to Jia Sixie's manual. Since he wrote at the time that Buddhists were coming to power, I suspect that his manual (including its direction for milk products) reflected Buddhist as well as traditional Chinese food-processing technologies. In any case, the monastic estates produced oil for votive lamps, tea for meditation, sugar, and mock meats. Serfs and slaves husked rice and worked the mills that crushed sugarcane and oil. Beginning in the mid-eighth century, flour was ground by water mills.[29]

The daily life of the monks, literate and from well-to-do backgrounds, was ordered according to Indian monastic rule books. The monks supervised the kitchen and, once the works of Caraka and Suśruta had been translated from the Sanskrit in the late fifth century C.E., arranged their menus according to a merged yin/yang "rajasic/sattvic" system. They began to shift from the traditional yang foods of north China—lamb, onions, and garlic—which were rajasic, to sugar, tofu, fish, oranges, cucumber, chrysanthemum petals, bean sprouts, and winter melon, which were sattva (yin) foods. Pure white steamed rice was thought to be more conducive to reflection than wheat pasta.[30]

Plants and ingredients important to Buddhists were introduced from India: the lotus, turmeric, and saffron (though whether preserved or fresh is unknown); the astringent fruits known as myrobalans; and asafetida, black pepper, and long pepper (*Piper longum*), believed to lengthen life.[31] Irrigated rice farming expanded during the seventh century, when Buddhist monasteries colonized areas close to the Buddhist and Hindu areas of Southeast Asia.

In 647, the emperor Taizong sent an envoy to India charged with learning the secrets of sugar making. He returned with six monks and two artisans, who established sugar manufacturing south of Hangchow, where the climate was favorable to sugarcane, so that it changed from the exotic plant of southernmost China mentioned by Jia Sixie to an increasingly important crop. Figure 3.5, an illustration from a dietetic herbal, probably from the fourteenth or fifteenth century, but depicting methods in use earlier, shows how sugarcane was pressed and the juice evaporated to sugar. Like the Indians, the Chinese used milk to whiten sugar, though they used their own edge-runner presses rather than the Indian ox-driven pestles and mortars. The Chinese produced several grades and kinds of sugar, most of them soft and brown. "Like amber (the sap of venerable pine trees embalmed by a spiritual preservative) presented on a crystal plate / Is there anything more beautiful than crystallized sugar?" wrote the poet Su Shi in 1074 on saying good-bye to a friend setting off for the cane-sugar area of Sichuan.[32]

Ghee, according to Jia Sixie's *Essential Skills,* was made by a three-stage process like that used in India. Milk and yogurt went into sauces or were drunk cultured, perhaps as buttermilk, perhaps as yogurt mixed with water.[33] Sugar and ghee continued to be magico-medical substances as much as foodstuffs. The text of the illustration in figure 3.5 describes sugar as sweet, cold, and nonpoisonous, cooling to the body (whereas in the West it was classified as slightly warm), killing parasites, and alleviating alcohol poisoning. Taken in excess it damaged the teeth,

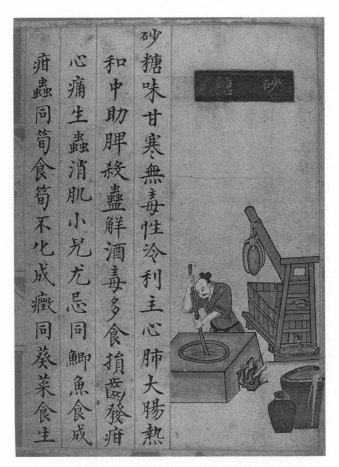

FIGURE 3.5. A laborer in Ming Dynasty China (1368–1644) stands behind a raised bench stirring a pot of boiling cane juice. Ready for use are a pottery jar of greenish cane juice and a pitcher. In the background, heavy weights pull down a beam expressing cane juice (probably a second pressing after a first pressing with an edge-runner mill), which pours into a second pottery jar from a spigot. From the dietetic herbal *Shiwu bencao,* author and artists unknown. Courtesy Wellcome Library, London (L0039388).

caused symptoms of malnutrition, and harmed the muscles. Sugar revived the weak, disguised the taste or enhanced the properties of other medicines, made syrup for anointing images of the Buddha, and was distributed to the faithful. Sugar brought out the sweetness of crab. It was combined with ghee and wheat flour to make pastries. It was made into lion-, duck-, or fish-shaped bonbons used as decorations in grand banquets.

Tea, one of China's most important contributions to Buddhism, began its trajectory from a medicinal herb, to an aid to meditation, to the centerpiece of a new social meetingplace, the teahouse. From the sixth century on, tea, simultaneously cool and stimulating, displaced yogurt and water drinks and substituted for the sweetened fruit drinks of India.[34] Buddhist and Taoist monasteries in southeastern China pioneered its large-scale production from the leaves of the evergreen bush *Camellia sinensis*, native to the mountains between northeast India and southwest China. Instead of using tea as a medical infusion, monks used it to stay awake during meditation. A legend describes how a monk cut off his eyelids to prevent himself from dropping off to sleep, only to see that from them sprouted the tea plant. The first major treatise on tea, the *Classic of Tea*, from 780 C.E., was written by Lu Yu, an orphan raised in a Buddhist monastery, who remained close to monks all his life.[35]

Tea then was not made with the loose leaves but with a powder. The leaves of the tea bushes were steamed, dried, powdered in a rotary mill, and pressed into cakes. When it was time to serve the tea, the cakes were pounded in a pestle and mortar, a little powder was placed in each tea bowl set on its own stand, boiling water was poured from a metal pot, and the beverage was mixed with a bamboo whisk to distribute the flavor. The process brought to mind the five phases: wood, water, fire, metal, and earth (table 1.4). Tea came from wood. During brewing, it met water, "the friend of tea." Fire, "the teacher of tea," brought out its character. The ewers for hot water were metal. Tea was served in ceramic cups—earth refined. Monks carried tea for their own use and as gifts across China. In spite of criticisms that tea, like alcohol, incited vice, and that it was grown on land that would be better used for grains, tea became an essential part of Chinese cuisine.[36]

Buddhists also seem to have had a large hand in the introduction of tofu, gluten, and other mock meats. Tofu, probably invented in the first couple of centuries C.E. with the spread of rotary grindstones and the knowledge of milk processing, appears to have become common by no later than the twelfth century. It was made by soaking soybeans, wet-grinding them in a mill, and filtering out the milk. The filtered milk was coagulated with vinegar, gypsum, or other chemicals, and the coagulant was pressed into a solid block. It was widely used in Buddhist and other ascetic cuisines. Gluten, wheat flour with the starch washed out, commonly known in America as seitan, was probably invented around the same period as a by-product of the making of wheat-flour noodles. By the thirteenth century, Marco Polo reported, it was established as a monastery specialty. Boiled, fried, pickled, smoked, and shredded, it was transformed to resemble chicken, fish, shrimp, and other meats. Buddhist monasteries remained famous for fine gluten dishes until the 1950s. Agar-agar, a gelatinous substance extracted from certain seaweeds, was fried in lard and substituted for dried meat. Mushrooms were called "chicken of the earth." Lotus roots and other tubers were turned into purees, perhaps resembling the vegetable kofta of India.[37]

Buddhist monks in China, as in India, apart from a light breakfast of rice gruel (congee) and pickles, ate one main meal, prepared by servants or slaves.[38] Between ten and eleven they assembled for their repast of rice gruel, rice, vegetable dishes, grains, and fruits. After this, solid food was forbidden for the rest of the day, though herbal infusions, fruits, sugarcane juice, and tea could be sipped. Visitors were offered good tea and light meals, famous for their elaborate presentations. The nun Fan Zheng was famed for reproducing the paintings of the eighth-century artist and poet Wang Wei, with vegetables, gourds, meat, and fermented fish.[39]

In the mid-ninth century, the heyday of official Chinese Buddhism came to an end. The state shut down the houses of foreign religions, mainly Buddhist monasteries, which had been exempt from tax. Between 842 and 845, a quarter of a million monks and nuns were returned to secular life, 4,660 monasteries and 40,000 smaller places of worship were destroyed or turned into public buildings, and the state confiscated their estates, the families of their serfs, the money, and the metals.[40] This was not, however, to be the end of Buddhist cuisine in China. Far from it. Buddhism was now firmly established as one of the three philosophies that shaped Chinese cuisine, along with Taoism and Confucianism. [41]

CONFUCIAN-TAOIST-BUDDHIST CUISINE
IN CHINA, 850–1350 C.E.

Not very long after the disestablishment of Buddhist monasteries in northern China, the focus of Chinese society moved south to a climate more favorable to rice, sugar, and tea. In 1127, the court relocated to Hangchow. Nomads cut off access first to the Silk Roads, then to the old trade routes linking Sichuan and the area between the Yangtze and Yellow Rivers. Now, rather than facing west along the Silk Roads, China looked south and east, to maritime trade with Japan. Hangchow grew to a city of a million people, capital of a territory that stretched 1,200 miles from west to east and 600 from the northern frontier to the southern coast, with several cities that approached a million, and another dozen with populations ranging from a quarter to half a million. The total population of the empire, according to official censuses, was more than sixty million, perhaps as high as a hundred million.

Twenty thousand scholar-bureaucrats, men of wealth and education, used the Confucian classics to run the country, observed the ritual occasions, and made offerings to the ancestors at the spring festival of Ching Ming. They used Buddhism and Taoism to order their lives and cultivated gastronomy as a mark of the Chinese gentleman, along with calligraphy, poetry, and the other great arts that satisfied the mind and the emotions as much as they pleased the senses. Together these three traditions led to a highly elaborated culinary philosophy, an ascetic cuisine for the scholar-hermit, and new forms of social life based on restaurants and teahouses. Steamed rice began to displace steamed millet as a staple. Wheat products were sufficiently common that the old single category of *bing* was divided into two: the term *bing* was used exclusively for bakery products, while noodles, an increasingly common food for all social classes, were now called *mein*. Milk products became less important, while sugar and tea, by contrast, formerly medicines or aids to spirituality or meditation, entered mainstream cuisine. This may also have been the period when the wok first entered the kitchen, though as yet we lack a good understanding of the history of the wok.[42]

According to the culinary philosophy of Chinese gastronomes, a civilized or cultured man was in harmony with the cosmic order, with everything working in balance while simultaneously obeying its own nature. The impartial, patterned cosmic order, watched over by heaven, was to be emulated by humans in all their activities. To cook well, a slow, steady fire was needed, not a smoky one, nor one that flared and died. This slow steady fire was a *wen* fire. The words for civilization, *wen ming*, and culture, *wen hua*, both derived from *wen*, or pattern.

Taste demanded intelligence as well as a good palate, an understanding of history as well as knowledge of market produce, a sense of how a well-made meal reflected the deepest cosmic harmonies, and the ability to wield a knife and handle a wok. The taste of food was like the meaning of a poem. In the latter part of the ninth century, Tsu-kung Tu commented of a friend's poem: "One cannot begin to speak of poetry if one has not learned to tell taste (*wei*). . . . People who merely eat to fill the stomach know only what is sour and what is salty, and not what perfection requires."[43] The natural taste of foodstuffs was revealed only after careful preparation.[44] If you touched your tongue to a raw chicken it tasted metallic, a raw fish insipid, and raw beef rank with the flavor of blood. Only with cooking were their true, natural flavors revealed. Edible plants and roots and mushrooms gathered in the mountains had to be coaxed to display their full flavors. The raw or very simply cooked foods that Xuan-zang had reported as being typical of China were being replaced by processed and cooked ones.

Those who fled from or were expelled from bureaucratic or political life created an ascetic cuisine that shows signs of being indebted to the Buddhists. The distinguished poet and statesman So Dongpo was banished to Hangchow in 1080 c.e., when it was still a small provincial town. He cooked for himself, his wife, and his favorite concubine, Zhaoyun, ignoring the old adage that "the gentleman keeps his distance from the kitchen" (credited to the Confucian scholar Mencius, who had lived about fifteen hundred years earlier). So Dongpo grew his own vegetables, relished the local oranges and persimmons, and delighted in the local fish. Besides preparing traditional meats such as mutton and venison, he popularized pork, and a pork dish is still named in his honor. He is remembered for his appreciation of the natural taste of carefully scrubbed cabbage, wild daikon, and shepherd's purse cooked into a soup with a little rice, fresh ginger, and oil.[45]

A couple of centuries later, around 1275 C.E., Lin Hong, a scholar-hermit who lived south of Hangchow, wrote a cookbook, *Simple Offerings of a Mountain Hermit*, which contained a hundred recipes for fruits, flowers, fungi, and bean curd.[46] Then, in the fourteenth century, one of the greatest Chinese painters, Ni Tsan, a master of deceptively simple ink paintings, wrote a short cookbook, the *Cloud Forest Hall Collection of Rules for Eating and Drinking.*[47] Its fifty-two recipes are mainly for fish and vegetables, with the sweet flavors of Shanghai dishes. Included are ways of flavoring tea and a gluten preparation.

> Use the fine wheat gluten (noodles or pieces) from Wuchung (Suchou), newly steamed and not cooked by water. Tear into thin slices. Cut licorice into inch-long pieces, put these in *chiu* and cook with water till the liquid boils off. Then use perilla leaf, tangerine peel slices, and ginger slices with gluten and cook. Let cool. Then mix in hot oil, soy paste, flower pepper, black pepper, and apricot kernel powder, so that the flavors are well blended. Dry under the sun and put in a sugar jar and seal. If it is left too long and gets hard, steam it when you want to eat it.

New forms of social life sprang up in the cities, centered on eating regional specialties, drinking wine, and taking tea in the overlapping categories of restaurants, wine shops and teahouses. Restaurants, particularly in Hangchow, offered homesick officials their home cuisine. Northern restaurants served wheat noodles, breads, and pancakes, as well as mutton and game. Sichuan restaurants were renowned for health-inducing herbs and fine-quality teas. Hangchow restaurants specialized in the foods of the Yangtze delta, rice, pork, fish, and frogs. Outside the city, on West Lake, diners ate at floating restaurants, where they could view the moon's reflection in the dark waters.

The best restaurants, or "wine shops," offered food that only the wealthiest official residences could rival, a far cry from that served in simple eateries or on the street. In teahouses, officials, literati, army officers on leave, and prosperous merchants enjoyed professional performances, played and sang, and commented on fine paintings hung for their appreciation. Written menus were posted. Diners called out their orders to the waiters, who scurried between the tables, rushing back and forth from the kitchen, trying to remember each diner's preferences. Many diners chose whole steamed shad, a summer favorite in that part of China. When fish were cooked without scaling, as the (perhaps apocryphal) Mrs. Wu suggested in her *Records of Home Cooking* around 1100 C.E., the fat under the delicate skin kept the flesh moist and tender. The word for fish, *ya*, resonated with the word for surplus, an apt closing to a sumptuous meal. Vendors pushed in, offering dishes that the restaurant or teahouse kitchen could not or had not prepared. Dancers and entertainers performed. After the meal, diners could retire to the back rooms, where courtesans offered further pleasures.

Sugar was now found in recipes, and confections were available as a street food. Sugar was, for example, used in a quarter of the recipes in Mrs. Wu's book. It sweetened pastries, was a seasoning for preserves, and was used with vinegar in a pickle of eggplant. It sweetened vegetable stuffings. Sugar topped deep-fried "donuts," tenderized duck flesh, reduced the acidity of wine, preserved mandarin oranges for the longest possible time, and deodorized smelly foods. For more humble folk, the twelfth-century artist Su Han-ch'en shows a sweetmeat vendor selling candied fruits and small pastries from tables adorned with peonies in a red lacquer vase shaded by a canopy.[48]

The cuisine of the imperial court was structured by Confucian doctrine on ritual, which, as in the past, was deliberately formal and archaic to emphasize continuity.[49] On less formal occasions, the court sipped cool grape wine, the color of bamboo leaves, from red bowls.[50] Or they had tea-tasting contests, seated on chairs, sipping the tea from cups of finely chased silver or exquisite porcelain.

The poor probably had some grasp of Buddhist and Taoist culinary philosophy because priests and monks attended major festivals in even the most remote villages.[51] It was one of the better times to be a peasant. Although most could not afford all the "seven necessities"—rice, salt, vinegar, soy sauce, oil, tea, and wood—in good times, after paying half their harvest in taxes, setting aside seed grain, and saving grain for themselves, many would go to the markets described by the poet Chou Mi:

> The small market—
> People with their bundles of tea or salt,
> Chickens cackling, dogs barking,
> Firewood being exchanged for rice
> Fishes being bartered for wine.[52]

The daily grind continued, though. Peasants raised rice seedlings and transplanted them one by one to the paddies, trod the steps of the waterwheel hour after hour to flood the fields, weeded, and added compost from the deep pit by the side of their house where they threw chaff from threshing rice, vegetable trimmings, and night soil. They threshed the rice to remove the husk. As soon as the rice harvest was done, they planted new strains of millet and wheat that could survive the southern heat. They perhaps also raised a pig on household scraps or planted a few cabbages, onions, garlic, and daikon radishes for themselves or, if they were near a city, for the market.

Peasant meals were based on steamed grain—millet in the north and the high-yielding but tough, chewy Champa (Vietnamese) rice, which the government insisted they grow, in the south. The less well-off depended on the old basics, yams and taro. On the side were steamed vegetables, usually some form of cabbage, and a scrap of pork or dried or salted fish from the rice paddies. A thin soup provided liquid. For special occasions, there might be white rice and a little tea or rice wine. In bad times, peasants resorted to the time-honored hierarchy of famine foods. First they ate the pig's wheat and rice bran. Then they ate bark and leaves. When those ran out they searched for roots and wild greens. Then it was handfuls of dirt. Finally, they consumed the bodies of the dead.

In Hangchow, the urban poor crowded the many take-out food shops that offered noodles, stuffed buns, bowls of soup, and deep-fried confections. Splendor amid poverty was the way Wu Tzu-mu described Hangchow in his *Dream of Happiness*. In 1276, Genghis Khan's grandson, Kublai Khan, conquered Hangchow, which sent many Chinese fleeing to Japan or Vietnam. At the Mongol court for a century or so, the Confucian-Buddhist-Taoist culinary tradition was merged with Mongol and Persian cuisines (chapter 4). When the Mongols left China in the mid-fourteenth century, it once again became the dominant tradition.

BUDDHISM TRANSFORMS THE CUISINES OF KOREA
AND JAPAN, 550 C.E.–1000 C.E.

Following their disestablishment in northern China, Buddhists had reorganized and created new sects that were to be particularly important in transporting Buddhist cuisine elsewhere in East Asia. China's neighboring states—Vietnam in the south, the Nanzhao kingdom in modern Yunnan, the kingdoms of the Liao, the Jin, and the Xi Xia on the steppe, as well as Korea and Japan—looked to their prosperous, stable trading partner as a model for the reform of their own social orders from the fifth century on. Chinese Buddhists and their patrons sponsored missions. A little is known about how this happened in Korea, a lot more about Japan. In both cases, a small number of monks immigrated with books, tools, and plants, struck alliances with the ruling dynasty, and founded monasteries.[53]

Buddhism was accepted by Korean rulers as the state religion in the mid-sixth century, a couple of centuries after its first introduction, and Buddhist cuisine flourished there for the better part of a millennium. The state forbade killing animals for meat. Buddhist monasteries accumulated estates, cultivated tea from the ninth century on, and offered visitors tea and light, sophisticated eatables. Aristocrats enjoyed elaborate tea ceremonies.[54]

In the sixth century, Korean Buddhists sailed the hundred miles to Japan. As is often the case with islands, Japan's native food resources were scanty: some root vegetables even now scarcely known elsewhere; some nuts and fruits; wild greens;

game, river and inshore fish; seaweeds; and a sweet syrup made from the amazura vine. Millets, rice, wheat, and barley, introduced from China, were probably processed by pounding to groats, not grinding to flour. A condiment (*hishio*) was made by fermenting meat, fish, and shellfish. Meals were predominantly one-pot gruels and porridges, and perhaps pounded cooked glutinous rice (*mochi*). The Japanese sacrificed to the spirits, both benevolent and malevolent, that they believed to have given birth to humans and that inhabited lakes and streams, trees and bushes, and every part of the house, including the cooking pots.[55]

To establish Buddhism and its cuisine in Japan, Korean artists and architects built temples and monasteries to house monks from Korea and China. Nineteen expeditions made the dangerous crossing to China in unstable, flat-bottomed boats between 600 and 850, returning laden with monks and scholars skilled in cuisine, literature, politics, and theology, with seeds and cuttings, including tea and sugar, ferments, rotary grindstones, pottery, lacquer, chopsticks, spoons, silk, art, musical instruments, and Jia Sixie's *Essential Skills for the Daily Life of the People* (quickly translated into Japanese). In April 675, the emperor Tenmu banned the consumption of cattle, horses, dogs, monkey, and chicken (though not wild birds or animals). Meat eating declined but, as elsewhere, never entirely disappeared. Aristocrats, for example, demanded meat for their health. Increasingly, though, fish and Chinese-style mock-meat products such as tofu and gluten were substituted.[56]

The Japanese court adopted the typical Buddhist trio of butter, sugar, and rice. The government bureau of milk production was producing cream, butter, and an unknown product known as *daigo*, which logic suggests may have been ghee, by the beginning of the seventh century, a practice that continued for at least three hundred years. Sugar was imported from China at great expense and in tiny quantities. The eighty bundles of sugarcane that the Chinese monk Chien-Chen reportedly imported in 743 did not grow in the cold climate. To increase short-grain rice production, river valleys were irrigated. Tofu almost certainly came with the Buddhists. According to legend, another missionary, Ganjin, introduced Chinese fermentation techniques to Japan in 754, when he imported gallons of fermented black beans. True or not, the manufacture of fermented products, carefully regulated and taxed by the government, increased. By the eleventh century, no fewer than twenty-two varieties were available, including miso. Tea was introduced, but it did not gain a foothold at this time.

Japanese court cuisine was modeled on the court cuisine of medieval China. Indeed, many culinary historians use it to assess what Chinese cuisine was like prior to the ninth century, a comparison that supports Xuan-zang's description of the Chinese eating fish and vegetables uncooked or lightly and simply cooked. The eleventh-century Japanese novel *The Tale of Genji* describes what a formal court meal was like. Diners knelt at individual trays (*zen*), using chopsticks, believed to be cleaner and more sophisticated than hands, to take morsels from Chinese-style lacquerware, using Chinese table manners.[57] In front of them were bowls of salt, vinegar, and *hishio* for dipping. They were treated to four kinds of food—dried foods, raw foods, fermented foods, and desserts—with as many as seven dishes of each. Dried fish or fowl were steamed or grilled. Red snapper, for example, might be grilled and served with *hishio*. Fresh foods were served raw and thinly sliced. Fermented foods might include salt-fermented fish, abalone miso, and miso-pickled eggplants.[58] Desserts were primarily fruits and nuts, though Chinese-style wheat pastries stuffed with sugar were also served.[59] Peasants contented themselves with miso soups, salt-pickled daikon, and porridge of millet or buckwheat, which the emperor had decreed in 722 should be grown in colder regions.

In the twelfth century, a second wave of Chinese Buddhist monks brought noodles, chopsticks, and tea to Japan. Chinese-style noodles made of wheat ground in water-driven rotary mills supplemented steamed millet.[60] Broad udon noodles became available in the fourteenth century. This time tea took hold. In the earliest Japanese tea treatise, the *Kissa Yojoki*, the Buddhist monk Eisai praised it as "the most wonderful medicine for nourishing one's health . . . the secret of long life," and an antidote for alcohol. He then presented the emperor, known for his fondness for alcohol, with a copy.[61]

As Japan devolved into a series of warring fiefdoms in the fifteenth century, monks developed an ascetic cuisine (*shojin ryori*) based on fresh, dried, fried, and processed tofu, wheat gluten, mushrooms, seaweed, sesame, walnuts, and vegetables, which they transformed into delicate dishes.[62] Meat, onions, and alcohol were shunned. Cooking was at once ethical and aesthetic. As the authors of a modern cookbook on Japanese temple cuisine explain, cooks have to have a "moral spirit," balancing the six flavors (bitter, sour, sweet, hot, salty, and delicate), the five cooking methods (boiling, grilling, deep-frying, steaming, and serving raw), the five colors (green, red, yellow, white, and purple—substituting for scarce, inauspicious black), and the three virtues of lightness, cleanliness, and freshness.[63]

Tea, as shown by the Chinese-style landscape in figure 3.6, painted in the sixteenth century, was associated with harmony with nature and contemplation far from the affairs of state. In the mid-seventeenth century, in the troubled times of the samurai, the tea ceremony, where art and the Buddhist path met, was brought to a high point by Rikyu, the most famous tea master. Inspiring exquisite pottery, textiles, and an ascetic collation of light confections to be eaten with the tea, the tea ceremony reconciled an idealized reclusive life (appealing in the turbulent world of seventeenth-century Japan) and an appreciation of high Chinese culture—ceramics, painting, lacquerware, brocades, and tea drinking.[64] A small group of men gathered for four hours or so in a small, simple hut. The host lit fresh charcoal, brought water to a boil, and then whisked powdered tea into the hot water.

FIGURE 3.6. In this portion of a Chinese-influenced six-panel Japanese folding screen, ca. 1530–73, pavilions for taking tea are situated so that the drinkers can view the landscape as it reflects the passage of the four seasons with their changing colors. Avery Brundage Collection (B68D58+). Copyright Asian Art Museum, San Francisco. Used by permission.

First the thick tea was taken in solemn silence. A second round of thinner tea encouraged a more buoyant mood and lively conversation.

By 1650 Buddhist cuisine had followed the pattern of earlier culinary expansions, crossing mountains, deserts, and oceans to become established, now with state support, in areas where radically different cuisines flourished, such as the wheat and ferment cuisine of northern China. Buddhist cuisines offered a new model for high cuisines: refined, restrained, and ascetic. They introduced a range of satisfying meatless dishes based on dhal, vegetables, and mock meats. Their confections of sugar and ghee and their nonalcoholic beverages based on sugar and fruit juices or on the leaves of the tea plant offered a sober alternative to alcohol. Where Buddhism spread, so did irrigated rice farming, sugarcane growing and refining, dairying, and the cultivation of a range of typical fruits and vegetables.

The fate of Buddhist cuisines had varied from region to region. In India, a probably similar Hindu cuisine had displaced Buddhist cuisine hundreds of years earlier. In Sri Lanka, Buddhist cuisine still flourished, as it did in Southeast Asia, often melded with Hindu cuisine. In Tibet, too, Buddhist cuisine, albeit adjusted to the extreme climate, was alive and well. In China, although Buddhism was no longer officially backed by the state, a Confucian-Taoist-Buddhist cuisine reigned. In Korea, Buddhist cuisine of a traditional kind had vanished with the Mongol invasion. Four thousand miles from India and almost two thousand years after Buddhist cuisine had first been created, Japanese Buddhists continued to believe that cooking paralleled the search for enlightenment, that the right cuisine encouraged contemplation, and that meat, smelly alliums, and alcohol should be eschewed in favor of meat substitutes and nonalcoholic beverages. Today, the cuisines of India, Southeast Asia, Tibet, China, Korea, and Japan seem totally distinct, thanks to the successive cultures and cuisines that have impinged on them, including Islamic and modern Western cuisines. Yet viewed on a global scale, features such as a reverence for rice and the modest use of meat can still be seen to link them.

Buddhist cuisines were to expand again in the late nineteenth century, when population pressure, war, and hunger sent people fleeing as indentured laborers from southern China and Japan, and again with the migration of Vietnamese and Thais in the latter half of the twentieth century. In Hawaii, Mary Sia, a Christian, in the cookbook she wrote in 1956 that introduced many Americans to Chinese cuisine, had to explain Buddhist culinary philosophy. "The Chinese connect the eating of meat with man's animal nature and think of a vegetable diet as more spiritual," she said. "It is customary that the first meal of the new year be completely vegetarian"—the dish called *jai,* or monk's delight, Buddha's delight, or Buddha's feast.[65]

4

Islam Transforms the Cuisines of Central and West Asia, 800–1650 C.E.

Islamic cuisines began their rapid expansion across western Eurasia at the time when Buddhist cuisines had almost vanished from India, were at their height in China, and were just reaching Japan. Christian cuisine, established in the first to third centuries C.E., had spread over large parts of the old Roman Empire and was the cuisine of the Byzantine Empire. I defer discussing Christian cuisine until chapter 5 because it did not spread as widely as Islamic cuisine until the fifteenth century, and when it did, it was heavily indebted to Islamic cuisine. Thus it makes sense to address Islamic cuisine first.

Islamic cuisine did not break as sharply with earlier sacrificial cuisines as Buddhist cuisine had done. Muslims esteemed meat and, for a long time, alcohol. They did not regard the pleasures of this world, dining included, with suspicion, but enjoyed them as a foreshadowing of Paradise. Building on the long tradition of high cuisine in what became the heartland of Islam, Islamic cuisines were based on an extraordinary variety of flat or lightly raised wheat breads and other wheaten products; aromatized, spicy dishes of lamb, goat, and game; and sweet confections.

The cuisines evolved in two separate stages. Perso-Islamic cuisines took shape in the eighth and ninth centuries, spreading from Mesopotamia west to North Africa and parts of southern Europe, and east to India. Innovations in chemical food processing, particularly sugar refining and distilling, allowed the development of a range of culinary-medical-alchemical syrups, drinks, and confections of sugar, fruit, nuts, and wheat flour as well as new distilled flavorings, such as rose and orange flower waters. In the thirteenth century, this stage came to an end with the Mongol invasions, although the Mongols drew on Perso-Islamic cuisine, among others, to create Mongol imperial cuisine. In the second stage, from the fifteenth century on, Turko-Islamic cuisine was refined in the Ottoman, Safavid, and Mughal empires. Among the important innovations were rice (and other granule dishes), cooked pilau-style, and the new hot drink, coffee. Islamic cuisines also penetrated the southern fringe of the Sahara in the west and Indonesia in the east.[1]

RIVERS OF WINE, RIVERS OF HONEY: PERSO-ISLAMIC CUISINES, 700–1250 c.e.

Muhammad died in 632 c.e. Within a couple of generations, his followers had taken the Middle East from the two powers that had long vied for supremacy over the area, Byzantium (the Christianized eastern half of the Roman Empire) and Sassanid Persia (a successor to the Achaemenid Empire). Under Muslim rule, the Near and Middle East, North Africa, and Spain—formerly parts of the Roman and Sassanid Persian empires—came to share a single culture, a sacred language—Arabic, the language of the Qur'an—and a cuisine (map 4.1). This was much more complex than that of the desert Arabs (described in chapter 1), which depended on barley and, occasionally, wheat breads, pottages and gruels, milk, butter, and cheese in multiple combinations with barley and dates, and mutton and goat meat.

In 762, the first caliph of the Abbasid Dynasty founded Baghdad on an empty site between the Tigris and the Euphrates. The circular city, a microcosm of the spherical cosmos, would, he promised, be the "crossroads of the universe . . . the most prosperous town on earth."[2] The Abbasids, not Arabs but Persians, were converts to Islam from Zoroastrianism, Christianity, or, in the case of one prominent family, Buddhism. Fifty years later, under Harun al-Rashid, Baghdad's population had soared to a million, two or three times the size of Constantinople, Damascus, or Cairo, and fifty times bigger than even the largest European city. The atmosphere of the city is best known to many from the One Thousand and One Nights (put in written form in the fourteenth century), although the tales about Harun al-Rashid himself are probably fictitious. In Baghdad, Perso-Islamic cuisine was brought to its highest level, recorded in manuals on etiquette, medical texts, histories and geographies, drinking poetry, the One Thousand and One Nights, and the most extensive collection of cookbooks yet created anywhere.[3] The most important of these, the Baghdad Cookbook, the common name for the Book of Dishes (Kitab-al-Tabik), exists as three remaining manuscripts and scraps of a fourth. It contains over three hundred recipes from late-eighth- to late-ninth-century Baghdad, including twenty from Harun al-Rashid's son and thirty-five from his poet brother. Although the cuisine is that of the court, the number of manuscripts strongly suggests that courtiers, and perhaps even merchants, emulated court cuisine.

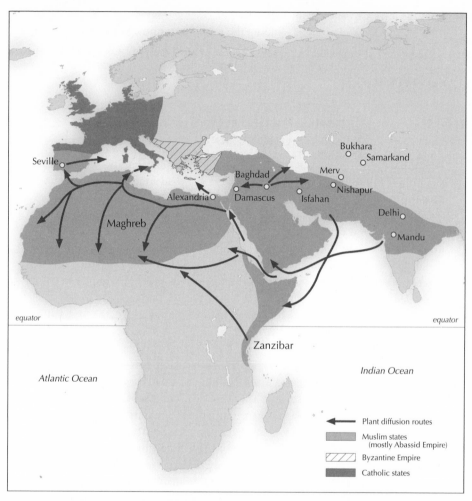

MAP 4.1. The expansion of Perso-Islamic cuisine, 700–1250. Arrows show the probable routes by which plants such as sorghum, Asian rice, sugarcane, citrus, watermelon, spinach, artichoke, and eggplant were transferred westward from India and north and south across the Sahara. The techniques for processing them would have followed the same routes. Thanks to the long border with Islamic states in the Mediterranean, the small Catholic states of Europe became aware of Perso-Islamic cuisine, adopting some aspects and repudiating others. Source: Watson, *Agricultural Innovation in the Early Islamic World*, 78.

FIGURE 4.1. A Sassanid Persian gilded silver wine jar from the sixth or seventh century, decorated with twirling vines, the birds of the vineyard, and naked boys gathering grapes. Probably from Mazanderan in Iran. Courtesy Trustees of the British Museum (124094).

Perso-Islamic cuisine owed much to Sassanid Persian cuisine, about which, unfortunately, little is known. As Zoroastrians, the Sassanids revered the sacred fire and the transformations it wrought in cooking, viewed the garden as an emblem of the world and the state, and valued chicken and eggs. A sixth-century description of a royal meal, in which King Khusrow cross-examines a young nobleman keen to serve him, mentions hot and cold meats, rice jelly, stuffed vine leaves, marinated chicken, and a puree of sweetened dates.[4] Soups of green vegetables thickened with flour, and thick purees of meat and grains (*harisa*), were popular. Black pepper, turmeric, saffron, cinnamon, fenugreek, and asa-fetida seasoned and tempered dishes. Sweets such as jams, almond pastries, dates stuffed with nuts, and a "Greek" sweet of eggs, honey, milk, butter, rice, and sugar (though the rice and sugar were surely Persian), as well as fruits were served on fine silver platters. Drinking wine, which was produced on a large scale and elegantly presented for the court in jars like the one in figure 4.1, was a religious duty.

Following their conquest, those Persians who did not convert to Islam were penalized politically and economically. Many fled to China or to India, where their descendants, the Parsis, still prepare a cuisine that reflects their long heritage, including, for example, many chicken and egg dishes.[5]

An evolving Muslim culinary philosophy reshaped Sassanid cuisine and incorporated elements from the Roman Empire, India, China, and the local humble cuisine of Syria and Iraq (dishes called Nabatean for the peoples of the region). God's creation was good, said the Qur'an, and good Muslims should enjoy it. A cuisine of fine dishes, beautifully presented, was believed to stimulate the appetite, contribute to a healthy and attractive body, and keep diners in tune with the cosmos. Food was the greatest of the six pleasures, more pleasing than drink, clothes, sexual intercourse, scent, or sound, according to the preface to the *Baghdad Cookbook*.[6] The Qur'an promised believers that in the afterlife, they would enter a garden with rivers of sweet water, rivers of milk that never soured, rivers of wine, and rivers of honey—fluids that paralleled the humors circulating in the human body. Water sustained life; milk stood for breasts and semen and new life; wine represented blood and hot, powerful male things; and honey exemplified sweetness, purity, and morality. The caliph, like kings in earlier Persian political thought, was responsible for tending to law and justice in the present world, as gardeners tended to ordering and cultivating the wild to a new level of beauty in their gardens.[7] Cultured courtly meals took place in gardens, reminding diners of the ordered, lawful state.

The Abbasid court recruited physicians, including Jews and Christians versed in the humoral theory and alchemy, from across the Islamic world and India.[8] The works of Hippocrates and Galen and alchemical treatises were translated into Arabic by Christians who were also fluent in Greek and Syriac. In the eleventh century, Ibn Sina, or Avicenna, one of the most distinguished court physicians, corrected and modified Galen in his *Canon of Medicine,* a treatise later eagerly perused by Europeans.

Eating meat was manly. Abstainers were suspected of heresy, guilty of the arrogant sin of "forbidding what God has made licit."[9] Those who could afford it sacrificed a sheep or goat on the annual festival of Eid al-Adha, echoing the long-ago sacrifice offered by Abraham, distributing the meat to the poor afterward. Only pork and blood were forbidden. To avoid the latter, animals were slaughtered by cutting their throats and allowing the blood to drain out. The Hindu prohibition on killing cattle confounded the Islamic scholar Abu Rayhan al-Biruni when he traveled to India in the eleventh century. After listening to various explanations, he decided that it was designed to protect the cattle needed to haul, plow, and give milk, not because, as some of his informants suggested, beef was indigestible or provoked lust.[10]

Wine, sold by Jews and by Christian monks, was esteemed in early Islam as it had been in Sassanid Persia and among pre-Islamic nomads. Poetry composed to be recited while drinking was used to express opinions that were otherwise prohibited.[11] Princes were depicted in Islamic paintings seated on the ground, the correct position for eating and drinking, with a glass of wine in the right hand, the correct hand for consuming, waiting to be transported to the land of bliss. Wine-drinking parties concluded courtly meals, with poets reciting verses, often ribald, but celebrating generosity, aristocracy, and the quest for freedom, and beseeching divine mercy for the caliph. Apart from the rivers of wine in Paradise, the Qur'an makes few references to wine.

On the other hand, in a couple of commentaries in the Hadith, the sayings of the Prophet assembled a couple of hundred years after his death, wine seemed to be suspect. One passage was understood to forbid making or storing fruit beverages in vessels in which they could ferment. The other observed that wine (construed as fermented beverages made from grapes, dates, honey, wheat, and barley, for example) obscured the intellect. The doctors were ambivalent. Wine taken prudently, according to Avicenna, was a friend; in excess, it was an enemy. A small amount was an antidote, but a large amount was a poison. Over the centuries, wine became prohibited, but it was a slow process.

Wheat was the most prestigious grain, praised by physicians as having the greatest nutritional value since it was slightly warm and moist and thus close to the ideal human temperament.[12] Many wheat products, such as bread, starch, and thick purees, had a long ancestry, and all were described in terms of the humoral theory. Rich, sedentary people in Islam, as earlier in the Roman Empire, insisted on eating digestible leavened bread, leaving heavy, unleavened bread to manual workers. Bread soaked in broth, a food that went back to Mesopotamia, became newly popular as the Prophet's favorite dish (*tharid*). Because of that, it is still made from Morocco to Xinjiang. Wheat flour was mixed with water to make a drink (*sawiq*) that was thought to be cooling and thus good for hot-tempered people, especially during the summer. Wheat kernels were simmered whole, often with meat, as they had been in Sassanid times and probably long before, to make the thick, creamy soup or puree known as harisa. It was warm, damp, and bland, slow to digest, especially when fats were added, and good for thin, dry people. The ground kernels might also be washed with water to extract starch, which was used to make custards and thicken sauces.

Important wheat-based innovations included a bread-based condiment (*murri*), complex pastries, and pasta. Murri was a tasty dark liquid made from moldy bread, which, though independently invented, added flavors similar to both soy sauce and the fish sauce (garum) of the Roman Empire. With added fat, eggs, and flavorings, wheat flour made pastries that could be baked in an oven or hot ashes, pan-fried into cakes, deep-fried into donuts or fritters, or stretched paper thin and baked on a griddle. A hard wheat (durum) with a higher gluten content than earlier varieties was used to make pasta, particularly thin noodles (*fideos, fidawsh*) and thick noodles (*atriyya*).[13]

Richly scented and colored dishes reflected the power and wealth of the diner, echoed sacred images, and helped balance the micro- and macrocosm. "Understanding spices is the cornerstone of the art of cooking," wrote the author of a cookbook from Islamic Spain. "They distinguish one dish from another, define flavor, and heighten taste." Moreover, "they promote well-being and prevent harm."[14] Cinnamon, cloves, cumin, black pepper, and saffron were particularly important spices, but there were a host of others. Anise, for example, was favored in sweet dishes. As aromatics, spices were joined by new distilled essences that kept alive the perfumes of roses and orange blossoms. Dishes were turned gold, the color of sunlight, power, and kingship, by incorporating saffron or turmeric, painting with egg yolks, or covering with gold leaf. White, evoking brightness, happiness, hope, the moon's restrained purity, and the color of the caliph's clothes in the mosque, was found in white bread, milk of almonds, breast of chicken, white rice, white sugar, and silver leaf. Green, bringing to mind birth, regeneration, and gardens irrigated with life-giving water, came from spinach and herbs.

"To enjoy sweets is a sign of faith," the Qur'an says, so it is not surprising that about a third of the recipes in the *Baghdad Cookbook* are for sweet dishes. Many of them went back to Roman, Sassanid, or Byzantine cuisine. Tiny leavened donuts (*luqum al-qadi*), fried pastry fritters (*zulabiya*), and fried pancakes with a nut filling (*qataif*) were all made by frying wheat doughs, often leavened, and adding sugar or syrup. A pudding was made by thickening syrup with starch. Cooked rice was sweetened and colored with saffron or turmeric (*zarda*). The new thin wheat noodles were served in syrup (*kunafa*). Soft drinks (sherbet or *sharab*) for women were sweetened with honey or costly sugar, tinted rose, green, or orange by pureed fruit or fruit juices or pure white by ground almonds, delicately spiced and perfumed with rose or orange blossom water, and cooled with snow or ice rushed from distant mountains to icehouses.

Jams, jellies, boiled-down fruit juices (*rubbs*) and syrups (*julabs*) straddled the boundary of cuisine and medicine. Quince paste (*membrillo*) made by cooking pounded quince with honey was opaque and red. Sugar, with its magical, alchemical properties, could be substituted for the honey, according to the author of an anonymous thirteenth-century Andalusian cookbook, and then quince paste could be "made by another, more amazing recipe: take it as said before, and cook it in water alone until its essence comes out, clean the water of its sediments, and add it to as much sugar, and make it thin and transparent, without redness, and what you have made will remain in this state."[15] After all these years, you can still sense his wonder. A paste that stayed pale and translucent, capturing the essence of quince, hinted at immortality.

The cities of Islam, like Rome earlier, had enough wealth to support commercial food processing and professional cooking (although the caliph's kitchen probably continued to take in and process raw materials). Bread was the basic food of the cities. Where there was sufficient water, water mills were used to grind wheat into flour, although animal-driven mills, which could be depended on inside the walls of a besieged city, remained in use. One water mill in Baghdad was said to have an output of thirty thousand tons a year.[16] Flour came in different grades: white for high cuisine, large-grained semolina for special purposes, whole meal for the urban poor, and the remaining bran for animals. In the cities, bread was baked in beehive ovens, white loaves for the higher ranks, and darker loaves for those lower on the social scale.

Rice was husked with pivoted pestles, perhaps introduced from China, and, later, with trip-hammer mills.[17] Oil from olives, sesame, poppy, and cottonseed was pressed in edge-runner mills (or presses in backward areas). Fish was salted. Poultry was raised in artificial incubators, meats and sausage were preserved, butter was clarified (*samn*), the fat from the fat-tailed sheep was rendered, cheese was prepared, vinegars were made, and fruits and vegetables were pickled in brine and vinegar. Wine shops run by non-Muslims dotted the major cities.

Sugar processing, probably adopted from India, was improved with new methods of crushing and boiling, particularly in Egypt, Jordan, and Syria. Cane was peeled and split, crushed first in an edge-runner mill, then netted and crushed again in a press, the juice from both pressings running into a single tank. Boiled and filtered three times, it was then allowed to drip through conical pots. The solids were dissolved and boiled with a little milk to clarify them to white refined sugar (*qand*). The syrup that dripped out was collected and reprocessed into lower-quality sugar. Fruits were dried and crystallized, then as now a specialty of Damascus.

Distilling too saw technical improvements and new uses. Small-scale wine distilling probably went back to classical antiquity, when flickering, cool-burning alcohol was used first in pagan and then in Christian religious ceremonies of purification by fire.[18]Alchemists in Islam, aided by the translation of Greek texts written in Egypt in the first century C.E., carefully purified themselves for their solemn quest for the spirits normally trapped in bodies and invented new kinds of apparatus to release them. A vessel often known as a pelican or cucurbit, because its long sidearm looked like a pelican's beak or the curved upper part of a gourd, released the essence of gently heated flower petals, which could be collected in the sidearm. By the ninth century C.E., the process had been commercialized. Factories in Spain, Damascus, Jur and Sabur in Persia, and Kufa in Iraq prepared and shipped rose and orange blossom water throughout Islam, as well as east to India and on to China. Wine in all likelihood was also distilled. The eighth-century poet Abu Nuwas is frequently quoted as describing a wine "that has the colour of rain-water but is as hot inside the ribs as a burning firebrand."

In the palace, huge kitchens prepared meals for the caliph's household, including his harem of several hundred women, slaves, freedmen, guards and officials, astronomers and physicians, goldsmiths and carpenters. Cooks, presumably Persian, transformed and refined raw materials just like alchemists, pounding meat and spices in pestles and mortars, baking in tannurs, preparing sweet dishes and eggs in small braziers, frying in iron pots, stewing and simmering in glazed and unglazed earthenware and soapstone, and dishing up in a wealth of specialized serving dishes, including locally made, Chinese-inspired porcelain.

The caliph, dressed in colorful Chinese silks, dined with his companions in the garden, seated on rugs or low cushions alongside canals that fed a central pool sheltered by vines and fragrant orange trees. Dishes of lamb or other meat simmered in a vinegar-and-sugar sweet-sour sauce flavored with herbs (*sikbaaj*) or pomegranate juice (*narbaaj*), or chicken sauced with nuts or chickpeas (*zirbaja*), were served. Many dishes were flavored with cinnamon, cloves, cumin, and black or other kinds of pepper. Caraway, asafetida, galangal (a root with overtones of mustard and ginger), and herbs such as mint, parsley, cilantro, basil, and tarragon added further flavor notes. Murri, the condiment made of fermented wheat or barley, introduced a rich, meaty taste. Rose and orange blossom water perfumed some dishes. Lamb, mutton, goat, and fowl, including chicken, partridge, squab, dove, small birds, ducks, and geese, were baked or roasted. Harisa was a favorite. Vegetables including artichokes, cardoons, asparagus, spinach, Swiss chard, and gourds were prepared individually or added to meat dishes. Eggplant, a new introduction, was not as popular as it would become later, once it had been bred to reduce the bitterness.

Following the meal, salaried poets, physicians, astrologers, alchemists, and other scholars and intellectuals celebrated the history and power of the state. Cuisine, like poetry, was a fine art and an adornment of the ruling dynasty and hence a worthy subject. The poet Ishaq ibn Ibrahim of Mosul chose the filling of a triangular meat dumpling (*sanbusak*, otherwise known as *samosa*, the first syllable from the Persian word for three) as his subject (echoing the earlier Chinese praise of stuffed dumplings). "Take first the finest meat, red, soft to touch, / and mince it with the fat, not overmuch / Then add an onion, cut in circles clean, / A cabbage, very fresh, exceeding green / and season well with cinnamon and rue."[19] On hearing the poem, the caliph ordered *sanbusak* from the kitchen, demonstrating his command of the resources to produce high culture.

The high Perso-Islamic cuisine of Baghdad, like its clothing and architecture, was disseminated along the trade routes of empire to other Islamic cities, including those of southern Spain. In 711, this area, where 200,000 Visigoths barely controlled eight million Hispano-Romans, fell to Arabs from Morocco, supported by Berber horse cavalry. The Arabs ruled, Berbers controlled the military and herded, and converts to Islam made up 80 percent of the population, the other 20 percent being Christian or Jewish.

Al-Andalus, as the Islamic part of Spain was called, could be a paradise like that described in the Qur'an, thought the conquerors—a garden watered by rivers, shaded by trees, and perfumed with flowers that bloomed in a climate more beneficent than that of the fearsome, arid deserts of Arabia and Africa.[20] In Seville, Granada, and above all Cordoba, the new rulers set about reproducing their cuisine. The first emir of Cordoba, Abd al-Rahman I, who had fled from Damascus when his family was ousted in the eighth century, was homesick for his familiar landscape and planted date palms, while his chief justice imported a fine variety of pomegranate. The second emir founded new towns on old Roman foundations and established Persian-style farming in the rich bottomlands. Artisans, including potters and probably cooks, were ordered to move from east to west. Persian ways of well making, water raising, and irrigation were introduced to upgrade older Roman installations. Water mills for grain were built along the larger rivers; the rural poor used hand querns and tannurs. Agricultural treatises were composed and Avicenna's medical works were copied.[21]

Perso-Islamic cuisine was adapted to its new setting. The olive oil of the Roman tradition substituted for the fat of the long-tailed sheep (which apparently never thrived in Spain), and cheese took the place of yogurt. Lamb and mutton were salted as pork had been salted in Roman days, and rabbit and cabbage were prominent in the cuisine. A stew of meatballs (*banadiq*, from *karyon pontikon*, the Byzantine Greek name for the filbert or hazelnut, the nut of the Black Sea) and cheese-filled baked dumplings (*mujabbanas*, a word that survives in Spanish as *almojavana*) were specific to the western Mediterranean. The Berbers are believed to have contributed a pie of layers of paper-thin pastry filled with a chicken ragout (*judhaba*) that still exists in Morocco (*bastilla*) and a soupy stew or pottage (*sinhaji*, a Berber term) of a variety of meats, including beef and mutton, chicken, partridges, sausages, meatballs, chickpeas, and seasonal vegetables, sometimes proposed as the origin of the similar Spanish dish often called *olla podrida*. Couscous, here made of coarsely ground particles of wheat or other grain rolled to form tiny balls, was a basic staple. By the twelfth and thirteenth centuries, the Perso-Islamic cuisine in al-Andalus rivaled that of Baghdad.

Central Asian cities such as Samarkand, Bukhara, and Merv in Central Asia, Nishapur in northeastern Iran, and Isfahan in west-central Iran became Islamicized between the end of the tenth century and the middle of the twelfth century, putting an end to earlier Buddhist (and to a lesser extent Christian) dominance of the Silk Roads. Much of India became ruled by Muslims from the tenth to eleventh centuries. In the Delhi sultanate from the twelfth to early sixteenth century, a distinctly Indian-Muslim courtly style was created that survived the destruction of Delhi by Timur in 1398. It is described in the *Book of Delights* written in the late

FIGURE 4.2. The sultan of Mandu in a garden overseeing the preparation of *sanbusak*, or dhal cakes (*vada*). He is being offered a sample, while one slave fries more and another places them in a dish. The recipe calls for dhal, onions, fresh ginger, pepper, and honey, palm sugar, molasses, or cane-sugar syrup as desired, and recommends frying "in ghee or sweet sesame oil or in almond oil or rape seed oil or in ghee flavoured with burnt asafetida." From the *Book of Delights* (ca. 1500). Courtesy British Library Board (I.O. ISLAMIC 149, f.83b).

fifteenth century at the order of Ghiyath Shahi, ruler of Malwa in central India.[22] In his capital, Mandu, he collected a female army of five hundred Abyssinian slave girls. His personal slave companions were trained in music, dancing, wrestling, and cooking, and some were permitted to share his meals. In his *Book of Delights*, recipes for food and drink jostle with those for perfumes and essences, aphrodisiacs, medicines, and betel quids. Most of them are illustrated with the sultan (fig. 4.2) overseeing (unusually) female cooks.

Humble cuisines were adequate or better throughout the Abbasid Empire and farther afield. In the crowded passageways of the covered bazaars and suqs that dotted the cities, vendors were arranged in groups. Shoppers could pick up cooked meats, bread, snacks, and drinks made from milk, yogurt, grapes, carrots, and lemons. In Baghdad, the urban poor bought barley bread, cooked meats, salt fish, fruit, and vegetables. They consumed so much chickpea soup that one vendor in 1000 C.E. bought sixteen hundred donkey loads of chickpeas each year, selling out by the end of the season.[23] In Basra in southern Iraq, a young man could buy enough bread and salt fish to survive for two dirhams a month, about a fifteenth of a rubbish collector's earnings.[24] The wealthy in al-Andalus, and probably elsewhere, grumbled that city dwellers ate too much wheat and meat. Although serious food shortages were rare, everyone understood that urban provisioning could not fall short.[25] In the middle of the tenth century, for example, the court in Baghdad was having serious financial difficulties. The army, short of pay, resorted to violence and damaged the fragile agricultural system, leading to greater shortages and more violence. People took to the streets demanding bread at reasonable prices.

Those shocked by the extravagant courtly life turned to the ascetics such as the Hanbalis, followers of the jurist Ibn Hanbal, who argued, like the Roman republicans, that the appetite, the strongest of the passions, had to be controlled. He softened old bread by sprinkling it with vinegar or water, eating it with nothing but salt, and bought only cheap fruits such as watermelons and dates, not the more expensive quinces and pomegranates, according to his son. In 935 C.E., his followers raided houses, pouring out wine wherever they found it. To guard against such eventualities, the government built granaries to hold emergency reserves of grain (as well as grain collected for tax).[26]

In the countryside, the peasants depended on soups, porridges, and flatbreads of barley, sorghum, and millet, grinding grain in hand mills and baking it in tannurs or over upturned pots.[27] In North Africa, coarsely ground bread made thick soups (*jashisha*), thought to be good for strengthening and fattening. In some areas, boiled taro corms, stems, and leaves and sorghum porridges, were backstops in times of hunger, along with the more traditional grape seeds and acorns.

Trade flourished as never before in the history of the world. Spices and sugar moved throughout the system, and Vikings brought honey from the north. Merchants made their way along the Silk Roads. The Indian Ocean and the Mediterranean were Islamic lakes dominated by Arab traders. Muslim traders sailed down the east coast of Africa as far as Madagascar, settling in the islands of Pemba and Zanzibar. Other traders and missionaries made their way from North Africa to West Africa by way of the Nile Valley, then across the Sudan, or directly across the Sahara.[28]

Islamic rulers and their agronomists, according to historian Andrew Watson, pulled off an agricultural revolution in the arid and often exhausted landscapes of the Islamic empires. They encouraged the westward transfer of "Indian" crops as they were then called—sorghum, rice, sugarcane, citrus (Seville oranges, lemons, limes, pomelos), banana, plantain, watermelon (from Africa via India), spinach, and eggplant.[29] In many areas, the imported crops ripened in the hot summers, adding a second crop to the one previously harvested in the winter. By 1400, sugar was being grown in Egypt, Syria, Jordan, North Africa, Spain, and probably Ethiopia and Zanzibar. Irrigation systems were mended or created for sugarcane and fruit trees; land was made de facto private property that could be worked as the owner wished and sold or mortgaged if he wanted; gardens were established for naturalizing and improving plants; fields were fertilized with dung, compost, and ash; farming manuals were written and distributed.

In the thirteenth century, Islam suffered setbacks. In the west, Cordoba fell to the Christians in 1236 (although they were not to take Granada, the last Islamic stronghold in Spain, until 1492). Twenty-two years later in 1258, Baghdad itself fell to the Mongols.

A SOUP FOR THE KHAN: TURKO-ISLAMIC AND MONGOL CUISINES, 1200–1350

In the early 1220s, Chinggis (Genghis) Khan had united the Mongol clans, who, like the related Turkic peoples, were nomads from Central Asia. By mid-century, the Mongols controlled northern China, Persia, and Russia, and then they went on to take Baghdad, and, by 1280, much of southern China as well. With an army of only ten thousand men drawn from a scattered population of a million people, they had created an empire the size of Africa, the largest to date. Within a generation, the empire devolved into four closely connected states, the Russian, Central Asian, Persian, and Chinese (the major focus here). In this middle ground between the Byzantine-influenced cuisine of Russia, Perso-Islamic cuisine, and the Confucian-Taoist-Buddhist cuisine of China, a high Mongol cuisine was created (map 4.2).[30]

The vast area ruled by the Mongols was traversed by the Silk Roads, which linked northern China with India, Persia, and Iraq, and by a new more northerly route from China to the Lower Volga. The Mongols established posts a day's journey apart, with garrisons, relay horses, pastures, and granaries, on the Chinese postal model. The roads were traveled by armies and captives, merchants, such as the Polos from Venice, missionaries, including Franciscans sent by European monarchs, Mongol rulers on their way to wed their relatives, and senior officials transferring their skills around the empire. The steward Bolad, for example, went as ambassador from China to Tabriz in Iran, where he became close friends with his counterpart, the steward Rashid-al-din. At Karakorum, a thousand miles out on the steppe from the Great Wall, the Mongols constructed their first capital. In the 1230s, anticipating their later culinary politics, they ordered Guillaume Bouchier, a French goldsmith, to construct a drinking fountain that spouted the alcohols of their empire: wine from Persia, mead from the northern forests, *chiu* from China, and their own *koumiss*—fermented mare's milk—from the steppes.

In 1267, the Mongols built their second capital, Khanbalik (the city of khans), where Beijing now stands. In their private capacity, the Mongol rulers, it is reported, were excessive drinkers and, in their new situation, eaters as well, which may, according to one historian, have contributed to infertility and early death.[31] In their public capacity as rulers, though, the khans used cuisine as a tool for ruling as expertly as earlier rulers, linking cuisine in time-honored fashion with politics,

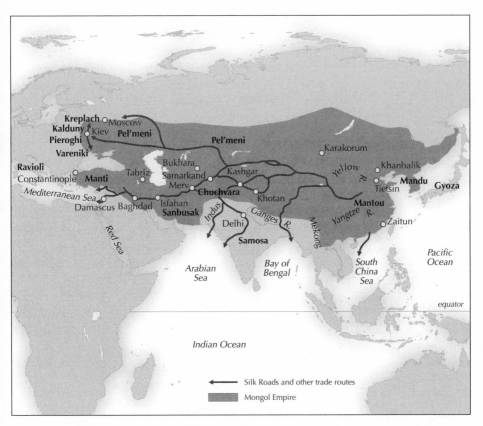

MAP 4.2. Stuffed boiled dumplings and the Mongol Empire, 1200–1350. Contemporary stuffed dumplings with dozens of different names and minor variations in preparation map onto the former extent of the Mongol Empire. They all have a wheat dough wrapper (which was sometimes leavened in China), a filling of meat (usually lamb) and onions, and a pleated seal. Although scholars still debate the origin and etymology of these dumplings, it is clear that the Pax Mongolica shaped the geography of their diffusion. Pierogi have a cheese filling. The Japanese gyoza was a later adoption from China. The relations with baked or fried dumplings, called *sanbusak* and samosa, and with ravioli are unclear. Sources: Buell and Anderson, *Soup for the Qan,* 113; Serventi and Sabban, *Pasta,* 327–29; personal communication Alice Arndt, Glenn Mack, Sharon Hudgins, Aylin Tan, and Fuchsia Dunlop.

the culinary cosmos, and religion. In 1271, Kublai Khan asked Chinese advisors to devise ceremonies for the conduct of the court, including the traditional sacrifices to sustain the balance of the cosmos and the stability of the country, and, doubtless, banqueting protocol.

Even on the steppe, the khans had asserted shaman-like powers, claiming that heaven-sent charisma justified their rule, as shown by a ray of light or halo around the head of the khan, an image they copied from the Persians. Following their conquests, the khans portrayed themselves as heirs to earlier emperors, calling themselves "Great King," "King of Kings," "Son of Heaven," and "Caesar," the titles of Indian, Iranian, Chinese, and Roman rulers, respectively. They situated themselves squarely in a world history that began with Adam, as recorded by Rashid al-Din, steward at the court of the il-khan (subordinate khan) in Tabriz. They accepted that justice involved balancing the interests of different groups, as laid out in a treatise originally written for Iran by the political theoriest Nasir al-Tusi but much more widely distributed in the thirteenth century.

From this political theory, it was a short step to the assumption that imperial cuisine had to draw on earlier imperial cuisines and balance the cuisines of different groups within the empire, as well as strengthening the diners physically and morally. The physicians to the Mongols drew on the sympathetic medicine of the steppe, Chinese nutritional theory (a synthesis of herbal medicine and the theory of correspondences with roots in Taoism and Indian Buddhism), and Perso-Islamic humoral theory (from Mediterranean and Indian sources via Avicenna and other physicians). They compiled an encyclopedia of Near Eastern medicine, of which, unfortunately, only fragments survive.

Imperial cuisines by tradition also meshed with official religion. Along the Silk Roads to their south, the Mongols, whose own shamanistic religion revolved around a sky god, had had plenty of opportunity to see what was on offer. A few, inspired by monks, merchants, and missionaries in the oasis towns of Merv, Balkh, Bukhara, Samarkand, Kashgar, Turfan, and Khotan, had converted to Buddhism or Christianity. In general, though, Mongol rulers patronized Muslims, Christians, Buddhists, and Taoists as it served their interests. In predominantly Islamic Persia, Ghazan, khan at the end of the thirteenth century, though born a Christian, flirted with Buddhism before prudently becoming a Muslim, as did his steward, Rashid al-Din. In China, Mongols felt no need to convert to Islam, which observed two culinary rules they found unappealing. Slaughtering by cutting throats spilt the lifeblood the Mongols revered; they issued edicts against Muslim slaughtering methods. Abstaining from alcohol would have put an end to the drinking and feasting that created bonds between Mongol warriors. So the khans favored first the Taoists, then the Buddhists. Both these groups, however, refrained from meat, also not something a Mongol happily contemplated. In the end, in 1250, they handed control of religious communities to Tibetan Buddhists, who held meat in such high esteem that a curved chopper with a point or hook at each end, modeled on the Indian butcher's flaying knife, was one of their sacred instruments.

Mongol stewards (*ba'urchis* in Mongolian, *ch'u-tzu* in Chinese) such as Ked Buqa, for example, who had led and provisioned the Mongol army in campaigns against the Persians in the 1250s, took over the Bureau of Imperial Household Provisioning.[32] These high-ranking ministers were expert quartermasters. Drawing on centuries of experience plotting their annual migration routes around the availability of food and water, the army stewards had planned how to feed and water an army of ten thousand, with as many as five horses apiece, as they campaigned across thousands of miles. So although in the popular imagination Mongols are famed for surviving on blood drawn from the necks of their horses, this was an emergency short-term strategy, the most dramatic aspect of a sophisticated if lessstriking set of strategies for collecting and processing food.[33]

In constructing an imperial cuisine for the Chinese khans, the stewards turned to the Confucian-Taoist-Buddhist cuisine of the conquered (chapter 3), Perso-Islamic cuisine, the Mongol cuisine of the steppe, and Turko-Islamic cuisine. Mongol cuisine, like other nomad cuisines, was simple. Soup (shülen), made by boiling meaty mutton and game bones in water to extract their strength and essences, and then thickening the broth with grains or flour, was the signature dish. Meat was also stewed, fried, or grilled as kebabs. The cuisine was rounded out with milk, yogurt, a drink of yogurt mixed with water, fermented mare's milk (koumiss), and breads and other grain dishes.

As steppe nomads, the Turkic people had had originally eaten a cuisine very like that of the Mongols. Then they settled in Turkey, pushing back the Byzantine Empire. By the eleventh century they had converted to Islam and were creating a more sophisticated Turko-Islamic cuisine. Scholars are reconstructing it from food words in a dictionary compiled at the end of the eleventh century to teach Arabs Turkish and descriptions of feasts and table service from the late eleventh-century Book of Knowledge. Early Turko-Islamic cuisine was based on grains, particularly wheat. These were turned into many different foodstuffs: toasted grain; porridge (talqan); wheat fried in butter (qawurmac); groats (yarmis); porridge of roasted millet, butter, and sugar (qawut); another kind of porridge (töp); boiled millet with butter flavoring (kürshäk); and an unsweetened flour pudding (bulgamac). They also made noodles, pancakes, and breads, including breads cooked in the ashes (kömäc and közmän); a round flatbread (ätmäk); a round, flat, fine bread (cöräk); very thin breads somewhat like filo (yuvqa, pöskäl); loaf bread (cuqmin); a breading or pastry used to cover chicken or meat (mamata); and long noodles (tutmajh).[34] Soups (ash) were as fundamental to Turkic cuisine as they were to Mongol cuisine. Sweets included syrups, jams, and candied nuts. From Perso-Islamic cuisine, Turko-Islamic cuisine adopted stews thickened with chickpeas, spiced meat stews, pastries, including a precursor of baklava, and sweetened fruit drinks (sherbets).

To process the foodstuffs for the new high cuisine in China (and to make the other necessities for an imperial court), the Mongols relocated captive Chinese, Tibetan, Korean, Russian, Persian, and Turkish artisans, whom they viewed as more trustworthy than the local population and "skillful in the laws and customs of cities." They were given their keep and the tools of their trade, but confined to special quarters and forbidden to change trades. Captives from Muslim lands milled wheat flour and oil about a hundred miles west of the future Khanbalik from the 1220s on. Others tended vineyards and made wine for the court, using techniques brought from Samarkand. Babylonians ran the sugar refinery at Yung-chun north of Zaitun (Quanzhou in southern Fujian), again probably introducing techniques from their home region, famous for its white sugar. Iraqis prepared sweet drinks and sherbets. In the Persian khanate, Chinese cooks worked in the kitchens and gardeners experimented with new varieties of rice. In 1313, a new treatise on agronomy appeared, the *Nung-shun.* Techniques for making blue-and-white glazed porcelain were exchanged between China and Persia.

The Mongols, like earlier conquerors, seized land, collected taxes, forcibly imported labor, transferred technologies, naturalized plants, and created the conditions for new trade routes to foster their cuisine. Some taxes came as coin, but others came as farm products, including 20,000 tons of cereal annually, according to an estimate by the Mongols' Chinese advisor in 1229.[35] Presumably, as in earlier empires, this was processed and paid in kind to the bureaucracy and the army. Roads, canals, and sea lanes were rerouted to supply Khanbalik. The Grand Canal having fallen into disrepair, a new canal to bring rice and other products north from the Yangtze was ordered. Rice from the Lake T'ai area was loaded onto boats for the thousand-mile trip on the Yangtze to the port of Tientsin (Tianjin) and then sent overland to the capital. According to Marco Polo, the port of Zaitun, whose residents included Muslims, Buddhists, Jains, Hindus, Manicheans, and Christians, could be compared only to the great Mediterranean port of Alexandria, receiving cargoes from Southeast Asia, India, and Iraq and sending ships laden with sugar on the two-thousand-mile journey to the capital. In 1330, Hu Szu-hui, the emperor's physician in the Bureau of Imperial Household Provisioning, wrote in the preface to the *Proper and Essential Things for the Emperor's Food and Drink,* a handsomely illustrated dietary manual and cookbook (fig. 4.3): "There is none, near or far, who does not come to court and offer tribute. Rare dainties and exotic things are all collected in the imperial treasury."[36]

Hu's *Proper and Essential Things* showed how the Mongol emperors in China gathered not just rare dainties from across the empire but also, in a deft piece of culinary politics, culinary philosophies and techniques to elaborate their own cuisine, making it an expression of their conquered territories and peoples. In parts one and two, Hu gave recipes for food and drinks. In the third, since dining on rare dainties from a different "wind and land" could be dangerous, Hu explained their nutritive values.

Twenty-seven soups (*shülen*) dominate the ninety-five food recipes. The centerpiece of Mongol cuisine, these soups could be quite liquid or thickened to become solid. The basic recipe went as follows:

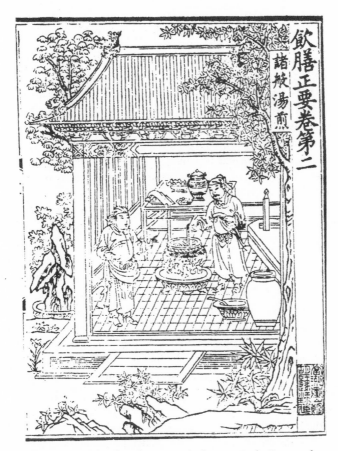

FIGURE 4.3. Hu Szu-hui, the emperor's physician in the Bureau of Imperial Household Provisioning, presented his *Proper and Essential Things for the Emperor's Food and Drink,* a handsomely illustrated dietary manual and cookbook, to the khan at an auspicious moment— the third day of the third month of the third year of T'ien-li (1330). The first image in the book shows a cook preparing a cauldron of soup, the signature dish of Mongol cuisine, over a brazier, with serving vessels and a water jar at hand. From Buell and Anderson, *Soup for the Qan,* 321. Courtesy Paul D. Buell.

1. Chop meat on the bone (usually mutton, but also game such as curlew, swan, wolf, snow leopard) into pieces. Boil in a cauldron of water until tender. Strain the broth and cut up the meat.
2. Boil the broth with a variety of thickeners, vegetables, and *tsaoko* cardamom [*Amomum tsao-ko*].

3. Add the meat.
4. Season to taste with salt, coriander, and onions (optional).

For a traditional Mongol taste, the thickeners might be chickpeas, hulled barley, or barley meal. To give the soup a Persian touch, it was thickened with aromatic rice or chickpeas, seasoned with cinnamon, fenugreek seeds, saffron, turmeric, asafetida, attar of roses, or black pepper, and finished with a touch of wine vinegar. For a Chinese taste, it was thickened with wheat-flour dumplings and glutinous rice powder or rice-flour noodles, with additions of Chinese radish, Chinese cabbage, and yams, and flavorings of ginger, orange peel, soybean sauce, and bean paste. In this way, the soup of the khans could be adjusted to the preferences of the peoples they had conquered.

The next-largest category of recipes described by Hu were pasta or noodle dishes. Turkic noodles (*tutmajh*) had a creamy yogurt-garlic sauce, similar to some still served in Turkey. Others were made Chinese-style of different "grains," including beans. Yet another noodle dish was thickened with blood. Assuming that cooks knew how to prepare the dough for stuffed pasta dumplings (*mantu*), praised as delicacies in Chinese and Persian gastronomic literature, Hu suggested a variety of traditional Chinese fillings combining mutton and mutton fat, onions, and fermented grain condiment. Some were square and ravioli-like, others curved like the borek still found in the Middle East. Other recipes included a kind of Middle Eastern potted meat (*kofte*), a couple of light Chinese dishes, and meat baked in an underground oven, an ancient technique in Siberia and elsewhere. Toasted flour (*tsampa*), useful for traveling, was typically Mongolian. So was the tersely described salt stomach: "Sheep's bitter bowel. Wash clean with water. Apply salt to ingredient. When it has dried in the wind, put into vegetable oil and fry."

In part two of *Proper and Essential Things*, drinks and liquid concentrates merited a hundred and fourteen recipes, including different kinds of water; distilled liquors, including arrack, called by its Arab name (*a-la-ji*); fruit punches, spiked and not; gruels and congees; herbal infusions; and sugar-based recipes, including the jams, jellies, julabs, and rubbs of Perso-Islamic cuisine. Tea Mongol-style with milk was included. From the eighth or ninth century on, the Mongols had traded horses for tea, for which they had developed a taste when Buddhism gained ground on the steppes. A couple of centuries later, the nomads and the Tibetans were buying between one and five million pounds a year between them, for a populace that only numbered about one and a half million.[37]

Although Chinese was the language of *Proper and Essential Things*, Hu dropped in Mongol, Turkish, and Arabo-Persian words, giving the baked and steamed breads of the Middle East, the *tutmajh* noodles, and the spices their Turkic names.[38] Following Chinese practice, he specified that ingredients in each dish be cut to the same size and shape. From Chinese cuisine, he picked out the noodle dishes and

stews most appealing to Mongol palates. He suggested Chinese flavorings for Turkic dishes and analyzed them using Chinese nutritional theory.

The khans now banqueted as befitted emperors of China.[39] As many as forty
thousand spectators gathered outside the dining hall, Marco Polo estimated,
including emissaries bringing tribute from the length and breadth of the empire.
Inside, the Great Khan and his primary wife sat at a raised table, their backs to the
north, the women below them on the left, the men on the right, with the heads of
the khan's sons, the highest ranking of the guests, on a level with the khan's feet,
and the heads of others lower yet. They waited expectantly, small, sharp steel dag-
gers, more costly than gold, at hand to cut their meat.[40]

Stewards, with silver and gold cloths swathed around their mouths and nostrils
so that the smell of their breath did not permeate the dishes, served the khan's
food. If a poisoned dish slipped past their inspection or if they were suspected, as
Rashid al-Din was suspected of poisoning the il-khan of Persia, they were sum-
marily executed. The instruments sounded. Drink was served from a huge golden
pot, not as spectacular as the fountain at Karakorum, but still big enough to hold
liquor for the company. The khan drank, his subjects kneeling, humbling themselves before his majesty.

The Pax Mongolica united the core of Eurasia and its cuisines for the better part
of a century. Then, in 1368, following unrest that had been fomenting for several
decades and plague in southwestern China in the 1330s, the Mongols left Khanbalik for the steppes. High Mongol cuisine, including grape wine, Turkic-style pasta
in yogurt-garlic sauce, and Persian techniques and dishes, vanished from southern
China. All that remained were techniques for candying and sugaring foods.

Yet, just as great empires leave traces in ruined palaces, old trading posts, forts,
and religious buildings, as well as in art and language, so they leave culinary traces.
In Korea, the court had abandoned Buddhist cuisine (unlike Japan, which was not
conquered), once again making meat central and using onions and spices. In Central Asia the Uzbeks still enjoy a Mongol-style cuisine. They bake, fry, and above
all boil wheat pasta as ravioli or dumplings (*chuchvara, manty*), they hold pilau
rice (variously called *polo* or *plov*) in high regard, and they make pancakes, flatbreads, fermented dairy products, and sweet confections such as candied almonds
and apricot seeds, strawberry, fig, and quince jams, sherbets, and a halvah of flour
toasted with fat and sugar.[41] In northern China, Muslims (Hui) of Ning-hsia, Kan-
su, and Shan-shi continue to prepare mutton and other meat soups, noodles,
and dumplings (*mantou*) with lots of Chinese onions and simple spicing.[42] In
Russia, the earlier cuisine based on the Christianized Hellenistic cuisine of
Byzantium to the south, was augmented with Mongol- or Turkic-style dumplings
(*pel'meni*), melons, lemons, dried fruits such as raisins, figs, and apricots, confections of root vegetables cooked in sugar or honey, halvah, rose-petal jam, caramel-
ized nut clusters, and fruit drops.[43] Under the Mongols, Chinese blue-and-white

porcelain, so good for serving liquid foods, became an export, setting off a craze for the product across the Old World and, following 1492, in the Americas as well.

In the last third of the fourteenth century, Timur conquered Central Asia, but that was to be the last time that nomads were to conquer a settled society. With the invention of gunpowder, the nomads lost the advantage of mobility. A long phase of culinary history, the to-and-fro between the cuisines of the nomads and the cuisines of the settled that went back to Mesopotamia, came to an end. From this point on, the history of high cuisines is exclusively the history of settled societies.

RAW, ROASTED, AND BURNED: TURKO-ISLAMIC CUISINES, 1450–1900

During the Mongol years, Islam had expanded east to Southeast Asia. Adding to and melding with the Hindu-Buddhist cuisines of the complex area, the Islamic cuisines made use of local ingredients such as rice, coconut, ginger, galangal, and tamarind. Islam had also expanded south of the Sahara. The empire of Mali, with its great cities of Timbuktu, Gao, and Jenne, became Muslim in the early fourteenth century.[44] According to Arab travelers, the cuisine was based on boiled rice or on couscous made of hulled and boiled millet or sorghum, which was similar in texture, though not in raw materials or technique, to the rolled semolina couscous made north of the Sahara. Cowpeas, meat and dairy products from the indigenous African cattle, guinea fowl, lamb, or goat accompanied the grain dishes. The poor, often slaves, had porridges frequently made of little more than the bran from the hulling of the millet.

Following the collapse of the Mongol empires, in the core area of Islam, three closely related Turko-Islamic cuisines evolved from earlier Perso-Islamic cuisine (map 4.3). Ottoman cuisine became the cuisine of what is now Turkey. Mughal cuisine was superimposed on the Hindu cuisines of northern India. Persian Safavid cuisine flourished under the rule of Shah Abbas, who reigned from his capital in Isfahan from 1588 to 1629. Little is known about the latter, so I shall focus on the Ottoman and Mughal cuisines. All the Turko-Islamic cuisines favored flat, lightly raised breads, lamb, mutton, and chicken soups and stews, skewered and grilled meats, meat dumplings or pastries, ground meat with spices, meats marinated in yogurt, sugar confections in wide variety, and sherbets and yogurt drinks.

Two important innovations were pilau rice and, in the Ottoman and Safavid empires, coffee. Pilau rice was not a staple like the boiled or steamed rice of Asia but an elaborate dish. Rice was washed, soaked, often sautéed, then boiled, drained, and steamed, so that the grains remained separate. Meat, nuts, dried fruits, vegetables, and colorings were frequently added before steaming. The steaming liquid was likely to be a broth enriched with fat. Pilau probably evolved from the many solid or semisolid dishes of grains and meat that went back to Mesopotamia and were widely found as tharid, harisa, or the near-solid soups beloved by Turkic and Mongol peoples. It had the advantage of retaining the granular structure, something that many diners found pleasing. The pilau technique was extended to other granule or pasta dishes.[45]

Coffee was closely associated with the Sufis, a mystic and often missionary wing of Islam that drew on elements of Christianity, Gnosticism, Buddhism, and Hinduism. Important not only for spreading coffee but for the diffusion of Turko-Islamic cuisines, Sufi culinary philosophy was developed in lodges that, like Buddhist monasteries, were simultaneously spiritual centers, guesthouses, and the nuclei of future settlements. Drawing on traditions going back to the ancient culinary cosmos, and also found in Buddhism, Sufis described the passage from a raw mortal to one who achieved mystic union with the divine as cooking: "No more than three words. I was raw, I roasted, and I burnt," said the Persian poet and philosopher Rumi, founder of an important Sufi order, who lived in Konya in central Turkey in the thirteenth century.[46]

The kitchen shaped the organization of Sufi orders. In Rumi's order, for example, the second most senior position was that of head cook (*sertabbah*). He trained initiates to the order, who spent a thousand and one days working in the kitchen. The keeper of the cauldron oversaw the sacred pots that symbolized loyalty to the ruler and the transformation of raw materials and initiates into fully cooked products. The table setter ensured that salt was the first thing placed on the eating cloth, followed by bread.

Sufi imagery was shot through and through with culinary metaphors. Bread and salt stood for the civilized life, reminding the diner of the labor, creativity, and wisdom required to bring them to the table and to keep peace in the world. Bread symbolized God's care in providing food for humans. The growing of wheat and the making of bread—from the dead grain in the earth, to the living wheat, to meal and flour ground in the mill, to living leavened bread, and finally to bread's dissolution in the human body—paralleled the stages of human life. Salt, pure and incorruptible, was used to seal covenants. A little was taken before and after every meal. A pinch taken from the large stone bowl of salt in the mausoleum of red stone that houses the tomb of Rumi's cook, Ates baz-i Veli, who died in 1285, is still believed to bring blessings to the tasters' kitchens, make them better cooks, and boost their health. Soup reminded diners that without water life could not exist; meat and vegetables recalled the earth that sustained life; and rice pilau and stuffed flaky pastries (*borek* made with phyllo or *yufka*) evoked fire's power to transform and perfect. Eggs brought to mind women's fruitfulness; salt meat (*pastirma*), men's power to impregnate. Sweet halvah and rice-flour puddings (*muhallebi* in Turkish and *muhallabiyya* in Arabic) conjured up images of human and divine community; milk and sweetened fruit drinks (*sherbet*), the food that angels gave the Prophet.

To achieve union with the divine, Sufis kept vigil, danced (and hence were named whirling dervishes by uncomprehending Europeans), and drank to achieve

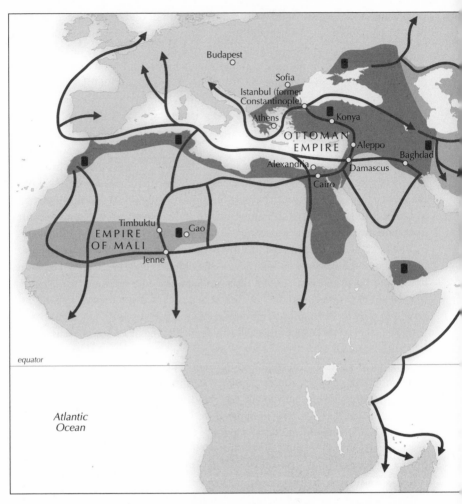

MAP 4.3. Tannurs, sixteenth-century trade routes, and Turko-Islamic cuisines. Beginning in the fifteenth century, the courts of the Ottoman, Safavid, and Mughal empires created variants of Turko-Islamic cuisines. Trade routes stretched across these empires and extended to other Islamic states south of the Sahara and in Indonesia. Throughout most of this area bread continues to be baked in the tannur oven of ancient Mesopotamia, as indicated by the black

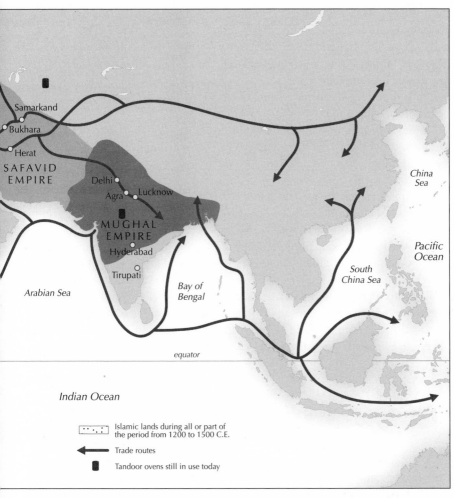

Samarkand

Bukhara

Herat

SAFAVID
EMPIRE

Delhi
Agra • Lucknow

MUGHAL
EMPIRE

Hyderabad

Tirupati

Arabian Sea

Bay of
Bengal

China
Sea

Pacific
Ocean

South
China Sea

equator

Indian Ocean

Islamic lands during all or part of
the period from 1200 to 1500 C.E.

Trade routes

Tandoor ovens still in use today

rectangles. Variants of the word—*tandoor, tennur, tandir, tandore, tamdir, tandur, tanir,* and others—are found in Farsi, Kurdish, Arabic, Aramaic, Assyrian, Persian, Tajik, and Turkish languages. Sources: Robinson and Lapidus, *Cambridge Illustrated History of the Islamic World;* Alford and Duguid, *Flatbreads and Flavors,* 35–37.

the drunkenness that symbolized divine intoxication. The twelfth-century Persian mathematician and philosopher Omar Khayyám, whom some believe to have been sympathetic to Sufism, may have been referring to sacred drunkenness when he wrote: "A jug of wine, a loaf of bread—and thou." In another verse, he said, "If I'm drunk on forbidden wine, so I am!/And if I'm a pagan or idolater, so I am! / Every sect has its own suspicions of me, / I myself am just what I am. . . . / To be free from belief and unbelief is my religion."[47]

Coffee, like wine, was an aid to union with the divine. Long before the time of the Sufis, coffee beans, the fruit of a bush native to the highland forests of southwestern Ethiopia, had been chewed like a nut or mixed with animal fat to make a portable, satisfying, and stimulating food for warriors.[48] Coffee plants were naturalized in Yemen perhaps as early as the sixth century B.C.E., when the Abyssinians invaded Arabia. Later, a new way of preparing coffee by toasting the beans, grinding them, and brewing them with hot water was developed, perhaps in Iran. The Arabic word for coffee, qahwah, probably derives from a word meaning to have little appetite and hence to be able to do without. It had first been applied to wine (which suppressed the desire for food) and later to coffee (which suppressed the desire to sleep). Sufi pilgrims, traders, students, and travelers consumed coffee to keep awake during ceremonies and to induce a sense of euphoria, spreading its use throughout the Islamic world between the thirteenth and fifteenth centuries. Finally, in a lighter mode, Sufi poets also used food in their humorous poetry. Abu Ishaq Shirazi (Bushaq At'imah) parodied the words of the fifteenth-century Sufi poet Shah Ni'matullah, "We are the songbird of the Beloved's rose bed / as her lover we sing the canticles of love," with "On the surface of the stew we are dollops of rich grease / and we befriend the yogurt-meatball soup."[49]

Ottoman Cuisine

In 1453, the Ottoman sultan Mehmed II took Constantinople from the Byzantine Christians. Mehmed's advisor, the Sufi physician and mystic poet Ak Şemseddin, preached the first Friday sermon in the former Orthodox patriarchal basilica of Agia Sofia, which had been converted into a mosque. The city, which encompassed "two lands" (Asia and Europe) and "two seas" (the Mediterranean and the Black Sea), was to be the successor to Rome, the center of the "empire of the world." Mehmed encouraged wealthy Greek Orthodox, Armenian, and Jewish merchants, the latter expelled from Spain, to settle in the city, which later became known as Istanbul. By the following century, Istanbul had a million people, more than any European city, 40 percent of them non-Muslims. The Ottoman Empire (named for Osman Bey, the founder of the dynasty) stretched across North Africa, Egypt, Syria, Mesopotamia, Greece, and the Balkans.

Ottoman cuisine, refined in the kitchens of the Topkapi Palace, almost certainly incorporated certain elements of Byzantine cuisine, such as confections and stuffed vegetables, though this is yet to be investigated.[50] Mehmed II issued a decree setting out the protocol to be followed when preparing and serving food and when dining. Physicians such as Zeyneladabidin bin Halil (d. 1647), physician to Murad IV, wrote nutritional tracts describing the humoral properties of grains, meats, fish, milk products, fruits, dried fruits, and vegetables. The enormous kitchens were divided into those that prepared food for the sultan, for his mother and high-ranking ladies in the harem, for the rest of the harem, and for the rest of the palace household. The kitchen staff, which grew from 150 in 1480 to around 1,500 by 1670, included specialists in baking, desserts, halvah, pickles, and yogurt (fig. 4.4). Pages levied from across the empire and from as far away as West Africa were highly educated in the palace arts, including the preparation and serving of the emperor's meals.[51]

Soups (çorba, from the Persian shorba) were prepared in great variety from lamb, noodles, yogurt, grains, and pulses, thickened with flour or with an emulsion of lemon and egg yolk (terbiye). Meat dishes included kebabs; balls of finely ground and pounded meat (kofte); steamed, stuffed dumplings (mantı); salted, spiced meat, or pastrami (pastırma); fricassees or ragouts (yahni). Pilau was held in high regard. Vegetable dishes, fried, braised and layered, stuffed, or combined with onions and with chopped meat, were one of glories of the cuisine. Eggplants were now the vegetable par excellence. Compared to Perso-Islamic cuisine, Ottoman cuisine tended to separate salt and sour tastes from sweet ones, used fewer fruits and less sugar and vinegar in savory dishes, and reduced the spices, even though Istanbul remained a key node in the spice trade.

Wheat-flour preparations continued to evolve. Deep-fried doughs of flour and water, some yeast-raised, some with eggs beaten into the dough (a kind of choux fritter), often soaked in syrup (lokma), were popular. Phyllo was used in both savory and sweet dishes, rolled or folded, stuffed with ground meat, fresh cheese, or vegetables in little pies (börek), or stuffed with chopped nuts, baked, and soaked in syrup (baklava and related pastries). A novelty was a sponge cake (revani), made from semolina (coarse ground wheat), eggs, and sugar and soaked in syrup.

Many other sweet dishes had a long history, including rice puddings, sweetened puddings of starch and milk, and halvahs. A sweetened dish of mixed grains of great antiquity, asure, was eaten in remembrance of the martyrdom of the grandson of Muhammad. Drinks included sherbets of pomegranate, cherry, tamarind, violet, and countless other flavors, as well as buttermilk or yogurt and water (ayran).

Sugar was fashioned into elaborate, extravagantly expensive sculptures. When, once or twice a century, a spectacular public festival was held, sculptures were commissioned from sugar workers, many of them Jewish.[52] Several hundred brightly colored sugar candy figures—stallions, camels, giraffes, elephants, lions, sea monsters, castles, fountains, and candelabra—were carried in procession in 1582, some so large that several bearers or even a wheeled cart was needed.

G. Scotin maj. sculp.

𝓑.

Beulouk-Bachi

Chef de Cuisine du Grand Seigneur.

11.

Avec Privil. du Roi.

FIGURE 4.4. Like head cooks in all early imperial courts, the *beulouk-bachi,* head cook to the Ottoman caliph, was a senior court official responsible for overseeing large institutional kitchens that turned out meals appropriate for the caliph and his harem, elite troops, and host of servants and slaves. His executive position is made clear by his dignified stance and fine robes. Engraving by Jean-Baptiste Scotin. From Charles Ferriol, *Recueil de cent estampes représentant différentes nations du Levant* (Paris: Le Hay, 1714–15), pl. 11. Courtesy New York Public Library. http://digitalgallery.nypl.org/nypldigital/id?94387.

Food was the hub between rulers and subjects, according to the oldest substantial surviving Islamic-Turkish writing, the eleventh-century *Mirror for Princes,* a treatise on kingship heavily indebted to the Perso-Islamic tradition. The ruler was advised to give bread and salt to nobles, scholars and religious men, and commoners. "Eating the sultan's bread" was the phrase for receiving a salary.[53] The janissaries, the sultan's infantry bodyguard core of the standing army, formed of children taken from Christian families, were converts to Islam and influenced by the Bektashi Sufi order. They took their bread and soup seated in order of precedence around a cloth laden with rich dishes into which they dipped with their own individual, precious spoons. At the end of the meal, the diners tasted a pinch of salt, praying, "May God grant abundance to our table." The cauldron, reflecting long-standing tradition, was the symbol of their loyalty to the sovereign. Their ranks were those of the kitchen: the soup maker at the top, then cooks, then scullions. Overturning the cauldron, rejecting the sultan's food, signaled rebellion.[54]

From the mid-fourteenth century on, the poor and travelers were fed in a variety of benevolent institutions, such as Sufi community kitchens and hostels (called tekkes in Turkey, from the word for a dervish monastery) and charitable institutions attached to certain mosques that served two meals a day to the employees of the mosque, students, travelers, and the poor. By the sixteenth century, each of the twelve in Istanbul served as many as four to five thousand people soup, bread, sometimes pilau or *asure,* and on special occasions a little meat.[55] Elsewhere noble and pious ladies endowed charitable foundations, an act that would bring them a place in Paradise. One in Jerusalem fed five hundred people daily, four hundred of them poor, from a cauldron so gigantic that it had to be lifted by four men using two beams crossed through the four handles.

Ottoman high cuisine spread beyond the palace kitchens to the households of high-ranking nobles, officials, and merchants, Jewish and Christian as well as Muslim, in cities such as Cairo, Alexandria, Damascus, Aleppo, Athens, Sofia, Baghdad, and Budapest. In Istanbul, so fine was the cuisine in the thousand mansions that entertained regularly that even the sultan accepted invitations to dine. Guilds of butchers, *pastirma* makers, sherbet makers, snow and ice merchants, and fishermen served the households.

In the sixteenth century, coffee drinking created a new social venue—the coffeehouse—marking a transition from the spiritual to the secular realm, as had happened earlier with tea in China.[56] In these establishments the literati discussed their work, played chess, danced, sang, and talked politics (fig. 4.5).The state suspected that coffeehouses, which existed outside the circle of benevolence that bound state and religious authorities to the people through gifts of food, were centers of sedition. Legal proceeding and penalties started in Mecca with a famous case in 1511, spread to Cairo in the succeeding twenty years, and were reenacted around the empire for the next century. It was to no avail. Lawyers such as Abd al-Quadir,

FIGURE 4.5. An Ottoman coffeehouse. Coffeehouses, more respectable than taverns, offered not only coffee but also a place to smoke tobacco, listen to storytellers and musicians, and gossip. From Henry J. Van Lennep, *Bible Lands: Their Modern Customs and Manners Illustrative of Scripture* (New York: Harper, 1875).

in his *Argument in Favor of the Legitimate Use of Coffee* (1587), defended coffee-houses, and patrons flocked to them. Coffee became the drink of the Arab-speaking part of the Ottoman Empire: Egypt, Syria, and Iraq in the east, Libya and Algeria in the west, and Turkish Hungary in the north, where the coffeehouse became a magnet for intellectuals and writers.[57] For all the problems imagined by the state, coffee brought in revenue. Having occupied Yemen in 1536, the Ottomans had a monopoly on this sought-after product that lasted until the end of the seventeenth century.[58]

Ottoman cuisine depended on, and stimulated, commerce and agriculture. In the mid-seventeenth century, two thousand ships a year docked in Istanbul laden with wheat, rice, sugar, and spices from Egypt; livestock, grain, fats, honey, and fish from north of the Black Sea; and wine from the Aegean islands. In conquered territories, the Ottomans set up market gardens to provide fresh vegetables for Turkish garrisons. The gardeners sold green beans, onions, chile peppers, cucumbers, and cabbage to the townspeople on the side. In the seventeenth century, market gardeners from Bulgaria were supplying European cities.[59] In the Balkans, the Ottomans introduced improved grape varieties for eating and for drying as currants and sultanas, as well as okra, filberts, spearmint, flat-leaved parsley, eggplants, durum wheat, improved forms of chickpeas, and the aromatic Damask rose for petals for jam and rose water.

American plants entered the Ottoman Empire as fast as or faster than they did Spain, perhaps because networks of Sephardic Jews expelled from Iberia stretched from the Ottoman Empire to the Americas. The first illustrated book published in Istanbul was Mehmet Efendi's *Book of the New World* (1583). Beans, squashes, and chiles came into use. Maize became an alternative food for the humble.

Ottoman cuisine continued to evolve until the breakup of the empire in the late nineteenth and early twentieth centuries. The cuisines of Turkey, the Levant, Egypt, the Balkans, and North Africa still show its influence. And as with earlier Perso-Islamic cuisine, its borders with the Christian cuisines were permeable: traces of Ottoman cuisine can be found along the northern Mediterranean and in central Europe, where rice pilau, pita bread (*lángos*), phyllo (*strudel*), honeyed drinks, and stuffed vegetables (although stuffed cabbage had been made earlier) entered the culinary repertoire from the Ottoman period in Budapest.

Mughal Cuisine

In 1523, Babur (the Tiger), a soldier of fortune of Turkic descent, led his men across the Afghan plateau and down the precipitous roads to the north Indian plain. Babur hailed from Turkestan (now Uzbekistan), which had been conquered by Timur, with Sufi advisors, in the 1360s. The cities of Bukhara, Samarkand, and Herat had splendid palaces and silken tents in gardens with channels of water dividing trees, flowers, fruits, and vegetables, according to an impressed Portuguese ambassador to Timur's court.

Babur took Delhi as his capital, but he always saw northern India and its food as second best to that of Central Asia. "India," he commented in his memoirs, "is a land of few charms." It lacked "grapes, melons and any good fruit; ice and cold water; good food or good bread in the markets."[60] Hindus didn't eat meat; their griddle-baked whole-wheat breads and barley bannocks compared unfavorably with tannur-baked puffy, slightly raised naan bread. Imperial advisor Abū al-Fazl, anticipating later British attitudes, opined that the wet heat of Bengal was the reason that its inhabitants were so weak, an implicit comparison with the dry cool of the Mughal's Central Asian homeland.[61] Nonetheless, India did possess "large quantities of gold and silver," farmers planted two crops of wheat a year in the dryer regions, two of rice in the wetter areas, and grew cotton, sugar, poppy, and hemp for the market. Babur and his men stayed.

The Mughal court was dominated by Persianized, Islamicized, Turko-Mongolian aristocrats. In 1595, about two-thirds of the nobles at the court of Akbar, the third Mughal emperor, were of Persian or Turkish ancestry, including Persian intellectuals and poets, Arab scholars, and military men of Turkic and Uzbek origin.[62] Akbar accepted the Persian political theory of power, virtue, and order radiating from a benevolent, semi-divine emperor supported by hierarchical ranks of soldier-administrators (*mansabdars*). He was familiar with Sufi theology and culinary philosophy, knowing much of Rumi's writing by heart.[63] The fourth Mughal emperor, Jahangir, enjoyed Sufi pursuits—cooking, especially noodles, and dervish dancing—in the gardens of Herat. The fifth Mughal emperor, Shah Jahan, called himself Second Lord of the Conjunction, after Timur, who had also been born at the conjunction of two favorable planets.

Like the Mongols, the Mughals frequently adopted the customs of the conquered, unlike the Ottomans, who, despite whatever Christian elements may have slipped into their cuisine, did nothing to officially acknowledge them. Akbar, to the horror of his more devout Muslim followers, adopted the Hindu customs of sitting on a raised platform and holding public audiences. He invited Rajput nobles, local nobility, mercenaries, missionaries, including Jesuits, and diplomats to court. He encouraged his sons to marry Hindus, particularly the powerful Rajputs: Jahanghir's mother was a Hindu princess from Rajastan; his wife, Nur Jahan of Taj Mahal fame, was the daughter of Persian immigrants. In addition to mosques, Akbar's palaces included Hindu temples and even Christian chapels. Hindu ayurvedic physicians received stipends, and a new literary language, Urdu (from a Turkic word for army encampment), which combined Hindi grammar with Arabic, Persian, and Turkish vocabulary, was used alongside the Persian of the court.[64]

Abū al-Fazl, advisor to Akbar and steward of the imperial kitchens, included a short but informative section on the kitchens in the imperial how-to manual, the *Ain-i-Akbari*.[65] Following the now-familiar pattern, Abū al-Fazl brought in cooks from different parts of the Islamic world to work in the kitchens in Delhi or in the sixteen large kitchen tents that were part of Akbar's train as he traveled constantly through his territories. Ingredients were imported from Afghanistan, Persia, and other Middle Eastern kingdoms. Butter or ghee cost by weight almost as much as white sugar (though oil and brown sugar were a little cheaper) and twice as much as mutton or goat meat. Saffron was the most prestigious and expensive spice, followed by cloves, cinnamon, and cardamom. Fine rice fit for the palace cost as much as butter or sugar and about ten times as much as wheat. Persian gardeners planted almonds, pistachios, and walnuts, pomegranates, grapes, melons (supposed to have restorative power), peaches, and apricots. Royal horses dined better than most humans on a daily ration of four pounds of grain and three pounds of sugar.[66] Ice, used in Persian cuisine for water and sherbets, and much in demand in steamy Delhi, was rushed from the Himalayas. An alternative was to suspend jugs of water in solutions of saltpeter, a magical substance that created hot, explosive gunpowder as well as cooling water.[67]

Abū al-Fazl began his treatise by reiterating the old truth that "the equilibrium of man's nature, the strength of the body, the capability of receiving external and internal blessings and the acquisition of worldly and religious advantages depend ultimately on the proper care being shown for appropriate food." The core of the cuisine remained Islamic. Fruits and nuts, a hallmark of Mughal cuisine, were eaten fresh, added to pilaus and meat and chicken dishes, made into sherbets, and incorporated into confections. Rice pilaus were taken to new heights of extravagance. In one dish, each grain was painted red and white to resemble pomegranate seeds. In another, rice was cooked with thin sheets of gold and silver beaten with egg yolk to look like pearls. In another, it was mounded, birds flying out when the mound was breached.[68]

In contrast to Perso-Islamic cuisine, the Mughals used ghee rather than the fat of the fat-tailed sheep. Hindu dishes, such as rice and beans (*kichiree*), were enriched with an amount of ghee equal in weight to the rice and legumes. Hindu confections joined Islamic ones. Milk puddings spanned the two traditions: toasted vermicelli pudding (*sivayan*) for the end of Ramadan, along with rice pudding (*kheer*) and ground rice pudding aromatized with rose water or orange flower water (*firni*), and the popular halva and *qulfi* (ice cream). Soup, so common in nomadic and other Turko-Islamic cuisines, disappeared, perhaps because it could not be eaten Hindu-style with the fingers. It was replaced by pilau and biryani, a pilau layered with a spicy, meaty sauce.

Under the light of the moon, Jahangir's son Shah Jahan served white banquets. His retinue, dressed in white, knelt on white carpets and cushions on the terrace of the Agra Fort decorated and perfumed with white flowers.[69] Spectacular vessels and eating utensils made in the palace workshops or imported from distant countries were set out: gold ladles encrusted with jewels, platters of Ming porcelain, elegant ewers, based on Persian models, and wine cups of gold, jade, and silver. Following

FIGURE 4.6. Shah Jahan drank wine from this milky white jade cup, perfectly sized to fit in his palm. The jade came from the borders of China and Central Asia. An unknown craftsman would have spent months cutting, grinding, and polishing it to the form of a gourd, with a lotus base and a handle shaped as the head of a wild goat. According to alchemists, jade calmed the soul, kept the humors circulating, prevented disease, and turned color in contact with poison. The cup was a world in miniature, symbolizing universal and immortal kingship. Courtesy Victoria and Albert Museum, London (12-1962).

Turkic custom, drinking now began before the meal, opium often being taken as well. After partaking of white dishes, like chicken in a sauce of almonds and yogurt (chicken korma), the drinking party and poetry recital began. The royal retinue, in Jahanghir's phrase, became intoxicated with the "wine of loyalty." Shah Jahan took his wine from a milky white jade wine cup (fig. 4.6), made in 1657.[70]

Mughal cuisine spread far beyond the imperial court, becoming the high cuisine across much of India. It was refined in the courts of the Nizams of Hyderabad and the Nawabs of Agra and Lucknow, who specialized in korma, as well as among the rulers of Kashmir and Rajastan, whose courts were known for their elaborate rice and meat preparations. It went beyond the Mughals to become a cuisine of the elite of other faiths.[71]

At its height, the Mughal dynasty ruled about one-seventh of the world's population, rivaled in that era only by the Qing dynasty in China. As in other successful empires, the poor were relatively well fed. To guard against shortage in the cities, public granaries were built into the walls. Delhi, unusual in the world's great cities for not being accessible by water, was surrounded by lightly populated arid lands so that the draft oxen of the hereditary migrant livestock herders (*banjaras*) could feed along the roads. An abundance of fertile arable land meant that the rural poor lived quite well on traditional dishes made from the lesser grains and a wide variety of beans and lentils. They turned to new plants from the Americas only for variety, enjoying, for example, fruits such as papaya, sapote, avocado, passion fruit, and above all guava, and the inexpensive piquancy added by chiles, "the ornament of the garden and the insurance for domestic happiness."[72] With the exception of maize, other American plants, such as cassava, peanut, tomato, and potato, remained unimportant until the nineteenth century.

Islamic cuisines by the sixteenth century were firmly entrenched across much of India, central and western Asia, and North Africa. The constant iteration of techniques in the huge palace kitchens of the region had raised the high cuisine to a level of great sophistication, and it would continue to evolve for centuries to come. In the cities, the high cuisine spread to the houses of the wealthy and even, in a simplified form, to the dishes offered by vendors in the market. Commercial food processing and the appearance of places to drink or eat open to all who could afford it offered an alternative to culinary benevolence, at once generous and a self-interested way of buying loyalty. In the country, people usually ate adequately, though the aromatic meat dishes and glowing confections of high cuisine were worlds away from their humble meals. And insecurity remained. In 1630, when Shah Jahan was imbibing from his jade wine cup and his retinue was feasting on exquisite dishes, a famine was devastating the people of Gujarat.[73]

On three occasions in succeeding centuries, Islamic cuisines, or at least aspects of them, expanded beyond the core area. From the twelfth century on, Europeans modified the cuisines to Christian tastes, and in the sixteenth century, the expansion of the Iberian empires transferred Islamic-influenced Catholic cuisines to the Americas, the Philippines, and trading posts in the Indian Ocean. In the late nineteenth century, the migration of Hindu indentured laborers to plantations in the Indian Ocean, Africa, the Caribbean, and the Pacific, and of Greeks, Lebanese, and others to the Americas and elsewhere transferred Mughal-influenced Indian cuisine and Ottoman cuisine to those regions. And in the second half of the twentieth century, the migration of Indians following the breakup of the British Empire made a Mughal-inspired cuisine popular in Britain.

Christianity Transforms the Cuisines of Europe and the Americas, 100–1650 C.E.

BREAKING BREAD: CONSTRUCTING A CHRISTIAN CULINARY PHILOSOPHY, 100–400 C.E.

"Jesus took bread, and blessed and brake it . . . and said, Take, eat: this is my body. And he took the cup, and . . . they all drank of it. And he said unto them, This is my blood of the new testament, which is shed for many."[1] According to three of the four Christian gospels, Jesus of Nazareth performed these acts at the Last Supper, eaten with his disciples before his crucifixion, probably in 33 C.E.

Backtracking a millennium and a half from the preceding chapter, I now turn to Christian cuisines, the third of our sample of cuisine families shaped by an alliance of universal religion and state. After sketching the early evolution of Christian culinary philosophy, I concentrate on the two most expansive branches of Christian cuisine prior to 1650: Byzantine cuisine, or the cuisine of the Eastern Orthodox Church; and Catholic cuisine, as I shall call the cuisine of the western church, first in Europe, then in its expansion in the sixteenth and seventeenth centuries. The cuisines of other Christian groups, such as the Egyptian Copts, Armenian Turks, Syrian Nestorians (who from about 450 C.E. to around 1000 C.E. expanded along the Silk Roads to China), Indians, and Cathars in twelfth-century southern France, I leave to one side, because in the absence of powerful state backing, they had less effect on global culinary history.

For ten centuries, following the dissolution of the kingdom of David and Solomon in the tenth century B.C.E., the Jews worshipped their god under different imperial rules: the Babylonians, the Achaemenids, the Alexandrians, the Seleucids, and, at the end of this period, the Romans.[2] Following the Roman destruction of the Second Temple in 70 C.E., the Jews could no longer perform the traditional Passover sacrifice of a lamb in remembrance of the flight from Egypt, when, to escape Moses's curse on the Egyptians that they would lose their first-born, the Jews had smeared lamb's blood on their doorposts. In many respects, Jewish cuisine in Palestine (though not in Babylonia), now resembled the cuisine of the Roman Empire, of which it was a part: the round slashed loaf (fig. 2.6), the garum, the culinary vocabulary, and the table manners. In the Passover meal, the participants washed their right hands, prayed, took wine from the communal cup, and then blessed and broke bread.

Nonetheless, Jewish cuisine had distinct features. The Torah laid down rules about slaughter, what was not edible (including blood and pork), how cooking should proceed, what foods were appropriate for celebrating Passover, and how the Sabbath should be set aside as a day of rest. The Jews' refusal to sacrifice to the emperor made them a thorn in the side of Rome, which, although generally tolerant of race and local religions, expected everyone to participate in this expression of membership in the empire.

In about 100 C.E., when Galen was advising his rich patients on diet and Seneca was writing about Stoic virtues and diet, little groups of Christians began gathering to eat simple meals together.[3] An increasing number were converts from the sacrificial religions of the Roman Empire. Many were artisans or traders, established, financially secure people, though not the elite. They lived in the same winding streets as their non-Christian neighbors, going to the same markets in Rome, Alexandria in Egypt, Ephesus or Antioch in Asia Minor, or Carthage in Tunisia.

Constructing a Christian cuisine distinct from both Jewish and Roman, yet not so strange, so unpalatable, or so difficult to prepare that it scared off potential converts, took the next couple of hundred years. It's worth remembering that in the ferment of the changing beliefs of late antiquity, other nascent religious groups were also creating cuisines. The Manicheans, headed by a Persian prophet, Mani (216–76), took elements from Christianity and Buddhism, attracting flocks of converts from North Africa to China. The Elect, his elite followers, ate only fragrant fruits and brightly colored vegetables. They abstained from meat, wine, and cooked foods (as well as sex), because Mani had explained that food and bodies, part of the dark material world, trapped the Divine Light that the sun and the moon rained down on the earth.[4] Christians struggled against the Manicheans until the end of the sixth century, Muslims until the end of the tenth, and farther east, the religion flourished for hundreds of years more.

Christian converts in Ephesus, Corinth, and Rome in the first century C.E. addressed queries about cuisine to Paul of Tarsus, who was raised a Jew but following his conversion grew hostile to Jewish customs, including dietary law. Food was not the point of Christianity, he insisted. Understanding the meaning of Christ's death through the eating of bread/body and the drinking of wine/blood was

FIGURE 5.1. In this drawing of a painting in the Roman catacombs, a family dines on a fish (symbol of Christ) and a shared goblet of wine, watched over by Peace (Irene) and Love (Agape). From Rodolfo Lanciani, *Pagan and Christian Rome* (Boston: Houghton Mifflin, 1896), 357.

sufficient. Christians need not follow Jewish dietary law or observe its feast days. On the other hand, they should not eat meat that had been sacrificed to the gods of the Roman Empire, nor should they participate in the sacrificial feasts at fraternity banquets, at funerals, or following state sacrifices.

A frugal meal celebrating community, the Eucharist of bread and wine, became the central Christian act (fig. 5.1). After eating, the participants lit the lamps, confessed their sins, and offered gifts of flour, grapes, lamp oil, bread, and wine at the altar. The apostle or other officiant broke the bread, consecrated the bread and wine, and then the baptized, chanting a hymn of thanks, received the bread and the wine.

Bread, the everyday staple, was used as a metaphor to explain Christian beliefs. Christians were united in the body of Christ as the grains of wheat were united in a loaf of bread. Christ was bread for hungering humans. Christ digested Christians, binding them to his body. Spiritual progress was like cooking, as Augustine explained in a much-quoted sermon in the fourth century, using symbolism similar to that found in Buddhism and Islam. "When you received exorcism you were 'ground.' When you were baptized, you were 'leavened.' When you received the fire of the Holy Spirit, you were 'baked.'"[5]

Blood, forbidden by Jewish law, was taken symbolically in the form of wine signifying the blood of Christ, the Lamb of God. The blood of slaughtered animals was not discarded in Christian lands but used to thicken sauces and make sausage. Pork, also forbidden to Jews, was permitted for "those who exercise the body"— presumably athletes and laborers—though it should be avoided by those "who devote themselves to the development of the soul," according to Clement of Alexandria (echoing the explanation that the Jewish theologian Philo, Clement's near contemporary, gave for Jewish pork avoidance). Jewish culinary cosmogony was adopted and reinterpreted by Paul and the church fathers. The expulsion of Adam and Eve from the Garden of Eden marked the change from a cuisine of fruit and vegetables to one with meat. Whereas God had earlier allowed Abraham to substitute a lamb for his son, Isaac, now he had given his own son in the Crucifixion.[6]

Drawing from Roman as well as Jewish culinary thought, the Christian fathers looked to republican or Stoic culinary philosophy, with its insistence on decent food and natural appetite in preference to the appetizers, sweets, and sauces said to lead to gluttony. The appetite of the belly and of the sexual organs that lay below the belly had to be controlled, asserted Clement, bishop of Alexandria toward the end of the second century C.E., in a book on Christian etiquette, *Paidagogus.* Christians should avoid high cuisine (which most of them could not have afforded in any case). They should eat plain, economical fare such as "roots, olives, all sorts of green vegetables, milk, cheese, fruits and cooked vegetables of all sorts—but without sauces. And should there be need for meat, [let it be] boiled or roasted."[7] They should not drink much liquid, which washed food through the system before it could be digested. Above all they should avoid lust-inducing wine. To escape becoming "captives of pleasure" they should avoid "sweet sauces" and a "multitude of new sweets" that provoked gluttony and left many "shipwrecked on pastries and honeycakes and desserts," as well as appetizers that led to eating without hunger.[8] They should chew thoroughly to promote digestion and minimize excrement, a reminder of the earthly body that provoked lust when it accumulated around the sex organs.

Fasting gradually became more stringent. Following Jewish custom, the early Christians had probably fasted on Wednesdays and Fridays. The church fathers gave fasting greater importance. Fasting "empties the soul of matter and makes it, with the body, clear and light for the reception of divine truth . . . [whereas excess food] drags down the intellectual part towards insensibility," according to Clement of Alexandria.[9] In Egypt and the Byzantine East, an ascetic movement developed, whose adherents, fearing that meat and wine provoked lust, withdrew to the desert, where they experimented with raw food and performed extraordinary acts of self-negation and abstention to control sexual desire.[10]

In the fourth century, monasteries presided over by abbots began to form, where such excessive fasting was regulated. Broadly similar dietary regimens were included in the rules for monastic life drawn up by a number of leading Christians, including Pachomius, the founder of important Egyptian monasteries (his were translated into Latin by Saint Jerome, who also translated the Bible), Saint Basil of Caesarea, Saint Augustine, and, most influential of all, Saint Benedict in the sixth century. All stipulated that monks should eat only one or two meals a day of bread, vegetables, and a little wine or ale, inasmuch as "nothing . . . is more contrary to being a Christian" than gluttony.[11] On Wednesdays, Fridays, Lent, and Pentecost, monks had only one meal a day. Dry eating—just bread, salt, water, and perhaps vegetables—was practiced in many monasteries. Garum was banned by Pachomius, followed by Jerome, possibly because it was fish transformed from cold and wet to hot and dry, and hence likely to evoke lust.[12] Gluttony—failure to control appetite—became one of the seven deadly sins.

By about 300 C.E., Christian cuisine had taken its first shape as a communal meal, actual or symbolic, of bread and wine, variously called in English the Eucharist, Holy Communion, or the mass, replacing the pagan sacrificial feast. Bread, wine, oil, fish, lamb, and pork were the Christians' signature foods. Fasting, which meant abstaining from meat, eggs, milk, butter, and animal fats, was required on close to half the days of the year. Non-Christians rumored that their secret meals might involve eating human flesh and drinking human blood. Subjected to harassment by mobs, Christians, still only about 10 percent of the population of the Roman Empire, were liable to summary execution.[13] Their culinary philosophy would have remained unimportant on the global scale had it not achieved official status in the eastern Roman Empire.

FROM THE CUISINE OF THE EASTERN ROMAN EMPIRE TO THE CUISINE OF THE BYZANTINE EMPIRE, 350–1450 C.E.

Christian culinary philosophy began its shift from that of a minority to that of the majority in the eastern Roman Empire when the emperor Constantine granted tolerance to Christians in 313, following this with laws in 352 and 356 that forbade the sacrifice of animals on pain of execution, exile, or dismissal from rank and office. In doing so, he heeded Eusebius, bishop of Caesarea, one of a small circle of court clerics, who argued in his *Ecclesiastical History* that Rome and Christianity were mutually supportive, that the monarchy of Constantine would bring the kingdom of God to men. Just as Ashoka's edict half a millennium earlier in India had initiated the slow disappearance of sacrificial religion there, in the Roman Empire, although reintroduced by the emperor Julian in the fourth century, it was now also on the way out.

Byzantium, renamed Constantinople, became the capital of the Roman Empire when political and economic problems in the late third century C.E. made it obvious that the east was where the wealth of the empire lay. Home to around a million people, it was situated at the crossroads of trade routes that brought spices from the east, grain from Alexandria, and honey and furs from northern Europe, connecting with Alexandria, Antioch and Trebizond in Asia Minor, and Thessalonica across the straits in Greece. As the western, Latin-speaking empire crumbled, Christianity became the official religion of the Greek-speaking Byzantine Empire, which comprised most of Asia Minor, the Balkans, Greece, Egypt, and much of North Africa. By the fifth century, Christians comprised almost half the population. Leavened bread, like that at elite tables, was also used for the mass, baked in its own oven and stamped with Christian symbols such as the fish and the cross.

In Byzantium, the imperial court forged Byzantine high cuisine. Unlike the simple communal meals shaped by Stoic dietary theory of the early Christians, this was based on the Hellenistic cuisine of the eastern Roman Empire and reshaped by Christian culinary philosophy, particularly the mass, the rules of fasting, and the preferred foods.[14] The emperor's meal showed his dominion over his peoples and over nature, his authority deriving from ancient tradition, his place at the top of the social hierarchy, and God. He reclined as Christ at the Last Supper, the meal that Christians remembered in the Eucharist, his companions on the dining couches representing the twelve apostles, a Christian version of Augustus's dining symbolically with the Greek gods.[15] On almost half the days of the year, following Christian principles, no meat and dairy products were allowed, though we know little about the alternatives. Meals were designed according to the theory of diet and nutrition taught in the medical school in Alexandria in the sixth century, based on the writings of the second-century physician Galen.[16] On nonfasting days, the court might dine on roast pork basted with honey wine; wild duck with wine, fish sauce, mustard, and cumin-salt; stuffed grape leaves (probably invented in this period); young suckling animals; small birds, game, fish, and other seafood; puddings of boiled grains, honey, and raisins; and jams and conserves of quince, pear, and lemon, eaten from a spoon with a glass of water on the side. There might also be sweetened fruity soft drinks. Wine flavored with aromatics such as mastic and aniseed spouted from fountains.

Byzantine court cuisine, for all its sophistication, now tasted strange to visitors from the west, where Greek wine and garum had largely vanished, and lard and other fats often substituted for olive oil, which was much in demand as a lubricant. When Bishop Liutprand of Cremona visited the Byzantine court as the ambassador of the Holy Roman Emperor Otto I, he complained that the wine tasted of resin, that the dishes had too much olive oil, and that they included "another very unpleasant liquid made from fish."[17]

Large landowners and monasteries (which owned large tracts of land) also served high cuisine to guests. They operated grist and oil mills, wineries, beehives, carts, and even ships. If their estates did not provide sufficient food, they could shop at the baker for the best grade of bread, at the grocer for cheese, olives, salt meat, vinegar, honey, pepper, cinnamon, cumin, caraway and salt, at the sheep or pork butcher for fresh meat. The hundred and fifty thousand monks in the seven thousand monasteries that had been established by 1000 would have dined on an ascetic cuisine based on wheat bread and wine.[18]

In the cities, ordinary people had the now-familiar cuisine of second-grade whole-wheat bread, "the bread of poverty," or barley bread made by bakers. They had meat with it only on festive occasions. The usual accompaniment was a soup of beans, onions, garlic, and vegetables. In the lesser taverns, they bought *posca*, essentially water with a little sour wine or vinegar added to make a refreshing, not particularly intoxicating, drink. In the countryside, people depended on millet porridge (*píston*) or on flatbreads they baked themselves. Soldiers carried a crock (the *klibanus*) to make flattish barley bread similar to that still prepared in the region.[19]

Supplying the high cuisine of Constantinople and the ascetic cuisine of the monasteries demanded the agricultural resources of the empire. As in other empires, manuals on farming were written. Part of Cassianus Bassus's *Eklogai peri georgias* (Selections on Farming), dating from around the sixth century C.E., for example, survives in a collection called the *Geoponika*, dedicated to the emperor Constantine VII Porphyrogennetos (r. 913–59). Landowners sent grain, cheese, oil, and wine to the capital.[20] Wheat was shipped in, first from Egypt (160,000 metric tons annually in the early sixth century), then, after Egypt was lost to the Arabs in the early seventh century, from the Balkans and the Black Sea region.[21]

In the late tenth century, Byzantine cuisine expanded northward to Slavic lands. According to *The Primary Chronicle,* a history composed a couple of centuries later, Grand Prince Vladimir of Kiev summoned Muslim, Jewish, western Christian, and Byzantine emissaries to explain their religions.[22] Food loomed large in all the reports. The Muslims reported that pork and alcohol were forbidden. "Drinking," retorted Vladimir, "is the joy of all the Russes. We cannot exist without that pleasure." The western Christians explained that they fasted. The fathers of Rus' saw no reason to fast, said Vladimir. The Jewish delegation said that pork and hare were prohibited, so they too were sent packing. Finally, the Byzantine Christians (presumably skirting the matter of fasting) proclaimed that they ate not the wafers of western Christianity (of which more soon) but the very bread and wine ordained by Jesus when he said "this is my body broken for you" and "this is the blood of the new testament." After prudently sending envoys to check these stories, in 988 Vladimir decided on Byzantine cuisine, with its bread, wine, and pork, for his people.

More legend than history, *The Primary Chronicle* is nonetheless telling, a reminder that rulers frequently declared what religion their people should adopt (often easier said than done), and that conversion brought with it a change of cuisine. In this case, converting justified banning the unpopular practice of casting lots for young sacrificial victims and enabled Vladimir to marry the emperor Basil II's sister, Anna, getting the benefits of trade with the great power and experience in how a major state was run.

The high cuisine of Kievan Rus' included wheat bread and grape wine. Wine, like spices and rice, had to be imported from the south and paid for in honey and furs. Pancakes, baked in the image of the sun to welcome its return, were transformed into yeast-raised blinis for Butter Week before the Lenten fast. Sweet dishes included simmered berries thickened with flour (*kissel*) and a spice cake of rye meal, honey, and imported spices.[23] Beets and onions cooked with honey made a sweet condiment. The environment yielded wildfowl, game such as bear and elk, and berries and honey from the forests or the buckwheat fields. Fasting dishes were freshwater fish, particularly the sturgeon, and its eggs (caviar) and sperm (milt), and mushrooms, dismissed in the Byzantine Empire as having "killed off many a large family."[24] The egg sac and eggs of the sturgeon were floured, fried, and served with a sauce of onion, berry, or saffron, or eaten cold, sliced, with herbed vinegar or mustard. Or the eggs were taken out of the sac by hand at near freezing temperatures and cured lightly with salt. Mushrooms were eaten fresh in the summer and fall and dried or pickled in the winter. Alcohols were made from fermented honey (mead) or lightly fermented grains (*kvass*).

Humble Slavs, particularly in the more northerly regions, ate gruels of oatmeal, barley, one or more of the millets (*Panicum miliaceum*), and buckwheat (*Fagopyrum*), the seed of a plant related to rhubarb. Their bread was a sourdough of rye (*Secale cereale*), which Pliny the Elder had spurned as a weed grain for times of famine. "Mother rye feeds all alike but wheat is choosey" said a Russian proverb, referring to the difficulty of growing the variety of wheat known as spelt, originally a hybrid of emmer and wild grass that had entered the peasant diet north of the Alps in 500 B.C.E.[25] Cabbage, beets, and onions went into soups.

Byzantine high cuisine continued to evolve for eight hundred years. Frustratingly, almost nothing is known about what it contributed to (and perhaps received from) Perso- and Turko-Islamic cuisines. In 1237, the Mongols invaded Kievan Rus'. For two hundred years they demanded tribute from the Slavs, whose culinary orientation turned east (chapter 4) instead of south. In 1453, the Turks, who beginning in the eleventh century had advanced slowly across Anatolia, took Constantinople. Something of the cuisine, however, survived wherever people worshipped in the Eastern Orthodox Church.

FROM ROMAN IMPERIAL CUISINE TO THE CATHOLIC CUISINE OF THE EUROPEAN STATES, 1100–1500

For five or six centuries, while Byzantine cuisine, Perso-Islamic cuisine, and Buddhist cuisine were at their height, high cuisine largely vanished in the former western Roman Empire, surviving only as remnants in courts and monasteries. The Germanic invaders of the fourth and fifth centuries, many of whom had been converted to Christianity, albeit to Arianism, a variant that denied the divinity of Jesus, were familiar with Roman cuisine but incapable of maintaining the commerce and agriculture to sustain it.[26] Roman villas decayed, mules no longer towed barges up the Rhône laden with sweet wine from Gaza, dried fruits from Turkey, fish sauce and olive oil from North Africa, and spices from the East. Viticulture and the raising of edible dormice (*Glis glis*), which were eaten as a snack by the Romans, and still are in Slovenia, vanished from northern Europe. Anthimus, a physician trained in Constantinople, in a letter to the Frankish king on "the observance of foods" tactfully praised butter, beer, mead, meat, and cured pork, while insinuating that Byzantine cuisine was vastly superior.[27]

Humble people depended on gruels, pottages, and flat or raised breads of the grains that grew best locally—millet in much of Italy, rye in much of central Europe, oats in cold, wet Scotland, barley in much of the rest of Britain—with dried peas or beans, onions and cabbages, a bit of salt pork fat, a fish from the river, a rabbit caught with a noose. They ate their meals from the communal bowl with fingers or spoons, accompanying them with mead, weak beer, or watery wine.

Bishops, who led the congregations in the remaining small towns, attacked non-Christian eating, particularly the sacrificial feast that still persisted. They forged alliances with the kings of small states, frowned on drinking and singing at feasts, forbade eating with non-Christians, whether they were pagans, Jews, or (just about as bad) Arian heretics, outlawed sacrificial feasts, and offered their own feasts at Easter, Christmas, and saints' days, prepared by large staffs in their ample kitchens. The Irish missionary monk Columbanus (540–615), who proselytized in the Frankish and Lombard kingdoms, prescribed forty days' bread and water and three years' penance for anyone who sacrificed "in worship of demons or in honour of idols."[28] Eating horsemeat, another sacrificial favorite, was a "filthy and abominable practice," Pope Gregory II said in a letter in 732 C.E. to Boniface, his apostle to the Germans. Gradually and reluctantly, and probably never completely, people gave up the easy-to-understand, time-honored sacrifice, which offered feasting, singing, and dancing and a welcome break from hard work, for a single, invisible, all-powerful god who demanded a tithe of their hard-earned farm produce. They stopped eating horsemeat (except for the Icelanders, who had a special dispensation) and, officially at least, fasted on half the days of the year.

Then, from the eleventh century on, Europe became more prosperous and a pan-European high Catholic cuisine was established. Although Europe was a patchwork of independent but tightly interconnected cities and city-states, small kingdoms, and principalities, a shared culinary philosophy, political and social connections, and social and commercial interchanges meant that the noble classes across Europe dined on a single Catholic cuisine, albeit with regional differences.[29]

A united Christendom, the Roman Empire recreated in a holy, Christian mold, was a dream nearly realized by Charlemagne in the eighth century, shared by Henry II of Germany in the early eleventh century, and almost pulled off by Philip II of Spain in the sixteenth century. Ruling families moved and intermarried. Anglo-Norman families settled in Ireland, Normans in Cyprus and Sicily, Germans in Pomerania, and Castilians in Andalusia, taking with them their cuisines.[30] The Portuguese Infanta Dona Maria, who took her cooks and cookbooks with her when she moved to Italy on her marriage in 1565, was following an old tradition. Merchants rode along the trade routes across the Alps. Venice, Barcelona, and Genoa in the Mediterranean were linked by trade, as were the cities of the Hanseatic League around the Baltic and North Sea. Papal delegates traveled between courts and the Vatican or Avignon. Catholic orders operated across state boundaries. None was more important for cuisine than the Cistercians, founded in 1098 by Robert, abbot of Molesmes, who in Cîteaux (hence Cistercian) in the Burgundy forests revived the rule laid down by Saint Benedict five hundred years earlier. Close to a thousand Cistercian monasteries had been founded from Hungary to Portugal and from Italy to Sweden by the mid-twelfth century. The Brothers of the German House of Saint Mary in Jerusalem, better known as the Teutonic Knights, rode through central and eastern Europe converting people at the point of the sword.

Catholic cuisine defined itself against the neighboring high cuisines: Byzantine or Eastern Orthodox to the east, and Perso-Islamic to the south. For many people, the tangible sign of the drawing apart of the Eastern Orthodox Church and the Catholic Church in the eleventh century was the difference in the bread served at mass: in the east, it was raised; in western Christendom, it was unleavened, a thin wafer baked between hinged irons.

Of the two neighboring cuisines, Perso-Islamic cuisine, particularly the cuisine of al-Andalus (now southern Spain), was the more important in shaping Catholic cuisine. Most of the Iberian Peninsula was in Muslim hands in the eighth century. In the tenth century, Palermo, Cordoba, and Seville were all Islamic towns. Many Mediterranean islands—Cyprus, Sicily, Malta, and the Balearics—as well as parts of southern Italy were Islamic for periods.[31] The Crusades of the eleventh to thirteenth centuries gave Europeans a further glimpse of Islamic cuisine. Genoa, Barcelona, and Venice made fortunes trading with Islam. Merchants traded not only luxury silks and spices but everyday kitchenware, North African pots being sold in southern Europe, for example. As Christians advanced across southern Spain, Morisco (converted Muslim) girls worked as servants in Christian households and followed their mistresses to monasteries. Morisco families were important in the bread trade.

Europeans adopted much from Islamic cuisine, just as earlier Alexander and the Romans borrowed from the cuisine of the conquered Persians, Islam drew from the Sassanids, and the Mongols appropriated from the Chinese and Persians. Given that traces of Roman culinary philosophy and cuisine persisted in Islamic lands as in Europe, this was easy to do, one more step in the entangling of the cuisines of Eurasia. Specifically, Europeans adopted the theory of the culinary cosmos; the techniques for working with sugar, distilling, and making pasta; and a whole series of specific dishes.

The theory of the culinary cosmos entered Christendom as translations of Arabic medical texts, which, as we have seen, were themselves translations of or further developments of earlier classical works. In the late tenth century, in Salerno, a small town outside Naples with a famed medical school, Constantine the African, a convert from Islam, translated Arabic versions of Galen. The *Regimen Sanitatis Salernitanum* (Salernitan Health Regimen), a Latin poem by a doctor of the Salerno school, popularized the humoral theory, offering advice such as: "Peaches, apples, pears, milk, cheese and salted meat,/ Deer, hare, goat, and veal,/ These engender black bile and are enemies of the sick." Following the Christian conquest of Sicily and central Spain, translations of Arab physicians, particularly Avicenna, followed.[32]

As in Islam, the correspondences (table 1.1) underpinned the choice of aromatic and colored dishes. Spices, whose aroma suggested a life that persisted after the plant or mineral from which they came had died, originated somewhere in the east, perhaps Paradise itself.[33] Although enormously expensive, they were an essential sign of status, inhaled as aromatics in grand houses and castles, wafted as incense in churches, and used in three-quarters of the recipes in medieval cookbooks. The familiar pepper, cinnamon, ginger, and saffron were the most important, with nutmeg and cloves coming close behind. In all, between twenty and thirty were commonly used, including some, such as galangal (still widely used in Southeast Asia) and grains of paradise (Guinea pepper, *Aframomum melegueta*), that are now scarcely known in Europe. As in Islamic cuisine, colors were endowed with significance. White in the form of almond milk symbolized holiness and purity. Yellow, from saffron, egg yolk, or gold leaf, suggesting the sun, gold, light, and hope, was an Easter color, like white. Green, from spinach and other herbs, was the color of Epiphany, suggesting nature and fertility. Brown and black, on the other hand, suggested the earth, poverty, and death.

In preparing food for their noble employers, cooks were as aware of the need to balance the humors as we are today of, say, the need to have all food groups represented. Root vegetables such as turnips were by nature earthy (dry and cold) and thus better left to peasants. Chard, onions, and fish were cold and wet, so that frying was appropriate. Mushrooms were so cold and wet that they were best avoided entirely. Melons and other fresh fruit were not much better, being very moist and thus thought likely to putrefy in the stomach. Grapes were best served dried as raisins, quinces were dried and cooked with extra sugar—warm in humoral theory—to make quince paste. Red wine tended to be cold and dry, so it was best served warm with added sugar and spices (as hypocras).

Sugar cookery was introduced from Islam in the twelfth century by a physician known as Pseudo-Messue. The English words "syrup," "sherbet," and "candy" all have Arabic roots. Medicinal electuaries, pastes of spices and drugs, and comfits, sugar-coated spices, were the distant forerunners of candy. Sugared spices did not break the fast, Thomas Aquinas said, because "although they are nutritious themselves, sugared spices are nonetheless not eaten with the end in mind of nourishment, but rather for ease in digestion."[34] It was an important decision, both because it gave medical respectability to sugar and because it foreshadowed later arguments about chocolate. A flurry of books in the mid-sixteenth century, including *De secreti* by Alexis of Piedmont (Venice, 1555) and the *Traité des fardemens et confitures* (Treatise on Cosmetics and Conserves) (1555) of the French physician and astrologer Nostradamus, disseminated the techniques for working with sugar.

In convent kitchens, nuns created Islamic-style confectionary to sell to eager customers, contributing to sugar's shift from a medicinal spice to an ingredient in confections and cakes. Islamic fruit pastes became the Portuguese quince paste *marmalada* (and later evolved into citrus preserves, such as marmalade). Deep-fried doughs drenched in honey or sprinkled with sugar (*luqam al qadi*), which were served to celebrate the end of Ramadan and the end of the Yom Kippur fast, again with roots in antiquity, became the family of deep-fried doughs (*buñuelos, beignets,* donuts) eaten on Catholic festive days, particularly before the Lenten fast.[35] Islamic sweetened drinks of nuts, fruits, and grains, such as barley water, often medicinal and often with roots going back to antiquity, also entered the repertoire. As in Buddhism and Islam, sugar was good. In 1666, the German chemist J. J. Becher explained that just as rainwater was transformed into grape juice and wine, and food was cooked and digested into blood, so the juices of cane were digested and cooked by the sun.[36] And in their laboratories, alchemists mastered Islamic methods of distilling and experimented with all kinds of plants and minerals, experiments that were to bear fruit in the distilled drinks and the culinary revolution of the seventeenth century (chapter 6).

The wheat- and rice-based dishes of Islam continued to be prepared, particularly in southern Europe. *Tharid,* bread moistened with broth and layered with meat, the Prophet's favorite dish, was renamed *capirotada* in Spain. Thin dried pasta (*itrya*) of durum wheat was traded around the Genoa-Barcelona network. The pilau method of rice cookery became Spanish paella. Couscous continued to be prepared in Sicily and Spain. The pottage of mixed meats, grains, and beans became the *olla podrida* (literally "rotten pot") of Spain. Harisa, the puree of grains and meat, reappeared as blancmange, a puree of rice and chicken.

In the early fourteenth century, cookbook manuscripts began appearing across Europe. One of the first, the early-fourteenth-century *Le Viandier,* is often and probably mistakenly attributed to Gillaume Tirel, or Taillevent, master cook to Charles V of France, but it certainly reflects dishes served at the court. It was followed in the mid-fourteenth century by *Das Buch von Güter Speise* and the *Libre de Sent Sovi* (Book of Sent Sovi), probably composed in Barcelona. In the late fourteenth century, a manuscript drafted by master cooks (given the name *Form of Cury* in the eighteenth century) gave recipes for the dishes at the court of Richard II of England (fig. 5.2), while *Le Ménagier de Paris* consisted of instructions from a bourgeois husband to his young wife. The *Libro de arte coquinaria* by Martino da Como dates from the early fifteenth century and the *Libre del coch* by the Catalan Ruperto de Nola from the early sixteenth. This sampling and others were recopied and attributed to different authors, and they were often excerpted, much as today housewives put together collections of recipes from other books, friends and relatives, and their own inventions. Rarely were these cookbooks step-by-step manuals, being, rather, testimonials to a ruler's fine cuisine or aide-memoires to professional cooks.

With the invention of printing, the number increased again. Particularly important for the expansion of Catholic cuisine was the *Arte de cocina, pastelería, bizcochería y conservería* (Art of Cooking, Cake Making, Biscuit Making, and Conserving), first published in 1611 by Francisco Martínez Motiño, master cook to several kings of Spain, most notably Philip III.

Islamic dishes were reworked in these cookbooks. *Al-sikbaj* was transformed into fried or poached fish (or chicken, rabbit, or pork) in an acid marinade of vinegar or orange (*escabeche*), perhaps the origin of aspic.[37] Ruperto de Nola's *Libre del coch* included thin noodles (*fideos*), bitter oranges, fried fish, *escabeche,* almond sauces, and almond confections. Martínez Motiño's *Arte de cocina* contained several recipes for meatballs (*albóndigas*) and *capirotada,* and one for couscous. It also had one for Moorish hen (*gallina morisco*): roast chicken cut into pieces, simmered with bacon, onion, broth, wine, and spices—which were not named, but probably included pepper, cinnamon, and cloves—and then enlivened with a final dash of vinegar. The bacon and wine were typically Christian, but the sour-spicy sauce justifies the name *morisco.*[38]

Just as, for all the borrowing, Roman cuisine was different from Hellenistic cuisine and Mongol cuisine was different from Chinese or Perso-Islamic, so Catholic cuisine was also different from Perso-Islamic. The mass, the fasting, and the preferred foods of Christianity gave Catholic cuisine its own character. Bread and wine were hallowed. The preferred bread for the mass was a flat wafer and that for fine dining was a raised wheaten manchet roll, rather than the flat or slightly puffy breads of Islam. The technique of cooking wafers between hinged, heated irons was to give rise to a variety of related baked goods, including waffles.

Fresh pork, cured pork, pork sausages (the old Roman Lucanian sausage) and blood products were ways of distinguishing Catholic from Islamic and Jewish

FIGURE 5.2. Richard II of England and the dukes of York, Gloucester, and Ireland are seated at a table set with personal knives, wine cups, and rolls of manchet (white wheaten) bread. In the center are platters of roast meat. Under the watchful eye of the steward with his staff of office, one courtier serves wine (or perhaps water for hand washing) and another brings in the nef, a table ornament in the form of a ship, often used to hold salt. The walls of the hall are covered with rich tapestries. Musicians sound trumpets. From *Chronique d'Angleterre*, vol. 2 (Bruges, Belgium, late fifteenth century). By permission of the British Library (Royal 14 E. IV, f.265v).

cuisines. Large roasts were popular. Butter and lard were used in cooking rather than mutton fat or olive oil. Gelatin-preserved meats (galatines) were favored. When tinted green with spinach, for example, these were understood in humoral theory as cold, dry jelly preserving hot, moist meat. Pies and tarts of all sizes were popular. Fasting gave rise to dishes without meat or dairy products, including fish dishes and sauces with almond milk, made by pouring water through ground almonds. Catholic cuisine delighted in conceits and disguised food: ground meat shaped like hedgehogs with colored spines, edible sculptures that resembled castles or the lamb of God, gilded boars' heads. Peacocks were cooked and then covered with their skin and iridescent feathers. Birds fluttered out when huge pies were cut.

The grand dishes included roasts, pottages (the *olla podrida* of Spain was one of the most famous), meats cooked in acid sauces or sauces thickened with nuts and spices, a carefully balanced puree of rice and chicken sprinkled with sugar (*blancmange*), and pies and tarts of all sizes, with a pastry made of flour, water, and salt, sometimes with added egg. The sauces of Catholic high cuisine were based on vinegar or verjuice (the acid juice of unripe grapes) flavored with spices, including sugar, to carefully balance the cool moistness of the vinegar with the hot, dry, pounded spices; the whole was thickened with breadcrumbs or nuts. One of the most popular sauces was cameline. "To make an excellent cameline sauce, take skinned almonds and pound and strain them; take raisins, cinnamon, cloves, and a little crumb of bread and pound everything together, and moisten with verjuice; and it is done.[39] Others were jance, a ginger sauce also with almonds, and a sharp black sauce heavy in pepper. Diners enjoyed hypocras, warm spiced wine, with meals that were taken seated on chairs or benches with knives and spoons as utensils. By the sixteenth century, Catholic cuisine was widely distributed across the royal and noble houses of Europe (with some regional variations) and highly refined.

Monasteries, particularly Cistercian ones, spread Catholic high cuisine to rural areas. The kitchens made up the fourth side of the monastery, the other three being the church, the chapter house (administrative building), and the sleeping quarters. One of the best-preserved kitchens, at Fontevrault on the Loire, has eight ovens arranged around one side of an octagonal base, rising to a square, topped by an octagonal roof. As with palace kitchens, there were separate areas for cooking for different groups: for the abbot and visiting dignitaries; for preparing meat for the sick (and, after rules were relaxed in the mid-fifteenth century, for the monks once or twice a week); and for the monks. Located in remote areas, Cistercian monasteries were largely self-sufficient, appropriate for an order that believed that "to work is to pray." The monks grew their own grain, beans, vegetables, fruit, and herbs, raised poultry and fish, brewed ale, made cheese and wine, if possible, and produced oil for cooking (and for the lamps in the church). Sales of processed foods and farm products supported the order. Clairvaux was known for its breeds of cattle, presumably for milk and cheese, Waldsassen in Sweden for its fish hatchery, while in England, Wensleydale cheese is frequently associated with the order. Cistercian monasteries were famous for their gardens and for the new varieties of fruit they bred. They excelled in making wine, ale, and cordials. The motherhouse of Cîteaux in Burgundy produced Clos-Vougeot, a wine that would become world famous. The abbey at Eberbach, a pioneer in growing vines on terraced hillsides, sent 53,000 gallons of wine down the Rhine in its own ships each year to be sold in cities such as Cologne.

Humble cuisines continued to be based on darker breads and pottages, with a bit of rabbit or small birds, with the occasional piece of butcher meat. The quality of the bread and the quantity of meat increased in the late fourteenth century after

FIGURE 5.3. God, his dominion over the world shown by the
cross-topped orb in his left hand, showers down bread (manchet rolls).
Miniature by Cunradus Schlapperitzi (1445). Courtesy New York
Public Library, http://digitalgallery.nypl.org/nypldigital/id?426487.

the population dropped by half following the Black Death, only to go down again
in the sixteenth century. Food tended to be more plentiful in the rich farmland of
northern Europe than around the Mediterranean with its often-rocky soils. The
humble may have dreamed of eating wheaten manchet rolls (fig. 5.3) but most
subsisted on grains lower in the hierarchy, and humble cuisines probably varied
more by region than high cuisines. In fifteenth-century Poland, the poor made
ashcakes, porridges, pottages of millet and buckwheat, and hemp grits. In times of

famine, they resorted to ashcakes of ground knotgrass seeds.[40] In Sedgeford, a village in the county of Norfolk in eastern England, laborers hired for the heavy work of harvest enjoyed white bread, fresh meat from animals too old to work or give milk, and nearly a gallon of ale a day. Two hundred years earlier, they had had a humbler repast: barley bread, cheese, a little bacon or salt herring, and ale, milk, or water to drink.[41]

In the cities, the state imposed strict rules and regulations to ensure that bakers did not shortchange customers on the weight of bread and that pies were not made with tainted meat. Purveyors of basic foodstuffs, such as butchers, fishmongers, and grain merchants, and producers of prepared foods, such as bakers, pastry cooks, sauce makers, and caterers, were members of guilds, their establishments and shops grouped together on specific streets. Markets bustled with customers, and taverns and simple eateries offered meals. Urban cuisines, like rural ones, varied from satisfying to barely adequate. In Barcelona, in relatively wealthy Catalonia, between 20 and 50 percent of the population of between 25,000 and 40,000 went hungry. The cathedral almshouse could help only about two hundred individuals, or 1 to 3 percent of the poor.[42]

Several innovations improved the culinary scene for the humble. Women in northern Europe spent less time grinding. The plentiful rainfall and many small rivers made the locale ideal for small water mills, most of them for grinding flour (fig. 5.4). In England, there was a water mill for every fifty households, according to the 1086 Domesday survey.[43] In my home village, the stream, although only a foot or so deep and a few feet wide, had sufficient power to drive three mills per mile in the twelfth century. Many resented laws requiring that grain be ground at the lord of the manor's mill. On the other hand, since grinding for a family of five with a rotary quern would have taken about an hour a day (chapter 2) or a full day's work a week, they now had time for other activities.

Again, the Cistercians may have helped diffuse this important technology. Every Cistercian monastery had a mill on a nearby river to grind the grain, sift the flour, and (in the south) crush olives. Mills were also used to grind malt for beer and to drive edge runners to crush poppy and mustard seeds. Not only did mills make the mechanical processing of food more efficient, but they had wider benefits, including disseminating mechanical knowledge through the population and encouraging new methods of financing these expensive installations in the form of precursors of joint stock companies.

Proteins other than meats became more widely available. One tantalizing possibility is that peasants literally became "full of beans," the historian Lynn White Jr. observes, a suggestive idea pursued by the novelist Umberto Eco, thanks to a change from cultivating two large fields to three, allowing the planting of peas, fava beans, and lentils as part of a regular rotation.[44] Unfortunately, no hard evidence has been produced to confirm an increase in the consumption of beans.

FIGURE 5.4. Engraving showing the workings of a water mill such as those found along the rivers of northern Europe. River water was piped (A) into buckets in a waterwheel (B), which turned a shaft (F) connected to gears (C and D) that rotated the millstone (G). Grain was fed into the millstones from a hopper above. Here a miller checks the outgoing flour as it enters a chute to be passed through a sieve (H) before filling sacks with flour. From Georg Andreas Böckler, *Theatrum Machinarum Novum* (Cologne: Sumptibus Pauli Principis, 1662), fig. XLV. Courtesy New York Public Library, http://digitalgallery.nypl.org/nypldigital/id?1691567.

Salted and dried fish from the North Sea and the Atlantic also added a new element to humble cuisines across Europe. These preserved fish could be traded long distances, unlike fresh fish, which, even if carried by relays of horses, could be taken no more than a hundred miles from the sea. Fish-rich northern Europe began supplying the fish-poor Mediterranean.[45]

Herring (*Clupea harengus*), so plentiful that it was said that their massed bodies would keep a halberd (fighting axe) upright in the water when they shoaled inshore, were fatty fish, difficult to preserve. So-called white herring, which were lightly salted in piles on the shore before packing into baskets, kept for only a few weeks. Red herring, hard smoked until reddish brown and pungent, lasted longer. Ten to twenty-five thousand tonnes were traded up the rivers of northern Europe annually. In the twelfth century, north German merchants reorganized the herring trade, present on a minor scale since the seventh century, making it one of the chief commodities of the Hanseatic League, a string of near-autonomous cities and guilds, headed by Lübeck, that stretched from southern England to the Russian border, from Hamburg in northern Germany to Bergen in Norway. In the thirteenth century, a better way of preserving herring by partially gutting the fish was invented, with consequences that we shall see in chapter 6. Pilchards (*Sardinas pilchardus*) were salted along the Atlantic Coast from Cornwall to northwestern Spain and Portugal for export to the Mediterranean (fig. 5.5).

Cod (family *Gadidae*) had long been gutted and hung to dry in the wind and sun of the northern summer by Norsemen. Its flesh, which dwindled to one-fifth its original weight, became as dry as a board. In Dutch, the product was called *stokvisch,* or "stick fish," translated into English as "stockfish." In Iceland, where it was too cold to grow even the tougher cereals, stockfish spread with sheep butter substituted for bread. It became an important resource for the poor in Spain and Portugal and later in West Africa, Brazil, and Mexico. Bergen shipped two to four thousand tonnes of it annually. In the fifteenth century, fishermen began salting cod (*bacalao*). John Cabot, a Genoese living in Bristol, discovered the Grand Banks of Newfoundland, perhaps already known to the Basques. By 1500, all the European fishing nations sent ships to fish there during the summer, returning loaded with bacalao to sell, particularly in the Mediterranean. To restore its succulent flesh, cooks soaked the stiff, white pieces in several changes of water before cooking.

As Catholic high cuisine flourished, so did the trade and farming to supply it. Grain was shipped to cities from increasing distances. From the twelfth century on, Tuscany imported grain from Sicily, North Africa, and northern Europe, and the Low Countries bought it from eastern Europe; later Spain and Portugal also imported grain. Fresh fish (usually freshwater, more prestigious than salt) was in great demand for fasting days. Tench, pike, and trout were caught in streams and rivers. Carp came from monastery and castle ponds (sometimes also from mill ponds), a

FIGURE 5.5. Fishmonger and customer depicted in a fourteenth- or fifteenth-century manuscript on health and well-being, known as the *Tacuinum Sanitatis,* based on an eleventh-century Islamic medical treatise by Ibn Butlân of Baghdad. In front of the counter are barrels, presumably packed with salt fish.

fish-farming technique about which we know little. Eels were trapped. In 1187, 264,000 eels were taken from the fishponds of the count of Flanders.[46] Cattle were walked from Hungary to northern Italy, from Scotland to London, from Poland and Denmark to the Low Countries. Lemons, capers, raisins, dates, figs, and nuts such as almonds came from Mediterranean countries.

The demand for sugar was met by Mediterranean growers and refiners. By the twelfth century, sugarcane was grown in the Levant and Sicily by Venetians and Normans, who copied Muslim techniques. When Muslims regained control of the Levant in the thirteenth century, crusaders used land grants in Cyprus to grow it.[47] It seems likely that in Sicily, from the fourteenth century on, the Jewish population, which traded with North Africa as well as Genoa and Venice, conveyed Muslim expertise in pasta and sugar to Europe, at least until the Jews were expelled from the island in 1493 by the ruling Spanish.[48] Venice and Bologna were the centers of the sugar-refining industry. The demand for spices motivated navigators to push out into the Atlantic in search of alternatives to the overland route, over which Europeans had no control.

THE GLOBAL EXPANSION OF THE CATHOLIC CUISINE OF THE IBERIAN EMPIRES, 1450–1650

In 1492, the Spaniards defeated the Muslim kingdom of Granada, several centuries after having driven the Moors out of the rest of Spain (though many Moors continued to live in Granada under Spanish rule). Thanks to marriage and inheritance, Charles V and Philip II of Spain, of the Spanish Hapsburg dynasty, became the most powerful rulers in Europe. They controlled Spain, the southern half of Italy and Sicily, Austria, parts of southern Germany, and the rich duchy of Burgundy, which stretched from what is now Belgium south into France and north into the southern Netherlands; its court outshone that of France.

The Spanish and the Portuguese colonized the Canary and Azores islands in the Atlantic (map 5.1.). Subsequently, the Portuguese sailed round the Cape of Good Hope and gained control of the Strait of Hormuz, which gave access to the Persian Gulf. They took Goa on the west coast of India in 1510; Malacca on the Malaysian coast, which was the transit point for cloves and nutmeg from the Spice Islands; Ternate in the Moluccas, the Spice Islands of eastern Indonesia; and Macao on the fringes of the Ming Empire. Mozambique, added at the end of the century, gave the Portuguese control of the East African coast. They also had possession of Brazil, or at least of much of its coastline.

In the early sixteenth century, the Spanish took Cuba, Mexico, and Peru, conquering Tenochtitlan, the Aztec capital, in 1521. In 1571, a Spanish conquistador established Manila as the seat of colonial rule in the Philippines. From 1568 on, what were called the Manila galleons, probably the largest ships ever launched up to that date, annually made the terrifying four-month voyage across the Pacific from Acapulco to Manila, with connections to Panama and Peru, with as many as a thousand passengers on board.[49]

Following the American conquests, Philip II ruled over more territory than the Romans had done. In Europe, it looked as if he might be able to create a united Holy Roman Empire. Even though this dream was thwarted, he inadvertently brought about the transformation of the cuisine of most of the Americas and the addition of Catholic elements to the Buddhist, Hindu, and Islamic cuisines of South, Southeast, and East Asia. In contrast to these imperial conquests, the Renaissance, the European cultural flowering following the recovery of classical knowledge, had relatively little effect on culinary history.

Particularly important for the introduction of Catholic cuisine to America and parts of Asia were the Catholic religious orders. The Council of Trent, a series of meetings between 1545 and 1563 during which the leaders of the Catholic Church formulated their response to reformers such as Martin Luther and John Calvin, concluded that the new overseas possessions of the Spanish and the Portuguese were a place to make up the ground that had been lost to Protestants in Europe. Franciscans, Augustinians, Dominicans, and Jesuits, and their female counterparts from all parts of Catholic Europe, established missions throughout the Spanish and Portuguese empires and beyond their borders. They constructed imposing baroque churches and impressive monasteries from Cordoba in Argentina to Saltillo in northern Mexico, from Goa on the coast of India to Manila in the Philippines. In particular, evidence suggests that the Jesuits and the Franciscan order of the Sisters of Santa Clara (Poor Clares), although their contribution has not yet been studied in detail, were as central to the dissemination of Catholic cuisine as monks had been for Buddhist cuisine or Sufis for Islamic cuisine.

The Jesuit order was established in 1534. Founding members seem to have cared little about food for themselves, though as with the militant orders of the Middle Ages, their dietary rules were less stringent than those of the monastic or mendicant orders. To fund the order, however, with support from the highest levels, they turned to plantation agriculture and food processing. Those who managed plantations were provided with the latest technical and managerial knowledge in the form of *Instrucciones* from a secretariat in Rome.[50] They exported sugar and cacao to Europe from their American plantations. They sold maize and cassava (American crops transplanted to Africa) from their plantations in Angola to slavers to provision their ships. In the southern part of the Americas, where tropical crops did not flourish, they dried the leaves of the local mate plant for brewing into a drink. For a couple of centuries it contended with coffee, tea, and chocolate as a favored hot beverage in Europe. It remains the beverage of choice in Argentina.

Catholic nuns, associated with many of the male Catholic orders, established convents across the Iberian empires. Like the Jesuits, the nuns had to support their orders, and they turned to food processing to do so. Well-to-do women entered convents in significant numbers, some sent by their families, others seeking an alternative to married life. By 1624, sixteen thousand women made up world networks of nuns.[51] Far from cut off from the outside world, nuns in New Spain for example, had their own apartments and their own servants or slaves, often converted Moorish slaves in the early years.[52] Within the walls, these educated, forceful women could rise to considerable power, managing the lands of the convent and seeking ways to increase the power and influence of the order. The Poor Clares, for instance, already well established in Europe, had a convent in Cusco, Peru, by 1549 and a major one in Querétaro, Mexico, by 1605; these were followed by others— in Manila in 1621, in Macao in 1633, and in Guatemala City in 1699. Sisters and

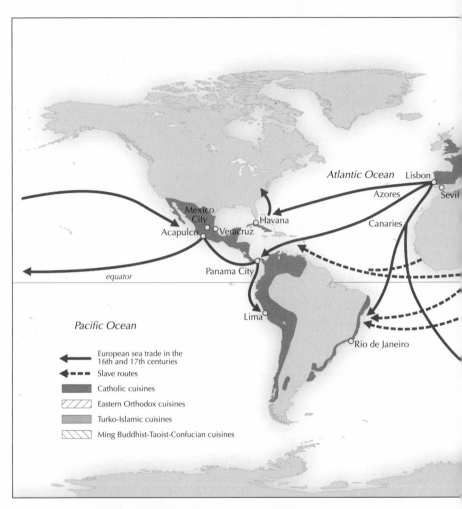

MAP 5.1. The globalization of Catholic cuisine, 1500–1650. Following the discovery of ways to navigate the Atlantic and Pacific oceans, colonists, clergy, and others transplanted Catholic cuisine to newly founded cities, convents, plantations, and haciendas on islands in the Atlantic and Caribbean, in the Americas, and across the Pacific in Guam and Manila. The Portuguese established it in trading posts around the Pacific, particularly Goa, Malacca, and Macao, and left traces in Japan (though not China). West Africans, transported to the Caribbean and the

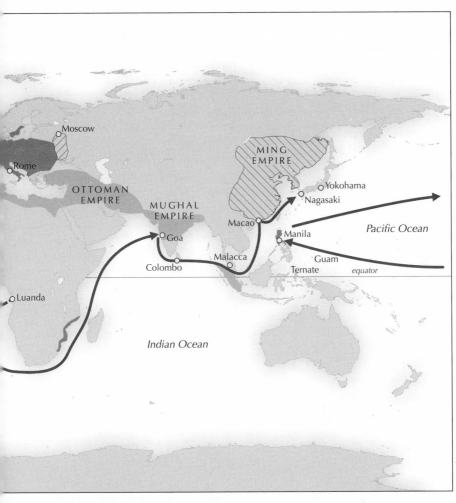

Americas as slaves (dashed arrows), tried to recreate the grain cuisines of the Sahel and the root and banana cuisine of the African coast in the most adverse of circumstances. Although many American plants were transplanted to the Old World, with the exception of the techniques for turning cacao beans into a drink, the cooking and dishes of New World cuisines did not reach the Old World. Source: Bentley and Ziegler, *Traditions and Encounters*, 599, 614, 635.

information, including about the confectionary in which they specialized, moved around this network.

Sephardic Jews also disseminated the techniques that became characteristic of Catholic cuisine.[53] After they were expelled from Spain in 1492 and Portugal in 1500, they found refuge in the Ottoman Empire, relatively tolerant Holland, and the Spanish and Portuguese colonies. They were involved in the booming trade and processing of sugar and cacao, transmitting skills across the Iberian and Ottoman empires. Others acted as gadflies to the prevailing Catholic culinary consensus. Garcia da Orta, for example, who was trained in medicine at the universities of Salamanca and Alcalá de Henares, arrived in Goa in the mid-1530s as the personal physician to the future Portuguese governor, Martim Afonso de Sousa. He engaged in trade, chatted about local customs with Islamic rulers, established a botanic garden, and published a dialogue on the plants of India, mocking the theories of Galen so central to Catholic culinary philosophy.

On arriving in the Americas, Cortés's chronicler Bernal Dias del Castillo, in a letter intended to impress Charles V with the richness of the territory that Cortés had found, enthused about a banquet that Montezuma offered the Spanish.[54] He described the game, including fowl, wattled fowl, pheasants, native partridges, quail, domestic and wild ducks, deer, peccary, reed birds and doves, and hares and rabbits; the variety of fruits; and the drink of royalty, cold, spiced, foamy chocolate. He did not know it, but this cuisine was the successor to that of Teotihuacan, described in chapter 2, to the ruins of which Montezuma made a pilgrimage on foot every year from the city of Tenochtitlan.

In fact, the Spanish and the Portuguese, in moving to these new lands and leaving their place in the culinary cosmos, perceived themselves to be running enormous risks. The sea voyages were bad enough. The ship's victuals were predominantly biscuit (twice-cooked hard bread), salt fish, and meat. Even on the Atlantic crossing, the biscuit could become ridden with weevils and the salt fish and meat turn rancid or rotten. The Pacific was yet more terrifying. Magellan's crew subsisted on breadcrumbs and rats, then only on rats. They felt weak, their flesh swelled with scurvy, their joints ached, their teeth loosened, and their gums turned black. They lanced the gums and rinsed them with urine, but it did little to help.[55]

They arrived in the tropics, thought to be dangerous to Europeans. To survive the "fricasseeing" sun, newcomers had to be "salted" or "seasoned," as beef had to be salted if it were to stay good. In the case of humans, this meant sweating, running fevers, and suffering bloody fluxes and diarrhea, which damped down the digestive fires. Physicians prescribed restorative foods, such as rum (served as punch, mixed with water, fruit juice, and spices), chile or pepper, and sugar. A few physicians had a different diagnosis. The digestive fires were burning out of control and needed to be controlled by taking a cup of cooling chocolate for breakfast and another in the afternoon, with the big meal at night, when the cooler temperatures made it safe to eat.

Because of their fervid growth, the local fruits—oranges, lemons, limes, watermelons, guavas, papayas, and mangoes (whether of American or Old World origin)—along with the meats, it was generally believed, offered "little substance and virtue." According to the English Dominican friar Thomas Gage, who traveled through the Spanish Americas in the early seventeenth century, they left the settlers' stomachs "gaping and crying, Feed, feed."[56] Whatever the theory, the fact of the matter was that the tropics were dangerous. Three centuries later, the British Army, on tallying the deaths of their troops in India, found them to be three times higher than in England, and the same was true in all tropical regions except the Pacific Islands.[57] Not knowing the causes of diseases such as malaria and yellow fever, and believing that individuals were best suited to the places in which they were reared in the culinary cosmos, the migrants blamed the cuisine.

Further, many Europeans suspected that the indigenous peoples of the Americas were less than fully human and were perhaps the natural slaves described by Aristotle. Europeans recoiled from their foods, including unfamiliar grains such as maize; starchy roots (although they did eat the cassava bread); the viscous, mildly alcoholic pulque prepared from the sap of the agave; and cactus paddles, eaten as a vegetable. They were horrified by the careful, ritual meals of human flesh following sacrifice. And they were disgusted by the thought of eating insects, a taboo that went back to Persian and Jewish thought several centuries before Christ. "They eat hedgehogs, weasels, bats, locusts, spiders, worms, caterpillars, bees, and ticks, raw, cooked and fried . . . and what is all the more amazing [even] when they have good bread and wine," the historian Francisco López de Gómara commented in 1552, suspicious of the food, even though he had never been to the Americas.[58]

Diplomatically, in his letter to Charles V, Bernal Díaz passed over the maize flatbreads or dumplings (tortillas and tamales), the pottery serving dishes, and the mats on the floor, which he, his fellow conquistadors, and Charles V would have thought unfitting to high cuisine. In the Americas, including the Caribbean, the Europeans had no intention of eating like the indigenous peoples. They took with them their favored plants and animals, cutlery, china, cooks, and iron cauldrons for stews (fig. 5.6). They built bench stoves to prepare stews and confectionary, domed ovens for baking, stills for preparing essences and alcohol, and mills for grinding wheat. They constructed Islamic-style granaries (*alhondigas*) and added the Islamo-Roman irrigation of southern Spain to existing Indian irrigation works. They also took Francisco Martínez Motiño's *Arte de cocina,* with its five hundred densely packed pages of recipes.[59]

Before looking at Catholic high cuisine in the Americas, I turn to Asia, with which Europeans had always had contact, even if distant, and where the Islamic cuisines in particular seemed somewhat familiar. There the Spanish and Portuguese

FIGURE 5.6. Spaniards unload breeding pairs of pigs, sheep, cattle, and horses under a rainbow (reminiscent of Noah's landfall after the Flood), in the title page to book 12 of the sixteenth-century *Historia general de las cosas de la Nueva España* (General History of the Things of New Spain), also known as the Florentine Codex, assembled by the Franciscan friar Bernardino de Sahagún. From Sahagún, *The Florentine Codex,* digital facsimile edition (Tempe, Ariz.: Bilingual Press, 2008). Reproduced with permission from Arizona State University Hispanic Research Center, Tempe.

were prepared to accept much from the cuisines they encountered. They also enthusiastically contributed to the transfer of techniques for processing and cooking sugar and for preparing drinks such as chocolate and palm wine across the Atlantic and the Pacific.

The Jesuits, whose Asian headquarters were in Goa, were the largest group of Catholics to go to East Asia. Beginning in 1555, a ship sailed annually from Goa to Macao and Nagasaki. Over the next couple of centuries, nine hundred Jesuits worked in China. They appear to have made no attempt to introduce Catholic cuisine, accepting the well-established high Confucian-Taoist-Buddhist cuisine, while relying on their science to make their way into the highest circles of Chinese society. In Japan, with its Buddhist cuisine, although the Jesuits did not stay so long, they left many traces, including deep-frying (*tempura*), cakes and confectionary *(kasutera, confeiti),* and the bread still called by the Iberian name *pan.*

In Goa, the Portuguese encountered both Hindu and Islamic cuisines (and they would have encountered similar mixes with Buddhist cuisines added in other trading posts such as Malacca and Macao). With the encouragement of the crown, they married local Hindu women, provided they had converted. The result was a mixed cuisine. From the Portuguese came the round raised loaves of Catholic cuisine, presumably with wheat shipped in from farther north in India, turned out by bakeries. Pork pickled in wine or vinegar with garlic (*carne de vinha d'alhos*), which cropped up everywhere in the Portuguese diaspora, became vindaloo, a curry offered by all Indian restaurants today. The everyday main meal, however, when the Dutchman Jan Huyghen van Linschoten arrived in Goa in the 1580s, consisted of boiled rice with a soupy sauce poured over it, salt fish, mango pickle, and a fish or meat sauce.[60] Sesame oil substituted for olive oil, pickled green mangoes for green olives. Coconut milk, more plentiful than cow or goat milk had ever been in Portugal, and much cheaper than almond milk, doubtless made fasting easier.

In the Philippines, criollos (people of Spanish descent born in Mexico) found a simple, rice-based local cuisine. They introduced Catholic-style stews, breads, empanadas (pies), escabeche, and hot chocolate drink as well as tamales, though not tortillas, which got no farther than Guam. They traded with China. Junks, crewed by two to four hundred men, left Guangzhou (Canton) on the seven-hundred-mile voyage to Manila laden with wheat flour, salt meat, and trade goods to be exchanged for Mexican silver.[61] Later the Spanish also traded with Japan, receiving wheat flour, salt meat, and fish, and sending fruit, honey, palm wine, grape wine that had been shipped from distant Castile, and large jars for storing tea. The Manila galleons returned to Mexico laden with spices, silks, porcelain, and other luxury goods, and plants such as the mango, tamarind tree, and coconut palm, as well as people from East, Southeast, and South Asia who for one reason or another had traveled to the ship-building entrepot, Manila.

In the course of this global exploration, the Spanish and Portuguese facilitated the exchange of sugar and confectionary and of a wide variety of drinks. Sugarcane processing was made both cheaper and of higher quality by the vertical roller mill (that is, a mill consisting of two or more rollers geared to move in different directions, through which the material to be crushed, in this case sugarcane, is moved), multiple boilers, and claying.[62] Although the origin of the vertical roller mill is not clear, the Catholic missionaries and the Manila galleon played a major role in its diffusion. To make a long and complicated story short, a horizontal roller mill probably went from India to China, where, in the sixteenth century, artisans geared it for vertical milling. The Augustinian Martin de Rada, on a mission to one of China's major sugar manufacturing areas, Fujian, reported on it to both Spain and Mexico.[63] Other missionaries studied sugar-making methods in India and China. The vertical mill was probably introduced to Mexico and Peru in the late sixteenth century (fig. 5.7). At some point, engineers devised more efficient two- and three-roller vertical mills. These cross-Pacific innovations became

FIGURE 5.7. In this composite picture of a Brazilian sugar plantation, small figures work cane fields in the distance. Two different mills are shown, the more distant driven by oxen, the other (left) by water. One of the most experienced workers is shown doing the dangerous work of feeding the cane through the first two rollers; a second, on the other side, draws it out and then feeds it back through. To the right, slaves skim impurities from the cane juice being boiled. Cones of sugar can be seen on the floor and in the background of the boiling house. From *Brasilise Suykerwerken* in Simon de Vries, *Curieuse aenmerckingen der bysonderste Oost en West-Indische verwonderens-waerdige dingen . . .* (Utrecht: J. Ribbius, 1682). Courtesy John Carter Brown Library at Brown University, Providence, Rhode Island.

standard worldwide in the seventeenth, eighteenth, and nineteenth centuries. Such mills were a signal technological invention, whose full potential was realized in the nineteenth century, when they transformed grain processing and were used to gin cotton, roll steel, and make paper.

The expressed cane juice was evaporated by being boiled in pans. *Muscovado* (still available in Latin America as *piloncillo*), a cone of golden brown sugar that needed further refining in Europe before it could be offered for sale, was made by pouring the concentrate into earthenware pots, where the molasses seeped to the bottom and was drained out after a couple of days, leaving a hard cone (loaf) of brown sugar. White and semirefined sugar, which fetched a higher price (and were subject to higher taxes), were produced by a variant of the same process known as claying. The top of each pot was covered with several inches of wet clay. As the moisture seeped through the sugar, it dissolved more of the molasses, leaving soft, whitish sugar. The molasses was either sold as a cheap sweetener or fermented and distilled into a potent alcohol, the best known being rum.

Plantations in the Americas grew larger. Funded by capital from Germany, Genoa, Florence, and London, sugar masters kept careful records of construction, machinery, boiling houses, distilleries, warehouses, and production. They imported slaves from West Africa (see chapter 6), as well as African cattle, which could haul loads and drive machinery in the tropics.[64] They shipped the raw sugar to refineries in Antwerp (then still in Spanish hands) and later Amsterdam, both of which were convenient to the Atlantic trade and the growing markets of northern Europe, unlike the declining refineries of Venice and Bologna. By the second half of the seventeenth century, Brazil dominated sugar production, with ten times the output of the Caribbean, Mexico, Paraguay, and the Pacific coast of South America.

Raw sugar's high value-to-bulk ratio made it worth shipping to Europe, where it fetched higher prices than other American products, such as hides and cheap stringy salt beef at the low end or turtles (for soup), turtle shells, indigo, cocoa, cotton, ginger, limes, pimento, or tobacco at the high end. Never in the history of the world (with the possible exception of spice islands such as the Moluccas) had there been units with more invested in long-distance trade, in terms of both production and consumption, nor had political control operated at such length or from such different societies.

Confectionary, a major use of sugar, was produced by convents around the world to offer to patrons and to sell. Many of the delicacies, such as a paste of ground almonds and sugar (*marzipan*), had roots in Islam. So did the fruit pastes and syrups made from imported quinces (*membrillo*), apples, and peaches or from American guavas, cherimoyas, and mamey sapote; fried, sugared doughs (donuts and *buñuelos*); creams of sugar, starch, and flavoring; and sweet drinks flavored with fruits or nuts (lemonade and horchata).

Other confections, such as those using eggs, were new inventions. Among them were sugar cooked to a soft paste with egg yolks (*ovos moles*) and egg threads (yolks drizzled into syrup to form threads). In Mexico, nuns made sheets and strips of egg yolks and soaked them in syrup or stuffed them with nuts or spices (*huevos moles, huevos reales, hojuelas, huevos hilados*). In Goa, Portuguese nuns imported cane sugar from China, since the sticky brown Indian palm sugar (*gur, jaggery*) did not work well.[65] In Mozambique, *ovos moles* were enriched with papaya. Today in Thailand, duck egg yolks are dropped into syrup to make threads, drops, and flowers. In Afghanistan (recalling that there was a Portuguese ambassador to the court of Timur), the threads of yolk are fried, rolled, and soaked in syrup.[66]

Another novelty in the Americas was a series of milk confections made by boiling down milk to a thick cream (*dulce de leche*), solid fudge, or toffee-flavored cream (*leche quemada*). Since these techniques are also used in Hindu cuisine, it is not out of the question that they were brought by migrants on the Manila galleon. Layered pancakes were popular. From Goa to the Philippines, variations of the layered pancake *bibingka* were enriched with coconut milk.[67] Flaky pastry was becoming popular in Europe and Mexico. Sponge cake (compare Ottoman *revani*, chapter 4), called *pan di Spagna* in Italian and *genoise* (from Genoa) in French, appeared in Japan as *castella* or *kasutera* (cake from Castile).

In Europe, Islamic-inspired confectionary made its way northward as sugar became more affordable. A Portuguese cook was the "chief counsellor" to ladies-in-waiting who wanted to make "delicate dishes" at the court of Queen Elizabeth I of England.[68] Expensive sugarwork, some of it designed to look like savory food, such as marzipan hams, sugar-paste bacon, and eggs of yellow and white jelly, became fashionable, served in special banqueting houses on the grounds of noble houses.[69] Although these confections are largely forgotten in the Anglo world, they remain favorites in Italy and Spain, where the Poor Clares sell such items in a chain of shops, and across Latin America.

The Iberian empires also served as clearinghouses for exotic drinks, foods, and smokes, often psychoactive, which were sought out as sources of revenue. Their variety is amazing. European distilled liquors; pulque (fermented agave juice from New Spain); palm liquor; coca (from the Andes); betel (from Southeast Asia); tobacco (from Mesoamerica); *bangue* (marijuana, from Asia); wine must (unfiltered grape juice); hypocras (hot spiced wine); lemonade (of Islamic origins); beer and cider; *aloxa* (a sweetened, cold medicinal drink); *chica* (maize beer, from the Americas); and *atole* (maize gruel, from Mexico) were all described in detail in the medico-theological treatise *Question moral si el chocolate quebranta el ayuno eclesiastico* (Moral Question of Whether Chocolate Breaks the Ecclesiastical Fast), written by Antonio de León Pinelo, who was born in Cordoba in what is now Argentina and raised as a Jesuit.[70] He could also have included *guamaná*, kola nut (from Africa), and mate (from South America). Two of these drinks are worth closer investigation: chocolate and palm liquor.

The Jesuits were the leading producers and promoters of chocolate, harvesting it in Guatemala and the Amazon jungle with indigenous labor and shipping it to their confreres in Southeast Asia, Spain, and Italy.[71] The market for drinking chocolate was greatly increased by the theological consensus, based on the same arguments that Saint Thomas Aquinas had used earlier for sugar, that chocolate was not a food and thus could be consumed while fasting, even though the Dominicans, always at odds with the Jesuits, dissented. It was thought to be cooling and thus calming for cholerics and lust-reducing for monks and nuns. Nuns sipped it to sustain themselves through night services in chilly churches.

FIGURE 5.8. Europeans struggled to understand the exotic New World chocolate drink, here shown being prepared by natives in feather headdresses. The shallow gourd cup (*jicara*) from which chocolate was sipped is correctly depicted, but the illustrator had clearly never seen how cacao beans were ground on a warm grindstone, and the stick used to whip up foam was a European introduction. In the Americas, foam was created by pouring from one vessel to another. From John Ogilby, *America: Being the Latest, and Most Accurate Description of the New World* (London: printed by the author, 1671), 241. Courtesy New York Public Library, http:// digitalgallery.nypl.org/nypldigital/id?1505018.

The Jesuits brought the Mesoamerican techniques of processing and preparing chocolate to Europe (fig. 5.8). The fermented beans had to be ground on a heated grindstone to prevent the oily chocolate from catching. Simple grindstones had been largely forgotten in Europe, having been replaced by rotary grindstones in Roman times, and if they had ever been heated, this technique had vanished. Thus grinding chocolate was done by specialists, frequently Sephardic Jews who traveled from house to house, dragging their grindstones with them. The drink that Mesoamericans had taken cold, spiced with chiles, and colored with reddish-orange annatto (the seeds of a small tropical tree) was Europeanized. Figure 5.8 notwithstanding, gourds were replaced with new, expensive fashionable ceramic cups, and the drink was heated with sugar and sweet spices on the model of hypocras. As chocolate became a social drink, particularly in Spain and Italy, it followed the same trajectory from sacred to secular earlier taken by tea and being simultaneously taken by coffee.

As a drink, chocolate remained largely in the Catholic world, including the Philippines. The historian Marcy Norton has rightly challenged the idea that Europeans became addicted to chocolate, pointing out that it had to be adopted first.[72] Yet although she is surely correct that the first users drank cold, spiced, and colored chocolate like Mesoamericans, daring to enter a world that meant witchcraft to them, I doubt that either the Jesuits or their customers continued to accept these meanings, just because of the effort that did go into Europeanizing the drink.

Palm liquor, another of the exotic drinks reported by León Pinelo in his *Question moral,* is less well known today. León Pinelo included it, however, because it was so important in Mexico in the sixteenth and seventeenth centuries. Landowners in the balmy Pacific state of Colima in Mexico imported coconut palms, stills, and workers from the Philippines to run them.[73] The workers shimmied up the palms and inserted tubes to catch the sap, which fermented naturally to a sweet, alcoholic drink. Since this went sour quickly, distilling it into palm liquor was a way to preserve it. The stills, very different from Islamic stills, were in essence an inverted bowl cooled by water, with spouts to lead off the distillate, placed over heated palm wine. They were probably of Chinese origin, since such stills were producing liquor on a commercial scale by the time of the Mongols.[74] The liquor was shipped across western and central Mexico, especially to the booming silver-mining towns of Zacatecas and Guanajuato. Production was finally stopped by the Spanish crown, after years of negotiation, at the beginning of the eighteenth century. It is likely, though, that this kind of still was used make mescal and tequila from the cooked, pounded hearts of agaves, a transfer of an Asian technique to a Mexican raw material.

New Spain, roughly corresponding to today's Mexico, is the best-studied example of the transfer of Catholic cuisine to the Americas. Similar patterns of transfer occurred across Spanish and Portuguese America, especially where there were riches to be made from silver mining (in Peru) or from plantations, particularly sugar plantations (in parts of Brazil and the Caribbean). The chief distinctions were to be found between the tropical areas, where the indigenous people depended heavily on root cuisines, and the higher or cooler areas, where maize was the predominant local staple. Adding to the complexity of the interaction between Catholic and local cuisines were the cuisines of two other groups of migrants, one brought as slaves from the west coast of Africa (the single largest group is discussed in chapter 6) and the other arriving on the Manila galleon from across Asia.

Following the discovery of rich deposits of silver in the mid-sixteenth century, the economy of New Spain boomed. In the kitchens of the vice-regal palace, where the cooks were from Europe, and in the convents, haciendas, and townhouses of the fabulously wealthy silver-mine owners, Catholic cuisine was prepared.[75] In spite of the European disdain for the cuisine of Mesoamerica, intermarriage and servants meant that the kitchens of the conquerors and the conquered could not be kept completely separate. In particular, the indigenous grindstone (*metate*) entered the Catholic-criollo kitchen, placed on the floor alongside the bench stoves and ovens of the south European kitchen. With the grindstone, making pureed sauces, meat pastes, and ground nuts and spices became a simple matter compared to the laborious pounding and sieving of the European kitchen. Well-to-do households had six or seven, for different uses—chiles and spices, meat, fish, cheese, nuts, and fruits— and the classic dishes of Catholic cuisine were further elaborated.

The first order of business was bread and wine. After all, Saint Thomas Aquinas had stipulated that only wheaten bread and grape wine could be used in the mass. Even where grapes could not grow, mulberry or pomegranate wine could not be substituted.[76] Although at first there was "neither flour nor wine nor clothing in the land," as a merchant in Veracruz complained, adding, "The earth lacks so much that they should sell stones," within a generation Europeans were growing wheat.[77] By the 1560s, bakers, who often used yeasts from local fermentations, such as pulque from the sap of the maguey, were selling the four main grades of bread: white (manchet), whitish, wholemeal, and coarse (*semitas*). They prepared biscuits (dry, twice-baked breads); fried breads (*buñuelos* and *rosquetes*); empanadas filled with fish; and ten-pound cakes (probably made with yeast dough) filled with meat or blancmange. Wine and oil were imported from Spain, which did not want to lose the revenue from these valuable products to growers in the Americas. Chorizo, longaniza, and blood sausage, which survived in Iberia from Roman times, were made in New Spain and Goa. Dry cured hams seem to have vanished. Lard continued to be the main fat.

Catholic-criollo cuisine continued to show Islamic elements apart from the confectionary already discussed.[78] Couscous from a recipe in Martínez Motiño's *Arte de cocina* was made at least until the nineteenth century, as well as a substitute made by crumbling tamale-like steamed ground maize. A press for making thin noodles was carried to the Augustinian fortress monastery in Yuriria in central Mexico, and the noodles (*fideos*) remain a favorite dish today. Pilau rice (one version being known as Spanish rice in the United States) and noodles became known as dry soups, soups from which all the water had evaporated. *Capirotada* (the successor to *tharid*) gradually lost its meats and became a sweet Lenten dish. Pork was often cooked in its own fat, rather like the fat-preserved meats of the later Islamic empires, though it was consumed immediately. Some indigenous ingredients also crept in. Turkey was substituted for stewed chickens or roasted partridges, and indigenous beans joined chickpeas. Acidic *tomatillos* and tomatoes made green sauces similar to those of Europe.

The formal dishes of high Catholic-criollo cuisine were stews in spicy or nut sauces, pies, fish soured with vinegar (escabeche), and chopped- or minced-meat dishes (gigots). A particularly interesting pair of recipes for braised fowl were called *morisco* and *mestizo* ("mixed race"), respectively, in the *Recetario de Dominga de Guzmán* (Recipe Book of Dominga de Guzmán), compiled around 1750. The first was copied from Martínez Motiño's recipe for *gallina morisco*. The writer specified the spices as oregano, mint, parsley, capers, garlic, cumin, and the typically Islamic cloves, cinnamon, and black pepper. The second, the *mestizo,* drops the spices and substitutes Mexican tomatoes and chiles.

At some point, the spicy brown sauces took on the collective name of mole (pronounced MO-lay), even though some of the older Spanish names, such as *almendrado,* also persisted. Mole had multiple resonances in the Mexican kitchen. In the Aztec Nahuatl spoken by many servants, *molli* meant sauce. In Portuguese, *mollo* (pronounced something like "molio" in English) meant sauce, and Martínez Motiño had many recipes by this name. *Moler* means to grind in Spanish, the crucial technique used in preparing these sauces. "Mole," therefore, was a word that made it easy for a mistress or nun to communicate with the servants who carried out menial tasks. The mole of Puebla, which added cooling chocolate and warming chiles to the standard range of spices, became the signature Catholic-criollo dish.

The Spaniards debated what to do about the cuisine of the indigenous. Speaking to them, Father Bernardino de Sahagún said they should eat "that which the Castilian people eat, because it is good food, that with which they are raised, they are strong and pure and wise. . . . You will become the same way if you eat their food."[79] Others disagreed, perhaps fearful that peoples who still outnumbered the Spanish almost twenty to one, even though the indigenous population had fallen by as much as 90 percent, would become too strong if they ate wheat and European meats.

In fact, the indigenous people preferred the taste of tortillas to wheat bread. Only gradually did Indian nobles emulate Europeans in eating wheaten bread; most of the population continued to make their tamales and tortillas and to cook their beans as they do to this day. Of the finer details, we know very little. It seems reasonable to believe that they rehydrated and then ground dried chiles to make sauces. Once the ban on beef, pork, lamb, and goat for the Aztecs was officially lifted at the end of the sixteenth century, they happily began eating the meat of European animals, adding lard to their tamales, and raising chickens, smaller versions of the native turkey.[80] With the old strict rules about sobriety gone, they consumed more alcohol: pulque produced on big Spanish or criollo-owned haciendas in arid areas near Mexico City; cane alcohol (*chiringuito*), cheap because it was so easy to produce; and palm liquor.[81]

By the mid-seventeenth century, New Spain (and the rest of Hispanic America) had a layered cuisine. Those of Spanish descent, or at least those with sufficient money, dined on Catholic-criollo high cuisine, most of the ingredients coming from animals and plants transferred from Europe and perhaps in some cases, such as long grain rice, from Asia or Africa. The indigenous peoples dined on their traditional Mesoamerican cuisine, most of their foodstuffs coming from local plants as well as animals and plants brought from Europe, Africa, and Asia. Coconut palms came across the Atlantic from the Cape Verde Islands and across the Pacific from the Philippines. Black-eyed peas and rice could have come from Spain, the Philippines, West Africa, or all three.

In 1972, Alfred Crosby described transfers of plants, animals, peoples, culture, and communicable diseases between the Old World and the New World as the Columbian Exchange. Many subsequent scholars have identified this as one of the major events in food history. Here is another point where it is important to tease apart different meanings of food history. The transfers of plants and animals undoubtedly made new raw materials for food available in both the Old and New Worlds. In the Old World tropics, maize and cassava became important new sources of calories. In the temperate zones, beans quickly entered the repertoire. Maize and later potatoes were introduced as food for the humble who could afford nothing else. Chiles were a cheap source of piquancy in the Mediterranean, the Balkans and Hungary, India, Southeast Asia, West Africa, and China. Tomatoes are now firmly established as beloved vegetables in Europe. And the New World had wheat, citrus, cattle, sheep, goats, and pigs, to name only the most obvious introductions.

This exchange of raw materials should not blind us to the fact that they all have to be processed to become food. European and Asian food-processing and cooking technology was transferred wholesale to the New World, whereas essentially no American food-processing technology was moved to the Old World. There are several possible reasons for this, including attitudes to the conquered in the Americas; the fact that, except for the vice-regal entourage, few Europeans returned to their homelands from the Americas and native American cooks did not travel to Europe or Asia; and the perception that the simple grindstone, pottery, and a fire on the floor were better suited to peasants than to cooks in noble houses, who now could count on water mills, iron pots, and bench stoves. The one major exception was grinding cacao for chocolate on the simple grindstone, something difficult to do on a rotary grindstone, because it gummed up, but the simple grindstone never gained popularity for uses other than chocolate.

Without a culinary exchange, the lessons gained from long experience in dealing with maize and chiles in Mesoamerica never made it across the Atlantic. As we have seen, cooking brings about culinary, gastronomic, and nutritional changes in foodstuffs. In the case of maize, treating with an alkali (a process called nixtamalization) produces a fluffy hominy that can be ground wet to create a dough that can be made into soft and flexible flatbreads (culinary change). These have a fragrance that is immediately appealing to most people (gastronomic change). And the process releases nutrients, creating a better outcome for some of those living largely on maize (nutritional change). In the nineteenth and early twentieth centuries, poor Italians and American southerners who did not nixtamalize suffered horribly from the deficiency disease pellagra, while Mexicans who did nixtamalize were left unscathed.[82]

Similarly, much that had been learned about chiles was ignored. In most places (except perhaps North Africa) the dried chiles were not rehydrated and sheared to produce a pureed sauce. As a result the color, texture, and fruity tastes they could contribute to dishes were not appreciated. And because they were not eaten in quantity as sauces, they did not add much vitamin C to the diet.

Other plants were transferred without the accompanying technology. Potatoes were adopted only slowly and reluctantly (chapter 7) and without Andean ways of preserving. Cactus paddles, which grow freely all around the Mediterranean, are rarely used as vegetables. Agaves are not exploited for their sap or their hearts. Tomatillos remain largely unknown. With the exception of the belatedly adopted tomatoes, which became important only in the late nineteenth century, when canning made them available year-round for sauces, the cuisines of the Mediterranean remain based on plants introduced in classical antiquity and by Islam. The transfer of the cuisines of Mesoamerica, the Andes, and the American tropics to the Old World was restricted, lop-sided, long-delayed and to this day radically incomplete. This was, in fact, typical of culinary transfers. In the case of Buddhist cuisines, the transfer was primarily from India to China; and in the case of Islamic cuisines, the transfer was from the Middle East to Europe and thence to the Americas. Islam never adopted, for example, the range of cured meats and fish found in Christendom. From a culinary perspective, then, as opposed to a biological or ecological one, there was no Columbian Exchange; there was yet one more largely one-way culinary transfer.[83]

By the 1530s and 1540s, Catholic cuisine was flourishing both in Europe and in the Americas, as a glance at three events shows. In England, Henry VIII's first act on taking over Hampton Court as his main residence in 1529 was to enlarge the solidly built brick kitchens (fig. 5.9). They occupied 36,000 square feet (as a point of comparison, the total size of the White House is 55,000 square feet), and catered to the establishment of between eight and twelve hundred people. Outside the palace were sculleries for plucking chickens and skinning rabbits, a wood store, and a bakery with multiple ovens that turned out about five hundred pounds of wholemeal bread for commoners and two hundred pounds of white bread for nobles daily.

Such kitchens also produced the royal banquets, which, with coronations and the ceremonial entries of rulers to their cities, were the great events of the sixteenth century, far more elaborate than even royal everyday meals. By our standards they were ruinously expensive, but they satisfied the imperatives of royal magnificence and the benevolent distribution of leftovers. The dishes were served up in a grand ceremony designed to show the ruler's place at the pinnacle of the natural order, sanctioned by God, echoing the mass at every stage.

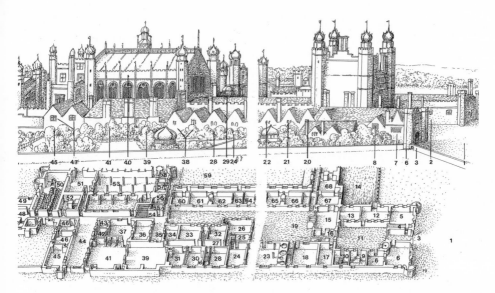

FIGURE 5.9. The well-preserved kitchens at Hampton Court in England give an idea of the scale of institutional court cooking from the earliest empires to the eighteenth century. Foodstuffs arriving at the gate were checked in through security (1–4). Senior kitchen management had a series of offices (5–15). To prevent waste and theft, officers reported daily on the use of supplies. Special rooms were used to store salt beef, raw meat, and fish and to prepare cold sauces (mustard being the most important), confectionary, and pasties, pies, and tarts (17–33). Servants and minor courtiers, nobles, and the royal family had separate kitchen-dining areas, with space for utensils and for cleaning up (33–58). Kitchen areas were equipped with serial open fireplaces and cauldrons for boiling, which, when full, had to be moved by crane, because they weighed as much as a quarter of a ton. The main dining hall could seat 350 people at a time. Original drawing from Peter Brears, *All the King's Cooks: The Tudor Kitchens of King Henry VIII at Hampton Court Palace* (London: Souvenir Press, 1999), 10–11. Courtesy Peter Brears.

Some of the most splendid of those banquets were served in the Holy Roman Empire. Charles V, the Holy Roman Emperor, was born in Ghent in the rich duchy of Burgundy. When he went to Spain, he took with him the Burgundian court ceremonial and, we may assume, his cooks.[84] Every detail of these great official banquets was carefully planned. In *Banchetti, composizioni di vivande e apparecchio generale* (1549), the Italian nobleman Cristoforo di Messisbugo supplied an inventory of the paraphernalia required, over three hundred up-to-the-minute recipes, and examples of fourteen actual feasts for a variety of different celebrations. In 1533, Charles V conferred on him the title of count palatine, one of the highest honors available, for his service as steward to the dukes of Este in Ferrara.

A banquet of the Burgundian style began with a processional entry like that of the prelates entering the church for mass. Just as the Byzantine emperor had reclined in remembrance of the Last Supper, the king's meal echoed the mass. He sat, often alone, at a high table, covered with a tablecloth like the altar in the church, arranged across the narrow end of a long room. Bread and wine were on the table, and the knives were arranged in a cross. The noblemen who served the king kissed the vessels and raised the cup on high, as the vessels for the mass were kissed and the chalice holding wine was raised. Hands were ritually washed as the dishes were uncovered for inspection. The napkin was presented by one of the most powerful courtiers in the land. The highest prelate present blessed the meal, and the cupbearer genuflected every time he served the king wine. Continuing to mimic the Eucharist, the meal concluded with wafers and hypocras. Spicy comfits helped ease digestion.

In New Spain in 1538, seventeen years after the Conquest, Hernán Cortés and the Spanish viceroy mounted a three-day fete in Mexico City's main plaza, right atop the old temples of the Aztecs. On the third day the banquet was served. Collations of marzipan, figures of sugar and starch paste, candied citron, almonds, comfits, and fruits were offered, accompanied by mead, spiced wine, and chocolate. Roasted kids and hams, quail pies, stuffed fowl and pigeons, blancmange, escabeche of chickens, partridges, and quail, empanadas of fish, fowl, and game, and boiled mutton, beef, pork, turnips, cabbages, and chickpeas followed. Live rabbits hopped out of some of the large empanadas; birds fluttered from others. At the very end, olives, cheese, and cardoons were served. Apart from the chocolate, nothing remained of the feast that Montezuma had offered Cortés.

GLOBAL CULINARY GEOGRAPHY AROUND 1650

When Mexico's leading writer and Nobel Prize Laureate Octavio Paz arrived in New Delhi to take up his post as ambassador to India, he asked, is mole "an ingenious Mexican version of curry, or is curry a Hindu [Indian] adaptation of a Mexican sauce"? How could this seeming coincidence in "global gastronomic geography" be explained? The answer, I suggest, lies in an overlapping and interconnected chain of traditional or theocratic cuisines between ten and fifty degrees north that had been created by 1650. At its core were the same regions that had made up the chain of ancient imperial cuisines based on wheat in 200 C.E. Now they extended farther: Buddhist cuisine in Japan; a Confucian-Taoist-Buddhist cuisine in the Chinese Ming Empire; a complex of Buddhist, Hindu, Islamic and Christian cuisines in kingdoms of Southeast Asia; largely Hindu cuisines in the kingdoms of south India; Islamic cuisines in the Mughal, Safavid, and Ottoman empires; and Islamic-influenced Catholic cuisine in Europe and the Spanish and Portuguese overseas empires. Together these areas accounted for about 70 percent of the world's population of well over five hundred million people.[85] Although far more people were now being fed, no major innovations had been made in the provisioning of cities and armies.

For a millennium and a half, traditional cuisines had been created by reworking ancient ones and had evolved in a series of interactions with each other, marked by emulation, repudiation, co-optation, and rejection of their culinary philosophies, cooks, techniques, dishes, ingredients, and raw materials. The Atlantic and Pacific oceans had joined the Silk Roads and the China Sea–Indian Ocean–Mediterranean route as the main passageways for commerce and transfers. Only Australasia and the Pacific Islands remained relatively isolated.

Wheat remained at the top of the grain hierarchy, now joined by rice, while the lesser grains and root vegetables were still relegated to the humble and marginal. At a guess, 10 percent of the world's population ate high cuisines, perhaps in all as many as thirty-five million people, while 80 percent, approximately three hundred million, worked the land and ate humble cuisines. Nomad cuisines, although they still existed, no longer had important effects on the cuisines of the settled. As in earlier periods, it did not follow from the expansion of wheat and rice cuisines that these were becoming more homogenized. As a result of the experimentation with new techniques and dishes, the differences in available ingredients, and the unevenness of transfers, cuisines were becoming more, not less, varied.

The changes in the mechanical, thermal, chemical, and biochemical processing and preparation of food had been incremental rather than revolutionary, as they had been between 200 B.C.E. and 200 C.E. The major innovation in mechanical processing was the vertical roller mill. Chemical processing had seen the mastery of sugar refining and boiling, improved distillation, the manipulation of soybeans and wheat to make tofu and gluten, and the mastery of the preserving of oily ocean fish. Little new seems to have appeared in biochemical processing or in changes of temperature except for the harvesting and preserving of ice and the gradual introduction of iron cooking equipment, though this history remains murky.

Within cooking, most meat dishes and sauces had evolved rather than seen dramatic changes. Gelatins and pies in Christian cuisines were novel. Sauces remained largely purees in Islamic and Christian cuisines, though eggs were creeping in as thickeners in the latter. New grain dishes included pilau in Islam, wafers and perhaps batters for frying in the Christian world, and the earliest signs of something resembling modern cakes. Sugar had overlapping uses as a medicine, a spice in savory dishes, and a spiritual aid (besides being used for sculptures), and its manipulation was one of the most innovative branches of cooking. Confections of sugar and grains, dairy products, or fruits, depending on the cuisine, were highly prized, as were sweetened fruit drinks made primarily for the religious and for women. Tea, coffee, and chocolate, associated with Buddhism, Islam, and Christianity, respectively, had moved from sacred settings to secular ones, providing new occasions to socialize. Though the public eating places of Islam and Christendom were limited and often for the urban poor, restaurants were well established in East Asia.

Today, the links in the chain of traditional cuisines have been obscured by subsequent developments. In Europe, for example, the dishes that were derived from or paralleled Islamic cuisine have largely disappeared. They crop up only occasionally, in, for example, the pounded nuts, garlic, herbs, spices, and toasted bread (*picada*) used to thicken sauces in Catalonia; pureed breadcrumbs cooked in milk (bread sauce), and chopped mint, sugar, and vinegar (mint sauce) in England; and the chopped-herb, oil, and vinegar sauce in Italy.

In the sixteenth century, when Charles V and Cortés were banqueting, there was no reason to think that this chain of traditional cuisines would not persist for centuries. Then around 1650, the early signs of very different cuisines, modern cuisines, began appearing in what had previously been a culinary backwater: northwestern Europe. They were precipitated, I argue in chapter 6, by new ideas about food and the natural world, food and the divine, and food and political economy fostered by chemical physicians, Protestants, and those who were searching for an alternative to divine kingship and the hierarchical principle.

6

Prelude to Modern Cuisines

Northern Europe, 1650–1800

The high cuisine of France, historians of food are agreed, changed dramatically in the mid-seventeenth century. As the first sign of that shift, most of them point to the publication in 1651 of Pierre François La Varenne's *Le cuisinier françois* (The French Cook) and the many translations and takeoffs that followed it.[1] They are equally of one mind that two factors were central to the change: the disappearance of spices and sugar from savory dishes and the appearance of new fat-based sauces, many thickened with flour. I suggest that this was not just a French affair. It was part of the replacement of traditional Catholic cuisines by modern Western cuisines in Europe. Like earlier culinary revolutions, modern Western cuisine was occasioned by a new culinary philosophy that followed from new ideas in chemistry, theology, and political theory in the sixteenth and seventeenth centuries. Chemists and natural philosophers abandoned the culinary cosmos, the four elements, and the theory of correspondences and proposed a new theory of nutrition and digestion. Protestants jettisoned the principle of an ascetic cuisine as a way to spiritual growth, arguing instead that all believers had equal access to the divine regardless of what they ate. Political theorists challenged monarchism with its high cuisines, proposing republican, liberal, and national alternatives.

Replacing one cuisine by another is not easy, so it is no surprise that the French, Dutch, and English all abandoned different aspects of Catholic cuisine. In France, the monarchy and the aristocracy changed cooking and dishes in light of the new theory of nutrition and digestion to create French high cuisine, which displaced Catholic cuisine as the pan-European high cuisine from 1650 on. In the Dutch Republic, the bourgeoisie kept many Catholic dishes but incorporated them into a middling republican cuisine consisting of ample, decent home-cooked food for most of the population. In England, the aristocracy dined on the new French cuisine. The gentry, by contrast, rejected this in favor of a middling bread-and-beef cuisine optimistically described as the national cuisine. All three of these first versions of modern Western cuisine, besides introducing new sauces and a separation of sweet and sour, emphasized bread and beef and experimented with fat, flour, and liquid combinations in sauces and sweet dishes. French high cuisine expanded among elites almost to the end of the twentieth century.

Middling cuisines, however, were the major innovation of the modern period. Middling in the sense of bridging high and low cuisine, not in the sense of being mediocre, rich in fats, sugar, and exotic foodstuffs, featuring sauces and sweets, and eaten with specialized utensils in dedicated dining areas, middling cuisine became available to an increasing proportion of the population in the following centuries. Changes in political and nutritional theory underwrote this closing of the gap between high and humble cuisines. As more nations followed the Dutch and British in locating the source of rulers' legitimacy not in hereditary or divine rights but in some form of consent or expression of the will of the people, it became increasingly difficult to deny to all citizens the right to eat the same kind of food. In the West, the appearance of middling cuisines ran in close parallel with the extension of the vote. Reinforcing this, nutritional theory abandoned the idea that cuisine determined and reflected rank in society in favor of a single cuisine appropriate for every class of people.

The growth of middling cuisines is what nutritionists call the "nutrition transition," the sequential global shift from diets composed largely of grains to diets high in sugar, oils, and meat.[2] Nutritionists worry that although the nutrition transition increases food security, it brings in its wake many associated health problems, including increased incidence of strokes, heart attacks, obesity, and diabetes, and with them increased costs for society. To reduce middling cuisines to a matter of nutrition alone is to miss their importance. Although the problems of the diseases of plenty should not be ignored, they are surely less appalling than the diseases of poverty. And the improved social, political, and economic status of the humble, inextricably linked to the increased choice and tastiness of middling cuisine, is a welcome end to millennia of inequality forcibly expressed by culinary distinctions. Nothing proclaims your equality more than eating the same as other people. Nothing shows your independence more than being able to choose what you eat.

Giving everyone the same cuisine meant bringing down the cost of food. The industrialization of food processing at the end of the nineteenth century, the most important change in cooking and processing since the mastery of grains, reduced prices. Cheaper transport and more efficient farming, both tied up with increased global commercial links as agriculture became specialized by region and grains were moved globally, also contributed. Urbanization made it easier to distribute the components of modern cuisine, so that urban cuisines improved faster than rural ones. Thus the growth of modern cuisines with the spread of modern nation-states, with ever-tighter global links, with industrialization and with urbanization, is an integral part of modernization.

What it means to be modern has been debated since the eighteenth century. The current discussion was shaped in the 1950s and 1960s by sociologists such as S. N. Eisenstadt, who argued that modernity meant nuclear as opposed to extended families, an urbanized world, industrialization, individual political rights, and the decline of a religious mentality. Since the 1980s, although every aspect of modernization theory has been attacked, there has nonetheless been widespread agreement that the contemporary world differs significantly from the world of four hundred years ago. For my purposes, what is important is to analyze the emergence of modern, middling cuisines without assuming that they always emerged in the same way. Thus I am quite happy to accept the broad definition suggested by the historian Chris Bayly that modernization is both a process in which those who aspire to be modern borrow from and emulate those they believe to be modern and a period in which the centralized nation-state, increasing global commercial and intellectual links, industrialization, and urban living go hand in hand.[3]

Until this point in the book, it has been possible, if somewhat simplistic, to structure chapters according to a distinction between high and humble cuisines in the major empires. From now on, with the growth of nation-state empires and the simultaneous spread of modern cuisines and the construction of distinct national variants, the story grows more complex. In this chapter, we look first at the origins of modern Western culinary philosophy; second at French cuisine as the high cuisine of Europe, a successor to Catholic high cuisine; third at Dutch bourgeois cuisine as an alternative to French cuisine; fourth at English gentry cuisine as the root of Anglo cuisines; fifth at different humble cuisines in the Europe and the Americas; and finally at the global culinary geography in 1840.

THE ORIGINS OF MODERN WESTERN
CULINARY PHILOSOPHY

In the 1530s, Luther, Calvin, and others broke with the Catholic Church. In one country after another, rulers resisted the efforts of the Hapsburg emperors Charles V and Philip II of Spain to secure Europe for Catholicism and the Holy Roman Empire. In England, Henry VIII declared himself head of a national church in 1534. In the United Netherlands, the leaders opted for a sober Calvinism and in 1581 declared their independence from Spain, prompting decades of war. In France, Protestants and Catholics fought bitterly until the Calvinist Henri IV converted to Catholicism and ascended the throne, thereafter establishing a degree of toleration. The many small German states that had chosen Protestantism, aided by the united Denmark-Norway and Sweden, fought the Holy Roman Empire and its allies in the devastating Thirty Years' War from 1618 to 1648. Refugees from these conflicts, both Catholic and Protestant, fled to different countries and different continents. In 1648, the treaties collectively known as the Peace of Westphalia were signed. It was in these turbulent years that philosophers, religious and political leaders, and scientists, particularly in France, England, and the Netherlands, propounded the ideas on which the earliest modern culinary philosophy was based.

To begin with food's place in the relations between humans and the divine, Protestant leaders rejected four aspects of Catholic culinary philosophy or practice. First, they gradually changed fasting from a matter of routine to a deliberate act of piety.[4] Luther, for example, argued that "our Lord God regards not what we eat, drink, or how we clothe ourselves; all such matters, being ceremonies or middle things."[5] Fasting dishes dwindled in number and appeared on the table less frequently. Pond fish, for example, ceased to be served as monastery fishponds were abandoned or turned into ornamental lakes by their new lay purchasers.[6] Almondmilk sauces vanished from the menu. Delicate wafers cooked between hot irons were secularized and nibbled or, if made with raised batter, eaten as waffles.[7]

Second, following arguments by scholars such as Thomas Cramer in *Of the Eating and Drinking* (1551) and Nicholas Ridley in *Reasons Why the Lord's Board should be after the Form of a Table*, a communal meal around a table replaced the ceremonial mass celebrated by priests at the altar. The imperial banquet that paralleled the mass had no place in Protestantism. Instead, Protestants preferred family meals preceded by grace, harking back to the early Christian meals described in chapter 5, as an expression of social and religious harmony.

Third, as religious houses were broken up, the charity they had offered the poor vanished, to be only partially replaced by aristocratic and noble largesse and later by state contributions. Fourth, Protestants proposed a new theory of the culinary cosmos to replace that of classical antiquity, which by this date was firmly associated with Catholicism, which I shall turn to when I discuss food, the body, and the environment.

With respect to the role of cuisine in political life, republicanism and liberalism, theories that were to have a long and intertwined history, were proposed as alternatives to monarchism and inherited power. Republicanism, generally believed to be possible only in small states, particularly city-states, depended on rule by a group of officials. Its most important culinary consequences followed from its emphasis in the eighteenth century, as in republican Rome, on replacing aristocratic values of magnificence and display with civic virtues, including frugality and, for women, domesticity. In particular, republicans, like Protestants, believed the family meal, where children imbibed both physical and moral nourishment, not the aristocratic banquet, was the foundation of the state. These beliefs were to be particularly important in the Dutch Republic and in colonial America and the early years of the United States.

Liberalism, a newer doctrine first promulgated by John Locke (and with a chameleon history), asserted that the state derived its legitimacy from some imagined social contract in the past wherein subjects assented to be ruled in return for the establishment of order. Emphasizing the rights of citizens and the importance of property, liberals, like republicans, tended to oppose aristocracy and aristocratic dining, advocating instead a state based on independent yeoman farmers and, at least in some versions, counting on private interests to produce public goods. In the eighteenth and nineteenth centuries, republicanism and liberalism fed into the growing nationalism that began emerging following the Peace of Westphalia and was reinforced by the independence of the European colonies in the Americas. Nationalism, at least in the West, became associated with democracy and with the expectation that all citizens were entitled to the same cuisine. The nation in which individuals lived was gradually to replace their status and rank as the chief determinant of the cuisine they ate.

Finally, radical new beliefs about food and the natural world, including the human body, were proposed after five millennia during which linked theories of a culinary cosmos driven by the fire of the sun, of four or five basic elements and humors, and of correspondences between different aspects of the natural world had prevailed. The first stage was an alternative theory of the culinary cosmos based on fermentation, not heat or fire, and of three principles instead of four elements. The culinary consequences of the theory were new ways of making sauces, a new respect for vegetables as health foods, a rationale for airy foods and drinks, and an end to the long-held belief that cold foods were dangerous. Although the culinary changes persisted, the theories on which they were based had only a brief life. In the eighteenth century, they were replaced by a theory that health depended on balancing acid and alkaline foods, and in the nineteenth, by an entirely new understanding of chemistry and nutrition.

Because the fermentation cosmos and the three principles had such far-reaching effects, we need to look at them in some detail. As already mentioned, they had their origins in Protestantism. In the 1560s, the Swiss Protestant preacher and chemist Paracelsus declared that it was time for chemistry and medicine to be rooted in the Bible.[8] On the one hand, he took aim at the university-trained, Galenic medical establishment, arguing that dietary cures should be replaced with chemical remedies (the ancestors of today's medicines), making him a "master at murdering folk with chemistry," according to Guy Patin, a member of the medical faculty of the University of Paris. On the other hand, Paracelsus promulgated such a promising alternative to the culinary cosmos and humoral theory that it was taken up by many Catholics as well as Protestants, who together formed a group I shall call the chemical physicians. By the late sixteenth century, European rulers were hiring chemical physicians instead of Galenist physicians, perhaps because they were frightened by new diseases such as syphilis, or perhaps because they were intrigued by alternative medicine. Joseph Duchesne, physician to Henri IV of France, jubilantly wrote to his friends in 1604 that chemical physicians had displaced Galenists in the courts of Protestants and Catholics alike, including those of the king of Poland, the duke of Saxony, the elector of Cologne, the margrave of Brandenburg, the duke of Brunswick, the landgrave of Hesse, the duke of Bavaria, and even the Holy Roman Emperor.

The world (and food), according to the chemical physicians, was composed not of the four elements of the classical culinary cosmos—earth, air, fire and water—but of three principles—salt, oil, and mercury. As evidence, they cited the fact that distilling, which alchemists had been busily working on, produced three, not four, products: a solid residue, an oily liquid, and an ethereal product that they variously called an air, spirit, gas, or vapor (it would take another hundred and fifty years to sort out what gases were). They named their three basic principles after substances found in nature. "Salt" was the solid residue that resisted the heat of distillation. "Sulfur," or oil, was the oily liquid. "Mercury" was the vapor, the pure essence of whatever was being distilled. Each had culinary properties. Salt or solids gave foodstuffs body and taste. Oil made them viscous or unctuous. Mercury—air or essence—gave them lightness and aroma.

Air, spirits, or essences were considered food for the brain. Sparkling mineral waters became popular, and spas where they could be sipped opened across Europe. Cakes were raised with beaten eggs, cream was whipped to airy lightness, and mousses became fashionable. Vaporous essences such as brandy, rum, whiskey, and vodka, often tellingly named water of life or firewater (eau de vie and aguardiente), became more popular. Less-powerful extractions, such as essences of nutritive foods like meat, were preferable for everyday use. Cooks had a new rationale for the old practice of simmering meat and fish to extract their essence in the form of stock, bouillon, and gelatin. Meat essences, said the French chemist Louis Lémery in a treatise that remained standard for much of the eighteenth century, were made from "musculous Flesh, which is of all [parts of the animal] the most nourishing, that which produces the best juice."[9] Land animals' juices were more nourishing than those of fish or birds, and beef produced the most nutritive.

Anticipating contemporary chefs' enthusiasm for food science and technology, cooks experimented with sauces based on the new chemical theory, which hypothesized that the oily principle, sulfur, bound together the solid principle, salt, and the vaporous principle, mercury, just as lime bound together water and stone to make a new substance, cement. Butter, lard, or olive oil, rich in the sulfur principle, cooks reasoned, could bind flour and salt, both rich in the salty principle, with wine, vinegar, spirits, or essences of meat or fish, which were rich in the mercury principle. The fat or oil joined and harmonized the jarring flavors of salt and spirituous essences (wine, stock, or vinegar) to produce a single delicious taste and,

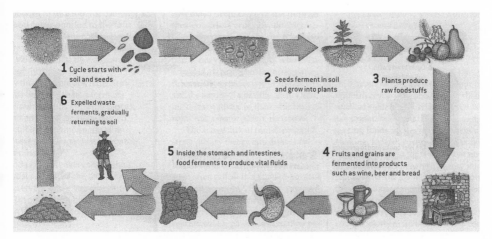

FIGURE 6.1. The cosmic culinary cycle ca. 1650. In the late sixteenth and seventeenth centuries, the theory of the cosmic culinary cycle was reworked with fermentation as the driving force. The theory justified serving raw vegetables, fruits, and cold foods, which had a profound impact on cuisine before it was replaced by newer theories of digestion. Courtesy Patricia Wynne.

more important, a perfectly balanced sauce. "To thicken the sauce," said La Varenne, "take a little diced salt pork, place it in the saucepan, and when it has melted down, take it out, and mix in a little flour that you allow to brown well and dilute it with bouillon and vinegar"—the first known recipe for a roux.[10] No one at the time would have guessed that this change, one that placed fat at the center of the menu, would shape both cuisine and health for the next three hundred and fifty years.

Digesting, said the chemical physicians, was fermenting, not cooking (fig. 6.1). The stomach was a brewer's vat, not a cauldron. Physicians in antiquity and in the Muslim world, notably Avicenna, had already played with the notion that digesting might be a form of fermenting. But what was this mysterious process, fermenting? Paracelsus suggested that "ferment" was spiritual, reinterpreting the links between the divine and bread in terms of his Protestant chemistry. When ferment combined with matter (*massa* in Latin, significantly also the word for bread dough), it multiplied. If this seems abstract, consider what happened in bread making. Bakers used a ferment or leaven (perhaps the foamy crust from fermenting beer or a bit of uncooked dough from the previous day) and kneaded it with flour and water. A few hours later, the risen dough was full of bubbles, or spirit. Ferment, close to the soul itself, turned lifeless stuff into vibrant, living bodies filled with spirit. The supreme example of ferment was Christ, described by the chemical physicians as *fermentum*, "the food of the soul."

At a more mundane level, ferments caused seeds to grow in the ground, fruits to mature, flour to turn into bread, malt to turn into beer, grapes to turn into wine, and foods in the stomach to change into flesh and blood. Babies were formed of ferment-like semen that swelled in women's bodies, and the earthly matter in the alchemist's vessel awaited transformation by the philosopher's stone. Putrefying, a process akin to fermenting and digesting, started the culinary cycle over again. "Vegetable putrefaction resembles very much Animal Digestion," said John Arbuthnot, physician to Queen Anne of England and a member of the Royal Society of London, in a popular handbook on foodstuffs that appeared in 1732.[11] Everything that classical physicians had attributed to cooking, chemical physicians attributed to fermenting.

Fermenting—dough rising, grape juices turning to wine, barley malt brewing— involved gentle heat and produced bubbles of air. This suggested that fermenting was, moreover, related to distilling and the mixing of acids and salts, other reactions that also involved gentle heat and bubbles. Acid, not fire, digested food, the Flemish chemist and physician Jan van Helmont argued (probably meaning one of the recently discovered strong ones, such as sulfuric acid or hydrochloric acid).[12] Leather gloves placed in acid turned into juice. By analogy, food in stomach acids would turn into a white, milky fluid. On passing to the intestine and mixing with alkaline bile, it would form bubbles of air and a salty liquid, the first going to the brain, the second becoming flesh and blood. Foods that did not ferment fast enough passed through the system without turning into flesh, blood, and spirit; foods that fermented too fast caused a fever.

Sugar, the chemical physicians believed, was a salt because it formed a solution in water that could be evaporated to crystals. This meant it would react violently with strong stomach acids, leading to uncontrolled fermentation. It probably caused the mysterious disease afflicting those with sugary urine (diabetes), argued both Joseph Duchesne and Thomas Willis, England's most successful physician and a member of the Royal Society. Sugar was demoted from its position in Catholic humoral or Galenist theory as a panacea for all kinds of sickness and a warming spice to temper savory dishes to an unhealthy and dangerous substance. In the circumstances, it is not surprising that it ceased to be used throughout the meal.

Fresh fruit, raw vegetables and herbs, mushrooms, oysters, and anchovies, in defiance of centuries of tradition, were heralded as health foods because they rotted or fermented so readily, suggesting they were easy to digest. Mushrooms were not poisons; they contained "much Oil and essential Salt."[13] Melons, Jacques Pons told Henri IV of France, his patron and patient, in his *Traité des melons* (1583; Treatise on Melons), did not in fact cause cholera and were not potentially lethal. Salads, "a composition of certain crude and fresh herbs, such as usually are, or may safely be eaten with some acetous juice, oyl, salt, etc.," John Evelyn explained in his *Acetaria: A Discourse on Sallets* (1699), were appetite-stimulating combinations of well-balanced sauce and readily digestible greens.[14]

For a brief period, this new theory of the culinary cosmos based on fermentation (fig 6.1) replaced the ancient culinary cosmos. Then Descartes, Newton, and Laplace proposed physical cosmogonies in which vortices or gravity, not heat or water, were the driving forces. In the infinite universe, there were no correspondences between location, rank, age, gender, humors, and colors delimiting what people should eat. Over the next couple of centuries, the idea that a person's place in the cosmos determined what he or she should eat gradually vanished. Before that, though, the new culinary possibilities opened up by the fermentation cosmos and the three principles were most thoroughly explored in the new French high cuisine.

FRENCH REPLACES CATHOLIC AS THE HIGH EUROPEAN CUISINE

Pierre de La Varenne's *Le Cuisinier françois* (1651) marks the turning point between Catholic high cuisine and the new French high cuisine. Reading the term "French cuisine," it is easy to assume that this was the cuisine of the citizens of France. Nothing could have been further from the case. Nations in the modern sense were only then taking shape. Rank in society remained far more important in determining a person's cuisine than nationality. French cuisine, like French couture or French furniture, was the cuisine of the European upper class, and this would be true until the late nineteenth or early twentieth century. It was far beyond the reach of most of the king's subjects.

In the preface to *Le Cuisinier françois,* La Varenne claims he had spent ten years in the employ of the marquis d'Uxelles and that he had served dishes to the leading members of the court, suggesting that his cookbook reflected changes that were occurring widely in aristocratic kitchens. As might be expected in a pioneering work, La Varenne continued to include plenty of recipes for the mainstays of Catholic cuisine, including roasts, big pies, pureed sauces, pottages, and fasting dishes. Similarly, *Le Pâtissier françois* (1653), possibly also by La Varenne, is full of traditional sweet pies, tarts, wafers, and waffles. Alongside the older recipes are ones for new kinds of dishes judged healthful by the chemical physicians. Among them are basic preparations such as liaisons, thickeners for sauces made with the new roux or egg yolks and almonds; bouillons, extracts of meat and fish to be turned into soups or sauces; herb mixes; and forcemeats (stuffings). There are many recipes for fashionable ragouts, thick flavorful stews used as garnishes, and mushrooms, cauliflower, artichokes, and peas. A recipe for a light, airy sponge cake (*biscuit*) very much like today's ladyfingers appears in the *Pâtissier françois.*

Ragouts, dishes flavored with fresh herbs, and light desserts were the kinds of delicacies served ten years later to Louis XIV during a fateful dinner on 17 August 1661. The king, a member of the Bourbon family, longtime rivals of the Hapsburgs, was then twenty-three and had taken control of the French government after long years as a minor. He and his entourage—his brother, his three favorite ladies, his mother, and, if gossip is to be believed, which it probably shouldn't be, six thousand others—made a three-hour trip from Fontainebleau to Château Le Vaux, the lavish residence of his finance minister and France's greatest patron of the arts, Nicolas Fouquet. In the classical-style building, hung with tapestries depicting Alexander the Great, Fouquet offered a banquet that evoked the magnificence (though not the specific dishes) of Hellenistic cuisine. Musicians played, processions of noble servers brought in the food, carvers slashed their knives through the air, fountains tinkled in the background, and the king sat at his own table. What exactly was served that night is not known, but Fouquet was famed for offering the latest novelties: "Sauces beyond compare, tarts of *fines herbes,* ragoûts in pastry, cakes, biscuits, and pâtés and superb chilled wine."[15] Such dishes could have come straight from La Varenne's *Cuisinier françois.*

It's hard to imagine what Fouquet was thinking. Angered by such a regal display, Louis XIV left early, not staying the night as planned. Three weeks later Fouquet, already suspected of skimming the state budget, was arrested and charged with treason and embezzlement. Louis XIV, meanwhile, had learned the lesson that cultural innovation combined with magnificence created an aura of power. He summoned Fouquet's architect, his landscape gardener, and his interior designer to turn Versailles, then just a hunting lodge, into a palace far grander, larger, and more splendid than Fouquet's château. Monarchs and aristocrats across Europe turned to the courtly life there as a model for the latest in deportment, fashion, and furniture and the new French cuisine.

Spanish aristocrats were not happy about the demotion of Catholic cuisine. In 1700, in the absence of a Hapsburg heir, the throne of Spain was claimed for the Bourbon dynasty in the form of Louis XIV's grandson, Philippe, the duke of Anjou. According to the memoirist Saint-Simon, a banquet was held at Figueras, just across the French border in Spain, on 3 November 1701, to celebrate Philippe's marriage to Maria Louisa, daughter of the duke of Savoy. In honor of a new French Bourbon king for the Spanish part of the Hapsburg Holy Roman Empire, half the items on the menu were part of the new French cuisine and half were part of the old Catholic cuisine. The noble Spanish courtiers, wanting neither a French king nor his cuisine, fumbled every one of the French dishes, allowing them to crash to the floor. The eighteen-year-old Philippe and his thirteen-year-old bride sat expressionless, suffering the humiliation in silence. The nobles had not won, however. On arrival in Madrid, the young king hired French cooks to run his court kitchens, a practice followed by the Bourbons for the rest of the century. In the Spanish colonies in the Americas, the viceroys followed suit, employing French chefs and alternating traditional Catholic and French menus.[16] In Paris in 1707, a formal dinner for the Spanish ambassador was clearly in the new French style (fig. 6.2), which now prevailed across Europe.

FIGURE 6.2. In this depiction of a dinner given for the Spanish ambassador in Paris in 1707, there is nothing of the earlier Catholic banquet, modeled on the mass. Everything is modern, from the light pouring in through large glass windows to the glass chandeliers, mirrors, opulent table settings, seated ladies, and milling courtiers. Engraving by Gérard Scotin from Paul Lacroix (pseud. Paul-Louis Jacob), *XVIIme siècle: Institutions, usages et costumes* (Paris: Firmin-Didot, 1880).

It might seem strange that France, a Catholic country, would embrace, indeed, carry to its highest level, a cuisine that had its origins in a Protestant physiology. Yet, as we have seen, the Protestant theory had already been accepted in most of the Catholic courts of Europe. Moreover, it was quite in line with French cultural policy. Wherever modern culture had surpassed that of antiquity, France embraced that culture, whether originally Protestant or Catholic. The half-century-long debate about whether contemporary art, music, rhetoric, literature, and sciences were better or worse than those of antiquity ended in a consensus that the sciences, at least, had progressed: Descartes's geometry outshone Euclid's, Newton's mechanics and astronomy surpassed those of Archimedes and Ptolemy. Progress in reason was paralleled by progress in taste; progress in chemistry was paralleled by progress in the taste of the cuisine based on that chemistry, that is, in French high cuisine.

Foodstuffs were processed and cooked to extract their essence, in a process likened to that of alchemists refining coarse hunks of mineral to yield shining pure silver. Using the language of the kitchen and the laboratory, Baron Melchior von Grimm complained in his correspondence of the kind of literary works that manipulated and condensed their subjects. "It looks as if we were out to quintessentialize everything, to put everything through a sieve; we *must* get at the quiddity, the rock-bottom of things."[17] François Marin, the presumed author of *Les Dons de Comus* (1739; The Gifts of Comus, in Greek mythology the god of festivities), explained that modern cookery was "a kind of chemistry." He continued, "The cook's science consists today of analyzing, digesting, and extracting the quintessence of foods, drawing out the light and nourishing juices, mingling and blending them together, so that nothing dominates and everything is perceived. . . . And making them homogeneous, so that from their different flavors result only a fine and piquant taste, and if I dare say it, a harmony of all the tastes joined together." Refined cookery was for refined, civilized people, leaders in taste, in morals, and in techniques. The French gave the long-standing association of high cuisine with civilization a new twist, using the word *civilité* to describe polite, polished, or indeed refined behavior.

Following the death of Louis XIV in 1715, the center of French cuisine shifted from Versailles to Paris. The aristocracy offered suppers in their fine stone houses (called *hôtels*), perhaps intimate suppers for a single couple, perhaps formal affairs for fifty or more, or perhaps open tables for guests. Hosts such as the sixth prince of Conti, Louis François I de Bourbon, planned menus, gave orders to the cooks, and oversaw the buffet-style service. For those who could not afford to hire a cook, restaurants that sold *restaurants*—"restoring broths"—began opening in France in the 1760s and 1770s.[18]

The cuisine French aristocrats offered, recognizably the ancestor of today's French cuisine, was constantly updated, as the old-fashioned pottages and pies included in La Varenne were phased out. Cookbooks continued to appear through the eighteenth century, addressed to the court and the aristocracy. Among the most important were François Massialot's *Le Cuisinier roïal et bourgeois* (1671; The Royal and Bourgeois Cook), which ran to many editions; Vincent La Chapelle's *The Modern Cook* (1733), published in English when the author was working for the duke of Newcastle, with a large proportion of the recipes taken straight from Massialot (the French translation, *Le Cuisinier moderne,* was published at the Hague in 1742, in five volumes, with folding plates several feet long); Menon's *Les Soupers de la cour* (1755; Court Suppers); Joseph Gilliers's *Le Cannameliste français* (1751; The French Sweet Maker); the later edition of Marin's *Les Dons de Comus,* now with recipes; and the anonymous *Traité historique et practique de la cuisine* (Historical and Practical Treatise on Cuisine), a work in two volumes published in 1758.

The favored ingredients were beef, chicken, butter, cream, sugar, fresh herbs, vegetables, particularly asparagus and peas, and fruits such as pears, peaches, and cherries. The flavors came not from spices but from meaty bouillons. *The Modern Cook* gives two dozen recipes for bouillon, mainly made of beef, veal, and chicken. A thin bouillon was the perfect restorative dish, suitable for civilized men of exquisite sensibility who could not possibly stomach the rough food of the peasantry.

Ragouts and fricassees, essentially interchangeable names, were meaty sauces served over meat or vegetables. Often they were based on a coulis, an extraordinarily rich, expensive, and time-consuming broth thickened with pureed meat. For four quarts, a couple of slices of ham might be browned with two pounds of veal, carrots, onions, parsley, and celery, then covered with stock, bouillon, or broth, simmered until done, and then thickened with a roux made with half a pound of butter and three or four large spoonfuls of flour. "White sauces," often called cream sauces or béchamel (though not in the contemporary sense), were also based on meat juices, which in this case were thickened with egg yolks, cream, and sometimes flour rolled in butter (*beurre manié*).[19] Mousses made of pounded meat, egg whites, butter, and cream slipped down the throat without the necessity of vulgar chewing. Cool wine was sipped from glasses, a matched set becoming a required sign of sophistication by the 1770s. For the final course, light, creamy desserts replaced the dense confections of the Catholic kitchen. Cold dishes, no longer believed to be dangerous, were popular, including ices, sorbets, iced custards, and ice creams. So were puff pastries filled with fruits and conserves and exotic fruits such as hothouse pineapples. Quick to pick up trends from across Europe, the French aristocracy experimented with the English habit of taking tea in the afternoon (fig. 6.3).

In no time, French cuisine, with its multiple ways of combining fat, flour, sugar, and liquids to make new kinds of sauces and sweets, its use of meat essences for flavoring, and its employment of whipped egg whites and cream to create light,

LE THÉ A L'ANGLAISE

FIGURE 6.3. In Michel Barthélemy Ollivier's painting *Le thé à l'anglaise dans le salon des quatre glaces au Temple, avec toute la cour du prince de Conti, écoutant le jeune Mozart* (1766), the prince of Conti, fifth from the left, in the corner, hosts an English tea party. The habit of drinking tea *à l'anglaise* was reportedly brought to Paris in 1755 by Madame de Vierville (seated in the middle of the group of three women below the long panel). The company nibbles on cakes while listening to the latest fashion in chamber music, performed by the young Mozart on the harpsichord. From Paul Lacroix (pseud. Paul-Louis Jacob), *XVIIme siècle: Institutions, usages et costumes* (Paris: Firmin-Didot, 1880).

airy textures, became the European high cuisine.[20] Catherine the Great insisted that the Russian court adopt it in preference to the previous hybrid Slav-Byzantine-Mongol-Dutch style of cooking, along with the French language, French fashion, and French balls, dinners, and salons.[21] Kitchens were equipped with bench stoves, metal saucepans, and griddles. Gardens and greenhouses were established to see whether salad greens (which many Russians, still of the traditional opinion that raw greens were food for animals, not humans, dismissed as little better than grass), asparagus, grapes, citrus, or pineapples would grow in the Russian climate. Elector Friedrich August I and Frederick the Great, rulers of Saxony and Prussia, the two richest German states, employed French cooks.[22]

Diplomats drawn from the aristocracy offered dinners in the French style, which helped spread French cuisine across Europe. Long important in international relations, diplomacy was formalized into an increasingly rigid system following the Peace of Westphalia. Permanent diplomatic residents at other courts had already been expected to display an "exaggerated magnificence" to echo and project the magnificence of their monarch, offering largesse and banquets at great expense. Now each state had a corps composed of aristocrats selected for their easy habit of command, impressive bearing, correct clothing, sophisticated manners, and mastery of French, the language of diplomacy. The worldly Cardinal de Bernis, ambassador in Rome, employed a hundred people, including French cooks.[23] By 1796, the word "diplomacy," of French origin, had been introduced into English by the political thinker Edmund Burke.

Other aristocrats snapped up French paintings and furniture, hired French valets and cooks for themselves and French dancing masters for their children, and installed them in palaces built or remodeled on the pattern of Versailles, such as Blenheim Palace in England. Gustaf Soop, one of the king of Sweden's state councilors, hired Romble Salé, a French cook, and it was he who translated *Le Cuisinier françois* into Swedish.[24] The Russian aristocracy built French-style dining rooms and held French-style open tables. Ivan Betskoi, a magnate with a palace on the Neva down from the Summer Garden, expected as many as fifty guests to show up daily for dinner. Count Brühl, the favorite and prime minister of the elector of Saxony, outdid his master, importing pastries from Paris and chocolates from Rome and Vienna, and decorating the table with sugar, caramel, and marzipan figures created by his confectioner, La Chapelle. He offered dinners for hundreds of guests seated at tables where eight-foot fountains sprinkled rose water.[25] The Whigs, the party in power in England at the end of the seventeenth century, competed to hire what we would today call celebrity chefs. Robert Walpole, prime minister from 1721 to 1742, hired Solomon Sollis; Lord Chesterfield, an associate of Montesquieu and author of *Letters to My Son,* an introduction to behavior in polite society, employed Vincent La Chapelle; and Pierre Clouet, who had formerly worked for Marshal Richelieu, cooked for the duke of Newcastle, another prime minister.

French cuisine did not come cheap. The cost of meaty reductions and fine wines offset any savings from the elimination of expensive imported spices. The salaries of well-known cooks, many of them now independent of the guilds, were sky-high. The duke of Newcastle, reputedly one of only five people in Europe to own a solid-gold dinner service, paid his French celebrity cook £105 a year, when most French cooks in England received £40 and an English woman cook only £4. The dining equipment could cost a small fortune. Silver cutlery, including the new forks, and crystal glasses had to be purchased for each guest. For serving coffee, one noble Swedish family spent about a thousand Swedish silver thalers (about U.S.$10,000 today) on a silver pot, Chinese porcelain cups (perhaps specially ordered from China), a painted and lacquered round table, a handheld steel grinder, a silver tray, and linen cloths.[26] Catherine the Great paid Josiah Wedgwood £2,700 (perhaps U.S.$250,000 today) for a set of enamel-painted creamware. It comprised 680 pieces for the main course, 264 pieces for dessert, and tureens, fruit baskets, and eight ice cream "glaciers" to serve as centerpieces, with domed lids crowned by female figures in antique dress and two handles on the sides. Each and every piece of this Frog Service, named for the repeated frog motif, was hand-painted with a different British landscape.[27] Even this extravagance paled into insignificance next to Count Brühl's Meissen Swan Service, which cost about three million in present-day dollars. Wine reportedly cost Thomas Jefferson, who had a taste for French cuisine, $3,000 a year, at a time when Merriwether Lewis, one of the leaders of the Lewis and Clark expedition, earned a very respectable $500 a year.[28]

French high cuisine was accessible to only a tiny minority, mainly aristocrats who lived off the income from their large estates—about 2 percent of the French population at the time of the Revolution, or about 400,000 individuals—and the upper bourgeoisie. The proportion of the population that could afford French cuisine was similar in Russia, lower in Germany, and a little higher in Poland and Hungary.[29] True, in all these countries, there was a small bourgeoisie that could enjoy a simplified version of French cuisine. In France, for example, Menon addressed this group in *La Cuisinière bourgeoise* (1746; The Urban Female Cook). Most French people, though, had no more tasted French high cuisine than they had earlier tasted high Catholic cuisine. Their worry was getting their daily bread.

Indeed, both in France and elsewhere, many people from diverse backgrounds and political points of view were of one mind that French cuisine, far from being the pinnacle of culinary progress that its advocates asserted, was instead the very symbol of the alliance between hereditary absolute monarchy and Catholicism, a visible sign of the luxury and corruption of aristocrats. It was attacked by physicians and cooks, mocked in the press and political tracts, lampooned by cartoonists, and derided in conversations in salons and coffeehouses. Today, when fine dining is greatly admired and luxury is associated with success, not corruption, this can seem simple philistinism or petty resentment of the upper class. To discount the critiques this way, though, is to miss the point that criticizing French cuisine was a way to dramatize deeply held reservations about aristocratic privilege and hierarchical, monarchical societies.

The French *philosophes,* men of learning including Diderot, Voltaire, and Rousseau, members of what was known as the republic of letters, turned to the Roman Republic, a strong state supposedly built on frugality and simplicity, as an alternative, reviving the classical argument that luxurious high cuisine was the first step on the slippery slope away from virtue and toward misery and war.[30] Since wealth was then believed to be a country's reserve of precious metals, a fixed quantity, spending on one thing meant scarcity in other areas. Spending on tea from China, when the Chinese bought nothing in return, bled the nation dry. Chevalier Louis de Jaucourt, author of the culinary articles in the manifesto of the *philosophes,* Diderot's multivolume *Encyclopédie,* reminded his readers that first the Athenians and then later the Romans in the imperial period had damaged their states and further impoverished their citizens by adopting luxurious cuisines. When the *philosophes* congregated, it was not to eat luxurious intimate suppers, but to share conversations in salons.

Ragouts, believed by critics to stimulate unnatural, out-of-control appetites, exemplified French cuisine. French ragouts and bouillons brought on a "national sickness" or "homelessness," complained Russians, a state that could be cured by cabbage soup. They joked that béchamel-induced gout would kill off the Russian ruling class long before a revolution became necessary. In a treatise written toward the end of the eighteenth century, *On the Corruption of Morals in Russia,* the conservative Prince Mikhail Shcherbatov lamented that Russian dining had become "a pleasure in its own right, casting aside its moral and religious significance."[31] The authors of the French *Encyclopédie* argued that the "combining and seasoning" characteristic of high cuisines encouraged "excessive eating" and was "dangerous to the health."[32] The abbé Pluquet calculated in 1786 that the foods reduced to essences for ten gourmets could have been used to feed three hundred hungry people.[33] Those who partook of indulgences that "all men might not enjoy," getting drunk on claret and consuming "whole joints . . . stewed down into essences," appalled the English poet and political thinker Samuel Taylor Coleridge.[34]

English cookbook author Eliza Smith repeated a Protestant commonplace when she turned to biblical history to attack luxury and ragouts. In the Garden of Eden, she said, "apples, nuts, and herbs, were both meat and sauce, and mankind stood in no need of additional sauces, ragoos, &c. to procure a good appetite." It was only after the Fall that humans began using seasonings and salt to preserve meat from "stinking and corruption" and to create appetite. Thus "luxury entered the world." Food and medicine drew apart, health now depending not on diet but on the ministrations of physicians, necessary because professional cooks and confectioners designed elaborate (and unhealthful) dishes to stimulate "depraved palates."[35]

The *philosophe* Jean-Jacques Rousseau argued in his treatise on education, *Émile,* published in 1762, that what was natural was as little altered as possible, not an essence achieved by lengthy processing and cooking.[36] Simply boiled vegetables, fresh fruit, and milk (a novel idea, since fresh milk was rightly thought to be dangerous) were natural. Children and country folk who enjoyed them did not need strong flavors to stimulate the appetite, nor sauces and desserts, nor butter, meat, and wine. Better to eat like a child outdoors in a garden, under a tree, or in a boat than like the rich with their "stoves and hot-houses," their "poor fruit and poor vegetables . . . for a very high price," and the "tedious flunkeys" who attended them, counting "every mouthful with greedy eyes." Rousseau's romantic vision of nature providing food that needed a minimum of further cooking became a major theme in succeeding centuries.

The critiques were made especially pointed by the deteriorating diets of the humble.[37] Every few decades, with monotonous regularity, people suffered real hunger when the harvests were bad. France had food crises in 1630, 1649–51, 1661, 1693, 1709–10, and the decade of the 1770s. Only the children of the rich grew up without experiencing or at least hearing about an empty table. This uncertainty, rather than average calorie intake, which optimists estimate at a generous four thousand calories a day, while others suggest two thousand, of which only about three hundred calories came from meat, butter, cheese, or milk, was what kept the poor so on edge about food.[38]

In 1789, bread was again in short supply, giving people a reason to rally in protest.[39] Angry crowds seized grain wagons, precipitating the French Revolution. Ordinary people interpreted the events in terms of the bread on which they depended. When the king and his family were brought back from Versailles, the women of Paris mocked them as "the baker, the baker's wife, and the baker's boy," who had their own interests at heart, not the fate of those hungry for bread. "Bread or death" was the chant of the crowds that broke into the Revolutionary Convention. In widely circulated cartoons, Louis XVI was depicted gorging, oblivious of his hungry people at the moment of his formal arrest on 13 August 1792. He was imprisoned in the Temple, where just sixteen years earlier the prince of Conti had been painted enjoying his English tea. From there, on 2 January 1793, Louis XVI was taken to the guillotine.

France was declared a republic.[40] Frugal republican fare was served at fraternal meals, where rich and poor assembled in public places to eat the same food at the same table.[41] A small chapbook appeared, very different from earlier lavish cookbooks, called *La Cuisinière républicaine* (1795; The Republican Woman Cook), consisting of simple and inexpensive recipes for potatoes. Had the republic continued, the high cuisine of the aristocracy would have disappeared. As it happened, the political scene soured, thousands were executed in the Reign of Terror, and by 1799 Napoleon was in power, declaring an empire in 1804. As French armies marched across Europe, taking Spain, Italy, and the German states, then moving farther east, riches poured into Paris.

In a sign of the times, Joseph Berchoux, in 1800, in a poem titled "La Gastronomie," repudiated republicanism and its plain food. The cuisine of the ancient Persian Empire was a triumph of civilized dining, a model for the French. The new rich went to the restaurants that opened across Paris, now serving high cuisine rather than restorative broths. The old rich continued to dine in private. One such was Charles Maurice de Talleyrand-Périgord, a master diplomat and expert in the culinary politics that accompanied diplomacy, who had first introduced Napoleon to French political society in a series of dinners. He hired an ambitious young cook, Marie-Antoine Carême, lending him out to Napoleon for events such as his marriage, the birth of his son, and victory celebrations. When Talleyrand lost confidence in Napoleon, he conspicuously dumped him at another dinner.[42]

Following the defeat of Napoleon, the European nations met at the Congress of Vienna in 1815 to redraw national boundaries and establish the European system of diplomacy based on internationally recognized rules and administered by a class of career (but still aristocratic) diplomats. Talleyrand represented France, taking Carême with him to prepare the dinners at which Talleyrand restored France's place among the other nations. Carême, who had done so well in Napoleon's empire, concluded that gastronomy "marches like a sovereign at the head of civilization . . . it vegetates during revolutionary times." His colleagues, such as the cook Antoine Beauvilliers, were equally ready to link French high cuisine and empire. The French were honored, he said in 1813, "to have their taste and cuisine reign, in the same imperial manner as their language and their fashion[,] [over] the opulent states of Europe from the North to the South."[43]

DUTCH BOURGEOIS CUISINE: A REPUBLICAN ALTERNATIVE TO FRENCH HIGH CUISINE

The Dutch Republic was founded in 1581 after three generations of struggle against the control of the Spanish Hapsburgs. Once the Spanish were gone, the Calvinists, referring to themselves as the chosen people, the Children of Israel, disbanded monasteries, convents, and almshouses, sending the wealthier Catholics fleeing, while welcoming French Huguenots and Spanish and Portuguese Jews escaping the Inquisition. The seven provinces of the republic became Europe's wealthiest and most urbanized area in the seventeenth century, the Dutch Golden Age. Almost a quarter of the two million Dutch lived in prosperous small towns and cities of between 10,000 and 200,000 people, in a sharp contrast with other European countries, where one or two large cities dominated a rural hinterland. Although the Dutch worried that the stadtholder (head of state) might have monarchical leanings, cities were governed by leaders of commerce and industry, not landed aristocrats.

The cosmopolitan and relatively tolerant Dutch cities were leaders in art and learning, home to humanists such as Erasmus, philosophers such as Descartes and Spinoza, and scientists such as Huygens. In Leiden, site of Europe's most famous medical school, physicians such as Sylvius and Boerhaave advanced the theories of physiology and nutrition pioneered by Paracelsus and van Helmont. The Dutch had the largest fleet of merchant ships in the world. They controlled the Baltic route, imported goods from the Levant, took over the spice trade from the Portuguese in the late sixteenth century, and were major participants in the new trade across the Atlantic. They founded the first modern stock market. The fact that as a republic they ranked lower than even the smallest principalities and duchies in the aristocratic diplomatic world was of little concern to them.

The Dutch created a middling bourgeois cuisine, ample but not luxurious, celebrating the family rather than the courtly meal or intimate supper, and a food-processing industry to support the cuisine. Bourgeois or gentry cuisines were to be found in other European countries as well. They are often described as middle class. In the sense that they were less lavish, often deliberately so, than old aristocratic high cuisines, they mark a step in the direction of the middling cuisines that most people in the rich world now eat. It is, however, an error to assume that the bourgeoisie were the kind of urban, salaried people we think of today as middle class. That group was not to appear until the nineteenth century. The bourgeoisie in the cities was likely to be made up of moneyed merchants, while the country gentry were those who had an income from land; both had substantial houses and employed a number of servants. Although the bourgeoisie and the gentry distinguished themselves from, and had different values from, the aristocracy, they certainly did not see themselves as representative of the vast majority of the population, being as careful to distinguish themselves from the humble (laborers, small artisans, small shopkeepers, or the indigent) as the aristocrats were.

In the Dutch Republic, citizens were exhorted to avoid luxury, which would precipitate the decline of the republic. On civic occasions, the fraternities (professional guilds) celebrated at hearty, unpretentious open-air feasts supposedly modeled on those of their imagined ancestors, the Batavians, toasting one another with pseudo-Teutonic drinking horns. These feasts implied a culinary cosmogony rooted in the locality, not in the imperial Alexandrine dining evoked at Fouquet's dinner for Louis XIV.[44]

Taking Calvin's word that God had created food not for necessity alone but also for "enjoyment and merriment," the prosperous urban burghers and rural gentry created an ample but moderate cuisine.[45] Gentry who quoted Cato's advice in *De Agricultura* on how to run their estates would have been familiar with his recipes for simple republican dishes. The bourgeois housewife, perhaps the wife of a merchant, brewer, or large farmer, oversaw a substantial household and did the cooking herself or supervised a couple of servant girls. For guidance she turned to housekeeping manuals (fig. 6.4) such as *De Verstandige Kock* (The Sensible Cook), which appeared in 1668, less than two decades after La Varenne's *Le Cuisinier français* (1651).[46] Others followed in the eighteenth century: the *Perfect Dutch Cook* (1746), the *Perfect Utrecht Cook* (1754), and the *Perfect Guelders Cook* (1756).[47] For the first time, the woman housewife was celebrated as a cook.

Dishes adapted from Catholic cuisine included delicately spiced stews (the pottage became *hutespot*), meatballs (*albóndigas* became *frikkadellen*), and sweet and savory pies and tarts of all sorts. The cook continued to thicken sauces with bread or eggs. She abandoned Catholic wine and lard for vinegar or verjuice and butter. Waffles and donuts were for special occasions and, like many deep-fried foods, were street rather than home food. The main family meal consisted of a vegetable

FIGURE 6.4. The well-equipped kitchen of a well-to-do Dutch housewife included the traditional northern European open hearth with spits, a beehive oven for baking, and a bench stove that needed little fire and allowed the preparation of delicate stews and sauces. This title page of *De Verstandige Kock, of Sorghvuldighe Huyshoudster* (The Sensible Cook, or Careful Housekeeper; Amsterdam: M. Doornick, Boeckverkooper, 1668) assures its readers that they will learn "how to cook, stew, roast, fry, bake, and prepare all sorts of dishes in the best and most able manner, with the appropriate sauces, very useful and profitable in all households." Courtesy New York Public Library, http:// digitalgallery.nypl.org/nypldigital/id?1111632.

or raw salad, a main dish, and a pie or tart. Secondary meals depended on commercially processed food, beer, bread, butter, herring, and cheese.

Dutch engravings of the period depict the family sitting around a cloth-covered table set with individual plates. It is a scene so familiar to us that it takes a moment to remember that, although representations of humble kitchens and meals were common in the Middle Ages, say, the bourgeois family meal has appeared only once (if at all) before in our story, in the early days of the Christian church. The contemporary belief that the family meal is a place where children learn to become members of a moral society owes much to the Dutch. The father at the head of the table said grace and read from the Bible while his wife, children, and other members of the household listened and a neatly dressed servant girl brought in platters laden with food. The meal was an occasion for both physical nourishment and education (*opvoeding*), a word with the same root as the verb "nourish" (*voeden*). Here children absorbed republican and Calvinist values and the manners advocated in Desiderius Erasmus's *De civilitete morum puerilium* (1530; On Civility in Children).

At its best, domestic cooking, as its advocates never failed to point out, created a welcoming home and a family table where all could share and where the values of the family, the state, and (often) religion could be inculcated in children. At its worst, the cooking was inept or hurried, the home a source of tension, and the family table something that children dreaded. In either case, expectations rose. Instead of eating a common pottage that varied according to what was in season, different dishes, often complex ones such as tarts, were expected on different days of the week. Two or three different courses were served at the main meal, requiring ceaseless gardening, preserving of fruits and vegetables, menu planning to avoid waste, and cooking and cleaning up for the housewife and her servants.

The other Dutch contribution to culinary history was the commercial processing of fish and dairy products to make easy meals affordable by most in society. At the beginning of the fifteenth century, the Dutch had figured out (or picked up from their Baltic neighbors) a new way of brining herring by pulling out the gills and part of the gullet and guts but leaving the tender and flavorful liver and pancreas.[48] By the seventeenth century, one in five people worked in the herring industry. Each May, two thousand herring-busses (*haringbuizen*), each with a crew of fifteen, sailed out of ports such as Rotterdam and Amsterdam for the two-month season when fat herring started breeding. The crew eviscerated the shining fish, one every twelve seconds, packed them in barrels, with one part salt for every twenty parts fish, and transferred them to ships waiting to take them back to harbor. Each ship carried four to five hundred wooden barrels, and every year the Dutch Grand Fishery inspected and branded over thirty thousand tons of herring. They were traded, along with Rhine wine and salt, around the Baltic and up rivers such as the Vistula (Poland), the Rhine (Germany), the Seine (France), and the Meuse and the Schelde (France and the Low Countries).

Herring bones, said the Dutch, were the foundation of Amsterdam. Herring lurks behind the paintings of Rembrandt, Vermeer, Franz Hals, and others who recorded the sailing ships, the gray skies with their scudding clouds, and the substantial, prosperous town houses. Herrings were depicted in still lifes, neatly arranged on small dishes in the form of a cross, drawing on the centuries-old association of fish with Christ and the Resurrection.[49] Pickled herring—affordable, ready to eat, and rich in protein, vitamin D, calcium, and mineral salts—enriched the diet of northeastern Europeans.

Herring was more important by far than the flashier imports of silk, spice, sugar, and coffee; it "determine[d] the destiny of empires," according to the French biologist Bernard Germain de Lacépède, whose phrase was quoted time and again.[50] In the case of the Dutch Republic and its empire, Lacépède was on to something. By processing highly perishable herring into a commodity that kept for a considerable period, the Dutch were able to lay the foundation of their commercial empire. In 1656, five years after La Varenne published Le cuisinier françois and within a decade of the Peace of Westphalia, the Dutch physician Jacob Westerbaen wrote a poem in praise of pickled herring: "A shiny pickled herring, corpulent, thick, and long, its head chopped off, its belly and back sliced neatly, its scales scraped, its guts removed, eat raw or fried, and don't forget the onion. And before the Sun sets in the evening, devour with relish."[51] If the French signature dish was the ragout, the Dutch equivalent was pickled herring and bread.

The Dutch also made butter, whole milk cheeses such as Gouda and Edam, and skimmed-milk cheese such as Leiden, aromatic with cumin, cloves, coriander, or caraway. "Our Holland overflows with butter, cheese and milk and . . . these blessings we receive from the hand of the Almighty," the Dutch exalted, well aware of echoes of the biblical promised land overflowing with milk and honey. They brushed aside both the objections of the stricter Calvinists that the new habit of having both butter and cheese on bread—dairy food on dairy food—was "the Devil's work" and English sneers that Dutch ships and the Dutch themselves were "butter boxes."[52] Wrapped in protective red wax, cheese was a product that, like herring, could be traded across Europe, and even farther afield to the colonies in South and North America. Herring and cheese were "the great levelers," enabling the whole nation to eat fast, tasty, nutritious, and relatively inexpensive preserved food.

Amsterdam became the center of the lucrative sugar trade, as Portuguese Jews fleeing the Inquisition brought with them know-how about sugar refining. There were three refineries in 1605, a number that had jumped to sixty by 1655. Coffee and tea were also principal imports, transported from Asia. By the eighteenth century, tea from China was the most valuable commodity in the return cargoes of Dutch East Indiamen, reaching three and a half million pounds a year by 1785.[53] The Dutch East India Company, it is rumored, underwrote the publication of Dr. Cornelis Bontekoe's Tractaat van het excellenste kruyd Thee (1678; Treatise on the Excellent Herb Tea), which promoted tea as a cure-all.

The Dutch walked a tightrope between the decent sufficiency appropriate to a republic and the luxurious cuisine that their wealth would have enabled many of them to enjoy. Dutch pastors followed John Calvin, who had worried that all too easily civilized humans would turn into pigs at a trough. Intemperance was a constant danger. People became "insatiable," so that even great abundance would not "extinguish the fire of a depraved appetite." The clergy attacked the two standard targets, sauces and sweets. Sauces disguised food as the equally dubious wigs and cosmetics disguised women. Sugar led to overeating. One minister, Belcampius, feared that citizens might become so shameless as to "found an Academy to which they would send all cooks and pastry bakers to teach them how to excel in the preparation of sauces, spices, cakes and confections, so that they should taste delicious."[54] On the other side, savants such as Abbé Jean-Baptiste Dubos argued that dry and warming sugar and spices were necessary in the northern climate. They corrected the beer soup, fish, and rain, which induced lethargy and phlegm and filled "the blood of a man of the North with animal spirits formed in Spain and in the most burning of climates."[55]

The evidence strongly suggests that the Dutch did in fact enjoy a "decent sufficiency." Unlike in other parts of Europe, with a tiny minority who dined lavishly and a vast majority whose food supply was insecure, if not invariably inadequate, even the poor who had to resort to the food handed out in the Leiden poorhouse had bread and milk or buttermilk for breakfast and supper, and a midday main meal that included vegetable soup and meat twice a week and on other days offered various porridges, grains, vegetables, and milk.

Dutch cuisine was copied by other nations and spread by colonists, merchants, and religious refugees. Young girls from southern Norway were sent across the sea to the Netherlands to learn housewifery and manners, returning to create the cookery recorded by Karen Bang in the first national cookbook, *The Complete Norwegian Cookbook* (1835).[56] Before Catherine the Great commanded that her court adopt French cuisine, Dutch cuisine had begun reshaping the cuisine of Russia. On his European tour in 1697–98, Tsar Peter the Great refused further invitations to the suppers given by the French regent, Philippe d'Orléans, "because he found the behavior too free."[57] On his return to Russia, he commissioned a translation of Erasmus's *De civilitete morum puerilium* (1530), renamed in Russian *The Honorable Mirror for Youth* (1717).[58] He ordered his nobles to follow the new manners he had observed among the upper classes on his tour, such as using individual bowls or plates instead of dipping into the communal bowl, drinking from shot glasses or goblets rather than drinking horns, and using napkins, not the edge of the tablecloth, to wipe their mouths. They were told to wear European clothes, shave their beards, and mingle with women. Dutch open-faced sandwiches with cheese (some of it imported from Holland), herring, smoked and salted fish, and, meat began meals. Sauces, fried dishes, waffles, and butter churned from fresh cream appeared on the menu. Russians were introduced to coffee, chocolate, and, most significantly, tea. It has been suggested that the invention of the Russian samovar was inspired by a Dutch wine cooler.[59]

Two chartered companies, the East India Company in Asia and the West India Company in the Americas, controlled Dutch long-distance trade, its early imperial ventures, and the spread of Dutch cuisine to Africa, Asia, and the Americas. By 1600, the East India Company had dislodged the Portuguese from Ceylon and the Moluccas and established a base in Indonesia. It had seized control of the Indian

Ocean spice trade and was importing sugar from Java and tea and porcelain from China. The last was copied as Delft, creating another product to export. To reprovision ships on the long haul round the Cape of Good Hope, the company sent Commander Jan van Riebeeck to establish a midway station in South Africa in 1652.[60] Within six months, he was offering visiting ships' officers a meal of chicken, peas, spinach, asparagus, and lettuce; within four years, fresh cheese and butter; and within seven years, breads and pies. The farthermost eastern reach of the Dutch extended to Dejima, or Deshima, a small artificial island in Nagasaki Bay, where they were allowed a tiny settlement. There a few Japanese learned something of Western medicine, including nutritional theory, and of Western cuisine, although even in the nineteenth century, these were still curiosities to most Japanese, as the woodcut by Yoshikazu Utagawa in figure 6.5 shows.

The West India Company had plantations in Guyana and the Caribbean. In North America, it had settlements in Manhattan and the Hudson River Valley (the New Netherlands), the latter intended to supply the plantations with wheat. In the Netherlands, bakers made bread, but when the Dutch moved to places with more fuel and fewer cities, this task fell to the housewife. Dutch elements entered American cuisine out of all proportion to the size of the colony, including a standard of decent plenty rather than luxury, the family meal, and foods such as waffles, donuts, cookies, and coleslaw.[61]

Some religious groups, for all the relative tolerance, still found the Netherlands repressive and fled. Mennonite refugees moved first to northern Germany, then, in the later eighteenth century at the invitation of Catherine the Great, to the newly opened territories of South Russia, and, at the beginning of the twentieth century, to Canada, Paraguay, Mexico, and the United States.[62] They took with them the custom of buttering their bread and eating it with jam, cheese, or sausage; their expertise in making white and rye bread, pancakes, and waffles; and the know-how to build windmills to grind grain.

The Netherlands retained a substantial colonial empire, particularly in Indonesia, until World War II. Traces of Dutch cuisine map its commercial and political reach. Pickled herring and open-faced snacks remain favorites around the Baltic. On 3 October every year, the people of Leiden eat bread and herring, "the food of liberty," to celebrate the end of the Spanish siege in 1574. Buttered bread and open-faced sandwiches have spread far beyond Holland. Dutch cheeses are traded worldwide, and Dutch-style cheeses are made in many different places. Waffles, pancakes, and cookies, although belonging to broader European traditions, are enjoyed in their Dutch versions. Because the Dutch traded Bengali and Javanese sugar from Persia to Japan, and because they ruled Indonesia (the Dutch East Indies) until after World War II, traces of Dutch food are found across much of Asia.[63] In Sri Lanka and in Indonesia, it is still possible to find Dutch (and originally Islamic) meatballs (called *krokete, croquettes* in the latter). The *rijsttafel,* or

FIGURE 6.5. This Japanese woodcut from 1861, after Japan had been "opened" to Western commerce, shows a Dutch kitchen with a man tightening the screws on a cheese press, a woman with a baby, and a second man watching something frying on a bench stove. Print by Yoshikazu Utagawa. Courtesy Chadbourne Collection of Japanese Prints, Library of Congress (LC-USZC4-10581).

rice table, that Dutch settlers created in nineteenth-century Indonesia is now served in Holland and is a tourist attraction in Indonesia.[64]

We are indebted to the Dutch for fine eating chocolate, thanks to the invention of defatting and alkalizing processes for cocoa. We also owe to them the commercialization of margarine, following the sale of the inventor's patent to the Dutch company Jurgens, which became part of Margarine Unie. In the 1930s, Margarine Unie amalgamated with the British soap-making firm Lever Brothers to form Unilever, now one of the world's largest food companies.

ENGLISH GENTRY CUISINE
AS THE NATIONAL CUISINE

The second half of the seventeenth century saw tumultuous changes in English politics and religion: the beheading of a king, a civil war, a republic, the restoration of the monarchy, the accession to the English throne of the Protestant Dutch stadtholder William III of Orange, and the Act of Union that united England and Scotland. Colonial and imperial expansion was under way, and the British had trading companies in India, settlements in Ireland, plantations in the Caribbean, colonies in North America, and, by the end of the eighteenth century, a toehold in Australasia and the Pacific.

The high cuisine of England, particularly of the leaders of the Whig Party, which ruled for much of the eighteenth century, was French high cuisine. At the same time, national sentiment was on the increase as the British fought the Dutch and the French throughout the century and around the globe. Important parts of the population began identifying with their nation rather than their region or others of their rank.[65]

National English cuisine had its roots in the cuisine of the rural gentry or squirearchy, who formed the backbone of the Country Party, a group of Tories and disaffected Whigs who distrusted the power of London with its court, bankers, and merchants. It included country lawyers, doctors, and parsons as well as smaller landlords whose income from rent or from farming was sufficient to give them local, though not national, political power and a substantial house, but not a second house in London. It was, in short, the society in Jane Austen's novels. When they saw Whig grandees buying Bordeaux wine, paying French cooks extravagant salaries, and dining on French sauces that required twenty-two partridges, such as one Clouet was rumored to have prepared for the duke of Newcastle at a time when England was at war with France, they concluded that the behavior verged on treason. At the very least, it caused ill health and fattened the pockets of doctors (fig. 6.6). An outpouring of cookbooks, cartoons, and essays contrasted the purported French combination of extravagant meals for the rich and thin soups for the poor with the English gentry cuisine of roast beef, bread, and pudding supposedly for all.[66]

England's leading physician, Dr. Cheyne, put the weight of his medical authority behind the distrust of French cuisine. Luxury (a code word for unwonted extravagance, including in cuisine) was the cause of the "English malady," or the vapors. Trying to cure them by sipping on French-style beefy restoratives would

FIGURE 6.6. A physician greets a stereotypically skinny French cook (the French were usually depicted as scrawny in English cartoons, since they supposedly lived on thin soups and wine, rather than beef and beer). Against a background of steaming pots on a bench stove, thought to be a French affectation compared to the English open hearth, the cook greets the doctor with the words "I make de frigcasse, de ragoo, and de Kickshaw!!!" The doctor tells him: "Your skill in kickshaws [a garbling of *quelques choses,* or "somethings," meaning small dishes] and the ingenious art of poisoning enables us medical men to ride in our carriages, without your assistance we should all go on foot." Charles Williams, *The Physician's Friend,* ca. 1815. Courtesy Wellcome Library, London (V0010928).

simply "rouze a sickly Appetite to receive the unnatural Load, [and] render a good one incapable of knowing when it has had enough," he said, drawing a discussion of the relation between appetite and luxury initiated in antiquity.[67] Instead, the British should turn to the products turned out in country houses: beef when they were healthy, chicken and milk when they ailed.

The medium-sized country house kitchen was run by a housewife, who oversaw the garden, supervised the dairy maids as they made milk and butter, preserved her own produce, and brewed ale or cider. She did her cooking over an open hearth, where spits in front of the fire produced superlative roasts. For more delicate dishes, she turned to a small brazier. A growing flood of cookbooks addressed these housewives, such as Eliza Smith's *The Compleat Housewife, or,*

Accomplished Gentlewoman's Companion (1727), Hannah Glasse's *The Art of Cookery Made Plain and Easy* (1747), and Elizabeth Raffald's *The Experienced English Housekeeper* (1769).[68] These authors were aware that although their readers might sniff about French cuisine, they wanted to set a modern, cosmopolitan table. Thus French recipes taken directly or indirectly from French authors such as La Chapelle and Massialot, usually without acknowledgment, appeared in these cookbooks. Simultaneously, the authors emphasized the kinds of dishes that an English female cook could produce without the staff and budget of the households that hired French male cooks. "So much is the blind folly of this age," said Hannah Glasse, "that [English gentlemen] would rather be impos'd upon by a French booby, than give encouragement to a good English cook!"[69]

Roast beef, not the game or the richly sauced dishes of the aristocrats, nor the rabbit and pig of the cottager, was the centerpiece of English cuisine. Parson James Woodforde, a meticulous chronicler of English cuisine, recorded everything he ate between 1758 and 1802 in his diary. The last entry before his death on Sunday, 17 October 1802, concluded with the words "Rost Beef."[70] Beefsteak theater clubs were established in major cities. Henry Fielding's song "The Roast Beef of Old England" became a favorite and remained so well into the twentieth century.

> Then, Britons, from all nice dainties refrain,
> Which effeminate Italy, France, and Spain;
> And mighty roast beef shall command on the main
> Oh the roast beef of England
> And Old England's roast beef!

The English prided themselves that even the poor could indulge in roast beef when an ox roast was offered, unlike the poor in France, who, they believed, subsisted on thin soups. In this community meal, a whole ox donated by a landlord was slowly roasted over a fire and then ceremoniously carved and served to a couple thousand people, along with bread and plum puddings donated by bakers.

White wheaten bread was taken for granted. Joining it was "pudding," usually based on flour and steamed. Sometimes it was baked, like the egg-and-flour batter enriched with the drippings from the roast known since the 1730s as Yorkshire pudding. Pudding straddled the sweet-savory boundary and could be plain or filled with a little meat or dried fruits (Christmas plum pudding being the most famous of these). It was the British equivalent of the homemade white-flour dishes—dumplings and noodles in Germany and central and eastern Europe, gnocchi and egg pasta in Italy—that supplemented white bread for the well-to-do, and was contrasted with French soups, which were derided as insubstantial. The older pottage became the hotpot.

For sauces, the English preferred gravy, meat juices, and an emulsion of melted butter known as butter sauce to the extravagant coulisses and ragouts of French high cuisine. Store sauces (sauces that kept a long time on the shelf and gave a rich flavor without the expense of the meaty reductions of high French cuisine) were eagerly adopted. Most derived from Asian sauces. Recipes for ketchup, an Anglicization of *ketap*, the fish sauce brought back by the India trade, appeared in cookbooks by the early nineteenth century. Thin, vinegary, and spicy brown liquids made from mushrooms, walnuts, or anchovies, they were more akin to their present-day successors—Worcestershire sauce, Harvey's sauce, and A1 Steak Sauce—than to modern tomato ketchup.[71] Indian-style fruit pickles and chutneys were known as "mangoed fruit." "Curry" (a word that may come from *karhi*, the Tamil term for sauce) described any stew-like dish made with Indian methods and flavored with spices associated with India, such as pepper, chile, turmeric, fenugreek, cumin, and coriander; these slipped naturally into the place of the older spiced dishes of Catholic cuisine.[72] Hannah Glasse's recipe "To make a Currey the India Way" used expensive chicken and butter and whole pounded spices.[73] Cakes were raised with yeast or eggs. Like the sauces, cakes incorporated fat and sugar into the menu, allowing greater variety and culinary inventiveness. Sugar was also turned into a growing range of candies. The more affordable port, not claret from Bordeaux, was the drink of gentry cuisine.

Coffeehouses proliferated in cities, many of them offering food as well as coffee, and a variety of services, from insurance to betting. Tea, still expensive, became the nonalcoholic drink of choice for women. A teashop for ladies was opened in 1717 by Andrew Twining (of Twining's Tea fame). Tea gardens, landscaped grounds where men and women could mingle, drink tea, and take refreshments, became the rage in England.[74] All these venues offered new places to meet others and discuss the affairs of the day.

"Groceries," stores selling sugar, spices, tea, and coffee, proliferated. Quaker families, such as Cadbury, Rowntree, and Fry, began offering cocoa powder, a step in the long transition of chocolate from a cold, spicy, sacred Mesoamerican drink to a confection.[75] Such tropical goods, which in mid-sixteenth-century England amounted to only 10 percent of the country's imports, made up a third in 1800, when the total volume of imports had grown much larger.[76] Between 1650 and 1800, British sugar consumption jumped 2,500 percent. The import taxes on coffee, tea, and sugar fattened the coffers of the government.[77] The revenue from the annual British duty on sugar in any year in the 1760s was enough to maintain all the ships in the Navy, while the customs duty on coffee alone in 1774 was enough to build five ships of the line. Taxes on tea rose to a tenth of overall British tax income. Smugglers flourished. In 1784, duties were lowered, smuggling ceased, the government insisted that the East India Company sell tea at reasonable prices, and tea consumption continued to rise.

Like French and Dutch cuisine, English cuisine expanded to the colonies. In trading posts in India, merchants hired both English and Indian cooks to prepare gentry and Mughal cuisine, respectively. In the Pacific, penal and free colonies were established in Australia from 1788 on, bringing it back into the world of culinary interchange. In 1778, Captain Cook reached Hawaii, where the cuisine, brought hundreds of years earlier by the first Polynesian settlers, was based largely on pounded taro (poi), seaweed, and small fish. British naval officer Captain George Vancouver, who had explored the Hawaiian Islands with Cook and returned again later, dropped off two cows, a bull, and some sheep so that they could multiply and provision future visiting ships. The Pacific ceased to be a Spanish lake, and the Manila galleon, for two hundred years the sole link between the Asian and American shores of the Pacific, sailed for the last time in 1815. From then on, the British, French, and Americans settled the Pacific Islands, introducing modern Western cuisine alongside the long-standing taro and breadfruit cuisines of the first inhabitants.

The eastern seaboard of the Americas from the Caribbean to Canada was the most important outpost of English cuisine. Because the colonists came from all social ranks, belonged to a variety of Christian denominations, and settled in climates ranging from tropical to frigid, the history of their cuisines is complex. The better off, mainly planters in the South and merchants in the middle colonies and north, dined on English gentry cuisine, seeing the English Country Party's repudiation of the luxurious cuisine of the court in London as a model for their repudiation of French cuisine. A republican strain, perhaps also drawing on the Dutch colonies, would permeate American culinary history throughout the nineteenth century. Those who, like Thomas Jefferson, could afford French cuisine were in a tiny minority. Most of the more prosperous settlers used English cookbooks such as those by Eliza Smith and Hannah Glasse.[78] In the middle colonies, which grew enough wheat to become the breadbasket of the West Indies, people had wheat breads. The typical English slightly sweetened yeast cake was also made, often as a "great cake" weighing as much as fifty pounds and served for public occasions, one version becoming known as election cake. Using their English cookbooks, housewives prepared ketchup and chutney. Instead of Indian mangoes they used sweet peppers, still called mangoes in parts of the South.[79] The drink of well-to-do Americans was rum or rum punch.

Like their criollo counterparts in Spanish America, the English in North America did not like to hear the culinary resources of the Americas criticized, even if they themselves dined on imported European cuisines. When, in the mid-eighteenth century, a series of European scholars, including Guillaume-Thomas Raynal, Cornelis de Pauw, and France's leading naturalist, Georges-Louis Leclerc, comte de Buffon, argued that the natural products of the Old World were superior to those of the New, they were stung.[80] Thomas Jefferson, in his *Notes on the State of Virginia* (1781), and the Jesuit Francisco de Clavijero, in his *Historia antigua de México* (1780; Ancient History of Mexico), retorted with praise for the riches of the New World.

Provoked by British legislation that threatened tax increases and less autonomy, such as the Molasses Act (1733), Sugar Act (1760), Revenue Act (1762), and Tea Act (1773), the thirteen colonies declared their independence from Great Britain in 1776. Four years later, in a letter, Thomas Jefferson envisaged that the young country would become an empire of liberty stretching across the continent and a bulwark against the British Empire. Twenty years later, in 1796, Amelia Simmons published the first American cookbook, *American Cookery.*[81] It was a manifesto advocating a cuisine that included American ingredients and an ample, decent diet. The book's long subtitle promised to teach the reader how to deal with meat, fish, poultry, and vegetables, how to make all kinds of pies, puddings, and preserves, and "all kinds of CAKES, from the imperial plumb *[sic]* to plain cake adapted to this country and all grades of life." She made a point of juxtaposing puddings and cakes made with expensive wheat flour and sugar with ones made with maize—an everyday American grain that Europeans considered food for cattle—and a common inexpensive sweetener, molasses. At a time when the bread question preoccupied Europe, when Marie Antoinette was being credited (falsely) with the unthinking "let them eat cake," when it was not clear whether further famines were to come (and they were, in the Hungry Forties), self-described orphan Amelia offered cake to all grades of life.

THE HUMBLE CUISINES OF THE EUROPEAN EMPIRES

Humble cuisines remained the lot of the majority in the French, Dutch, and British empires. With the growth of empires overseas and of population in Europe, the nature and quality of humble cuisines were becoming more diverse. I begin with three cases linked to the growth of empire—enslaved Africans, ordinary free people in the Thirteen Colonies, and seamen in the British Navy—and then turn to the rural poor in Europe.

Enslaved Africans were the single largest group of immigrants to the Americas—three out of four prior to the 1820s. Sugar plantations required about one worker for every acre.[82] To staff them and other agricultural enterprises, as many as twelve million Africans were forcibly moved to the New World between the sixteenth and early nineteenth centuries, most to the lowland tropics, about half to Brazil, and a high proportion of the rest to the Caribbean.[83] In Africa, the enslaved would have depended on one of two overlapping major cuisines, descended from the cuisine families described in chapter 1. In the Sahel, the savannah region in a belt from the Senegal River to the tropical forests, the typical cuisine was based on steamed grains or fermented grain porridges, including rice, millet and sorghum, beans, vegetables, and a little meat. In the tropical forests that stretched to the Gulf of Guinea, the cuisine was based on mashed cooked yams, bananas, beans, vegetables, and a little meat. Contemporary drawings of a flourishing market at Cabo Corso on the coast of what is now Ghana (fig. 6.7) suggest a standard of living similar to that in rural Europe.

FIGURE 6.7. A market in Africa, showing the house of the market governor (A), the granary (B), stalls for bananas and other fruit (C), a palm wine store (D), poultry and fish markets (E and F), women selling firewood, rice, sorghum, millet, and fresh water (G, H, and I), sugarcane (K), foreign cloth (L), prepared food (M), a fetish table (N), visiting Dutchmen (O), guard (P), roads to the coast and inland, and women bringing products for sale (Q, R, S). From Pieter de Marees, *Beschryvinhe ende historische verhael van het Gout Koninckrijck van Gunea . . .* [Description and Historical Account of the Gold Kingdom of Guinea . . .] (1602, reprinted, The Hague: M. Nijhoff, 1912), 62.

In the British, French, Dutch, and Spanish empires in the Americas, Africans, like other migrants forced or voluntary, tried to replicate their cuisines. Maroon communities of escaped slaves perhaps came closest. On the plantations, the slaves had to depend on rations handed out by slave owners and on what they could grow in their gardens. Many of the available plants were unfamiliar. To import and naturalize plants familiar to them in Africa was more or less impossible. Insofar as these plants arrived in the Americas, they were probably salvaged from leftover ship's provisions. The slaves worked long days in the field, leaving little energy for the laborious, time-consuming processing methods needed to prepare, for example, American cassava. Yams and bananas, high yielding and less laborious to process, crept into the slave gardens. Africans from the rice belt made their traditional pestles and mortars for pounding rice and other grains, their winnowing baskets, and perhaps even their cooking pots. They prepared couscous. Those from the tropical belt made a pounded root dish (now known as fufu in Nigeria). This might be eaten with sauces of palm oil, dried fish, sesame, and hibiscus or the native American amaranth leaves. Stews of meat or fish with okra (called callaloo, or gumbo) accompanied rice. On the Brazilian plantations, Africans had rice, beans, manioc meal, and dried beef (*carne sêca* or *charque*), and were given the last even on fast days, to fuel them for the hard labor.[84]

African cuisines (like indigenous cuisines or humble European cuisines) had little appeal for the slave owners, given the prevailing belief in culinary determinism. The African women who cooked in the kitchens of the great houses on the plantations were taught to prepare Catholic or Western cuisine, depending on the owner and the location. Even so, certain dishes did cross the boundary through the kitchens of plantation houses or through purchases of street food. The dishes of rice cuisines, because they were based on grains, probably crossed over more frequently than the pastes of the root cuisines. The many rice-and-bean dishes in the Americas are almost certainly of African origin. Pilau-style rice steamed in an aromatic liquid in Mexico and South Carolina may have had an origin in the ancestor of today's jollof rice of Nigeria or in Mediterranean rice dishes, or both. Tamales in former plantation regions, such as Puerto Rican *pasteles*, have Afro-Caribbean elements. Infusions of hibiscus flowers probably had a West African origin, while those of tamarind pulp might have reflected the same, Mediterranean, or Asian origins. Black-eyed pea fritters (called *akara* balls in Igbo-speaking parts of Nigeria) became street food in Brazil and elsewhere. In the Bahia of Brazil, in Columbia, and in Panama, African women mastered Catholic egg yolk and sugar confectionary, selling it in the market.[85] In South Carolina, they created the sesame seed benne wafers that became a favorite in the region.

By the late eighteenth century, campaigners in Latin America and Europe were arguing against the slave trade and slavery itself. In 1787, an alliance of Quakers, Unitarians, and other groups established the Society for the Abolition of the Slave Trade. Those in favor of abolition bought sugar from East India (Indonesia), and displayed it in sugar bowls stamped with a calculation of how many souls could be saved in this way.[86] In 1833, legislation was passed that began the end of slavery in British and other colonies. The heritage of slavery, however, continued to cloud the African contribution to the cuisines of the Americas.

The ordinary free people, including the five million Anglo settlers, in the Thirteen Colonies were mainly small farmers who owned their own property. In their homeland, they would not have eaten gentry cuisine. They would have had a much simpler cuisine, based on flatbreads or porridges of the lesser grains. In America, they did well.[87] Fuel for cooking, waterpower for grinding, and meat, all in short supply in Europe, were abundant in the New World. "All Europe is not able to afford so great Fires as New England," wrote one settler triumphantly, perhaps remembering that in England, villagers went to prison to defend their right to gather wood from the only remaining woodlands, the forests where the lord hunted.[88] The many rivers and creeks of the eastern United States were ideal for water mills, so that in most areas grinding or pounding was not a domestic chore.

Most could afford meat, frequently boiled salt beef or pork.[89] They prepared maize as they had prepared oats or barley in the British Isles. Oat porridge was replaced with cornmeal mush or grits, the daily staple across much of the Thirteen Colonies. Oat or barley cakes were superseded by hoe cakes (maize flatbreads). The settlers did adopt some Native American techniques, notably the use of lye (or ashes in water) to remove maize hulls to make hominy. Hard cider was the common drink, the barley and wheat for beer not doing well in many parts of the colonies. In short, although from the European perspective having to eat maize was a step down the culinary hierarchy, the relative abundance and availability to all of food, particularly meat, was a sharp contrast to Europe. In his *Letters from an American Farmer* (1781), Hector St. John de Crèvecoeur compared the situation of rural families in the American colonies to those in Europe. "Wives and children, who before in vain demanded from him a morsel of bread, now, fat and frolicsome, gladly help their fathers to clear those fields whence exuberant crops are to arise to feed ... them ... without any part being claimed, either by a despotic prince, a rich abbot, or a mighty lord."[90] Although in his boosterism he probably overstated his case, his description held an essential kernel of truth.

Back in Europe, seamen in the British Navy enjoyed an ample and wholesome diet by the late eighteenth century, the result of a more than century-long effort by the Victualling Board to improve the cuisine and reduce the incidence of scurvy, which killed more sailors than did battle. The cuisine was based on hard wheat-flour biscuits (often called pilot bread or hardtack), a protein such as salt beef or pork (or salt cod or cheese on non-meat days), and beer, a trio that mirrored the ordinary British diet, with biscuits standing in for bread.[91] Rounded out with oatmeal or peas cooked to a mush (called loblolly or burgoo), butter for the biscuits, and vinegar as a condiment, this, in theory at least, provided four to five thousand calories a day. Over the years, the unpopular, often rotten, salt cod was banished, fresh beef and fresh baked bread were offered in port instead of salt meat and biscuit, and root vegetables and greens were added. At sea, salt meat still had to be used. It was inspected before being put on board. If it was not up to standard it was discarded. Greater care was taken with the casks in which beef, butter, and beer were stored. Citrus juice was introduced to counteract scurvy in the late eighteenth century. A regular tot of brandy or rum cheered the sailors. Naturally, seamen grumbled, but a daily hot meal, meat four times a week, biscuits or bread of wheaten flour, plentiful beer, and fruit and vegetables on occasion was much better fare than they had had in their villages and small towns.

Indeed, sailors stayed so much healthier that time at sea increased from two weeks in 1700 to three months by 1800. This gave the Royal Navy an important edge over both the Dutch and the French, who could not stay at sea so long. The French in particular were plagued with corrupt managers and, in the West Indies at least, forced to obtain their beef from Ireland. The British naval historian N. A. M. Rodger concludes that "It was . . . above all the Victualling Board, which transformed the operational capabilities of British fleets at sea. . . . Only when ships could be kept at sea with healthy crews for long periods could the possibilities of naval power be fully exploited. . . . Britain had incontestably gained the real command of the ocean."[92]

On the other hand, the rural poor in Europe, including Britain, struggled as their numbers grew and access to land and fuel for cooking grew ever tighter. At times there was serious shortage, even famine. Continental Europe had poor wheat and rye harvests in 1770, followed by famine.[93] In 1756 and 1773, farmers across Sweden lay dying, and "what is even more gruesome, hear their little children's whimpering, suffering and death agonies."[94] Even when hunger did not threaten, the rural poor worried that they might lose their staple bread of whatever grain. The English were largely eating wheaten bread by the late eighteenth century. The Welsh and the Cornish ate barley bannocks; the Scots, oatmeal or oatcakes. Many northern Europeans had rye bread and buckwheat groats. The French had dark bread, made of rye, oats, barley, maize, or chestnuts (the bread of the forest). To save fuel, they baked as rarely as once every six months.[95] Sometimes so tough that having the strength to cut it with an axe was a sign of manhood, the bread was softened in soup, the most basic of foods, cooked in a cauldron hanging over the fire.

Bread, though, of any kind was something to sink the teeth into, to eat with cheese or a bit of preserved fish, or to dip into soup. It was easily carried to the fields and did not have to be heated before it was eaten. Many believed that it was the gift of God, and that it was the duty of rulers to provide it (fig. 6.8). People had eaten it since time immemorial and thought of it as synonymous with food itself.

And bread was increasingly in short supply as populations rose. Traditional systems of monarchical and church benevolence were disintegrating. Physicians, economists, and politicians debated how to feed the poor, whom many regarded as little more than animals. "Many people see little difference between this class of men and the animals they use to farm our lands," said an article in the French *Encyclopédie* published in the middle of the eighteenth century. George Cheyne concluded, "Ideots, peasants, and mechanics have scarce any passions at all, or any lively sensations, and are incapable of lasting impressions."[96]

Adam Smith and Thomas Malthus inclined to the view that high bread prices would have the advantage of keeping the population under control by deterring the poor from having so many babies. Others thought that the shortfall of bread could be made up for by water or broth. Water, which "acts as a much more important Part

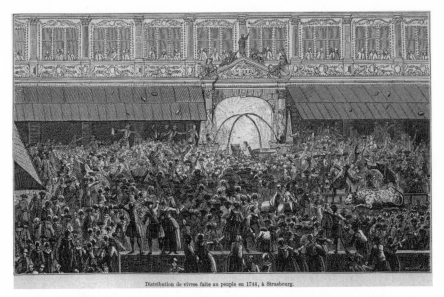

Distribution de vivres faite au peuple en 1744, à Strasbourg.

FIGURE 6.8. This engraving shows food and drink being distributed to the populace in Strasbourg in October 1744 to celebrate Louis XV's recovery from illness and entry into the city. What appears to be bread is being tossed from the balcony, people by the fountains are raising tankards, and on the right a butcher is about to slaughter an ox. Engraving by Jacques-Philippe Le Bas after a drawing by Johann Martin Weis. From Paul Lacroix (pseud. Paul-Louis Jacob), *XVIIme siècle: Institutions, usages et costumes* (Paris: Firmin-Didot, 1880).

in Nutrition than has hitherto been generally imagined," could replace part of the bread, said the Massachusetts-born scientist Benjamin Thompson, Count Rumford. "A surprisingly small Quantity of solid Food [is] necessary, when properly prepared, for all the Purposes of Nutrition." Sir Frederick Eden, of Maryland, a follower of Adam Smith, agreed in a pioneering study titled *The State of the Poor*, published in 1797. Water combined with the proper solid ingredients, such as salep (a flour made from the roots of orchids), hartshorn (roasted and powdered deer horns), or barley, formed a superior nutrient. Consequently, the Scottish diet of oatmeal and barley meal with water and salt, the Irish diet of potatoes, or the slave diet of three barrels of Indian corn (maize) a year (admittedly supplemented with garden produce) was perfectly adequate.[97]

Efforts were made to ensure the bread supply. Frederick the Great in Prussia, for example, stockpiled grain so that bread could still be made following poor harvests. The French government offered prizes for improvements in milling, hoping to increase the yield of quality flour from grain. Most radically, liberals such as Anne-Robert-Jacques Turgot and the Physiocrats in France and Adam Smith in

England proposed that government controls on the wheat trade and wheat prices be replaced by free trade. When in the 1760s the French government acted on this, the poor felt their traditional security had been pulled from under them. The "moral economy," as the historian E. P. Thompson called the belief in the right to food at a fair price, had been abrogated.[98] Although the policy was reversed within a few years, the added insecurity was not.

For those who could not feed themselves, most European countries had "hospitals," poor houses, or later workhouses, founded largely by the contributions of the urban middle class, which took the poor off the streets and put them to work, if they were fit enough, in return for giving them food and shelter. To combat hunger in Sweden, almanacs, sermons, and vernacular pamphlets recommended famine foods. Some, such as tulip bulbs cooked with butter and pepper; black currants mashed with sugar; asparagus; and cherry-tree resin, seem out of touch with what was likely to have been available. Others were more practical, time-honored fallbacks such as fir bark, nettles, burdock, acorns, Iceland moss, seaweed, bog myrtle, and thistles.[99]

The solution to the bread problem, the elite came to hope from the 1770s on, was the potato. It had been known in Europe since the late sixteenth century and grown in fields from the mid-eighteenth century, but it was still not a significant part of the diet. Accustomed as we are to potatoes, it is hard to realize that they were stranger to Europeans than taro and cassava are to modern Americans.[100] As roots, potatoes seemed like turnips, which were thought of as winter cattle feed and thus for animals, not humans. They were often small and tasted bitter because breeding had not yet produced the varieties that we enjoy. Once harvested, they had to be kept cold or eaten quickly, or they went green and sprouted. When cooked they formed a bland, soft mass rather than aromatic, toothsome bread. The only place where potatoes were adopted with enthusiasm was in distant New Zealand. The Maoris, accustomed to the subtropical roots that they had introduced to the North Island, welcomed them when introduced by Europeans in the 1770s, because they grew in the colder South Island. Trading potatoes for muskets with European whalers and sealers enabled the Maoris to resist the British army from the 1840s to the 1870s.

In the Old World, people rejected potatoes as a staple. "The things have neither smell nor taste, not even the dogs will eat them," Germans complained. "What use are they to us?" Russian Old Believers objected that the potato was "that forbidden fruit which the first two human beings ate; therefore, whoever eats it disobeys God, violates the holy testament and will never inherit the Kingdom of Heaven."[101] Even potatoes' promoters admitted their shortcomings. Gabriel-François Venel described them as causing flatulence in his 1765 article "Pommes de Terre" in the Encyclopédie, but added a phrase that was to be much quoted: "What is a bit of wind for the vigorous organs of peasants and labourers?" The Russian agronomist

Andrei Bolotov found them insipid and mealy in the mouth, without the textured chewiness of bread or kasha. No one would have guessed that modern scholars would argue that potatoes would reduce the incidence of the fungal disease ergotism, caused by eating moldy rye.

Unpopular as potatoes were, with the population growing and bread shortages threatening, the ruling classes saw no option but to urge the rural poor to eat them. To make them a little more acceptable the French chemist and potato promoter, Antoine-Augustin Parmentier, published *Manière de faire le pain de pommes de terre, sans mélange de farine* (Way of Making Potato Bread without Adding Flour) in 1779. No one was convinced. Frederick the Great sent a load of potatoes to relieve famine in Kolberg in 1774. The Russian College of Medicine recommended growing "earth apples, which in England are called potatoes," especially in Siberia and Finland, when famine followed harvest failure. Similar initiatives were undertaken across Europe.[102] In the 1790s, widespread hunger as a result of bad harvests, urbanization, and the revolutionary and Napoleonic wars (1792–1815) forced the poor finally to accept them. In southern Europe, the poor already relied on maize polenta. Now in northern Europe, the poor began to rely on boiled potatoes.

GLOBAL CULINARY GEOGRAPHY IN 1840

By 1840, high Western cuisine was established across Europe and Russia. Middling Western cuisine was to be found in the Low Countries and Britain; it was also established in modified form on the eastern seaboard of the United States and Canada and had a toehold on the coast of Australia and in New Zealand. In the newly independent states of Latin America, a long, drawn-out contest between modern Western high cuisine and Catholic-criollo high cuisine was under way. *El cocinero mexicano* (The Mexican Cook, 1831), the first Mexican cookbook to be published after independence from Spain, included French and English recipes.

Modern Western cuisine had new kinds of rich, fatty sauces, a wide range of vegetables, and foods and drinks with air incorporated, whether in mousses, bubbling spa waters, or fizzy drinks such as tonic (quinine) water, now possible as a result of research on airs and gases. Sugar had vanished from savory courses. It was on its way from being a spice and medicine to becoming a staple food, supplying a significant proportion of the calories in the diet. Sweetmeats, formerly nibbled by the nobility in special banqueting rooms or edifices, were moving down the social scale to become everyday candies. A whole range of less densely sweet cakes, pies, cookies, puddings, and desserts was beginning to emerge. Sugar made bitter tea, coffee, and drinking chocolate more palatable.

The steam engines of the Industrial Revolution were being used in the manufacture of the new, dark, bitter, inexpensive porter beer and ship's biscuits.[103] The latter were now baked on a conveyor belt running through the oven (continuous-process baking), Admiral Sir Isaac Coffin of the British Navy taking out the earliest patents for this important invention at the beginning of the nineteenth century. Indeed, provisioning militaries played an important role in the growth of modern cuisines. By the 1760s, the British Navy, for example, with 16,000 men to feed, had its own breweries, mills, and meatpacking plants in its victualing yards in the southern ports of Portsmouth and Plymouth. As the largest single purchaser of British farm products, it created a stable national market and stimulated international trade.

Religion still permeated Western culinary philosophy, although few Western states demanded that their subjects follow religious culinary rules. Hierarchical, monarchical cuisines had been challenged in the Netherlands, France, and the United States. Even so, monarchies lived on, and with them high French cuisine. As for the poor, governments still thought that their main responsibility was simply providing the humble with enough to eat.

Ottoman, Safavid, and Mughal cuisines continued to evolve. In Qing China, a high cuisine, as yet little studied, flourished among the well-to-do, whose consumerism paralleled that of Europe.[104] In Japan, Buddhist high cuisine based on rice and fish thrived in Kyoto and Edo (now Tokyo), which by the early eighteenth century had a million people, twice the population of Paris. It was one of the largest and most prosperous cities in the world.[105] The Sumida River in Edo was lined with restaurants, teahouses, and houses of entertainment. Pleasure boats offered food, music, and hostesses. Snack shops offered rolled soba buckwheat noodles, which had become popular in the sixteenth century. Commercial establishments produced and sold sake, soy, miso, and dried bonito for stock.

Global patterns of commerce and agriculture had been transformed by Western cuisine, particularly the demand for wheat, beef, wine, tea, coffee, and sugar. Long-distance trade in food was increasing.[106] Grocer's shops in Paris, London, Saint Petersburg, and other capital cities sold sugar, tea, coffee, spices, and other tropical goods.[107] In Saint Petersburg, a city of 250,000 people, the aristocracy bought butter from Prussia, wines and brandies from France, sweet wines from Hungary,[108] and fresh apples, pears, lemons, and watermelons from across Europe, while turning to their own country for honey, sturgeon, grains, and salt. The Dutch imported wheat and rye from the plains of Poland and the Ukraine, paying with profits from the herring trade. Amsterdam was the biggest wheat market in the world.[109] Cattle were driven from eastern Europe, the Alps, Denmark, Scotland, and Ireland to Paris and London.[110] The English liked to drink wines from Bordeaux, but to avoid buying from France, with whom they were more or less constantly at war, they tried unsuccessfully to establish vineyards in Virginia and imported wines from Madeira and Portugal. By the late seventeenth century, wines were being produced under Dutch East India

Company rule at the Cape of Good Hope, aided by an influx of French Huguenot refugees.

Sugar for the Dutch came from Guyana and the Dutch West Indies, for the French, from the French West Indies and Louisiana, and for the British, from the British West Indies. Coffee, once the Dutch had smuggled slips of the coffee plant from South India to Indonesia, was grown on plantations on the island of Réunion in the Indian Ocean, as well as Martinique, Jamaica, Haiti, Guadeloupe, Puerto Rico, and Cuba. Tea came from China.[111] To stem the drain on the Swedish currency, the botanist Carl Linnaeus urged his countrymen to "Bring the Tea-tree here from China!"[112] When he realized that tea was not going to adapt to the dark Swedish winter, even in a heated greenhouse, he suggested that patriotic Swedes drink infusions of sloes, arctic raspberries, and bog myrtle instead. In place of coffee, they should sip boiled water mixed with toasted "peas, beechnuts, almonds, beans, maize, wheat or toasted bread." There is no evidence that anyone paid the slightest attention. To explore the potential of tropical plants, botanic gardens were established by the Dutch at the Cape of Good Hope, by the French in Mauritius, and by the British in Jamaica, St. Vincent, and later Calcutta and Penang, with Kew Gardens in London coordinating the work of the gardens in the British colonies.[113] Other circles of commerce had been established to feed the slaves. By the mid-seventeenth century, the Jesuits had ten thousand slaves on fifty plantations in Angola growing maize and cassava to provision slave ships. Salt beef from South America and salt cod from North America went to plantations in Brazil, Mexico, and the Caribbean.[114]

The world population had doubled since 1650, reaching about 1.2 billion. Wheat and rice continued to be the prestige grains for those who could afford them. Many could not. First in China and then in India, the humble turned to grains lower in the grain hierarchy, such as maize, or even to roots such as taro, yams, sweet potatoes, and potatoes.[115] Industrial cities in England, peopled by those who had fled or been pushed off the land, were growing. In Europe, economic depression in the mid-1830s made it harder for the poor to eat well. In 1845–46, the Hungry Forties, crops failed across Europe. A fungus-like blight turned potatoes in the ground black and slimy. The rural poor suffered horribly and bore the brunt of the crisis. In Belgium, where the cottage linen industry had slumped, the unemployed and starving wandered over the northern provinces in search of food, while the state suppressed protests, imposed price controls, expropriated uncultivated land, and lowered taxes on imported foodstuffs.[116] In Ireland, one million perished and another million emigrated. It looked as if the old distinction between high and humble cuisines, blurred by the appearance of middling cuisines, would harden once again.

7

Modern Cuisines

The Expansion of Middling Cuisines, 1810–1920

The years between 1880 and 1914 marked the greatest turning point in culinary history since the mastery of grains and the divergence of high and humble cuisines millennia earlier, the culmination of changes that had begun in the mid-seventeenth century and haltingly accelerated from 1810. Middling cuisines, rich in wheat bread or other preferred carbohydrate staples, beef and other meats, and fats and sugars, expanded from the bourgeoisie to two new and rapidly growing social groups: the salaried middle classes and the wage-earning working classes. These formed the majority of the population in the cities of the industrializing countries—particularly, though not exclusively, in the nations of northern Europe; European settlement colonies overseas, including Canada, Australia, New Zealand, South Africa, and Algeria; the United States; and Japan. High and humble cuisines did not disappear. The rich and powerful everywhere accepted French high cuisine as their own, while humble cuisines remained the lot of the rural poor.

Middling cuisines spread rapidly to become the predominant cuisines in the wealthier parts of the world. Their foodstuffs, dishes, kitchens, special areas and implements for dining, and the literature describing them meant that middling cuisines had more in common with high cuisines than with humble cuisines. They differed in not being used to express hierarchical political and religious power. Thus the changes that gave citizens more say in the political process in modern states were paralleled by the shifts that gave them access to cuisines formerly reserved for a powerful minority. Although the choice of dishes and the manner of serving and eating could signal minute distinctions in status, the yawning gap between the food of the rich and the powerful and the food of everyone else within the state was diminishing. It was replaced by a different gap, a gap between the states where the shift to middling cuisines had occurred and the states that retained a sharp distinction between high and humble cuisines.

The explosion of middling cuisines would still have seemed impossible in the 1840s—the Hungry Forties, as they were called—when it looked as if in spite of all the political turmoil of the previous half century in Europe and the Americas, the aristocracy would continue to dine on high cuisines while the poor barely subsisted on a starchy cuisine. Thomas Malthus had warned as early as 1798, in his *Essay on Population,* that given a limited supply of land, and thus of food, periodic famines were to be expected. Instead, in significant parts of the world, middling cuisines (a term I prefer to "nutrition transition," since it indicates that social and political changes were involved as well as nutritional ones) were created.

As in the past, cuisines spread with the empires or expansive states with which they were associated, notably the European, Russian, and Japanese empires, and the United States. Settlers, migrants, militaries, missionaries, merchants, and the new multinational corporations all contributed to the process. The pattern was complicated, however, by nationalism, which was incipient in northern Europe in the eighteenth century and began to appear in the Americas, Japan, Russia, and other countries in the late nineteenth century. The new middling cuisines became identified as national cuisines, making the world's culinary geography in 1920 radically different from that in 1840. In 1820, national cuisines scarcely existed. The older pattern of imperial high cuisines for the elite and regional cuisines for the poor persisted. By 1920, diners tended to identify cuisines as national, not imperial, even though national cuisines were constantly in flux as nations coped with changing boundaries and local or immigrant minorities.

Particularly important in the shift to middling cuisines was the Anglo world— the world of those who spoke English, whatever their ethnicity. In 1830, Britain had a population of about twenty-three million. By 1914, this had grown to forty million, and Britain ruled over an empire of nearly four hundred million, an increase of over 500 percent. By 1920, it held sway over one-fifth of the world's population and a quarter of its land area. The other great Anglo power, the United States, spread across a continent and grew from thirteen million people in 1830 to a hundred and six million in 1920. Altogether there were perhaps two hundred million English speakers. Although other empires were growing in population and often in size, the rate of expansion was not comparable. France, for example, with a home population similar to Britain's, ruled just over sixty million people overseas. The population of Latin American countries, formerly part of the Spanish Empire, almost quadrupled from twenty-five million to ninety million. The huge populations of the Chinese Qing Dynasty and the old Indian Mughal Empire each doubled from two hundred million to four to five hundred million.[1]

Anglo cuisines, since the eighteenth century identified with white bread and beef, were thus the most rapidly expanding cuisines in the world. At the end of the eighteenth century, perhaps twelve million people in the world ate some form of Anglo cuisine. Only the aristocracy and the bourgeoisie could afford high Anglo cuisine of white bread, beef, sugar, and tea or coffee. Most depended on a humble cuisine of coarse wholemeal bread, or breads and porridges made of grains regarded as less desirable, such as oats, barley, rye, or, in America, maize, accompanied by salt pork and probably beer or cider. At the beginning of the twentieth century, two hundred million, about 10 percent of the total world population of two billion, ate a middling Anglo cuisine: white bread, fresh meat, sugar and fats in cakes and biscuits, and tea or coffee. Many were in the United States or were settlers in the overseas dominions, such as Australia and Canada. "Cookery in the Southern Hemisphere is largely British in character," wrote the anonymous author of the Australasian *Cookery Book* in 1913, echoing the Ladies of Toronto, who had noted in their 1878 *Home Cook Book* that Canadians had "no national dish to distinguish themselves from the British."[2] By contrast, although Anglo cuisine left traces in the societies that Anglos had colonized in India, Southeast Asia, or the Philippines, it did not become dominant.

For the shift to middling cuisines to take place when the population was growing rapidly was surprising. That it occurred when people were moving to the cities is more astonishing yet. One in five people in Britain lived in a town in 1801, one in two by 1851, and two out of three in 1881. By the 1890s, both London and New York contained over a million people. Chicago had grown from almost nothing to nearly a million inhabitants in a generation, while other American cities, such as Cincinnati, Saint Louis, Pittsburgh, and San Francisco, had populations of around half a million. Manchester, Liverpool, and Glasgow in Britain, Toronto in Canada, Melbourne and Sydney in Australia, and Buenos Aires in British-influenced Argentina also had populations that were huge by world-historical standards. As in the past, all of these cities had to be provisioned with two pounds of grain (or the equivalent calories in other foodstuffs) per day for every inhabitant.

Because the Anglo world urbanized and grew both in population and in territory as it shifted to middling bread-and-beef cuisines, many politicians, economists, doctors, and intellectuals, both Anglos and others, asked themselves whether there was a connection. Was it bread and beef that underlay the increase in population? Was it bread and beef that gave these nations the power to dominate huge areas of the globe? Was it bread-and-beef cuisine, backed by a philosophy of thrift, domesticity, and modern nutritional theory, that created national unity, ensured strong citizens, workers, and soldiers, and laid the groundwork for imperial expansion? After all, it was widely agreed that "the fate of nations depends on how they are fed," as the French gastronome Jean-Anthelme Brillat-Savarin had put it in the early nineteenth century. "The various races have distinct characters, and whether they are strong or niggardly, or great or weak, depends in large part upon the foods they eat," echoed the Italian poet Olinda Guerrini, quoted in Pellegrino Artusi's

How the British Empire spells Bovril

and illustrates the close association of this Imperial British Nourishment with
the whole of King Edward's Dominions at Home and Beyond the Seas.

How many parts can you name?

NOTE.—The shapes are correct, but the sizes are not in proportion.   Each number indicates a separate part of the
Empire.   A complete key will later on be published in the Newspapers and on the Hoardings.

VIROL is recommended by Bovril, Ltd., as a fat food for the young.

FIGURE 7.1. "How the British Empire Spells Bovril." Bovril was one of the many commercial
beef extracts created in the nineteenth century following the pronouncement by the German
chemist Justus Liebig that these concentrates of broths made from meat and bones were as
nutritious as beef itself. Bovril was developed by John Lawson Johnston, who had received a
contract from the French Army to supply it with preserved beef products. Johnston chose
the name from *bovis* (genitive of *bos*), Latin for "cow, bull, or ox," and "Vril," a fictional
all-penetrating energy harnessed by a subterranean master race in a cult book, *The Coming
Race* (1871), by the English politician and novelist Edward Bulwer-Lytton. Thanks to canny
advertising, Bovril became synonymous with intrepid explorers, soldiers at the front, and
the British Empire. Each number in the advertisement represents a different part of the
empire. From *Illustrated London News,* 2 February 1902. Courtesy Mary Evans Picture
Library, London.

best-selling Italian cookbook, *La scienza in cucina e l'arte di mangiare bien* (1891;
The Science of Cooking and the Art of Eating Well).[3] That diet determined a
nation's strength became a commonplace, picked up time and again, for example,
in World War I in the state of Kansas by the compilers of the *Coffeyville Cook Book,*
who quoted Brillat-Savarin's epigram as their frontispiece.[4] Many accepted this
culinary determinism. A British advertisement from 1902 (fig. 7.1) associates
"Imperial British Nourishment," in the form of hot meaty broths made from a
sticky, black, industrially produced beef extract called Bovril, the precursor of
today's stock cubes, with the spread of the British Empire; the ad depicts the sixty-
eight countries in "King Edward's Dominions."

Members of elites worldwide were attracted to the theory of culinary determinism, which linked political and economic expansion with cuisine, because it offered a strategy for competing with the Anglo world and the European empires. If the source of Anglo strength lay in racial character or perhaps in the bracing climate of Britain or the northeastern United States, as some theorized, then there was little to be done. If, on the other hand, a bread-and-beef cuisine were fueling Western imperial expansion, then by switching their populations to bread and beef, countries could stem the Anglo tide. Consequently, members of the Japanese, Mexican, Brazilian, Italian, Indian, and Chinese elites who thought there was something to the bread-and-beef theory decided that their countries must either modernize their cuisine along Western lines or fall behind economically and politically. The Islamic world, long dependent on wheat bread and keen on meat, was the least concerned, but even there, many argued for modernizing the kitchen. Around the world, reformers, including home economists, nutritionists, physicians, politicians, and military men, embarked on programs to persuade their citizens or subjects to change their diets and to introduce the commerce and farming to make that possible. The debates between those promoting modern bread-and-beef cuisines and those arguing for the retention of traditional cuisines were central to modernization worldwide in the late nineteenth century.

THE MIDDLING CUISINES
OF THE URBAN SALARIED CLASSES

Because Britain had a substantial urban salaried middle class earlier than most other countries, it is the focus of this chapter. Examples from the rest of the industrializing world will be included to stress how widely the shift to a middling cuisine occurred, how the appropriate culinary philosophy was shared, and yet how the different traditions and aspirations in each nation created distinct national cuisines. The new salaried middle class, like today's emerging middle classes in China, India, and Mexico, was largely composed of people whose parents or grandparents owned a small farm or worked as farmhands. People left the farm and moved to the city for many reasons—because the farm was not profitable or the oldest son had inherited it, because they could no longer find farmwork or had married a townsperson, or just in search of a better life. Men established themselves as small shopkeepers or took jobs as clerks or bureaucrats; women became housewives.

The urban salaried middle class, like the old agrarian bourgeoisie, occupied a social position intermediate between the aristocrats and the humble. Unlike the bourgeoisie, those who depended on salaries did not have rental income to live off, nor positions as clergy, lawyers, or doctors, nor income from successful businesses. They rarely had gardens where they could grow produce, let alone farms that supplied milk or pork, nor ample kitchens, sculleries, pantries, attics, and cellars for storing food. Their salaries left no room for luxuries, and they depended on groceries that they purchased daily. In houses without electricity or central heating, they did the laundry, tended the fires or ranges, and cared for children. Housework was heavy, unremitting labor, made worse by the necessity of preparing three meals a day. Although their culinary philosophy was closer to that of eighteenth-century Dutch burghers or English gentry than to that of the aristocracy who dined on high cuisine, the urban salaried classes placed more emphasis on thrift, respectability, and the safety of the food they purchased.

Because money was so tight and food consumed such a large portion of the household budget, to maintain the respectability demanded of middle-class life the housewife had to make thrift a priority in running the household, and particularly in planning meals. It was key to domesticity. "Of all those acquirements, which more particularly belong to the feminine character . . . none . . . take on a higher rank . . . than such as enter into a knowledge of household duties; for on these are perpetually dependent the happiness, comfort, and well-being of a family," said Mrs. Beeton in the introduction to her *Book of Household Management* (1861, better known as *Mrs. Beeton's Cookery Book*). This and subsequent editions were to shape the aspirations of middle-class British, Canadian, Australian, and New Zealand housewives in the running of the household, including management of servants, childcare, entertaining, and above all cooking, for the rest of the nineteenth century.

In the United States, domesticity was often seen as a religious duty. "The family state is then, the aptest earthly illustration of the heavenly kingdom, and in it woman is its chief minister," Catharine Beecher and Harriet Beecher Stowe argued in *The American Woman's Home* (1869).[5] The careful housewife avoided being distracted by activities outside the home, such as clubs or (worse) feminist organizations, preferring instead to create a happy nest for her husband and children (fig. 7. 2). In Russia, the ladies of the Smolensk Society declared that not one of their members was "emancipated from domestic work. For us the rational thriftiness of bees is more appealing." The meals that came from their well-run kitchens kept their husbands away from cafés and restaurants, drinking, and other women.[6]

From newspapers, magazines, and advertisements, the housewife picked up the latest nutritional advice. This was no longer only for the rich, who had a personal physician to advise them on diet, but for all members of society now that their health contributed to a strong nation. Chemists had been analyzing the components of foodstuffs and come to the conclusion that only nitrogenous and carbonaceous foods (our proteins, fats, and carbohydrates), a few minerals, and water were needed to maintain health (fig. 7.3). Nitrogenous foods built and repaired the body, while carbonaceous foods supplied heat and energy. Foods should not be mixed up together, as they had been in the old pottages and stews, but served separately to ease digestion.

FIGURE 7.2. The maid works in the kitchen and the immaculate housewife, unbesmirched by the enclosed coal range, presents a roast chicken to her family. They are seated in a respectable dining room, with flowers and a clock on the mantel, a hanging gas lamp, and individual glasses, plates, and cutlery on the cloth-covered table. This was one of a series of cartoons that appeared in the satirical magazine *Puck* contrasting the poorly run homes of emancipated women with the "duties and dignities of the old-fashioned American home." *Puck,* no. 1288 (6 November 1901).

Fruits and vegetables, said the experts, caused fever or, worse, cholera, and thus were dangerous as well as a waste of the housewife's scarce resources—a fall from favor compared to their prestigous position in the first modern nutritional theory in the late nineteenth century. Spices and condiments, although they tasted good and helped digestion, could be addictive. Children in particular should not be allowed to eat them. If children developed cravings for pickles at a young age, they were likely to crave alcohol as adults.

Chemical research thus appeared to confirm the well-established idea, at least in the West, that wheat and beef were particularly nutritious. Wheat now headed the hierarchy of grains because analyses showed it contained more "nitrogenous matter," and hence more protein, than other grains, something suggested by the strings of gluten, reminiscent of meat fibers, that were observed in bread making. Mrs. Beeton ranked the cereals according to "their respective richness in alimentary elements." After wheat came other northern grains—rye, barley, and oats.

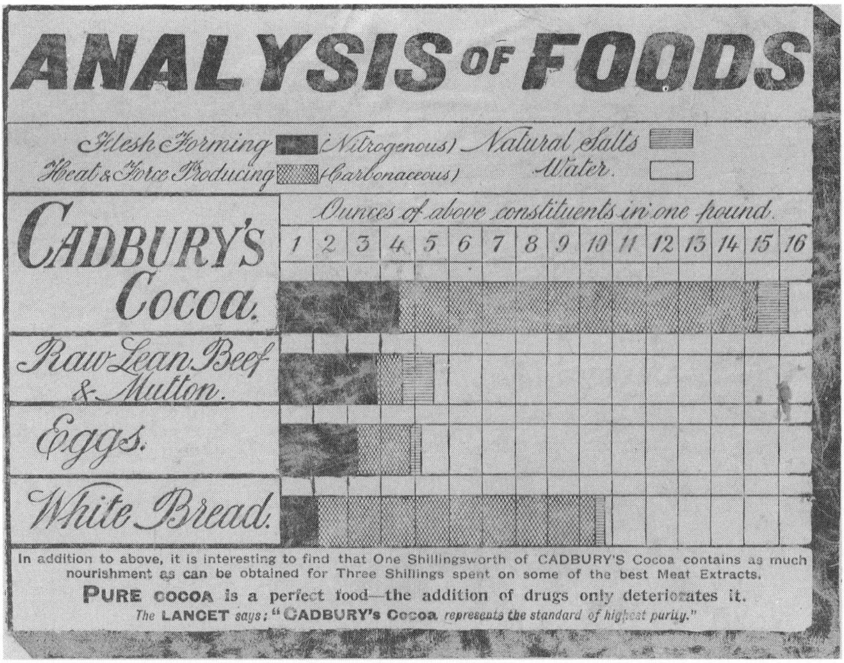

FIGURE 7.3. This "Analysis of Foods," an advertisement for cocoa produced by the English Quaker firm Cadbury and printed on the back of a children's book, compares the "flesh-forming nitrogenous and heat-producing carbonaceous constituents" of raw beef, white bread, and cocoa. In the late nineteenth century, these constituents were thought to be the most important nutrients, apart from mineral salts and water. The "analysis" cites the medical journal *The Lancet* in support of the purity of cocoa and points out how thrifty it is, giving as much nourishment for a shilling as three shillings' worth of beef extracts such as Bovril. From *Doggie's Doings and Pussy's Wooings: A Picture Story Book for Young People* (London: S.W. Partridge, n.d.). In the author's possession.

Rice and maize were at the bottom. Wheat bread became a necessity among "civilized peoples" because, according to Mrs. Beeton, it "constitutes of itself a complete life-sustainer, the gluten, starch and sugar, which it contains, representing azotized [another term for nitrogenous] and hydro-carbonated nutrients, and combining the sustaining powers of the animal and vegetable kingdoms in one product."[7]

Wheat bread was thus ideally the main item in the carbonaceous part of the diet. Everywhere it was a bakery bread, round, oval, or, if baked in a pan, oblong. Alternatives were potatoes, sugar, and fats. Formerly despised, potatoes appeared regularly alongside main dishes now that better varieties had become available and a range of ways of cooking them had been found. Sugar was now back in favor with nutritionists, who regarded its abundant calories as more important than the linkage to diabetes, which had caused scientists to condemn it in the late seventeenth century. "A most excellent nutritive article of the diet," its calories could be substituted for those of wheat flour.[8] "Sugar and treacle," opined the editor of the 1888 edition of *Mrs. Beeton's Cookery Book,* "are good foods and replace starch."[9] The preferred fats were solid animal fats, such as butter, lard, and suet.

Proteins, which are high in nitrogen and provide the basis for life, might be the only true nutrients, the German chemist Justus von Liebig argued in his hugely influential *Animal Chemistry* (1842).[10] Scientists, home economists, cookbook authors, and politicians all urged consumers to eat the recommended four ounces (about 113 grams) of protein a day. The chorus of enthusiasm for protein all but drowned out the voices of scientists who disagreed, such as the Dutch physiologist Jacob Moleschott, who contended in his *Science of Foodstuffs for the People* (1850) that the protein enthusiasts had overstated the case. Only two ounces of protein, or about 55 grams, were needed daily, added Russell Chittenden, professor at Yale. (Today, the recommendation for a man weighing 150 pounds is about 60 grams if sedentary, twice that if very active. Most people in the nineteenth century would have been very active by our standards.)

Beef was at the top of the meat hierarchy, "the most excellent food, the prince of foods, the food of virility, good sense and exacting taste," according to Giovanni Rajberti, a Milanese doctor and author of *L'arte de convitare* (1850–51; The Art of Inviting), who echoed general opinion.[11] "Those races who have partaken of animal food are the most vigorous, most moral, and most intellectual of races," said English surgeon, naturalist and science writer Edwin Lankester in 1860.[12] If beef was not available, beef broth, which we now know contains almost no nutrients, was then thought to be a fully adequate substitute. It was an "excellent, complete, and invigorating food," said Artusi in *La scienza in cucina,* adding that doctors who denied this were going "counter to common sense."[13] Digestible and strengthening, broth was thought to be beneficial for healthy and invalid alike. Beef extract dissolved in hot water made broth for a quick meal. For the middle class, it made lashings of gravy to accompany the Sunday roast beef. For those who could afford high cuisine, beef extract made consommé and *sauce espagnole* possible even where there was no beef, in New Delhi or Tokyo, for example.

Nutritional theory, integral to the culinary philosophy of middling cuisines, spread with the cuisines. Following the signing in 1858 of the treaty that established formal diplomatic relations with the United States, the Japanese quickly adopted the theory, along with other aspects of Western culture, such as the legal system, a quasi-parliamentary system, and science and technology. On 24 January 1872, it was publicly announced that the Japanese emperor Meiji ate beef on a regular basis. Although some meat eating had continued throughout the period when the thousand-year-old Law Prohibiting Killing was in force, this put the emperor squarely in the Westernizing, meat-eating wing of Japanese opinion. The government published a booklet on how to cook beef and set up an office, the Cattle Company, to coordinate the sale of beef and dairy products. Fukuzawa Yukichi, an intellectual and educator, wrote an open letter to the company praising beef's nutritional qualities. One of his pupils, Takahashi Soan, later to become a leading tea master, promoted beef and milk consumption in his book *The Improvement of the Japanese Race* (1884). In 1871, in a book of monologues, *Aguranabe* (Sitting around the Stewpan) by the playwright Kanagaki Robun, a "young man fond of the West" says "even people like ourselves can now eat beef, thanks to the fact that Japan is steadily becoming a truly civilized country. Of course, there are some unenlightened boors who cling to their barbaric superstitions and say that eating meat defiles you so much that you can't pray any more before the Buddha and the gods."[14]

In the West, those who did not eat bread and beef were frequently viewed as second-class citizens or even not citizens at all. In the United States, immigrants were urged to adopt these foods. Those who did not were open to attack. The American Federation of Labor, led by Samuel Gompers, published a pamphlet entitled *Some Reasons for Chinese Exclusion: Meat vs. Rice, American Manhood against Asiatic Coolieism* in 1902, calling for an extension of the 1882 Chinese Exclusion Act. It quoted the Hon. James Blaine's testimony to the Senate when it considered Chinese immigration in 1879. "You can not work a man who must have beef and bread . . . alongside of a man who can live on rice. In all such conflicts, and in all such struggles, the result is not to bring up the man who lives on rice to the beef-and-bread standard, but it is to bring down the beef-and-bread man to the rice standard."[15] The argument that bread and beef eating was a condition for citizenship resonated in a country that for a century had followed the practice, inherited from England, of celebrating national events with ox roasts. Following the ratification of the U.S. Constitution in 1778, for example, American butchers marched with their cleavers in a "grand federal procession" in Philadelphia. At the end of the march, they slaughtered two oxen that had been paraded with a banner between their horns, one reading "Anarchy," the other "Confusion," metaphorically killing the Antifederalists. The threat dismissed, the strengthening beef was roasted and fed to the assembled company.[16] Ox roasts continued to be part of political life until after World War II.

Cookbooks and magazines, cooking schools, entertaining, and simple meals out, as well as imperial encounters, gave urban salaried workers a shared sense that theirs was the national cuisine. Housekeeping manuals, bossy but encouraging compendia of household management that were almost always directed at a national audience, began appearing in the 1830s. Cooking took up the bulk of these texts, as it took up most of the housewife's time. Their authors happily rooted through earlier cookbooks intended for the aristocracy and bourgeoisie to find recipes. Their readers, judging by the pristine manuals in my possession, rarely opened them to cook from, except to check the odd special recipe for, say, Christmas pudding, or to look up the proportions of fruit and sugar for making jam or marmalade. Instead, they turned to these books for a vision of how the housewife could organize her home and family, and of the dinners she might give if she and her husband ever became wealthy. In every urbanizing country, different authors contended for the market, and the more successful saw their books go through dozens of printings over decades. To give a sampling, some of the more popular were Henriette Davidis's *Praktisches Kochbuch für die gewöhnliche und feinere Küche* (Practical Cookbook for Home and Fine Cooking) in Germany (first published in 1844 and going through seventy-six editions by 1963); Isabella Beeton's *Book of Household Management* in Great Britain (1861); Tante Marie's *La veritable cuisine de la famille* in France (1890; The Complete Tante Marie Cookery Book); Hildagonda Duckitt's *Hilda's Where Is It?* in South Africa (1891); Fannie Farmer's *Boston Cooking School Cook Book* in the United States (1895); Kristine Marie Jensen's *Miss Jensen's Cookbook* in Denmark (1901); Olga and Adolf Hess's *Viennese Cooking* in Austria (1916); Marja Ochorowicz-Monatowa's *Polish Cooking* in Poland (1910); and Nikolaos Tselementes's *Guide to Cooking* in Greece (1910). For housewives in British India, there was Flora Annie Steel and G. Gardiner's *Complete Indian Housekeeper and Cook* (1890); for Indonesia, Mrs. Catenius's *New Complete East-Indies Cookbook* (1902), which included recipes for rijsttafel, relishes, cakes, puddings, preserves, and ices. For the French in Algeria, A. Galian's *L'art de bien cuisiner* (1933; The Art of Cooking Well) gave advice on cooking French food with local ingredients, as well as a few Algerian and Moroccan recipes such as couscous. In Southeast Asia, the *Guide du français arrivant en Indochine* (Hanoi, 1935; Guide for French People Arriving in Indochina) suggested French cuisine with a few exotic ingredients. In the United States, community cookbooks helped codify middle-class cuisine; they were particularly well stocked with recipes for the baked goods that were so important to Anglo cuisines. (These little local cookbooks, usually compiled by Presbyterian churchwomen and prefaced by ministers, were originally sold at bazaars as fundraisers to raise money to improve the medical conditions in Civil War field hospitals.)[17] In Japan, cookbooks and women's magazines such as *The Western Cooking Expert* (1892), *Practical Home Cookery* (1903), *Western Home Cooking* (1905), and the *Western Cookery Textbook* (1910) flew off the presses.

Cooking schools to instruct the aspiring housewife proliferated. In London, Mrs. Marshall, a tireless culinary entrepreneur—publisher of a weekly magazine, *The Table,* from 1886, author of four cookery books, and vendor of branded products, such as beef consommé, colorings, icing sugar, and curry powder, as well as jelly and cream molds—opened the Marshall School of Cookery in 1883. In Paris, Marthe Distel, founder of *La Cuisinière cordon bleu: Revue illustrée de cuisine bourgeoise,* wanted to drum up more business for the magazine. In 1895, she invited professional chefs to give classes to middle-class women. Le Cordon Bleu, a school that instructed housewives in high French cuisine was the result.[18] In Tokyo, the Akabori family began teaching Western as well as Japanese and Chinese cuisine in 1882. By 1962, their school had graduated eight hundred thousand students and published more than forty cookbooks.[19]

Entertaining and eating out were done on a modest scale. The British, for example, might invite family to tea, a respectable but inexpensive meal. Similarly, when they went out, they avoided restaurants that served French cuisine, which were perceived as extravagant and intimidating, preferring more affordable meals chosen from menus in a language they understood, an experience that helped shape their sense of the cuisine of their nation. They headed to teashops for light bread-based meals not very different from those they ate at home. London had chains such as the ABC, run by the Aerated Bread Company, and Jo Lyons and Co., which opened in Piccadilly in 1894 and fifteen years later could seat a thousand customers in its Strand Corner House. The public liked the inexpensive and familiar food, the cheery waitresses, the lack of alcohol (unlike in pubs), and the elegant marble-and-gilt surroundings. By 1926, nearly five hundred Lipton Tea Shops were scattered across England and Wales.[20] In the United States, those who traveled by rail found that the dining cars and the Harvey House restaurants that dotted railroad stops in the West offered high-quality regional food in a nice setting, with efficient service, and at a reasonable price, from the 1870s onward.[21]

Outside Europe and the United States, a variety of establishments introduced diners to simple Western-style dishes adapted to local taste. In Japan, many people, men especially, first tasted Western cuisine in restaurants, coffee shops, and milk bars. From the 1880s on, Japanese diners could sample beef at any one of nearly five hundred specialist restaurants in Tokyo.[22] Sliced thin, it was simmered with vegetables and tofu in a sauce of water, sugar, soy, and sake—the precursor of sukiyaki. By the 1920s, street stands, restaurants, and takeout places offered omelets, croquettes, *hayashi* rice (hashed beef rice), *tonkatsu* (breaded pork cutlets), and curry rice. The prosperous could indulge in sugar candies or in syrups poured over mixed fruits, jellies, and beans or over containers of shaved ice offered by street vendors on hot summer days, driving sugar consumption to twelve pounds per head per annum in 1903, twice what it had been fifteen years earlier.[23] Coffee shops offered new opportunities for conversation and glimpses of different worlds: the Café Paulista in the Ginza, for example, flew the Brazilian flag outside and had waiters in naval uniforms inside.[24]

Life in the overseas colonies made housewives aware of how much their cuisines differed from those of the colonized. Following the opening of the Suez Canal in 1869, which reduced the passage to India on a P&O steamship to less than a month, more wives joined their husbands in India, Indochina, or Indonesia. Where previously single men had happily accepted the local high cuisine, many

Europeans came to believe that they were bringing civilization, including cuisine, to the less-civilized world. European women feared that native hands were dirty and that death lurked everywhere. They ran their own kitchens, so far as they could, on European lines. "We do not wish to advocate an unholy haughtiness but an Indian household [meaning a British household in India] can no more be governed peacefully, without dignity and prestige, than an Indian Empire," Flora Annie Steel advised in her *Complete Indian Housekeeper*.[25] The curries and other Anglo-Indian dishes of the first half of the century were now relegated to breakfast or lunch. The main evening meal was British.

The British spent between 38 and 60 percent of their income on food, according to seven contributors to the short-lived *Family Oracle of Health, or Magazine of Domestic Economy, Medicine and Good Living, Adapted to All Ranks of Society, from the Palace to the Cottage*, when asked in 1824 to estimate what percentage of their income was spent on food. Additional funds went toward fuel for cooking and wages for a girl servant.[26] These figures were typical of new urban salaried workers. Penny-pinching on food and cooking fuel, the largest items of disposable income, allowed families to save for a nest egg to invest in a business, send their sons to high school or even university, give their daughters a dowry, or splurge on a few luxuries, such as chairs for the front room, a magazine subscription, a nice dress, or a day trip by rail to the seaside. In the 1850s, the German economist Ernst Engels formalized this strategy as Engels's law: the proportion of income spent on food fell with rising incomes, even though the absolute amount increased.

Respectability (and the sheer hard work of keeping the house going) meant that in Britain in the 1880s, a quarter of all town housewives employed a servant girl in spite of the expense. Propriety also impelled the housewife, unlike her rural grandmother, who relied on one-pot meals, to prepare different meals for different times of day and different days of the week, and two or three distinct courses for the main meal. She attempted recipes, especially for sweet dishes, more complicated than anything her mother had cooked, requiring more exact timing, standardized ingredients, and precise weights. She scrimped so that she could buy individual sets of cutlery, china plates, a sideboard, table, chairs, and a wall clock for the dining room.

Shopping was a new experience. Where her mother or grandmother went to a market, garden or storeroom, the housewife bought almost everything from shops or deliverymen. Fishmongers, greengrocers, and milkmen came to the door. Butcher shops cut family-size portions of mutton, lamb, beef, and pork to order from carcasses hung behind the counter. Bakers offered breads, sweet and savory pies, and cakes. When shopping, the housewife had to be constantly vigilant, trying to make sure the food she bought was safe. Milk was rumored to be adulterated with sheep's brain to thicken and whiten it. Coffee was said to be stretched with chopped baked horse liver. Everything from cocoa to pepper was bulked out with potato flour in the 1850s, according to the British magazines *Punch* and the *Gardener's Chronicle.*

Scientists pinned down just how bad food adulteration was. In the 1820s, Frederick Accum, who had worked with the famous chemist Sir Humphry Davy at the Royal Institution, had published *The Adulteration of Food and Culinary Poisons,* with a cover portraying snakes writhing around food. The medical journal *The Lancet* appointed Dr. Arthur Hill Hassall, a chemist and physician with special interests in food safety, to look into the purity of foods for its Analytical Sanitary Commission in the early 1850s. Although he found no evidence of sheep's brain in the samples of milk he analyzed, he confirmed horse liver (and acorns, sawdust, and burnt sugar) in coffee and concluded that adulteration was a common practice. In the 1870s, investigators found that chocolate manufacturers were using oils and fats other than cocoa butter and thickening their products with potato starch and arrowroot. Housewives responded gratefully to Cadbury, which advertised that its chocolate was "Absolutely Pure, Therefore Best." By skillfully manipulating the public's fear to its advantage, Cadbury became the world's largest chocolate manufacturer by the end of the century.

Similar antiadulteration campaigns were waged elsewhere.[27] In 1851 and 1855, France updated its penal code to strengthen the laws against selling bad or adulterated food. Britain followed in 1860, Germany in 1879, and soon the Netherlands, Belgium, Italy, Austria, Hungary, Australia and Canada had enacted similar legislation. In the United States, where food purity had been a state matter, the federal government passed the Pure Food and Drug Act in 1906 after years of campaigning by the chief chemist of the U.S. Department of Agriculture, Harvey Washington Wiley. This extended traditional governmental regulations of market standards to food processed in factories and mills. Regulations were of little use without inspectors or methods for detecting adulterants. Only in the 1930s, when governments began to employ the necessary personnel and when scientists developed efficient methods for identifying adulterants, did the problems of unsafe and adulterated food decline.

In the meantime, housewives did what they could to buy foods that were sanitary. Adulterants were harder to disguise in white bread and sugar than in brown, one reason for the preference for white foods. Flour or crackers packaged in paper or cardboard seemed likely to be safer than those scooped out from barrels. Foods bought in the new grocery stores had not been exposed to the filth often found around outdoor markets.

Kitchens changed more in the late nineteenth century than they had in hundreds of years.[28] They were used for a much smaller range of tasks than formerly, as factories took over many of the chores of processing and preserving food formerly done in the home. At the same time, they became better lit, easier to keep clean, and more efficient. To take Britain as an example once more, by 1900 most town kitchens had running water and gas lights. Coal-burning ranges had appeared in the mid-nineteenth century, and though they were unreliable and dirty and required constant feeding with as much as fifty pounds of coal a day, as well as clearing of ashes, they did allow several different cooking operations to be carried out simultaneously. The cleaner and more convenient gas ovens, which once lit were ready to cook in an instant, quickly displaced ranges when they became available at the end of the nineteenth century. One in four urban households in Britain had a gas oven by 1898, a number that jumped to one in three by 1901. New gadgets such as meat grinders and egg beaters made short work of chopping left-over roast meat or beating eggs or cream, so that croquettes, shepherd's pie, and cakes became everyday options. These changes occurred throughout Europe, the United States, Canada, and Australasia between 1880 and 1920, as well as in cities across Latin America. In Japan, Western-style kitchens began to appear after the great Kantō earthquake of 1923.

By the end of the century, national cuisines were established in the Anglo world, Europe, Latin America, and Japan and were being discussed in China, India, and different parts of the Ottoman Empire. The British, Canadians, Australians, and New Zealanders might try out a recipe or two from French high cuisine when they wanted to impress the family, but they generally favored Anglo plain cooking, especially for the young. Indeed, the boarding schools for the children of Britons overseas in the colonial service or the military prided themselves on serving a spartan cuisine to toughen up their pupils. The main meal was taken in the middle of the day. Respectability demanded that a roast be served on Sunday, more often lamb or mutton than the desirable but very expensive beef. This was accompanied by a savory pudding or stuffing, boiled or roast potatoes, and vegetables, followed by dessert. "Cold meat cookery" simplified meal planning and used up the left-overs, the housewife converting cut-up beef into ragout, sliced beef into beef olives, and minced beef into rissoles, hash, and croquettes. Curry, which in the eighteenth century had been prepared with fresh spices, much as it might have been in India, was assimilated into the cold-meat cookery of Western cuisine by adding a commercially prepared mix of spices known as curry powder to a roux. Making stock from meat and bones, especially with wine, was costly, so house-wives, like many professional cooks, substituted meat essences in their gravies and soups. Bottled sauces that added flavor and kept for a long time became available in the 1820s. Worcestershire sauce, named for a county in England, was a variation on Asian fish sauce. It spread wherever the British went: "Everywhere in the Argentine, even in the most primitive inn, Worcester sauce, called salsa inglesa, is placed on the table," a traveler wrote.[29]

Bread, toast, or sandwiches with cheese, bacon, butter, or jam were quick and easy to set out for breakfast and tea. Housewives, reluctant to experiment with the expensive meaty sauces of French high cuisine, poured their ingenuity into producing a staggering range of pies, puddings, cookies, and cakes, the glory of middle-class Anglo cuisine, made possible by the properties imparted to the doughs and batters by sugar and fat. In the colonies, where bread was unavailable except in major cities such as Calcutta, Delhi, Madras, and Saigon, crackers and sweet biscuits (cookies) packed in tins by British companies such as Peek, Frean and Co., and Huntley & Palmers might be substituted. In India, Yeatman's baking powder went into a quick bread that served as a substitute. (The French resorted to hardtack in the backcountry of Southeast Asia, and to flatbreads of maize on the island of Réunion.) European wafers, maries, and custard-filled biscuits were quickly imitated by entrepreneurs in the tropics.

Sugar sweetened hot, bitter drinks such as tea and coffee as well as fruit drinks and carbonated beverages. Cocoa powder, developed by Quakers looking for an alternative to alcohol, made it easy to prepare a hot chocolate drink. Jam moved down the social scale, becoming a spread for bread instead of a luxury dessert. Sweets and candies in glowing colors, no longer luxuries, were sold in penny packages to eager children. Chocolate candy became available at the end of the century, again made by Quakers such Rowntree and Cadbury. Fancy boxes of bonbons became a necessary part of courtship. Ice cream was an occasional affordable luxury.

Without inexpensive bread and wheat flour, this middle-class cuisine would have been impossible. In Britain, bread had become more affordable from mid-century on following the repeal of the Corn Laws, which had protected wheat prices for British landowners. Wheat could be produced more cheaply overseas than in England, where farms had to support laborers, farmers, and landlords. Canals, railroads, and steamships lowered the price of shipping. As a consequence, the price of wheat bread, a large proportion of the budget, fell. The British middle and working classes embraced the Free Trade movement that had released them from hunger and poverty as the very foundation of peace, prosperity, progress, and democracy.[30]

In the United States, a cuisine of beef, sugar, and wheat bread displaced the older one of salt pork, molasses, and corn mush in the late nineteenth century, when greater acreages of wheat, cattle ranching, and railroads to move flour and beef to the eastern cities made these foodstuffs accessible to all. The 1876 centennial and the colonial revival, rapid urbanization, and the need to integrate old and new immigrants all encouraged discussion of what constituted the national cuisine. With their long republican tradition, middle-class Americans were even more suspicious of French high cuisine than the British.

German immigrants, particularly refugees from the failed 1848 uprisings, were especially important in differentiating American cuisine from British cuisine. One in ten Americans spoke German at the end of the nineteenth century, five million in all, as many as the total number of whites at the time of independence. Many of these were people of substance, unlike the Irish, who were fleeing dire poverty.

Henriette Davidis's cookbook from 1844, *Praktisches Kochbuch,* was translated into English in 1879. It even-handedly praised the dishes and products of "our American homeland," including catsup (an alternative name for ketchup, which by that date had become a thick, sweet, tomato-based sauce), baking-powder quick breads, and cakes, pies, and cookies, while extolling the excellence, wholesomeness, and taste of German cuisine.

In their new country, German butchers, bakers, brewers, grocers, cooks, and restaurateurs established food businesses. German families, such as the Clausens and Entenmanns, dominated commercial baking in many cities.[31] They adapted sweet rolls and sweet yeast breads to American taste, the latter coming to be called coffee cakes. Butchers and sausage makers in Texas smoked meats, which gradually merged with other traditions to become barbecue. The Wiener schnitzel, a breaded, fried piece of meat, entered Texas cooking as chicken-fried steak. Noodle casseroles made their appearance. Schlitz, Blatz, Pabst, and Miller introduced industrialized lager beer, which displaced hard cider. Heinz was a leader in canning. Beer gardens serving sausages and potatoes and offering entertainment flourished. German restaurants, found in almost every city, not just German-dominated Milwaukee and Saint Louis, offered wider menus.

Away from the Anglo world, in Italy, a national cuisine had to be forged from very disparate traditions following the unification of the country, a process that was more or less complete by the 1870s. Wheat bread had been the staff of life for those who could afford it since Roman times. The alternative form of wheat—pasta—although found in other parts of Europe, such as Catalonia and the German-speaking regions, was widely regarded as the Italian contribution to middle-class cuisine, whether or not Garibaldi had declared, "It will be maccheroni [the term for all pasta except for sheet pasta and ravioli], I swear to you, that will unite Italy." Middle-class Italians and Italians who had emigrated to the United States and Argentina and were doing well enthusiastically adopted industrially produced dried pasta, which lasted seemingly forever and made a tasty and filling first course in a matter of minutes, particularly when sauced with the canned tomatoes that became available by the end of the century.[32]

In Japan, leaders looked to English and American culture, including cuisine, as a model, since China, its polestar for centuries, seemed directionless, torn apart by famines and civil wars, and defeated by the Japanese in the war of 1894–95. "As democratic as American homes are, and as unsophisticated as the English homes are," announced Tetsuka Kaneko, home economics instructor at the Japan Woman's College, their food is "extremely simple . . . and easily adaptable for Japanese homes."[33] French cuisine was too "labour-consuming and troublesome" for the home kitchen. Housewives began shopping and preparing family meals, activities formerly reserved for maids or professional cooks. At the Akabori cooking school, women learned that the meals they prepared were the "sole source of energy" for the family, keeping women from idleness and promoting their independence and the "independence of our country."[34] Novels such as *Gourmet's Delight* (1903), by the popular and prolific author Murai Gensai, reinforced the message. Japan's moral and social reform started in the kitchen, with protein-rich recipes, a wide variety of ingredients, and thoroughly cooked, easy-to-digest meals that conserved the energy of family members so that they could turn Japan into a civilized nation.

Townspeople and the poorer samurai began to eat more complex meals. The main meal consisted of the rice, soup, and side dishes already eaten by the elite. Factory-made miso ended the tricky, tedious, and heavy job of making it by hand. Combined with hot water and a garnish, it made an instant soup, so that by 1936, miso consumption had risen to about twenty pounds per capita per annum. The family dinner in the evening provided energy and nutrients as efficiently as possible and taught children proper behavior. Seated on the floor at a round table (*chabudi*) about an arm's length in diameter, perhaps using newly affordable porcelain (instead of the traditional lacquerware for important meals and plain wood for everyday meals), families might substitute "I partake" and "It was a feast" for grace. They ate in silence, backs straight, legs tucked under them, chopsticks handled correctly, starting with a little rice, a sip of soup, and then bites of fish, meat, or vegetables alternated with bites of rice, while Father offered homilies on school performance.

The salaried Japanese middle classes tried coffee, black tea, milk, lemonade, beer, whiskey, ice cream, packaged cookies, macaroni, crackers, and Western cakes and sweets for the first time. Canned sardines and tuna, along with fresh tuna, beef, pork, cabbage, and onions, were all affordable. Housewives learned to cook breaded pork cutlets, beef croquettes (*korokke*), and a dish of potatoes seasoned with *dashi* (the traditional Japanese stock of kelp and dried bonito flakes), sugar, and soy, then mashed and rolled in seaweed (an adaptation of Japanese rice rolled in seaweed). Others made quick main meals such as sukiyaki and omelets. Bread, available at a hundred bakeries in Tokyo, including one in the Ginza that filled rolls with sweetened red bean paste (*an pan*), lasted longer than cooked rice and was thus good for snacks. Japanese migrants spread the popular treat of flavored syrup poured over shaved ice to Hawaii, the Philippines, and Southeast Asia.

In China, the Qing Dynasty, which had ruled China for three centuries, was overthrown in 1912. Reformers wanted to modernize both households and cuisine. In 1893, the educator Wu Rulun had published a book translated from the Japanese on how to run the home, titled *Home Governance*. It asserted that "if the home is in order, the commandery and county will be calm. If the commandery and county are calm . . . the kingdom will be ordered. Therefore, a kingdom's virtue and education springs from the virtue and education of the home." The words echoed the

FIGURE 7.4. Chinese women eating a Western meal. Here Wu Youru (d. 1893), one of the most talented illustrators in late-nineteenth-century China and editor of the major Chinese-language newspaper *Dian Shi Studio Pictorial,* depicts courtesans eating in a dining room that is a near replica of the American dining room shown in figure 7.2, from the flowers and clock on the mantel to the hanging lamps, cutlery, and glasses. From *Wu Youru hua bao* [A Treasury of Wu Youru's Illustrations] (1916; Shanghai: Shanghai gu ji shu dian, 1983), vol. 1.

opening words of Mrs. Beeton: "As with the commander of an army, or leader of any enterprise, so it is with the mistress of a house. Her spirits will be seen through the whole establishment."[35]

Most Chinese were not so keen on modern Western cuisine, which they encountered in bakeries, gardens, import grocery stores, brothels offering foreign prostitutes, and restaurants and hotels for foreigners in the port cities where foreigners were allowed to settle, particularly Shanghai. Among the first to experiment with eating Western-style were Chinese courtesans (fig. 7.4). Gingerly, other Chinese tried these rank-smelling dishes that had not been cooked with wine and ginger or that included beef, not a proper meat for humans, coming as it did from man's work companion, the ox. The author of *Entertainment,* a Shanghai tabloid, suggested that the Western cuisine sold in restaurants did not represent it at its best. Quoting Confucius, he said, "Eating choice quality can cultivate the person, cooking crudely can harm the person."[36] For all the efforts of the reformers, the Chinese, unlike the Japanese, adopted little from modern Western cuisine at this time.

In India, ruled by the British, many prosperous and educated Indians had experienced British middle-class cuisine. In Bengal, radical intellectuals such as Henry Vivian Derozio, leader of a group of free thinkers in the first years of the twentieth century, argued that Hindus should shift to modern Western cuisine.[37] He relished beef and downed pegs of whiskey and rum in public. Others sought a middle way between Hindu and Western cuisines, arguing that Indians should not blindly ape the West but instead take what was most useful, perhaps using Western etiquette and Indian cuisine, perhaps eating Western cuisine in Western company and Indian cuisine at home, perhaps selecting particular elements of Western cuisine. Spoons, forks, and tables were deemed "convenient and decent." Meat, far from robbing Indian women of their identity, would make them "healthy and civilized members of society." The author of a text on physical education suggested avoiding foods "soaked in ghee or oil, sweets and unripe fruit," which were all like "poison to the child."[38] Still others wanted to retain their own traditions unchanged.

Thus, in rapid succession, urban middle-class cuisines, based on a philosophy of thrift, domesticity, and respectability, were created around the world. New kinds of kitchens and dining rooms, new forms of culinary literature, and new ways of organizing the household were quickly and widely accepted. So were foodstuffs previously restricted to high cuisine: white bread, beef and other meats, fats, and sugar. Sweet dishes in particular multiplied in number and complexity, dining became more formal, with individual place settings, and different meals were served at different times of day. The new dishes and meals of the urban salaried class appeared to citizens to be the national cuisines.

THE MIDDLING CUISINES
OF THE URBAN WORKING CLASSES

By the end of the nineteenth century, in Britain, the United States, Germany, and other industrializing countries, the urban working classes were also eating middling cuisines, rich in wheat bread, beef (or at least the beef extract believed to be equivalent), sugars, and fats. The traditional benevolent concern with preventing hunger and starvation among the poor was being replaced with a broader concern about the quantity and quality of the cuisine of the poor, or at least the urban poor. Political leaders wanted to avoid food riots or, worse, repeats of the French Revolution or the revolutions of 1848. The military and the factory owners wanted tall, tough soldiers for conscript armies and resilient laborers to work in factories and mines. Lawyers and criminologists feared that poor diets were responsible for degeneracy, a supposed decline in human quality that was widely feared in the nineteenth century, not least because it was thought to lead to criminality. More bread and meat to eat, less alcohol to drink, and home cooking and family meals like those of the middle class were the way to solve all these problems, crusaders thought.

The poor, from their standpoint, at least in Europe, also wanted more wheat bread or rice, fats, sugar, and meats. Many had left the countryside in search of work in factories or domestic service in the cities. Others had emigrated to Australasia, Canada, Argentina, or the United States, where they hoped to have the dignity of being able to eat like other citizens. In America they found food available "at a price and in quantities which staggered the imagination of women and men who had been hungry," wrote Hasia Diner, a historian of migration. "Meat, sugar, fat, fruit, vegetables, soft and fine white bread, ice cream, beer, coffee were within their grasp at last."[39] However, given how little time working women had to cook and how limited their kitchens were, if they had kitchens at all, the frugal cooking and family dining of the middle class were rarely an option. The urban poor turned instead to ready-made and takeout or street foods such as hot dogs or fish and chips.

Governments were alarmed by the first surveys of health and poverty, by the number of conscripts who could not be accepted into the military because of short stature or physical defects, and by food riots. International comparisons of health and diet were made, using the data on height and health collected by militaries and physicians and the new lists of calorific values of different foodstuffs painstakingly compiled, first by the German-trained chemist Wilbur Atwater at Wesleyan University in the United States, and then by chemists and home economists elsewhere. In Britain, B. Seebohm Rowntree's book *Poverty: A Study of Town Life* (1901) concluded that social conditions in the slums, including the inadequate diet, explained the poor physique and lack of stamina of British working-class troops recruited to fight the Second Anglo-Boer War (1899–1902). The Inter-Departmental Committee on Physical Deterioration set up by the British Parliament estimated in 1904 that a third of all working-class children were undernourished. In France, leaders worried about their defeat by the Prussians in 1871, after a war that had lasted less than two years. Many feared that the French citizenry was degenerating due to bad living conditions, particularly their substandard diet. In Japan, after wartime inflation led to soaring rice prices, riots broke out across the country in the summer of 1918, raising the specter that Japan might face its own version of the Russian Revolution. The government fiercely suppressed the riots and immediately put into place measures to assure cheap rice for city dwellers.

In countries where the poor, rural as well as urban, depended on rice, maize, millet, or cassava, governments initiated efforts to increase consumption of supposedly more nutritious wheat. Contemplating the success of the United States in the Spanish-American Wars, Francisco Bulnes, a Mexican intellectual and foreign secretary, stated in *The Future of the Hispano-American Nations* (1899) that there were three races—wheat eaters, rice eaters, and maize eaters. Wheat eaters had founded the great Egyptian, Vedic, Greek, and Roman civilizations of antiquity, had overthrown the Aztec and Inca empires, and now ruled Irish potato eaters and Asian rice eaters. Mexico's peasants still consumed maize, salt, beans, and pulque, so the country had no hope of competing with the wheat-eating United States. To get the 113 grams of protein recommended by physicians from a staple grain, Mexicans would have to eat 2,300 grams of maize daily (seventy tortillas). Wheat eaters could get this protein from only 1,400 grams of wheat bread (three one-pound loaves)—a lot, but perhaps possible.

From then until the middle of the twentieth century, Mexican leaders, worried that the maize diet of the Indians was holding back national progress, tried to reduce dependence on maize. This effort had counterparts in other Latin American countries, including Colombia, Venezuela, and Brazil.[40] The anthropologist Manuel Gamio, although he denounced Bulnes as a racist, suggested replacing maize with soybeans. In 1901, the criminologist and sociologist Juan Guerrero described tamales (stuffed maize dumplings) as "an abominable outcome of the Mexican popular cooking tradition" and urged Mexicans to adopt French or Spanish cuisine instead. José Vasconcelos Calderón, minister of education from 1921 to 1924 and architect of Mexico's system of rural schooling, also believed Mexicans should give up maize for wheat. From 1921 on, at least some schoolchildren received free breakfasts of bread, beans, and coffee. Schoolteachers and social workers instructed rural women in the arts of making wheat bread and macaroni and cheese, and in the 1940s, sociologists used tortilla eating to assess how backward rural areas were.[41] Poor Mexicans resisted, preferring their tortillas to bread. Meanwhile, in the United States, those living in the South and the Appalachians were urged to give up corn bread for more healthful and refined biscuits of wheat flour.[42]

In India, English physicians and military officers compared the supposed nutritional quality of the diets of different Indian groups. A diet of wheat-flour flatbreads (chapatis) made the Rajputs of Rajputana and the Sikhs of the Punjab as strong as Europeans, according to Field Marshal Sir Colin Campbell, commander-in-chief of the Indian Army during the Sepoy Mutiny of 1857.[43] On the other hand, a rice diet meant that the people of Bengal exhibited none of the manly virtues, but "slackness, want of vigour, tonelessness . . . self absorption, . . . little power of attention, observation, or concentration of thought," according to Major David McCay, professor of physiology at the Medical College in Calcutta.[44] Even worse, the sorghum, millets, and barley that most Indians subsisted on had only 7 to 8 percent nitrogen compared to the 11.5–14.2 percent in Indian whole wheat, McCay explained in his book *The Protein Element in Nutrition* (1912).

Reluctantly, McCay rejected Russell Chittenden's doctrine that two ounces of protein a day was sufficient, even though it would have led to such savings "in the feeding of prisoners, famine camps, plague camps, hospitals, and even armies in the field, with their crowds of followers . . . [that it would] fill the heart of any Chancellor of the Exchequer with delight." The best way to provide the necessary higher levels of protein, McCay thought, was to encourage the consumption of "the poor man's beef," the legumes collectively known as dhal in India, which had about 20 percent nitrogenous matter, even though he thought the body's capacity to absorb protein in this form was limited. In a departure from general opinion, McCay said that maize, already the diet of the rural poor in the United States, Italy, and China, was an excellent cheap alternative food.[45]

Beef substitutes to increase dietary protein were eagerly sought by scientists and philanthropists in Europe and the United States as well. Horsemeat was reintroduced in many parts of Europe, a reversal of hundreds of years of Christian tradition. Zoological societies held dinners featuring exotic animals, hoping that some of them would prove palatable and could be domesticated. Offal, cheap fish, and shellfish often substituted for muscle meat. In Britain, salted and smoked herrings, such as kippers and bloaters, were economical and plentiful and saved on fuel since they cooked quickly. In the Mediterranean, dried fish continued to be a standby of the poor. In the United States, the working class turned to inexpensive, if not very safe, farmed oysters during the Depression, until typhoid scares led to the decline of the oyster business.

Militaries set about improving the diet of conscripts, conscription having been introduced in all major European nations except Britain after 1871. Many young men from the countryside first had white bread, fresh meat, canned goods, and coffee on a regular basis, or even at all, in the army. "Every day, meat and soup / Without working, without working / Every day, meat and soup / Without working in the army" went a Flemish song. In the 1870s, French military rations included over half a pound of meat a day, half a pound of bread, often white, and two pounds of vegetables, including potatoes, making French soldiers healthier and longer-lived than the average civilian, including the very wealthy. Coffee, wine, and sugar were sometimes offered, and some commanders introduced mess halls, benches, plates, and glasses.[46] In Italy, military diets included about half a pound of canned meat, a pound of dry biscuit, bottles of meat sauce for pasta, meat extract, powdered milk, and coffee substitutes.[47]

In the 1920s and 1930s, the Japanese military Westernized rations, offering meat, lard, potatoes, fried dishes, and oil-dressed salads adapted to Japanese tastes. Military cooks were trained in Western nutritional theory and provided with calorie counts in the 1924 *Reference Book of Military Catering;* in 1937, *Military Catering Methods* included protein counts as well. With this meaty, fatty Western diet, the military aimed to feed enlisted men four thousand calories a day, twice the estimated daily peasant intake of 1,850 calories and close to the American army standard. Hamburgers (*hikiniku*), ground beef with chopped onions fried in lard, with boiled potatoes on the side; croquettes of canned salmon and mashed potatoes dipped in egg yolk and bread crumbs and deep-fried in lard; macaroni beef (*macaroni bifu*) with potatoes, onions, and carrots in a white sauce; curried rice (*kari meshi*), a mixture of rice, barley, and sweet potatoes in a sauce of minced beef, carrots, and onions flavored with curry powder; boiled potatoes in a sauce of mustard, sugar, miso, and vinegar; and ship's biscuits deep-fried in sesame oil and sprinkled with sugar were some of the meals that a young country conscript could expect. They were frequently a reason for enlisting.[48]

Children were the next beneficiaries of state wheat-and-meat diets. In the first decade of the twentieth century, as it became clear that hungry children did not do well in the newly compulsory primary education schools, states began providing lunches, at least to poor children. Led by Italy, countries offering lunch programs included the United States, Britain, Holland, Switzerland, Austria, Belgium, Denmark, Finland, Norway, Sweden, Germany, Spain, and Russia.

Even in the United States, with its comparative plenty, nutritionists such as Wilbur Atwater, businessmen such as Edward Atkinson, and home economists such as Ellen Richards—a pioneer in the home economics movement who had trained as a chemist and become an instructor at the Massachusetts Institute of Technology—campaigned to get the urban poor to eat more healthful food.[49] They urged them to purchase cheaper but equally nutritious cuts of meat, to cook them long and slowly, to serve meat, potatoes, bread, and vegetables separately for easier digestion, and to avoid pickles and spices, suggestions that usually fell on deaf ears.

The working class wanted cheap, quick food, not home-prepared meals that took hours to cook, needed expensive fuel, and required more pantry and kitchen space than most of them had in their tiny living quarters. When they had a little extra cash, they preferred to spend it on a nice piece of meat instead of beans or other worthy foods. For men, a drink at a bar was a way to escape from a family crowded into a single room or the tedium of a boardinghouse existence.

Bread, unlike gruels and porridges, could be bought warm from the bakery to make a comforting meal. It could be carried to the mine or the factory, be divided into equal portions, eaten with the fingers, used as a plate for a bit of fat, cheese, pickle, or bacon, or made into a sandwich. The British poor, who spent as much as 40 to 80 percent of their weekly income on bread, knew exactly why they preferred it white.[50] Whiteness suggested purity, desirable when so much food was adulterated. White bread was easy to chew and palatable even without expensive accompaniments. Unlike wholemeal bread, with its indigestible bran and fiber that loosened the bowels, it was easy to assimilate—important as farm laborers took less active jobs as spinners, weavers, and clerks—and probably yielded more calories. When wheat's weight per volume, its ease and yield in

FIGURE 7.5. Australian drovers sharing tea and "damper"—unleavened campfire bread—in the Australian bush. Drovers received rations of white flour, sugar, and tea to sustain them, together with meat from stock they killed, for the months they would spend working in the outback. They prepared damper with flour and water and baked it in the ashes. From Troedel & Co., *Australasian Sketcher*, supplement, June 1883. Courtesy Australian National Library.

grinding, and its relatively low cost of baking compared to, say, barley, were taken into account, white bread worked out to be only slightly more expensive than coarser breads. White bread, in sum, was desired not simply because it was the food of the rich and powerful, but because it had many virtues as a staple, virtues long recognized by anyone who could afford it. British demand for bread, the major item in the diet, increased fourfold in the hundred years between 1770 and 1870; three-quarters of this increase was due to a threefold growth in population, and one part to people switching from other grains to wheat bread. In the 1770s, wheat made up 60 percent of Britain's breadstuffs; by the 1860s, it had reached 90 percent.

Bread, meat, sugar, and tea or coffee were standard fare for pioneers, settlers, overlanders, and farmhands in Canada, the United States, Argentina, Australia, and New Zealand (fig. 7.5). Bakers migrated around the world to supply the demand for white bread and hardtack. In Argentina, Italian bakers led the labor movement. In Honolulu, Hawaii, two Chinese bakers from Canton, known as Sam and Mow, used flour shipped from the East Coast of the United States to bake bread and hardtack to supply the American whalers who wintered there in the 1840s.

Urban wage earners turned to street foods and takeout. In the United States, the frankfurter, which used the by-products of the meat-packing industry and was precooked in the factory, required only a quick turn on a grill or a dunk in boiling water before being served on a bun. In Britain, tripe and meat pies were popular in northern cities, and eels, pie and mash, baked potatoes, and sausages were favorites in the south. By the 1920s, fish and chips had become the most popular takeout, particularly in the industrial cities of the midlands, north, and Scotland.[51] More than thirty thousand fish and chip shops turned out batter-dipped fish fillets and soft fried potatoes seasoned with malt vinegar and salt, with a side of big, mushy canned peas, reminiscent of pease pudding. Bundled up in layers of newspaper, the food stayed hot as people ate it on the street or took it home.

Fish and chips probably originated in London's East End in the 1860s, when an unknown entrepreneur offered deep-fried potatoes alongside typical Sephardic Jewish fried fish. From London, the combination spread north, often prepared by Italian immigrants looking for a way to make a living. Measured by the number of outlets opened, fish and chip shops became the fastest-growing branch of the retail trade (corner sweet shops were the nearest competitors). More than half the fish caught in British waters and about one-sixth of British potatoes went into fish and chips. Newly invented steam trawlers stayed out for weeks at a time in the bitter waters of the North Sea and North Atlantic, shipping cheap plaice and haddock back to Hull, Grimsby, and other ports to be sent by rail to the cities. The proprietors of fish and chip shops bought frying ranges, refrigerating equipment, and potato washing, peeling, and chipping machines from British manufacturers, coal from British mines, cheap cottonseed oil from Egypt and the United States, and cheap beef fat from Argentina. While the middling and upper classes derided fish and chips as unpalatable, indigestible, and a waste of good money that should have gone for plain home cooking, the working class disagreed. Fish and chips warmed the insides, kept Father out of the pub and home with the family, and, many believed, helped win World War I and prevented a revolution. They may well have been right.

Consumption of bread, meats, fats, sugar, and tea soared in the industrializing countries. British meat eating increased by 20 percent between 1880 and 1900; German consumption went from 59 pounds a year per person in 1873 to 105 in 1912.[52] The French ate 50 percent more butter in 1884 than in 1870.[53] Margarine, half the price of butter, became the staple fat of the working class in Europe and beyond. After World War I, one-pound packages and brand names increased margarine's popularity, and consumption jumped from 550,000 tons in 1913 to 1 million tons in 1925, and 2½ million tons in 1965.[54]

Until midcentury, British annual sugar consumption stood at about twenty pounds a head. The poor had obtained much of their sugar in the form of by-products such as molasses or treacle, but when the British government removed the duty on sugar in 1874, it became cheap enough for most people to enjoy in their tea or coffee, or in the form of candy or jam. Britons consumed twice as much beet as cane sugar. By the 1880s, beets provided two-thirds of the world supply, much of it produced by government-supported programs in central and eastern Europe.[55] The British consumed a third more sugar in 1900 than in 1880, while the Germans, who consumed twelve pounds per person per annum in 1870, were putting away thirty-four pounds in 1907. Australians consumed eighty-five pounds for every man, woman and child in 1882 and a hundred pounds by 1900. Housewives spent as much as 8.4 percent of the family budget on sugar.[56] Around 1900, tea in London cost approximately half what it did in Saint Petersburg, supposedly the trend-setter for one of the world's great tea-drinking countries, and as a result, Britons used seven pounds of tea leaves a head per annum to Russians' one pound.[57]

To conclude these sections on middling cuisines, it is worth noting that few cuisines have been so roundly condemned as nutritional and gastronomical disasters as British cuisine, and that there is near-unanimity about the causes of these presumed failings. According to historian Avner Offer, Britain had "the worst dietary heritage in Europe" in the nineteenth century, while anthropologist Sidney Mintz dismisses the sugar that the British enjoyed as "one of the people's opiates." The historian of British food Colin Spencer attributes the supposed poor quality of the cuisine to the lack of peasant cooking, urbanization, and the industrial kitchen with its canning, packaging, and freezing. Michael Symons, a historian of Australian cuisine, similarly bemoans "the lack of a peasant experience—or our total history of industrialization." Economist Paul Krugman points to England's "early industrialization and urbanization" as the reason that British food, with its greasy fish and chips and mushy peas, was "deservedly famous for its awfulness."[58]

It is time to reassess this consensus, not as a matter of national pride in the country in which I was raised, but because the judgments above are as much part of a wider distrust of modern cuisine, the nutrition transition, and middling cuisines as they are about British cuisine. To begin with, there was no single British cuisine at the end of the nineteenth century. Aristocrats, like aristocrats everywhere, dined on French cuisine. The bourgeoisie continued to eat gentry cuisine. And the cuisines of the urban salaried class, the working class, and the rural poor were distinct too. Moreover, the surveys, contemporary reports, and experience of more recent visitors on which these judgments are based, are questionable. Because Britain, like most nations until recently, did not have a restaurant tradition, the public food most accessible to visitors was working-class fare such as fish and chips. Well prepared, this can be excellent, but it is necessarily limited. Bourgeois and middle-class cuisine, confined to the home, and upper-class Anglo-French cuisine, prepared in grand houses and clubs, were almost impossible to sample. Turn-of-the-twentieth-century surveys and reports are taken at face value rather than as documents informed by the point of view of the wealthy. Since these documents had neither an earlier baseline for the diet nor a comparison with the diet of parallel groups in other parts of the world, their conclusions have to be taken with a pinch of salt.

Nutritionally, considerable research suggests that by the end of the century, the British poor had enough calories. After a couple of decades of scholarly debate in the latter half of the twentieth century, historians now agree that the working-class standard of living, of which food was a key part, may have declined in the early part of the Industrial Revolution, from about 1780 to 1850, causing considerable suffering, but that from then on it became markedly better than it had been in the eighteenth century. Economic historian Robert Fogel, after an incisive review of the recent research on the effect of infectious diseases on absorption of calories, stature, mortality, and mortality crises, concludes that both prior to and during the early Industrial Revolution, the humble in both country and city suffered from such chronic malnutrition that they had little energy for work. This accords with the judgment of historians Peter Garnsey, Piero Camporesi, and Steven Kaplan, discussed in chapter 1, that humble diets in classical antiquity, medieval Italy, and eighteenth-century France were so insecure that they seriously affected work and health. Fogel argues that it was "the huge increases in English productivity during the later part of the nineteenth and the early twentieth centuries that made it possible to feed even the poor at relatively high caloric levels."[59] So in terms of regular access to enough calories, the late-nineteenth-century British working-class diet was better than it had been at least in the eighteenth and nineteenth centuries. It was also better than the diets of working people in most other parts of the world, the United States, Canada, and Australasia excepted. Imported wheat, sugar, and oils processed into easily digestible and highly calorific white flour, white sugar, and fat gave the British working class enough to eat, something not to be sniffed at.

By our standards, the diet of the working poor was nutritionally unbalanced, lacking in fruits and vegetables. By the standards of the late nineteenth century, it was just what chemists and physicians advocated, supplying the carbohydrates, fats, protein (carbonaceous and nitrogenous elements), minerals, and water that were then believed, on the basis of the latest research, to be all that was needed for growth and health.

So far as gastronomy was concerned, middle- and working-class cuisine could not compare with high cuisine. The middle-class culinary philosophy that rejected the extravagance and snobbery associated with French cuisine and the pressure of preparing three meals a day for a large family could all too easily lead to a lack of care in the kitchen. The belief that middle-class children should be raised not to fuss over food but to eat what was on offer to prepare themselves for the exigencies of a life in the military or the colonial service could result in appalling food being served in schools. Moreover, both working- and middle-class cooks were trying to prepare more varied meals and more complicated dishes using previously unknown ingredients and unfamiliar kitchen equipment, undoubtedly resulting in many failed experiments.

Nonetheless, from the perspective of the urban salaried and working classes, the cuisine was what they had wished for over the centuries: white bread, white sugar, meat, and tea. A century earlier, not only were these luxuries for much of the British population, but the humble were being encouraged to depend on potatoes, not bread, a real comedown in a society in which some kind of bread, albeit a coarse one, had been central to well-being for centuries. Now all could enjoy foodstuffs that had been the privilege of the aristocracy just a few generations earlier. Indeed, the meal called tea came close to being a true national cuisine. Even though tea retained traces of class distinctions, with snobberies about how teacups should be held, or whether milk or tea should be put into the cup first, everyone in the country, from the royal family, who were painted taking tea, to the family of a textile worker in the industrial north of the country, could sit down to white bread sandwiches or toast, jam, small cakes, and an iced sponge cake as a centerpiece. They could afford the tea that accompanied the meal. Set out on the table, tea echoed the grand buffets of eighteenth-century French high cuisine. Middle- and working-class cooks rightly prided themselves on the quality of their offerings. What seemed like culinary decline to those Britons who had always dined on high or bourgeois cuisine was a vast improvement to those enjoying those ampler and more varied cuisines for the first time.

Finally, urbanization and industrial food processing, far from causing a decline, were largely responsible for the improved nutritional and gastronomic quality of Anglo cuisine. Cities, with their ability to import foodstuffs from far afield, had always had cuisines superior to those of the countryside. With railroads and steamship lines converging on the cities, the difference in the culinary options for urban dwellers and rural folk became yet more marked. Food processing provided new, more affordable, easier-to-use ingredients and freed up cooks at all levels of society, including the cooks who prepared French high cuisine, to spend more time on meal preparation, creating the sauces and sweet dishes long associated with high cuisines. For all the problems involved in this major historical change, on balance the shift to modern, middling cuisines was a big nutritional and gastronomic step up for the majority of people in the industrializing world. That is why so many other countries wanted to emulate Anglo cuisine.

Just as important, or perhaps even more so, this majority no longer had to suffer the indignity of watching the rich and powerful eat a high cuisine they could only dream of. Instead, most people could afford the same white bread and sugar, indulge in the same meats, at least on special occasions, and enjoy the same kinds of sauces and sweet dishes as the wealthy. Although to this day food continues to be used to reinforce minor differences in status, the hierarchical culinary philosophy of ancient and traditional cuisines was giving way to the more egalitarian culinary philosophy of modern cuisines.

THE HUMBLE CUISINES OF THE RURAL POOR

In contrast to the improved diet, nutrition, and cuisine of those living in the cities of Britain and other industrializing countries, the cuisines of the rural poor deteriorated almost everywhere as the world population increased. Most of those who worked the land were farmhands, sharecroppers, or indentured laborers rather than independent, landowning peasants. This segment remained the largest proportion of the population in most parts of the world, constituting 75 percent of the French population, 65 percent of Germans, and 82 percent of Austrians in 1850. In 1900, 80 percent of Japanese and 88 percent of Russians were still struggling to make a living on small plots.[60] When they grew wheat, sugar, or coffee, these went to the cities or were exported to the wealthier countries. In Italy through the 1930s, dried pasta was too expensive for 80 percent of the people. "Our Christmas treat was store-bought Neapolitan pasta, dry, in a box," explained a sharecropper about his childhood before World War II. "That was a special, rare treat. You see, most of our wheat was sold. We didn't eat pasta very much; we lived on polenta."[61] In Japan, a country short of land and with a population that doubled between 1870 and 1950 and grew from about thirty-four million people to about seventy million, peasants ate one-pot meals, usually low-quality brown rice mixed with lesser grains and root vegetables such as taro, daikon, and burdock and flavored with seaweed.[62] Tax collectors seized their rice. "You can always squeeze peasants and beans a little harder" went the saying. In China, where the population grew by two-thirds during the same period, between half and four-fifths of family spending went to food, mainly millet, sorghum, sweet potatoes, or maize. Meat, especially in the country, was a special treat reserved for festivals.[63] Famines continued to kill millions. Droughts between 1876 and 1879 and again between 1886 and 1900 claimed a terrible toll in places as far apart as India, China, Morocco, and Brazil.[64]

Two million people, most of them from India and China, but also from Japan and the Pacific, fled the harsh conditions of food shortage, political unrest, and outright famine by signing up as indentured laborers (map 7.1). They traveled to work on plantations from Southeast Asia to Australia. Wherever they settled, priests, small traders, and others followed to attend to their needs. Like other migrants, they took with them what was necessary to recreate their cuisine, including plant seeds and cuttings and cooking equipment. As a result, in much of Latin America, eastern and southern Africa, the Caribbean, and islands in the Indian and Pacific oceans, Indian, Cantonese, or Japanese cuisines jostled with those of the original inhabitants and of

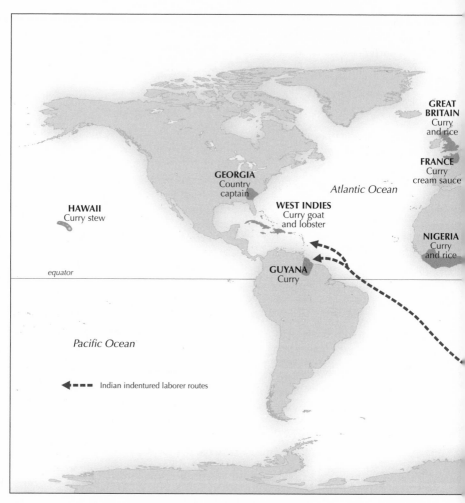

MAP 7.1. Curry and the expansion of Anglo cuisine. British colonists and Indian indentured laborers transferred curries (stews flavored with Indian spices) around the Anglo world in the nineteenth century in two distinct but overlapping routes. Anglo merchants offered curry powder to enliven stews in the Western world, its colonies, Hawaii, and Japan. Indian

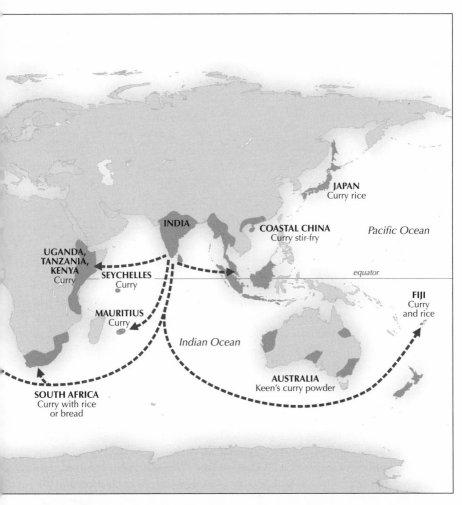

indentured laborers brought with them their traditional spiced stews, now identified as "curries." Arrows show Indian indentured-labor migrations. Sources: For curry: Sen, *Curry*. For migration routes of Indian indentured laborers: Northrup, *Indentured Labor in the Age of Imperialism,* map 1.

the Spanish, English, French, or Dutch settlers. In Hawaii, for example, the Japanese indentured laborers were guaranteed white rice in their contracts, and they and the Chinese quickly converted taro patches into rice paddies.[65]

New World crops continued to be urged on the poor, who rarely welcomed them with enthusiasm, though they staved off famine. The global acreage of potatoes increased with every war through World War II. Potatoes fed the populations of Germany and Russia, along with beer, beets, bread, and cabbage. During the Great Famine in Ireland (1840–41), the English bought maize from the United States to feed the hungry. The maize, however, was of a very hard variety known as flint corn, which had to be ground twice, not easy to do in potato-eating Ireland, where mills were scarce. Even when ground, it was not something the Irish knew how to cook, nor something they wanted to eat, since it was regarded as cattle feed. When they did cook it, they found it gave them diarrhea. They called it brimstone. Maize porridge, beer, and other preparations (*kenkey*) became staples in East and Central Africa.[66] On the plains of Bihar (on the Ganges in India), where fuel was scarce, the poor roasted maize and barley periodically and ground it to a powder (*sattu*) that they could eat cold with chiles, onions, and salt.[67] Maize, sweet potatoes, and potatoes were the fallbacks of Japanese peasants when famine threatened. Maize polenta was the food of poor Italians and Romanians. It had become "nine-tenths of the entire daily food" in much of northern Italy, according to a report to the Milan Academy of Sciences in 1845.[68] Compared to the poor in the industrial cities, the rural poor in many parts of the world were reduced to eating ever more humble cuisines.

THE GLOBALIZATION OF FRENCH HIGH CUISINE

At the other end of the social scale, French high cuisine continued to spread around the globe. It was the preferred cuisine of monarchies—including the new ones created in Greece, Belgium, and Hawaii—and of aristocrats and monied people everywhere, at least on those occasions when demonstrating membership in a cosmopolitan global elite was required. In courts and clubs it could be experienced only by invitation or membership. In restaurants, hotels, railroad dining cars, and steamship dining rooms, it could be purchased at a price.

To eat French cuisine was to be civilized. "France has been the center, the focus of European civilization," announced François Guizot, France's leading historian and soon-to-be minister of the interior, in a series of packed public lectures at the Sorbonne in 1828. Guizot's *Histoire de la civilisation en Europe* (published in 1828 and translated by William Hazlitt in 1846 as *The History of Civilization in Europe*) became part of the French heritage, read by successive generations of French schoolchildren. France was the crossroads of "the civilized peoples" said Paul Vidal de La Blache, the star of France's outstanding group of geographers, at the end of the century. France excelled in both food and civilization—high cuisine was "a school of courtesy and a system of cooking," said Maurice Sailland, France's most famous writer on gastronomy, who was usually known by his pen name, Curnonsky. Germany and the United States, on the other hand, were "barbaric," as was their cuisine.[69] Monarchs and aristocrats worldwide, who felt they had more in common with other ruling classes than with the middle and working classes of their own nations, formed an international upper caste united by their culture, including French cuisine, and by a shared vision of progress toward the kind of civilization that many granted that France had achieved.[70] When the Japanese, following their forcible opening to the West in 1854, decided to adapt Western culture, including cuisine, to their own ends, their slogan was "civilization and enlightenment."

French cuisine, its promoters insisted, was the culmination of a heritage that stretched back through the Middle Ages to Greece and Rome (ignoring the intervening pan-European Catholic cuisine), just as aristocrats were the product of family trees that went back to the mists of time. Wine, for example, France's second-largest export after textiles, its production revolutionized by science and technology in the late nineteenth century, was marketed as owing its excellence to the soil in which it grew (the *terroir*) and centuries of aristocratic tradition. In 1850, only one of the leading Bordeaux wines (Margaux) was prefixed with the word "Château." Then French vineyard owners began tacking gothic-looking towers onto substantial farmhouses, calling them châteaus and, taking advantage of the new technique of color lithography, placing their pictures on their bottle labels. By 1900, every leading Bordeaux producer used the word "château," leading one historian to comment that there are "few better examples of the invention of tradition than the process that some wines underwent in this period."[71] As a marketing strategy, promoting wine that was produced using the most modern of techniques as ancient and handmade was such a successful ploy that it was soon copied by cheese makers and, in the later twentieth century, by the food industry more generally.

French scientists and technologists, seen as leading contributors to the nation's progress and civilization, were also celebrated as contributing to its cuisine. Louis Pasteur, who loved wine, discovered it could be prevented from souring, a problem for the wine industry, by gently heating it to 50 degrees Centigrade. Scientists at the Académie des sciences and the University of Montpellier led the fight against phylloxera, the aphid that was destroying French vineyards. Marcellin Berthelot, the leading French chemist at the end of the nineteenth century, contributed to food science by showing that all chemical phenomena, including sugars and fats, depended on physical forces, not on a mysterious and nonreproducible life force. Nicolas Appert, a Parisian chef and confectioner, invented canning, making it possible to serve French cuisine anywhere. In the much-quoted phrase of the early-nineteenth-century gastronome Brillat-Savarin, cooking was "the most important of the arts [in the sense of skill, craft, industry] . . . the art which has rendered the most important services to civic life."[72]

French cuisine, as Carême, the leading chef in the first half of the nineteenth century, had said, was the "escort to European diplomacy." A French chef, Monsieur Cloup, was an essential member of the retinue of Lord Auckland, governor-general of India, when he met the ruler of Afghanistan in 1837 in Simla in the Himalayan foothills to make sure he favored British interests, not Russian ones.[73] When the Mexicans wanted to celebrate victory over the French in 1862, they dined on French cuisine. When King Rama V of Thailand held state functions for Western diplomats and advisors, partly as a courtesy, partly because the ordered sequence of courses lent itself to diplomacy, he served French cuisine.[74] When the emperor of Japan invited eight hundred guests to dinner in his new European-style palace in Tokyo in 1889, once again it was French cuisine that was offered. The event was, said Mary Fraser, wife of the British ambassador, just like "official dinner parties in Rome or Paris or Vienna." The tricky utensils, glasses, porcelain, silver, and linen were perfectly handled. Another guest reported that since conversation was impossible, her companions entertained her by using their bread to model tiny men and horses.[75] To Mary Fraser, it was self-evident that a state dinner, even in a nation such as Japan, with its own high cuisine and no previous exposure to French cuisine, would be French. A rare exception seems to have been the imperial palace in Beijing. Although the emperor Qianlong may have tasted a Western meal prepared by Jesuits in 1753, the imperial kitchens continued to serve high Chinese cuisine.[76]

The newly rich modeled their lifestyles on those of the old aristocracy. In Paris, where money poured in when Napoleon imposed heavy taxes on his huge, if short-lived, European empire, the beneficiaries dined at expensive restaurants with mirrored walls, chandeliers, and small tables set with fine linens and tableware, where they made their selections from fixed-price menus. These French restaurants soon appeared in other cities. In Moscow in the 1860s, the Russian-Belgian chef Lucien Olivier presided over the Hermitage restaurant, serving French burgundy, sturgeon in champagne, saddle of lamb, salads, and *bombe surprise*. In Mexico City, the well-to-do went to the Maison Dorée and Prendés, in Melbourne to the Union Hotel, in New York to the eight Delmonico's restaurants, and in London to the Ritz, reigned over by Auguste Escoffier, whose modernization of Carême's elaborate style made him one of the most influential of all French chefs in the late nineteenth century.[77] In Kyoto, Itani Ichirobe opened a French restaurant in his house in 1910, after being sent to the West to learn how to cook after a recession hit his textile-manufacturing family. He covered tatami mats with plush carpeting, installed tables and chairs, and set the tables with Mappin & Webb silverware, purchased with the fruits of a lucky win while gambling in Monte Carlo.[78] In London, and later in many other cities, clubs, an outgrowth of London coffeehouses, hired French chefs so that their members could dine in the company of like-minded members rather than in restaurants open to anyone who could pay.[79] Clubs serving French high cuisine were soon found in large cities everywhere (table 7.1).

TABLE 7.1 Examples of the Global Spread of French High Cuisine

	Royal court	Restaurant, hotel, or club	Chef	Bakery, patisserie, or high-end grocery
Paris	—	Grand Hôtel, Café Anglais, La Tour d'Argent, Jockey Club	Marie-Antoine Carême, Jules Gouffé, Joseph Favre, Prosper Montagné, Edouard Nignon	Fauchon, Le Bon Marché
London	Queen Victoria of England	Ritz Hotel, Savoy Hotel, Claridges Hotel, Crockfords Club, Athaneum Club, Reform Club	Louis Eustache Ude, Marie-Antoine Carême, Antoine Beauvilliers, Alexis Soyer, Chales Elmé Francatelli, Edouard Nignon, Auguste Escoffier	Harrods, Fortnum & Mason, Army & Navy Stores
Berlin	King Friedrich Wilhelm IV of Prussia	Central Hotel, Hotel Adler	Urban Dubois, Emile Bernard, Joseph Favre	Kaufhaus des Westens
Vienna/Budapest	Emperor Franz Josef I of Austria	Gundel, Hotel Grand Sacher, István Foherceg Hotel, Jockey Club, Casino Club	József Marchal, József Dobos, Károly Gundel, Eduoard Nignon	—
Saint Petersburg/ Moscow	Emperor Alexander I of Russia	Hermitage Restaurant	A. Petit, Urban Dubois, Lucien Olivier, Edouard Nignon	The Passage
New York	—	Delmonico's, Waldorf-Astoria, Hoffman House	—	—
Mexico City	Emperor Maximilian I of Mexico	Tívoli, Prendés, Maison Dorée, Café Colon, Jockey Club	Sylvain Daumont, Mauricio Porraz	El Globo, Palacio de Hierro, Deverdun
Saigon	—	Hotel Continental, Bodega Restaurant, Le Cercle Sportif	—	La Civette
Calcutta/ Bombay/ Madras/New Delhi	Lord Curzon, Viceroy of India	Taj Mahal Hotel, Bengal Club, Calcutta Club	—	Peliti, Whitely, Tulloh & Co.
Tokyo/Kyoto	The Meiji Emperor	Tsukiji Hotel, Imperial Hotel, Seiyoken Hotel, Fujimiken, Manyoken	—	Meidi-ya, Mitsukoshi, Shirokiya, Takashimaya

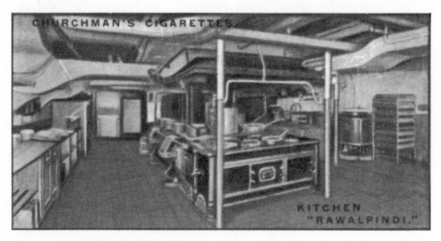

FIGURE 7.6. The modern professional kitchen, such as the one shown here for the SS *Rawalpindi,* a British ocean liner launched in 1925, was spacious and carefully organized. The *Rawalpindi* kitchen, with sinks on the left, stoves in the center, and trays for baked goods on the right, produced meals for over three hundred passengers in first class and two hundred and eighty-eight in second class. Cooks, hired at one port and leaving the ship at another, helped disseminate French cuisine, which was served even on Japanese lines. From Churchman's Cigarette Cards, 1930. Courtesy New York Public Library http://digitalgallery.nypl.org/nypldigital/id?1803781.

The professional kitchens of French high cuisine were places of cast and forged iron: closed iron ranges, metal pans, and steel knives (fig. 7.6). The workers were organized in assembly lines. Departing from the practice of assigning one team to one dish, Escoffier assigned each team to a specific station, where they prepared sauces, cooked meats, and assembled the final dish. The chef, the head of the team, gave orders to the sous-chef, who in turn bossed the apprentices, or *commis,* who did the drudge work of forcing mixtures through sieves and straining liquids through cheesecloth and were in turn senior to the dishwashers and cleaners.

White flour, butter, sugar, meat stocks and reductions, eggs, and wine were the bases of the sauces and sweets of French high cuisine, combined in a variety of different ways. Sauces, now made separately instead of as part of individual dishes, were adjusted with different seasonings, then served with meat or fish. "Mother" sauces with a codified series of names were established. *Sauce espagnole,* made with a dark brown roux, meat stock, and seasonings, was the foundation for all brown sauces. Béchamel and velouté, made with a light roux and either milk or veal or fish stock, were used for lighter sauces. Mixed with eggs, they became the basis for soufflés, mixed with gelatin, the basis for chaudfroids for coating cold dishes. Ragouts and fricassees came to mean, respectively, stews and lightly sau-téed meats cooked in a white sauce.

Crème anglaise, a custard of milk, sugar, and egg yolks, could be used as a des-sert sauce or as a filling for *pâte à choux,* or it could be combined with whipped cream and whipped egg whites to make a *crème bavaroise.* Minor differences in technique produced different textures: fat and flour made *pâte brisée, pâte à choux,* or *pâte feuilletée* (puff pastry), which could be used in savory dishes with roux-based sauces or in sweet dishes with crème anglaise. Thus from a few basic prepa-rations, the cooks could prepare a vast assortment of dazzling dishes.

The most popular meats were beef, lamb, veal, game, and the very expensive chicken, with pork being relegated mainly to pâtés. Fish included turbot, halibut, and sole. Along with the appropriate sauce, meats and fish were also accompanied by carefully cut but simply cooked vegetables, such as carrots, small onions, pota-toes, peas, and asparagus. Favored fruits were pears, cherries, peaches, strawber-ries, and raspberries.

Consistent with their commitment to progress, science, and technology, French chefs enthusiastically welcomed processed foods such as white flour and white sugar, as well as canned goods. Escoffier used commercially prepared stocks and essences, endorsed Maggi's ham, anchovy, and mushroom essence (for a fee), and found canned carrots, green beans and peas, peaches, and cherries a boon when these fruits and vegetables were out of season. Alexis Soyer, the most celebrated French chef in Victorian England, was one of many who produced a branded essence. Indeed, without canned goods, it would have been difficult to replicate French cuisine around the world. Canned butter from France or Denmark made it possible to make French sauces and desserts even where there was no dairy indus-try. Canned caviar, paté, and salmon were staples of the well-to-do pantry. Canned asparagus was available in Tokyo, Madras, and Saigon (a soup of crab and canned asparagus remains a Vietnamese specialty). When His Highness Nawab Sir Sadiq Muhammad Khan Abbasi V was installed as ruler of Bahawalpur State in northern India in 1907, a meal of soup, pâté, salmon in béchamel sauce, roast game birds, crème caramel, a savory on toast, and coffee was served.[80] Except for the game birds, the béchamel sauce, and the toast, the Goan cooks brought in to prepare it had only to open cans.

Explaining and teaching French cuisine became a growth industry, with Paris firmly at the center, ensuring that its cuisine did not devolve into many subcui-sines. Cookbooks multiplied. Carême published *Le Patissier royal parisien* (The Royal Parisian Pastry Chef) in 1815, *Le Cuisinier parisien* (The Parisian Chef) in 1828, and, with Plumery, *L'Art de la cuisine française* (The Art of French Cooking) in 1833. Then came *La Cuisine classique* (Classic Cuisine) by Urbain Dubois and Émile Bernard in 1856 and Jules Gouffé's *Le Livre de cuisine* (The Book of Cuisine) in 1867. At the beginning of the twentieth century, three more magisterial tomes appeared: *Le Grand livre de cuisine* (The Great Book of Cuisine) by Prosper Montagné and Prosper Salles (1900 and 1929), *Le Guide culinaire* (The Culinary Guide) by Escoffier in 1903, and the *Larousse gastronomique,* by Montagné in partnership with Alfred Gottschalk, in 1938.

Other cookbooks explained how to prepare French high cuisine in foreign countries. In Britain, such books appeared every few years, some of the more important being Beauvillier's *Art of French Cookery* (1825), Soyer's *Modern Housewife* (1852), and Escoffier's *Complete Guide to Modern Cookery* (translated from the French in 1903). Russians could turn to A. Petit's *Gastronomy in Russia* (Paris, 1860), Hungarians to the *Hungarian-French Cookbook* (not dated but early twentieth century) by József Dobos (of the eponymous torte), and Americans to Charles Ranhofer's thousand-page *Epicurean* (1894). In 1885, *Culinary Jottings: A Treatise . . . on Reformed Cookery for Anglo-Indian Exiles* by "Wyvern," aka Colonel A. R. Kenney-Herbert, presented the "enlightened system of [French] cookery."

The new rich, not having been raised in households where comportment and gastronomy were part of the routine, turned to critics and etiquette guides. In 1803, Alexandre Grimod de la Reynière began publishing critical reviews of restaurants in his *Almanach des gourmands,* which continued until 1812 in annual volumes. Just over a decade later, in a last attempt to gain recognition, Jean-Anthelme Brillat-Savarin, an aging intellectual, published his *Physiologie du goût* (1825; *Physiology of Taste*), which the diplomat Talleyrand found full of handy aphorisms. In 1887, the Japanese court hired Ottmar von Mohl, formerly in the service of Emperor Wilhelm in Berlin, to teach the courtiers how to dress and behave at a French dinner, including putting them through a full dress rehearsal without any other foreigners present.

The globalization of French cuisine depended on hundreds of cooks willing to travel. Ten thousand cooks emigrated from Paris, by one count. Young peasant boys apprenticed themselves in large kitchens and put up with years of drudgery. Once trained, they leaped at well-paying overseas positions, hoping to save enough to open a small restaurant on return to their homeland.[81] There were five thousand French cooks in London alone in the 1890s. Swiss, Belgians, Armenians, Italians, English, Hungarians, Russians, and Japanese apprenticed in Paris before returning to their homelands.

The observation of the English gourmet Lieutenant Colonel Nathaniel Newnham-Davis that "all the great missionaries of cuisine have gone forth from Paris" was not quite correct, however. Many aspiring to be French cooks mastered the art in the new Swiss hotel schools. Others in London, Saint Petersburg, and Vienna learned from French or French-trained cooks, Escoffier himself claiming to have trained thousands of English cooks. In Saint Petersburg and Moscow, French cooks trained Russian serfs so that their masters could sell them for a high price. In Tolstoy's *War and Peace,* Count Rostov boasts of paying a thousand rubles for the serf who prepared hazel grouse sautéed in Madeira on the name day of his daughter Natasha.[82] In Italy, French cooks in the great baronial houses trained Sicilian cooks, who came to be called *monzu,* from the French "monsieur."

Two thousand Escoffier students emigrated from England, and many taught others the skills in their new locations. Cooks from Moscow or Saint Petersburg went to work in Kiev and Odessa, or, after the 1917 revolution, in Istanbul and Paris.[83] Cooks trained in Vienna or Budapest went to Athens, like the Greek Nikolaos Tselementes, who returned home to work in the Austrian embassy, or to Mexico City, like the Hungarian Tüdös, cook to Emperor Maximilian. The French-Belgian Genin family ran the Casa Deverdum in Mexico City. The French cook of the governor of Calcutta earned a little extra by giving cooking classes. Italian cooks trained in the French style worked in the kitchens of British steamships, training Goans, who as Christians had no qualms about eating beef and pork, and who then set up restaurants and cake shops in Bombay.[84] Cooks in the British and French enclaves in China sent their trainees to work in Japan. Many Vietnamese picked up French culinary techniques when serving French troops, watching French cooks, or washing dishes in French cafés.[85] In his *Culinary Jottings,* Colonel Kenney-Herbert, quartermaster at Madras (now Chenai) in southern India, relates how he used Jules Gouffé's *Book of Cuisine* (1867) to teach "Ramasámy" (a widely used name for an Indian cook) French cooking.[86] He had to get rid of his grindstone, scrub the soot off the kitchen walls, use canned vegetables from French or American companies (never British), become proficient with patty pans, fish kettles, and Warren's cooking pot (a kind of bain-marie), and master white and brown sauces.

Also necessary for French cuisine to spread worldwide were waiters, butchers, and bakers as well as shops in which to buy china, cutlery, dining room furniture, and canned goods. Waiters traveled from summer resorts and spas to city restaurants and from country to country. French butchers and bakers practiced their trades in Saigon. Chinese who had learned Western-style baking opened bakeries in Shanghai, Saigon, and Honolulu.[87] Bakers from Germany and Italy arrived in Rio with the Portuguese court in 1808.[88] By the end of the nineteenth century, shoppers could go to department stores in Paris, London, New York, Calcutta, Mexico City, Tokyo, and other major cities to buy all the European goods needed to put on a dinner.

Outside France, and particularly outside Europe, French cuisine, like all earlier high cuisines, was adapted to local tastes, while local dishes were refined to be more like the high cuisine, a process that can be traced through a multitude of cookbooks.[89] "French cooking has invaded our kitchens," said the author of a major nineteenth-century Mexican culinary dictionary, who found it "indispensable to Mexicanize" the recipes.[90] French cuisine was not simply Mexicanized but, depending on location, Austrianized, Russianized, Greekized, Indianized, and Siamized.[91] One way to do this was to serve small boneless cuts or shaped ground-meat patties that in much of the world were commoner than the roasts and steaks of Europe, including France. Cutlets, croquettes, and escalopes spread around the world as thin pieces of meat, or ground meat or fish mixed with béchamel or mashed potatoes, and breaded and fried. In Latin America, they are called *milanesas;* in Persia, they are *kotlets* flavored with saffron and turmeric, wrapped in fresh greens, and served with flatbread; in India, they are *cutlis;* in Indonesia, they are *kroke;* in Japan, *korokke.* Another move was to add a discreet hint of local spicing or a local ingredient to a dish. Omelets, for example were flavored with coriander or bulked up with chickpea flour in India (*amlates*), while in Persia they were stuffed with dates (*omlets*).

To refine local dishes and make them taste more French, cooks reduced the spices and used butter instead of mutton fat, lard, or vegetable oil. In the most popular Greek cookbook, *Odigos Mageirihes* (1910; Guide to Cooking), which sold 100,000 copies by the author's death in 1958, Nikolaos Tselementes recommends cutting down on oil and spices to rid Greek dishes of "the influence and contamination they suffered trying to conform to the taste of the Eastern peoples, so that they don't appear too greasy, over spiced and unappealing."[92] In Russia, cooks anointed kasha with butter.[93] Adding French sauces was a sure way to make a dish seem French. A vinaigrette (*vinagrety* in Russian, French dressing in the United States) was essential to a French green salad; mayonnaise turned cold meats, fish, and cooked vegetables into something French.[94] Béchamel was by far the most useful sauce for making a dish appear French. Béchamel, parmesan, and mushrooms transformed Russian *pirozkhi* into "little Caucasian pastries." A puree of béchamel, made with milk, cream, or egg yolks (*sup-pyur*) made cabbage soup (*shchi*) and (*borscht*) acceptable for fine dining. Local vegetables (eggplant, moringa, and pumpkin in India) or fish (snapper in Mexico) became respectable when covered with béchamel.[95] Pastries, both sweet and savory, lent a refined French touch. So too did French-style desserts such as a mousse or soufflé. Light, airy vol-au-vents filled with oysters (probably from a can) were a favorite entrée from Mexico to Vietnam.[96]

Cooks also invented new dishes that combined local ingredients with French techniques. Russian salad (cooked chopped vegetables in mayonnaise) and beef Stroganov (thin strips of beef quickly sautéed with mushrooms and cream) were Russian French-style inventions. Moussaka topped with egg-enriched béchamel, which we think of as typically Greek, and likewise Greek pastitsio (pasta, béchamel sauce, and ground beef) were Tselementes's modifications of dishes previously served without the béchamel. Lasagna (sheet pasta, meat sauce, and béchamel) was a northern Italian French-style invention. Kenney-Herbert reinvented Indian chicken curry (probably the white, nut-thickened korma that was the pride of Mughal cuisine) "as a *fricassée* or a *blanquette à l'Indienne.*" Siamese court cooks had mastered French cuisine to the point of playing culinary jokes: their chicken chaudfroid gleamed in a creamy white gelatinous sauce just like the French original of béchamel and gelatin. It was made, though, of minced chicken flavored with lemon grass and coated with coconut agar-agar (a gelatin made of seaweed).[97] Back in Europe, the Westernization of curry was completed by Escoffier, whose *emincé de volaille au curry* was chicken in a béchamel sauce flavored with a hint of curry powder.[98]

Diners often combined courses or meals from their own cuisine with French high cuisine. English aristocrats ate English breakfasts and afternoon teas, and added a savory course after dessert. Japanese ended French meals with green tea poured over hot rice. Romanians began French dinners with sour soup (*borsch*) and ended with rice and meat (*pilaf*).[99] Mexicans, at least at home, could not resist placing a bowl of chiles on the table so that they could add a touch of piquancy to French dishes. Sometimes these additions became central to high cuisine even in France. What would celebrations have been without Russian caviar?

New French-style dishes were created in and disseminated from countries other than France. Russians introduced Russian salad to Turkey, where it is now established in well-to-do home cookery, *cottlets* to Iran, and, by the mid-twentieth century, beef Stroganov from New York to Kathmandu.[100] Austro-Hungarians spread their variant of French cuisine to Prague, Bucharest, and Belgrade. Recipes for a buttery macedoine of vegetables, roast beef, roux, béchamel sauce, and *crème patisserie* jostle alongside classics of Ottoman high cuisine such as yogurt and garlic sauces and baklava in Balkan cookbooks.[101] In Athens, Cairo, and Alexandria cooks also turned out ragouts, mayonnaise, and soufflés.[102]

French cuisine appealed for its cachet—as a badge of belonging to the international elite—but not necessarily for its taste. What Europeans praised as creamy, Japanese disliked as cloying and greasy. What Europeans appreciated as subtle, Indians thought lacked the sophisticated spicing of their palace cooks. Chinese preferred eating with spoons and chopsticks, Turks with spoons, and Indians with their fingers. The jangle of metal on porcelain sounded crude to Japanese; being accustomed to eating in silence, they found it hard to keep up the required flow of small talk.[103] So that they could serve both French cuisine and their own cuisine, those who could afford to often maintained two kitchens, one for each. Nawaab Sadaat Ali Khan of Lucknow had two kitchens as early as 1800.[104] A century later, the gaekwar of Baroda (India) employed a French cook and an English butler, while his Indian cooks prepared Maratha cuisine. The Japanese imperial court, wealthy samurai, and merchants in Edo and Osaka reserved Western cuisine (*yôshoku*) for state occasions and kept it fastidiously separate from Japanese high cuisine (*washoku*), which was based on white rice, fish, and vegetables.

The price of adopting French cuisine, thus declaring that you were a modern, progressive, civilized nation, could be high. On 12 February 1883, David Kalākaua, Hawaii's king, offered a coronation banquet. On a world tour, Kalākaua had noticed that U.S. president Chester Arthur and modern monarchs in Japan, Siam, Egypt, Italy, and England all served French dinners as part of diplomatic protocol. To show that his government was on a par with theirs, he decided to serve French cuisine. By doing so, he distanced himself from the traditional meal of Hawaiian chiefs—an all-male affair with women excluded on pain of death if they broke the taboo, taken seated on the ground around a calabash of cooked pounded taro (poi). French dinners, though, could not be offered without the correct serving utensils, dining room, and splendid building to house the dining room. Prior to the coronation, he hired architects and builders to construct a palace, ordered oak Gothic Revival furniture from the Davenport Company in Boston, sent to Paris for blue-bordered porcelain with the Hawaiian coat-of-arms, and imported crystal from Bohemia. His subjects gave him a solid silver centerpiece from Germany, and he hung the portraits and clock that European monarchs had given him.[105] The Anglo-French menu began with mulligatawny, turtle, Windsor, and à la Reine soups. The fish was largely Hawaiian. Wild duck, pheasant, fillet of veal, turkey with truffle sauce, beef à la mode, ham, roast goose, and curry followed, the wild duck and pheasant, at least, imported since they are not found in Hawaii. They were served with potatoes, peas, tomatoes, corn, asparagus, spinach, and taro, many of which must have been canned. For dessert there were wine jelly, sponge cake, and strawberries and ice cream. All this was washed down with sherry, hock, claret, champagne, port, liqueurs, tea and coffee.

The palace, which cost over $360,000, the dining paraphernalia, and the coronation were paid for from taxes levied on sugar plantation owners, at a time when the island population was about 57,000 and the total exports about $5 million a year.[106] The plantation faction, most of them New Englanders, had little use for the idea that lavish monarchical displays were modern, being rather of the persuasion that the future lay with republicanism, including modest republican dining. They preferred middle-class thrift to royal magnificence. By 1893, the monarchy had been overthrown and Hawaii had been declared a republic, and by 1898 it had been annexed to the United States. Although much more was at stake in the overthrow than a lavish coronation dinner, it is a poignant reminder of the seriousness of the issues behind debates about monarchical versus republican dining.

INDUSTRIAL KITCHENS

The expansion of middling cuisines and the globalization of French high cuisine went hand in hand with the greatest revolution in cooking since the mastery of grains—the culmination of a change that had been going on ever since the first commercial grain mills, bakeries, and sugar refineries: a division into processing in industrial kitchens and final meal preparation in domestic, restaurant, and institutional kitchens. Both kitchens were now powered by fossil fuels. The industrial kitchen benefitted from the latest food science and technology. The new urban and working classes who ate middling cuisines provided a market big enough to support large-scale processing. Conversely, the economies of scale of industrial processing freed up domestic labor and brought down food prices, enabling more people to take jobs and to afford middling cuisine. The key period in the industrialization of food processing occurred late in the Industrial Revolution, between the 1860s and the beginning of World War I. Germany, a leader in science and engineering by this stage, the Low Countries, Britain, the United States, Japan, and France were the first countries to undergo this transition.

The French refinery depicted in figure 7.7, which converted sugar-beet juice into fine granulated sugar, is typical of the new industrial kitchen, owned by a multinational business, using fossil fuel, benefitting from government-sponsored scientific research, and producing affordable foodstuffs for the market rather than luxury foodstuffs for the court.[107] The research leading to the extraction of sugar from beets had been carried out a century earlier by the chemist Andreas Marggraf, who was working at the Prussian Academy of Sciences in Berlin. Chopped sweet root vegetables such as carrots, skirrets (water parsnips), and mangel-wurzels were macerated in water and the impurities precipitated with limewater; sugar was crystallized from the remaining solution. Nineteenth-century engineers scaled up the process using condensing pans to speed evaporation, centrifuges to spin the sugar crystals out of the solution, chlorine to bleach it a snowy white, and steam engines to power the process. Sugar could now be made from roots, not cane. The energy came from fossil fuels, not from oxen, wind, or water. The work was done by men paid salaries or wages, not by slaves or indentured laborers. The sugar was produced in northern Europe, not in tropical colonies. And the price was one all Europeans could afford.

Mechanical, thermal, chemical, and biochemical processing became both more powerful and more controlled with the help of coal-fueled steam engines instead of human, animal, or water power. Steam engines, and later electric motors, pushed stalks of sugarcane through horizontal metal rollers to extract the juice, ran grains of rice through belts that polished off the brown husk, and pummeled chocolate until it was no longer coarse and grainy. They spun centrifuges that separated sugar crystals from their solution, yeast from the liquid in which it grew, and cream from milk. They powered the conveyor belts along which hog and cattle carcasses were disassembled; flour was turned into bread, crackers, and cookies; and meats, vegetables, milk, and fruits were canned. Mechanical drills drove pipes into underground saltwater reservoirs, and the brine that was pumped out was evaporated using fossil fuels. Salt, which until then had been a scarce and expensive commodity for cooking and manufacturing, as well as a symbol of constancy and loyalty, plummeted in price so that cooks used it without a second thought. Pumps reduced the air pressure in vacuum pans, evaporating sugar solutions more

FIGURE 7.7. In the late nineteenth century, some three hundred sugar-beet refineries, such as this one in Abbeville, dotted the landscape of Picardy in northern France. After the beets in the surrounding fields were harvested, the juice was extracted, treated with quicklime to remove the impurities, and then pumped through pipelines up to twenty miles long to a refinery. Each was capable of refining, concentrating, and granulating the juice of ninety thousand tons of beets during the three-month harvest period. This refinery belonged to the Compagnie de Fives-Lille, which by World War I had offices or refineries for beet or cane sugar in Java, Réunion, Brazil, the Caribbean, Egypt, the Austro-Hungarian Empire, Russia, Italy, Argentina, Mexico, the Philippines, Australia, China, and the United States. From Edward H. Knight, *Knight's New Mechanical Dictionary* (Boston: Houghton, Mifflin, 1884), pl. XLVII, opp. p. 873.

rapidly, converting salt solutions into flowing white table salt, and turning milk into evaporated, condensed, and dried forms. Fossil fuel drove the compressors that made refrigeration without natural ice possible.

Scientific research made it easier to understand and hence control tricky biochemical processes. Beer fermentation was studied at the Carlsberg breweries. Wine was investigated by French scientists, and Asian ferments by a Polish biochemist, Ferdinand Cohn, working in Japan, who identified *Aspergillus oryzae* in the 1880s. Research on sake, miso, and soy by Western and Japanese scientists followed. By 1936 industrial miso production had risen to 660,000 tons annually.[108]

The processing of wheat, rice, beef, and animal fats, and the production of wheat flour, pasta and noodles, starch, sweeteners, condiments, artificial flavors, and drinks—the major Western foodstuffs, and some of the Asian ones—became industrialized. Roller milling increased the proportion of white flour that could be extracted from wheat. The grain was passed through a series of rollers that crushed it, the white flour was sieved out, and the remainder was passed through the rollers and sieved again, a process that was repeated multiple times.[109] Roller mills were invented in Hungary in 1865, where there was a large market for fine flour made from hard wheat, which stone mills did not handle well. Over three hundred mills were set up there in the next couple of decades. In 1875, the roller mill was adapted to use in the United States. Within a couple of decades the new mills were being built in the United States (by, for example, the Pillsbury-Washburn Flour Company), Britain (by Joseph Rank Limited), India, China, and wherever else flour was used.[110] In Shanghai, Sun Duosen invested $25,000, a significant sum, in a roller mill from a Milwaukee manufacturer, Edward Allis & Company, in 1898.[111] Others followed, the most important being the six Fuxin flour mills founded by the Rong brothers from 1913 on. Roller mills were established in Mexico in the first half of the twentieth century, before mills for processing maize. Bakeries, though, remained small-scale, especially outside the United States.

Dried pasta and noodle factories, which used steam power to push white wheat flour dough through holes to form different shapes and heated chambers to dry the dough, were built in Naples, Alsace, and Barcelona. In the United States, pasta manufacturers such as La Rosa, La Perla, Caruso, and Ronzoni had a national presence by the 1920s. In Argentina, on 17 August 1912, Vicente Fagnani opened a small pasta factory in Plata del Mar, a port town on a railway line that sped the pasta to Buenos Aires, 250 miles to the northeast.[112] Within five years, the Italians had awarded his pasta a gold medal. Noodle makers in China and Japan used machines to produce fresh *saimin* noodles (enjoyed by the wealthy perhaps since the fifteenth century) from wheat flour. Flour mills and noodle machines brought down the price, making noodle soups and dumplings everyday foods in China and in Chinese communities in Southeast Asia and the United States.

Rice processing was also transformed. Power mills polished the grain to a shining white, replacing the hand mills invented in the eighteenth century. In Southeast Asia, Western steam-powered mills began taking over traditional rice milling in the 1850s and 1860s. The Chinese began ordering English mills in the 1870s. They introduced Anglo-American rice-milling technology in Hawaii and the Philippines, where they owned three-quarters of all rice mills in the early twentieth century.

After Orlando Jones, an Englishman in the United States, discovered that grinding maize when wet and treating it with alkali made starch extraction easy, industrial cornstarch production began simultaneously in England and America. Starches from wheat, rice, potato, arrowroot (initially from a West African plant, later from a variety of tropical plants), sago (from a Southeast Asian palm), and tapioca (from cassava) were used to thicken sauces, custards and puddings.

The industrialization of meat began with beef extract. Justus von Liebig, who had lent scientific respectability to the ancient idea that meat was a powerful food, joined forces with George Christian Giebert, an engineer, to exploit the carcasses of cattle killed for their hides in South America. In 1863, they opened a factory on the banks of the Uruguay River in Fray Bentos, which became the company name, where they were producing five hundred tons of extract annually by 1875. Other companies, such as Bovril, soon followed. Marmite, made from yeast extract, a by-product of the brewing industry, was added to the list of dark, salty, tasty gravy additives or substitutes in 1902. Canning was the next industrial technology to be applied to meat, though the fibers turned stringy and unappealing. Canned salt beef (corned beef) was the most successful. Then, in the late nineteenth century, mechanical refrigeration made it possible to take cattle and hogs to central locations, slaughter them, disassemble them on a production line, and ship the dressed and chilled parts by railroad to the cities. Fresh beef displaced salt meats, growing by 66 percent between 1904 and 1925 in the U.S. Chicago declared itself "The Great Bovine City of the World," though Fray Bentos could have competed for the title.[113] Edible side products included lard, suet, sausages, and gelatin. Sausage production tripled, as the hot dog became America's favorite cheap street food. Gelatin leaves or powder, a side product of boiling bones for glue, made jellies and aspics, formerly restricted to high cuisine, accessible to any cook beginning in the 1870s.

Margarine and shortenings, such as Crisco and artificial ghee, were invented as substitutes for butter, which was too expensive for most people. In 1870, for example, a Polish miner had to work for half a day to earn enough to buy a pound of butter.[114] The French, whose chemists had been working on fats, offered a prize for the best artificial butter at the Paris World Exhibition in 1866. Hippolyte Mège Mouriès, a chemist, secured a patent for margarine three years later. In Dutch, German, Austrian, Norwegian, American, Swedish, Danish, and British factories, margarine was made with beef tallow (fat) combined with skimmed milk. Following the invention of hydrogenation, which turned liquid fats solid, and deodorization, which killed disgusting smells, shortening could be made from fish oil, whale oil from Antarctic waters, and tropical vegetable oils, such as West African palm oil. Jewish housewives found Crisco a good substitute for lard for pastries, while Indian housewives snapped up artificial ghee. By World War I, the British oil and fat industries, the largest in the world, were worth over £50 million a year.

Other innovations made foods and drinks more appealing. Carbon dioxide was added to soft drinks to make them fizzy and to bread to make it light and fluffy. Bottled condiments such as ketchup, mustard, and Worcestershire sauce offered a convenient way to perk up dishes. Dried peppers ground in a mill made goulash laden with paprika possible. Flavors such as vanillin, extracted from the wood pulp used to make paper, and taste enhancers such as monosodium glutamate, discovered by the Tokyo Imperial University chemist Kikunae Ikeda in the first decade of the twentieth century, made food tastier and more palatable. Preservatives prevented food from spoiling quickly.

The manufacture of ready-to-eat foods such as crackers, sweet biscuits and wafers (cookies), jams, and candies also became industrialized. Soda crackers, ship's biscuit, slightly sweet arrowroot or Marie-type cookies, ginger snaps, and cream-sandwich cookies rolled off production lines in many countries, including Britain, Australia, the United States, and India.[115] Jams and pickles, equally widely produced, were welcome enhancements to bread and main dishes.

Canning, which grew out of earlier techniques for extending the lives of food, including sealing meat in fat and preserving fruit in sugar syrup in glass jars, was used to preserve a greater variety of foodstuffs. It made seasons irrelevant and added new items to the diet. In the eighteenth century, the Dutch had shipped roast beef packed in fat in sealed tin cans to the East Indies.[116] Nicolas Appert, in his *Art de conserver* (1810; The Art of Conserving), described how he extended the know-how of the head cooks of great houses by experimenting with placing sealed jars of foodstuffs without added sugar in hot water baths. The delicacies of the French table were canned: cauliflower, spinach, artichokes, green peas, pears, meat stock, and jellies. Gourmands were delighted. "The peas above all," enthused the gastronome Grimod de la Reynière in his *Almanach des gourmands* (1806) of the bottles in Appert's shop window, "are green, tender and more flavorful than those eaten at the height of the season."

Working out the technical problems of canning and getting around the health dangers took the better part of a century. Should the containers be glass—easy to sterilize and with the contents serving as their own advertisement—or metal— unbreakable, and not as heavy, but tricky to open and subject to corrosion and bursting? In 1852, when 2,707 canisters of food purchased by the Royal Navy were opened, only 197 were fit to eat. Glass won out for the luxury market. Metal cans were subsidized first by military and exploring expeditions, then by Europeans in the colonies willing to pay high prices. Inventors initially tried heating cans unsealed in boiling water, then sealed in a calcium chloride bath where, unfortu- nately, they were liable to explode, and finally in an autoclave or retort (a vessel with steam under pressure). Special cans were created for different products, such as a tapered can that allowed corned beef to slide out whole, a rounded rectangular can for sardines, and a paper-lined can that prevented crab from turning black.

Urban housewives began using cans in the 1870s. Country people preferred to preserve their own foods until the second half of the twentieth century. In every industrializing country, small companies began production. Those that survived became household names. In England, Crosse & Blackwell was famous for pickles and sauces, Robertson and Chivers for fruits and jams; in the United States, Swift and Armour canned meats, Heinz canned vegetables and sauces, Hunt and Dole canned fruits, and Eagle canned milk; the French had Amieux-Frères, the Italians, Cirio, and the Mexicans, Herdez. The fifty-seven varieties made famous by Heinz were more than matched by Amieux-Frères, whose three thousand employees produced one hundred sixty products in twelve different factories by the end of the nineteenth century.[117]

Canning introduced novel foods. The name "sardine," originally applied to small fish of the Clupeid family caught off Sardinia, was now applied to any species in the family caught anywhere in the world. Tuna, previously little eaten in the United States, was advertised as chicken of the sea, and American sandwiches were never the same. Salmon, formerly reserved for the very rich, was now canned in the American northwest and became a special treat for middle-class families. Plants were reengineered for canning. Sweet kernels from young field corn were so popular that maize was bred to produce cobs that were sweet when mature. Something similar happened with the pea and the tomato, whose success owes much more to the canning industry than to beefsteak tomatoes in Grandmother's backyard.

Natural ice to cool foods and drinks had long been harvested. In the nineteenth century, this became big business in the United States, from whence it was shipped around the country and to the tropics. Looking for an alternative, scientists and technologists experimented with artificial refrigeration, which became economical, for brewers at least, in the 1870s, opening up the possibility of year-round brewing of lager, formerly made only in the winter because the yeasts require low temperatures. Following the identification of the lager yeast in 1883 by Emil Christian Hansen at the Carlsberg Brewery in Denmark, lager breweries were set up in many different parts of the world, from China to Latin America. Lager displaced ale, except in Britain and some of its colonies, and local alcoholic drinks such as pulque in Mexico. The major meat packers in the United States and elsewhere used artificial refrigeration to cool storage facilities, railroad cars, and the holds of ships, so that fresh meat replaced salt meat in industrializing countries.

As food corporations grew, they added research staffs of food scientists and technologists to regularize the innovation of new products, hired home economists to develop recipes and work in the testing and cooking laboratories, and created professional sales staffs. Scientists such as William Tibble, author of *Foods: Their Origin, Composition and Manufacture* (London, 1912), wrote texts that synthesized information from government bulletins, physiological chemistry, and food analysis.

To persuade German, British, and other European biologists and biochemists to come to the new Imperial University of Tokyo in the 1870s, the Japanese government offered high salaries and senior positions.[118] It hired experts to set up steel roller mills, bakeries, breweries, and canneries. Foreign contractors taught skills such as canning in Japanese Encouragement of Industry offices. In late-nineteenth-century China, reformers adopted "Chinese learning at base, Western learning for use" as their slogan.[119] Well-to-do Chinese traveled to the United States or Japan to study, while Protestant missionaries arrived in China, teaching Western medicine and nutrition. China, having overthrown the Qing Dynasty, was proclaimed a republic in January 1912. "Chinese people should consume Chinese products!" became a rallying call.[120] Chinese products were exhibited, consumers who bought foreign goods condemned, Chinese captains of industry praised, and foreign imports boycotted. Foodstuffs manufactured in China became symbols of hope and survival. The monosodium glutamate manufacturer Wu Yunchu was lauded in his biography and in the popular imagination as a "patriotic producer."

In a century that had seen the introduction of baking powder that made possible light, spongy cakes, carbon dioxide that added fizz to soft drinks, margarine and shortening that made fats for spreading and cooking available to everyone, vanillin to flavor drinks, cakes, and ice cream, and cold beers to sip in the heat of summer, it is not surprising that chemists thought they were on the brink of a world of synthetic foods. Before dismissing this as disgusting, it is worth recalling that many traditional food-processing techniques, such as treating maize with lye to make the dough for tortillas, letting bread or beans go moldy in the process of making murri or soy sauce, or allowing fish to rot to create fish sauce, also must once have seemed unappealing and potentially dangerous. In 1894, in the course of a widely reported speech about what food would be like in the year 2000, the distinguished French chemist and historian of the alchemists and their dreams, Marcellin Berthelot, predicted that soon beefsteaks would be made from coal and the earth would become a garden again, as it had been in the Golden Age.[121] This sense of wonder and possibility has since been lost, though we are all the beneficiaries of the nineteenth-century revolution in food processing.

ANYTHING BUT BEEF, BREAD, AND DOMESTICITY: COUNTERCUISINES

A wide variety of critics, including religious groups, conservatives, socialists, and feminists, attacked modern, middling cuisines. Some wanted the egalitarianism of modern culinary philosophy but rejected other aspects. For example, many reformers turned their backs on meat, white bread, and alcohol, developing alternative physiologies and nutritional theories to explain why vegetarianism or whole grains were superior. Others attacked domesticity, liberalism and free trade, proposing alternative ways of organizing modern cooking, commerce, and farming. Yet others hoped that it might be possible to return to an imagined egalitarian past, invoking agrarian and romantic traditions to criticize modern, industrialized cuisines.

Many Western religious or quasi-religious groups rejected meat eating in favor of vegetarianism, a term coined in the 1840s. They included the Seventh-Day Adventists, Bible Christians, the Salvation Army, the Doukhobors (a Russian dissident group who eventually emigrated to Canada after being treated severely by the tsarist regime), and followers of Leo Tolstoy, for whom meat eating symbolized everything that was wrong with society.[122] Vegetarians tended to be opposed to industrialism and urbanization and supportive of naturopathy, anthroposophy, land reforms that encouraged small-scale independent farmers, and the garden city movement. Between them, different groups put forward a variety of arguments for vegetarianism. It was healthier, they said, because meat harbored animal parasites, spread diseases such as tuberculosis, and, if from animals that had been artificially fed, retained excretory substances that caused gout and cancer-inducing uric acid deposits. It was economical because fruits, nuts, grains, and vegetables cost less than meat. It made the best use of the land, which produced far more food when sown with grains than when used to feed cattle. It was good for the nation because if everyone switched to eating vegetable foods, the number of independent yeomen farmers, the backbone of society, would increase. And it was morally preferable to extend sympathy to animals.

By the beginning of the nineteenth century, vegetarians had founded over thirty societies and were opening restaurants and sanatoria. The most famous was the Seventh Day Adventist sanitarium in Battle Creek, Michigan, which opened in the mid-nineteenth century and was later led by John Harvey Kellogg (fig. 7.8). Advocates of vegetarianism published weeklies, such as the English *Vegetarian*, and monthlies, such as the American *Vegetarian* and the English *Herald of the Golden Age*; wrote tracts, such as Henry Salt's *A Plea for Vegetarianism*, Howard Williams's *The Ethics of Diet*, and Anna Kingsford's *The Perfect Way in Diet*; and Percy Bysshe Shelley published his poem *Queen Mab* (1813) with an accompanying essay on vegetarianism. They compiled cookery books to help those raised on meat to cope with a meatless regime, such as *The Vegetable Diet* (1849) by the American educator and physician William Allcott and the *New System of Vegetable Cookery* (1821) by the British Bible Christian Mrs. Brotherton. To show that they could trounce meat eaters, they competed in walking matches, cycling races, racquets, and tennis.

In India, an organized cow protection movement began in the Punjab in the 1870s. Riots protesting Muslim slaughter of cows occurred throughout the 1880s, and the movement gained strength after 1888, when the North-Western Provinces High Court decreed that the cow was not a sacred object. Further violence broke out in different parts of the country in the three following decades. Hindu nationalists were able to use these events to focus political feeling against British and Muslims who ate beef.[123] Later, Gandhi, who had joined the Vegetarian Society when he was studying in London, also advocated cow protection.

White bread was another target of critics of modern Western cuisine (map 7.2). Professor Tournier at the Faculté de Paris warned that children who ate white bread would suffer from dyspepsia, convulsions, and problems with the nervous system, prompting *Le petit journal* to begin a "Return to the Grindstone" campaign in 1895. A few years later, a similar campaign was launched in England for

BATTLE CREEK SANITARIUM

HEALTH FOODS

The line of health foods manufactured by the **SANITARIUM HEALTH FOOD CO.** is so well and favorably known, that little needs to be said as to their quality and genuineness.

The demand for these foods originated at the Battle Creek Sanitarium, itself a pioneer in reforms, where was felt the necessity of providing suitable dietetic preparations of a special character.

The standard raised at the inception of the enterprise has been maintained and elevated by scrupulous attention to details and the utilization of the unequaled facilities afforded by the extensive laboratories of the Sanitarium ; hence, all foods produced by this company can be relied upon as being

STRICTLY PURE, and Made with Special Reference to Healthful Properties, rather than to command a sale. Prominent among the different foods may be mentioned

Granola, highly nutritious and toothsome. The process of preparation is such that every element of an irritating character is eliminated. Thoroughly cooked and **READY FOR USE.** One pound more than equals three pounds of best beef in nutrient value.

Granose. A NEW CEREAL FOOD, thoroughly sterilized. Its use clears the tongue and stomach of germs. **CURES** constipation, biliousness, sick-headache, and indigestion. A capital food for sedentary people. Good for everybody, both sick and well.

GRANOSE is the invention of a physician of many years' experience. GRANOLA received highest award at the Columbian and Atlanta Expositions, and GRANOSE a special gold medal at the latter. For circular describing complete line of Health Foods address,

BATTLE CREEK SANITARIUM HEALTH FOOD CO.,
Battle Creek, Mich.
1897

FIGURE 7.8. John Harvey Kellogg, director of the Seventh-Day Adventist Battle Creek Sanitarium, opened the Battle Creek Sanitarium Health Food Co. in 1890 to offer a line of "health foods." Kellogg rejected meat, sugar, alcohol, caffeine, and white bread, the foundations of the modern Western diet, arguing that instead of sending missionaries abroad, they should be sent to the poor and miserable in American cities to promote the "Gospel of Health." This advertisement from 1897 claims that one pound of the company's "granola," a mixture of several baked cereals, was equivalent to three pounds of beef. The sanitarium, resembling a first-class hotel, counted William Howard Taft, John D. Rockefeller, George Bernard Shaw, and Thomas Edison among its many famous clients. Kellogg's Corn Flakes, introduced at the very end of the nineteenth century, came to replace ham and eggs as the American breakfast. Courtesy New York Public Library, http://digitalgallery.nypl.org/nypldigital/id?833916.

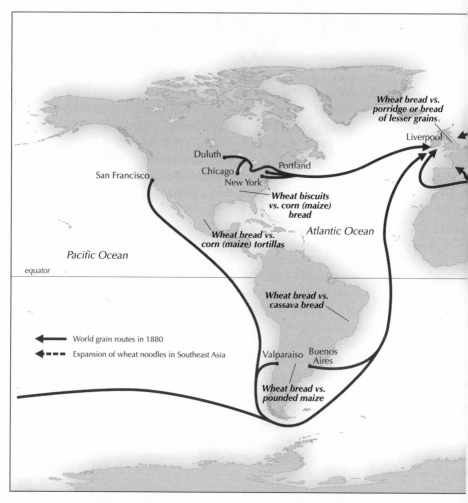

MAP 7.2. The bread debates at the turn of the twentieth century. In one modernizing nation after another, factions arose that argued that to compete globally its citizens had to shift to eating wheat bread. Arrows show the major world wheat trade routes in the 1880s, most leading to Britain. Source: Morgan, *Merchants of Grain*, frontispiece.

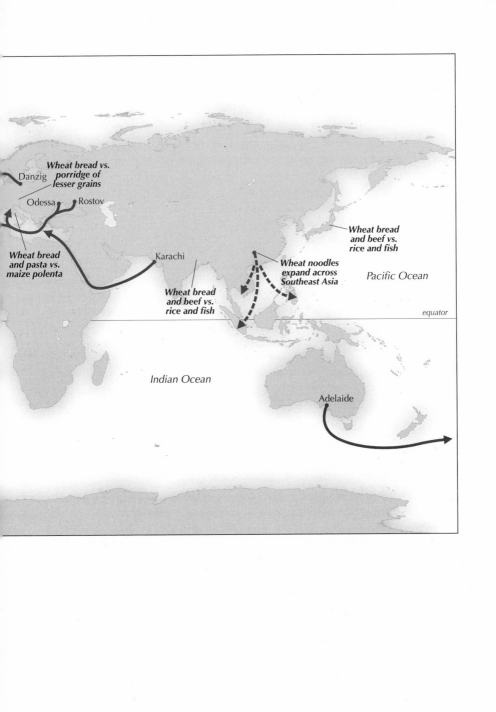

Wheat bread vs.
porridge of
lesser grains

Danzig

Odessa   Rostov

Wheat bread
and pasta vs.
maize polenta

Karachi

Wheat bread
and beef vs.
rice and fish

Wheat bread
and beef vs.
rice and fish

Wheat noodles
expand across
Southeast Asia

Pacific Ocean

equator

Indian Ocean

Adelaide

"standard bread." The campaigns were short-lived, and stone-ground bread gave way to roller-milled white bread.[124] In the German-speaking world, Adam Maurizio, who had studied milling technology in Berlin before becoming a professor of botany and commerce at the Technical University of Lemberg (Lvov), worked with Anni Gamerith, an Austrian teacher and ethnologist. They recorded traditional techniques of pounding millet by hand, for example, which they believed created healthier, tastier products than the wheat flour from modern roller mills. In his *Die Geschichte unserer Pflanzen-Nahrung* (The History of Our Vegetable Diet, 1927), Maurizio charged that rich countries that attempted to shift the diet of ethnic minorities to white bread were guilty of "dietary imperialism."[125]

Maize and rice found their defenders. In Mexico, the sociologist Andrés Molina Enríquez, in *Los grandes problemas nacionales* (The Great National Problems; 1909), argued that national unity was impossible unless the indigenous peoples were fully incorporated into the nation, making maize tortillas and tamales "absolutely without doubt the national cuisine." In Japan, the nativist political thinker Hirata Atsutane asserted that Japanese rice was the backbone of the nation, making it the great regional power, whereas Chinese rice made its people "weak and enervated." Rice fields against the backdrop of the perfect cone of Mount Fuji, the symbol of Japanese identity, figured in all of Hiroshige's prints depicting Japan's central thoroughfare from the political capital, Kyoto, to the economic capital, Edo. Sumo wrestlers heaved bulging sacks of rice high over their heads in 1901 in the open area between the Imperial Palace and Japan's first Western-style hotel, the massive Victorian gingerbread Imperial Hotel. Japanese rice, composed of 80 percent food and only 20 percent water, made them strong enough to carry out this feat, making it superior to Western beef, which was 70 percent water and only 30 percent food, they explained to the Japanese and American press.[126]

Alcohol was a third point of contention. British Quakers proposed cocoa as an alternative drink. Fry's, founded in 1761, Cadbury in 1824, and Rowntree in 1862 then moved from cocoa to making chocolate confectionary. Milton Hershey, an American with Mennonite roots, followed their lead. Russian reformers touted mildly alcoholic kvass, made by natural fermentation of rye bread, as a temperance drink.[127] According to the Russian Society for the Preservation of the Population's Health, kvass "removes the desire to touch beer or spirits" and in addition "tones you up physically without getting you drunk." In Australia, those who argued on moral grounds for temperance, called wowsers, accused those who did not agree with them of putting individual rights and the search for profits above community building and social responsibility. By the beginning of the twentieth century, the prohibition movement was international.

Even if the critics of nineteenth-century nutritional theory did not persuade society as a whole (except for the temporary success of the American temperance movement with Prohibition), they did introduce many new foods to the diet.

From Sweden came crispbreads. From Switzerland came Bircher muesli, named for Max Otto Bircher-Benner, a Swiss doctor who pioneered the uncooked foods movement. From the United States came Graham crackers, named for the Presbyterian minister Sylvester Graham. Kellogg turned the English-speaking world back into breakfast porridge eaters, at least once the original name for his product, Elijah's Manna, had been changed to Kellogg's Corn Flakes. Health foods might be made of whole grains, but by 1900, they were manufactured and marketed just like any other industrialized food, such as Cadbury's cocoa or Bovril.

Communal meals and kitchens, argued utopians, socialists, and feminists, should replace the family meal and the domestic kitchen. A number of utopian communities were set up in the United States. Members of the Amana Colonies, built in the 1860s, ate at one of over fifty kitchens, each overseen by a senior woman cook, who arranged the preparation of three meals and two snacks daily, as well as the tending of the gardens. The houses themselves had no kitchens (though families gradually began taking meals at home). Those in the Zoar settlement in northeastern Ohio dined communally from its foundation in 1817 until the end of the nineteenth century. Grand communal eating halls figured in books by the Russian revolutionary socialist Nicolai Chernyshevsky (*What Is to Be Done?*, 1863) and the American socialist Edward Bellamy (*Looking Backward*, 1888).

Feminists saw communal dining as a way to escape domesticity. In Australia, for example, Maybanke Wollstenholme, an advocate of women's education and women's suffrage, argued for it in the magazine she briefly edited and produced in the mid-1890s, *Woman's Voice*. The views of American feminist and sociologist Charlotte Perkins Gilman differed sharply from those of her aunts, Catherine Beecher and Harriet Beecher Stowe, who were leading proponents of domesticity. Gilman neatly inverted the usual argument that republican dining, which she characterized as eating to live rather than living to eat, depended on home cooking. The housewife as an amateur, she declared, never acquired a high level of culinary expertise. Unlike professional cooks, she purchased in small quantities, making it impossible to insist on high-quality ingredients. And dependent on her husband for every cent, she pandered to his likes and dislikes instead of cooking fine, healthful meals. Cooking, thought Gilman, should be a "reputable, well-paid profession."[128]

Finally, a diffuse movement of intellectuals, writers, farmers, and others in Europe, Japan, and the United States rejected the modern, urban, industrial world, including its cuisine and its farming, yearning instead for an idealized rural past. They contrasted dirty, artificial cities with the pure, natural countryside. In the late nineteenth century, in the modernizing countries, groups of ramblers took to the hills and mountains, pausing on their walks to admire the buildings of the preindustrial past, and schools of painters depicted the sublime beauty of unspoiled nature.[129] Many followed the Romantic tradition ushered in by Rousseau in identifying peasant food as the freshest, most healthful, and delicious and rejecting the widely held belief that nineteenth-century Western cuisine, particularly French high cuisine, was the pinnacle of culinary progress. Maurizio and Gamerith, who explored folk cooking traditions in the German-speaking world, had their equivalents elsewhere. The food writer Florence White founded the English Folk Cookery Association in 1928. The following year, the Scottish folklorist Marian McNeill published *The Scots Kitchen,* while the English social historian Dorothy Hartley started work on *Food in England,* published in 1954. In the first part of the twentieth century, the French Right (the affiliation of most, though by no means all, gastronomes) and the French Left both emphasized rural France and its peasantry. The Right had masterminded the canonization of Joan of Arc, the fifteenth-century peasant girl who saw visions and inspired the French to resist British occupation, in 1920. The very substantial Left, many of them socialist and a significant number communist in the 1930s, thought that the older feudal system, although flawed, was kindlier than capitalism. In 1929, the historians Marc Bloch and Lucien Febvre, professors at the University of Strasbourg in Alsace, founded the pioneering journal *Annales* to promote the study of everyday life, including food, publishing empirical studies of what people, particularly peasants, had actually eaten. This was the background to the identification of French peasant cuisine as the foundation of French high cuisine.

Dovetailing with the reevaluation of peasant cuisine was an agrarian movement, which was particularly strong in the United States. Yeoman farmers, asserted Thomas Jefferson, were the nation's most valuable citizens—strong, independent, and virtuous. Henry David Thoreau took up the theme of the virtues of a simple rural life in *Walden; or Life in the Woods* (1854). In England, Richard Jefferies, a journalist who himself was the son of a farmer, eloquently described the life of the disappearing yeoman farmers, gamekeepers, and laborers of rural England in a series of books published in the 1880s. The botanist Albert Howard drew on his experience as head of the Institute of Plant Industry at Indore in central India to criticize modern farming methods; instead he advocated composting and other organic farming practices. The grassland specialist George Stapledon, who taught at the Royal Agricultural College, argued for small farms that rotated grassland and cereals. Howard's and Stapledon's ideas, picked up by many British farmers, were endorsed in mid-twentieth-century America by the Rodale Institute and the organic movement. Although the agrarian-romantic vision of culinary history remained confined to a minority until well after World War II, it provided the underpinnings for the majority late-twentieth-century understanding of culinary history.

GLOBAL CULINARY GEOGRAPHY CA. 1910

By 1920, in the cities of Great Britain and its dominions, the United States, northern Europe, Japan, and other industrializing countries, new middling cuisines had been created by members of the new urban salaried and wage-earning classes. High French cuisine was the cuisine of the global elite, while middle-class and working-class cuisines were quickly becoming the national cuisines of their respective countries. All three cuisines were based on the most prestigious grains—wheat or rice—and meat, particularly beef. Crackers and cookies, candy, sugar, canned goods, Worcestershire sauce, curry powder, cocoa, coffee, tea, and beer were available globally.

The industrialization of food processing and the creation of corporations (along with cheaper transport and more efficient farming) had contributed to falling prices of food and strong national economies. Families in the industrialized world spent a smaller proportion of their budgets on food than ever before. In 1800, about two-thirds of the British were close to subsistence; a century later, only a third of the population was at that level. In the 1890s, the French spent only 60 percent of their average budget on food. Grinding, which in the earliest states had been the daily chore of 20 percent of the population, was now handled by such an insignificant number of workers that it did not figure in occupational statistics. Flour milling was the leading American industry in 1860, its product worth twice that of the cotton industry and three times that of the iron and steel industries. In the forty years following, while general manufacturing multiplied only sixfold, food manufacturing grew fifteenfold, accounting for 20 percent of all manufacturing in 1900.[130] In Japan, food processing accounted for 40 percent of economic growth in the 1880s and 1890s.[131]

The shift to middling, national cuisines in the industrializing regions makes a stark contrast to developments in other parts of the world. Famines, while declining in the West, were more serious than ever in unindustrialized regions of the world. This was due to increased population, bad harvests as a result of changes in world ocean currents, a shift to export crops, a lack of transport infrastructure, and the failure of colonial policy to anticipate or ameliorate the hunger and starvation that killed millions. Potatoes, cassava, and maize, in addition to yams, taro, and sorghum, continued to increase in importance in rural diets. In the American South and Italy, diets high in maize untreated with lime meant that many suffered and died from pellagra. In plantation economies, machines imported from England or the United States were used for milling sugar, not for relieving women of the labor of processing their food.

Agriculture had become globally specialized. Wheat for Britain came from the prairies of Canada and the United States, the plains of the Punjab, and the pampas of Argentina. In Britain, one in six (17 percent) of the ships in the merchant marine carried wheat. In 1880–81, six hundred ships sailed from San Francisco and Oregon alone, laden with wheat for the British Isles. In the United States, most of the food came from within its own vastly expanded territory. The South and the industrial Northeast of the United States imported wheat from other parts of the nation. China, as its supply of wheat dwindled due to severe flooding in wheat-producing regions, imported wheat from the Pacific Northwest via Pacific Coast flour corporations.[132] Steamships from Seattle made their way up the muddy estuary of the lower Yangtze in spite of an anti-American boycott in 1905.

In Europe, sugar-beet acreage soared, one ton of beets producing as much sugar as one ton of cane, in addition to leafy greens for animal feed. The acreage devoted to growing wine grapes and a widening array of fruits and vegetables, sold either fresh or canned, expanded in areas with Mediterranean climates—warm, dry summers and cool, wet winters—including the Mediterranean nations, California, and the Western Cape in South Africa. When tunnels through the Alps opened in 1871, Italian entrepreneur Francesco Cirio built warehouses near railroad stations so that his refrigerated carriages could whisk fresh fruits and vegetables to the cities of northern Europe. By the 1870s, canned goods had taken over, and Cirio's firm was producing a million kilograms of canned asparagus, artichokes, peaches, and peas annually.[133] The tropics in Africa, India, Southeast Asia, the Caribbean, and Central America supplied European colonial powers with spices, sugar, coffee, tea, and cacao. "Without sugar, there is no country," said Cuban sugar planter José Manuel Casanova.[134] This region also supplied the more durable tropical fruits—bananas and oranges—or fruits that could be canned, such as pineapple from Hawaii, as well as palm oil from West Africa. Southeast Asia exported rice to feed plantation laborers.

Farming became a little less laborious and more efficient with the introduction of machines to do the backbreaking job of threshing grains and nitrogenous fertilizers to increase plant yields. Plants and animals essential to Western cuisine—wheat, dairy and beef cattle, apples, potatoes, even microorganisms such as the lactobacilli for cheddar cheese and sourdough bread and the yeasts for bread and beer—were transferred to other temperate and even tropical zones. Botanic gardens, natural history museums, and agricultural experiment stations were set up by big companies such as U.S.-owned sugar companies in the Caribbean and the United Fruit Company, and to a lesser extent by governments, to increase the productivity of export crops.

For all the successes in the industrializing world, modern cuisine faced a series of problems. There were signs that a diet entirely of bread, noodles or rice, beef, sugar, and fat was inadequate. A large proportion of the Japanese military and even the emperor suffered from beriberi, and debates raged about whether this was caused by germs or diet. In the American Midwest, people suffered from scurvy and goiter, in the South, from pellagra. Children in British cities had the bowlegs typical of rickets. Why were the new cuisines not creating healthier citizens?

The rapid changes in farming that accompanied the shift to middling cuisines also had some deleterious consequences. Old wheat-growing areas such as lowland England and the Shenandoah Valley in Virginia were in decline. Unprotected by tariffs, British wheat production dropped 50 percent between 1870 and 1914, at a time when the population doubled. Although farms shifted to producing meat, milk, and vegetables, British agriculture did not recover until World War II. In Latin America, Italy, and parts of Africa and Asia, growing export crops took precedence over modernizing the diet, causing suffering for the rural poor.

The decline of hierarchical cuisines and their replacement by national cuisines that had followed from the globalization of trade and agriculture also rendered the industrializing regions vulnerable to changing economic policies and war. Free trade was being replaced by neomercantilism and trade protection. Bismarck had established high tariffs to protect the large landowners of Germany's eastern provinces, who created revenue for the central German government. From the 1880s on, agriculture was supported by Germany's manufactured exports. In France, although neither population growth nor industrialization was as rapid, the Third Republic wanted to win the support of conservative Catholic farmers. Serious criticisms of imperial policies were voiced in Britain and the United States.

By the outbreak of World War I, Britain, Germany, and the Low Countries, all of which depended on imported food, feared starvation. England received chilled beef from the United States and Argentina, mutton from Australia and New Zealand, canned meat from the River Plate in South America, and bacon from Denmark. Butter and margarine came from Denmark and Holland. Sugar came from eastern Europe and the Caribbean. Potatoes, cheese, tea, and apples came from various parts of the British Empire. The country imported 50 percent of its foodstuffs by value, 58 percent in terms of calories, as well as fertilizer for its fields and fodder for its animals.[135] Joseph Chamberlain, a liberal, began campaigning for tariffs. "If tomorrow it were possible . . . to reduce by a stroke of the pen the British Empire to the dimensions of the United Kingdom, half at least of our population would be starved."[136] Rudyard Kipling, an astute observer of Britain at the height of its empire, explained to schoolchildren how Britons were fed:

> "Oh, where are you going to, all you Big Steamers,
> With England's own coal, up and down the salt seas?"
> "We are going to fetch you your bread and your butter,
> Your beef, pork and mutton, eggs, apples and cheese!"

> "And where will you fetch it from, all you Big Steamers,
> And where shall I write you when you are away?"
> "We fetch it from Melbourne, Quebec and Vancouver,
> Address us at Hobart, Hong-Kong and Bombay."[137]

In the ominous last line, the steamers say: "And if anyone hinders our coming, you'll starve."

Modern Cuisines

The Globalization of Middling Cuisines, 1920–2000

"You can find your way across [the United States]," said Charles Kuralt, journalist for CBS News, "using burger joints the way a navigator uses the stars. We have munched Bridge burgers in the shadow of the Brooklyn Bridge and Cable burgers hard at the Garden Gate, Dixie burgers in the sunny South and Yankee Doodle burgers in the North. . . . We had a Capitol burger—guess where. And, so help us, in the inner courtyard of the Pentagon, a Penta burger."[1]

By the end of the twentieth century, thirty years after Kuralt's pronouncement, you could navigate the entire globe via hamburgers (fig. 8.1), in place of the roots and grains of chapter 1, or the Buddhist, Islamic, and Christian cuisines of chapters 3–5, or the French dinners of chapter 7.[2] A bulgogi burger? Seoul. A rice-bun Mos-burger? Tokyo. A McTempeh burger? Jakarta. A McPork burger with Thai basil? Bangkok. A mutton burger? Delhi. A shammi kebab burger? Pakistan. A burger on a bap? Edinburgh. A McGarden burger? Stockholm. And a McHuevo? Well, it must be Montevideo, Uruguay.

In burger joints more brightly lit than any monarch's dining room, ordinary people in many parts of the world could feast on grilled beef on fluffy white bread, accented by a creamy sauce and fresh lettuce and tomato, with perfect French fries on the side. With the meal went a tall, icy drink, perhaps a shake of milk and ice cream or perhaps a sparkling cola. Three generations earlier, white bread, beef, fresh vegetables out of season, ice cream, and chilled drinks were restricted to the very wealthiest in the Western world. French fries, made crispy by frying twice at different temperatures, and so very different from English chips, which were only fried once, were the acme of French high cuisine. The French gourmet Curnonsky, writing in the 1920s, called *pommes frites*, "the Parisian *plat*

FIGURE 8.1. Egyptians eating the white-flour buns and beef hamburgers that epitomize modern Western cuisine in a McDonald's in downtown Cairo in the late twentieth century. Photo by Dick Dougherty / SaudiAramcoWorld / SAWDIA.

par excellence." The French magazine *Paris Match* reported that they were requested by General Christian Marie Ferdinand de la Croix de Castries following the signing of the armistice that brought the First Indochina War to an end in 1954. He instinctively understood, commented the French intellectual Roland Barthes, that they were the "alimentary sign of Frenchness."[3] Little did he know that within a decade they would become a staple of middling cuisines. In 1965, when John Richard Simplot sold McDonald's on his discovery that frozen potatoes made an excellent French fry, this formerly expensive and labor-intensive delicacy became an everyday treat.

Where the British had made tea, with its white bread and cakes, the national meal, the Americans made the burger, with its beef and bread, fries, and shake, their national meal, eaten by people of all ages, occupations, and classes, alone or with friends or family. President Clinton had no qualms about being photographed stopping for a hamburger. On 25 June 2010, President Obama chose to treat Russian president Dmitry Medvedev to this American delicacy. McDonald's, half of whose profits come from outside the United States, offers a taste of the cuisine and culture of the world's most powerful nation, as French restaurants had earlier offered a taste of the high cuisine and culture of the European empires.

No wonder hamburgers became the touchstone for judging modern Western cuisine and its relation to political economy, nutrition, and religion. In Moscow, the opening of a McDonald's prefigured, some suggest hastened, the end of the Soviet Union.[4] In Iran, where international fast food chains are forbidden, local imitations such as MashDonalds and McMashallah fill the gap.[5] In India, the McSpicy Paneer made with fresh cheese brought a beef burger chain in line with Hindu beef avoidance. Morton Spurlock chews his way through Big Macs at every meal in the documentary *Supersize Me* to suggest a link between fast food and obesity. The *Economist* uses the price of a Big Mac to value the world's currencies, while McDonaldization, a term coined by the sociologist George Ritzer, has became synonymous with efficiency, predictability, and work done by nonhumans.[6] The rise of fast food, said Eric Schlosser, hastened "the malling of our landscape, widened the chasm between rich and poor, fueled an epidemic of obesity, and propelled the juggernaut of American imperialism abroad." He urged Americans to "turn and walk out the door."[7] To raise awareness of McDonald's use of hormone-treated beef, the French farmer José Bové dismantled one being constructed in Millau in southern France in 1999, calling it McMerde. And the Slow Food movement, dedicated to opposing fast food and preserving regional cuisines, took its name in protests against the opening of a McDonald's near the Spanish steps in Rome in 1986.[8]

For those for whom the bread, beef, fries, and shakes of McDonald's were too expensive, including the emerging middle class in most of the world, there was an alternative quick modern meal in the form of instant ramen. It had the key combination of modern ingredients: wheat flour, fat, and meat (or at least a meaty flavor, like the Bovril and meat essences of the nineteenth century), and a hint of vegetable in the specks of green floating on the liquid soup. Instant ramen was the latest manifestation of the pasta invented in China more than two thousand years earlier and introduced to Japan in the early twentieth century. After World War II, the thin wheat-flour noodles were peddled from small pushcarts in Japan by Chinese and Koreans from former Japanese colonies. Momofuku Ando, a Taiwanese Japanese, thought an instant industrial version might be sold to the school lunch program initiated by the occupying authorities, in practice the Americans, using donations from American charitable organizations. He invented a way of deep-frying and then drying the noodles so that they could be prepared with boiling water in less than five minutes.[9]

In 1958, Ando's company, Nissin, sold thirteen million packets of ramen, and the following year, sixty million. In 1971, in a marketing masterpiece, the dried noodles were offered in a Styrofoam cup. By the 1990s, 4.5 billion servings of instant ramen were sold annually in Japan, forty servings per head per year. Japanese companies exported them worldwide. They became part of Japanese food aid to Indonesia, Thailand, and the Soviet Union. In Mexico, workers bought instant ramen in convenience stores and markets, heating it in on-site microwaves. In refugee camps, it made an instant hot meal. In England, Prince Harry was one of many students who brewed up bowlfuls. By the year 2000, 53 billion packets of instant noodles were sold annually.

By the end of the twentieth century, American cuisine was the most rapidly expanding branch of modern Western cuisine, and Japanese of non-Western cuisine. The global spread of hamburgers and instant ramen cannot be read, anti-American protests notwithstanding, as the irresistible advance of American (or to a lesser extent Japanese) culinary imperialism. Both were constantly adjusted to appeal to local tastes. Ramen sells better if it is kimchi-flavored in Korea, garam masala–flavored in India, and dried shrimp–flavored in Mexico. Cooks don't feel constrained by the instructions on the package but create dishes unthought-of in corporate headquarters, giving rise to cookbooks like *Everybody Loves Ramen, Ramen to the Rescue, Oodles and Oodles of Ramen Noodles,* and *Low Cost Gourmet Meals Using Ramen Noodles.*

Similarly, diners adapt McDonald's to their own purposes, which are quite different from those in its American homeland. It is a place for children to play while women shop in Mexico City, to enjoy a date with candlelight and champagne in Rio de Janeiro, to work in a study group in Seoul, to do homework in Tokyo, and to eat alone if one is a respectable single woman in Vietnam.[10] In Beijing, the upwardly mobile sit behind the huge plate-glass window of KFC, confident that their passing friends will admire their sophistication. They take their dates to a McDonald's to sit in the private service area with tables for two, the "lover's corner," secure in the knowledge that the bill will not be an unpleasant surprise. They read the newspaper, conduct business meetings, celebrate farewells, graduations, scholarships, or the end of term, or enjoy a weekend family meal together.

Furthermore, everywhere that Japanese ramen and American fast food chains have gone, they have provoked local competition. In Indonesia, Indofoods owns the three main Indonesian noodle brands—Indomie, Sarimi, and Supermi—exporting them to thirty countries, including Saudi Arabia, Nigeria, Australia, and the United States. Around 2000 C.E., Indonesians were consuming ten billion packets of noodles a year. In Nepal, not known for growing wheat or for industrial food processing, the Chaudhary Group began manufacturing Wai Wai Noodles in 1980 and had 60 percent of the local market and 15 percent of India's in the 1990s. Since 1972, MOS Burger has sold hamburgers, teriyaki burgers, pork cutlet burgers, hamburgers with rice buns, lemon- and honey-flavored *konnyaku* drinks (thickened with powder made from a starchy corm), and "curry chicken fokaccha" (a sandwich made with a version of focaccia, a flatbread) in Japan. Since 1981, the French have been buying hamburgers from the Belgian chain Quick. In New Delhi, Indians go to Nirula's for a spicy grilled chicken burger, paneer walnut burger, and ice cream. Koreans go to Lotteria for hamburgers and fried chicken. In the Philippines, McDonald's has had to yield to Jollibee, a family-owned company, whose clean restaurants and burgers seasoned with garlic and soy sauce have enabled it to become the largest fast-food chain in the nation. Jollibee, which proudly calls itself "a stronghold of heritage, a monument of Filipino victory," moved on to open outlets wherever Filipino expatriates clustered in Hong Kong, the Middle East, and California.[11]

Indeed, all Western culinary products, processes, and stores face competition. As Coca-Cola expanded globally, other soft drinks, such as the Indian Thums-Up or the Peruvian Inca Kola, became local favorites, outselling Coca-Cola. General Foods, although one of the world's largest food-processing companies, was out-ranked by Anglo-Dutch Unilever and Swiss-based Nestlé, the biggest giant of them all. The sliced, wrapped white-bread loaf, invented in the United States, was most widely sold by a Mexican company, Bimbo, which dominated the market by the end of the first decade of the twenty-first century, moving into fourth place among food corporations. The leading food retailer, and one of the world's largest employers, Walmart, had English Tesco and French Carrefour hot on its heels. All three found it hard to break into Japan, Korea, and Indonesia. In Hong Kong, in spite of offering live frogs, turtle blood, and whole roasted suckling pigs, Carrefour lost $400 million between 1996 and 2000 and had to close its operations.[12]

This global plenty and culinary competition would not have been expected at the beginning of the twentieth century, when European political leaders worried about their growing dependence on imported foods, or even after World War II. World War I brought severe deprivation, and in some areas near starvation, to Europe. In the 1920s, the world pulled back from globalization.[13] Even Britain questioned free trade, with many leaders advocating trade within the empire instead. Other European countries, the United States, and the British Dominions never embraced it. Italy, for example, established tariffs on wheat in 1925, France in 1926. The Russian Revolution introduced a socialist alternative to the prevalent market economy. The Depression created long bread lines in even the richest countries. Migration to the Americas slowed, but fifty million migrants went to Manchuria, Siberia, Central Asia, and Japan, many in search of better food or to grow food to support the Russian and Japanese empires.[14] Then World War II dev-astated many of the world's economies.

Following World War II, the pace of culinary change picked up again. The global culinary geography shifted in three ways, obscuring the older pattern of empires with high cuisines for an urban minority, and humble cuisines for the urban and rural poor. First, globally, Western and socialist culinary philosophies reflected for forty years, from about 1950 to 1990, the divisions of the Cold War and the sustained military and political tension between the United States—which now had the greatest agricultural production and strongest economy—and its allies and the Eastern Bloc, dominated by the Soviet Union. Second, the number of nations, each staking out its own cuisine, rose to around two hundred as the British, French, Dutch, and other European empires broke up. Third, in the richer nations, humble rural cuisines, for millennia the most meager and least varied of all cuisines, disappeared as humble urban cuisines had done in the late nineteenth century. Like those in the cities, country people now enjoyed a cuisine prepared from the better grains, meat, fat, and sugar. Mechanization reduced the number of poorly paid farmhands (except in fruit and vegetable farming); remote villages and farms became linked to cities by telephones, buses, and cars; and rural kitchens had running water and electricity. In the place of empires with high and humble cuisines came a division, incipient in the nineteenth century, between rich nations, where everyone, even in rural areas, ate middling cuisines, and poor nations, with high cuisines for a tiny minority and humble cuisines for the rest. Last but not least, world population continued to climb, tripling from two billion in 1927 to six billion in 2000.

The changes in cuisine in the post–World War II period have been so sweeping that some food scholars have argued that culinary rules have vanished and, with them, distinct cuisines and the identities they conferred.[15] In light of the number of nations that claimed to have their own cuisine, the variety of political forms—including liberal democracies, socialist states, empires, monarchies, fascist states, theocracies, and dictatorships—that flourished and competed, migration, and multinational food corporations, it might seem that making sense of the late twentieth century is an impossible task. Nonetheless, certain themes stand out in the history of modern middling cuisines, all of which show the same tension between global convergence and divergence as hamburgers and ramen.

WESTERN VERSUS SOCIALIST MODERN CUISINES

Following World War II, many different agents, including militaries, multinational corporations, nongovernmental organizations, missionaries, and migrants, contributed to extending modern middling cuisines around the globe. None were more important, though, than powerful states with global influence, the subject of this section. Especially during the Cold War, they offered two different concepts of modern cuisine—Western and socialist—creating two different culinary spheres. Japan, also an imperial power in the first half of the century, along with other traditional empires, debated whether there was not a third concept of modern middling cuisine.[16]

Modern Western cuisine, already discussed in chapter 7, had taken shape by the 1920s. It was based, though never consistently or without contest, on the family meal and domesticity, the family farm, free trade, corporate capitalism, nationalism, religious tolerance, and modern nutritional theory. Following World War II, American cuisine became its fastest expanding branch. Like other Western cuisines, American cuisine now included milk, vegetables, and fruit as well as bread, beef, fat, and sugar.[17] Meals were based on hot or cold cereal for breakfast, soup and a sandwich for lunch, and meat and two vegetables for dinner. Ingredients and dishes of turn-of-the-century immigrants, particularly pasta, began entering the American culinary mainstream in mid-century.

Socialist cuisine took shape in the Soviet Union. In 1917, following a decade of civil unrest and protests, women in Petrograd, who had to spend as many as forty hours a week queuing for bread, rioted, starting the series of events that led to the fall of the Russian Empire. The Soviet Union introduced collective farming, state control of food processing and distribution, communal dining, the suppression of religious culinary rules, and modern nutritional theory.[18] Following World War II, socialist cuisines extended across much of eastern and central Europe. State-run canteens throughout the USSR served standardized meals of soup, usually with cabbage (*shchi*) or beetroot (*borscht*), a meat dish such as a cutlet, a sausage, a stuffed dumpling, or grilled beef or pork, with a starch such as bread, kasha, or macaroni, something to drink, such as tea, coffee, or a yogurt or fruit drink, and a sweet of some kind. Ice cream was the sweet treat of choice. Collective agriculture and communal dining, though not specific foodstuffs and dishes, were widely emulated in Mexico following the Mexican Revolution, in Cuba following the Cuban Revolution, and in communist China prior to economic reform. They also offered a model for protest movements in the West.

Japan, Turkey, and other countries tried to find ways to modernize their cuisine without accepting modern Western cuisine wholesale. In the late nineteenth century, as racism hardened in the West, many intellectuals and politicians in other parts of the world began to search for an alternative to Western modernization, from which they were increasingly excluded. In 1905, Japan defeated Russia, a Western country. This encouraged Turkey, which then declared itself a republic in 1923, Iran, and China to institute reforms along Japanese lines.[19] In the 1930s, Japan withdrew from the League of Nations. Pan-Asianism and pan-Islamicism were widely debated. The culinary philosophy was to take from the West what was useful while retaining local cultural characteristics, often including religious rules. The Japanese, for example, accepted modern food processing but turned their attention to the rich tradition of Asian ferments and Asian flavors. A Japanese-Western-Chinese cuisine was created between the 1920s and 1960s (with a pause during the hard war years of the 1940s). The Japanese component (*washoku*) consisted of soup, rice, pickle, and a steamed or boiled fish or meat dish, known as rice and three, a much more complicated meal than ordinary Japanese housewives had previously prepared. The Western component (*yoshoku*), most commonly encountered in department-store restaurants, included sandwiches, mayonnaise salads, and the like. The Chinese component (*Shina ryori*) derived from the pasta culture of northern China, notably *gyoza* dumplings and *shina soba*, the noodles renamed ramen in the 1950s and 1960s. Western, socialist, and nonaligned cuisines, like earlier ones, faced the same three issues: what was the relation between cuisine and the natural world, including the diner's own body? What was the relation between cuisine and religion or morality? And what was the relation between cuisine and the state?

To begin with cuisine and the natural world, as an explanation of the links between cuisine and health, at the state level modern nutritional theory became as ubiquitous as humoral theory had once been. (Individuals in many parts of the world continued to accept the humoral theory.) The correspondence between cuisine, environment, and health had been replaced by the abstract concepts of modern nutritional theory.[20] The idea that plentiful protein, particularly meat, was necessary to growth and strength remained an item of faith through most of the century, cropping up everywhere from popular thought to academic theories. In his *Autobiography*, first published in 1927 and frequently reprinted, Gandhi, famously a vegetarian, quoted the Gujarati poet popularly known as "Narmad" on the British and meat eating: "Behold the Mighty Englishman / He rules the Indian small / Because being a meat eater / He is five cubits tall."[21] Shortly afterward, Dr. Cecily Williams, a British physician working in the Gold Coast (now Ghana), introduced the idea that there was a global and endemic deficiency of protein, based on her identification of kwashiorkor, a fatal condition in children, which arose from malnutrition caused by a diet primarily of maize. Following World War II, John Waterlow of the London School of Tropical Medicine and Hygiene, and Nevin Scrimshaw of the Massachusetts Institute of Nutrition in Cambridge, formalized the concept of a "protein gap" between richer and poorer countries. Shortage of protein owing to the absence of large domesticated animals, postulated anthropologists, had driven Mesoamericans to sacrifice and eat humans.[22] The protein gap loomed large in official thinking until the last third of the century. Then it faded away as studies found that indigenous diets were much more nutritious than formerly assumed, thanks to proteins in the staples. As early as 1942, for example, Francisco de Paula Miranda, director of the Institute of Nutrition in Mexico, and his American colleagues judged the indigenous Otomi diet, based on maize, beans, and chiles, to be basically adequate. Scholars pointed out that game, birds, fish, and insects as well as maize and beans provided more than sufficient protein.[23] Official thinking aside, for many individuals, protein remains the centerpiece of the meal if they can afford it. By comparison, carbohydrates and fats, so highly valued in the late nineteenth century for their calories, fared less well in the twentieth. Sugar once again came under attack, this time as a source of empty calories. Fats were revealed to be complex and much research went into trying to assess the healthfulness of different kinds.

Once vitamins were identified in the first half of the twentieth century, "protective foods," that is, vitamin-rich foods such as fruits and vegetables, formerly thought to be unnecessary luxuries, were promoted as essential to good health. Diseases that could not be explained by the germ theory, such as beriberi, rickets, and pellagra, were found to be curable with changes in diet. Finally, liquid milk, formerly consumed transformed into yogurt, butter, or cheese, depending on the society, was declared nature's perfect food. Compared to those who did not drink milk, "The peoples who have made liberal use of milk as a food, have ... attained greater size, greater longevity, and have been much more successful in the rearing of their young. They have been more aggressive ... and have achieved much greater advancement in literature, science and art," Elmer McCollum, one of America's leading nutritionists, asserted in 1918.[24]

Governments in the West, the Eastern Bloc, and the unaligned world offered nutritional advice, hoping to improve the health of the citizenry. The U.S. Department of Agriculture published its first dietary recommendations in 1894 and its first food guide for young children in 1916, laying out five food groups (milk and meat, cereals, vegetables and fruits, fats, and sugars). In 1943, it came up with its "Basic Seven," the outcome of a National Nutrition Conference convened at the suggestion of President Franklin D. Roosevelt. By the end of the century, nations were publishing dietary pyramids, circles, houses, and pagodas, depending on their cultural preferences. Earlier in the century, home economists in the United States, Japan, and elsewhere disseminated nutritional theory. By 1915, American home economists were teaching in China, by 1920, in Turkey, and by 1930, overseas students were traveling to the United States to study nutritional science. Nutritional theory shaped rationing in Great Britain, Germany, and the United States in World War I, and in all combatant countries in World War II. Official cookbooks were published, advertisements were taken out, and health and safety regulations were promulgated. Institutes of nutrition were opened in Japan in 1920, in the Soviet Union in 1930, and in Mexico in 1944. Soviet nutritionists, harking back perhaps unconsciously to the long tradition that criticized luxurious eating, decried diets heavy in rich sauces and in spices as leading to excessive appetite, overeating, gluttony, and moral dissolution. "An excessive amount of salt, pepper, mustard, vinegar, and other flavorings and spices harms not only the alimentary organs but the whole organism," M. P. Dubianskaia explained in *Healthful Food and How to Prepare It* (1929). To maximize the nutritional benefit of the food, Soviet citizens were advised to eat slowly, chew thoroughly, and drink limited amounts of water.[25] In the late twentieth century, China sought to achieve improved "population quality" (*renkou sushi*) by bettering children's diets. Information on breast-feeding and children's diets was disseminated in rural China, and "baby-friendly" hospitals that encouraged breast-feeding (enthusiastically supported by the World Health Organization and the United Nations Children's Fund) were established in China's cities.[26] When First Lady Michelle Obama told Americans that "[t]he physical and emotional health of an entire generation and the economic health and security of our nation is at stake" in the first decade of the twenty-first century, promoting her "Let's Move" initiative, she was expressing the characteristically modern belief that governments were responsible for the well-being of their citizens, a significant expansion of the older obligation to prevent hunger.[27]

As far as relations between cuisine and religion were concerned, government policies diverged as widely as they converged in the case of nutrition. The clear pattern of imperial-religious alliances with associated cuisines, typical from a couple of hundred years B.C.E. until the seventeenth century, had now vanished. In the West, the state left individuals free to observe religious culinary rules or not as they wished. Muslims in Europe, and Mormons and Jews in the United States, although minorities, were numerous enough to organize their own food supplies. In the United States, for example, kosher slaughterhouses, specialized lines of merchandise, produced by companies such as Manischewitz, and special dishes for religious festivals, such as the Passover bitter herbs, lamb, and charoset (a dark paste of fruits and nuts), were available. Most Protestants had relatively few religious rules, though they continued to favor plain cuisine and debated the hygiene of drinking communion wine from a common cup.[28] Evangelicals, the fastest-growing branch of Christians in Yucatán, Mexico (and in many other parts of the world), were told by missionaries to stop eating their traditional maize dishes since the growing of maize had been accompanied by syncretic pre-Hispanic-Catholic religious ceremonies. They had to resort to processed flour tortillas, snack foods, and soft drinks from tiny local mom-and-pop stores.[29]

Socialist states considered religion, including religious cuisines, as backward. On taking power, the Soviet government decreed that from that point on, the Orthodox Church, with its fast days when fish and mushrooms replaced meat and religious holidays celebrated with special dishes such as the rich breads of Easter, was to have no part in shaping Russian cuisine. In Central Asia, the USSR suppressed Islam and introduced vodka. In 1926, the Mexican state, populist if not actually socialist, took the properties of the Catholic Church and restricted the activities of priests. Following the Cuban Revolution in 1957, the state curtailed religious practices. In China, Buddhism was banned between 1949 and the 1980s.

Notwithstanding, traditional religious practices tended to reappear once socialist states relaxed their grip. Following the breakup of the Soviet Union, Russians turned to programs such as the Christian Church of Moscow Soup Kitchen for food.[30] In the late twentieth century, many Mexicans continued to observe Lent, flocking to buy the fish and meatless empanadas offered in all grocery stores, even though the state was secular and the Catholic Church no longer insisted on most of the rules. And in China, Buddhist restaurants reopened once the ban on Buddhism was lifted, and traditional offerings reappeared on the graves of the departed.

In those states aligned neither with the West nor with the Soviet Union, religious cuisines continued to hold sway. In India, Hinduism was the dominant faith following Independence and Partition in 1947. "The central fact of Hinduism is cow protection," Gandhi said in 1954, and periodic riots and hunger strikes were held in support of a national ban on cow killing. There was great public uproar in 2001, when the Hindu nationalist Bharatiya Janata Party was in office, over the publication of *Holy Cow: Beef in Indian Dietary Traditions* by Dwijendra Narayan Jha, a senior historian at the University of Delhi who argued that early Indians had eaten beef and that the practice had not been introduced by Muslims. In Islamic nations, Muslims continued their traditional methods of slaughter, food avoidances, and festival days.[31] In Iran, where an Islamic republic replaced the regime of westernizing Shah Mohammad Reza Pahlavi following the revolution of 1979, the state enforced Islamic culinary rules. Clerics banned caviar, an important export, reportedly harvested from a non-halal fish without scales. Faced with cans of the valuable foodstuff piling up in warehouses, the administration ordered clerics and biologists to investigate the matter. When they found that the fish had nonstandard scales, exports resumed.[32] In East Asia, Buddhist cuisine permeated the lives of millions through rules for cooking and eating, meals at vegetarian restaurants, prayers before Japanese kindergarteners opened their bento boxes (lunch boxes), and offerings to the deceased in graveyards.

Turning to relations between cuisine and political economy, the socialist world diverged sharply from America and its allies in taking state control of food production, processing, and, in many cases, cooking and dining. Communal meals were to be eaten in communal dining halls, prepared in communal kitchens, with foodstuffs produced on communal farms.[33] The USSR rejected domesticity. "We are still not free from the family burden," one of the delegates at the Women's Congress in 1927 pleaded; "it is clear that women factory workers are still forced to stand by the stove and fiddle around with the pots."[34] As Trotsky had said in 1923, "If a woman is tied to her family, to cooking, washing and sewing, then by that very fact her chances of influencing the life of society and the state are reduced to a minimum." It was hoped that communal dining with tablecloths, fresh flowers on the table, classical music from a pianist in the background, and original paintings hung on the wall would also bring civilization and culture to those formerly denied it. Unlike earlier restaurants, characterized as exemplifying the class structure with cringing waiters and imperious diners, these communal dining rooms were to be open to all. Because they economized on ingredients and fuel, they would be more efficient than domestic kitchens (fig. 8.2). The state, Stalin proclaimed in a Soviet cookbook in 1939, *The Book of Healthy and Delicious Food,* would give "the people not only freedom, but also material goods and an opportunity for a wealthy and civilized life."[35]

The communal dining movement had its fits and starts and was always underfunded. It seems likely that it did improve dining for the urban poor, or at least alleviate the worst of the food shortages (even as six to eight million Ukrainians

FIGURE 8.2. *Down with Kitchen Slavery: A New Way of Life.* In a kitchen steamy from drying laundry and cooking, the traditional woman is up to her elbows in soapy water, washing clothes by hand, while a meal simmers in a pot on a tiny burner. The modern Soviet woman throws open the door to a new life, her children happily playing, a fancy cafeteria with a balcony for eating outside in good weather, and a club to go to after work. Poster by Grigory Mikhailovich Shaga (1931). Courtesy Glenn Mack.

who resisted collectivization starved). It has been estimated that 25.5 million people were being fed in these facilities by 1933.[36] It was an enormous task for a young state, so the inadequate, overcrowded, dingy kitchens and facilities frequently served unappetizing food. Home dining continued alongside community dining. Many women wanted to use their new knowledge of nutrition to feed their own children. Others were driven back to the kitchen garden as cheap new canning equipment made preserving fruits and vegetables economical and prudent. With poor harvests and grains in short supply, ration cards were issued, allocating one pound of black bread a day to manual workers, half a pound to white collar or "brain workers," and one quarter of a pound to housewives and the elderly (fig. 8.3).[37] Black markets and soaring prices became the pattern of everyday life.

Other nations followed the Soviet lead in community processing and dining. In Israel, the early kibbutzim founded before World War II, fired up by socialist ideals, had communal dining areas and communal kitchens. In China, communists began taking over the rice trade and the flourishing food-processing industry in Shanghai in the summer of 1949, shortly after Mao's army took the city. Members of the party debated whether austerity, essential for revolutionary will, or the promise of prosperity that the revolution was to provide should guide culinary policy as they struggled to make sure the city was provisioned. Banqueting and expensive restaurant meals were discouraged. Small food vendors were encouraged and communal and workplace cafeterias set up.[38] Earlier in the 1940s, Uruguay, Argentina, Chile, Peru, and Mexico established public dining halls for the poor (whereas in the West, soup kitchens for the poor were usually run by churches or private charities). In Mexico, the foods offered were fish, hamburger, macaroni bolognaise, Hungarian casserole, Scotch meat, and grilled beefsteak. Although the names often do not convey exactly what the dish was, they do indicate that most of them were made of wheat flour and beef, the foods approved by Western nutritionists. Because few maize tortillas, the basis of the Mexican diet, were served, the mechanical tortillerias in the public dining facilities being still primitive, the dining halls were not a great success.[39]

High cuisine, so closely associated with monarchies, was suspect in Western democracies and socialist countries alike. In the United States, for example, presidents were expected to identify with citizens, not to offer the lavish feasts of the past. Will Rogers, a leading political satirist of the Progressive Era and a highly paid Hollywood movie star, tore into French cooks in 1931, saying they could "put a liquid overcoat, and a non-pronounceable name, on a slice of horse meat and have an American wondering if it's breast of veal or Angel food cake. It's that gravy those Frogs pour on there that does the dirty work."[40] Probably without knowing it, he was echoing the thoughts of English Protestants and French *philosophes*, notably Jean-Jacques Rousseau, themselves indebted to Cato, Seneca, and other republicans of the ancient world. A few years later, Henrietta Nesbitt, housekeeper

FIGURE 8.3. *Labor Is Bread: Who Doesn't Work Doesn't Eat.* In this poster, created between 1917 and 1921, a worker in a Russian shirt and boots claims the bread on the table in the face of a presumably Jewish banker, an aristocrat and his wife, and a priest. Courtesy New York Public Library, http://digitalgallery.nypl.org/nypldigital/id?1216178.

to the Roosevelt White House, explained, "With so many Americans hungry, it was up to the head house of the nation to serve economy meals and act as an example." Diplomats and politicians complained about the plain American meals the president dished up, but to no avail.[41] When Nancy Reagan raised private money to buy a new set of 4,400 pieces of china for the White House for $210,000, a public outcry over the expense followed. Catherine the Great's comparable purchase in late-eighteenth-century Russia could not have elicited a response like that. The $4,000 dinner served to the *New York Times* critic Craig Claibourne and his fellow columnist chef Pierre Franey in Paris in 1975 epitomized high cuisine for many Americans. "This calculated evening of high-class piggery," as one commentator put it, "offends an average American's sense of decency."[42]

Although still the primary cuisine of diplomacy, French high cuisine had ceased to be mandatory. Following the lead of President Roosevelt, American presidents began serving alternatives from time to time. American regional specialties were offered to guests by President Ronald Reagan at an international economic summit in Williamsburg, Virginia, in May 1983, while in May 2010, President Obama offered President Felipe Calderón a Mexican dinner cooked by American restaurateur and cookbook author Rick Bayless.

High-end restaurants and hotels toned down the elaborate haute cuisine of Escoffier and other predecessors. In 1922, Fernand Point, who had trained at the prestigious Parisian Bristol and Majestic hotels, opened La Pyramide in Vienne, just south of Lyon on the route to the Riviera. He offered the "food of liberty," supposedly light and easily digestible dishes that tasted of themselves, including some French provincial dishes, as well as "foreign" dishes acceptable to French tastes, such as beef Stroganoff (invented by French chefs in Russia). La Pyramide was less exclusive than earlier establishments, but it hardly offered the cuisine of the people and was patronized by socialites like the duke and duchess of Windsor, Sir Sultan Muhammed Shah, Aga Khan III (the president of the League of Nations), and the playwright Jean Cocteau. French gastronomes distanced themselves from expensive global French or international cuisine. The gourmet and critic Curnonsky lambasted the offerings of the big hotels, the "dreadful thermochemical and doctored food served in the American Palace-Hotels."[43] That of Germany was "barbaric," he declared, its fried potatoes so disgusting that "the Treaty of Versailles should have forbidden their fabrication across the Rhine."[44] Following World War II, Point's pupils carried on developing a less extravagant version of French high cuisine.

In its turn, the USSR banned the cookbook that had come to symbolize the hierarchical tsarist state, *A Gift to Young Housewives,* by Elena Molokhovets, first published in 1861.[45] During the Cultural Revolution, the Chinese Communist government, early sympathetic to preserving China's culinary heritage, closed all except state-run restaurants, and the Red Guard systematically destroyed menus and other memorabilia.[46] "Sumptuous feasts are generally forbidden," declared the Communist-led Peasants' Association as early as the 1920s. "In the town of Chia-mo, Hziang-Hsiang country, people have refrained from eating expensive foods and use only fruit when offering ancestral sacrifices."[47]

High cuisine was reinvented once again in the West at the end of the twentieth century by a group of star or celebrity chefs in Spain and France. Although many of the chefs repudiate the term, the style is best known as molecular gastronomy. By presenting themselves as artists or celebrities, chefs repositioned themselves from personnel serving the court to cultural innovators. They sought out local, even foraged, ingredients, frequently presenting their dishes as refinements of regional or national cuisines, even while using the latest techniques of the industrial kitchen.[48] The tiny tastings they offered circumvented the charges of extravagance and gluttony. Although the well-heeled guests traveled globally to enjoy these destination restaurants, they did not engage in the conspicuous consumption traditionally associated with high cuisine. In short, the new style served more as a gold standard for middling cuisine than as a flamboyant demonstration of high social rank.

In the area of foreign policy, food aid was now offered beyond national boundaries. Although its geographic reach was greater, like earlier culinary benevolence practiced by powerful states such as the Achaemenid and Ottoman empires, it was simultaneously generous and self-interested, idealistic and hardheaded, and incidentally served to disseminate the ingredients and often the cuisine of the state powerful enough to offer it. Take the case of the United States and wheat. During World War I, when there were widespread food shortages in Europe, Herbert Hoover arranged for the shipment of 700 million pounds of wheat flour to feed eleven million Belgians. In 1918, under the auspices of the new Food Research Institute at Stanford, he published a "Hunger Map of Europe" and organized a campaign for Americans to cut back. Millions of Americans, appalled by the suffering, did so. Twenty million tons of wheat were shipped to Europe. Grateful Belgians embroidered flour sacks with Belgian and American flags, symbols of peace, the American eagle, and messages of thanks. This was the moment when Americans ceased to see Europe as a model to follow, historian Helen Veit has argued, and began to think of it as dependent and in need of help.[49]

Under the Lend-Lease program in World War II, the United States shipped food and matériel to Britain, France, the Soviet Union, and China. Presumably searching for historical antecedents, someone in the U.S. Department of Agriculture condensed Xenophon's longish discussion of Socrates's theory of food and the state into the pithy statement, "No man can be called a statesman who is ignorant of problems of wheat." It has been regularly cited in U.S. Department of Agriculture documents ever since. In 1954, President Dwight D. Eisenhower signed Public Law 480 into effect, enabling the United States to send food as aid to countries it wanted as friends.[50] At the height of the Cold War, U.S. Secretary of Agriculture Earl Butz famously stated, "Food is a weapon." The recipients of aid, who had been debating the relations between bread and political power for the better part of a hundred years, were primed to accept wheat. More than a hundred million tons of wheat were shipped overseas, including to Asia, Africa, Egypt, and Middle Eastern oil-producing countries, which did much to bring about the global shift to wheat-based cuisines.

By the 1990s, socialist cuisines were in retreat. Western multinational food-processing and food-service corporations began operating in Russia and China. Socialist cuisines left their mark in foodstuffs previously unavailable to the poor, such as ice cream and, in some, a nostalgia for communal dining. Beyond their borders, their heritage was a turn to culinary benevolence in the form of social welfare and a continued sense among many, particularly in the counterculture, that alternatives to corporate capitalism had to be found.

THE PROLIFERATION OF NATIONAL CUISINES

As the number of nations in the world soared following the breakup of the European empires and later the Soviet Union, national cuisines proliferated, adding to those that had already taken shape in the nineteenth century, such as the cuisines of Britain and the Americas. For citizens, cuisines (along with national clothing, monuments, currency, stamps, and sports teams) were an easier way to grasp their own and other nations than abstract theories about legitimacy. Something typical was "as American as apple pie." Foreign nations might be dismissed with derogatory food-related epithets (e.g., calling Germans "Krauts" and Mexicans "Beaners"). For states, national cuisines now attracted tourists and their revenue, in addition to creating national identity and producing strong citizens and soldiers. Yet few aspects of culinary history are more fraught with problems, ironies, and contradictions than the simple equation between one nation, one national territory, one national people, and one national cuisine.

A national cuisine is usually thought to be one which is familiar to all citizens, eaten by all of them, at least on occasion, and found across the entire national territory, perhaps with regional variations. It is assumed to have a long continuous history and to reflect and contribute to the national character. In fact, national cuisines, like nations themselves, have been created in the last two hundred years, and often in the last fifty or sixty. They have been forged from hierarchical traditional imperial cuisines, particularly Christian, Islamic, and Buddhist-Confucian, in which rank, not nation, determined what an individual ate. Or they have resulted from the breakup of modern empires, particularly British, French, and Dutch, which, at least in the areas they had conquered, had done little to change the hierarchical cuisines already in place. So how did hierarchical cuisines, in which class was more important than territory, get transformed into territorial national cuisines? How were territories with very different culinary histories (say Provence, Alsace, and the Paris region in France) made subordinate to some national whole? How did these new national cuisines survive or get reworked following civil wars? And how did they deal with changing national boundaries and the influx of migrants?

What follows is simply a sampling of the many factors shaping, changing, and eroding national cuisines. Cookbooks, menus, gastronomic treatises, cooking magazines, and cartoons, as we have already seen, established typical ingredients, archetypal national dishes, national culinary philosophy, and stories about the nation's culinary evolution, a theme culinary historians have taken from Benedict Anderson's idea of the nation as an imagined community in which print media constructed and disseminated a vision of the nation.[51] In the twentieth century, radio, movies, television, and the Internet joined the media that shaped cuisines. Important as media were, so too were festival meals, restaurants and hotels, grocery stores, industrial foodstuffs, school lunches, army canteens, and political and cultural policies.

Creating a national French cuisine was no simple matter, since it involved connecting the transnational high cuisine with regional provincial and peasant cuisines. Rural France, with its multiple regional languages spoken by up to 50 percent of the population, remained a foreign country to bourgeois Parisians at the beginning of the twentieth century.[52] As car ownership climbed to a million in the late 1920s (France had about forty million people at the time), the urban well-to-do went for drives on the weekend and motoring vacations to visit Gothic cathedrals, Loire châteaux, and winemaking regions. After a long day of sightseeing, they wanted good food. When I returned from a holiday in Provence in the 1960s, Parisian friends worried about the food I had encountered: "All that garlic! Such a heavy hand with the tomatoes and herbs!" and prepared me a restorative meal of smooth, creamy, mild Parisian food. In the early twentieth century, much provincial food had been yet more different, including thick stews of root vegetables cooked in an iron cauldron, or buckwheat cakes, red peppers, lard, and garlic. The Michelin tire company actively encouraged the revival, or perhaps invention, of regional dishes. Louis Baudry de Saunier, editor of a promotional periodical, the *Revue mensuelle* (Monthly Review), invited readers to submit details of regional specialties so that they could be inventoried, "not only for our well-being and our reputation but also for our financial recovery." He argued that regional dishes "still occasionally exist in the country and ... should be resurrected in our tourist hotels."[53]

Cooks refined peasant dishes as nineteenth-century chefs had refined foreign dishes. They put more meat in the cassoulet, added creamy sauces to make blanquette of veal, and substituted butter for lard in the potato gratins. "Nothing can replace butter," Curnonsky insisted.[54] By the end of the 1920s, the more popular tourist regions all had their signature dishes. Sometimes they were made from local ingredients (the cream and cider of Normandy, the red wine of Burgundy, the fish of the coasts). Sometimes, one particular region claimed what must have been a widespread dish, such as beef stewed in red wine, as its own. Sometimes, as in the case of the pâté de foie gras and sauerkraut of Alsace and Lorraine, which by 1914 had been in German hands for almost two generations, they were re-described as French. Neither had anything to do with Germany, the *Revue mensuelle* explained. They were "eminently national and contrary to common belief, not a German dish."[55]

Regional associations found that food-related festivities stimulated the local economy. Entrepreneurs opened inns (auberges) and rural restaurants. Manufacturers in Paris, Lille, and Lyon made rustic furniture for restaurants, local potteries turned out colorful dishes, hand-painted in primitive styles, waitresses dressed up in local costume. The Touring Club de France organized village beautification contests. To promote the wines of Burgundy, for example, the Confrérie des Chevaliers du Tastevin (Brotherhood of the Knights of Tastevin) was founded in the 1930s, claiming to be able to trace its heritage back to the Ordre de la Boisson founded in 1703. Clad in red robes, silk sashes, and special headdresses, the chevaliers performed ceremonies and drinking songs that they had composed.

The 1937 World's Fair in Paris celebrated an alternative to the American model of a centralizing, industrial, modern nation, suggesting that modernizing could mean producing high-quality luxury goods on a small scale, encouraging regional specialization and honoring the French countryside, its peasantry, folklore, artisanal foods, and regional dishes.[56] By creating, preserving, refining, homogenizing, and packaging provincial and peasant cuisines to the tastes of the Parisian elite, the French abandoned the earlier culinary history of an aristocratic cuisine continually improved by modern science and technology, adopting instead Rousseau's romantic vision of fresh and natural rural cuisine as the basis of their national cuisine.

In Mexico, the nation's culinary history was rewritten and its cuisine redefined following the revolution (1910–1920) that tore the country apart. Artists and intellectuals turned their backs on the nineteenth-century conception of Mexican cuisine as high French cuisine, with Spanish, English, and Mexican touches, and on the eighteenth-century conception of it as a criollo version of the Islamic-inspired cuisine of medieval Spain. They declared instead that it was a blending of indigenous and Spanish cuisine, which had been going on since the Conquest. Frida Kahlo put on a meal of corn tortillas and Mexican dishes served in clay pots arranged on a hand-woven cotton tablecloth to greet Trotsky on his arrival in Mexico in 1929.[57] The upper classes, who had hitherto sipped wine and brandy, cautiously tried the tequila of small independent landowners, celebrated by moviemakers. On 12 December 1926, the national newspaper *Excelsior* ran a story on how Sor Andrea de la Asunción had created mole poblano, the national dish, in the Dominican Santa Rosa convent in Puebla by combining European nuts, cloves, and pepper with Mexican chiles and chocolate. Thus a dish that derived from Islam and was the high cuisine of Mexican-born Spaniards, sharply distinguished from the cuisine of the indigenous peoples, was reinterpreted as a result of the seamless mixing of races.

In many countries, restaurant menus and decor suggested the range and nature of the national cuisine to diners. Coffee shops, department stores, and small eateries in Japan, canteens in Russia, tea shops in England, and diners, roadhouses, and department-store cafés in the United States all created shared experiences. In China, particularly in Shanghai, with its multitude of restaurants catering to immigrants from all parts of the republic (1912–49), eating places were a way to comprehend China's culinary heritage and to unify a diverse nation.[58] Similarly, widely reported meals taken by political leaders served to establish national dishes. The Empire Christmas Pudding served to George V and his family by their French chef André Cédard in 1927, on the urging of the Empire Marketing Board, became the most requested British recipe ever.[59] Including ingredients from all parts of the empire, such as currants from Australia, cloves from Zanzibar, rum from the West Indies, brandy from Cyprus, and pudding spice from India, it showed the power of

FIGURE 8.4. Hot dog stand, New York City, 1936. A street vendor
advertising ice-cold lemonade and red-hot frankfurters waits for
customers at the corner of West Street and North Moore Street in
Manhattan. Photographed by Berenice Abbott for the Federal Art
Project of the Works Progress Administration. Courtesy New York
Public Library, http://digitalgallery.nypl.org/nypldigital/id?1219152.

Britain to command global resources. In America, hot dogs completed their transformation from ethnic German street food to national dish when, in a much-pub-
licized informal picnic in June 1939, FDR served them to King George VI and
Queen Elizabeth of England (who were, ironically, visiting to request American
help in the war against Germany). The queen ate them with a knife and fork, while
the king manfully ate them American-style, with his fingers (fig. 8.4).

In India, cookbook authors contributed to the debate about what should be the
national cuisine following Independence in 1947. "Mr. Gandhi repeatedly declared
that a common countrywide diet was a 'necessity for our national well-being and

for our political unity,'" reported Shanta Ranga Rao, a Hindu author from southern India, in 1968. Speculating about what dishes might emerge as national, she suggested that when "a diet of the country comes, one can be sure that the korma [one of the jewels of Islamic Mughal cuisine, a dish of meat or chicken in a creamy sauce of yogurt and ground nuts] will be there," even though this would involve "outrageous breaking of caste."[60] As it turned out, her prediction was only partially correct. The growing urban middle class began abandoning some of the stricter rules of caste, experimenting with foods from outside their own region, using gadgets and prepared foods to speed preparation in the kitchen, and eating in railway stations, neighbors' houses, and affordable restaurants or picking up takeout foods. In the north, these included tandoori chicken and kebabs prepared by refugees from the Punjab in what is now Pakistan in traditional tannur bread ovens. By the early 1960s, some entrepreneurs had accumulated enough capital to open restaurants, such as Gaylords and Kwality in Delhi and other major cities, that offered menus with Punjabi, Mughal, and Anglo-Indian dishes. By the sixties, eating out meant eating Punjabi cuisine, which, argues economist and culinary entrepreneur Camellia Panjabi, became the national cuisine by default.

In Africa, leaders of some of the new nations created following the withdrawal of the European colonial powers advocated replacing Western cuisines with African ones. "Do you not know where imperialism is to be found?" Thomas Sankara, former president of Bukino Faso, asked rhetorically. "Just look at your own plate." He was presumably referring to the French-style baguettes and coffee that were popular for breakfast in this one-time French colony in West Africa. Zaire, the former Belgian Congo, instituted an official "authenticity" campaign in 1971, encouraging elites to abandon Western cuisine. Goat, catfish, porcupine, and monkey were to replace filet mignon on menus.[61] Egypt, under the anti-Western Nasser regime, banned many foreign imports and expelled thousands of Greeks, Italians, and Jews, and with them European cuisine. As cookbooks began appearing in newly independent African colonies, many continued the tradition established by European residents of offering a mix of local and Western recipes (fig. 8.5). Others, particularly those authored by African Americans and published in the United States, such as Bea Sandler's *African Cookbook* (1970) or Jessica Harris's *The Africa Cookbook* (1998), downplayed European recipes and ascribed dishes to specific nations.

When the "-stans" were under Soviet rule, cookbooks had been structured to show the diversity of cultures that made up the brotherhood of Soviet nations. Following independence in the 1990s, first the Uzbeks, then the Tajiks and Kazaks, began publishing national cookbooks with foreign recipes removed and national differences accentuated to strengthen national identity and present their culinary traditions to others.[62]

In Persian cookbooks and restaurants created by Iranian refugees around the world in the 1980s and 1990s, kebabs and white rice had much more prominence

FIGURE 8.5. An East African housewife in Western dress consults a
cookbook offering recipes for traditional African dishes of maize,
sweet potatoes, dried meat, and insects; Asian samosas, pilau, and
tandoori chicken; and European foods, including pot roast, Irish stew,
barbecue, and avocado pear with prawns. One recipe, for mushroom
and rice casserole with packaged mushroom soup, shows how quickly
food trends could spread. Mary Ominde, *African Cookery Book*
(Nairobi: Heinemann, 1975).

than they did in Iranian home cooking. Because during Reza Shah's push to modernize and westernize Iran in the 1920s, the Teheran municipal authorities decreed that restaurants that served kebabs and white rice should present them in a European style, they were easier to introduce to the West than home-cooked stewed dishes eaten with the fingers. In Thailand, pad thai, a dish with plentiful inexpensive vegetables and protein (bean sprouts, onions, eggs, and peanuts), was popularized, codified, and quite probably invented in the 1940s, when the prime minister of Thailand, Plaek Pibulsonggram, attempted to simultaneously improve the diet and create a sense of Thai-ness. Though it includes Chinese noodles and is prepared using the Chinese technique of stir-frying, it is now the dish most closely associated with Thai cuisine in much of the world.[63]

"Ethnic" restaurants run by migrants introduced diners to new dishes, which often became identified as national. In the first third of the twentieth century, 2 percent of the world's population was foreign-born. Italian migrants opened restaurants in Western cities (fig. 8.6). Chinese restaurants exemplified the storefront "ethnic" restaurant; run by hard-working family members, they had exotic decor and long menus adjusted to local tastes. Australia, with a Chinese population dating back over a century, had over eight thousand Chinese restaurants by the end of the twentieth century.[64] France, Britain, Germany, and Belgium each had at least a thousand Chinese restaurants, with Italy catching up rapidly. In most of these countries, up to 90 percent of the Chinese population was involved in one way or another with the restaurant business. For Peruvians, Chinese cuisine was spicy and served in restaurants known as *chifas*. For the Japanese, Chinese cuisine comprised sweet-and-sour dishes, tofu with spicy sauce, or pork and garlic-chive dumplings, served with Japanese rice. For the Americans and British, it was first chop suey and chow mein, then General Tso's chicken and hot and sour soup. Japanese diners progressed from Chinese food to Korean barbecue, Italian pasta, and Mexican and Thai food. In Moscow, Russians went out for the pilau of Central Asia, *lobio*, a spicy bean dish from Georgia, lamb soup with saffron, and steamed dumplings.[65] Urban Mexicans, by the end of the twentieth century, enthusiastically ate sushi, its rolls filled with cream cheese, in the Mexican chain Sushi Itto.

In the West, cookbooks from the 1960s on promised their readers authentic reproductions of foreign cuisines. *Mediterranean Food* (1950) and *French Country Cooking* (1951) by Elizabeth David inspired cooks weary of modern English food. The two volumes of *Mastering the Art of French Cooking* (1961, 1970) by Simone Beck, Louisette Bertholle, and Julia Child made high French cuisine acceptable by explaining in detail how to prepare it with American ingredients. Other cookbooks followed, written by highly educated middle- or upper-class women. Marcella Hazan, Claudia Roden, Madhur Jaffrey, Irene Kao, and Diana Kennedy interpreted high Italian, Middle Eastern, Indian, Chinese, and Mexican food for American or British readers, their writings codifying these cuisines in the same

FIGURE 8.6. Menu for a dinner sponsored by the Roman Spaghetti House, one of eighty restaurants participating in the 1939–40 New York World's Fair. Others included Old Prague, Heineken's on the Zuiderzee, Café Tel Aviv, and Merrie England. Courtesy New York Public Library, http://digitalgallery.nypl.org/nypldigital/id?1687367.

FIGURE 8.7. The Gawharet el Nil (Jewel of the Nile) was the main dining room of the Nile Hilton, which opened in Cairo in 1958 as part of Conrad Hilton's "World Peace through International Trade and Travel" program. In addition to offering American comforts, Hilton Hotels attempted to introduce guests to the local culture and food. Guests could order American roasts or steak Diane flambé from the brass-bound menu or opt for Egyptian stuffed pigeon with *fereek* (wheat harvested while green and then charred). Courtesy Hospitality Industry Archives, Conrad N. Hilton School of Hotel and Restaurant Management, University of Houston.

way French cuisine had been codified earlier, to make them reproducible outside the country. Because readers often assumed that they were learning about the everyday fare of humble folk, "ethnic" cookbooks contributed to the modern urban myth of the excellence of premodern peasant cuisine.

Hotels, especially resort hotels, increasingly featured not only French cuisine but also the local cuisine. In Hawaii, the luau was invented for the tourist trade in the early 1930s when the four liners of the Matson steamship line began plying regularly between the West Coast and Honolulu, taking wealthy Americans to holiday in the Matson luxury hotels—the Moana and the Royal Hawaiian.[66] Just as Parisians driving to the provinces could experience local culinary festivities or dine on local dishes served by waitresses in local costumes, so Americans sipped mai tais from coconut shells and ate baked pork, long rice, and lomi lomi salmon while they watched Hawaiian girls dressed in sarongs performing songs and dances. And just as the regional French festivities and meals had been adjusted to Parisian tastes, so the luau had been created for tourists; the long rice was Chinese, the lomi lomi salmon was composed of salted salmon imported from the Pacific Northwest and included tomatoes and onions, neither of which was native to the Hawaiian islands, and the sarongs were a recent introduction. In Turkey, the Divan

Hotel began presenting Turkish cuisine in 1956. About the same time, Conrad Hilton was opening hotels overseas, offering guests a taste of the local cuisine (fig. 8.7). At the time, no cookery schools taught local non-European cuisines, and the staff of grand hotels, including the restaurant staff, were almost always from Switzerland and the United States.[67] In response to the new demand, however, hotel management and catering schools began training cooks to prepare non-European cuisines. In India, for example, the government founded twenty catering colleges to teach urban Punjabi cuisine.[68]

Foreign dishes made their way into national cuisines, though rarely in their original form. Pasta was probably the commonest, with "spag bol" becoming a popular Sunday dish in Britain and lasagna a staple of the American table. The British had Balti curry, the Americans, chop suey, the Japanese, *kari raisu* ("curry rice"), and the Thais, Lao food. When Japanese children were asked to evaluate the foods in the national school lunch program in 1982, they ranked curry rice as their favorite.[69] Even a beginning cook could prepare it using instant curry roux, which resembled fat little chocolate bars, with indentations to allow for easy separation; these were sold by two of the biggest Japanese food companies, S&B Foods and House Foods Corporation. Many dishes, like curry rice in Japan and ramen noodles in the United States, lost their foreign associations. Other dishes remained faintly exotic: flaming pupu platters and sushi in the United States, fondue in Mexico, tandoori in the United States and Great Britain. Dishes from former colonies became part of the national cuisines of the former colonial powers. In England, curry and chicken tikka masala (invented in England) came close to being national dishes, easy to find in cheap restaurants or to make at home using packaged mixes from firms such as Pataks, and in France, Algerian couscous became a standard side dish. In China, children quickly accepted enticingly advertised foreign foods. As economic reforms proceeded, children went to convenience stores or supermarkets with their allowances and picked out Snickers bars, M&Ms, McVitie's digestive biscuits, Keebler cookies and crackers, Coca-Cola, and Sprite, often modified for the Chinese market with, say, mango flavoring in the sandwich cookies.[70] In the big cities, children frequently made 70 percent of the family's buying decisions (compared to 40 percent in the United States), instructing their parents about new foods.[71]

By the end of the century, confusion about national cuisines was rife. Foreigners frequently identified street foods, working-class dishes, or dishes created for tourists as typical. Europeans, knowing nothing of pot roast or corn bread, thought American cuisine consisted of hot dogs and hamburgers. Americans thought all Britons ate fish and chips. India was the land of tandoori chicken, China of chop suey and fried rice, Italy of pasta and pizza, and Mexico of fajitas and nachos. These dishes were sometimes exported to their purported homelands, such as fajitas and nachos to Mexico and American-style pizza to Italy. Diners worried about whether they were cooking or eating the authentic cuisine of Mexico, China, Thailand or Greece, not aware that the cuisines of those countries were sharply divided by class and region and were changing as they absorbed foreign foodstuffs, techniques, and dishes.

By the end of the century, many Westerners and Japanese, among others, had abandoned the assumption central to ancient and traditional culinary philosophy that the cuisine of one's birthplace was the most healthful and the most delectable of cuisines. They also discarded the belief at the core of nineteenth-century culinary philosophy that bread and beef was the tastiest as well as the most strengthening diet. Instead, a new culinary philosophy according to which every nation had a long-standing traditional cuisine worth exploring for its delicious taste was coming to the fore.

THE GLOBALIZATION OF WHEAT FLOUR, CONVENIENT MEATS, MILK, FRUITS, AND VEGETABLES AND THE SPECIALIZATION OF COOKING

By the late twentieth century, the foods available to consumers had changed in multiple ways. Far more fresh, or apparently fresh, foodstuffs were now available compared to the salted and dried foodstuffs that had prevailed throughout much of history. Fresh meat displaced salted meat. Bread and snack cakes, such as Hostess Twinkies in the United States and Gansitos in Mexico, remained soft rather than going hard and stale. Ultrapasteurized milk kept for months. Orange juice, milk, eggs, fruit, and vegetables were sold year-round instead of only in a limited season. Fruits and vegetables lasted longer with new forms of packaging and refrigerated transport from field to store. Far more flavored foods lined the shelves, including pepper-, vinegar-, and barbecue-flavored potato chips and hazelnut- and chocolate-flavored coffee. Foods commonly contained more fat, although the typical Western fat-flour-sugar combination made it invisible in, say, cakes and cookies. More foods were available as individual or family-sized portions, which could be consumed as snacks or instant meals.[72] Many packaged foods were on offer, some of which, like frozen concentrated orange juice, fish sticks, Kool-Aid, salad dressing mixes, toaster pastries, Miracle Whip, nondairy creams, and TV dinners, were accepted, while others, such as canned deep-fried hamburgers, were rejected. Above all, consumers around the globe were eating more white bread, pasta, and other wheat-flour products, meats in convenient forms, fats, sweeteners, milk, and fruits and vegetables.

White bread in the United States finally became as soft and fluffy as people had wished it could be for centuries once baking was industrialized in the late 1920s. Flour delivered at the entrance to the factory was kneaded by machine. Yeast, fat, milk, sugar, and vitamins were automatically added to the dough, which was weighed, divided, and shaped by machine. It then passed through the oven on conveyor belts. On emerging at the other end, it was wrapped by machine. Small bakers almost disappeared, their market share in 1939 down to less than 4 percent of the total ($20 million, compared to the $514 million earned by industrial bakeries). The slicing machine and the electric toaster, invented in the 1930s, made sandwiches a popular American lunch. When, in 1942, in an effort to save steel for the war effort, the U.S. government banned bread-slicing machines, public outcry made it back down.[73] Bread supplied about 40 percent of American calories during World War II, when Americans ate white bread at every meal, for a total of about a pound and a half a week (much more than now, but less than their European grandparents ate daily). By the 1950s, the calories supplied by white bread had fallen to about 25–30 percent, and by the end of the century to about 9 percent, less than either sweet cakes and cookies or meat.[74]

By the time Americans were moving on to foods other than the white bread that had been the object of desire for so long, puffy white bread wrapped in plastic had become a staple in places as diverse as Japan, Nigeria, and Mexico. In Japan, at the end of the 1940s, the Supreme Commander for the Allied Powers announced that the school lunch program would provide children with nearly a quarter of a pound of bread a day, along with butter.[75] Housewives embraced store-bought bread, which, unlike rice, did not have to be cooked daily and thus was ideal for a quick snack. Toast for breakfast with eggs and thinly sliced cabbage instead of rice meant they could sleep in a little later. Bread became so important that it was the Japanese, in the 1980s, who invented the bread machine.

The Nigerian bread industry, still tiny in 1946, grew nineteenfold by 1960, to become the country's third largest indigenous industry, after clothing manufacturing and woodworking.[76] Nigerians who had learned to bake from West Indians or trained at their own expense in Britain set up bakeries in the south of the country. They used flour ground from American wheat in a Greek-run mill financed by American loans. They sold it to well-to-do urban Nigerians—senior civil servants, professionals, richer merchants—who had become used to it when studying in Britain. Because it was from three to eight times more expensive than cassava, however, and twice as expensive as yams, most Nigerians continued to eat pounded yam or cassava (fufu) in the south and sorghum and millet in the north, buying bread only as a snack food when traveling on the buses that now careened along the roads.

Then, in the 1970s, bread consumption climbed, as drought decimated the sorghum and millet crop of the northern regions and earnings from oil exports made it possible to purchase large amounts of wheat. By the 1980s, food imports, largely from the United States, had grown sevenfold; 90 percent of the wheat consumed in Nigeria, 50 percent of the rice, and 20 percent of the maize was imported, and per capita food output had fallen nearly 20 percent. The number of bakeries in Kano, one of the country's two biggest cities, jumped from 5 to 226. The average Nigerian now consumed ninety-five pounds of wheat bread a year, as opposed to eleven pounds in the late 1960s. "Tea sellers" went around to offices selling bread, tea, and evaporated milk. "Bread has become the cheapest staple food of our people," the Nigerian head of state announced in 1984.

In Mexico, wealthier citizens had eaten crusty oval rolls since the Conquest in the sixteenth century. In the 1940s, the Servitjes, an immigrant family from Catalonia, imported American baking machinery to produce square, fluffy white bread that competed neither with tortillas nor with the traditional rolls. They quickly added American-style cookies and snack cakes. At the beginning of the twenty-first century, their trucks showed a young boy standing in a wheat field with a pyramid in the background. The slogan read, "The power of wheat." By then, Mexico's Grupo Bimbo was the biggest baker in the world, selling bread throughout Latin America, Spain, and (under other names) in the United States.

Despite the popularity of bread, the cake, particularly the baking powder cake, another wheat-flour product, was the Anglo tradition's greatest contribution to cuisine. It took its present form in the 1920s and 1930s, when all the elements necessary to make it were in place: enclosed home ovens, metal pans, readily available and inexpensive fine white flour and sugar, butter or margarine, eggs, and baking powder (fig. 8.8). The United States, Britain, Canada, Australia, and New Zealand all had their own specialties. American cooks, for example, developed a multitude of variations on the basic butter cake made of butter, sugar, eggs, raising agents, and white flour: yellow cake, white cake, chocolate cakes of various kinds, cakes flavored with orange or lemon, startling red velvet cake, pineapple upside-down cake, and towering layers of Lady Baltimore cake. Millers and chemical leavening companies promoted home baking. "Any one can bake," said a cookbook put out by Royal Baking Powder. "The American layer cake is . . . your best work in the kitchen, the highest thing you can offer to someone you love, the most emotionally laden thing." Making cakes could be tricky though. This opened the door for cake mixes, and companies launched advertising campaigns to promote their brands: Procter & Gamble (taking over Nebraska Consolidated Mills) hired the well-known restaurant critic Duncan Hines, Pillsbury invented Ann Pillsbury, and General Mills created the ever-youthful Betty Crocker. By the end of the century, 60 percent of American housewives used mixes. Outside the Anglo world, cakes were purchased from bakeries or pastry shops.

Wheat pasta sales, including ramen in Asia and Italian-style pasta in the West, grew as fast as those of fluffy white bread. In 2011, an Oxfam survey declared pasta the world's favorite food, consumed in quantity in Venezuela, the Philippines, South Africa, Mexico, Argentina, and Bolivia, as well as in Italy and the United States.[77] By the end of the twentieth century, one-fifth of the world's calories came from wheat, another fifth from rice.[78] Except for the potato, which grew in popularity when transformed into the French fry, the lesser grains and roots and tubers declined in relative share of the market.

FIGURE 8.8. An African American servant puts the finishing touches on a cake icing. Made with processed wheat flour, sugar, butter, and eggs and baked in a home oven, cake was the high point of home cooking in Western cuisine. The cook is a reminder of the crucial role of servants in the preparation and dissemination of cuisines. Courtesy New York Public Library, http://digitalgallery.nypl.org/nypldigital/id?1212151.

Consumption of liquid cow's milk also skyrocketed. Over the course of history, like all milks, it had rarely been drunk fresh because with good reason it was perceived to be dangerous. Instead, it was consumed in safer forms, as yogurt, cheese, butter, or milk sweets. This began to change in the West when the eighteenth-century French intellectual Jean-Jacques Rousseau declared it to be the best of all foods, a pure, strengthening, pastoral antidote to the over-processed food of the cities.[79] In the nineteenth century, reformers repeated the message, arguing that milk, from cows that frolicked in green pastures, as in the Nestlé advertisement in figure 8.9, should replace the long-time safe drinks—beer, cider, and wine. Milk, they suggested, was the perfect complement to red beef, which, not coincidentally came from the same animal. It was "a model of what a nutritious substance ought to be, and the most perfect of all elementary aliments," according to the English scientist William Prout, who worked on its chemical constitution.[80] Milk promoters invented an

FIGURE 8.9. This advertisement for Nestlé's Swiss Milk, signed by the prominent illustrators Dudley Hardy and John Hassall and probably created in the 1920s, shows a frisky cow kicking over a churn on a flower-speckled meadow. Rural imagery obscured the manipulations that milk went through before it reached the consumer. Courtesy New York Public Library, Miriam and Ira D. Wallach Division of Art, Prints and Photographs, http://digitalgallery.nypl.org/nypldigital/id?1259071.

ancient heritage for their favored beverage. Prout's followers asserted that it had created sturdy Roman citizens, while Robert Hartley, an American religious temperance reformer, postulated in *An Historical, Scientific and Practical Essay on Milk* (1842) that it went back to biblical times. By the end of the century, five million Londoners were consuming sixty million gallons of milk annually. In 1926, Americans consumed a third more dairy products than they had only seven years previously.[81] Public health officials worried because milk drinking was associated with scarlet fever, typhoid, diphtheria, and one of the most dreaded diseases of the epoch, tuberculosis. Moreover, contrary to the rural image of milk, in the cities, much of the milk came from cows kept in filthy stalls and fed on swill, the mash left over from brewing.[82]

Gradually industrial processing transformed liquid cow's milk into the safe, palatable, durable products that are now consumed around the globe by people of all ages, sexes, classes, and nations: canned milk, baby formula, pasteurized milk, ice cream, homogenized milk, yogurt, dried milk, and long-life (UHT) milk. Few foods are more industrialized, more regulated, and less natural.

Canned milk was invented simultaneously in different parts of the world and from the 1860s on, canned condensed and evaporated milk was sent to soldiers, travelers, and Europeans in the tropics. Dairy farming became profitable far from cities, for example, in Switzerland, Wisconsin, and Toogoolawah in South Queensland, Australia. Gail Borden in the United States patented a process for condensing and canning milk in 1856, a lucky stroke of timing, because after 1861, there was great demand from the Union Army for the products of his New York Condensed Milk Company. By the 1880s, the Anglo-Swiss Condensed Milk Company (later Nestlé) was turning out twenty-five million cans a year, and during World War I, it bought condenseries in the United States to fulfill government contracts in Europe. Baby formula, introduced in 1867 by Justus von Liebig, better known as the promoter of beef extract, came to be regarded as preferable to mother's milk.[83]

In the tropics, condensed milk was bought first by the wealthy and then by ordinary local people. In India and Latin America, it was welcomed as an inexpensive alternative to traditional condensed-milk sweets, such as khoya (milk boiled down to one-fifth of its volume) in India and dulce de leche (sweetened, boiled-down milk) in Latin America. In all parts of the tropics, syrupy condensed milk was spread on crackers or spooned over ice and canned fruit, two other new industrial products.[84] More controversially, watered condensed milk and baby formula were used as substitutes for mother's milk, instead of, say, rice or sweet potato pap. Because these products do not contain all the nutrients of breast milk, governments promoted breast-feeding instead of formula. For that reason, and because the water with which they were mixed was often polluted, advocacy groups in the 1970s organized a boycott of Nestlé, the major distributor, and launched a campaign to persuade mothers to breast-feed.[85] In China, condensed milk was probably responsible for soy milk's sudden popularity after it had languished for two thousand years since its invention in the Han era. When boiled like cow's milk, it lost its beany taste, became more digestible, and was sought after for the first time.[86]

Liquid milk drinking received a boost following World War I, when nutritionists such as Elmer McCollum and geographers such as Ellsworth Huntington and Eduard Hahn argued that milk produced "virile stock."[87] Western nations began experimenting with co-ops, regulations, and milk-marketing boards to prevent the shortages, seasonal variations in supply, and health scares associated with milk.[88] After prolonged debates about whether milk should be certified or pasteurized, pasteurized milk that had been heated to 144 degrees Fahrenheit slowly became the norm. Milk, military dieticians announced, had overtaken coffee, the favorite drink of GIs in World War I, as the new favorite in World War II.[89] One can only assume they were excluding alcohol. In the latter half of the century, the United States made milk the cornerstone of the four essential food groups, and it became an essential part of school milk programs. At this point it was homogenized by being forced through a nozzle at high pressure to distribute the fat globules and prevent creaming.

Other milk products also grew in popularity in the second half of the twentieth century. In the 1980s, manufacturers began to add flavors and sweeteners to yogurt, changing it from a health food that lengthened life to a favorite low-fat dessert for dieters in Western countries. Today pots of yogurt far outnumber cartons of milk in, for example, Mexican supermarket coolers. Ice cream spread globally. The United States defined it as a necessary and thus unrationed food during World War I, boosting its consumption. The Soviet Union invested in the infrastructure to make it readily available as evidence that the state could deliver the good life.[90] In Cuba, Fidel Castro declared that the state must produce quality ice cream, in 1966 setting up the Coppelia ice cream parlor, which still operates today.[91] In India, traditional milk products were industrialized by companies such as Amul. They adjusted milk condensers and dryers to make powdered milk, baby food, and condensed milk from water buffalo milk. They drained yogurt in laundry centrifuges for a sweetened condensed treat (*shrikand*). And they shaped dried milk balls (*gulab jamun*) in meatball-forming machines and cooked them in doughnut fryers before soaking them in the traditional syrup.[92]

Milk's triumphant rise continued when, toward the end of the century, governments worldwide, including those of India, Indonesia, Mexico, Argentina, and even China, where milk drinking had always been rare, encouraged their citizens to drink milk, which was assumed to be what made Westerners tall and strong. By now, improved methods of drying milk made it easy to rehydrate to make yogurt and UHT milk (ultra-high-temperature processed milk with a shelf life of six to nine months), both convenient forms in which to consume milk. Indian annual consumption rose to thirty-nine liters a head, a 240 percent increase between 1970 and the end of the century. To avoid raising concerns among the 14 percent of the population who were Muslim, milk was described as increasing physical and mental health, not as embedded in Hindu culture and associated with Mother India. Chinese advertising associated milk with tall athletes, suggesting that it would overcome "growth retardation" and make more powerful citizens. Twenty factories produced baby formula, and a school milk program was established in 1999.[93] Chinese consumption increased 1,700 percent in the last thirty years of the century, with average consumption reaching twelve liters a head.

Meat and fish, the centerpiece of the main meal in Western cuisine, were now often processed to yield uniform, convenient products that could be eaten without having to separate bone from flesh.[94] Beef ground by machine rose in popularity in America during World War II, providing cooks with an inexpensive substitute for steak (hamburger) or an economical meatloaf. Frankfurter consumption soared in the 1960s, first in the United States, then in many other parts of the world, as new ways were found to emulsify the bits of meat and send them along conveyor belts, where they were automatically packed into artificial casings. The average American ate eighty hot dogs a year by the end of the twentieth century.[95] Today supermarkets in Mexico, Spain, and Panama are full of wieners; the Chinese too now eat packed meats. Chicken became a cheap meal as new methods of rearing, killing, and chilling brought its price below that of steak.[96] No longer did families have to buy a whole chicken and cut it up. Boneless chicken breasts, known in the 1950s as expensive luxury morsels that had to be cut from a whole carcass, by the end of the century had become a go-to item for the harried housewife and the restaurateur looking to keep costs under control. By then, Americans consumed chicken as "nuggets" and Mexicans as *milanesa,* thin, breaded and pounded, ready-to-fry cutlets. Fish fingers, sold frozen, breaded, and boneless, became standard children's fare. The Japanese found ways to shape, flavor, and color ground white fish to make *surimi,* sold in the United States as ersatz crab and lobster, and in Spain as ersatz elvers (baby eels). The Nestlé brand Maggi carefully tailored chicken and beef stock cubes to the tastes of local consumers: *sinigang* in the Philippines, *cocido* in Spain, and halal for Muslims.

Fruits and vegetables appeared in new guises, such as orange juice in cartons, and ready-cut celery, broccoli, and carrots. Wrapping and refrigeration allowed vegetables to be shipped by rail, container ship, or air to consumers in the United States and Europe from Florida, California, the Mediterranean, Chile, and African countries. Out-of-season and exotic fruits and vegetables became commonplace, fresh as well as canned.

Fats and sugars were transformed. The solid animal fats of the Western tradition were displaced by new kinds of cooking oils. Soy cooking oil, less expensive than olive oil, appeared in the 1930s, followed by inexpensive canola and corn oil. By the 1970s, 65 percent of all the edible oils in the United States came from soybeans. Other important vegetable oils included palm, coconut, rapeseed, corn, and cottonseed. Public revulsion against cholesterol and solid animal fats, aided by skillful marketing, boosted the oil, shortening, and margarine market. Every kitchen came to have a bottle of vegetable oil waiting to be poured into the frying pan. Sugar consumption worldwide was six times greater in 1964 than in 1900, a bigger increase than for any other foodstuff, except possibly dried and canned milk. Sugar substitutes became available from the late nineteenth century on, most of them directed at the dieting market.[97] In the early 1980s, American food scientists picked up a Japanese innovation, a way of extracting high fructose corn syrup (HFCS) from wet-milled maize. With its low prices, it captured the expanding soft drinks wing of the beverage industry. By 2000, it almost equaled sugar in sales.

Ready-prepared appetizers, sweets, and sauces, formerly available only to those who could afford high cuisines, were available to all in the West. Shoppers could buy salty nuts, pretzels, potato chips, tortilla chips, salami, cheese, and olives. Children and office workers enjoyed the candy bars—whole meals in a wrapper—that appeared in the 1930s, and the snack cakes that arrived after World War II, as well as an increasing range of packaged cookies.[98] Americans in the 1960s and 1970s welcomed the introduction of canned soup bases, which saved the trouble of making and flavoring white sauces from scratch (though these never caught on in Europe). Later, white sauces fell out of favor as too heavy and calorific, replaced by bottled pasta sauces and canned broths. Mayonnaise, ketchup, and mustard remained widely used, the first two spreading globally. Chinese-made sauces entered the world market when the Lee Kum Kee Company became a global distributor. After World War II, the company moved its headquarters to Hong Kong. In 1972, it launched Panda Oyster Sauce, helping make what was a relatively recent addition to southern Chinese food well known internationally. Moving swiftly with the gourmet market, it launched XO sauce in 1992. Today the Lee Kum Kee Group distributes over 220 sauces and condiments to over 100 countries and regions across five continents.[99] In 1944, Kikkoman developed a way to make a semi-chemical soy using fermentation and hydrolyzed vegetable protein. In the 1950s, miso was made using automated equipment, new ingredients, continuous-process technologies, new packaging, and modern merchandising and advertising.[100] Many of these appetizers, sauces, and sweets were perked up with artificial flavors produced by the distilling industry of western Europe and the fermentation techniques of Japan.[101]

Fizzy sweetened beverages, particularly Coke, went global in the twentieth century, as lager beer had in the late nineteenth. By the 1980s, Coca-Cola was the world's most widely distributed product, available in 145 countries. In Japan, Coca-Cola's most profitable market, consumers of its products quickly developed their own preferences. By 1995, excluding Japan, "brand Coke" amounted to only 64 percent of the company's sales. Nonfizzy drinks, such as canned tea, made up the rest.[102]

Alternatives to basic foods were eagerly sought by scientists in Europe, the Soviet Union, and the United States as populations soared and famines continued in many parts of the world. Some, cognizant of successes synthesizing vanillin, say, tried to extend the technique to proteins. Others, particularly German and

Russian scientists, dusted off old lists of famine foods. They suggested making bread from mashed potatoes, apples, or beets, eating seal flesh and fat, raising rabbits, and using soybeans. Despite widespread hunger, Russians never took to the recipes in *130 Soybean Dishes* (1930) or *The Mass Preparation of Vegetable and Soybean Dishes* (1934). Converted into textured vegetable protein, soy had more success and can now be found in animal foods and packaged hamburger mixes, and can be purchased in health food stores and markets in countries such as the United States and Mexico. Algae-based foodstuffs, one of the major research initiatives of the 1950s and 1960s, failed as much because they disgusted people as because they were more expensive than predicted.[103]

The transformation of the domestic kitchen, already under way in the West, spread to other parts of the world. For the middle classes, water and fuel, expensive commodities in earlier times, became essentially free. Kitchens had hot and cold running water, often pure enough to drink from the tap. In the West, stoves with enclosed ovens heated by electricity or gas, both safer to use and less time-consuming to tend than coal-fired ranges, became standard kitchen equipment. In other parts of the world, where baking and roasting were not part of the culinary tradition, the ovens were often used for storage. Refrigerators, promoted by electric companies, became common in the United States before World War II, as well as in Europe and in wealthier homes in Latin America in the 1950s and 1960s, and then spread elsewhere as a sign of middle-class membership (fig. 8.10). Used at first for beer, soft drinks, and ice cream, refrigerators gradually became pantries in which to keep milk, meat, fresh fruit, vegetables, and even condiments, especially when cars made shopping a once-a-week rather than daily chore.

After World War II, first in the United States and then in Europe, small electric gadgets, such as plug-in kettles, toasters, and mixers, made traditional tasks easier and allowed new tasks to be taken on. Countertop models of the microwave oven, patented by Percy Spencer, a scientist at the American defense contractor Raytheon, were first produced for home kitchens by a subsidiary, Amana, in the 1960s. Aluminum foil, cling wrap, and detergent were handy for storage and cleanup. In a famous incident in 1959, Vice President Richard Nixon toured a model American home at the American National Exhibition in Moscow with Soviet premier Nikita Khrushchev. Nixon lauded the kitchen equipped with labor-saving devices as a symbol of American accomplishments, while Khrushchev dismissed it as unimportant to a nation's development. Whether the "kitchen debate" was as widely known in the USSR as it was in the United States and whether it contributed to dissatisfaction with the regime is not clear. What is clear is that home kitchens in the richer parts of the world were streamlined and filled with gadgets by the latter part of the twentieth century. Rice cookers were welcomed in Japan, blenders for salsas and pressure cookers for high-altitude cooking in Mexico, and yogurt makers in India.

FIGURE 8.10. A gleaming white Zenith refrigerator would keep food fresh, just as the gleaming white Taj Mahal kept the memory of Shah Jahan's wife from fading, or so this advertisement suggested. From Vila Patik, *The Finest Recipe Collection: Kashmir to Kanyakumari* (Bombay: Rekka Supra, n.d. [1970s?]). In the author's possession.

The home kitchen ceased to be a place where dirty, dangerous, smelly processing was carried out and became a place for final meal preparation. Standards went up again. Now the cook was expected to turn out a variety of different meals from different culinary traditions, instead of the nineteenth-century pattern of a weekly sequence of meals, or the yet-earlier pattern of a series of minor variations on a pottage. It became a room for living, "the heart of the home." Lavishly equipped with marble counters and industrial-strength stoves, it was a place for entertaining as well as cooking.

Grocery stores linked domestic and industrial kitchens. In the first half of the century, emporia such as the Great Atlantic and Pacific Tea Company (fig. 8.11) added processed foods to traditional imported luxuries such as tea, sugar, dried fruit, and spices. Flour, self-raising flour, baking powder, custard powder, blanc-

FIGURE 8.11. This window of the A&P (Great Atlantic and Pacific Tea Company) at 246 Third Street in Manhattan in 1936 is crowded with industrially produced canned food and crackers as well as the coffee and tea that had been the earlier staples of grocery stores. A&P was the first grocery chain in the United States, in the late nineteenth century, and one of the first to adopt self-service in the 1930s. Photographed by Berenice Abbott for the Federal Art Project of the Works Progress Administration. Courtesy New York Public Library, http://digitalgallery.nypl .org/nypldigital/id?1219150.

mange powder, concentrated egg powder, starches, bottled gelatin, powdered gelatin, and bottled sauces and pickles appeared in sanitary cardboard boxes and shiny cans, offering hitherto unheard-of shortcuts. The tin can, said Poppy Cannon, food editor in the 1950s of *Ladies' Home Journal* and *House Beautiful,* was "The open sesame to wealth and freedom. . . . Freedom from tedium, space, work and your own inexperience."[104] Advertisements implied stories about the origin and use of foodstuffs. Buitoni pasta showed a smiling, buxom girl standing with a sheaf of wheat against a background of golden grain and blue skies. Chocolate was advertised with roses and kittens. Japanese girls who graduated from higher schools for women between 1922 and 1937 received MSG in a perfume-shaped bottle.[105]

In the second half of the twentieth century, grocery stores changed again; counter service was replaced by self-service. As the demand for fresh, natural products increased, perishables were added, such as meat, milk, and fruit and vegetables in refrigerated cases. In-store bakeries promised fresh bread, and rotisseries a ready meal to take home. By the end of the century, huge hypermarkets such as Walmart and Carrefour sold both groceries and the types of goods found in department stores.

Housewives happily submitted recipes to corporate competitions, while home economists were hired to develop recipes for company products. For example, in 1928, *Better Homes and Gardens* set up a "Testing-Tasting Kitchen," where its home economists embarked on a campaign to "nudge the American public into a new, more scientific era of cooking," giving precise recipes instead of vague general directions, and trying out new products and new appliances that were coming on the market.

The industrial kitchen continued to grow, in war and peace, with and without government help, in Europe, former European colonies, Japan, and the United States. The British, who had generally preferred to keep manufacturing, including food processing, at home, found themselves in World War II with the task of feeding a two-million-strong volunteer Indian army and Allied troops gathering to attack the Japanese in Burma and the Far East. They set up 134 factories to produce crackers, dehydrated potatoes, clear molasses, ground coffee, salt, curry powder and other powdered condiments, chutney, lemon and lime juice cordials, dried and canned fruit, and vegetable ghee.[106] After Independence in 1947, the Indian government moved swiftly to establish a food-processing industry, founding the Central Food Technological Research Institute at Mysore, the city of palaces, in southwestern India. Researchers developed new uses for Indian products, found substitutes for expensive imported goods such as baby food, organized conferences for the United Nations, and trained chemists and engineers from India and from some forty foreign countries to work in the food-processing industries.

In the United States, food corporations, which had provided rations for American troops around the globe, introducing or popularizing Coca-Cola, Nescafé, Spam, cake mixes, and packaged macaroni and cheese, turned their attention to the domestic market. By the end of the century, about 70,000 food scientists were working in the United States, about two-thirds in private industry, the other third in government education and research. The Institute of Food Technologists, with 28,000 members, was the main professional group. Their work was eagerly perused both by chefs interested in molecular gastronomy and by the development personnel in the fast-food industry.

In 1985, American food processing was an over $300 billion a year industry, substantially larger than automobile manufacturing, at $188 billion a year, or petroleum refining, at $167 billion. Archer Daniels Midland (grains), Kraft Foods, Cargill, Pepsi, Coke, Mars, General Mills, Anheuser-Busch, Swift, and Dairy Farmers of America were all among the top thirty world food businesses by 2008.[107] Although convenience foods are the best-known product of the industrial kitchen, its basic achievement in the second half of the twentieth century was the creation of starches, sweeteners, oils, and flavors from a few basic sources, particularly maize, soy, yeast, and fermented products. Starch-sweet-fat combinations were fundamental to Western cuisine. Now they became even more affordable than ever. Specialized starches were created to use as thickeners and stabilizers in soup, sauces, salad dressings, puddings, and pie fillings as well as for making noodles and pasta (and for many industrial purposes, particularly paper making).

Many European flavor and fragrance companies, especially those owned by big chemical companies such as Roche, Bayer, and Unilever, moved to New Jersey following World War II. In the late 1940s, monosodium glutamate (MSG) was welcomed by the American military and food corporations for its ability to enhance the taste of inexpensive foods; large-scale production began in the 1950s. In the 1960s, the mass spectrometer and gas chromatography made it easier to isolate the flavor-giving chemicals in liquids and solids, respectively. In the 1970s, the University of California at Davis introduced a diagram resembling a spider web, with a particular flavor attribute along each axis, to record the flavors detected by humans. By the 1990s, chefs were being hired to match natural and man-made flavors. By the end of the century, the fragrance and flavor industry was making $16 billion in sales annually.

American and other food processors moved into China following the shift there to a market economy in the 1980s. Wall's, owned by the Anglo-Dutch multinational Unilever, made ice cream, French Danone made Lu cookies and dairy products, Chinese Amoy and Wahaha made soy sauce, dim sum, and children's food, and American Heinz, Chinese United Food Enterprise of Guandong, and Nestlé all made baby foods (map 8.1). Coca-Cola, dismissed by Mao in his *Little Red Book* as "the opiate of the running dogs of revanchist capitalism," applied for and was granted the right to operate in China in 1979.[108] By the late 1990s, Coke had twenty-three plants in China, was the most widely recognized brand name in the country, and had almost 60 percent of the soft drink market.[109] Chinese entrepreneurs went back into food processing as they had in the earlier twentieth century, increasing beer production and flour milling, industrializing the production of gluten, and canning and refrigerating mock abalone, shrimp, and chicken to export to Chinese communities in the United States and Europe.[110]

Food service kitchens to supply restaurants and hotels, hospitals and universities, stadiums and sporting events appeared in the second half of the twentieth century, bringing down the cost of eating out. New companies were created, such as Sysco, Compass, and Aramak in the United States and the giant Sodexo in France, with 380,000 employees worldwide, working in eighty different countries, delivering foodstuffs and prepared meals to its customers. Fast-food chains succeeded in creating menus for outlets that had only one or two appliances, a griddle, and a deep fryer for hamburger restaurants, or an oven in the case of pizza restaurants, and a young staff with minimal kitchen experience.

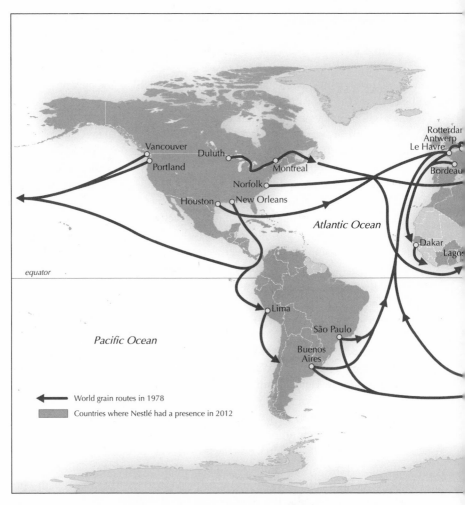

MAP 8.1. Culinary nationalism and transnationalism, ca. 2000. By the year 2000, empires had broken up into about two hundred different nations, almost all of them claiming to have their own cuisine. Countervailing forces such as supranational culinary philosophies, aid, NGOs, and multinational corporations crossed these boundaries. Shaded nations are ones in which Nestlé had factories or a sales force, selling condensed and dried milk and dozens of other products from stock cubes to spaghetti, often adjusted to suit national tastes.

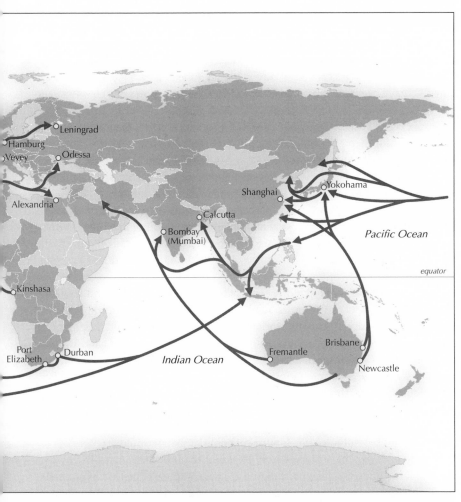

The arrows show the main routes for wheat and other grains in the 1980s, dominated by four major companies—ADM, Bunge, Cargill, and Louis Dreyfus—now supplying many more parts of the world than a century earlier, including the Middle East, Japan, China, Russia, and Southeast Asia. Sources: www.nestle.com/AboutUs/GlobalPresence/Pages/Global_Presence .aspx; Morgan, *Merchants of Grain*.

COUNTERCUISINES

The agrarian and romantic criticisms of modern food processing and mechanized farming examined in chapter 7 continued until the onset of World War II.[111] Once the war was over, a succession of new critiques appeared. In 1959, the American physiologist Ancel Keys, who had conducted important studies on starvation, and his wife, Margaret, published *How to Eat Well and Stay Well the Mediterranean Way.* A cuisine with lots of fresh fruit and vegetables, pasta, fish, and wine was more healthful than Western cuisine, with its saturated fats, was their message. The International Olive Oil Council, set up under UN auspices in 1959, was soon able to capitalize on this in an exceptionally successful advertising campaign, enlisting some of America's best food writers and cookbook authors to address the virtues of the Mediterranean diet. Coming at a time when foreign, particularly Mediterranean, foods were growing in popularity, the promise that they were also healthier tipped many diners into abandoning the white bread, beef, butter, and lard of northwestern Europe for olive oil and the bold flavors and bright colors associated with the Mediterranean.

In the 1960s, the counterculture repudiated what it termed the food establishment: the network of nutritionists, food scientists and technologists, bureaucrats, journalists, and advertisers who worked for large universities, food corporations, news organizations, or the government, who were seen as working hand-in-glove with the military-industrial complex. It favored the organic (a new word) movement and communal farms run on principles described in Rodale Press publications, founding over three thousand communes between 1965 and 1970 and setting up cooperative groceries. It embraced ecology, feminism, Rachel Carson's attack on DDT, and Adele Davis's onslaught on additives. It worried that if the atom bomb did not kill millions, the population bomb probably would.[112]

Ethnic and regional cuisines were explored to find alternatives to "plastic" foods, plastic now being seen as industrial, ersatz, and nasty instead of as a fascinating novelty, as it was in the 1930s. Brown bread and brown foods were thought preferable to white, slow food to fast, vegetables to meats, and ethnic dishes to Anglo cuisine. In her 1971 best seller *Diet for a Small Planet,* Frances Moore Lappé introduced the idea that two complementary vegetable proteins, grains and beans, provided an adequate substitute for animal protein. Alice Waters, inspired by time in France and the English cookbook writer Elizabeth David, set up her restaurant, Chez Panisse, in Berkeley, California, to offer cuisine based on fresh, local produce. The following year, Mollie Katzen published *The Moosewood Cookbook,* a handwritten cookbook of vegetarian recipes, which still sells today.

At the end of the 1970s, the American counterculture lost steam as it failed to expand beyond its youthful middle-class roots. Like earlier countercuisines, it left its mark on Western cuisine. Yogurt, 2 percent milk, herbal tea, bulk grains in grocery stores, sprouts, and sunflower seeds, as well as Whole Foods Market, the Institute for Food and Development Policy, and the Center for Science in the Public Interest, are just some of its bequests.

In Japan, a wave of nostalgia for the rural past was part of a backlash against foreign foods such as pizza, McDonald's, Dairy Queen, Kentucky Fried Chicken, and A & W Root Beer. Agricultural museums propagated an agrarian myth, as did restaurants and inns offering traditional Japanese food, scholars seeking the origins of Japanese cuisine, and magazines and cookbooks showing beautifully photographed Japanese dishes.[113]

In the 1990s, a new food movement gathered strength in the United States and Europe as consumers felt increasingly distanced from their food supply. Many activists argued for a return to home cooking (though not just by women) and welcomed government regulation of the food industry in the interest of improving the safety, healthfulness, and quality of food systems in their own countries. They continued to campaign against large food corporations and against what was now called industrial agriculture, expressed hostility to food science and technology, especially to scientists working on genetically modified organisms, and advocated fair trade and tariff barriers to protect small farmers. A host of voices, some of the most prominent being those of Michael Pollan, Eric Schlosser, Marion Nestle, the Center for Science in the Public Interest, and the *New York Times,* warned that modern Western food threatened consumers with obesity and was destroying the environment, hastening the demise of the small family farm, and opening Americans to food terrorism.

The food movement pointed to a series of food scares—*E. coli,* mad cow disease, salmonella—as indications of the dangers of the long global food chains, which could mean untraceable contamination and new dangers. Too many calories from cheap fats and sugars, without enough micronutrients from a balanced diet, led to obesity. In 1994, Barry Popkin, a nutritionist at the University of North Carolina, identified America's nutrition problem as "the increasing number of people who consume the types of diets associated with chronic diseases."[114] In the United States, Oldways, an organization founded by Dun Gifford in Boston, promoted a return to premodern cuisines, though some alternatives—the taro and seaweed diet of the Hawaiians, for example—were less appealing than the generalized Mediterranean cuisine.

In Italy, Carlo Petrini formed the brilliantly named Slow Food movement. He urged followers, instead of saving the world by eating vegetarian fare, to save traditional foodways by supporting peasants, who were advised to upgrade their cheeses, vegetables, and sausages to suit gourmet tastes and to sell them internationally.[115] In France, the food elite revived older, slower methods of making sourdough loaves. The artisan baker Lionel Poilâne, who inherited his father's bakery on the Left Bank in Paris, grew the business by using traditional techniques and by the end of the century was producing 15,000 loaves a day, many of which were shipped overseas by Federal Express. In Japan, traditional handmade misos were sought out, aficionados tasting them from five-gallon cedar kegs before picking out the preferred flavor and variety. Doing good by eating well was how food journalist Corby Kummer summed up the movement.[116]

By the early twenty-first century, among wealthier people in the Western world, a new consensus about cuisine had emerged. Modern Western cuisine, now taken for granted, was thought to be unhealthful and unsafe, processed and marketed by corporations who cared more about profits than about the consumer and produced by industrial agriculture in the hands of the multinational biotechnology company Monsanto—in short, a cuisine that should be abandoned in the West. In its place, there should be a return to home cooking, natural, unprocessed foods, short food chains, and small farmers, all with the aid of government. The poorer parts of the world, with the help of nongovernmental organizations, should be encouraged to retain their traditional cuisines.

This consensus is underpinned by the agrarian-romantic story about culinary history, now linked with domesticity and nationalism. Repeated time and again in cookbooks, magazine articles, travelogues, and newspapers, it tells how the fresh, natural, and healthful bounty of the earth, lovingly prepared by peasant women, was refined in the cities to become the cuisine of the region or the nation. It is the latest in a series of stories that every society has told itself about the origins and evolution of cooking. It is, of course, a myth, just like older stories of cooking being taught by the gods, or forced on humans on leaving the Garden of Eden, or discovered by accident when a pig was roasted in a house fire. It does, however, as we shall see, have significant consequences.

GLOBAL CULINARY GEOGRAPHY, 2000

By 2000, the world's population had risen to six billion; a decade later it had reached over seven billion. Over half of all human beings lived in cities, many in megacities in Asia, Africa, and Latin America. They consumed what at first sight is a complex patchwork of national and regional cuisines. In most parts of the world that have been inhabited for a long time, the complexity can be untangled by checking off the stages of culinary history. Working backward, in the twentieth century, most cuisines were changed by three overlapping realignments: a division into Western, socialist, and nonaligned countries; a splintering into two hundred national cuisines; and a global shift to a division between a rich world with middling cuisines and a poor world with high and humble cuisines. In the eighteenth and nineteenth centuries, most parts of the world came under the sway of modernizing, expansive empires or states, particularly the British, French, Dutch, Russian, Japanese, or American. In the two thousand years before that, Eurasia and large parts of Africa were ruled by one or more traditional empires in alliance with a universal religion, such as Buddhism, Islam, or Christianity. Prior to that, Eurasia was divided up into empires that practiced sacrificial religions. And before that, and still faintly discernible, were the expansions of the peoples who learned to process roots and grains into food.

In Italy, for example, the porridge (polenta) of early farmers persists, now usually prepared from maize, not barley or millet. The bread of the Roman Empire is found across the whole peninsula. The sweet and sour dishes of Sicily, as well as the risotto of the north, are there because of the presence of traditional Islamic states in the Mediterranean. The sweet pastas of the traditional Renaissance Catholic states have largely been transformed into savory ones. The mousses, béchamel, dried pasta, and canned tomatoes of the middle classes date from eighteenth- and nineteenth-century modern cuisines. And in the second half of the twentieth century, all Italians began eating middling cuisines, with a consequent blossoming of rural dishes.

A visit to an Indian restaurant in the United States will reveal the tandoori chicken of the modern Indian nation, the *jalfreezi* of the British Empire, the vindaloo of the traditional Catholic Portuguese Empire, the korma of the traditional Islamic Mughal Empire, and the chapatis that have been the bread of Hindus for thousands of years. Or in a city in southern Nigeria, the middle class will eat the puffy white bread popularized in the second half of the twentieth century, stews made with dried fish, introduced in the days of the European slave trade, and pounded yam (fufu), which has been made for millennia (fig. 8.12). The culinary past, with its earlier global interactions, is still very much with us in spite of the rapid change of the last hundred years.

Those lucky enough to eat middling cuisine, with plentiful meat, fat, and sugar, are probably about one in three of the world's population, a higher proportion than ever before. Those in this group enjoy hot meals at least once a day and often more. They eat soft, creamy, crispy, crunchy, and often sweet foods, or foods with the rich flavors of meat. Simple dishes, such as polenta, have been upgraded with rich toppings unimaginable to the laboring poor in the past. An older friend told me, as he ordered polenta with butter and gorgonzola, that he did so in memory of his Italian-born parents, who, on coming to America, refused ever again to eat plain polenta, the monotonous food of the poverty they had escaped. Festival dishes, once reserved for high days and holidays, such as roast chicken, lasagna, mole, korma, and layer cake, are now everyday fare. Going out to eat is a pastime, a form of entertainment or travel, pursued to enjoy new surroundings and taste new or luxurious foods.

Children in countries with middling cuisines grow up taller and heavier than their parents who ate humble cuisines. Botulism is no longer the threat that it once was. It is unusual to see people with legs bowed with rickets, throats bulging with

FIGURE 8.12. This photograph shows a Nigerian on a visit to purchase stockfish (dried cod) from a dealer in Bergen, Norway, around 1960, the time of independence. Nigerians were beginning to eat the white bread of the modern West but continued to flavor dishes with the dried fish and chiles introduced during the sixteenth and seventeenth centuries, and they still relished their native palm oil and yam fufu. Photo Atelier KK, Bergen, picture collection of Bergen University Library.

goiter, and skin blotched and stained with scurvy and pellagra, all problems that were common even in wealthy countries such as the United States at the beginning of the twentieth century. Mexican women no longer have muscled shoulders and arthritic knees from hours spent grinding. As a nutritionist for the World Health Organization points out, many of the problems that crippled people earlier, such as kwashiorkor in rice-eating areas, have vanished with better diets.[117] In England and Wales, according to the Office for National Statistics, deaths from gastrointestinal infections dropped from over a hundred per hundred thousand of the population in 1900 to practically zero by 2000, even though reporting has probably increased.[118]

The 13.7 million people in the United States, or one in ten people in the workforce (leaving aside the military), who worked in food processing, marketing, or the restaurant business in 1997 did so, in most cases, by choice and were paid to do so, instead of having no option in life but to spend their days pounding or grinding or cooking three meals a day for a large family. Multinational corporations, such as McDonald's and Walmart, specializing in retailing and food service, joined existing multinationals focusing on food processing. They have opened new opportunities for work and for social life, as well as raising the standards of agriculture and distribution. New methods of shipping, such as long-distance trucking, refrigerated trucking, and airfreight, brought down prices or made exotic out-of-season delicacies accessible. The introduction of containers by a North Carolina trucking magnate in the 1950s reduced the cost of transfers between trucking, rail, and shipping.

Mechanized farming is now the rule in the richer parts of the world. Grain is farmed in former grasslands in the temperate parts of the Americas from Canada in the north to Argentina in the south, in Australia, India, China, Europe, and parts of the former Soviet Union. Soybeans and maize are grown in many of these areas to feed the growing number of cattle. Adequate grain supplies have been made available by the opening of new farmland, the introduction of tractors, fertilizers, and hybrid maize, and new strains of wheat, rice, and maize. The Green Revolution, sparked by Rockefeller-funded research in the 1960s, averted famine on a massive scale. Dairying has been transformed by effective milking machines, artificial insemination, careful attention to lactation cycles, and new ways of feeding cattle, providing safe, fresh, affordable milk year-round. In India, a White Revolution followed the Green Revolution. The world's largest dairy farm is in China. Areas with hot Mediterranean climates, including Mediterranean countries, the Central Valley of California and the Bajio of Mexico, Chile, south Australia, and even parts of Africa, supply fruits and vegetables to the world's cities. Although much farm labor is still carried out by the poorest, often or even usually not on their own land, human muscle power is increasingly replaced by machines powered by fossil fuels.

For all the advances, some old problems remain, and new ones have arisen. For much of the twentieth century, famines occurred on a scale greater than ever before, often the result of deliberate policies, inadvertence, or failure to act. In 1932, between 2.4 and 7.5 million Ukrainians died of famine. The death toll in the Bengal Famine of 1943 exceeded that of all Allied Forces in the course of World War II. In China, Mao's Great Leap Forward in 1958 resulted in between 20 and 45 million dead of hunger. The Biafran Civil War that divided Nigeria in 1970 left a million dead from fighting and famine. In the past generation, in spite of skyrocketing populations, famines have been fewer, though they could all too easily recur. In the poorer countries, the old pattern of a small elite eating a high cuisine (though not as ostentatiously, perhaps, as in the ancient empires) and a large rural population laboring to process and cook a humble cuisine persists. Many of the poor still suffer from chronic malnutrition. Others are succumbing to the health problems caused by the abundance of middling cuisines.

In richer countries, rooting out inadequate diets has proved harder than expected. Obesity and the diseases of affluence, such as heart attacks and diabetes, are on the rise in rich countries and not-so-rich countries alike, usually attributed to middle-class cuisines, which are high in meat, fat, and sugar, as well as to a sedentary lifestyle. Long supply chains and a higher consumption of milk, processed meats, and fresh fruit and vegetables, all ideal for the growth of bacteria, mean new dangers from *E. coli* and salmonella. Research in improving horticultural productivity has lagged behind that of increasing the productivity of grains. The grain trade is consolidated in a few, secretive companies. And demand for meat and milk continues to grow.

SOME FINAL THOUGHTS

I began by saying that I intended to take seriously that humans are the animals who cook, who transform the plants and animals that are the raw materials of our food. All seven billion people in the world eat food that has been processed and cooked. The traditional virtues of grains—the fact that they are dense in calories and nutrients, can be turned into a great variety of foodstuffs, and ship and store well—make them as important as raw materials for food as they have been for thousands of years. Foods made from wheat, rice, and maize still provide most of the world's calories, and the lesser grains and the roots still feed the poor. We depend basically on the same seeds, roots and tubers, nuts, fruits, and vegetables, albeit in many cases much altered by breeding, that humans depended on when the first cities and states were being formed. If anything, the range of animals and plants that we eat has decreased. We depend less on wild plants and creatures and more on the domesticated ones whose breeding (and thus flavor) we can control.

Yet drawing on the same raw materials, we have access to a vastly greater range of foodstuffs, dishes, meals, and cuisines than our ancestors had. Over the centuries, we have discovered how to change the gastronomic, culinary, and nutritional properties of plants and animals by cooking. Maize that has been treated with alkali and ground to a paste forms a cohesive dough, unlike maize that has been simply ground. When baked on a griddle it makes a flexible flatbread (tortilla), again unlike maize that has not been treated with alkali. Meat that has been sliced thinly or ground can be cooked in a flash, and flour that has been mixed with yeast rises. With cooking, diverse new flavors and textures are created. Tortillas taste quite different from cornbread, raised bread from flatbread, and salt meat from fresh meat. Cocoa beans that have been conched (ground for hours) have a creamy texture, while those that have been processed on a simple grindstone remain gritty. Cooking often improves safety and nutrition. Many varieties of taro and cassava are toxic when raw, maize is less nutritious and more likely to have poisonous fungi, and everything is harder to digest. It is true that cooking is not invariably beneficial, because it may improve some culinary, gastronomic, and nutritional properties at the cost of worsening others. As an ingredient, white sugar has a range of wonderful properties and almost everyone likes its taste, but many worry that although it supplies calories, it does not offer a complex range of nutrients. Brown rice may be more healthful than white, but many rice eaters like neither the way it cooks nor the way it tastes.

Over the centuries, though, the benefits of cooking have far outweighed the costs. Chinese noodles and soy sauce, Roman sauces and raised bread, Islamic distillation, Western cakes and chocolate are technological achievements that stand alongside Chinese bronzes, Roman hydraulic engineering, Islamic ceramics, and Western steam engines. When the chef Emeril assured the viewers of his television show that cooking was not rocket science, he was wrong. Using cooking techniques may be easy. Developing them in the first place *was* rocket science.

However, the agrarian-domestic-national story about the history of cooking obscures how cooking has transformed human life. By emphasizing farming, which produces the raw materials, it passes over the work required to turn these resources into food. Instead, the implication is that the farther from the farm gate, the less natural and virtuous the food. By arguing that home-cooked food is tastier and healthier than industrially produced food, it downplays how the large-scale, efficient bakeries and fish sauce manufactures in Rome, tea-processing facilities in Buddhist monasteries, herring-packing plants in Holland, sugar-beet refineries in France, and roller mills around the world have improved diets, reduced heavy manual labor, and enhanced the range of tasty foods. Indeed, home cooking and industrial processing form a continuum, using mechanical, thermal, chemical, and biochemical methods to make farm products into something edible. By focusing on national cuisines, the agrarian-domestic-national story underestimates how important long-distance transfers of culinary innovations have been. If our vision of the way to have better food is to have less processing, more natural food, more home cooking, and more local food, we will cut ourselves off from the most likely hope for better food in the future.

Although cooking improved the variety, quality, healthfulness, and sheer deliciousness of the food we eat, until recently these benefits have been very unequally distributed. Those who cooked had lives of unremitting, time-consuming, backbreaking labor, as many in the world still do. Culinary philosophy assumed and reinforced an inequitable world, with food as the most tangible aspect of that inequality. Peasants and artisans dined well after the harvest but braced for hunger before it. Those in institutions, such as servants, apprentices, courtiers, soldiers, and sailors, probably had better and more regular food, but at the price of having to eat what was provided and be grateful for it. Because the culinary philosophies that inspired innovation in cooking and processing were so often focused on providing magnificent food for the court or refined food for religious elites, they did little to improve food for the vast majority. Even the choices of the wealthy were restricted because of the need to maintain hierarchy. Women were frequently excluded from fine dining—expected to drink fruit beverages, not wine, in Persia, and tea, not coffee, in England. Kings and emperors had to eat in public, to eat lavishly, and to eat what custom and ritual demanded. As the duke of Edinburgh is reported to have complained, "I never see any home cooking. All I get is the fancy stuff."

Only in the nineteenth century, with the advent of more-inclusive political theories, did food processing come to be directed at providing decent, affordable food for whole populations. The vast increase in power offered by fossil fuels, which enable control of heat, cold, and pressure, and the understanding of biochemical processes in the past couple of hundred years were essential to the creation of middling cuisines. Industrialized food processing was as necessary to the weakening of social hierarchy as the mastery of grains had been to its appearance. It reduced the human labor needed to process food even as it brought down prices, so that more people could afford a varied diet. The distinction between high and humble cuisines, if it did not disappear entirely in the richer parts of the world, became comparatively insignificant.

For the richer part of the world today, dining on high or humble cuisines is not a matter of class determined by one's birth, but a matter of choice: a quick piece of toast for breakfast, pizza on a hurried night, a home-cooked meal for the family, a visit to a restaurant with friends, or a night at a fine restaurant for a once-in-a-lifetime treat. It's a fine world where princes eat ramen noodles and presidents eat hamburgers, where real men eat quiche and real women drink whiskey, and where dining on high cuisine, if only very occasionally, is a quite-achievable goal.

As I was finishing this book, I walked ten minutes to my local grocery store in Mexico City, a Walmart, as it happens, though it could have been a Mexican chain such as Chedraui. As always, it was busy, filled with a mix of shoppers from the very wealthy neighborhood to the west, the middle-class neighborhoods to the east, and the working-class neighborhood to the south. They were picking up fluffy white Bimbo bread for after-school snacks, reasonably decent artisanal breads from the bakery, and maize tortillas—not the best, but not bad either—fresh and hot from the tortilleria. Those with time to cook could choose from half a dozen different dried chiles with which to make salsa, pig's feet and three kinds of tripe, mole pastes from huge tubs, half a dozen varieties of beans to put in the *olla*, and a couple of dozen kinds of vegetables, including the traditional huazontle. Those who did not want to cook could select from prepared foods, including roast chicken, salsas, Spanish jamon serrano, stuffed grape leaves, kibbeh, *tortillas arabe* (pita bread), Gouda, goat cheese, a range of salad greens, and ready-cut fruit. And small entrepreneurs with stands in the streets outside carried out foot-high stacks of thin-sliced beef and bulging sacks of rolls to make *tortas* to sell to passersby.

Many of the mothers and a high proportion of the grandmothers of the shoppers in the Mexico City supermarket once spent hours grinding every day. Now they could pick from this cornucopia with foods of all price ranges and from many parts of the world, middling cuisines far more various than the traditional ones. The same day that I walked to Walmart, I had a letter from a graduate student at Stanford. Working with women in Mozambique, he had been appalled at the amount of time they had to spend pounding maize. He was trying to find a mechanical mill that would free them from this exhausting chore and give them more time to care for their children, take paid work, and perhaps even have access to the culinary choice now available in much of Mexico.

Yet many worry about the loss of older cuisines and about the diseases of abundance that follow on the shift to modern middling cuisines. "Fortunately fast foods and soft drinks are beyond the reach of the poor, who, for this reason, will be spared" from the problems of Western cuisine, said the same World Health Organization nutritionist who was pleased to see the disappearance of the diseases of poverty.[119] Yet it is precisely the ability to make those choices that is at stake. On 2 January 2005, twenty-three-year-old Shin Dong-hyuk escaped from a prison camp in North Korea and made his way to the West. As the story in the *Wall Street Journal* put it, "Freedom . . . was just another word for grilled meat."[120] It is easy to see this as a trivialization of high ideals. But it isn't. Good food, food freely chosen, is part of living your own life. Although this choice brings with it the responsibility of choosing your food wisely, the alternative is a world where the powerful constrain what you can eat, in the name of health, religion, or political and economic expediency.

The challenge is to acknowledge that not all is right with modern cuisines without romanticizing earlier ones; to recognize that contemporary cuisines have problems with health and equity without jumping to the conclusion that this is new; to face up to new nutritional challenges of abundance without being paternalist or authoritarian; to extend the benefits of industrialized food processing to all those who still labor with pestles and mortars; and to realize that the problem of feeding the world is a matter not simply of providing enough calories but of extending to everyone the choice, the responsibility, the dignity, and the pleasure of a middling cuisine.

NOTES

INTRODUCTION

1. Our term "cuisine" derives from the French word *cuisine,* for kitchen, which by metonymy came to mean style of cooking, as did the related Spanish *cocina,* the Portuguese *cozinha,* the Italian *cucina,* the German *Küche,* and the Russian *kukhnya.* "Cuisine" has been used in a number of different ways by food scholars. The anthropologist Jack Goody sharply distinguishes the "cooking" of reputedly nonhierarchical societies from the high cuisines of hierarchical ones in *Cooking, Cuisine, and Class,* 97–153. Trubek, *Haute Cuisine;* Korsmeyer, *Making Sense of Taste;* and Ferguson, *Accounting for Taste,* 3, 19, all use the term "cuisine" primarily for high cuisines. My use of it is closer to that of Belasco, "Food and the Counter-culture," and Cwiertka, *Making of Modern Culinary Tradition in Japan,* 11. I differ from them, however, in treating culinary philosophy as crucial to cuisine.

2. Although much used in diverse historiographical traditions, the concept of "the modern" is regarded with great suspicion by historians and social scientists because it is so ambiguous and, when applied globally, so suggestive of Eurocentrism. For all the debate, though, most scholars agree that some things have changed since the seventeenth century. I want to explore the culinary dimensions of these changes, thus contributing to the debate about "modernity."

1. MASTERING GRAIN COOKERY

1. Wrangham, *Catching Fire;* for the debate about cooking, diet, and human evolution, see Aiello and Wells, "Energetics"; Aiello and Wheeler, "Expensive-Tissue Hypothesis"; M. Jones, *Feast,* chap. 4; Leonard, "Dietary Change." For earlier work on fire and cooking in prehistory, see Perlès, *Préhistoire du feu.*

2. Wrangham, *Catching Fire*, chap. 1; Freidberg, *Fresh*. In passing, it is worth noting that centuries of breeding also mean that the "Paleo diet," based on works such as Eaton and Konner, "Paleolithic Nutrition," is unlikely to resemble what Paleolithic humans actually ate.

3. In placing emphasis on the multiple operations involved in cooking, I differ from Wrangham, *Catching Fire*, chap. 3. It may be that fire was particularly important in getting humans started on cooking. For understanding the evolution of cuisines, though, it is essential to consider all post-harvest transformations, not just the use of heat. See Stahl, "Plant-Food Processing," for nutritional changes following cooking; McGee, *On Food and Cooking*, for the science of cooking.

4. For the variety and sophistication that can be achieved with hearth cooking, see Rubel, *Magic of Fire*; for pit cooking, Wandsnider, "Roasted."

5. Piperno et al., "Processing of Wild Cereal Grains"; Revedin et al., "Thirty Thousand-Year-Old Evidence."

6. Archaeologists sift the soil of digs to find tiny plant remains, identify the proteins, blood, and fats on cooking vessels using spectroscopes, experiment with ancient food-processing techniques, and extract small amounts of DNA from plant and human remains to trace the history of plants and peoples. Traditional sources included paintings and sculptures, literary texts such as tax records, recipes, epics and orders of service, household accounts, cooking equipment, and the rare foods preserved by volcanic eruptions, in funeral offerings, and in the stomachs of bodies preserved in ice or acid bogs, or in dehydrated feces (coprolites). See Samuel, "Approaches."

7. For the millet cuisine of the Yellow River Valley, see Chang, "Ancient China"; Anderson, *Food of China*, chaps. 1 and 2; Nelson, "Feasting the Ancestors"; Sterckx, ed., *Of Tripod and Palate*, chaps. 1–5; Yates, "War, Food Shortages, and Relief Measures"; and for general background, Gernet, *History*, chaps. 1–5.

8. Fuller, "Arrival of Wheat in China."

9. Legge, *Chinese Classics*, 4: 171–72.

10. These Asian wines were made from grains by a process quite unlike either beer-making from malt or wine-making from fruit, and I call them by their Chinese name, *chiu*, to emphasize the difference. For details, see Huang, *Fermentations and Food Science*, 149–68, 457–60.

11. Puett, "Offering of Food."

12. Knechtges, "Literary Feast," 51.

13. Chang, "Ancient China," 37.

14. Sterckx, ed., *Of Tripod and Palate*, 38.

15. For the Pacific spread of Southeast Asian root cuisine, see Kirch, *On the Road of the Winds*; Holmes, *Hawaiian Canoe*, chap. 2; Bellwood, "Austronesian Dispersal"; Pollock, *These Roots Remain*; Skinner, *Cuisine of the South Pacific*; Titcomb, *Dog and Man*.

16. Fuller, "Debating Early African Bananas" and "Globalization of Bananas."

17. Fuller et al., "Consilience."

18. Achaya, *Oilseeds and Oilmilling*, 142.

19. Bottéro, *Oldest Cuisine in the World*; Pollock, "Feasts, Funerals, and Fast Food." In the past one hundred and fifty years, archaeologists have turned up a wealth of evidence about the cuisine, including lists of quantities of foodstuffs for royal meals, quantities of

barley paid in wages, business letters mentioning food, treatises on how to divine the future, dictionaries, forty recipes in Akkadian from about 1600 B.C.E., and the *Epic of Gilgamesh*, its clay tablets collected in a library in Nineveh.

20. Potts, "On Salt and Salt Gathering."

21. Sandars, ed., *Epic of Gilgamesh*, 109, 93.

22. Bottéro, *Oldest Cuisine in the World*, 30. "Little" and "pastry" in parentheses in original Bottéro translation, [heart and liver] and [untranslatable] my interpolations. See also Ellison, "Diet in Mesopotamia," and "Methods of Food Preparation in Mesopotamia."

23. Katz and Voight, "Bread and Beer," 27; Katz and Maytag, "Brewing and Ancient Beer."

24. Zeder, *Feeding Cities*, 34–42.

25. Forbes, R. J., *Studies in Ancient Technology*, 3: 175–76; Potts, "On Salt and Salt Gathering," 266–68.

26. Edens, "Dynamics of Trade."

27. For general background, see Barfield, *Nomadic Alternative; Encyclopedia Judaica*, s.v. "Food"; Cooper, *Eat and Be Satisfied*, chaps. 1–4.

28. Achaya, *Indian Food*, chap. 3; Fuller and Boivin, "Crops, Cattle and Commensals," 21–22.

29. Quoted in Achaya, *Indian Food*, 28.

30. Cunliffe, *Europe Between the Oceans*, 94–96, 239–45; Unwin, *Wine and the Vine*, chap. 4; Dalby, *Siren Feasts*, chap. 2.

31. Homer, *Iliad* 9.202–17. For the probable method of making barley bread (*maza*), Braun, "Barley Cakes and Emmer Bread," 25–32; Kaufman, *Cooking in Ancient Civilizations*, 82–83.

32. The first Greek to write about the Celts was Polybius, sometime around 140 B.C.E. Soon thereafter Posidonius, who came from western Syria and settled in Rhodes, gave a fuller account; his writings have not survived, but Diodorus of Sicily and Strabo drew on them, as did Julius Caesar. Powell, *Celts*, 108–9, 139, 53; Herm, *Celts*, chap. 4. McCormick, "Distribution of Meat."

33. Carney and Rosomoff, *Shadow of Slavery*, chap. 1; Fuller and Boivin, "Crops, Cattle and Commensals," 23; Ricquier and Bostoen, "Retrieving Food History." The earliest written records we have come from much later. See Lewicki, *West African Food*.

34. Mackie, *Life and Food*, 32–36.

35. Coe, *America's First Cuisines*, chaps. 12 and 13.

36. Ibid., chaps. 2 and 3; Pool, *Olmec Archaeology and Early Mesoamerica*, 146; Mann, *1491*, 194, 213; Pope et al., "Origin and Environmental Setting"; Diehl, *Olmecs*.

37. Zarrillo et al., "Directly Dated Starch Residues."

38. Huang, *Fermentations and Food Science*, 18; Achaya, *Indian Food*, 31.

39. Johns, *With Bitter Herbs*, chaps. 3 and 8; appendices 1 and 2.

40. On toxicity, see Johns, *With Bitter Herbs*, and Schultz, "Biochemical Ecology"; on molds and contamination, see Matossian, *Poisons of the Past*, and Lieber, "Galen on Contaminated Cereals."

41. Hillman, "Traditional Husbandry." For the labor of producing bread and beer in Egypt, see Samuel, "Ancient Egyptian Bread and Beer," "Ancient Egyptian Cereal Processing," "New Look at Bread and Beer," "Investigation of Ancient Egyptian Baking

and Brewing," and "Bread in Archaeology"; Samuel and Bolt, "Rediscovering Ancient Egyptian Beer."

42. See Coe, *America's First Cuisines*, 15, for an eighteenth-century engraving of grinders; for grinding slaves, Hagen, *Handbook of Anglo-Saxon Food*, 4; for time to grind, Bauer, "Millers and Grinders," and my personal experience; for early grinding, Stork and Teague, *Flour for Man's Bread*, chaps. 2–5; for the number of grindstones at an ancient village, Hole et al., *Prehistory and Human Ecology of the Deh Luran Plain*, 9.

43. Meyer-Renschhausen, "Porridge Debate."

44. Concepción, *Typical Canary Cooking*, 89–92.

45. Dorje, *Food in Tibetan Life*, 61–65.

46. Maurizio, *Histoire de l'alimentation végétale*, pt. 3; Meyer-Renschhausen, "Porridge Debate."

47. For early breads, Rubel, *Bread*, chaps. 1 and 2; for ember and bakestones, Rubel, *Magic of Fire*, 154–64.

48. Grocock and Grainger, trans. and eds., *Apicius*, 73–83.

49. The active agent is almost always a mold of either the Aspergillus or the Rhizopus family, rather than the yeasts and lactobacillae that are common in the West. Ssu-hsieh, "Preparation of Ferments and Wines"; Huang, *Fermentations and Food Science*, 149–282. For India, Kautilya, *Arthashastra*, 805–6.

50. Samuel, "Investigation of Ancient Egyptian Baking and Brewing."

51. Katz and Voight, "Bread and Beer"; Thomas Kavanagh, a brewer, doubts that it would have been possible to maintain the necessary temperatures without pottery. Kavanagh, "Archaeological Parameters."

52. Messer, "Potatoes (white)," 197.

53. The standard medieval ration was 2–3 pounds of bread and a gallon of ale a day (Scully, *Art of Cookery in the Middle Ages*, 36–37). In Italy in the Middle Ages and early modern period, 2½ pounds of bread a day was standard, reduced to about 1 pound if meat was available (Montanari, *Culture of Food*, 104–5). A French family of four in the eighteenth century needed 6 pounds of bread, 2½ for the father, 1½ for the mother, and the remainder for the two children (Morineau, "Growing Without Knowing," 374–82). "[T]he Chinese in the last six or seven centuries have been producing enough grain to supply each person with about 300 kilograms a year [1.8 pounds a day]" (Mote, "Yuan and Ming," 200). See also the figures on Roman army rations in chapter 2.

54. Engels, *Alexander the Great*, 14–18 for packhorses, 26 for ships; Thurmond, *Handbook of Food Processing in Classical Rome*, 2; A. H. M. Jones, *Later Roman Economy*, 841–42. In nineteenth-century Germany, which I'll take as a suggestive example, since we don't have figures for the ancient world, grain could be hauled fifty to sixty miles before the cost of transport equaled its value. Roots (in this case, mangolds, sugar beets, and potatoes) could be hauled only four to ten miles. Landers, *Field*, 89. For the complexities of provisioning, see the study of medieval London by Campbell et al., *A Medieval Capital*.

55. Adshead, *Salt and Civilization*, 7, 8, 24.

56. McGee, *On Food and Cooking*, 581.

57. "Waxworks."

58. For Tirel, see Scully, *Art of Cookery in the Middle Ages*, 252, and for Vatel, see Wheaton, *Savoring the Past*, 143–47.

59. For water, see C. Davidson, *Woman's Work Is Never Done*, 14. For fuel, see Braudel, *Mediterranean*, 1: 173–74.

60. K. D. White, "Farming and Animal Husbandry," 236; McGee, *On Food and Cooking*, 226; Bray, *Agriculture*, 4.

61. Torres, *Catalan Country Kitchen*, 104.

62. Hanley, *Everyday Things in Premodern Japan*, 91.

63. Bray, *Agriculture*, 378; Yates, "War, Food Shortages, and Relief Measures"; Garnsey, *Food and Society*, chap. 3.

64. Garnsey, *Famine and Food Supply*, 28–29; Zhou, ed., *Great Famine in China*, 69–71.

65. Camporesi, *Bread of Dreams*, 122.

66. Garnsey, *Food and Society in Classical Antiquity*, 39; "Steven Kaplan on the History of Food" discussing Camporesi, *Bread of Dreams*.

67. P. Brown, *World of Late Antiquity*, 12.

68. Crone, *Pre-Industrial Societies*, 8

69. Sutton, "Language of the Food of the Poor," 373.

70. Adshead, *Central Asia in World History*, 67–68.

71. Many of these works were put in written form after centuries of oral transmission. The *Book of Songs*, the hymns to be sung at the sacrifice, by tradition attributed to Confucius in the sixth century B.C.E., almost certainly had older roots. The texts were not actually established until the Han Dynasty (approx. 200 B.C.E.–200 C.E.), when scholars reconstructed them from fragments that survived a book burning.

72. According to documents from 570 C.E. (Stathakopoulos, "Between the Field and the Plate," 27–28).

73. Shaw, "Fear and Loathing," 25.

74. Herodotus, *Histories* bk. 4 For a more sympathetic account, see Cunliffe, *Europe between the Oceans*, 302–9.

75. Homer, *Odyssey* 20.108.

76. *Encyclopedia Judaica*, 1415; Braun, "Barley Cakes and Emmer Bread," 25; Kaneva-Johnson, *Melting Pot*, 223; Field, *Italian Baker*, 11; Delaney, *Seed and the Soil*, 243; Hanley, *Everyday Things in Premodern Japan*, 163.

77. Loha-unchit, *It Rains Fishes*, 17–19.

78. Grimm, *From Feasting to Fasting*, 44–53.

79. Temkin, "On Second Thought," 192.

80. Chakravarty, *Saga of Indian Food*, 11.

81. R. Eaton, *Rise of Islam and the Bengal Frontier*, 163.

82. Lévi-Strauss, *Introduction*, 3. *The Origin of Table Manners*, 486; Ramiaramanana, "Malagasy Cooking," 111.

83. Chang, *Food in Chinese Culture*, 51.

84. Briant, *From Cyrus to Alexander*, 302–23. The idea that the ruler had to provide a basic diet for the poor has persisted. E. P. Thompson described the expectation of the poor that at least they would have food as belief in a moral economy. See Thompson, "Moral Economy."

85. Singer, *Constructing Ottoman Beneficence*, 142.

86. Yates, "War, Food Shortages, and Relief Measures in Early China," 154.

87. MacMullen, *Christianity and Paganism,* chap. 2; Puett, "Offering of Food."

88. Bray, *Agriculture,* 80; George, trans., *Epic of Gilgamesh,* 901.

89. Detienne and Vernant, *Cuisine of Sacrifice,* 21–26.

90. Lev. 2:13.

91. Lincoln, *Priests, Warriors, and Cattle,* 65.

92. Gen. 32.

93. Finley, *Ancient Sicily,* 54–55.

94. Kierman, "Phases and Modes," 28.

95. Feeley-Harnik, *Lord's Table,* 64–66.

96. Bradley, "Megalith Builders," 95; Finley, *Ancient Sicily,* 54–55 and 46; *Encyclopædia Britannica,* 11th ed., vol. 6, s.v. "Cocoma."

97. Dalby, *Siren Feasts,* 2, quoting from Menander, *Bad-Tempered Man,* 447–53.

98. Zimmermann, *Jungle,* 128. John Milton describes in *Paradise Lost,* Book 5, 320–450, how in the Garden of Eden, Eve mixed and perfected foodstuffs to offer to the Angel Gabriel.

99. Chang, *Food in Chinese Culture,* 31.

100. Sterckx, *Of Tripod and Palate,* 47.

101. Huang, *Fermentations and Food Science,* 97.

102. Laudan, *From Mineralogy to Geology,* 20–32, for how the mineral world fits into the culinary cosmos.

103. *Hippocrates on Diet and Hygiene,* 36.

104. For cultivated plants as cooked, see Detienne, *Gardens of Adonis,* 11–12. See, e.g., Aristotle, *Meteorologica* 4.3; the Aristotelian *Problemata* 10.12 and 22.8; Xenophon, *Oeconomica,* 16.14–15; Lissarrague, *Aesthetics of the Greek Banquet,* 5, for wine-making as cooking.

105. Lévi-Strauss, *Introduction,* 1: 335–36.

106. Sabban, "Insights," 50.

107. For the Chinese, Unschuld, *Medicine in China,* chap. 3; for the classical world, Siraisi, *Medieval and Early Renaissance Medicine,* 97–106, and Albala, *Eating Right in the Renaissance,* chaps. 2 and 3; for India, Zimmermann, *Jungle,* esp. chap. 3; for Persia, Lincoln, "Physiological Speculation," 211, 215; and for Mesoamerica, López Austin, *Cuerpo humano,* 59, 65; Ortiz de Montellano, *Medicina,* 44–45.

108. For the correspondences, see Porter, ed., *Medicine,* 20–21; chap. 4; and Lincoln, "Physiological Speculation and Social Patterning." López Austin, *Cuerpo humano,* 58–62, and Ortiz de Montellano, *Medicina,* 60–64, argue that the New World system evolved independently. Albala, *Eating Right in the Renaissance, Postscript,* tends to the view that it was either brought by the Spanish or so heavily influenced by the Spanish that it is impossible to determine what the pre-Hispanic theory was.

109. Stathakopoulos, "Between the Field and the Plate," 27–28.

110. Sterckx, *Of Tripod and Palate,* 47.

111. Kuriyama, "Interpreting the History of Bloodletting," 36.

112. R. J. Forbes, *Studies in Ancient Technology,* 8: 157–95.

113. P. Colquhoun, *Treatise on Indigence,* 7–8.

2. THE BARLEY-WHEAT CUISINES OF THE ANCIENT EMPIRES

1. The word "empire" comes from the Latin *imperium*, the authority given to a magistrate to act on Rome's behalf. Gradually it changed to mean ruling over multiple dominions. For a general discussion of empires, see Doyle, *Empires;* Lieven, *Empire.*

2. Bottéro, *Oldest Cuisine in the World,* 99–101.

3. Briant, *From Cyrus to Alexander,* draws on recent research to reassess older interpretations based on Greek travelers' tales (particularly those of Xenophon, who wrote a biography of Cyrus after serving as a mercenary in the Persian army), the Avesta, the sacred text of the Zoroastrians, and tablets found at Persepolis (the Elamite Fortification tablets). For dining in particular, see 200–203. For a simpler introduction to the Persians, see Cook, *Persian Empire.* For the continuity of Assyrian and Achaemenid cuisine, see Parpola, "Leftovers of God and King," and for links with China, Laufer, *Sino-Iranica.* For recipes set in a sweeping survey of the long culinary tradition in what is now Iraq, see Nasrallah, *Delights from the Garden of Eden.*

4. Rüdiger Schmitt, "Cooking in Ancient Iran," www.iranicaonline.org/articles /cooking#pt1 (accessed 16 August 2012).

5. Briant, *From Cyrus to Alexander,* 124–28; Lincoln, "À la recherche du paradis perdu"; Lincoln, *Religion, Empire, and Torture,* esp. chaps. 3 and 4. Scholars are teasing out the complex relations between Achaemenid and Zoroastrian philosophy. For example, the assertion that in their ideal primeval state plants and fruits were without skins and thorns is first documented in the Sassanian period (224–651 C.E.). See Touraj Daryaee, "What Fruits and Nuts to Eat in Ancient Persia?" http://iranian.com/History /2005/September/Fruits/Images/TheFruitOfAncientPersia.pdf (accessed   January   6, 2013).

6. Kozuh, *Sacrificial Economy,* abstract.

7. M. Harris, *Good to Eat,* 67–87; Soler, "Semiotics of Food in the Bible"; Douglas, *Purity and Danger,* chap. 3. For a measured account of food taboos, see Simoons, *Eat Not This Flesh.*

8. "Garden," www.iranicaonline.org/articles/garden-i (accessed 16 August 2012).

9. For water, see Briant, *Cyrus to Alexander,* 263; for numbers of cooks, ibid., 292–93; for typical camp followers, Engels, *Alexander the Great,* 1.

10. Crone, *Pre-Industrial Societies,* 40.

11. Bentley and Ziegler, *Traditions and Encounters,* 1: 143–44. Since 800,000 liters hold about 1,200,000 pounds of grain, assuming that each individual needed two pounds of grain daily, this would have sustained about 1,650 people for a year.

12. Lewis, "King's Dinner"; Sancisi-Weerdenburg et al., "Gifts."

13. www.sacred-texts.com/zor/sbe31/sbe31025.htm (accessed December 16, 2012).

14. Xenophon, *Cyropaedia* (Life of Cyrus), 8.2.

15. Quoted from Athenaeus, *Deipnosophistae,* 12.1516d, in Wilkins and Hill, "Sources and Sauces," 437; see also Harvey, "Lydian Specialties."

16. Xenophon, *Cyropaedia* (Life of Cyrus), 8.2.

17. Basic sources for the cuisines of classical antiquity include Garnsey, *Food and Society in Classical Antiquity, Peasants and Food in Classical Antiquity,* and *Famine and Food Supply in the Graceco-Roman World,* and Wilkins et al., *Food in Antiquity.* For the Greeks in

particular, see Dalby, *Siren Feasts.* For recipes and menus, see Dalby and Grainger, *Classical Cookbook,* and Kaufman, *Cooking in Ancient Civilizations.*

18. Dalby, "Alexander's Culinary Legacy," 88, quoting Athenaeus 130e, quoting Aristophanes.

19. Renfrew, "Food for Athletes and Gods," 174–81, including quotation from Pindar *Ol.* 10.73–87; Detienne and Vernant, *Cuisine of Sacrifice,* 3–13; Schmitt-Pantel, "Sacrificial Meal."

20. Spencer, *Heretic's Feast,* chaps. 2 and 4; Sorabji, *Animal Minds;* Grimm, *From Feasting to Fasting,* 58–59.

21. Dalby, *Siren Feasts,* 126.

22. Garnsey, *Famine and Food,* chaps. 1 and 2, esp. 28; Forbes and Foxhall, "Ethnoarcheology and Storage," 74–75.

23. Hadjisavvas, *Olive Oil;* Amouretti, *Le pain et l'huile.*

24. Lissarrague, *Aesthetics of the Greek Banquet,* for Greek attitudes to wine and p. 5 for Euripides, *Bacchae* 274–83, trans. William Arrowsmith.

25. Lombardo, "Food and 'Frontier.'"

26. Dalby, *Siren Feasts,* chap. 5.

27. Murray, *Sympotica,* especially Schmitt-Pantel, "Sacrificial Meal," 14–33; Fisher, "Greek Associations."

28. For sauces, Harvey, "Lydian Specialties," 277; for couches, Boardman, "Symposion Furniture," 122–31.

29. J. Davidson, *Courtesans and Fishcakes,* chap. 1; and for the scarcity of fish, A. Davidson, *Mediterranean Seafood,* 13–16, 48–52. For the menu, Dalby and Grainger, *Classical Cookbook,* 42–55.

30. Dalby, *Siren Feasts,* 121–24.

31. Plato, *Timaeus* 72.

32. Wilkins et al., *Food in Antiquity,* 7–9, quotes and explains Plato, *Republic* 2.372a–3c. Quotation slightly modified.

33. Aristotle, *Nichomachean Ethics* 2.7; *Rhetoric* 1.9.

34. The source of my facts and my interpretation is Dalby, "Alexander's Culinary Legacy."

35. Engels, *Alexander,* 18–22, 35–36.

36. Lane Fox, *Alexander the Great,* 175.

37. For an early Hellenistic meal, see Dalby and Grainger, *Classical Cookbook,* 70–81.

38. Dalby, "Alexander's Culinary Legacy," and Ambrosioli, *Wild and the Sown,* 4.

39. Mauryan cuisine can be reconstructed from passages in Achaya, *Indian Food,* esp. chaps. 3, 5, 6, 7, 8, and 9; for Vedic ideas about food, see Zimmermann, *Jungle.*

40. Achaya, *Indian Food,* 98ff.

41. What *soma/haoma* actually was has been the subject of much debate, well summed up at http://en.wikipedia.org/wiki/Soma (accessed July 17, 2012).

42. Achaya, *Indian Food,* 54–56.

43. Zimmermann, *Jungle,* 171, 181, and esp. 183.

44. Achaya, *Indian Food,* 54; dishes from a picnic described in the Sanskrit epic the *Mahabharata,* whose oldest parts date from 400 B.C.E., put in final form in the fourth century C.E.

45. Zimmermann, *Jungle*, 171.

46. Kautilya, *Arthashastra*, 805–6.

47. Basic secondary sources for Roman cuisine include those in note 17; Gowers, *Loaded Table*, and Faas, *Around the Roman Table*. Background can be found in Dupont, *Daily Life in Ancient Rome*, esp. chap. 16, and Montanari, *Culture of Food*, chap. 1. Basic techniques are described in Thurmond, *Handbook of Food Processing*; Grocock and Grainger, *Apicius*, is an annotated translation of the major Roman cookbook.

48. Gowers, *Loaded Table*, 13.

49. Rosenstein, *Rome at War*, Introduction.

50. Cicero, *Tusculan Disputations*, 199 (5.34).

51. Ibid., 198 (5.34).

52. Celsus, *Of Medicine*, 77ff. (19).

53. Cato, *De agricultura*, Introduction.

54. Roth, *Logistics of the Roman Army*, 57; Vegetius, *De militaris*, 3.26.

55. Roth, *Logistics of the Roman Army*, 333.

56. Ibid., 43.

57. Ibid., and personal observation. I doubt that army bread was leavened.

58. Cato, *De agricultura*; Gozzini Giacosa, *Taste of Ancient Rome*, 149–50. For the meal, see Dalby and Grainger, 82–96. For the long debate about cooking and morality, see Laudan, "Refined Cuisine or Plain Cooking?"

59. Grimm, *From Feasting to Fasting*, 103.

60. Quoted in ibid., 129.

61. Speake and Simpson, eds., *Oxford Dictionary of Proverbs*.

62. Symons, *Pudding*, 98, quoting Seneca, Epistle 95: 15, 23; 67, 73.

63. Livy, *Ab urbe condita*, 39.6.

64. Grimm, *From Feasting to Fasting*, 103.

65. Ibid., 129, quoting Seneca, *Epistulae morales*, 110.18–20.

66. Malmberg, "Dazzling Dining."

67. "Roman Empire Population." www.unrv.com/empire/roman-population.php (accessed 15 August 2012).

68. Grant, *Galen on Food and Diet*, Introduction.

69. Grant, *Anthimus, De observatione ciborum*, 40, quoting Galen, *On Prognosis* 11.1–9.

70. See Grocock and Grainger, *Apicius*, 79–83, for a description of cooks and kitchens; C. Kaufman, *Cooking in Ancient Civilizations*, for recipes adapted to modern kitchens.

71. Quoted by Clutton-Brock, *Domesticated Animals*, 75–76.

72. Cutting, "Historical Aspects of Fish," 4–5.

73. Curtis, *Garum and Salsamenta*, esp. chap. 4.

74. Faas, *Around the Roman Table*, 48–75.

75. For such dishes, see Dalby and Grainger, *Classical Cookbook*, 97–113; Dupont, *Daily Life*, 275–78; Grocock and Grainger, *Apicius*; and Kaufman, *Cooking in Ancient Civilizations*, 127. For sauces, Solomon, "Apician Sauce." For red mullet and sow's udder, see Martial, *Epigrams*, 3.77 and 11.37.

76. Dalby and Grainger, *Classical Cookbook*, 68.

77. Ibid., 101–2.

78. Lieven, *Empire*, 9.

79. Alcock, "Power Lunches."

80. Grimm, *From Feasting to Fasting*, 3.

81. Quoted by P. Brown, *World of Late Antiquity*, 11; Reynolds, "Food of the Prehistoric Celts," 303–15;

82. J. Robinson, *Oxford Companion to Wine*; Cool, *Eating and Drinking in Roman Britain*, chaps. 8–15.

83. Montanari, *Culture of Food*, 11.

84. Cool, *Eating and Drinking in Roman Britain*, 38–41.

85. Wilson, *Food and Drink in Britain*, 72–73, 114–15, 193–97, 276–79, 325–27.

86. Cool, *Eating and Drinking in Roman Britain*, 53–55.

87. Adshead, *Salt and Civilization*, chap. 2.

88. Thurmond, *Handbook of Food Processing*, Introduction.

89. Garnsey, *Famine and Food Supply*, 51, quoting Galen, *De facultatibus naturalibus* 6.513.

90. For the higher quality and low cost of professionally baked bread, see Petersen and Jenkins, *Bread and the British Economy*, chap. 2. Thurmond, *Food Processing*, chap. 1, for Roman bread.

91. "Buying Power of Ancient Coins," http://dougsmith.ancients.info/worth.html (accessed July 20, 2012).

92. Robinson, *Oxford Companion to Wine*, 203. Thurmond, *Food Processing*, chap. 3.

93. Curtis, *Garum and Salsamenta*, chaps. 1 and 3.

94. Déry, "Milk and Dairy Products in the Roman Period"; Thurmond, *Food Processing*, 189–206.

95. Crane, *Archaeology of Beekeeping*, chap. 4.

96. Crone, *Pre-Industrial Societies*, 14.

97. Cool, *Eating and Drinking in Roman Britain*, 17.

98. P. Brown, *World of Late Antiquity*, 16.

99. Cunliffe, *Europe between the Oceans*, 426.

100. Mathieson, "Longaniza."

101. Basic sources for Han Chinese cuisine include Chang, *Food in Chinese Culture*, chap. 2; Anderson, *Food of China*, chap. 3; Bray, *Agriculture*; Huang, *Fermentations and Food Science*; and the papers by Sabban listed in the bibliography. For background, see Gernet, *History of Chinese Civilization*, and Waley-Cohen, *Sextants of Beijing*.

102. Confucius, *Analects*, 82.

103. These numbers, as Knechtges points out in "Literary Feast" (49) are idealized, but they convey an idea of the scale and importance given to kitchen operations.

104. Elvin, *Pattern of the Chinese Past*, 37–38.

105. Waley-Cohen, *Sextants of Beijing*, chap. 1.

106. Laufer, *Sino-Iranica*, 185–467.

107. Gernet, *History of Chinese Civilization*, 143.

108. Yates, "War, Food Shortages, and Relief Measures in Early China," 150. Levi, "L'abstinence des céréales chez les Taoistes," esp. 5–15.

109. Graham, *Disputers of the Tao*, pt. 1, chap. 1, and pt. 4, chap. 1; Unschuld, *Medicine in China*, 4 and 6.

110. Pirazzoli-t'Serstevens, "Second-Century Chinese Kitchen Scene."

111. See Sabban, "Système des cuissons" and "Savoir-faire oublié."

112. Huang, *Fermentations and Food Science*, 436–461.

113. Sabban, "Insights"; Huang, *Fermentations and Food Science*, 149–418.

114. Huang, *Fermentations and Food Science*, 462–66. As always, technology transferred is technology transformed. The Chinese also adapted the rotary grindstone to hulling by making the "stones" from sun-dried or baked clay or wood and fitting the grinding surfaces with teeth of oak or bamboo; when grains were fed through, the bran was stripped off. More than a millennium later, this method would be adapted to sugarcane. Daniels and Daniels, "Origin of the Sugarcane Roller Mill," 525.

115. Huang, *Fermentations and Food Science*, 462–96; Serventi and Sabban, *Pasta*, chap. 9. I follow Sabban's terminology.

116. Knechtges, "Literary Feast," 59–63; quotation is on 62.

117. Rickett, *Guanzi*, 428.

118. Bray, *Agriculture*, 314.

119. Ibid., 416–23.

120. Gernet, *History of Chinese Civilization*, 111.

121. Bray, *Agriculture*, 378–79; Will et al., *Nourish the People*, 2–5.

122. Gernet, *History of Chinese Civilization*, 144–45.

123. Coe, *America's First Cuisines*, describes how American cuisines had evolved at the time when Europeans arrived. See also, on health and the cosmos, Ortiz de Montellano, *Medicina*; on the intertwining of maize with the cosmic worldview, Clendinnen, *Aztecs*, 30, 181, 188–89, 251; on the archaeology, Sugiura and González de la Vara, *Cocina mexicana*, vol. 1: *México antiguo*, and González de la Vara, *Cocina mexicana*, vol. 2: *Época prehispánica*.

124. Alarcon, "Tamales in Mesoamerica."

125. MacDonough et al., "Alkaline-Cooked Corn Products."

126. Clendinnen, *Aztecs*, 30–35, 181, 188–89, 251.

3. BUDDHISM TRANSFORMS THE CUISINES OF SOUTH AND EAST ASIA

1. For the new religions, see Bentley, *Old World Encounters*, chaps. 2 and 3, for their spread and contact; Foltz, *Religions of the Silk Roads*, for their tangled history in Central Asia, a key area for culinary transfer; the historical sections in *Handbook of Living Religions*, ed. Hinnells, for basic information.

2. Shaffer, "Southernization."

3. No overview of the history of Buddhist cuisine in India exists. Achaya, *Indian Food*, 55–57, 70–72, discusses it briefly and has longer sections on other, probably similar, post-Vedic cuisines. Although primarily about China, Kieschnick, *Impact of Buddhism*, and Kohn, *Monastic Life in Medieval Daoism*, chap. 5, have discussions of Indian Buddhist cuisine.

4. Keay, *India*, 105.

5. Jha, *Holy Cow*, chap. 2, discusses the rejection of animal sacrifice at length.

6. Ibid., 68; Mather, "Bonze's Begging Bowl," 421.

7. Wujastyk, *Roots of Ayurveda*, Introduction.

8. Kieschnick, *Impact of Buddhism*, 251–52.

9. Achaya, *Indian Food,* 65 for milk as cooked, and 102–3 for milk processing.

10. On milk in Indian religions, see Apte and Katona-Apte, "Religious Significance of Food Preservation"; on churning the ocean, Achaya, *Oilseeds and Oil Milling,* 133–34.

11. On processing sugar, Achaya, *Indian Food,* 112–14; *Oilseeds and Oil Milling,* chap. 10; Mazumdar, *Sugar and Society in China,* 20–22.

12. Kieschnick, *Impact of Buddhism,* chap. 4.

13. To reconstruct Buddhist ascetic cuisine, see Achaya, *Indian Food:* for the ethos, 70; for sweets, 37–39 and 85; for cereals and pulses, 81–83; for milk products, 83–84; for beverages, 39; for physicians' ideas, chap. 7; and for utensils and processing, chap. 8. See also Mather, "Bonze's Begging Bowl," 421; Kieschnick, *Impact of Buddhism,* 250.

14. Daniels and Menzies, *Agro-Industries and Forestry,* 278; Kieschnick, *Impact of Buddhism,* 249–51.

15. Watson, *Agricultural Innovation in the Early Islamic World,* 77–78; Randhawa, *History of Agriculture in India,* 1: 379–81; Achaya, *Indian Food,* 82–83.

16. For the quotation, see Santa Maria, *Indian Sweet Cookery,* 15; for Hindu food, Achaya, *Indian Food,* esp. 61–70 and 88–91; for the foods of the pilgrimage temples, see Breckenridge, "Food, Politics and Pilgrimage in South India."

17. Eaton, *Rise of Islam and the Bengal Frontier,* 10.

18. Owen, *Rice Book,* 63.

19. Mrozik, "Cooking Living Beings."

20. Kieschnick, *Impact of Buddhism,* 252, 250.

21. Xinru, *Ancient India and Ancient China.*

22. Basic references for Buddhism and its cuisine in China are Waley-Cohen, *Sextants of Beijing,* 18–21; Gernet, *Buddhism in Chinese Society;* Kieschnick, *Impact of Buddhism;* Kohn, *Monastic Life in Medieval Daoism;* Saso, "Chinese Religions"; Ebrey and Gregory, "Religion and Society in Tang and Sung China." Anderson, *Food of China,* chap. 4, and Schafer, "T'ang," comment on the cuisine without paying special attention to Buddhism.

23. Gernet, *History of Chinese Civilization,* 210–232.

24. Dunlop, *Sichuan Cookery,* 121.

25. Wriggins, *Xuanzang.*

26. Schafer, *Golden Peaches,* 140.

27. Achaya, *Indian Food,* 148.

28. Gernet, *History of Chinese Civilization,* 241.

29. Elvin, *Pattern of the Chinese Past,* 113; T. Reynolds, *Stronger Than a Hundred Men,* 115.

30. Unschuld, *Medicine in China,* 132–44.

31. Anderson, *Food of China,* 73; Schafer, *Golden Peaches,* chaps. 7, 9, and 10.

32. Mazumdar, *Sugar and Society in China,* 1 for quotation; see also 20–33; Sabban, "Sucre candi" and "Savoir-faire oublié," 51; Kieschnick, *Impact of Buddhism,* 254–62.

33. Sabban, "Savoir-faire oublié."

34. Huang, *Fermentations and Food Science,* 503–61.

35. Lai, *At the Chinese Table,* chap. 9.

36. For background on tea, Gardella, *Harvesting Mountains,* chap. 1; Blofeld, *Chinese Art of Tea;* Kohn, *Monastic Life in Medieval Daoism,* chap. 6; Kieschnick, *Impact of Buddhism,* 262–75.

37. For meat substitutes, Sabban, "Viande en Chine"; Serventi and Sabban, *Pasta*, 324–25; Huang, *Fermentations and Food Science*, 497–502.

38. Kohn, *Monastic Life in Medieval Daoism*, chap. 5.

39. So, *Classic Food of China*, 16–17.

40. Gernet, *History of Chinese Civilization*, 295.

41. For the continued importance of Buddhism, see Sen, *Buddhism, Diplomacy, and Trade*, and Foulk, "Myth."

42. For overviews of the cuisine, see Freeman, "Sung"; Anderson, *Food of China*, chap. 5.

43. Kwok, "Pleasures of the Chinese Table," 48; Lai, *At the Chinese Table*, 8–12.

44. Freeman, "Sung," 171–72; Lin and Lin, *Chinese Gastronomy*, 12–13.

45. So, *Classic Food of China*, 3–4; Freeman, "Sung," 172–73.

46. Ibid., 27–28.

47. Wang and Anderson, "Ni Tsan and His 'Cloud Forest Hall Collection of Rules for Drinking and Eating'"; quotation, 30.

48. Tannahill, *Food in History*, 139. See also the sources in note 32.

49. Schafer, "T'ang," 132; Freeman, "Sung," 165–66.

50. Frankel and Frankel, *Wine and Spirits*.

51. Saso, "Chinese Religions," 349–51, 360.

52. Elvin, *Pattern of the Chinese Past*, 169.

53. Gernet, *History of Chinese Civilization*, 277–81.

54. Chon, "Korean Cuisine and Food Culture," 2–3; Pettid, *Korean Cuisine*, does not mention Buddhism.

55. Ishige, *History and Culture of Japanese Food*, chaps. 1 and 2. See Yoshida and Sesoko, *Naorai*, for fine illustrations of Japanese foods from all periods.

56. For the impact of Buddhism in Japan, see Ishige, *History and Culture of Japanese Food*, chap. 3. For milk, 61–62.

57. Isao, "Table Manners Then and Now," 58.

58. Ishige, *History and Culture of Japanese Food*, 73–75.

59. Ibid.

60. Hiroshi, "Japan's Use of Flour."

61. Castile, *Way of Tea*, 22–23.

62. Hosking, *Dictionary of Japanese Food*, Appendix.

63. Laudan, "Refined Food or Plain Cooking," 157.

64. *Wind in the Pines*, 21.

65. Sia, *Mary Sia's Chinese Cookbook*, 108.

4. ISLAM TRANSFORMS THE CUISINES OF CENTRAL AND WEST ASIA

1. See the introduction to Claudia Roden's *Book of Middle Eastern Food* for an overview of the history of the multilayered cuisines of the Middle East. *A Taste of Thyme*, edited by Sami Zubaida and Richard Tapper, offers a more scholarly perspective. For general background, see Lapidus, *History of Islamic Societies;* Robinson, ed., *Cambridge Illustrated History of the Islamic World;* and Chaudhuri, *Asia before Europe*, esp. chap. 6.

2. Clot, *Harun Al-Rashid*, 151.

3. For Perso-Islamic cuisine, I have used Perry et al., *Medieval Arab Cookery*, which collects and comments on classic texts. Zaouali, *Medieval Cuisine of the Islamic World*, is an accessible overview. Nasrallah, *Delights from the Garden of Eden*, weaves together the history and recipes of the region. See also Ahsan, *Social Life under the Abbasids*. For the long history of connections between China and Persia, Laufer, *Sino-Iranica*, is classic.

4. Christensen, *Iran sous les Sassanides*, 471–75.

5. For Parsi cuisine today, see King, *My Bombay Kitchen*.

6. Perry et al., *Medieval Arab Cookery*, 37.

7. R. Eaton, *Rise of Islam and the Bengal Frontier*, 29–30.

8. Rosenberger, "Dietética y cocina en el mundo musulmán occidental," 16–22; Achaya, *Indian Food*, 80.

9. Charles Perry, personal communication.

10. Achaya, *Indian Food*, 56–57.

11. See Gelder, *God's Banquet*, chaps. 1–4, for gastronomic poetry; Hattox, *Coffee and Coffeehouses*, chap. 4, and "Islam," in Robinson, *Oxford Companion to Wine*, for intoxicants in Islamic law and theology; and Matthee, *Pursuit of Pleasure*, chaps. 2, 3, 6, and 7, for the same issues in later Iran.

12. Grewe, "Hispano-Arabic Cuisine in the Twelfth Century," 143–44; Rosenberger, "Dietética y cocina en el mundo musulmán occidental," 22–40.

13. Serventi and Sabban, *Pasta*, 29–34; A. Watson, *Agricultural Innovation in the Early Islamic World*, chap. 4.

14. Rosenberger, "Arab Cuisine," 213. For the Qur'an on sweets, see Arsel, Pekin, and Sümer, *Timeless Tastes*, 266.

15. "An Anonymous Andalusian Cookbook of the 13th Century," translated by Charles Perry, in www.daviddfriedman.com/Medieval/Cookbooks/Andalusian/andalusian10.htm#Heading521 (accessed 2 January 2013).

16. For Perso-Islamic food processing, Wulff, *Traditional Crafts of Persia*, chap. 5; al-Hassan and Hill, *Islamic Technology*, chap. 8. For water mills, al-Hassan and Hill, *Islamic Technology*, 214; T. Reynolds, *Stronger Than a Hundred Men*, 116–18; Stathakopoulos, "Between the Field and the Plate," 34–35.

17. Glick, *Islamic and Christian Spain in the Early Middle Ages*, 2.

18. For distillation, al-Hassan and Hill, *Islamic Technology*, 133–46; R. J. Forbes, *Short History of the Art of Distillation*, chap. 3; Wilson, *Water of Life*, 91–93.

19. Perry et al., *Medieval Arab Cookery*, 29.

20. Basic references for the cuisine of al-Andalus are Bolens, *La cuisine andalouse*; Rosenberger, "Dietética y cocina en el mundo musulmán occidental," and for agriculture, Glick, *Islamic and Christian Spain in the Early Middle Ages*, 76–83 and chap. 7. For historical background, see Fletcher, *Moorish Spain*. For the Arabs in Sicily, see Simeti, *Pomp and Sustenance*, chap. 2.

21. Glick, *Islamic and Christian Spain*, 221–23.

22. Titley, *Ni'matnama Manuscript*, introduction.

23. Le Strange, *Baghdad*, 81–82.

24. Beg, "Study of the Cost of Living and Economic Status of Artisans in Abbasid Iraq."

25. Ashtor, "Essai sur l'alimentation des diverses classes sociales dans l'Orient médiéval."

26. Hurvitz, "From Scholarly Circles to Mass Movements," 992.

27. Rosenberger, "Arab Cuisine," 10.

28. For trade, see Abu-Lughoud, *Before European Hegemony.*

29. Watson, *Agricultural Innovation in the Early Islamic World.*

30. On Mongol cuisine, see Buell and Anderson, *Soup for the Qan;* Mote, "Yuan and Ming"; Sabban, "Court Cuisine." For background on the Mongol Empire, see Golden, *Nomads and Sedentary Societies;* Adshead, *Central Asia in World History;* and Allsen, *Culture and Conquest,* esp. chap. 15 on cuisine.

31. J. M. Smith, "Dietary Decadence."

32. Allsen, *Culture and Conquest,* chap. 15.

33. J. M. Smith, "Mongol Campaign Rations."

34. Perry et al., "Grain Foods of the Early Turks."

35. Gernet, *History of Chinese Civilization,* 365.

36. Buell and Anderson, *Soup for the Qan,* 192; for soups, 275–95; for sheep's bitter bowel, 307; for drinks including liquid soups, 373–433; for Mongol pasta, Serventi and Sabban, *Pasta,* 327–33.

37. Gardella, *Harvesting Mountains,* 27. The figure he gives is two to five million *jin* (500 jin is 665 pounds).

38. Perry, "Grain Foods of the Early Turks"; Buell and Anderson, *Soup for the Qan* (2010), appendix.

39. Marco Polo, *Description of the World,* 1: 209, 218–20.

40. Mote, "Yuan and Ming," 207.

41. Glenn Mack, personal communication.

42. Buell and Anderson, *Soup for the Qan,* 159.

43. Goldstein, "Eastern Influence on Russian Cuisine."

44. Lewicki, *West African Food in the Middle Ages.* For couscous, Franconie et al., *Couscous, boulgour et polenta.*

45. Zaouali, *Medieval Cuisine of the Islamic World,* xiii. Charles Perry dates plain pilau to twelfth-century Iran, personal communication. Fragner, "From the Caucasus," argues that flavored pilau was invented in sixteenth-century Iran.

46. Halici, *Sufi Cuisine,* introduction and 199–224. Quotation on 208.

47. "Omar Khayyám," in Robinson, *Oxford Companion to Wine.*

48. Hattox, *Coffee and Coffeehouses,* chap. 2.

49. www.superluminal.com/cookbook/essay_bushaq.html (accessed 16 October 2012).

50. On Ottoman cuisine, see Arsel et al., *Timeless Tastes,* 13–89.

51. Segal, *Islam's Black Slaves,* 151.

52. Evans, "Splendid Processions."

53. Singer, *Constructing Ottoman Beneficence,* 145, 155.

54. Ibid., 140.

55. Ibid., chap. 5 for Istanbul, chap. 4 for Jerusalem.

56. Hattox, *Coffee and Coffeehouses,* is classic.

57. Lang, *Cuisine of Hungary,* 30–32.

58. Hattox, *Coffee and Coffeehouses,* chaps. 6–8 for the transformation of social life.

59. Mehmet Genç, "Ottoman Industry in the Eighteenth Century," in *Manufacturing in the Ottoman Empire and Turkey,* ed. Quataert, 59–85; Faroqhi, *Towns and Townsmen of Ottoman Anatolia;* and Kaneva-Johnson, *Melting Pot,* 7–8.

60. Babur, *Bābur-nāma*, 2, 518.
61. Eaton, *Rise of Islam and the Bengal Frontier*, 169–70.
62. Ibid., chap. 7.
63. Balabanlilar, "Lords of the Auspicious Conjunction," 24.
64. Ibid.
65. Basic references for Mughal cuisine are Achaya, *Indian Food*, chap. 12; Collingham, *Curry*, chap. 2; Husain, *Emperor's Table*. For background, see Richards, *Mughal Empire*.
66. See Abū al-Fazl ibn Mubārak, *Ain-i-Akbari*, 59–68, for quotation and specific quantities.
67. Collingham, *Curry*, 31–32.
68. Sharar, *Lucknow*, 162.
69. Westrip, *Moghul Cooking*, 25–26; Collingham, *Curry*, 30; Panjabi, *50 Great Curries*, 88 and 106.
70. Khare, "Wine-Cup in Mughal Court Culture," 143–88.
71. Collingham, *Curry*, chap. 4; Westrip, *Moghul Cooking*, 27; Sharar, *Lucknow: The Last Phase of an Oriental Culture*, chaps. 28–31.
72. Mazumdar, "New World Food Crops," 70–74; Randhawa, *History of Agriculture in India*, 2: 49, 51, 188–89.
73. Collingham, *Curry*, 39.

5. CHRISTIANITY TRANSFORMS THE CUISINES OF EUROPE AND THE AMERICAS

1. Matthew 26:26, AV.
2. For Jewish cuisine, see Cooper, *Eat and Be Satisfied*, chap. 4, which draws on research by the early twentieth-century scholar Samuel Krauss; for the transition to Christianity, see Feeley-Harnik, *Lord's Table*, chaps. 2–5.
3. For Christianity and Christian cuisines in late antiquity, see P. Brown, *World of Late Antiquity* and *Body and Society*; MacMullen, *Christianizing the Roman Empire*; Grimm, *From Feasting to Fasting*; and Galavaris, *Bread and the Liturgy*.
4. Brown, *Body and Society*, 199; Grimm, *From Feasting to Fasting*, 185.
5. "Augustine on the Nature of the Sacrament of the Eucharist," www.earlychurchtexts.com/public/augustine_sermon_272_eucharist.htm (accessed 17 August 2012).
6. 1 Cor. 5:7–8.
7. Clement, *Paidagogus* 2.1.15, quoted in Grimm, *From Feasting to Fasting*, 106, 103.
8. Ibid., 100.
9. Quoted in Musurillo, "Problem of Ascetical Fasting," 13.
10. P. Brown, *Body and Society*, 92–93, 97, 181–82, 256–57.
11. Benedict, *Rule*, 80.
12. Curtis, *Garum and Salsamenta*, 188.
13. P. Brown, *World of Late Antiquity*, 16.
14. The basic references for Byzantine cuisine are Dalby, *Siren Feasts*, chap. 9; Dalby, *Flavours of Byzantium*; Brubaker and Linardou, *Eat, Drink, and Be Merry*, chaps. 7–20; Galavaris, *Bread and the Liturgy*, 14, 44.
15. Malmberg, "Dazzling Dining," 82.

16. Siraisi, *Medieval and Early Renaissance Medicine*, 5.

17. Dalby, *Siren Feasts*, 190 for stuffed grape leaves, 192 for flavored wine, 191–92 for sweets, and 199 for meat dishes and for Liutprand's comment.

18. Charanis, *Social, Economic and Political Life in the Byzantine Empire.* Thomas and Hero, eds., *Byzantine Monastic Foundation Documents*, 5: 1696–1716, detail different monastic rules.

19. Dalby, *Siren Feasts*, 196–97.

20. Magdalino, "Grain Supply of Constantinople."

21. Cunliffe, *Europe between the Oceans*, 425–26.

22. The basic references for this story are Cross and Sherbwitz-Wetzor, *Russian Primary Chronicle*, 96–119; Lunt, "On Interpreting the Russian Primary Chronicle," 17 and 26.

23. For food in Kievian Rus', see Lunt, "On Interpreting the Russian Primary Chronicle"; Smith and Christian, *Bread and Salt*, 1–15; Goldstein, "Eastern Influence."

24. Dalby, *Flavours of Byzantium*, 76.

25. Smith and Christian, *Bread and Salt*, 255.

26. For the Christianization of Europe and its cuisine, see Effros, *Creating Community with Food and Drink in Merovingian Gaul;* Fletcher, *Barbarian Conversion;* Hagen, *Anglo-Saxon Food and Drink.*

27. Anthimus, *De observatione ciborum*, trans. Grant, 27.

28. Effros, *Creating Community with Food and Drink in Merovingian Gaul*, 10.

29. The literature on high Catholic cuisine is enormous. On the relation to dietetics, see Scully, *Art of Cookery in the Middle Ages.* For cuisine in what are now France and Italy, see Wheaton, *Savoring the Past*, chaps. 2–5; Scully and Scully, *Early French Cookery;* and Redon et al., *Medieval Kitchen.* For Poland, see Dembińska, *Food and Drink in Medieval Poland.* For the Mediterranean, see Santich, *Original Mediterranean Cuisine.* For an overview, see Albala, *Cooking in Europe, 1250–1650.*

30. Bartlett, *Making of Europe*, 306–8.

31. For Islamic cuisine in Sicily, see Simeti, *Pomp and Sustenance*, chap. 3.

32. Siraisi, *Medieval and Early Renaissance Medicine*, 58–59.

33. Freedman, *Out of the East*, 4–5, chaps. 1 and 3.

34. Wheaton, *Savoring the Past*, 39–41; Mazumdar, *Sugar and Society in China*, 25.

35. Cathy Kaufman, www.academia.edu/1592459/The_Roots_of_Rhythm_The_Medieval_Origins_of_the_New_Orleans_Mardi_Gras_Beignet (accessed 1 November 2012).

36. P. H. Smith, *Business of Alchemy*, 167. Becher, a Protestant, was here expressing an opinion that was rapidly becoming dated.

37. Wright, *Mediterranean Feast*, 392; Redon et al., *Medieval Kitchen*, 117–18; http://language offood.blogspot.com/2009/11/ceviche-and-fish-chips.html (accessed 2 November 2012).

38. Martínez Motiño, *Arte de cocina*, 63, 407.

39. Redon et al., *Medieval Kitchen*, 170, 188–91.

40. Dembińska, *Food and Drink in Medieval Poland*, 106–14.

41. Dyer, "Changes in Diet in the Late Middle Ages."

42. Wheaton, *Savoring the Past*, chap. 4; Brodman, *Charity and Welfare*, chap. 2.

43. T. Reynolds, *Stronger Than a Hundred Men*, chap. 2.

44. White, *Medieval Technology and Social Change*, chap. 2; Albala, *Beans*, 48.

45. L. Hoffmann, "Frontier Foods"; Cutting, "Historical Aspects of Fish."

46. Scully, *Art of Cookery,* 74.

47. Curtin, *Rise and Fall of the Plantation Complex,* 5–8.

48. Simeti, *Pomp and Sustenance,* 101–4.

49. Pacey, *Technology,* 66–68.

50. Daniels and Daniels, "Origin of the Sugarcane Roller Mill," 529.

51. Coe and Coe, *True History of Chocolate,* 143.

52. Domingo, "Cocina precolumbina en España," 24; Loreto López, "Prácticas alimenticias."

53. For Jewish cuisine in Spain and New Spain, see Gitlitz and Davidson, *Drizzle of Honey.*

54. On New Spain, see Coe, *America's First Cuisines,* 74–76; Pilcher, *Que Vivan Los Tamales!* chap. 2; Long, ed., *Conquista y comida;* Super, *Food, Conquest, and Colonization in Sixteenth-Century Spanish America;* Laudan and Pilcher, "Chiles, Chocolate, and Race"; Laudan, "Islamic Origins."

55. Boileau, "Culinary History," 85–107; Hughes, *Fatal Shore,* 49.

56. Kupperman, "Fear of Hot Climates"; Thomas Gage quoted, 230.

57. Curtin, *Death by Migration,* chap. 1.

58. Earle, "'If You Eat Their Food . . .'"

59. Stoopen, "Simientes del mestizaje"; Suárez y Farías, "De ámbitos y sabores virreinales."

60. Boileau, "Culinary History"; Laudan, *Food of Paradise,* 140–46; Collingham, *Curry,* chap. 3.

61. Schurz, *Manila Galleon.*

62. On sugar plantations, see Daniels and Daniels, "Origin of the Sugarcane Roller Mill." See also Schwartz, *Tropical Babylons;* Dunn, *Sugar and Slaves,* chap. 6; Curtin, *Rise and Fall of the Plantation Complex,* chap. 5; Mintz, *Sweetness and Power,* chaps. 2 and 3.

63. Daniels and Daniels, "Origin of the Sugarcane Roller Mill," 527–30.

64. Carney and Rosomoff, *In the Shadow of Slavery,* 162–63.

65. Sabban, "Industrie sucrière."

66. Thompson, *Thai Food,* 603–7; Saberi, *Afghan Food and Cookery,* 144–45.

67. Laudan, *Food of Paradise,* 89.

68. Davidson and Pensado, "Earliest Portuguese Cookbook"; Couto, *Arte de cozinha,* 77–85; Aikin, *Memoirs of the Court of Queen Elizabeth,* 506.

69. Mason, *Sugar-Plums and Sherbet,* 22–25.

70. León Pinelo, *Question moral,* 120–23.

71. Coe and Coe, *True History of Chocolate,* chaps. 1–5.

72. Norton, *Sacred Gifts, Profane Pleasures,* 1–12.

73. Zizumbo-Villarreal and Colunga-García Marín, "Early Coconut Distillation"; Chávez, "Cabildo, negociación y vino de cocos."

74. Huang, *Fermentations and Food Science,* 203–31.

75. Laudan and Pilcher, "Chiles, Chocolate, and Race in New Spain."

76. Thomas Aquinas, *Summa Theologica,* pt. 3, question 74, www.newadvent.org /summa/4074.htm (accessed 18 August 2012).

77. Mijares, *Mestizaje alimentario,* 44.

78. Laudan, "Islamic Origins"; www.rachellaudan.com/2008/12/fideos-and-fideu-more-on-the-mexican-islamic-connection.html; www.rachellaudan.com/2010/09/couscous-cant-miss-festival-and-origins-of-mexican-couscous.html (accessed 2 November 2012).

79. Quoted in Burkhart, *Slippery Earth,* 166.

80. Lockhart, *Nahuas,* 278.

81. W. Taylor, *Drinking,* 34–40; Corcuera de Mancera, *Del amor al temor,* pt. 3; Lozano Arrendares, *Chinguirito vindicado.*

82. Warman, *Corn and Capitalism;* for Africa, see McCann, *Maize and Grace.*

83. Crosby, *Columbian Exchange.* As examples of the many historians who see the Columbian Exchange as a key turning point in food history, see, e.g., Kiple, *Movable Feast,* chap. 12; Standage, *Edible History of Humanity,* chap. 7.

84. Wheaton, *Savoring the Past,* chap. 3; Strong, *Feast,* 203–8; Kamen, *Spain's Road to Empire,* 78.

85. Bayly, *Birth of the Modern World,* Introduction.

6. PRELUDE TO MODERN CUISINES

1. Wheaton, *Savoring the Past,* chap. 6, describes the transition as the beginning of fine dining, comparing it to the rational philosophy of Descartes and the formalization of the rules of architecture; Flandrin, *Chroniques de Platine,* chaps. 4, 5, and 6, suggests new medical theory is responsible for the increase in green vegetables, butter, and cool wine; Fink, *Les liaisons savoureuses,* discusses change in aesthetics and the elevation of dining to a fine art; Peterson, *Acquired Taste,* chap. 10, puts the change down to the Renaissance recovery of Graeco-Roman traditions; Mennell, *All Manners of Food,* attributes it to the French courtly tradition in France; and Albala, *Cooking in Europe, 1250–1650,* and Pinkard, *Revolution in Taste,* part 2, judge it to be due to a combination of different factors.

2. Popkin, "Nutrition Transition."

3. Bayly, *Birth of the Modern World,* 9–12.

4. Albala, "Ideology of Fasting"; Spencer, *British Food,* 101–6.

5. Luther, *Table Talk,* ed. Hazlitt, DCCVI.

6. Bérard, "Consommation du poisson." Freshwater river fish such as trout, eel, roach, and carp were still eaten.

7. Moor, "Wafer."

8. For sources for the following section, see Laudan, "Kind of Chemistry" and "Birth of the Modern Diet." For an overview of the chemical physicians, see Debus, *The French Paracelsans.*

9. Lémery, *A Treatise of All Sorts of Foods,* 251–52.

10. La Varenne quoted in Wheaton, *Savoring the Past,* 251. For a different translation, see La Varenne, *The French Cook,* 41.

11. Arbuthnot, *Essay,* 10.

12. Pagel, "Van Helmont's Ideas on Gastric Digestion."

13. Lémery, *A Treatise of All Sorts of Foods,* 95, 129, and 224.

14. Evelyn, *Acetaria,* 4.

15. Young, *Apples of Gold*, for Fouquet's dinner, chap. 6; for the quotation, p. 313. Basic references for French cuisine from 1650 until 1840 include Wheaton, *Savoring the Past*, chaps. 6–12; Mennell, chap. 5 and 134–56, 266–72; Trubek, *Haute Cuisine*, chap. 1; Spang, *Invention of the Restaurant*, chaps. 1–3; and Pinkard, *Revolution in Taste*, parts 2 and 3. Fink, *Les liaisons savoureuses*, excerpts key texts.

16. Louis de Rouvroy, duc de Saint-Simon, *Mémoires, 1701–1707*, ed. Yves Coirault, *Bibliothèque de la Pléiade* (Paris: Gallimard, 1983), 2: 55–56, cited in Pérez Samper, "Alimentación," 533–34; for the reception of French cuisine in Italy and New Spain, Kasper, *Splendid Table*, 7; Curiel Monteagudo, *Virreyes y virreinas*, 119, 153.

17. Baron Grimm, *Correspondance littéraire*, 2: 187–88, quoted by Wheaton, *Savoring the Past*, 200; *Les dons de Comus; ou, Les délices de la table* (Paris: Prault, 1739), xx, trans. Wheaton, *Savoring the Past*, 197.

18. Spang, *Invention of the Restaurant*, chaps. 1 and 2.

19. Kaufman, "What's in a Name?"; Lehmann, "Rise of the Cream Sauce."

20. Drewnowski, "Fat and Sugar."

21. Munro, "Food in Catherinian St. Petersburg."

22. Wheaton, *Savoring the Past*, chap. 9.

23. Ibid., 163.

24. Valeri, "Création et transmission."

25. C. Young, *Apples of Gold*, chap. 7.

26. Koerner, "Linnaeus' Floral Transplants," 156.

27. Dolan, *Wedgwood*, 229–32.

28. www.salon.com//2011/07/02/jefferson_culinary_history (accessed 2 November 2012).

29. Stearns, *European Society in Upheaval*, 26; Bayly, *The Birth of the Modern World*, 425.

30. Bonnet, "Culinary System."

31. Goldstein, "Gastronomic Reforms," 16.

32. Bonnet, "Culinary System," 142–43.

33. Pluquet, *Traité philosophique et politique sur le luxe*, 2: 330.

34. Sherman, *Fresh from the Past*, 304.

35. E. Smith, *Compleat Housewife*, preface, unpaginated.

36. Chamberlain, "Rousseau's Philosophy of Food."

37. Kaplan, "Provisioning Paris: The Crisis of 1738–41," 72.

38. Morineau, "Growing without Knowing Why: Production, Demographics, and Diet," 382, for the more optimistic figure; Hemardinquer, *Pour une histoire de l'alimentation*, for earlier, less optimistic ones.

39. On bread in France, Kaplan, *Bread, Politics and Political Economy in the Reign of Louis XV*; Kaplan, *Provisioning Paris*; Kaplan, *The Bakers of Paris and the Bread Question, 1700–1775*.

40. Spary, "Making a Science of Taste."

41. Spang, *Invention of the Restaurant*, chap. 4.

42. Young, *Apples of Gold*, chap. 9; Ferguson, *Accounting for Taste*, 55–59.

43. Trubek, *Haute Cuisine*, 67 and passim, for further imperial language.

44. For Dutch cuisine, see Schama, *Embarrassment of Riches*, chap. 3, inc. 168–71 for the ample diet enjoyed even by small artisans and laborers; and Riley, *The Dutch Table*. For the

Dutch economy, see J. Vries, *Dutch Rural Economy in the Golden Age,* and for its empire, Boxer, *Dutch Seabourne Empire.*

45. Moor, "Dutch Cookery and Calvin," 97–98.

46. Rose, *Sensible Cook.*

47. Ibid., 61; Meijer, "Dutch Cookbooks Printed in the 16th and 17th Centuries."

48. Cutting, "Historical Aspects of Fish," 8–13.

49. Riley, "Fish in Art"; Riley, *The Dutch Table,* 19–22.

50. *Histoire naturelle des poissons,* 5: 429.

51. Riley, *Dutch Table,* 19.

52. Moor, "Farmhouse Gouda," 111.

53. Boxer, *Dutch Seaborne Empire,* 198.

54. For Calvin, see Moor, "Dutch Cookery and Calvin," 98; for Belcampius, see Rose, *Sensible Cook,* 29; for wigs and cosmetics, see Schama, *Embarrassment of Riches,* 165.

55. Abbé Jean-Baptiste Dubos, *Réflexions critiques sur la poésie,* 1: 306.

56. Dege, "Norwegian Gastronomic Literature: Part II, 1814–1835."

57. Wheaton, *Savoring the Past,* 157.

58. Smith and Christian, *Bread and Salt,* 173–78; Goldstein, "Gastronomic Reforms under Peter the Great."

59. R. Smith, "Whence the Samovar?"

60. Coetzee, *South African Culinary Tradition,* chap. 1.

61. Rose, *Sensible Cook,* 34–35.

62. E. Kaufman, *Melting Pot of Mennonite Cookery, 1874–1974*; Voth, *Mennonite Food and Folkways from South Russia.*

63. Mazumdar, *Sugar and Society in China,* 83–90.

64. www.sriowen.com/rijsttafel-to-go (accessed 4 November 2012).

65. Colley, *Britons* (1992), a work influenced by Anderson, *Imagined Communities* (1983).

66. For the architectural setting of English cuisine, see Girouard, *Life in the English Country House;* for the kitchens, see Sambrook and Brears, *Country House Kitchen* (though some of their kitchens are grander); for history, Spencer, *British Food,* chap. 8, and Colquhoun, *Taste,* chaps. 12–17; Paston-Williams, *Art of Dining,* 140–263; for the perspective of an agricultural historian, Thirsk, *Food in Early Modern England;* for cookbooks and their authors, Lehmann, *British Housewife;* and for theories on the divergence of English and French cuisines, as well as reminders not to romanticize the past, Mennell, *All Manners of Food,* chap. 5; for recipes to try, Sherman, *Fresh from the Past;* and for glorious recreations of English meals, Day, "Historic Food."

67. Cheyne, *English Malady,* 51. See also Guerrini, *Obesity and Depression in the Enlightenment.*

68. Lehmann, *British Housewife.* Although published a century later, in 1861, Elena Molokhovets's *Gift to Young Housewives,* which sold 295,000 copies by 1917, belongs to the genre of gentry rather than middle-class cookbooks.

69. Mennell, *All Manners of Food,* 96–98.

70. Rogers, *Beef and Liberty,* chaps. 1–5; Woodforde, *Diary of a Country Parson,* 500. For ox roasts, see www.foodhistoryjottings.blogspot.com/2012/08/a-jubilee-ox-roast.html (accessed 4 November 2012).

71. A. Smith, *Pure Ketchup,* chaps. 1 and 2.

72. Wilson, *Food and Drink in Britain,* 294.

73. Glasse, *First Catch Your Hare,* 52.

74. Ehrman, *London Eats Out,* 62–64.

75. Coe, *True History of Chocolate,* chap. 8.

76. Schamas, "Changes in English and Anglo-American Consumption," 179; Walvin, *Fruits of Empire,* 121, 169.

77. Bickham, "Eating the Empire," 72.

78. Basic references for colonial American cuisine are Eden, *Early American Table,* for culinary philosophy; Oliver, *Food in Colonial and Federal America;* Stavely and Fitzgerald, *America's Founding Food;* McWilliams, *Revolution in Eating,* and K. Hess, *Martha Washington's Booke of Cookery,* 8. For republican sentiment in British America, see Wood, *Creation of the American Republic.*

79. Wilson, *Food and Drink in Britain,* 294–95; A. Smith, *Pure Ketchup,* chaps. 1–3.

80. Juárez López, *La lenta emergencia,* 9–15.

81. Ridley, "First American Cookbook."

82. Curtin, *Rise and Fall of the Plantation Complex,* 11–14; Parish, *Slavery: History and Historians.*

83. Carney and Rosomoff, *In the Shadow of Slavery,* 51, and chaps. 3, 5, and 10.

84. Freyre, *Masters and the Slaves (Casa-Grande and Senzala),* 433.

85. Silva, *Farinha, feijão e carne-seca,* 47–54.

86. Mason, *Sugar-Plums and Sherbet,* 34.

87. In addition to the earlier references, see A. Taylor, *American Colonies,* part 2, and Fischer, *Albion's Seed.*

88. Cronon, *Changes in the Land,* 25.

89. Ibid., and Levenstein, *Revolution at the Table,* 26–28.

90. Crèvecoeur, *Letters from an American Farmer,* 55.

91. For Navy food, Wilkinson, *The British Navy and the State in the Eighteenth Century,* 107; Stead, "Navy Blues"; Rodger, *Command of the Ocean,* 304–7, 583; and Rodger, *Wooden World,* 82–86.

92. Rodger, *Command of the Ocean,* 583.

93. Salaman, *History and Social Influence of the Potato,* 459, and generally for the potato.

94. Koerner, "Linnaeus' Floral Transplants."

95. Weber, *Peasants into Frenchmen,* 130–43.

96. Weber, *Peasants into Frenchmen,* 6; Cheyne, *Essay of Health,* 135.

97. Rumford, *Essays,* 1: 105.

98. E. Thompson, "Moral Economy of the English Crowd in the Eighteenth Century."

99. Koerner, "Linnaeus' Floral Transplants."

100. Salaman, *History and Social Influence of the Potato,* esp. 115 and chaps. 5 and 9; Fitzpatrick, "Peasants, Potatoes and the Columbian Exchange"; on decline of ergotism, Matossian, *Poisons of the Past,* chap. 2.

101. Smith and Christian, *Bread and Salt,* 200.

102. Ibid., 200.

103. Matthias, *Brewing Industry,* part 1; Nye, *War, Wine and Taxes,* esp. chaps. 2 and 6.

104. Waley-Cohen, "Taste and Gastronomy."

105. McClain et al., *Edo and Paris*, chaps. 5, 8 and 9.

106. E. Jones, *European Miracle*, 81–82.

107. Walvin, *Fruits of Empire*, chap. 10.

108. Unwin, *Wine and the Vine*, 245.

109. Slicher van Bath, *Agrarian History of Western Europe A.D. 500–1850*, 157; J. Vries, *Dutch Rural Economy in the Golden Age, 1500–1700*, 171.

110. B. Thomas, "Food Supply in the United Kingdom during the Industrial Revolution."

111. Smith and Christian, *Bread and Salt*, 231.

112. Koerner, "Linnaeus' Floral Transplants," 155–57.

113. Drayton, *Nature's Government*, part 2.

114. Carney, *In the Shadow of Slavery*, 52–55, 67–69.

115. Mazumdar, "Impact of New World Food Crops"; for the high quality earlier in the Lower Yangtze Valley, Pomeranz, *Great Divergence*, 38–40.

116. Scholliers, "From the 'Crisis of Flanders' to Belgium's 'Social Question.'"

7. MODERN CUISINES, 1810-1920

1. For population numbers, see Belich, *Replenishing the Earth*, 3–4. I use Belich's useful term "Anglo" and extend it to cuisines.

2. D. Burton, *Two Hundred Years of New Zealand Food and Cookery*, 28; Ladies of Toronto, *Home Cook Book*, preface.

3. Artusi, *Art of Eating Well*, 35, quoting Olinda Guerrini, who wrote under the pen name Lorenzo Stecchetti, from a conference at the Turin Exposition of 1884.

4. Episcopal Church, Coffeyville, Kansas, *Coffeyville Cook Book*.

5. Beeton, *Mrs. Beeton's Book of Household Management*, 1; Beecher and Beecher Stowe, *American Woman's Home*, 19.

6. Toomre, *Classic Russian Cooking*, 12–13.

7. Beeton, *Mrs. Beeton's Book of Household Management*, 830–32. For an overview of late nineteenth century nutritional theory, see, for example, Drummond and Wilbraham, *The Englishman's Food*, chap. 20. For pickles as unsuitable for children, see Gabaccia, *We Are What We Eat*, 124 and 128.

8. Trentmann, *Free Trade Nation*, 56, quoting from *The Quarterly Leaflet of the Women's National Liberal Association*, no. 32 (July 1903): 8.

9. Beeton, *Mrs. Beeton's Book of Household Management*, 105.

10. Carpenter, *Protein and Energy*, chaps. 3, 4, and 6.

11. Quoted in Camporesi, *Magic Harvest*, 197.

12. Lankester, *On Food*, 173.

13. Artusi, *Art of Eating Well*, 15, 29, 35.

14. Quoted in Cwiertka, *Making of Modern Culinary Tradition*, 99–100.

15. Levenstein, *Revolution at the Table*, 24, 218n6.

16. Waldstreicher, *In the Midst of Perpetual Fetes*, 1–2.

17. Longone, "Mince Pie."

18. Trubek, *Haute Cuisine*, 84.

19. Cwiertka, *Making of Modern Culinary Tradition*, 110–12, 192–94.

20. Ehrman et al., *London Eats Out,* 92–95.

21. Haber, *From Hardtack to Home Fries,* chap. 9; Porterfield, *Dining by Rail.*

22. Cwiertka, *Modern Japanese Cuisine,* 30–34.

23. Mazumdar, *Sugar and Society in China,* 81.

24. M. White, *Coffee Life in Japan,* 45–46.

25. Steel, *Complete Indian Housekeeper,* 17.

26. Petersen and Jenkins, *Bread and the British Economy,* 4.

27. Atkins et al., *Food and the City in Europe since 1800,* pt. B.

28. C. Davidson, *Woman's Work Is Never Done,* chap. 9; R. S. Cowan, *More Work for Mother,* chaps. 3 and 4.

29. Tschiffely, *This Way Southward,* 61.

30. Trentmann, *Free Trade Nation,* Part 1.

31. Gabaccia, *We Are What We Eat,* 112.

32. Heltosky, *Garlic and Oil;* Gabaccia, *We Are What We Eat;* Anderson, *Pleasures of the Italian Table,* 75.

33. Quoted in Cwiertka, *Making of Modern Culinary Tradition in Japan,* 88–89.

34. Ibid., 110.

35. Swislocki, *Culinary Nostalgia,* 135; Beeton, *Mrs. Beeton's Book of Household Management,* 1.

36. Swislocki, *Culinary Nostalgia,* 125.

37. Ray, *The Migrant's Table,* 44.

38. Rangalal Bandyopadhyay, *Sarissadhani Vidyar Gunokirtan* (Calcutta, 1869?) titled in English *On the Importance of Physical Education,* 5, 38, 43, 46–47, trans. in Chakrabarty, "The Difference," 377–78.

39. Diner, *Hungering for America,* 229.

40. Pilcher, *Que vivan los tamales!* chap. 9; Freyre, *The Masters and the Slaves,* 45–70.

41. Aguilar-Rodríguez, "Cooking Modernity," 177.

42. Englehardt, *Mess of Greens,* chap. 2.

43. Spencer, *Vegetarianism,* 269.

44. McCay, *Protein Element in Nutrition,* 178, 51.

45. Ibid., 54–57, 153.

46. E. Weber, *Peasants into Frenchmen,* 300–301, 144–45. Heltosky, *Garlic and Oil,* 15, 133, argues that Italian peasants in many regions drank little wine, in many cases as late as the 1950s. Phillips, *Short History of Wine,* 238–41, relies on studies by the French social scientist Frédéric Le Play to suggest that although the French middle and upper classes drank wine in the nineteenth century, peasants and workers drank it regularly or scarcely at all depending on the region.

47. Capatti, "Taste for Canned and Preserved Food," 497. See also Heltosky, *Garlic and Oil,* 46.

48. Cwiertka, *Making of Modern Culinary Tradition,* 126–32.

49. Levenstein, *Revolution at the Table,* chap. 4.

50. Petersen and Jenkins, *Bread and the British Economy,* chaps. 2 and 4.

51. Walton, *Fish and* Chips, esp. 148.

52. Stearns, *European Society in Upheaval,* 190–91.

53. Ibid.

54. W. G. Hoffman, "100 Years," 13–18.

55. Headrick, *Tentacles of Progress*, 240–43.

56. Stearns, *European Society in Upheaval*, 222; Griggs, "Sugar Demand."

57. Dix, "Non-Alcoholic Beverages in Nineteenth Century Russia," 24.

58. Mintz, *Sweetness and Power*, 174; Burnett, *Plenty and Want*, chap. 11; Offer, *First World War*, 333; Oddy, *From Plain Fare to Fusion Food*; Spencer, *British Food*, 291–92; Symons, *One Continuous Picnic*, 12; Krugman, http://web.mit.edu/krugman/www/mushy .html (accessed 5 December 2012).

59. Griffin, *Short History*, chap. 9; Colgrove, "McKeown Thesis"; Fogel, *The Escape from Hunger and Premature Death*, chaps. 1 and 2, esp. p. 42.

60. Stearns, *European Society in Upheaval*, 16–17.

61. Kasper, *Italian Country Table*, 61–62, 171.

62. Hanley, *Everyday Things in Premodern Japan*, 85–94; Homma, *Folk Art of Japanese Country Cooking*, 15–17, 28–53, 91–92.

63. Jing, *Feeding China's Little Emperors*, 8.

64. M. Davis, *Late Victorian Holocausts*, preface.

65. Laudan, *Food of Paradise*, pt. 2.

66. Warman, *Corn and Capitalism*, chaps. 4, 5 and 6; McCann, *Maize and Grace*, chaps. 3–5.

67. Mazumdar, "Impact of New World Food Crops."

68. Camporesi, *Magic Harvest*, 119–20.

69. Quoted in Ferguson, *Accounting for Taste*, 55.

70. For the upper caste, see Bayly, *Birth of the Modern World*, 46–47.

71. Phillips, *Short History of Wine*, 236.

72. See also Zeldin, *France, 1848–1945*, 732–33.

73. Collingham, *Curry*, 123.

74. Thompson, *Thai Food*, 29 and 54.

75. Cwiertka, *Modern Japanese Cuisine*, 19–20.

76. Chuen, *À la table de l'empereur de Chine*, 152–53.

77. Chamberlain, *Food and Cooking of Russia*, 293–95; Symons, *One Continuous Picnic*, 112–15.

78. Hosking, "Manyoken, Japan's First French Restaurant."

79. Ehrman et al., *London Eats Out*, 68–85.

80. Tandon, *Punjabi Century*, 177. For the use of cans in Vietnam, see Peters, *Appetites and Aspirations*, 153–56.

81. Zeldin, *France, 1848–1945*, chap. 14.

82. Toomre, *Classic Russian Cooking*, 21.

83. Arsel and Pekin, *Timeless Tastes*, 118.

84. Panjabi, "Non-Emergence of the Regional Foods of India," 145–46.

85. Burton, *French Colonial Cookery*, 145; Peters, *Appetites and Aspirations*, 207.

86. Kenney-Herbert, *Culinary Jottings*, 3.

87. Peters, *Appetites and Aspirations*, 156–62.

88. Couto, *Arte de cozinha*, 119–32.

89. See, e.g., Bak-Geller, "Los recetarios afrancesados"; Peters, *Appetites and Aspirations*, chap. 6; Andrade, *Brazilian Cookery*, 240, 277–82; Kochilas, *Glorious Foods of Greece*,

245–46, 288; Kaneva-Johnson, *Melting Pot,* 157, 342, 353; Shaida, *Legendary Cuisine of Persia,* 304; Cwiertka, *Modern Japanese Cuisine,* chaps. 1 and 2; and other sources listed below.

90. *Nuevo cocinero mejicano,* prospecto.

91. Van Esterik, "From Marco Polo to McDonald's," 184–87; Thompson, *Thai Food,* 53–58.

92. Kremezi, "Nikolas Tselementes," 167.

93. Chamberlain, *Food and Cooking of Russia,* 175.

94. S. Williams, *Savory Suppers and Fashionable Feasts,* 113.

95. Mexican cookbooks of the late nineteenth century contain as many recipes for French sauces such as béchamel as they do for the tomato- and chile-based ones associated with the country today. See, e.g., *Nuevo cocinero mexicano,* 751–67.

96. Peters, *Appetites and Aspirations,* 177

97. Thompson, *Thai Food,* 31.

98. D. Burton, *Raj at Table,* 77.

99. Vaduva, "Popular Rumanian Food," 100.

100. Shaida, *Legendary Cuisine of Persia,* 94; Chamberlain, *Food and Cooking of Russia,* 127–28.

101. Kaneva-Johnson, *Melting Pot,* 102, 342.

102. Kochilas, *Glorious Foods of Greece,* 4.

103. Kumakura, "Table Manners Then and Now," 58.

104. Collingham, *Curry,* 171–73.

105. Dye, "Hawaii's First Celebrity Chef."

106. See www.hawaiihistory.org/index.cfm?fuseaction=ig.page&pageid=164 and http://en.wikipedia.org/wiki/Iolani_Palace (both accessed 18 August 2012).

107. http://fr.wikipedia.org/wiki/Fives_%28entreprise%29 (accessed 5 August 2012).

108. Shurtleff and Aoyagi, *Book of Miso,* 520–22.

109. Giedion, *Mechanization,* chap. 9; Storck and Teague, *Flour for Man's Bread,* 290ff.; Tann and Glynn, "Technology and Transformation."

110. Achaya, *Food Industries of British India,* 124–29.

111. Gernet, *History of Chinese Civilization,* 611; Meissner, "Business of Survival"; Arias, *Comida en serie,* 20–23.

112. www.grupoberro.com/2011/02/24/don-vicente (accessed 14 October 2012).

113. Cronon, *Nature's Metropolis,* 211 and chaps. 3 and 5. See also Horowitz, *Putting Meat on the American Table,* 32.

114. W. G. Hoffman, "100 Years of the Margarine Industry."

115. Achaya, *Food Industries of British India,* 196.

116. Thorne, *History of Food Preservation,* 25; May, *Canning Clan;* Mollenhauer and Froese, *Von Omas Küche zur Fertigpackung;* Capatti, "Taste for Canned and Preserved Food."

117. *Bonne cuisine pour tous,* 355.

118. Cwiertka, *Modern Japanese Cuisine,* 120.

119. Jing, *Feeding China's Little Emperors,* 125.

120. Gerth, *China Made,* Introduction and chap. 8.

121. Belasco, *Meals to Come,* 27.

122. Spencer, *Vegetarianism,* chap. 9; Goldstein, "Is Hay Only for Horses?"

123. Jha, *Holy Cow,* 19.

124. Dupaigne, *History of Bread,* 90.

125. Meyer-Renschhausen, "Porridge Debate."

126. Ohnuki-Tierney, *Rice as Self*, 105–7; K. Hess, *Carolina Rice Kitchen*, 7–9.

127. Dix, "Non-Alcoholic Beverages in Nineteenth Century Russia," 22.

128. Gilman, *Women and Economics*, chap. 11.

129. Ohnuki-Tierney, *Rice as Self*, chap. 9; Trentmann, "Civilization and Its Discontents"; Cronon, *Nature's Metropolis*, chap. 1.

130. Gabaccia, *We Are What We Eat*, 55–56; Cowan, *Mother's Work*, 48.

131. Landes, *Wealth and Poverty of Nations*, 378.

132. Meissner, "Business of Survival."

133. Pedrocco, "Food Industry and New Preservation Techniques."

134. McCook, *States of Nature*, 1.

135. Offer, *First World War*, 81.

136. Chamberlain, *Foreign and Colonial Speeches*, 202.

137. Kipling, "Big Steamers," 758.

8. MODERN CUISINES, 1920-2000

1. Kuralt, *On the Road*, 276.

2. For background, see Love, *McDonald's*; J. L. Watson, *Golden Arches East*.

3. Curnonsky and Rouff, *Yellow Guides for Epicures*, 20; on de Castries, Wilkins et al., *Food in Antiquity*, 5; see also http://fr.wikipedia.org/wiki/frite (accessed 5 December 2012).

4. Boym, "My McDonald's."

5. Chehabi, "Westernization of Iranian Culinary Culture," 60.

6. Ritzer, *McDonaldization of Society*.

7. Schlosser, *Fast Food Nation*, 270.

8. Laudan, "Slow Food."

9. Solt, "Ramen and US Occupation Policy."

10. J. L. Watson, *Golden Arches East*, Introduction.

11. Micklethwait and Wooldridge, *Future Perfect*, 127–28.

12. Jim Erickson, "Attack of the Superstore," *Time Asia Magazine* 159, no. 16 (29 April 2002).

13. Trentmann, *Free Trade Nation*, part 2.

14. McKeown, "Global Migration."

15. Scholliers, "Meals, Food Narratives, and Sentiments"; Warde, *Consumption, Food and Taste*; Fischler, "Food, Self and Identity." For modern cuisines in the twentieth century, Belasco, *Food*, offers a balanced and thought-provoking introduction to (largely American) cuisine. Warde, *Consumption, Food and Taste*, is oriented to Europe; Belasco and Scranton, *Food Nations*, and Belasco and Horowitz, *Food Chains*, offer excellent introductions to their topics. Belasco, *Meals to Come*, Fine et al., *Consumption in the Age of Affluence*, and Nütznadel and Trentmann, *Food and Globalization*, cover many themes of post–World War II culinary philosophy and practice. Wilk, *Home Cooking in the Global Village*, chaps. 7 and 8 show how a small nation like Honduras experiences these global forces.

16. The fascist cuisines of Germany, Italy, and Spain were a fourth, though less studied, alternative. Gordon, "Fascism, the Neo-Right, and Gastronomy."

17. Basic overviews of the history of twentieth-century American food include the *Oxford Encyclopedia of Food and Drink in America*; Levenstein, *Paradox of Plenty*; Shapiro,

Perfection Salad and *Something from the Oven;* Schenone, *A Thousand Years Over a Hot Stove,* chaps. 8–10; and Pillsbury, *No Foreign Food,* chaps. 4, 5, 8, 9.

18. For surveys of Russian cuisine, see Mack and Surina, *Food Culture in Russia and Central Asia;* Caldwell, "Taste of Nationalism," "Domesticating the French Fry," *Not by Bread Alone,* and "Tasting the Worlds of Yesterday and Today"; Caldwell et al., *Food and Everyday Life in the Postsocialist World.*

19. For the construction of non-Western modernization, see Aydin, *Politics of Anti-Westernism in Asia.* For shifts in modernization reflected in cafés, Merry White, *Coffee Life in Japan,* 3–4, 161–62. See also Cwiertka, *Modern Japanese Cuisine.*

20. For overviews of modern nutritional theory, see Carpenter, *History of Scurvy;* Carpenter, *Protein and Energy;* Carpenter, *Beriberi, White Rice, and Vitamin B;* McCollum, *Newer Knowledge of Nutrition;* McCollum, *History of Nutrition;* Apple, *Vitamania;* Crotty, *Good Nutrition?* For government involvement, see esp. *Food, Science, Policy and Regulation,* ed. Smith and Phillips, and *Order and Disorder,* ed. Fenton.

21. Gandhi, *Autobiography,* 21.

22. M. Harris, *Good to Eat,* which popularized a theory earlier advanced by Michael Harner.

23. Miranda et al., *El maíz,* 6, 20–25.

24. McCollum, *Newer Knowledge of Nutrition,* 150–51; Valenze, *Milk,* 251.

25. Rothstein and Rothstein, "Beginnings of Soviet Culinary Arts," 185.

26. See the essays in Jing, *Feeding China's Little Emperors.*

27. "First Lady Michelle Obama Launches Let's Move: America's Move to Raise a Healthier Generation of Kids." www.whitehouse.gov/the-press-office/first-lady-michelle-obama-launches-lets-move-americas-move-raise-a-healthier-generation (accessed 10 August 2012).

28. Sack, *Whitebread Protestants,* chaps. 1 and 3.

29. A. O'Connor, "Conversion in Central Quintana Roo."

30. Caldwell, *Not by Bread Alone,* esp. chap. 3.

31. For a schoolgirl's perception of food changes during Partition, see Jaffrey, *Climbing the Mango Trees,* chap. 22. And see Pankaj Mishra, "One Man's Beef . . . ," *The Guardian,* 12 July 2002.

32. Chehabi, "Westernization of Iranian Culinary Culture"; Chehabi, "How Caviar Turned Out to Be Halal."

33. Rothstein and Rothstein, "Beginnings of Soviet Culinary Arts."

34. Goldman, *Women, the State, and Revolution,* 131. The following quotation from Trotsky is translated in Rothstein and Rothstein, "Beginnings of Soviet Culinary Arts," 178.

35. Mack and Surina, *Food Culture in Russia and Central Asia,* 28–31.

36. Goldman, *Women at the Gates,* 294.

37. Lih, *Bread and Authority in Russia,* 243–45; Sorokin, *Hunger,* xxxii.

38. Swislocki, *Culinary Nostalgia,* chap. 5.

39. Aguilar-Rodríguez, "Cooking Modernity," 192–93.

40. Beverly Hills Women's Club, *Fashions in Foods in Beverly Hills,* foreword.

41. Haber, *From Hardtack to Home Fries,* chap. 5.

42. Hess and Hess, *Taste of America,* 157.

43. Curnonsky and Rouff, *Yellow Guides for Epicures,* 13.

44. Ibid., 20.

45. Toomre, *Classic Russian Cooking,* 3–4.

46. Chong, *Heritage of Chinese Cooking,* 19.

47. Chang, *Food in Chinese Culture,* 15.

48. Pujol, "Cosmopolitan Taste."

49. Veit, *Victory over Ourselves,* chap. 3.

50. Thanks to Jim Chevallier for figuring out the origin of the quotation attributed to Socrates. Cullather, "Foreign Policy of the Calorie" and *Hungry World.*

51. Anderson, *Imagined Communities.* For an Andersonian interpretation of the construction of French high cuisine in the nineteenth century, see Ferguson, *Accounting for Taste,* and for Indian cuisine, see Appadurai, "How to Make a National Cuisine."

52. Harp, *Marketing Michelin,* chap. 7; Csergo, "Emergence of Regional Cuisines."

53. Harp, *Marketing Michelin,* 240 and 244.

54. Curnonsky and Rouff, *Yellow Guides for Epicures,* 206.

55. Thanks to Adam Balic for conversations on boeuf bourguinon. Harp, *Marketing Michelin,* 241.

56. Peer, *France on Display,* 2–3, chaps. 1 and 3.

57. Pilcher, *Que Vivan Los Tamales!* chaps. 3 and 6; Laudan and Pilcher, "Chiles, Chocolate, and Race in New Spain."

58. Swislocki, *Culinary Nostalgia,* chap. 4.

59. O'Connor, "King's Christmas Pudding."

60. Ranga Rao, *Good Food from India,* Appadurai, "How to Make a National Cuisine," from which the quotation from the Hindu author comes; Panjabi, "Non-Emergence of the Regional Cuisines of India."

61. Cusack, "African Cuisines," 207; www.dianabuja.wordpress.com/2012/02/21/the-french-in-egypt-and-the-belgians-in-the-congo (accessed 5 December 2012).

62. Cusack, "African Cuisines"; Mack and Surina, *Food Culture in Russia and Central Asia,* 62–63.

63. Greeley, "Finding Pad Thai"; Chehabi, "Westernization of Iranian Culinary Culture," 43, 50.

64. Tang, "Chinese Restaurants Abroad."

65. Goldstein, "Eastern Influence on Russian Cuisine," 24.

66. K. O'Connor, "Hawaiian Luau." On culinary tourism generally, see Long, *Culinary Tourism.*

67. Arsel and Pekin, *Timeless Tastes,* 9–12.

68. Panjabi, "Non-Emergence of the Regional Foods of India," 144–49.

69. Ohnuma, "Curry Rice."

70. Jing, *Feeding China's Little Emperors,* 79.

71. Ibid., Introduction, 6.

72. On fresh foods, mainly in the United States, see Freidberg, *Fresh.* On packaged convenience foods, see Shapiro, *Something from the Oven,* 55–84.

73. Giedion, *Mechanization,* 169–201.

74. Bobrow-Strain, *White Bread,* 4, 123.

75. Ibid., chap. 5, for Japan and Mexico.

76. Kilby, *African Enterprise,* chaps. 2 and 3.

77. See www.bbc.co.uk/news/magazine-13760559 (accessed 12 August 2012).

78. "Rust in the Bread Basket," *Economist*, 1 July 2010.

79. Crumbine, *Most Nearly Perfect Food*; DuPuis, *Nature's Perfect Food*; Mendelson, chap. 2; Valenze, *Milk*, chaps. 8–14.

80. Prout quoted in DuPuis, *Nature's Perfect Food*, 32.

81. *Encyclopædia Britannica*, 11th ed., s.v. "Dairy and Dairying"; McCollum, *History of Nutrition*, 120.

82. Block, "Purity, Economy, and Social Welfare," 22; Atkins, "London's Intra-Urban Milk Supply"; Atkins, "Milk Consumption and Tuberculosis."

83. Bentley, "Inventing Baby Food."

84. Frantz, *Gail Borden*; Heer, *First Hundred Years of Nestlé*; Laudan, "Fresh From the Cow's Nest" and *Food of Paradise*, 61–65, 73–79; Levenstein, *Revolution at the Table*, 10, 12.

85. Hartog, "Acceptance of Milk Products"; Wiley, "Transforming Milk in a Global Economy."

86. Huang, *Fermentations and Food Science*, 322.

87. Crumbine, *Most Nearly Perfect Food*, 8.

88. Trentmann, "Bread, Milk and Democracy"; Block, "Purity, Economy, and Social Welfare."

89. Levenstein, *Paradox of Plenty*, 94.

90. Caldwell et al., *Food and Everyday Life in the Postsocialist World*.

91. "Castro's Revolutionary Cry: Let Them Eat Ice Cream!" http://articles.latimes .com/1991-11-05/news/wr-1156_1_ice-cream (accessed 5 December 2012).

92. Kamath, *Milkman from Anand*, 327–28.

93. DuPuis, *Nature's Perfect Food*; Aguirre, "Culture of Milk in Argentina."

94. On modern meat, see Horowitz, *Putting Meat on the American Table*, and Lee, *Meat, Modernity and the Rise of the Slaughterhouse*.

95. Horowitz, *Putting Meat on the American Table*, 102.

96. Dixon, *Changing Chicken*.

97. Peña, *Empty Pleasures*.

98. Dahl and Dahl, *Memories with Food at Gipsy House*, 150–55.

99. Lee Kum Kee, http://usa.lkk.com/Kitchen (accessed 18 August 2012).

100. Shurtleff and Aoyogi, *Book of Miso*, 484–85.

101. Schlosser, *Fast Food Nation*, 120–29; Katchadourian, "Taste Makers."

102. Pendergrast, *For God, Country, and Coca-Cola*, 99; "Debunking Coke," *Economist*, 12 February 2000, 70.

103. Rothstein and Rothstein, "Beginnings of Soviet Culinary Arts," 186–88; Belasco, "Algae Burgers."

104. Poppy Cannon, *Can-Opener Cookbook*, quoted by Hine, *Total Package*, 19. See also Shapiro, *Something from the Oven*.

105. Sand, "Short History of MSG."

106. Knight, *Food Administration in India*, chap. 17.

107. Connor, *Food Processing*, 4.

108. Pendergrast, *For God, Country, and Coca-Cola*, 208, 311.

109. Jing, *Feeding China's Little Emperors*, 190.

110. Huang, *Fermentations and Food Science*, 502.

111. Trentmann, "Civilization and Its Discontents."

112. Belasco, *Appetite for Change.*

113. Ohnuki-Tierney, *Rice as Self,* 107–8; Cwiertka, *Making of Modern Culinary Tradition in Japan,* 1–4, 35–36.

114. Popkin, "Nutrition Transition."

115. Laudan, "Slow Food."

116. Corby Kummer, "Doing Good by Eating Well," *Atlantic* 283, no. 3 (1999): 102–7.

117. Gopalan, *Nutrition,* 15.

118. www.economist.com/news/business/21571907-horse-meat-food-chain-wake-up-call-not-calamity-after-horse-has-been-bolted (accessed 20 February 2013).

119. Gopalan, *Nutrition,* 15.

120. http://online.wsj.com/article/SB10001424052702304724404577295463062461978.html (access 12 February 2013).

BIBLIOGRAPHY

Abū al-Fazl ibn Mubārak. *The Ā'īn-i Akbarī*. 2nd ed. Calcutta: Asiatic Society of Bengal, 1927.

Abu-Lughod, Janet L. *Before European Hegemony: The World System A.D. 1250–1350*. New York: Oxford University Press, 1989.

Achaya, K. T. *The Food Industries of British India*. New York: Oxford University Press, 1994.

———. *Indian Food: A Historical Companion*. New York: Oxford University Press, 1994.

———. *Oilseeds and Oilmilling in India: A Cultural and Historical Survey*. New Delhi: Oxford and IBH Publishing, 1990.

Adshead, Samuel Adrian M. *Central Asia in World History*. New York: St. Martin's Press, 1993.

———. *China in World History*. New York: St. Martin's Press, 1988.

———. *Salt and Civilization*. New York: St. Martin's Press, 1992.

Aguilar-Rodríguez, S. "Cooking Modernity: Nutrition Policies, Class, and Gender in 1940s and 1950s Mexico City." *The Americas* 64, no. 2 (2007): 177–205.

———. "Nutrition and Modernity Milk Consumption in 1940s and 1950s Mexico." *Radical History Review*, no. 110 (2011): 36–58.

Aguirre, P. "The Culture of Milk in Argentina." *Anthropology of Food* [online], no. 2 (2003). www.aof.revues.org/322 (accessed 4 November 2012).

Ahsan, M. M. *Social Life under the Abbasids, 170–289 AH, 786–902 AD*. London: Longman, 1979.

Aiello, Leslie C., and Jonathan C. K. Wells. "Energetics and the Evolution of the Genus *Homo*." *Annual Review of Anthropology* 31 (2002): 323–38.

Aiello, L. C., and P. Wheeler. "The Expensive-Tissue Hypothesis: The Brain and the Digestive System in Human and Primate Evolution." *Current Anthropology* 36, no. 2 (1995): 199–221.

Aikin, Lucy. *Memoirs of the Court of Queen Elizabeth*. London: Longman, Hurst, Rees, Orme, and Brown, 1818.

Alarcon, C. "Tamales in Mesoamerica: Food for Gods and Mortals." *Petits Propos Culinaires* 63 (1999): 15–34.

Albala, Ken. *The Banquet: Dining in the Great Courts of Late Renaissance Europe*. Urbana: University of Illinois Press, 2007.

———. *Beans: A History*. New York: Berg, 2007.

———. *Cooking in Europe, 1250–1650*. Westport, Conn.: Greenwood Press, 2006.

———. *Eating Right in the Renaissance*. Berkeley: University of California Press, 2002.

———. "The Ideology of Fasting in the Reformation Era." In *Food and Faith in Christian Culture*, edited by Ken Albala and Trudy Eden, 41–57. New York: Columbia University Press, 2011.

Albala, Ken, ed. *Food Cultures of the World Encyclopedia*. Santa Barbara, Calif.: Greenwood Press, 2011.

Albala, Ken, and Trudy Eden, eds. *Food and Faith in Christian Culture*. New York: Columbia University Press, 2011.

Alcock, Susan E. "Power Lunches in the Eastern Roman Empire." *Classical Studies Newsletter* 9 (Summer 2003). www.umich.edu/~classics/news/newsletter/summer2003/power-lunches.html (accessed 14 August 2012).

Alford, Jeffrey, and Naomi Duguid. *Flatbreads and Flavors: A Baker's Atlas*. New York: William Morrow, 2008.

Allison, A. "Japanese Mothers and Obentōs: The Lunch-Box as Ideological State Apparatus." *Anthropological Quarterly* 64, no. 4 (1991): 195–208.

Allsen, Thomas T. *Culture and Conquest in Mongol Eurasia*. New York: Cambridge University Press, 2001.

Ambrosioli, Mauro. *The Wild and the Sown: Agriculture and Botany in Western Europe, 1350–1850*. Cambridge: Cambridge University Press, 1977.

Amouretti, Marie-Claire. *Le pain et l'huile dans la Grèce antique: De l'araire au moulin*. Paris: Les Belles Lettres, 1986.

Anderson, Benedict R. O'G. *Imagined Communities: Reflections on the Origin and Spread of Nationalism*. London: Verso, 1983.

Anderson, Burton. *Pleasures of the Italian Table*. London: Viking Press, 1994.

Anderson, Eugene N. *Everyone Eats: Understanding Food and Culture*. New York: New York University Press, 2005.

———. *The Food of China*. New Haven, Conn.: Yale University Press, 1988.

Andrade, Margarette de. *Brazilian Cookery*. Rutland, Vt.: Charles E. Tuttle, 1965.

"An Anonymous Andalusian Cookbook of the 13th Century." Translated by Charles Perry. In *A Collection of Medieval and Renaissance Cookbooks*. 6th ed. N.p.: n.p. [David Friedman, 1993].

Anthimus. *De observatione ciborum = On the observance of foods*. Translated by Mark Grant. Blackawton, Totnes, Devon, UK: Prospect Books, 1996.

Apicius: A Critical Edition with an Introduction and English Translation. Translated and edited by Christopher Grocock and Sally Grainger. Totnes, Devon, UK: Prospect Books, 2006.

———. *The Roman Cookery Book*. Translated by Barbara Flower and Elizabeth Rosenbaum. London: Harrap, 1958.

Appadurai, A. "How to Make a National Cuisine: Cookbooks in Contemporary India." *Comparative Studies in Society and History* 30, no. 1 (1988): 3–24.

Appadurai, Carol. "Food, Politics and Pilgrimage in South India, 1350–1650 A.D." In *Food, Society and Culture: Aspects in South Asian Food Systems,* edited by R.S.Khare and M.S.A. Rao, 21–53. Durham, N.C.: Carolina Academic Press.

Appert, Nicolas. *L'art de conserver, pendant plusieurs années, toutes les substances animales et végétales.* Paris: Patris, 1810. Also known as *Le livre de tous les ménages.*

Apple, Rima D. *Vitamania: Vitamins in American Culture.* New Brunswick, N.J.: Rutgers University Press, 1996.

Apte, Mahadev L., and Judit Katona-Apte. "Religious Significance of Food Preservation in India: Milk Products in Hinduism." In *Food Conservation: Ethnological Studies,* edited by Astri Riddervold and Andreas Ropeid, 89. London: Prospect Books, 1988.

Arbuthnot, John. *An Essay Concerning the Nature of Aliments.* London: Tonson, 1732.

Arias, Patricia. *Comida en serie.* Vol. 9 of *La cocina mexicana a través de los siglos,* edited by Enrique Krauze and Fernán González de la Vara. México, D.F.: Clío; Fundación Herdez, 1997.

Arnold, David. *Colonizing the Body: State Medicine and Epidemic Disease in Nineteenth-Century India.* Berkeley: University of California Press, 1993.

Arsel, Semahat, Ersu Pekin, and Ayşe Sümer, eds. *Timeless Tastes: Turkish Culinary Culture.* 2nd ed. Istanbul: Vehbi Koç Vakfı: DiVan, 1996.

Artusi, Pellegrino. *The Art of Eating Well.* Translated by Kyle M. Phillips III. New York: Random House, 1996.

Ashtor, Eliyzhu. "Essai sur l'alimentation des diverses classes sociales dans l'Orient médiéval." *Annales: Économies, Sociétés, Civilisations* 23, no. 5 (1968): 1017–53.

Assmann, Stephanie, and Eric C. Rath, eds. *Japanese Foodways, Past and Present.* Urbana: University of Illinois Press, 2010.

Atkins, P. J. "Fattening Children or Fattening Farmers? School Milk in Britain, 1921–1941." *Economic History Review* 58, no. 1 (2005): 57–78.

———. "The Glasgow Case: Meat, Disease and Regulation, 1889–1924." *Agricultural History Review* (2004): 161–82.

———. "The Growth of London's Railway Milk Trade, c. 1845–1914." *Journal of Transport History* 4 (1978): 208–26.

———. "London's Intra-Urban Milk Supply, circa 1790–1914." *Transactions of the Institute of British Geographers,* n.s., 2, no. 3 (1977): 383–99.

———. "Milk Consumption and Tuberculosis in Britain, 1850–1950." In *Order and Disorder: The Health Implications of Eating and Drinking in the Nineteenth and Twentieth Centuries; Proceedings of the Fifth Symposium of the International Commission for Research into European Food History, Aberdeen 1997,* edited by Alexander Fenton. East Linton, UK: Tuckwell, 2000.

———. "The Retail Milk Trade in London, c. 1790–1914." *Economic History Review* 33, no. 4 (1980): 522–37.

———. "Sophistication Detected; or, The Adulteration of the Milk Supply, 1850–1914." *Social History* 16, no. 3 (1991): 317–39.

———. "White Poison? The Social Consequences of Milk Consumption, 1850–1930." *Social History of Medicine* 5, no. 2 (1992): 207–27.

Atkins, P. J., Peter Lummel, and Derek J. Oddy, eds. *Food and the City in Europe Since 1800*. Burlington, Vt.: Ashgate, 2007.

Aydin, Cemil. *The Politics of Anti-Westernism in Asia: Visions of World Order in Pan-Islamic and Pan-Asian Thought*. New York: Columbia University Press, 2007.

Aykroyd, Wallace Ruddell, and Joyce Doughty. *Wheat in Human Nutrition*. Rome: Food and Agriculture Organization of the United Nations, 1970.

Babur, emperor of Hindustan [Zahiru'd-dīn Muhammad Bābur Pādshāh Ghāzī]. *The Bābur-nāma in English (Memoirs of Babur)*. Translated by Annette Susannah Beveridge. London: Luzac, 1921.

A Baghdad Cookery Book: The Book of Dishes (Kitāb al-Ṭabīkh). Translated by Charles Perry. Totnes, Devon, UK: Prospect Books, 2006.

Bailyn, Bernard. *The Peopling of British North America: An Introduction*. New York: Vintage Books, 1988.

Bak-Geller Corona, Sarah. "Los recetarios 'afrancesados' del siglo XIX en México." *Anthropology of Food* [online], S6 (December 2009). http://aof.revues.org/6464 (accessed 16 October 2012).

Balabanlilar, L. "Lords of the Auspicious Conjunction: Turco-Mongol Imperial Identity on the Subcontinent." *Journal of World History* 18, no. 1 (2007): 1–39.

Barfield, Thomas J. *The Nomadic Alternative*. Englewood Cliffs, N.J.: Prentice Hall, 1993.

Barthes, Roland. *Mythologies* (1957). Translated by Annette Lavers. New York: Hill and Wang, 1972.

Bartlett, Robert. *The Making of Europe: Conquest, Colonization, and Cultural Change, 950–1350*. Princeton, N.J.: Princeton University Press, 1993.

Basan, Ghillie, and Jonathan Basan. *Classic Turkish Cooking*. New York: St. Martin's Press, 1997.

Basu, Shrabani. *Curry: The Story of the Nation's Favourite Dish*. Stroud, UK: Rupa & Co., 2011.

Bauer, Arnold J. "Millers and Grinders: Technology and Household Economy in Meso-America." *Agricultural History* 64, no. 1 (1990): 1–17.

Bayly, C. A. *The Birth of the Modern World, 1780–1914*. Malden, Mass.: Blackwell, 2004.

Beecher, Catharine Esther, and Harriet Beecher Stowe. *The American Woman's Home*. New York: Ford, 1869.

Beeton, Isabella. *Mrs Beeton's Book of Household Management*. 1861. Facsimile edition. London: Jonathan Cape, 1977.

Beg, M. A. J. "A Study of the Cost of Living and Economic Status of Artisans in Abbasid Iraq." *Islamic Quarterly* 16 (1972): 164.

Belasco, Warren James. "Algae Burgers for a Hungry World? The Rise and Fall of Chlorella Cuisine." *Technology and Culture* 38, no. 3 (1997): 608–34.

———. *Appetite for Change: How the Counterculture Took on the Food Industry, 1966–1988*. New York: Pantheon Books, 1989.

———. "Ethnic Fast Foods: The Corporate Melting Pot." *Food and Foodways* 2, no. 1 (1987): 1–30.

———. "Food and the Counterculture: A Story of Bread and Politics." In *The Cultural Politics of Food and Eating*, edited by James L. Watson and Melissa L. Caldwell, 217–34. Malden, Mass.: Blackwell, 2005.

———. *Food: The Key Concepts*. New York: Berg, 2008.

———. "'Lite' Economics: Less Food, More Profit." *Radical History Review*, nos. 28–30 (1984): 254–78.

———. *Meals to Come: A History of the Future of Food*. Berkeley: University of California Press, 2006.

———. "Toward a Culinary Common Denominator: The Rise of Howard Johnson's, 1925–1940." *Journal of American Culture* 2, no. 3 (1979): 503–18.

Belasco, Warren James, and Roger Horowitz, eds. *Food Chains: From Farmyard to Shopping Cart*. Philadelphia: University of Pennsylvania Press, 2009.

Belasco, Warren James, and Philip Scranton, eds. *Food Nations: Selling Taste in Consumer Societies*. New York: Routledge, 2002.

Belich, James. *Replenishing the Earth: The Settler Revolution and the Rise of the Angloworld, 1783–1939*. New York: Oxford University Press, 2009.

Bellwood, P. "The Austronesian Dispersal and the Origin of Languages." *Scientific American* 265, no. 1 (1991): 88–93.

Benedict, Saint, abbot of Monte Cassino. *The Rule of St. Benedict*. Edited and translated by Anthony C. Meisel and M. L. del Mastro. Garden City, N.Y.: Image Books, 1975.

Bentley, Amy. *Eating for Victory: Food Rationing and the Politics of Domesticity*. Urbana: University of Illinois Press, 1998.

———. "Inventing Baby Food: Gerber and the Discourse of Infancy in the United States." In *Food Nations: Selling Taste in Consumer Societies*, edited by W. J. Belasco and Philip Scranton. London: Routledge, 2002.

Bentley, Jerry H. *Old World Encounters: Cross-Cultural Contacts and Exchanges in Pre-Modern Times*. Oxford: Oxford University Press, 1993.

Bentley, Jerry H., and Herbert F. Ziegler. *Traditions and Encounters: A Global Perspective on the Past*. Boston: McGraw-Hill, 2000.

Bérard, L. "La consommation du poisson en France: Des prescriptions alimentaires à la prépondérance de la carpe." In *L'animal dans l'alimentation humaine: Les critères de choix; Actes du colloque international de Liège, 26–29 novembre 1986*, edited by Liliane Bodson, special no. of *Anthropozoologica* (Paris, 1988): 171–73.

Beverly Hills Women's Club. *Fashions in Foods in Beverly Hills*. Beverly Hills, Calif.: Beverly Hills Citizen, 1931.

Bickham, T. "Eating the Empire: Intersections of Food, Cookery and Imperialism in Eighteenth-Century Britain." *Past & Present* 198, no. 1 (2008): 71–109.

Bīrūnī, Muḥammad ibn Aḥmad. *Alberuni's India*. London: K. Paul, Trench, Trübner, 1914.

Block, D. "Purity, Economy, and Social Welfare in the Progressive Era Pure Milk Movement." *Journal for the Study of Food and Society* 3, no. 1 (1999): 20–27.

Blofeld, John Eaton Calthorpe. *The Chinese Art of Tea*. Boston: Allen & Unwin, 1985.

Boardman, J. "Symposion Furniture." In *Sympotica: A Symposium on the Symposion*, edited by Oswyn Murray, 122–31. Oxford: Oxford University Press, 1990.

Bobrow-Strain, Aaron. *White Bread: A Social History of the Store-Bought Loaf*. Boston: Beacon Press, 2012.

Boileau, Janet. "A Culinary History of the Portuguese Eurasians: The Origins of Luso-Asian Cuisine in the Sixteenth and Seventeenth Centuries." PhD diss., University of Adelaide, 2010.

Bolens, Lucie. *La cuisine andalouse, un art de vivre—XIe–XIIIe siècle*. Paris: Albin Michel, 1990.

La bonne cuisine pour tous d'après les préceptes de la grand-mère Catherine Giron et les formules modernes des meilleurs cuisiniers . . . recueillies par Gombervaux; publiées par "Le Petit journal." 1909. Facsimile reprint, Paris: Presses de la Renaissance, 1979.

Bonnet, Jean-Claude. "The Culinary System in the *Encyclopédie*." Translated by Elborg Forster in *Food and Drink in History: Selections from the "Annales,"* edited by Robert Forster and Orest Ranum, 139–65. Baltimore: Johns Hopkins University Press, 1979.

Borgstrom, Georg, ed. *Fish as Food*, vol. 1: *Production, Biochemistry, and Microbiology*. New York: Academic Press, 1961.

Borrero, H. "Communal Dining and State Cafeterias in Moscow and Petrograd, 1917–1921." In *Food in Russian History and Culture*, edited by Musya Glantz and Joyce Toomre, 162–76. Bloomington: Indiana University Press, 1997.

Bottéro, Jean. *The Oldest Cuisine in the World: Cooking in Mesopotamia*. Chicago: University of Chicago Press, 2004.

Boxer, C. R. *The Dutch Seaborne Empire: 1600–1800*. London: Penguin Books, 1973.

Boym, C. "My McDonald's." *Gastronomica: The Journal of Food and Culture* 1, no. 1 (2001): 6–8.

Bradley, Richard. "The Megalith Builders of Western Europe." In *People of the Stone Age: Hunter-Gatherers and Early Farmers*, edited by Göran Burenhult. St. Lucia, Queensland: University of Queensland Press, 1993.

Braidwood, R. J., J. D. Sauer, H. Helbaek, P. C. Mangelsdorf, H. C. Cutler, C. S. Coon, R. Linton, J. Steward, and A. L. Oppenheim. "Symposium: Did Man Once Live by Beer Alone?" *American Anthropologist* 55, no. 4 (1953): 515–26.

Braudel, Fernand. *The Mediterranean and the Mediterranean World in the Age of Philip II*. New York: Harper & Row, 1972–73.

Braun, T. "Barley Cakes and Emmer Bread." In *Food in Antiquity*, edited by John Wilkins, David Harvey, and Mike Dobson, 25–37. Exeter, UK: University of Exeter Press, 1995.

Bray, Francesca. *Agriculture*. Part 2 of vol. 6 of *Science and Civilization in China*, edited by Joseph Needham, *Biology and Biological Technology*. Cambridge: Cambridge University Press, 1984.

Breckenridge, Carol Appadurai. "Food, Politics and Pilgrimage in South India, 1350–1650 AD." In *Food, Society and Culture*, edited by R. S. Khare and M. S. A. Rao, 21–53. Durham, NC: Carolina Academic Press.

Briant, Pierre. *From Cyrus to Alexander: A History of the Persian Empire*. Winona Lake, Ind.: Eisenbraun, 2002.

Brodman, James William. *Charity and Welfare: Hospitals and the Poor in Medieval Catalonia*. Philadelphia: University of Pennsylvania Press, 1998.

Brown, Catherine. *Broths to Bannocks: Cooking in Scotland, 1690 to the Present Day*. London: John Murray, 1991.

Brown, Peter. *The Body and Society: Men, Women, and Sexual Renunciation in Early Christianity*. New York: Columbia University Press, 1988.

———. *The World of Late Antiquity, AD 150–750*. New York: Harcourt Brace Jovanovich, 1971.

Brownell, S., J. L. Watson, M. L. Caldwell, et al. "Food, Hunger, and the State." In *Cultural Politics of Food and Eating* edited by James L. Watson and Melissa Caldwell, 251–58. Oxford: Blackwell, 2005.

Brubaker, Leslie, and Kallirroe Linardou, eds. *Eat, Drink, and Be Merry (Luke 12:19): Food and Wine in Byzantium; Papers of the 37th Annual Spring Symposium of Byzantine Studies, in Honour of Professor A. A. M. Bryer.* Burlington, Vt.: Ashgate, 2007.

Buell, P. D. "Mongol Empire and Turkicization: The Evidence of Food and Foodways." In *The Mongol Empire and Its Legacy,* edited by Reuven Amitai-Preiss and David O. Morgan, 200–223. Leiden: Brill, 1999.

Buell, Paul D., and Eugene N. Anderson. *A Soup for the Qan: Chinese Dietary Medicine of the Mongol Era as Seen in Hu Sihui's Yinshan Zhengyao.* New York: Kegan Paul International, 2000.

Buffon, Georges-Louis Leclerc, comte de. *Histoire naturelle des poissons.* Paris: Firmin Didot, 1799–1804.

Burkhart, Louise M. *The Slippery Earth: Nahua-Christian Moral Dialogue in Sixteenth-Century Mexico.* Tucson: University of Arizona Press, 1989.

Burnett, John. *Plenty and Want: A Social History of Diet in England from 1815 to the Present Day.* London: Nelson, 1966.

Burton, Antoinette M. *At the Heart of the Empire: Indians and the Colonial Encounter in Late-Victorian Britain.* Berkeley: University of California Press, 1998.

Burton, David. *French Colonial Cookery.* London: Faber & Faber, 2000.

———. *The Raj at Table: A Culinary History of the British in India.* London: Faber & Faber, 1993.

———. *Two Hundred Years of New Zealand Food and Cookery.* [Wellington]: Reed, 1982.

Caldwell, M. L. "Domesticating the French Fry: McDonald's and Consumerism in Moscow." *Journal of Consumer Culture* 4, no. 1 (2004): 5–26.

———. "A New Role for Religion in Russia's New Consumer Age: The Case of Moscow 1." *Religion, State and Society* 33, no. 1 (2005): 19–34.

———. *Not by Bread Alone: Social Support in the New Russia.* Berkeley: University of California Press, 2004.

———. "The Taste of Nationalism: Food Politics in Postsocialist Moscow." *Ethnos* 67, no. 3 (2002): 295–319.

———. "Tasting the Worlds of Yesterday and Today: Culinary Tourism and Nostalgia Foods in Post-Soviet Russia." In *Fast Food/Slow Food: The Cultural Economy of the Global Food System,* edited by Robert Wilk, 97–112. Plymouth, UK: Altamira, 2006.

Caldwell, Melissa L., Elizabeth C. Dunn, and Marion Nestle, eds. *Food and Everyday Life in the Postsocialist World.* Bloomington: Indiana University Press, 2009.

Campbell, B. M. S., J. A. Galloway, D. Keene, and M. Murphy. *A Medieval Capital and Its Grain Supply: Agrarian Production and Distribution in the London Region c. 1300.* London: Institute of British Geographers, 1993.

Camporesi, Piero. *Bread of Dreams: Food and Fantasy in Early Modern Europe.* Translated by David Gentilcore. Chicago: University of Chicago Press, 1996.

———. *The Magic Harvest: Food, Folklore, and Society.* Cambridge, UK: Polity Press, 1993.

Capatti, A. "The Taste for Canned and Preserved Food." In *Food: A Culinary History from Antiquity to the Present,* edited by J. L. Flandrin and Massimo Montanari, translated by Albert Sonnenfeld. New York: Columbia University Press, 1999.

Carney, Judith A. *Black Rice: The African Origins of Rice Cultivation in the Americas.* Cambridge, Mass.: Harvard University Press, 2002.

Carney, Judith A., and Richard Nicholas Rosomoff. *In the Shadow of Slavery: Africa's Botanical Legacy in the Atlantic World.* Berkeley: University of California Press, 2009.

Carpenter, Kenneth J. *Beriberi, White Rice, and Vitamin B: A Disease, a Cause, and a Cure.* Berkeley: University of California Press, 2000.

———. *The History of Scurvy and Vitamin C.* New York: Cambridge University Press, 1986.

———. *Protein and Energy: A Study of Changing Ideas in Nutrition.* New York: Cambridge University Press, 1994.

Carson, Barbara G. *Ambitious Appetites: Dining, Behavior, and Patterns of Consumption in Federal Washington.* Washington, D.C: American Institute of Architects Press, 1990.

Castile, Rand. *The Way of Tea.* New York: Weatherhill, 1971.

Cato, Marcus Porcius. *Cato on Farming: De agricultura; A Critical English Translation.* Translated by Andrew Dalby. Totnes, Devon, UK: Prospect Books, 1998.

Celsus, Aulus Cornelius. *Of Medicine: In Eight Books.* Cambridge, Mass.: Harvard University Press, 1971.

Chakrabarty, Dipesh. "The Difference-Deferral of a Colonial Modernity: Public Debates on Domesticity in British Bengal." In *Tensions of Empire: Colonial Cultures in a Bourgeois World,* edited by Frederick Cooper and Ann Laura Stoler, 373–405. Berkeley: University of California Press, 1997.

Chakravarty, Indira. *Saga of Indian Food: A Historical and Cultural Survey.* New Delhi: Sterling, 1972.

Chamberlain, Joseph. *Foreign and Colonial Speeches.* London: Routledge, 1897.

Chamberlain, Lesley. *The Food and Cooking of Russia.* London: Allen Lane, 1982.

———. "Rousseau's Philosophy of Food." *Petits Propos Culinaires* 21 (1985): 9–16.

Chandler, Alfred Dupont. *The Visible Hand: The Managerial Revolution in American Business.* Cambridge, Mass.: Belknap Press of Harvard University Press, 1977.

Chang, Kwang-chih, ed. *Food in Chinese Culture: Anthropological and Historical Perspectives.* New Haven, Conn.: Yale University Press, 1977.

Charanis, Peter. *Social, Economic and Political Life in the Byzantine Empire.* New ed. London: Variorum Reprints, 1973.

Chastanet, M., F.-X. Fauvelle-Aymar, and D. Juhé-Beaulaton. *Cuisine et société en Afrique: Histoire, saveurs, savoir-faire.* Paris: Karthala, 2002.

Chaudhuri, K. N. *Asia Before Europe: Economy and Civilisation of the Indian Ocean from the Rise of Islam to 1750.* New York: Cambridge University Press, 1990.

Chávez, C. P. M. "Cabildo, negociación y vino de cocos: El caso de la villa de Colima en el siglo XVII" [Government, Negotiation, and Coconut Liquor: The Town Council of Colima During the Seventeenth Century]. *Anuario de Estudios Americanos* 66, no. 1 (2009): 173–92.

Chehabi, H. E. "How Caviar Turned Out to Be Halal." *Gastronomica* 7, no. 2 (2007): 17–23.

———. "The Westernization of Iranian Culinary Culture." *Iranian Studies* 36, no. 1 (2003): 43–61.

Chen, Helen. "Hangzhou: A Culinary Memoir." *Flavor and Fortune* 3, no. 1 (1996): 11, 13, 21.

Ch'en, Kenneth Kuan Sheng. *Buddhism in China.* Princeton, N.J.: Princeton University Press, 1972.

Cheyne, George. *An Essay of Health and Long Life*. Bath, UK: Strahan, 1724. Gale ECCO, Print Editions, 2010.

Chon, Deson. "Korean Cuisine and Food Culture." *Food Culture: Kikkoman Institute* 4 (2002): 1–6.

Chong, Elizabeth. *The Heritage of Chinese Cooking*. New York: Random House, 1993.

Christensen, Arthur. *L'Iran sous les Sassanides*. Copenhagen: Munksgaard, 1936.

Chuen, William Chan Tat. *À la table de l'empereur de Chine*. Arles: P. Picquier, 2007.

Cicero, Marcus Tullius. *Cicero's Brutus; or, History of Famous Orators*. Edited by Edward Jones. London: B. White, 1776.

———. *Tusculan Disputations: On the Nature of the Gods, and on the Commonwealth*. New York: Cosimo, 2005.

Cipolla, Carlo M. *Before the Industrial Revolution: European Society and Economy, 1000–1700*. New York: Norton, 1976.

Civitello, Linda. *Cuisine and Culture: A History of Food and People*. Hoboken, N.J.: Wiley, 2004.

Clark, Colin, and Margaret Rosary Haswell. *The Economics of Subsistence Agriculture*. New York: Macmillan, 1970.

Clendinnen, Inga. *Aztecs: An Interpretation*. New York: Cambridge University Press, 1991.

Clot, André. *Harun Al-Rashid and the World of the Thousand and One Nights*. London: Saqi, 1989.

Clutton-Brock, Juliet. *Domesticated Animals from Early Times*. London: British Museum; Austin: University of Texas Press, 1981.

Coe, Sophie D. *America's First Cuisines*. Austin: University of Texas Press, 1994.

Coe, Sophie D., and Michael D. Coe. *The True History of Chocolate*. New York: Thames & Hudson, 1996.

Coetzee, Renata. *The South African Culinary Tradition: The Origin of South Africa's Culinary Arts during the 17th and 18th Centuries, and 167 Authentic Recipes of This Period*. Cape Town: C. Struik, 1977.

Colgrove, James. "The McKeown Thesis: A Historical Controversy and Its Enduring Influence." *American Journal of Public Health* 92, no. 5 (2002): 725–29.

Colley, Linda. *Britons: Forging the Nation, 1707–1837*. New Haven, Conn.: Yale University Press, 1992.

Collingham, Lizzie. *Curry: A Tale of Cooks and Conquerors*. New York: Oxford University Press, 2006.

Colquhoun, Kate. *Taste: The Story of Britain Through Its Cooking*. London: Bloomsbury, 2007.

Colquhoun, Patrick. *A Treatise on Indigence*. London: Hatchard, 1806.

Concepción, José Luis. *Typical Canary Cooking: The Best Traditional Dishes, Sweets and Liquors*. La Laguna, Tenerife: José Luis Concepción, 1991.

Confucius. *The Analects (Lun yü)*. Translated by D. C. Lau. Hong Kong: Chinese University Press, 1983.

Connor, John M. *Food Processing: An Industrial Powerhouse in Transition*. Lexington, Mass.: Lexington Books, 1988.

Cook, J. M. *The Persian Empire*. New York: Schocken Books, 1983.

Cool, H. E. M. *Eating and Drinking in Roman Britain.* Cambridge: Cambridge University Press, 2006.

Cooper, John. *Eat and Be Satisfied: A Social History of Jewish Food.* Northvale, N.J.: Jason Aronson, 1993.

Corcuera de Mancera, Sonia. *Del amor al temor: Borrachez, catequesis y control en la Nueva España (1555–1771).* México, D.F.: Fondo de Cultura Económica, 1994.

Couto, Cristiana. *Arte de cozinha.* São Paulo: Senac, 2007.

Cowan, Brian William. *The Social Life of Coffee: The Emergence of the British Coffeehouse.* New Haven, Conn.: Yale University Press, 2005.

Cowan, Ruth Schwartz. *More Work for Mother: The Ironies of Household Technology from the Open Hearth to the Microwave.* New York: Basic Books, 1983.

Crane, Eva. *The Archaeology of Beekeeping.* Ithaca, N.Y.: Cornell University Press, 1984.

Crèvecoeur, J. Hector St. John de. *Letters from an American Farmer.* Applewood, 2007.

Critser, Greg. *Fat Land: How Americans Became the Fattest People in the World.* Boston: Houghton Mifflin, 2003.

Crone, Patricia. *Pre-Industrial Societies.* New York: Blackwell, 1989.

Cronon, William. *Changes in the Land: Indians, Colonists, and the Ecology of New England.* Rev. ed. New York: Hill & Wang, 1983.

———. *Nature's Metropolis: Chicago and the Great West.* New York: Norton, 1991.

Crosby, Alfred W. *The Columbian Exchange: Biological and Cultural Consequences of 1492.* Westport, Conn.: Greenwood, 1972.

Cross, Samuel H., and Olgerd P. Sherbitz-Wetzor. *The Russian Primary Chronicle.* Cambridge, Mass.: Medieval Academy of America, 2012.

Crotty, Patricia A. *Good Nutrition? Fact and Fashion in Dietary Advice.* St. Leonards, N.S.W.: Allen & Unwin, 1995.

Crumbine, Samuel J. *The Most Nearly Perfect Food: The Story of Milk.* Baltimore: Williams & Wilkins, 1929.

Csergo, Julia. "The Emergence of Regional Cuisines." In *Food: A Culinary History from Antiquity to the Present,* edited by J. L. Flandrin and Massimo Montanari, translated by Albert Sonnenfeld, 500–515. New York: Columbia University Press, 1999.

Cullather, N. "The Foreign Policy of the Calorie." *American Historical Review* 112, no. 2 (2007): 337–64.

———. *The Hungry World: America's Cold War Battle Against Poverty in Asia.* Cambridge, Mass.: Harvard University Press, 2010.

Cunliffe, Barry W. *Europe Between the Oceans: Themes and Variations, 9000 BC–AD 1000.* New Haven, Conn.: Yale University Press, 2008.

Curiel Monteagudo, José Luis. *Virreyes y virreinas golosos de la nueva españa.* México, D.F.: Porrúa, 2004.

Curnonsky [pseud. Maurice Edmond Sailland], and Marcel Rouff. *The Yellow Guides for Epicures.* New York: Harper, 1926.

Curtin, Philip D. *Cross-Cultural Trade in World History.* New York: Cambridge University Press, 1984.

———. *Death by Migration: Europe's Encounter with the Tropical World in the Nineteenth Century.* New York: Cambridge University Press, 1989.

———. *The Rise and Fall of the Plantation Complex: Essays in Atlantic History.* New York: Cambridge University Press, 1990.

Curtis, Robert I. *Garum and Salsamenta: Production and Commerce in Materia Medica.* Leiden: Brill, 1991.

Cusack, I. "African Cuisines: Recipes for Nationbuilding?" *Journal of African Cultural Studies* 13, no. 2 (2000): 207–25.

Cutting, C. L. "Historical Aspects of Fish." In *Fish as Food,* edited by Georg Borgstrom, 2: 1–15. New York: Academic Press, 1962.

Cwiertka, Katarzyna Joanna. *The Making of Modern Culinary Tradition in Japan.* Leiden: n.p., 1998.

———. *Modern Japanese Cuisine: Food, Power and National Identity.* London: Reaktion Books, 2006.

Dahl, Felicity, and Roald Dahl. *Memories with Food at Gipsy House.* London: Viking Press, 1991.

Dalby, Andrew. "Alexander's Culinary Legacy." In *Cooks and Other People: Proceedings of the Oxford Symposium on Food and Cookery,* edited by Harlan Walker, 81–93. Totnes, Devon, UK: Prospect Books, 1996.

———. *Flavours of Byzantium.* Totnes, Devon, UK: Prospect Books, 2003.

———. *Siren Feasts: A History of Food and Gastronomy in Greece.* New York: Routledge, 1996.

Dalby, Andrew, and Sally Grainger. *The Classical Cookbook.* Los Angeles: J. Paul Getty Museum, 2002.

Daniels, Christian, and Nicholas K. Menzies. *Agro-Industries and Forestry.* Part 3 of vol. 6 of *Science and Civilization in China,* edited by Joseph Needham, *Biology and Biological Technology.* Cambridge: Cambridge University Press, 1996.

Daniels, J., and C. Daniels. "The Origin of the Sugarcane Roller Mill." *Technology and culture* 29, no. 3 (1988): 493–535.

Darby, William J., Paul Ghalioungui, and Louis Grivetti. *Food: The Gift of Osiris.* New York: Academic Press, 1977.

Davidson, Alan. *Mediterranean Seafood.* Totnes, Devon, UK: Prospect Books, 2002.

———. "Sherbets." In *Liquid Nourishment,* edited by C. Anne Wilson. Edinburgh: Edinburgh University Press, 1993.

Davidson, Alan, and Tom Jaine, eds. *The Oxford Companion to Food.* Oxford University Press, 2006.

Davidson, Alan, and Eulalia Pensado. "The Earliest Portuguese Cookbook Examined." *Petits Propos Culinaires* 41 (1992): 52–57.

Davidson, Caroline. *A Woman's Work Is Never Done: A History of Housework in the British Isles, 1650–1950.* London: Chatto & Windus, 1982.

Davidson, James N. *Courtesans and Fishcakes: The Consuming Passions of Classical Athens.* New York: St. Martin's Press, 1998.

Davis, Audrey B. *Circulation Physiology and Medical Chemistry in England.* Lawrence: University of Kansas Press, 1973.

Davis, Mike. *Late Victorian Holocausts: El Niño Famines and the Making of the Third World.* New York: Verso, 2001.

Day, Ivan. "Historic Food." www.historicfood.com/portal.htm (accessed 14 August 2012).

Debus, Allen George. *The French Paracelsians: The Chemical Challenge to Medical and Scientific Tradition in Early Modern France.* Cambridge: Cambridge University Press, 2002.

Deerr, Noël. *The History of Sugar.* London: Chapman & Hall, 1949.

Dege, Hroar. "Norwegian Gastronomic Literature: Part II, 1814–1835." *Petits Propos Culinaires* 21 (1985): 23–32.

Delaney, Carol Lowery. *The Seed and the Soil: Gender and Cosmology in Turkish Village Society.* Berkeley: University of California Press, 1991.

Dembińska, Maria. "Fasting and Working Monks: Regulations of the Fifth to Eleventh Centuries." In *Food in Change: Eating Habits from the Middle Ages to the Present Day,* edited by Alexander Fenton and Eszter Kisbán, 152–60. Edinburgh: John Donald, 1986.

———. *Food and Drink in Medieval Poland: Rediscovering a Cuisine of the Past.* Edited by William Woys Weaver. Philadelphia: University of Pennsylvania Press, 1999.

Déry, C. A. "Milk and Dairy Products in the Roman Period." In *Milk: Beyond the Dairy; Proceedings of the Oxford Symposium on Food and Cookery, 1999,* edited by Harlan Walker, 117. Totnes, Devon, UK: Prospect Books, 2000.

Detienne, Marcel. *The Gardens of Adonis: Spices in Greek Mythology.* Atlantic Highlands, N.J.: Humanities Press, 1977.

Detienne, Marcel, and Jean Pierre Vernant. *The Cuisine of Sacrifice among the Greeks.* Chicago: University of Chicago Press, 1989.

De Vooght, Daniëlle. *Royal Taste: Food, Power and Status at the European Courts After 1789.* Burlington, Vt.: Ashgate, 2011.

Diamond, Jared. *Guns, Germs, and Steel: The Fates of Human Societies.* New York: Norton, 2005.

———. "The Worst Mistake in the History of the Human Race." http://discovermagazine.com/1987/may/02-the-worst-mistake-in-the-history-of-the-human-race (accessed 14 August 2012).

Diehl, Richard A. *The Olmecs: America's First Civilization.* London: Thames & Hudson, 2006.

Diner, Hasia R. *Hungering for America: Italian, Irish, and Jewish Foodways in the Age of Migration.* Cambridge, Mass.: Harvard University Press, 2001.

Dix, Graham. "Non-Alcoholic Beverages in Nineteenth Century Russia." *Petits Propos Culinaires* 10 (1982): 21–28.

Dixon, Jane. *Changing Chicken: Chooks, Cooks and Culinary Culture.* Sydney: University of New South Wales Press, 2002.

Dolan, Brian. *Wedgwood: The First Tycoon.* New York: Viking Press, 2004.

Domingo, Xavier. "La cocina precolumbina en España." In *Conquista y comida: Consecuencias del encuentro de dos mundos,* edited by Janet Long, 17–30. 1st ed. México, D.F.: Universidad Nacional Autónoma de México, 1996.

Dorje, Rinjing. *Food in Tibetan Life.* London: Prospect Books, 1985.

Douglas, Mary. *Purity and Danger: An Analysis of Concepts of Pollution and Taboo.* New York: Praeger, 1966.

Doyle, Michael W. *Empires.* Ithaca, N.Y.: Cornell University Press, 1986.

Drayton, Richard Harry. *Nature's Government: Science, Imperial Britain, and the "Improvement" of the World.* New Haven, Conn.: Yale University Press, 2000.

Drewnowski, A. "Fat and Sugar in the Global Diet: Dietary Diversity in the Nutrition Transition." In *Food in Global History,* edited by Raymond Grew. Boulder, Colo.: Westview Press, 1999.

Dreyer, Edward L., Frank Algerton Kierman, and John King Fairbank. *Chinese Ways in Warfare.* Edited by Frank A. Kierman Jr. and John K. Fairbank. Cambridge, Mass.: Harvard University Press, 1974.

Drummond, J. C., and Anne Wilbraham. *The Englishman's Food: A History of Five Centuries of English Diet.* London: Jonathan Cape, 1939.

Dubos, Jean-Baptiste, abbé. *Réflexions critiques sur la poésie et sur la peinture.* 1719. New rev. ed., Utrecht: E. Néaulme, 1732. 6th ed., Paris: Pissot, 1755.

Dunlop, Fuchsia. *Sichuan Cookery.* London: Michael Joseph, 2001.

Dunn, Richard S., and Institute of Early American History and Culture. *Sugar and Slaves: The Rise of the Planter Class in the English West Indies, 1624–1713.* Chapel Hill: University of North Carolina Press, 1972.

Dupaigne, Bernard. *The History of Bread.* New York: Harry N. Abrams, 1999.

Dupont, Florence. *Daily Life in Ancient Rome.* Cambridge, Mass.: Blackwell, 1993.

DuPuis, E. Melanie. *Nature's Perfect Food: How Milk Became America's Drink.* New York: New York University Press, 2002.

Dye, Bob. "Hawaii's First Celebrity Chef." In *We Go Eat: A Mixed Plate from Hawaii's Food Culture,* 55–60. Honolulu: Hawaii Council for the Humanities, 2008.

Dyer, Christopher. "Changes in Diet in the Late Middle Ages: The Case of Harvest Workers." *Agricultural History Review* 36, no. 1 (1988): 21–37.

Earle, Rebecca. "'If You Eat Their Food . . .': Diets and Bodies in Early Colonial Spanish America." *American Historical Review* 115, no. 3 (2010): 688–713.

Eaton, Richard M. *The Rise of Islam and the Bengal Frontier, 1204–1760.* Berkeley: University of California Press, 1993.

Eaton, S. B., and M. Konner. "Paleolithic Nutrition." *New England Journal of Medicine* 312, no. 5 (1985): 283–89.

Economic Research Service. "USDA Food Cost Review, 1950–97." www.ers.usda.gov /media/308011/aer780h_1_.pdf (accessed 14 August 2012).

Eden, Trudy. *The Early American Table: Food and Society in the New World.* Dekalb: Northern Illinois University Press, 2008.

Edens, Christopher. "Dynamics of Trade in the Ancient Mesopotamian 'World System.'" *American Anthropologist* 94, no. 1 (1 March 1992): 118–39.

Effros, Bonnie. *Creating Community with Food and Drink in Merovingian Gaul.* New York: Palgrave Macmillan, 2002.

Ehrman, Edwina, Hazel Forsyth, Jacqui Pearce, Rory O'Connell, Lucy Peltz, and Cathy Ross. *London Eats Out, 1500–2000: 500 Years of Capital Dining.* London: Philip Wilson, 1999.

Eisenstadt, S. N. *Modernization: Protest and Change.* Englewood Cliffs, N.J.: Prentice Hall, 1966.

Ellison, Rosemary. "Diet in Mesopotamia: The Evidence of the Barley Ration Texts (c. 3000–1400 B.C.)." *Iraq* 43, no. 1 (1 April 1981): 35–45.

———. "Methods of Food Preparation in Mesopotamia (c. 3000–600 BC)." *Journal of the Economic and Social History of the Orient* 27, no. 1 (1 January 1984): 89–98.

Elvin, Mark. *The Pattern of the Chinese Past: A Social and Economic Interpretation.* Stanford, Calif.: Stanford University Press, 1973.

Encyclopædia Britannica, 11th ed., 1910–11.

Encyclopedia Judaica. New York: Macmillan, 1972.

Engelhardt, Elizabeth Sanders Delwiche. *A Mess of Greens: Southern Gender and Southern Food.* Athens: University of Georgia Press, 2011.

Engels, Donald W. *Alexander the Great and the Logistics of the Macedonian Army.* Berkeley: University of California Press, 1980.

Episcopal Church, Coffeyville, Kansas, Ladies' Guild. *Coffeyville Cook Book.* Coffeyville: Journal Press, 1915.

Escoffier, Auguste. *Souvenirs inédits: 75 ans au service de l'art culinaire.* Marseille: J. Laffitte, 1985.

Esterik, Penny van. "From Marco Polo to McDonald's: Thai Cuisine in Transition." *Food and Foodways* 5, no. 2 (1992): 177–93.

Evans, Meryle. "The Splendid Processions of Trade Guilds at Ottoman Festivals." In *Food in the Arts: Proceedings of the Oxford Symposium on Food and Cooking, 1998,* edited by Harlan Walker, 67–72. Totnes, Devon, UK: Prospect Books, 1999.

Evelyn, John. *Acetaria: A Discourse on Sallets.* London: Tooke, 1699.

Faas, Patrick. *Around the Roman Table.* New York: Palgrave Macmillan, 2003.

Faroqhi, Suraiya. *Towns and Townsmen of Ottoman Anatolia: Trade, Crafts, and Food Production in an Urban Setting, 1520–1650.* New York: Cambridge University Press, 1984.

Feeley-Harnik, Gillian. *The Lord's Table: The Meaning of Food in Early Judaism and Christianity.* Washington, D.C.: Smithsonian Institution Press, 1994.

Fenton, Alexander, ed. *Order and Disorder: The Health Implications of Eating and Drinking in the Nineteenth and Twentieth Centuries: Proceedings of the Fifth Symposium of the International Commission for Research into European Food History, Aberdeen, 1997.* East Linton, UK: Tuckwell, 2000.

Ferguson, Priscilla Parkhurst. *Accounting for Taste: The Triumph of French Cuisine.* University of Chicago Press, 2004.

———. "A Cultural Field in the Making: Gastronomy in 19th-Century France." *American Journal of Sociology* 104, no. 3 (1 November 1998): 597–641.

Fernández-Armesto, Felipe. *Near a Thousand Tables: A History of Food.* New York: Free Press, 2002.

Field, Carol. *The Italian Baker.* New York: William Morrow, 1985.

Fine, Ben, Michael Heasman, and Judith Wright. *Consumption in the Age of Affluence: The World of Food.* New York: Routledge, 1996.

Fink, Beatrice, ed. *Les liaisons savoureuses: Réflexions et pratiques culinaires au XVIIIe siècle.* Saint-Étienne: Université de Saint-Étienne, 1995.

Finlay, M. R. "Early Marketing of the Theory of Nutrition: The Science and Culture of Liebig's Extract of Meat." *Clio medica* 32 (1995): 48–74.

Finley, M. I. *Ancient Sicily.* 1968. Rev. ed. London: Chatto & Windus, 1979.

Fischer, David Hackett. *Albion's Seed: Four British Folkways in America.* New York: Oxford University Press, 1989.

Fischler, Claude. "Food, Self and Identity." *Social Science Information* 27, no. 2 (June 1988): 275–92.

Fisher, N. R. E. "Greek Associations, Symposia, and Clubs." In *Civilization of the Ancient Mediterranean: Greece and Rome,* edited by Michael Grant and Rachel Kitzinger. New York: Scribner, 1988.

Fitzpatrick, John. "Food, Warfare and the Impact of Atlantic Capitalism in Aotearoa/New Zealand." www.adelaide.edu.au/apsa/docs_papers/Others/Fitzpatrick.pdf (accessed 14 November 2012).

Flandrin, J. L. *Chronique de Platine: Pour une gastronomie historique.* Paris: Odile Jacob, 1992.

———. "Le goût et la nécessité: Sur l'usage des graisses dans les cuisines d'Europe occidentale (XIVe–XVIIIe siècle)." *Annales: Économies, Sociétés, Civilisations* 38, no. 1 (1983): 369–401.

Flandrin, Jean-Louis, and Massimo Montanari, eds. *Food: A Culinary History from Antiquity to the Present.* Translated by Albert Sonnenfeld. New York: Columbia University Press, 1999. Originally published as *Histoire de l'alimentation* (Paris: Fayard, 1997).

Fletcher, R. A. *The Barbarian Conversion: From Paganism to Christianity.* 1st American ed. New York: Holt, 1998.

———. *Moorish Spain.* London: Weidenfeld & Nicolson, 1992.

Fogel, Robert William. *The Escape from Hunger and Premature Death, 1700–2100: Europe, America, and the Third World.* New York: Cambridge University Press, 2004.

Foltz, Richard. *Religions of the Silk Roads: Premodern Patterns of Globalization.* New ed. Palgrave Macmillan, 2010.

Forbes, H., and L. Foxhall. "Ethnoarcheology and Storage in the Mediterranean beyond Risk and Survival." In *Food in Antiquity,* edited by John Wilkins, David Harvey, and Mike Dobson, 69–86. Exeter, UK: University of Exeter Press, 1995.

Forbes, R. J. *Short History of the Art of Distillation from the Beginnings up to the Death of Cellier Blumenthal.* Leiden: Brill, 1948.

———. *Studies in Ancient Technology.* Leiden: Brill, 1955.

Foulk, T. Griffith. "Myth, Ritual, and Monastic Practice in Sung Ch'an Buddhism." In *Religion and Society in T'ang and Sung China,* edited by Patricia Buckley Ebrey and Peter N. Gregory. Honolulu: University of Hawaii Press, 1993.

Fragner, B. "From the Caucasus to the Roof of the World: A Culinary Adventure." In *Culinary Cultures of the Middle East,* edited by Sami Zubaida and Richard L. Tapper, 49–62. New York: I. B. Taurus, 1994.

Franconie, H., M. Chastanet, and F. Sigaut. *Couscous, boulgour et polenta: Transformer et consommer les céréales dans le monde.* Paris: Karthala, 2010.

Frankel, Edith J., and James D. Frankel. *Wine and Spirits of the Ancestors: Exhibition and Sale March 22nd Through April 28th 2001.* New York: E & J Frankel, 2001.

Frantz, Joe Bertram. *Gail Borden, Dairyman to a Nation.* Norman: University of Oklahoma Press, 1951.

Fraser, Hugh, and Hugh Cortazzi. *A Diplomat's Wife in Japan: Sketches at the Turn of the Century.* New York: Weatherhill, 1982.

Freedman, Paul H., ed. *Food: The History of Taste.* Berkeley: University of California Press, 2007.

———. *Out of the East: Spices and the Medieval Imagination.* New Haven, Conn.: Yale University Press, 2008.

Freeman, Michael. "Sung." In *Food in Chinese Culture: Anthropological and Historical Perspectives,* edited by Kwang-chih Chang, 141–76. New Haven, Conn.: Yale University Press, 1977.

Freidberg, Susanne. *French Beans and Food Scares: Culture and Commerce in an Anxious Age.* New York: Oxford University Press, 2004.

———. *Fresh: A Perishable History.* Cambridge, Mass.: Belknap Press of Harvard University Press, 2009.

Freyre, Gilberto. *The Masters and the Slaves (Casa-Grande & Senzala): A Study in the Development of Brazilian Civilization.* Translated by Samuel Putnam. 2nd rev. ed. Berkeley: University of California Press, 1987.

Fuller, Dorian Q. "The Arrival of Wheat in China." *Archaeobotanist,* 9 July 2010. http://archaeobotanist.blogspot.mx/2010/07/arrival-of-wheat-in-china.html (accessed 14 August 2012).

———. "Debating Early African Bananas." *Archaeobotanist,* 19 January 2012. http://archaeobotanist.blogspot.com/2012/01/debating-early-african-bananas.html (accessed 14 August 2012).

———. "Globalization of Bananas in 3 Acts: Recent Updates." *Archaeobotanist,* 19 January 2012. http://archaeobotanist.blogspot.com/2012/01/globalization-of-bananas-in-3-acts.html (accessed 14 August 2012).

Fuller, Dorian Q., and Nicole Boivin. "Crops, Cattle and Commensals across the Indian Ocean: Current and Potential Archaeobiological Evidence." In *Études Océan Indien,* no. 42–43: *Plantes et sociétés,* 13–46. Paris: Institut national de langues et civilizations orientales, 2009.

Fuller, Dorian Q., Yo-Ichiro Sato, Cristina Castillo, Ling Qin, Alison R. Weisskopf, Eleanor J. Kingwell-Banham, Jixiang Song, Sung-Mo Ahn, and Jacob Etten. "Consilience of Genetics and Archaeobotany in the Entangled History of Rice." *Archaeological and Anthropological Sciences* 2 (18 June 2010): 115–31.

Gabaccia, Donna R. *We Are What We Eat: Ethnic Food and the Making of Americans.* Cambridge, Mass.: Harvard University Press, 1998.

Galavaris, George. *Bread and the Liturgy: The Symbolism of Early Christian and Byzantine Bread Stamps.* Madison: University of Wisconsin Press, 1970.

Gandhi, Mahatma. *An Autobiography: The Story of My Experiments with Truth.* London: Jonathan Cape, 1966.

Gardella, Robert. *Harvesting Mountains: Fujian and the China Tea Trade, 1757–1937.* Berkeley: University of California Press, 1994.

Gardner, Bruce L. *American Agriculture in the Twentieth Century: How It Flourished and What It Cost.* Cambridge, Mass.: Harvard University Press, 2002.

Garnsey, Peter. *Cities, Peasants and Food in Classical Antiquity: Essays in Social and Economic History.* New York: Cambridge University Press, 1998.

———. *Famine and Food Supply in the Graeco-Roman World: Responses to Risk and Crisis.* New York: Cambridge University Press, 1988.

———. *Food and Society in Classical Antiquity.* New York: Cambridge University Press, 1999.

Garrido Aranda, Antonio, ed. *Cultura alimentaria Andalucía-América.* México, D.F.: Universidad Nacional Autonóma de México, 1996.

Gelder, G. J. H. van. *God's Banquet: Food in Classical Arabic Literature.* New York: Columbia University Press, 2000.

Genç, Mehmet. "Ottoman Industry in the Eighteenth Century: General Framework, Characteristics, and Main Trends." In *Manufacturing in the Ottoman Empire and Turkey, 1500–1950,* edited by Donald Quataert, 59–85. Albany, N.Y.: State University of New York Press, 1994.

George, Andrew, ed. and trans. *The Epic of Gilgamesh.* London: Penguin Books, 1999.

Gernet, Jacques. *Buddhism in Chinese Society: An Economic History from the Fifth to the Tenth Century.* Translated by F. Verellen. Columbia University Press, 1998.

———. *A History of Chinese Civilization.* Translated by J. R. Foster. New York: Cambridge University Press, 1982.

Gerth, Karl. *China Made: Consumer Culture and the Creation of the Nation.* Cambridge, Mass.: Harvard University Asia Center, 2003. Distributed by Harvard University Press.

Giedion, Sigfried. *Mechanization Takes Command: A Contribution to Anonymous History.* New York: Oxford University Press, 1948.

Gilman, Charlotte Perkins. *Women and Economics: A Study of the Economic Relation between Men and Women as a Factor in Social Evolution.* 1898. Reprint. Berkeley: University of California Press, 1998. http://classiclit.about.com/library/bl-etexts/cpgilman/bl-cpgilman-womeneco-11.htm (accessed 6 August 2012).

Girouard, Mark. *Life in the English Country House: A Social and Architectural History.* London: Penguin Books, 1980.

Gitlitz, David M., and Linda Kay Davidson. *A Drizzle of Honey: The Lives and Recipes of Spain's Secret Jews.* New York: St. Martin's Press, 1999.

Glants, Musya, and Joyce Toomre, eds. *Food in Russian History and Culture.* Bloomington: Indiana University Press, 1997.

Glasse, Hannah. *First Catch Your Hare : The Art of Cookery Made Plain and Easy (1747).* Edited by Jennifer Stead and Priscilla Bain. Totnes, Devon, UK: Prospect Books, 2004.

Glick, Thomas F. *Islamic and Christian Spain in the Early Middle Ages.* Princeton, N.J.: Princeton University Press, 1979.

Golden, P. B. *Nomads and Sedentary Societies in Medieval Eurasia.* Washington, D.C.: American Historical Association, 2003.

Goldman, Wendy Z. *Women at the Gates: Gender and Industry in Stalin's Russia.* New York: Cambridge University Press, 2002.

———. *Women, the State, and Revolution: Soviet Family Policy and Social Life, 1917–1936.* New York: Cambridge University Press, 1993.

Goldstein, Darra. "Domestic Porkbarreling in Nineteenth-Century Russia; or, Who Holds the Keys to the Larder?" In *Russia—Women—Culture,* edited by Helena Goscilo and Beth Holmgren, 125–51. Bloomington: Indiana University Press, 1996.

———. "The Eastern Influence on Russian Cuisine." In *Current Research in Culinary History: Sources, Topics, and Methods,* 20–26. Boston: Culinary Historians of Boston, 1985.

———. "Food from the Heart." *Gastronomica* 4, no. 1 (2004): iii–iv.

———. "Gastronomic Reforms Under Peter the Great." *Jahrbücher für Geschichte Osteuropas* 48 (2000): 481–510.

———. "Is Hay Only for Horses? Highlights of Russian Vegetarianism at the Turn of the Century." In *Food in Russian History and Culture*, edited by Musya Glants and Joyce Toomre, 103–23. Bloomington: University of Indiana Press, 1997.

———. "Russian Dining: Theatre of the Gastronomic Absurd." *On Cooking: Performance Research* 4, no. 1 (2001): 64–72.

González de la Vara, Fernán. *Época prehispánica*. Vol. 2 of *La cocina mexicana a través de los siglos*, ed. id. and Enrique Krauze. México, D.F.: Clío; Fundación Herdez, 1996.

Goody, Jack. *Cooking, Cuisine, and Class: A Study in Comparative Sociology*. New York: Cambridge University Press, 1982.

Gopalan, C. *Nutrition in Developmental Transition in South-East Asia*. SEARO Regional Health Paper no. 21. New Delhi: World Health Organization, 1992.

Gordon, B. M. "Fascism, the Neo-Right, and Gastronomy: A Case in the Theory of the Social Engineering of Taste." In *Oxford Symposium on Food and Cookery*. London: Prospect Books, 1987.

Gowers, Emily. *The Loaded Table: Representations of Food in Roman Literature*. New York: Clarendon Press, Oxford University Press, 1993.

Gozzini Giacosa, Ilaria. *A Taste of Ancient Rome*. Chicago: University of Chicago Press, 1992.

Graham, A. C. *Disputers of the Tao: Philosophical Argument in Ancient China*. La Salle, Ill.: Open Court, 1989.

Grainger, Sally. *Cooking Apicius: Roman Recipes for Today*. Totnes, Devon, UK: Prospect Books, 2006.

Grant, Mark. *Galen on Food and Diet*. New York: Routledge, 2000.

———. "Oribasius and Medical Dietetics or the Three P's." In *Food in Antiquity*, edited by John Wilkins, David Harvey, and Michael J. Dobson, 371–79. Exeter, UK: University of Exeter Press, 1995.

Greeley, Alexandra. "Finding Pad Thai." *Gastronomica* 9, no. 1 (2009): 78–82.

Grewe, Rudolf. "Hispano-Arabic Cuisine in the Twelfth Century." In *Du manuscrit à table: Essais sur la cuisine au Moyen Âge et répertoire des manuscrits médiévaux contenant des recettes culinaires*, edited by Carole Lambert. Montréal: Presses de l'Université de Montréal, 1992.

Griffin, Emma. *A Short History of the Industrial Revolution*. New York: Palgrave, 2010.

Griggs, Peter. "Sugar Demand and Consumption in Colonial Australia." In *Food, Power and Community: Essays in the History of Food and Drink*, edited by Robert Dare, 74–90. Adelaide: Wakefield Press, 1999.

Grimm, Veronika E. *From Feasting to Fasting, the Evolution of a Sin: Attitudes to Food in Late Antiquity*. New York: Routledge, 1996.

Grivetti, Louis E. *Chocolate: History, Culture, and Heritage*. Hoboken, N.J.: Wiley, 2009.

Guan, Zhong. *Guanzi: Political, Economic, and Philosophical Essays from Early China: A Study and Translation = [Kuan-Tzu]*. Translated by W. Allyn Rickett. Princeton, N.J.: Princeton University Press, 1985.

Guerrini, Anita. *Obesity and Depression in the Enlightenment: The Life and Times of George Cheyne*. Norman: University of Oklahoma Press, 2000.

Guthman, Julie. *Agrarian Dreams: The Paradox of Organic Farming in California*. Berkeley: University of California Press, 2004.

Guyer, Jane I., ed., *Feeding African Cities: Studies in Regional Social History.* Bloomington: Indiana University Press in association with the International African Institute, London, 1987.

Haber, Barbara. *From Hardtack to Home Fries: An Uncommon History of American Cooks and Meals.* New York: Free Press, 2002.

Haden, Roger. *Food Culture in the Pacific Islands.* Santa Barbara, Calif.: Greenwood Press, 2009.

Hadjisavvas, Sophocles. *Olive Oil Processing in Cyprus: From the Bronze Age to the Byzantine Period.* Nicosia: P. Åström, 1992.

Hagen, Ann. *A Handbook of Anglo-Saxon Food: Processing and Consumption.* Pinner, England: Anglo-Saxon Books, 1992.

Halici, Nevin. *Sufi Cuisine.* London: Saqi Books, 2005.

Hanley, Susan B. *Everyday Things in Premodern Japan: The Hidden Legacy of Material Culture.* Berkeley: University of California Press, 1997.

Hardyment, Christina. *Slice of Life: The British Way of Eating Since 1945.* London: BBC Books, 1995.

Harlan, J. R. *Crops and Man.* 1985. 2nd ed. Madison, Wisc.: American Society of Agronomy, 1992.

Harp, Stephen L. *Marketing Michelin: Advertising and Cultural Identity in Twentieth-Century France.* Baltimore: Johns Hopkins University Press, 2001.

Harris, David R., and Gordon C. Hillman, eds. *Foraging and Farming: The Evolution of Plant Exploitation.* Boston: Unwin Hyman, 1989.

Harris, Marvin. *Good to Eat: Riddles of Food and Culture.* New York: Simon & Schuster, 1985.

Harrison, William. *The Description of England.* Ithaca, N.Y.: Folger Shakespeare Library, 1968.

Hartog, Adel P. den. "Acceptance of Milk Products in Southeast Asia: The Case of Indonesia." In *Asian Food: The Global and the Local,* edited by Katarzyna Joanna Cwiertka and Boudewijn Walraven, 34–45. Honolulu: University of Hawai'i Press, 2001.

Harvey, David. "Lydian Specialties, Croesus' Golden Baking-Women and Dogs' Dinners." In *Food in Antiquity,* edited by John Wilkins, F. D. Harvey, and Michael J. Dobson, 273–85. Exeter, UK: University of Exeter Press, 1995.

al-Hassan, Ahmad Y., and Donald R. Hill. *Islamic Technology: An Illustrated History.* New York: Cambridge University Press, and Paris: Unesco, 1986.

Hattox, Ralph S. *Coffee and Coffeehouses: The Origins of a Social Beverage in the Medieval Near East.* Seattle: University of Washington Press, 1985.

Hayward, Tim. "'The Most Revolting Dish Ever Devised.'" *Guardian,* 30 June 2009. www .guardian.co.uk/lifeandstyle/2009/jul/01/elizabeth-david-food-cookbook (accessed 14 August 2012).

Headrick, Daniel R. *The Tentacles of Progress: Technology Transfer in the Age of Imperialism, 1850–1940.* New York: Oxford University Press, 1988.

Heer, Jean. *First Hundred Years of Nestlé.* Vevey, Switzerland: Nestlé Co., 1991.

Heim, Susanne. *Plant Breeding and Agrarian Research in Kaiser-Wilhelm-Institutes, 1933–1945: Calories, Caoutchouc, Careers.* Dordrecht: Springer, 2008.

Heine, Peter. *Weinstudien: Untersuchungen zu Anbau, Produktion und Konsum des Weins im arabisch-islamischen Mittelalter.* Wiesbaden: Otto Harrassowitz, 1982.

Helstosky, Carol. *Garlic and Oil: Food and Politics in Italy.* Oxford: Berg, 2004.

Hemardinquer, Jean-Jacques. *Pour une histoire de l'alimentation: Recueil de travaux présentés par Jean-Jacques Hemardinquer.* Paris: Colin, 1970.

Herm, Gerhard. *The Celts: The People Who Came out of the Darkness.* New York: St. Martin's Press, 1977.

Hess, John L., and Karen Hess. *The Taste of America.* New York: Grossman, 1977.

Hess, Karen. *The Carolina Rice Kitchen: The African Connection.* Columbia: University of South Carolina Press, 1992.

———. *Martha Washington's Booke of Cookery and Booke of Sweetmeats.* New York: Columbia University Press, 1996.

Hillman, G. C. "Traditional Husbandry and Processing of Archaic Cereals in Modern Times: Part I, the Glume Wheats." *Bulletin on Sumerian Agriculture* 1 (1984): 114–52.

Hine, Thomas. *The Total Package: The Evolution and Secret Meanings of Boxes, Bottles, Cans and Tubes.* Boston: Little, Brown, 1995.

Hinnells, John R., ed. *A Handbook of Living Religions.* Harmondsworth, UK: Viking Press, 1984.

Hiroshi, Ito. "Japan's Use of Flour Began with Noodles, Part 3." *Kikkoman Food Culture,* no. 18 (2009): 9–13.

Hocquard, Édouard. *Une campagne au Tonkin.* Paris: Hachette, 1892. Reprint, edited by Philippe Papin, Paris: Arléa, 1999. Originally published in *Le Tour de Monde,* 1889–91.

Hoffmann, R. C. "Frontier Foods for Late Medieval Consumers: Culture, Economy, Ecology." *Environment and History* 7, no. 2 (2001): 131–67.

Hoffmann, W. G. "100 Years of the Margarine Industry." In *Margarine: An Economic, Social and Scientific History, 1869–1969,* edited by Johannes Hermanus van Stuyvenberg, 9–36. Liverpool: Liverpool University Press, 1969.

Hole, Frank, Kent V. Flannery, and J. A. Neely. *Prehistory and Human Ecology of the Deh Luran Plain: An Early Village Sequence from Khuzistan, Iran.* Vol. 1. Ann Arbor: University of Michigan, 1969.

Holmes, Tommy. *The Hawaiian Canoe.* 2nd ed. Honolulu: Editions Limited, 1993.

Homma, Gaku. *The Folk Art of Japanese Country Cooking: A Traditional Diet for Today's World.* Berkeley, Calif.: North Atlantic Books, 1991.

Horowitz, Roger. *Putting Meat on the American Table: Taste, Technology, Transformation.* Baltimore: Johns Hopkins University Press, 2006.

Hosking, Richard. *A Dictionary of Japanese Food: Ingredients and Culture.* Boston: Tuttle, 1997.

———. *At the Japanese Table.* New York: Oxford University Press, 2000.

———. "Manyoken, Japan's First French Restaurant." In *Cooks and Other People: Proceedings of the Oxford Symposium on Food and Cookery, 1995,* edited by Harlan Walker, 149–51. Totnes, Devon, UK: Prospect Books, 1996.

Huang, H. T. *Fermentations and Food Science.* Part 5 of vol. 6 of *Science and Civilization in China,* edited by Joseph Needham, *Biology and Biological Technology.* Cambridge: Cambridge University Press, 2001.

Hughes, Robert. *The Fatal Shore.* New York: Knopf, 1987.

Hurvitz, N. "From Scholarly Circles to Mass Movements: The Formation of Legal Communities in Islamic Societies." *American Historical Review* 108, no. 4 (2003): 985–1008.

Husain, Salma. *The Emperor's Table: The Art of Mughal Cuisine.* New Delhi: Roli & Janssen, 2008.

Irwin, Geoffrey. "Human Colonisation and Change in the Remote Pacific." *Current Anthropology* 31, no. 1 (1 February 1990): 90–94.

Ishige, Naomichi. *The History and Culture of Japanese Food.* London: Routledge, 2001.

Jaffrey, Madhur. *Climbing the Mango Trees: A Memoir of a Childhood in India.* Vintage Books, 2007.

Jahāngīr, emperor of Hindustan. *The Tūzuk-i-Jahāngīrī; or, Memoirs of Jahāngīr.* London: Royal Asiatic Society, 1909. http://persian.packhum.org/persian/main?url=pf%3Fauth%3Dno110%26work%3Doo1 (accessed 17 August 2012).

Jasny, Naum. *The Daily Bread of the Ancient Greeks and Romans.* Bruges, Belgium: St. Catherine Press, 1950.

Jeanneret, Michel. *A Feast of Words: Banquets and Table Talk in the Renaissance.* Translated by Jeremy Whiteley and Emma Hughes. Chicago: University of Chicago Press, 1991.

Jenkins, D. J. A., C. W. C. Kendall, L. S. A. Augustin, S. Franceschi, M. Hamidi, A. Marchie, A. L. Jenkins, and M. Axelsen. "Glycemic Index: Overview of Implications in Health and Disease." *American Journal of Clinical Nutrition* 76, no. 1 (2002): 266S–73S.

Jha, D. N. *Holy Cow: Beef in Indian Dietary Traditions.* New Delhi: Matrix Books, 2001.

Jing, Jun. *Feeding China's Little Emperors: Food, Children, and Social Change.* Stanford, Calif.: Stanford University Press, 2000.

Johns, Timothy. *With Bitter Herbs They Shall Eat It: Chemical Ecology and the Origins of Human Diet and Medicine.* Tucson: University of Arizona Press, 1990.

Jones, A. H. M. *The Later Roman Economy, 284–602.* Oxford: Blackwell, 1964.

Jones, Eric. *The European Miracle: Environments, Economies and Geopolitics in the History of Europe and Asia.* 3rd ed. Cambridge: Cambridge University Press, 2003.

Jones, Martin. *Feast: Why Humans Share Food.* New York: Oxford University Press, 2007.

Juárez López, José Luis. *La lenta emergencia de la comida mexicana: Ambigüedades criollas, 1750–1800.* México, D.F.: M. A. Porrúa Grupo Editorial, 2000.

Kamath, M. V. *Milkman from Anand: The Story of Verghese Kurien.* 2nd rev. ed. Delhi: Konark, 1996.

Kamen, Henry. *Iron Century: Social Change in Europe, 1550–1660.* New York: Praeger, 1971.

———. *Spain's Road to Empire: The Making of a World Power, 1492–1763.* London: Allen Lane, 2002.

Kaneva-Johnson, Maria. *The Melting Pot: Balkan Food and Cookery.* Totnes, Devon, UK: Prospect Books, 1995.

Kaplan, Steven L. *The Bakers of Paris and the Bread Question, 1700–1775.* Durham: University of North Carolina Press, 1996.

———. *Bread, Politics and Political Economy in the Reign of Louis XV.* 2 vols. The Hague: Nijhoff, 1976.

———. *Provisioning Paris: Merchants and Millers in the Grain and Flour Trade During the Eighteenth Century.* Ithaca, N.Y.: Cornell University Press, 1984.

———. "Provisioning Paris: The Crisis of 1738–41." In *Edo and Paris: Urban Life and the State in the Early Modern Era,* edited by James A. McLain, John M. Merriman, and Kaoru Ugawa. Ithaca, N.Y.: Cornell University Press, 1994.

———. "Steven Kaplan on the History of Food." http://thebrowser.com/interviews/steven-kaplan-on-history-food (accessed 15 August 2012).

Kasper, Lynne Rossetto. *The Italian Country Table: Home Cooking from Italy's Farmhouse Kitchens.* New York: Scribner, 1999.

———. *The Splendid Table: Recipes from Emilia-Romagna, the Heartland of Northern Italian Food.* New York: William Morrow, 1992.

Katchadourian, Raffi. "The Taste Makers." *New Yorker,* 23 November, 2009, 86.

Katz, S. H., and Fritz Maytag. "Brewing an Ancient Beer." *Archaeology* 44, no. 4 (1991): 24–33.

Katz, S. H., and M. M. Voight. "Bread and Beer." *Expedition* 28 (1987): 23–34.

Katz, S. H., and William Woys Weaver, eds. *Encyclopedia of Food and Culture.* New York: Scribner, 2003.

Kaufman, Cathy K. *Cooking in Ancient Civilizations.* Westport, Conn.: Greenwood Press, 2006.

———. "What's in a Name? Some Thoughts on the Origins, Evolution and Sad Demise of Béchamel Sauce." In *Milk: Beyond the Dairy; Proceedings of the Oxford Symposium on Food and Cookery, 1999,* 193. Totnes, Devon, UK: Prospect Books, 2000.

Kaufman, Edna Ramseyer, ed. *Melting Pot of Mennonite Cookery, 1874–1974.* 3rd ed. North Newton, Kans.: Bethel College Women's Association, 1974.

Kautilya. *The Arthashastra.* New Delhi: Penguin Books India, 1992.

Kavanagh, T. W. "Archaeological Parameters for the Beginnings of Beer." *Brewing Techniques* 2, no. 5 (1994): 44–51.

Keay, John. *India: A History.* 1st American ed. New York: Atlantic Monthly Press, 2000.

Kenney-Herbert, A. R ["Wyvern"]. *Culinary Jottings: A Treatise in Thirty Chapters on Reformed Cookery for Anglo-Indian Exiles.* Madras: Higginbotham; London: Richardson, 1885. Facsimile reprint. Totnes, Devon, UK: Prospect Books, 2007.

Keremitsis, D. "Del metate al molino: La mujer mexicana de 1910 a 1940." *Historia mexicana* (1983): 285–302.

Khaitovich, P., H. E. Lockstone, M. T. Wayland, T. M. Tsang, S. D. Jayatilaka, A. J. Guo, J. Zhou, et al. "Metabolic Changes in Schizophrenia and Human Brain Evolution." *Genome Biology* 9, no. 8 (2008): R124.

Khare, Meera. "The Wine-Cup in Mughal Court Culture—From Hedonism to Kingship." *Medieval History Journal* 8, no. 1 (2005): 143–88.

Kierman, Frank A., Jr. "Phases and Modes of Combat in Early China." In Edward L. Dreyer et al., *Chinese Ways in Warfare,* edited by Frank A. Kierman Jr. and John K. Fairbank, 27–66. Cambridge, Mass.: Harvard University Press, 1974.

Kieschnick, John. "Buddhist Vegetarianism in China." In *Of Tripod and Palate: Food, Politics, and Religion in Traditional China,* edited by Roel Sterckx, 186–212. New York: Palgrave Macmillan, 2005.

———. *The Impact of Buddhism on Chinese Material Culture.* Princeton, N.J.: Princeton University Press, 2003.

Kilby, Peter. *African Enterprise: The Nigerian Bread Industry.* Stanford, Calif.: Hoover Institution on War, Revolution, and Peace, Stanford University, 1965.

Kimura, A. H. "Nationalism, Patriarchy, and Moralism: The Government-Led Food Reform in Contemporary Japan." *Food and Foodways* 19, no. 3 (2011): 201–27.

———. "Remaking Indonesian Food: The Processes and Implications of Nutritionalization." PhD diss., University of Wisconsin–Madison, 2007.

———. "Who Defines Babies' 'Needs'? The Scientization of Baby Food in Indonesia." *Social Politics: International Studies in Gender, State & Society* 15, no. 2 (2008): 232–60.

Kimura, A. H., and M. Nishiyama. "The Chisan-Chisho Movement: Japanese Local Food Movement and Its Challenges." *Agriculture and Human Values* 25, no. 1 (2008): 49–64.

King, Niloufer Ichaporia. *My Bombay Kitchen: Traditional and Modern Parsi Home Cooking.* Berkeley: University of California Press, 2007.

Kiple, Kenneth F. *A Movable Feast: Ten Millennia of Food Globalization.* Cambridge: Cambridge University Press, 2007.

Kiple, Kenneth F., and Kriemhild Coneè Ornelas, eds. *The Cambridge World History of Food.* New York: Cambridge University Press, 2000.

Kipling, John Lockwood. *Beast and Man in India: A Popular Sketch of Indian Animals in Their Relations with the People.* London: Macmillan, 1891.

Kipling, Rudyard. *The Collected Poems of Rudyard Kipling.* Ware, Herts., UK: Wordsworth Editions, 1994.

Kirch, Patrick Vinton. *On the Road of the Winds: An Archaeological History of the Pacific Islands before European Contact.* Berkeley: University of California Press, 2002.

Klopfer, Lisa. "Padang Restaurants: Creating 'Ethnic' Cuisine in Indonesia." *Food and Foodways* 5, no. 3 (1993): 293–304.

Knechtges, David R. "A Literary Feast: Food in Early Chinese Literature." *Journal of the American Oriental Society* 106, no. 1 (1986): 49–63.

Knight, Harry. *Food Administration in India, 1939–47.* Stanford, Calif.: Stanford University Press, 1954.

Knipschildt, M. E. "Drying of Milk and Milk Products." In *Modern Dairy Technology,* edited by R. K. Robinson, 1: 131–234. New York: Elsevier, 1986.

Kochilas, Diane. *The Glorious Foods of Greece.* New York: William Morrow, 2001.

Koerner, L. "Linnaeus' Floral Transplants." *Representations,* no. 47 (1994): 144–69.

Kohn, Livia. *Monastic Life in Medieval Daoism: A Cross-Cultural Perspective.* Honolulu: University of Hawai'i Press, 2003.

Korsmeyer, Carolyn. *Making Sense of Taste: Food and Philosophy.* Ithaca, N.Y.: Cornell University Press, 2002.

Kozuh, M. G. *The Sacrificial Economy: On the Management of Sacrificial Sheep and Goats at the Neo-Babylonian/Achaemenid Eanna Temple of Uruk (c. 625–520 BC).* Chicago: Oriental Institute, 2006.

Kremezi, Aglaia. "Nikolas Tselementes." In *Cooks and Other People: Proceedings of the Oxford Symposium on Food and Cookery, 1995,* edited by Harlan Walker, 162–69. Totnes, Devon, UK: Prospect Books, 1996.

Krugman, Paul. "Supply, Demand, and English Food." http://web.mit.edu/krugman/www /mushy.html (accessed 15 August 2012).

Kumakura, Isao. "Table Manners Then and Now." *Japan Echo,* January 2000.

Kupperman, Karen Ordahl, "Fear of Hot Climates in the Anglo-American Colonial Experience." *William and Mary Quarterly* 41, no. 2 (1984): 213–40.

Kuralt, Charles. *On the Road with Charles Kuralt*. New York: Ballantine Books, 1986.

Kuriyama, Shigehisa. "Interpreting the History of Bloodletting." *Journal of the History of Medicine and Allied Sciences* 50, no. 1 (1995): 11–46.

Kurmann, Joseph A., Jeremija Lj Rašić, and Manfred Kroger, eds. *Encyclopedia of Fermented Fresh Milk Products: An International Inventory of Fermented Milk, Cream, Buttermilk, Whey, and Related Products*. New York: Van Nostrand Reinhold, 1992.

Kwok, Daniel. "The Pleasures of the Chinese Table." *Free China Review* 41, no. 9. (1991): 46–51.

Ladies of Toronto. *The Home Cook Book*. Toronto: Belford, 1878.

Lai, T. C. *At the Chinese Table*. Hong Kong: Oxford University Press, 1984.

Landers, John. *The Field and the Forge: Population, Production, and Power in the Pre-industrial West*. New York: Oxford University Press, 2003.

Landes, David S. *The Wealth and Poverty of Nations: Why Some Are So Rich and Some So Poor*. New York: Norton, 1998.

Lane Fox, Robin. *Alexander the Great*. London: Penguin Books, 2004.

Lang, George. *Cuisine of Hungary*. New York: Bonanza, 1971.

Lankester, Edwin. *On Food: Being Lectures Delivered at the South Kensington Museum*. London: Hardwicke, 1861.

Lapidus, Ira M. *A History of Islamic Societies*. Cambridge: Cambridge University Press, 2002.

Laudan, Rachel. "Birth of the Modern Diet." *Scientific American* 283, no. 2 (2000): 76.

———. "Cognitive Change in Technology and Science." In *The Nature of Technological Knowledge: Are Models of Scientific Change Relevant?*, edited by Rachel Laudan, 83–104. Dordrecht, Holland: Reidel, 1984.

———. *The Food of Paradise: Exploring Hawaii's Culinary Heritage*. Honolulu: University of Hawai'i Press, 1996.

———. "Fresh from the Cow's Nest: Condensed Milk and Culinary Innovation." In *Milk: Beyond the Dairy; Proceedings of the Oxford Symposium on Food and Cookery, 1999*, edited by Harlan Walker, 216–24. Totnes, Devon, UK: Prospect Books, 2000.

———. *From Mineralogy to Geology: The Foundations of a Science, 1650–1830*. Chicago: University of Chicago Press, 1987.

———. "A Kind of Chemistry." *Petits Propos Culinaires* 62 (1999): 8–22.

———. "The Mexican Kitchen's Islamic Connection." *Saudi Aramco World* 55, no. 3 (2004): 32–39.

———. "A Plea for Culinary Modernism: Why We Should Love New, Fast, Processed Food." *Gastronomica: The Journal of Food and Culture* 1, no. 1 (2001): 36–44.

———. "Refined Cuisine or Plain Cooking? Morality in the Kitchen." In *Food and Morality: Proceedings of the Oxford Symposium on Food and Cookery, 2007*, edited by Susan R. Friedland, 154–61. Totnes, Devon, UK: Prospect Books, 2008.

———. "Slow Food: The French Terroir Strategy, and Culinary Modernism: An Essay Review." *Food, Culture and Society: An International Journal of Multidisciplinary Research* 7, no. 2 (2004): 133–44.

Laudan, Rachel, and J. M. Pilcher. "Chiles, Chocolate, and Race in New Spain: Glancing Backward to Spain or Looking Forward to Mexico?" *Eighteenth-Century Life* 23, no. 2 (1999): 59–70.

Laufer, Berthold. *Sino-Iranica: Chinese Contributions to the History of Civilization in Ancient Iran, with Special Reference to the History of Cultivated Plants and Products.* Chicago: Field Museum of Natural History, 1919.

La Varenne, François Pierre. *Le cuisinier françois, enseignant la manière de bien apprester et assaisonner toutes sortes de viandes . . . légumes, . . . par le sieur de La Varenne.* Paris: P. David, 1651.

———. *The French Cook: Englished by I.D.G., 1653.* Intro. by Philip and Mary Hyman. Lewes, East Sussex: Southover Press, 2001.

Lee, Paula Young. *Meat, Modernity, and the Rise of the Slaughterhouse.* Hanover, N.H.: University Press of New England, 2008.

Legge, James. *The Chinese Classics.* 2nd ed., rev. Oxford: Clarendon Press, Oxford University Press, 1893.

Lehmann, Gilly. *The British Housewife: Cookery Books, Cooking and Society in Eighteenth-Century Britain.* Totnes, Devon, UK: Prospect Books, 2003.

———. "The Rise of the Cream Sauce." In *Milk: Beyond the Dairy; Proceedings of the Oxford Symposium on Food and Cookery, 1999,* edited by Harlan Walker, 225–31. Totnes, Devon, UK: Prospect Books, 2000.

Lémery, Louis. *A Treatise of All Sorts of Foods, Both Animal and Vegetable: Also of Drinkables: Giving an Account How to Chuse the Best Sort of All Kinds; Of the Good and Bad Effects They Produce; The Principles They Abound With; The Time, Age, and Constitution They Are Adapted To.* London: W. Innys, T. Longman and T. Shewell, 1745.

Leonard, W. R. "Dietary Change Was a Driving Force in Human Evolution." *Scientific American* 288 (2002): 63–71.

León Pinelo, Antonio de. *Question moral si el chocolate quebranta el ayuno eclesiastico; Facsímile de la primera edición, Madrid, 1636.* México, D.F.: Condumex, 1994.

Le Strange, Guy. *Baghdad During the Abbasid Caliphate from Contemporary Arabic and Persian Sources.* Oxford: Clarendon Press, Oxford University Press, 1900.

Levenstein, Harvey A. *Paradox of Plenty: A Social History of Eating in Modern America.* New York: Oxford University Press, 1993.

———. *Revolution at the Table: The Transformation of the American Diet.* New York: Oxford University Press, 1988.

Levi, J. "L'abstinence des céréales chez les Taoistes." *Études Chinoises* 1 (1983): 3–47.

Lévi-Strauss, Claude. *Introduction to a Science of Mythology,* vol. 1: *The Raw and the Cooked.* Translated by John and Doreen Weightman. London: Jonathan Cape, 1970.

———. *Introduction to a Science of Mythology,* vol. 3: *The Origin of Table Manners.* Translated by John and Doreen Weightman. New York: Harper & Row, 1978.

Lewicki, Tadeusz. *West African Food in the Middle Ages According to Arabic Sources.* New York: Cambridge University Press, 2009.

Lewis, D.M. "The King's Dinner (Polyaenus IV 3.32)." *Achaemenid History* 2 (1987): 89–91.

Lieber, Elinor. "Galen on Contaminated Cereals as a Cause of Epidemics." *Bulletin of the History of Medicine* 44, no. 4 (1970): 332–45.

Lieven, D.C.B. *Empire: The Russian Empire and Its Rivals.* New Haven, Conn.: Yale University Press, 2001.

Lih, Lars T. *Bread and Authority in Russia, 1914–1921*. Berkeley: University of California Press, 1990.

Lin, Hsiang-ju, and Ts'ui-fêng Liao Lin. *Chinese Gastronomy*. New York: Harcourt Brace Jovanovich, 1977.

Lincoln, Bruce. "À la recherche du paradis perdu." *History of Religions* 43, no. 2 (2003): 139–54.

———. *Death, War, and Sacrifice: Studies in Ideology and Practice*. Chicago: University of Chicago Press, 1991.

———. "Physiological Speculation and Social Patterning in a Pahlavi Text." *Journal of the American Oriental Society* 108, no. 1 (1988): 135–40.

———. *Priests, Warriors, and Cattle: A Study in the Ecology of Religions*. Berkeley: University of California Press, 1981.

———. *Religion, Empire, and Torture: The Case of Achaemenian Persia*. Chicago: University of Chicago Press, 2007.

Lissarrague, François. *The Aesthetics of the Greek Banquet: Images of Wine and Ritual*. Princeton, N.J.: Princeton University Press, 1990.

Lockhart, James. *The Nahuas after the Conquest: A Social and Cultural History of the Indians of Central Mexico, Sixteenth through Eighteenth Centuries*. Stanford, Calif.: Stanford University Press, 1994.

Loha-unchit, Kasma. *It Rains Fishes: Legends, Traditions, and the Joys of Thai Cooking*. San Francisco: Pomegranate Communications, 1995.

Lombardo, Mario. "Food and 'Frontier' in the Greek Colonies of South Italy." In *Food in Antiquity*, edited by John Wilkins, F. D. Harvey, and Michael J. Dobson, 256–72. Exeter, UK: University of Exeter Press, 1995.

Long, Janet, ed. *Conquista y comida: Consecuencias del encuentro de dos mundos*. México, D.F.: Universidad Nacional Autónoma de México, 1996.

Long, Lucy M. *Culinary Tourism*. Lexington: University Press of Kentucky, 2004.

Longone, Jan. "'As Worthless as Savorless Salt'? Teaching Children to Cook, Clean, and (Often) Conform." *Gastronomica: The Journal of Food and Culture* 3, no. 2 (2003): 104–10.

———. "Early Black-Authored American Cookbooks." *Gastronomica: The Journal of Food and Culture* 1, no. 1 (2001): 96–99.

———. "The Mince Pie That Launched the Declaration of Independence, and Other Recipes in Rhyme." *Gastronomica: The Journal of Food and Culture* 2, no. 4 (2002): 86–89.

———. "Professor Blot and the First French Cooking School in New York, Part I." *Gastronomica: The Journal of Food and Culture* 1, no. 2 (2001): 65–71.

———. "What Is Your Name? My Name Is Ah Quong. Well, I Will Call You Charlie." *Gastronomica* 4, no. 2 (2004): 84–89.

Long-Solís, Janet. "A Survey of Street Foods in Mexico City." *Food and Foodways* 15, no. 3–4, 2007: 213–36.

López Austin, Alfredo. *Cuerpo humano e ideología: Las concepciones de los antiguos Nahuas*. 1st ed. México, D.F.: Universidad Nacional Autónoma de México, Instituto de Investigaciones Antropológicas, 1980.

Loreto López, Rosalva. "Prácticas alimenticias en los conventos de mujeres en la Puebla del siglo XVIII." In *Conquista y comida: Consecuencias del encuentro de dos mundos*, edited by Janet Long, 481–504. México, D.F.: Universidad Nacional Autónoma de México, 1996.

Love, John F. *McDonald's: Behind the Arches*. New York: Bantam Books, 1986.

Lozano Arrendares, Teresa. *El chinguirito vindicado: El contrabando de aguardiente de caña y la política colonial*. México, D.F.: Universidad Nacional Autonóma de México, 1995.

Luchetti, Cathy. *Home on the Range: A Culinary History of the American West*. New York: Villard Books, 1993.

Luckhurst, David. *Monastic Watermills: A Study of the Mills within English Monastic Precincts*. London: Society for the Protection of Ancient Buildings, 1964.

Lunt, H. G. "Food in the Rus' Primary Chronicle." In *Food in Russian History and Culture*, edited by Musya Glants and Joyce Toomre, 15–30. Bloomington: Indiana University Press, 1997.

Luther, Martin. *The Table Talk of Martin Luther*. Edited by William Hazlitt and Alexander Chalmers. London: H. G. Bohn, 1857.

Lynn, John A. *Feeding Mars: Logistics in Western Warfare from the Middle Ages to the Present*. Boulder, Colo.: Westview Press, 1993.

Lysaght, P., ed. *Milk and Milk Products from Medieval to Modern Times: Proceedings of the Ninth International Conference on Ethnological Food Research, Ireland, 1992*. Edinburgh: Canongate Academic in association with the Department of Irish Folklore, University College Dublin and the European Ethnological Research Centre, Edinburgh, 1994.

MacDonough, Cassandra M., Marta H. Gomez, Lloyd W. Rooney, and Servio O. Serna-Saldivar. "Alkaline Cooked Corn Products." In *Snack Foods Processing*, edited by Edmund W. Lusas and Lloyd W. Rooney, chap. 4. Boca Raton, Fla.: CRC Press, 2001.

Mack, Glenn Randall, and Asele Surina. *Food Culture in Russia and Central Asia*. Westport, Conn.: Greenwood Press, 2005.

Mackie, Cristine. *Life and Food in the Caribbean*. New York: New Amsterdam Books, 1991.

MacMillan, Margaret. *Women of the Raj*. London: Thames & Hudson, 1988.

MacMullen, Ramsay. *Christianity and Paganism in the Fourth to Eighth Centuries*. New Haven, Conn.: Yale University Press, 1997.

———. *Christianizing the Roman Empire (A.D. 100–400)*. New Haven, Conn.: Yale University Press, 1984.

Magdalino, Paul. "The Grain Supply of Constantinople, Ninth–Twelfth Centuries." In *Constantinople and Its Hinterland*, ed. Cyril A. Mango et al., 35–47. Brookfield, Vt.: Variorum, 1995.

Malmberg, Simon. "Dazzling Dining: Banquets as an Expression of Imperial Legitimacy." In *Eat, Drink, and Be Merry (Luke 12:19): Food and Wine in Byzantium; Papers of the 37th Annual Spring Symposium of Byzantine Studies, in Honour of Professor A. A. M. Bryer*, ed. Leslie Brubaker and Kallirroe Linardou, 75–91. Burlington, Vt.: Ashgate, 2007.

Mann, Charles C. *1491: New Revelations of the Americas Before Columbus*. New York: Knopf, 2005.

Maria, Jack Santa. *Indian Sweet Cookery*. Boulder, Colo.: Shambhala, 1980.

Martial [Marcus Valerius Martialis]. *The Epigrams*. Bohn's Classical Library. London: George Bell & Sons, 1888.

Martínez Motiño, Francisco. *Arte de cozina, pasteleria, vizcocheria y conserveria.* Madrid: Luis Sánchez, 1611. Reprint of emended 1763 edition. Valencia: Paris-Valencia, 1997.

Mason, Laura. *Sugar-Plums and Sherbet: The Prehistory of Sweets.* Totnes, Devon, UK: Prospect Books, 2004.

Matejowsky, Ty. "SPAM and Fast-Food 'Glocalization' in the Philippines." *Food, Culture and Society: An International Journal of Multidisciplinary Research* 10, no. 1 (2007): 23–41.

Mather, Richard B. "The Bonze's Begging Bowl: Eating Practices in Buddhist Monasteries of Medieval India and China." *Journal of the American Oriental Society* 101, no. 4 (1981): 417–24.

Mathias, Peter. *The Brewing Industry in England, 1700–1830.* New ed. Cambridge: Cambridge University Press, 1959.

Mathieson, Johan. "Longaniza." *Word of Mouth: Food and the Written Word* 8 (1996): 2–4.

Matossian, Mary Kilbourne. *Poisons of the Past: Molds, Epidemics, and History.* New Haven, Conn.: Yale University Press, 1991.

Matthee, Rudolph P. *The Pursuit of Pleasure: Drugs and Stimulants in Iranian History, 1500–1900.* Princeton, N.J.: Princeton University Press, 2005.

Maurizio, A. *Histoire de l'alimentation végétale depuis la préhistoire jusqu'à nos jours.* Translated by Ferdinand Gidon. Paris: Payot, 1932.

May, Earl Chapin. *The Canning Clan: A Pageant of Pioneering Americans.* New York: Macmillan, 1938.

Mazumdar, Sucheta. "The Impact of New World Food Crops on the Diet and Economy of China and India, 1600–1900." In *Food in Global History,* edited by Raymond Grew, 58–78. Boulder, Colo.: Westview Press, 1999.

———. *Sugar and Society in China: Peasants, Technology, and the World Market.* Cambridge, Mass.: Harvard University Asia Center, 1998.

McCann, James. *Maize and Grace: Africa's Encounter with a New World Crop, 1500–2000.* Cambridge, Mass.: Harvard University Press, 2005.

McCay, David. *The Protein Element in Nutrition.* London: E. Arnold; New York: Longmans, Green, 1912.

McClain, James L., John M. Merriman, and Kaoru Ugawa, eds. *Edo and Paris: Urban Life and the State in the Early Modern Era.* Ithaca, N.Y.: Cornell University Press, 1997.

McCollum, Elmer Verner. *A History of Nutrition: The Sequence of Ideas in Nutrition Investigations.* Boston: Houghton Mifflin, 1957.

———. *The Newer Knowledge of Nutrition: The Use of Food for the Preservation of Vitality and Health.* New York: Macmillan, 1918.

McCook, Stuart George. *States of Nature: Science, Agriculture, and Environment in the Spanish Caribbean, 1760–1940.* Austin: University of Texas Press, 2002.

McCormick, Finbar. "The Distribution of Meat in a Hierarchical Society: The Irish Evidence." In *Consuming Passions and Patterns of Consumption,* edited by Preston Miracle and Nicky Milner, 25–31. Cambridge: McDonald Institute, 2002.

McGee, Harold. *On Food and Cooking: The Science and Lore of the Kitchen.* New York: Scribner, 1984.

McGovern, Patrick E., Stuart J. Fleming, and Solomon H. Katz, eds. *The Origins and Ancient History of Wine.* Philadelphia: Gordon & Breach, 1995.

McKeown, A. "Global Migration, 1846–1940." *Journal of World History* (2004): 155–89.

McWilliams, James E. *A Revolution in Eating: How the Quest for Food Shaped America.* New York: Columbia University Press, 2005.

Meijer, Berthe. "Dutch Cookbooks Printed in the 16th and 17th Centuries." *Petits Propos Culinaires* 11 (1982): 47–55.

Meissner, D. J. "The Business of Survival: Competition and Cooperation in the Shanghai Flour Milling Industry." *Enterprise and Society* 6, no. 3 (2005): 364–94.

Mendelson, Anne. *Milk: The Surprising Story of Milk Through the Ages.* New York: Knopf, 2008.

———. *Stand Facing the Stove: The Story of the Women Who Gave America the Joy of Cooking.* New York: Holt, 1996.

Mennell, Stephen. *All Manners of Food: Eating and Taste in England and France from the Middle Ages to the Present.* Oxford: Blackwell, 1985.

Messer, Ellen. "Potatoes (white)." In *The Cambridge World History of Food,* edited by Kenneth F. Kiple and Kriemhild Coneè Ornelas. New York: Cambridge University Press, 2000.

Metcalf, Thomas R. *Ideologies of the Raj.* New York: Cambridge University Press, 1994.

Meyer-Renschhausen, Elizabeth. "The Porridge Debate: Grain, Nutrition, and Forgotten Food Preparation Techniques." *Food and Foodways* 5, no. 1 (1991): 95–120.

Mez, Adam. *The Renaissance of Islam.* Delhi: Idarah-i Adabiyat-i Delli, 1979.

Micklethwait, John, and Adrian Wooldridge. *A Future Perfect: The Challenge and Hidden Promise of Globalization.* New York: Times Books, 2000.

———. *God Is Back: How the Global Revival of Faith Is Changing the World.* New York: Penguin Press, 2009.

Mijares, Ivonne. *Mestizaje alimentario: El abasto en la cuidad de México en el siglo XVI.* México, D.F.: Facultad de Filosofía y Letras, Universidad Nacional Autonóma de México, 1993.

Miller, James Innes. *The Spice Trade of the Roman Empire, 29 B.C. to A.D. 641.* Oxford: Clarendon Press, Oxford University Press, 1969.

Mintz, Sidney Wilfred. *Sweetness and Power: The Place of Sugar in Modern History.* New York: Viking Press, 1985.

Miranda, Francisco de Paula, et al. *El maiz: Contribución al estudio de los alimentos mexicanos, ponencia presentada al tercer Congreso de Medicina en colaboración con la Comisión del Maiz y el Departamento de Nutriología de la S.S.A.* México, D.F., 1948.

Mollenhauer, Hans P., and Wolfgang Froese. *Von Omas Küche zur Fertigpackung: Aus der Kinderstube der Lebensmittelindustrie.* Gernsbach: C. Katz, 1988.

Monson, Craig A. *Nuns Behaving Badly: Tales of Music, Magic, Art, and Arson in the Convents of Italy.* Reprint. Chicago: University of Chicago Press, 2011.

Montanari, Massimo. *The Culture of Food.* Oxford: Blackwell, 1994.

———. *Food Is Culture.* New York: Columbia University Press, 2006.

Moor, Janny de. "Dutch Cookery and Calvin." In *Cooks and Other People: Proceedings of the Oxford Symposium on Food and Cookery, 1995,* edited by Harlan Walker, 94. Totnes, Devon, UK: Prospect Books, 1996.

———. "Farmhouse Gouda: A Dutch Family Business." In *Milk: Beyond the Dairy; Proceedings of the Oxford Symposium on Food and Cookery, 1999,* edited by Harlan Walker, 107. Totnes, Devon, UK: Prospect Books, 2000.

———. "The Wafer and Its Roots." In *Look and Feel: Studies in Texture, Appearance and Incidental Characteristics of Food: Proceedings of the Oxford Symposium on Food and Cookery, 1993*, edited by Harlan Walker, 119–27. Totnes, Devon, UK: Prospect Books, 1994.

Morgan, Dan. *Merchants of Grain*. New York: Viking Press, 1979.

Morineau, Michel. "Growing without Knowing Why: Production, Demographics, and Diet." In *Food: A Culinary History from Antiquity to the Present*, edited by Jean Louis Flandrin and Massimo Montanari, translated by Albert Sonnenfeld, 374–82. New York: Columbia University Press, 1999.

Mote, Frederick W. "Yuan and Ming." In *Food in Chinese Culture: Anthropological and Historical Perspectives*, edited by K. C. Chang, 193–257. New Haven, Conn.: Yale University Press, 1977.

Mrozik, S. "Cooking Living Beings." *Journal of Religious Ethics* 32, no. 1 (2004): 175–94.

Multhauf, Robert. "Medical Chemistry and the Paracelsians." *Bulletin of the History of Medicine* 28, no. 2 (1954): 101–26.

Munro, G. E. "Food in Catherinian St. Petersburg." In *Food in Russian History and Culture*, edited by Musya Glantz and Joyce Toomre, 31–48. Bloomington: Indiana University Press, 1997.

Murray, Oswyn, ed. *Sympotica: A Symposium on the Symposion*. Oxford: Oxford University Press, 1990.

Musurillo, Herbert. "The Problem of Ascetical Fasting in the Greek Patristic Writers." *Traditio* 12 (1956): 1–64.

Nasrallah, Nawal. *Delights from the Garden of Eden: A Cookbook and a History of the Iraqi Cuisine*. Bloomington, Ind.: 1stBooks, 2003.

Needham, Joseph, and Ho Ping-yu. "Elixir Poisoning in Medieval China." In Joseph Needham et al., *Clerks and Craftsmen in China and the West*, 316–39. Cambridge: Cambridge University Press, 1970.

Needham, Joseph, Gwei-djen Lu, Ho Ping-Yü, Tsuen-hsuin Tsien, Krzysztof Gawlikowski, Robin D. S. Yates, Wang Ling, Peter J. Golas, and Donald B. Wagner. *Chemistry and Chemical Technology*. Vol. 5 of *Science and Civilisation in China*, edited by Joseph Needham. Cambridge: Cambridge University Press, 1974.

Needham, Joseph, and Ling Wang. *Mechanical Engineering*. Part 2 of vol. 4 of *Science and Civilisation in China*, edited by Joseph Needham, *Physics and Physical Technology*. Cambridge: Cambridge University Press, 1965.

Nelson, Sarah Milledge. "Feasting the Ancestors in Early China." In *The Archaeology and Politics of Food and Feasting in Early States and Empires*, edited by Tamara L. Bray, 65–89. New York: Kluwer Academic/Plenum, 2003.

Newman, J. M. *Chinese Cookbooks: An Annotated English Language Compendium/Bibliography*. New York: Garland, 1987.

Northrup, David. *Indentured Labor in the Age of Imperialism, 1834–1922*. Cambridge: Cambridge University Press, 1995.

Norton, Marcy. *Sacred Gifts, Profane Pleasures: A History of Tobacco and Chocolate in the Atlantic World*. Ithaca, N.Y.: Cornell University Press, 2008.

Nuevo cocinero mejicano en forma de diccionario. 1858. Paris: Charles Bouret, 1888.

Nützenadel, Alexander, and Frank Trentmann. *Food and Globalization: Consumption, Markets and Politics in the Modern World*. New York: Berg, 2008.

Nye, John V. C. *War, Wine, and Taxes: The Political Economy of Anglo-French Trade, 1689– 1900.* Princeton, N.J.: Princeton University Press, 2007.

O'Connor, A. "Conversion in Central Quintana Roo: Changes in Religion, Community, Economy and Nutrition in a Maya Village." *Food, Culture and Society: An International Journal of Multidisciplinary Research* 15, no. 1 (2012): 77–91.

O'Connor, Kaori. "The Hawaiian Luau: Food as Tradition, Transgression, Transformation and Travel." *Food, Culture and Society: An International Journal of Multidisciplinary Research* 11, no. 2 (2008): 149–72.

———. "The King's Christmas Pudding: Globalization, Recipes, and the Commodities of Empire." *Journal of Global History* 4, no. 1 (2009): 127– 55.

Oddy, Derek J. *From Plain Fare to Fusion Food: British Diet from the 1890s to the 1990s.* Rochester, N.Y.: Boydell Press, 2003.

Offer, Avner. *The First World War: An Agrarian Interpretation.* New York: Clarendon Press, Oxford University Press, 1989.

Ohnuki-Tierney, Emiko. *Rice as Self: Japanese Identities Through Time.* Princeton, N.J.: Princeton University Press, 1993.

Ohnuma, Keiki. "Curry Rice: Gaijin Gold; How the British Version of an Indian Dish Turned Japanese." *Petits Propos Culinaires* 52 (1996): 8–15.

Oliver, Sandra. *Food in Colonial and Federal America.* Westport, Conn.: Greenwood Press, 2005.

Orlove, Benjamin S. *The Allure of the Foreign: Imported Goods in Postcolonial Latin America.* Ann Arbor: University of Michigan Press, 1997.

Ortiz Cuadra, C. M. *Puerto Rico en la olla: Somos aún lo que comimos?* Puerto Rico: Ediciones Doce Calles, 2006.

Ortiz de Montellano, Bernardo. *Medicina, salud y nutrición aztecas.* México, D.F.: Siglo Veintiuno, 1993.

Owen, Sri. *The Rice Book: The Definitive Book on Rice, with Hundreds of Exotic Recipes from Around the World.* New York: St. Martin's Griffin, 1994.

The Oxford Encyclopedia of Food and Drink in America. Edited by Andrew F. Smith. New York: Oxford University Press, 2004.

Pacey, Arnold. *Technology in World Civilization: A Thousand-Year History.* Cambridge, Mass.: MIT Press, 1991.

Pagden, Anthony. *Lords of All the World: Ideologies of Empire in Spain, Britain and France c. 1500–c. 1800.* New Haven, Conn.: Yale University Press, 1998.

Pagel, Walter. "J. B. van Helmont's Reformation of the Galenic Doctrine of Digestion, and Paracelsus." *Bulletin of the History of Medicine* 29, no. 6 (1955): 563–68.

———. "Van Helmont's Ideas on Gastric Digestion and the Gastric Acid." *Bulletin of the History of Medicine* 30, no. 6 (1956): 524–36.

Panjabi, Camellia. *50 Great Curries of India.* London: Kyle Cathie, 1994.

———. *The Great Curries of India.* New York: Simon & Schuster, 1995.

———. "The Non-Emergence of the Regional Foods of India." In *Disappearing Foods: Studies in Foods and Dishes at Risk; Proceedings of the Oxford Symposium on Food and Cookery, 1994*, 144. Totnes, Devon, UK: Prospect Books, 1995.

Parish, Peter J. *Slavery: History and Historians.* New York: Harper & Row, 1989.

Parpola, Simo. "The Leftovers of God and King: On the Distribution of Meat at the Assyrian and Achaemenid Imperial Courts." In *Food and Identity in the Ancient World,* edited by Cristiano Grottanelli and Lucio Milano, 281–99. Padua: S.A.R.G.O.N. editrice e libreria, 2003.

Paston-Williams, Sarah. *Art of Dining.* London: National Trust Publications, 1993.

Pearson, M. N. *Spices in the Indian Ocean World.* Brookfield, Vt.: Variorum, 1996.

Pedrocco, G. "The Food Industry and New Preservation Techniques." In *Food: A Culinary History from Antiquity to the Present,* edited by J. L. Flandrin and Massimo Montanari, translated by Albert Sonnenfeld, 485–86. New York: Columbia University Press, 1999.

Peer, Shanny. *France on Display: Peasants, Provincials, and Folklore in the 1937 Paris World's Fair.* Albany: State University of New York Press, 1998.

Peloso, Vincent C. "Succulence and Sustenance: Region, Class and Diet in Nineteenth-Century Peru." In *Food, Politics and Society in Latin America,* edited by John C. Super and Thomas Wright, 46–64. Lincoln: University of Nebraska Press, 1985.

Peña, Carolyn Thomas de la. *Empty Pleasures: The Story of Artificial Sweeteners from Saccharin to Splenda.* Chapel Hill: University of North Carolina Press, 2010.

Pendergrast, Mark. *For God, Country, and Coca-Cola: The Unauthorized History of the Great American Soft Drink and the Company That Makes It.* New York: Scribner, 1993.

Pérez Samper, M. Á. "La alimentación en la corte española del siglo XVIII." In *Felipe V y su tiempo,* edited by Eliseo Serrano, 529–583. Zaragoza: Diputación de Zaragoza, 2004.

Perlès, Catherine. *The Early Neolithic in Greece: The First Farming Communities in Europe.* New York: Cambridge University Press, 2001.

———. *Prehistoire du feu.* Paris: Masson, 1977.

Perry, Charles, A. J. Arberry, and Maxime Rodinson. *Medieval Arab Cookery: Papers by Maxime Rodinson and Charles Perry with a Reprint of a Baghdad Cookery Book.* Totnes, Devon, UK: Prospect Books, 1998.

Perry, Charles, Paul D. Buell, and Eugene N. Anderson. "Grain Foods of the Early Turks." In *A Soup for the Qan: Chinese Dietary Medicine of the Mongol Era as Seen in Hu Sihui's Yinshan Zhengyao.* 2nd ed., rev. Leiden: Brill, 2010.

Peters, Erica J. *Appetites and Aspirations in Vietnam: Food and Drink in the Long Nineteenth Century.* Lanham, Md.: AltaMira Press, 2012.

———. "National Preferences and Colonial Cuisine: Seeking the Familiar in French Vietnam." In *Proceedings of the . . . Annual Meeting of the Western Society for French History* 27 (1999): 150–59.

Petersen, Christian, and Andrew Jenkins. *Bread and the British Economy, c. 1770–1870.* Aldershot, UK: Scolar Press; Brookfield, Vt.: Ashgate, 1995.

Peterson, T. Sarah. *Acquired Taste: The French Origins of Modern Cooking.* Ithaca, N.J.: Cornell University Press, 1994.

Pettid, Michael J. *Korean Cuisine: An Illustrated History.* London: Reaktion Books, 2008.

Phillips, Rod. *A Short History of Wine.* New York: HarperCollins, 2000.

Pilcher, Jeffrey M. *Que Vivan Los Tamales! Food and the Making of Mexican Identity.* Albuquerque: University of New Mexico Press, 1998.

Pillsbury, Richard. *From Boarding House to Bistro: The American Restaurant Then and Now.* Boston: Unwin Hyman, 1990.

———. *No Foreign Food: The American Diet in Time and Place.* Boulder, Colo.: Westview Press, 1998.

Pinkard, Susan. *A Revolution in Taste: The Rise of French Cuisine, 1650–1800.* Cambridge: Cambridge University Press, 2009.

Pinto e Silva, Paula. *Farinha, feijão e carne-seca: Um tripé culinário no Brasil colonial.* São Paulo: Senac, 2005.

Piperno, Dolores R., Ehud Weiss, Irene Holst, and Dani Nadel. "Processing of Wild Cereal Grains in the Upper Palaeolithic Revealed by Starch Grain Analysis." *Nature* 430, no. 7000 (5 August 2004): 670–73.

Pirazzoli-t'Serstevens, M. "A Second-Century Chinese Kitchen Scene." *Food and Foodways* 1, no. 1–2 (1985): 95–103.

Pitte, Jean-Robert. *French Gastronomy: The History and Geography of a Passion.* New York: Columbia University Press, 2002.

Platina, Bartholomaeus. *On Right Pleasure and Good Health.* Edited by Mary Ella Milham. Tempe, Ariz.: Medieval & Renaissance Texts & Studies, 1998.

Pluquet, François-André-Adrien, abbé. *Traité philosophique sur le luxe.* 2 vols. Paris: Barrois, 1786.

Pollock, Nancy J. *These Roots Remain: Food Habits in Islands of the Central and Eastern Pacific Since Western Contact.* Laie, Hawaii: Institute for Polynesian Studies, 1992.

Pollock, S. "Feasts, Funerals, and Fast Food in Early Mesopotamian States." In *The Archaeology and Politics of Food and Feasting in Early States and Empires,* edited by Tamara L. Bray, 17–38. New York: Kluwer Academic/Plenum, 2003.

Polo, Marco. *The Description of the World.* Translated by A. C. Moule and Paul Pelliot. London: Routledge, 1938.

———. *The Travels of Marco Polo.* Edited by Manuel Komroff. New York: Modern Library, 1926.

Pomeranz, Kenneth. *The Great Divergence: China, Europe, and the Making of the Modern World Economy.* Princeton, N.J.: Princeton University Press, 2001.

Pool, Christopher A. *Olmec Archaeology and Early Mesoamerica.* Cambridge: Cambridge University Press, 2007.

Pope, K. O., M. E. Pohl, J. G. Jones, D. L. Lentz, C. von Nagy, F. J. Vega, and I. R. Quitmyer. "Origin and Environmental Setting of Ancient Agriculture in the Lowlands of Mesoamerica." *Science* 292, no. 5520 (2001): 1370–73.

Popkin, B. M. "The Nutrition Transition in Low-Income Countries: An Emerging Crisis." *Nutrition Reviews* 52, no. 9 (1994): 285–98.

Porter, Roy, ed. *The Medical History of Water and Spas.* London: Wellcome Institute for the History of Medicine, 1990.

———. *Medicine: A History of Healing.* London: Michael O'Mara, 1997.

Porterfield, James D. *Dining by Rail: The History and the Recipes of America's Golden Age of Railroad Cuisine.* New York: St. Martin's Press, 1993.

Potts, Daniel. "On Salt and Salt Gathering in Ancient Mesopotamia." *Journal of the Economic and Social History of the Orient/Journal de l'histoire économique et sociale de l'Orient* 27, no. 3 (1984): 225–71.

Powell, T. G. E. *The Celts.* New York: Praeger, 1958.

Prakash, Om. *Food and Drinks in Ancient India.* Delhi: Munshi Ram Manohar Lal, 1961.

Precope, John. *Hippocrates on Diet and Hygiene.* London: Zeno, 1952.

Puett, Michael. "The Offering of Food and the Creation of Order: The Practice of Sacrifice in Early China." In *Of Tripod and Palate: Food, Politics and Religion in Traditional China,* edited by Roel Sterckx, 75–95. New York: Palgrave Macmillan, 2004.

Pujol, Anton. "Cosmopolitan Taste: The Morphing of the New Catalan Cuisine." *Food, Culture and Society: An International Journal of Multidisciplinary Research* 12, no. 4 (2009): 437–55.

Ramiaramanana, B. D. "Malagasy Cooking." In *The Anthropologists' Cookbook,* edited by Jessica Kuper. London: Universe Books, 1977.

Randhawa, M. S. *A History of Agriculture in India.* New Delhi: Indian Council of Agricultural Research, 1980.

Ranga Rao, Shanta. *Good Food from India.* 1957. Bombay: Jaico Pub. House, 1968.

Ray, Krishnendu. *The Migrant's Table: Meals and Memories in Bengali-American Households.* Philadelphia: Temple University Press, 2004.

Read, Jan, Maite Manjon, and Hugh Johnson. *The Wine and Food of Spain.* Boston: Little Brown, 1987.

Redon, Odile, Françoise Sabban, and Silvano Serventi. *The Medieval Kitchen: Recipes from France and Italy.* Chicago: University of Chicago Press, 1998.

Renfrew, Wendy J. "Food for Athletes and Gods." In *The Archaeology of the Olympics: The Olympic and Other Festivals in Antiquity,* edited by Wendy J. Raschke. Madison: University of Wisconsin Press, 1988.

Renne, Elisha P. "Mass Producing Food Traditions for West Africans Abroad." *American Anthropologist* 109, no. 4 (1 December 2007): 616–25.

Revedin, Anna, Biancamaria Aranguren, Roberto Becattini, Laura Longo, Emanuele Marconi, Marta Mariotti Lippi, Natalia Skakun, Andrey Sinitsyn, Elena Spiridonova, and Jiří Svoboda. "Thirty-Thousand-Year-Old Evidence of Plant Food Processing." *Proceedings of the National Academy of Sciences* 107, no. 44 (2 November 2010): 18815–19.

Reynolds, P. "The Food of the Prehistoric Celts." In *Food in Antiquity,* edited by John Wilkins, David Harvey, and Mike Dobson. Exeter, UK: University of Exeter Press, 1995.

Reynolds, Terry S. *Stronger Than a Hundred Men: A History of the Vertical Water Wheel.* Baltimore: Johns Hopkins University Press, 1983.

Richards, John F. *The Mughal Empire.* New York: Cambridge University Press, 1993.

———. *The Unending Frontier: An Environmental History of the Early Modern World.* Berkeley: University of California Press, 2006.

Rickett, Allyn W. *Guanzi: Political, Economic and Philosophical Essays from Early China.* Princeton, N.J.: Princeton University Press, 1985.

Ricquier, Birgit, and K. Bostoen. "Retrieving Food History Through Linguistics: Culinary Traditions in Early Bantuphone Communities." In *Food and Language: Proceedings of the Oxford Symposium on Food and Cookery, 2009,* edited by Richard Hosking, 258. Totnes, Devon, UK: Prospect Books, 2010.

Riddervold, A., and A. Ropeid. "The Norwegian Porridge Feud." In *The Wilder Shores of Gastronomy: Twenty Years of the Best Food Writing from the Journal "Petits Propos Culinaires,"* edited by Alan Davidson et al., 227. Berkeley, Calif.: Ten Speed Press, 2002.

Ridley, G. "The First American Cookbook." *Eighteenth-Century Life* 23, no. 2 (1999): 114–23.

Riley, Gillian. *The Dutch Table: Gastronomy in the Golden Age of the Netherlands.* San Francisco: Pomegranate, 1994.

———."Fish in Art." *Petits Propos Culinaires* 56 (1997): 10–15.

Risaluddin, Saba. "Food Fit for Emperors—The Mughlai Tradition." *Convivium* 1 (1993): 11–17.

Ritzer, George. *The McDonaldization of Society*. 1993. Thousand Oaks, Calif.: Pine Forge Press, 2004.

Robinson, Francis, ed. *The Cambridge Illustrated History of the Islamic World*. New York: Cambridge University Press, 1996.

Robinson, Jancis, ed. *The Oxford Companion to Wine*. New York: Oxford University Press, 1994.

Roden, Claudia. *A Book of Middle Eastern Food*. New York: Knopf, 1972.

Rodger, N. A. M. *The Command of the Ocean: A Naval History of Britain, 1649–1815*. New York: Norton, 2006.

———. *The Wooden World: An Anatomy of the Georgian Navy*. New York: Norton, 1986.

Rodinson, Maxime. "Ghidha." In *Encyclopedia of Islam*. 2nd ed. Vol. 2: 1057–72. Leiden: Brill, 1965.

Rogers, Ben. *Beef and Liberty*. London: Chatto & Windus, 2003.

"Roman Empire Population." www.unrv.com/empire/roman-population.php (accessed 15 August 2012).

Rose, Peter G. *The Sensible Cook: Dutch Foodways in the Old and the New World*. Syracuse, N.Y.: Syracuse University Press, 1989.

Rosenberger, Bernard. "Arab Cuisine and Its Contribution to European Culture." In *Food: A Culinary History from Antiquity to the Present*, edited by Jean Louis Flandrin and Massimo Montanari, translated by Albert Sonnenfeld, 210. New York: Columbia University Press, 1999.

——— . "Dietética y cocina en el mundo musulmán occidental según el Kitab-al-Tabiji, recetarior de época almohade." In *Cultura alimentaria Andalucía-América*, edited by Antonio Garrido Aranda. México, D.F.: Universidad Nacional Autonóma de México, 1996.

Rosenstein, Nathan. *Rome at War: Farms, Families, and Death in the Middle Republic*. Chapel Hill: University of North Carolina Press, 2004.

Roth, Jonathan P. *The Logistics of the Roman Army at War (264 B.C.–A.D. 235)*. Leiden: Brill, 1999.

Rothstein, H., and R. A. Rothstein. "The Beginnings of Soviet Culinary Arts." In *Food in Russian History and Culture*, edited by Musya Glantz and Joyce Toomre, 177–94. Bloomington: Indiana University Press, 1997.

Rouff, Marcel. *The Passionate Epicure: La vie et la passion de Dodin-Bouffant, Gourmet*. Translated by Claude. 1962. New York: Modern Library, 2002.

Rubel, William. *Bread: A Global History*. London: Reaktion Books, 2011.

———. *The Magic of Fire: Hearth Cooking; One Hundred Recipes for the Fireplace or Campfire*. San Francisco: William Rubel, 2004.

Rumford, Benjamin. *Essays: Political, Economical and Philosophical*. 5th ed. London: Cadell, 1800.

Sabban, Françoise. "Court Cuisine in Fourteenth-Century Imperial China: Some Culinary Aspects of Hu Sihui's Yinshan Zhengyao." *Food and Foodways* 1, nos. 1–2 (1985): 161–96.

―――. "L'industrie sucrière, le moulin à sucre et les relations sino-portugaises aux XVIe–XVIIIe siècles." *Annales: Économies, Sociétés, Civilisations* 49, no. 4 (July–August 1994): 817–61.

―――. "Insights into the Problem of Preservation by Fermentation in 6th Century China." In *Food Conservation,* edited by Astri Riddervold and Andreas Ropeid, 45–55. London: Prospect Books, 1988.

―――. "Un savoir-faire oublié: Le travail du lait en Chine ancienne." *Zinbun: Memoirs of the Research Institute for Humanistic Studies* (Kyoto University) 21 (1986): 31–65.

―――. "Sucre candi et confiseries de Quinsai: L'essor du sucre de canne dans la Chine des Song (Xe–XIIIe siècles)." *Journal d'agriculture traditionnelle et de botanique appliquée* 35, special issue, *Le sucre et le sel* (1988): 195–215.

―――. "Le système des cuissons dans la tradition culinaire chinoise." *Annales: Économies, Sociétés, Civilisations* 38, no. 2 (March–April 1983): 341–69.

―――. "La viande en Chine: Imaginaire et usages culinaires." *Anthropozoologica* 18 (1993): 79–90.

Saberi, Helen. *Afghan Food and Cookery: Noshe Djan.* New York: Hippocrene Books, 2000.

Sack, Daniel. *Whitebread Protestants: Food and Religion in American Culture.* New York: St. Martin's Press, 2000.

Salaman, Redcliffe N. *The History and Social Influence of the Potato.* 1949. 2nd ed., rev. Cambridge: Cambridge University Press, 1985.

Sallares, Robert. *The Ecology of the Ancient Greek World.* Ithaca, N.Y.: Cornell University Press, 1991.

Sambrook, Pamela. *Country House Brewing in England, 1500–1900.* Rio Grande, Ohio: Hambledon Press, 2003.

Sambrook, Pamela A., and Peter C. D. Brears, eds. *The Country House Kitchen, 1650–1900: Skills and Equipment for Food Provisioning.* Stroud, UK: Sutton, 1996.

Samuel, D. "Ancient Egyptian Bread and Beer: An Interdisciplinary Approach." In *Biological Anthropology and the Study of Ancient Egypt,* edited by W. V. Davies and Roxie Walker, 156–64. London: British Museum Press, 1993.

―――. "Ancient Egyptian Cereal Processing: Beyond the Artistic Record." *Cambridge Archaeological Journal* 3, no. 2 (1993): 276–83.

―――. "Approaches to the Archaeology of Food." *Petits Propos Culinaires* 54 (1996): 12–21.

―――. "Bread in Archaeology." *Civilisations: Revue internationale d'anthropologie et de sciences humaines,* no. 49 (2002): 27–36.

―――. "Investigation of Ancient Egyptian Baking and Brewing Methods by Correlative Microscopy." *Science* 273, no. 5274 (1996): 488–90.

―――. "A New Look at Bread and Beer." *Egyptian Archaeology* 4 (1994): 9–11.

Samuel, Delwen. "Brewing and Baking." In *Ancient Egyptian Materials and Technology,* edited by Paul T. Nicholson and Ian Shaw. New York: Cambridge University Press, 2000.

Samuel, Delwen, and P. Bolt. "Rediscovering Ancient Egyptian Beer." *Brewers' Guardian* 124, no. 12 (1995): 27–31.

Sancisi-Weerdenburg, H., Pierre Briant, and Clarisse Herrenschmidt. "Gifts in the Persian Empire." In *Le tribut dan l'Empire perse: Actes de la table ronde de Paris, 12–13 décembre 1986,* ed. Pierre Briant and Clarisse Herrenschmidt, 129–46. Paris: Peeters, 1989.

Sand, J. "A Short History of MSG: Good Science, Bad Science, and Taste Cultures." *Gastronomica* 5, no. 4 (2005): 38–49.

Sandars, N. K, ed. *The Epic of Gilgamesh*. Baltimore: Penguin Books, 1964.

Santa Maria, Jack. *Indian Sweet Cookery*. Boulder, Colo.: Shambhala, 1980.

Santich, Barbara. *The Original Mediterranean Cuisine: Medieval Recipes for Today*. Chicago: Chicago Review Press, 1995.

Saso, Michael. "Chinese Religions." In *Handbook of Living Religions*, edited by John R. Hinnells. London: Penguin Books, 1985.

———. *Taoist Cookbook*. Boston: Tuttle, 1994.

Schaeffer, Robert K. *Understanding Globalization: The Social Consequences of Political, Economic, and Environmental Change*. Lanham, Md.: Rowman & Littlefield, 1997.

Schafer, Edward H. *The Golden Peaches of Samarkand: A Study of T'ang Exotics*. Berkeley: University of California Press, 1985.

———. "T'ang." In *Food in Chinese Culture*. New Haven, Conn.: Yale University Press, 1977.

Schama, Simon. *The Embarrassment of Riches: An Interpretation of Dutch Culture in the Golden Age*. New York: Knopf, 1987.

Schamas, Carole. "Changes in English and Anglo-American Consumption from 1550 to 1800." In *Consumption and the World of Goods*, edited by John Brewer and Roy Porter, 177–89. London: Routledge, 1993.

Schenone, Laura. *A Thousand Years over a Hot Stove: A History of American Women Told through Food, Recipes, and Remembrances*. New York: Norton, 2003.

Schivelbusch, Wolfgang. *Tastes of Paradise: A Social History of Spices, Stimulants, and Intoxicants*. New York: Vintage Books, 1992.

Schlosser, Eric. *Fast Food Nation: The Dark Side of the All-American Meal*. New York: Perennial/HarperCollins, 2002.

Schmitt-Pantel, Pauline. "Sacrificial Meal and Symposium: Two Models of Civic Institutions in the Archaic City?" In *Sympotica: A Symposium on the Symposion*, edited by Oswyn Murray, 14–26. Oxford: Oxford University Press, 1990.

Scholliers, P. "Defining Food Risks and Food Anxieties Throughout History." *Appetite* 51, no. 1 (2008): 3–6.

———. "From the 'Crisis of Flanders' to Belgium's 'Social Question': Nutritional Landmarks of Transition in Industrializing Europe (1840–1890)." *Food and Foodways* 5, no. 2 (1992): 151–75.

———. "Meals, Food Narratives, and Sentiments of Belonging in Past and Present." In *Food, Drink and Identity: Cooking, Eating and Drinking in Europe Since the Middle Ages*, edited by P. Scholliers, 3–22. Oxford: Berg, 2001.

Schultz, J. C. "Biochemical Ecology: How Plants Fight Dirty." *Nature* 416, no. 6878 (2002): 267.

Schurz, William Lytle. *The Manila Galleon: With Maps and Charts and This New World*. New York: Dutton, 1939.

Schwartz, Stuart B. *Tropical Babylons: Sugar and the Making of the Atlantic World, 1450–1680*. Chapel Hill: University of North Carolina Press, 2004.

The Science and Culture of Nutrition, 1840–1940. Edited by Harmke Kamminga and Andrew Cunningham. Wellcome Institute Series in the History of Medicine, vol. 32. Amsterdam: Rodopi, 1995.

Scully, Terence. *The Art of Cookery in the Middle Ages*. Rochester, N.Y.: Boydell Press, 1995.

Scully, Terence, and D. Eleanor Scully. *Early French Cookery: Sources, History, Original Recipes and Modern Adaptations*. Ann Arbor: University of Michigan Press, 1995.

Segal, Ronald. *Islam's Black Slaves: The Other Black Diaspora*. New York: Farrar, Straus and Giroux, 2001.

Seligman, L. "The History of Japanese Cuisine." *Japan Quarterly* 41, no. 2 (1994): 165–80.

Sen, Colleen Taylor. *Curry: A Global History*. London: Reaktion Books, 2009.

Sen, Tansen. *Buddhism, Diplomacy, and Trade: The Realignment of Sino-Indian Relations, 600–1400*. Honolulu: University of Hawai'i Press, 2003.

Serventi, Silvano, and Françoise Sabban. *Pasta: The Story of a Universal Food*. New York: Columbia University Press, 2002.

Shaffer, Lynda. "Southernization." *Journal of World History* 5 (1994): 1–21.

Shaida, Margaret. *The Legendary Cuisine of Persia*. New York: Interlink Books, 2002.

Shapiro, Laura. *Perfection Salad: Women and Cooking at the Turn of the Century*. New York: Farrar, Straus and Giroux, 1986.

———. *Something from the Oven: Reinventing Dinner in 1950s America*. New York: Viking Press, 2004.

Sharar, 'AbdulḤalim. *Lucknow: The Last Phase of an Oriental Culture*. London: Paul Elek, 1975.

Shaw, Brent D. "'Eaters of Flesh, Drinkers of Milk': The Ancient Mediterranean Ideology of the Pastoral Nomad." *Ancient Society*, no. 13 (1982): 5–32.

———. "Fear and Loathing: The Nomad Menace and Roman Africa." In *L'Afrique romaine: Les Conferences Vanier 1980 = Roman Africa: The Vanier Lectures 1980*, edited by Colin Wells, 29–50. Ottawa: University of Ottawa Press, 1982.

Sherman, Sandra. *Fresh from the Past: Recipes and Revelations from Moll Flanders' Kitchen*. Lanham, Md.: Taylor Trade Publishing, 2004.

Shurtleff, William, and Akiko Aoyagi. *The Book of Miso*. Berkeley, Calif.: Ten Speed Press, 1983.

Sia, Mary. *Mary Sia's Chinese Cookbook*. 3rd ed. University of Hawai'i Press, 1980.

Simeti, Mary Taylor. *Pomp and Sustenance: Twenty-Five Centuries of Sicilian Food*. New York: Knopf, 1989.

Simoons, Frederick J. *Eat Not This Flesh: Food Avoidances from Prehistory to the Present*. 2nd ed., rev. and enl. Madison: University of Wisconsin Press, 1994.

———. *Food in China: A Cultural and Historical Inquiry*. Boca Raton, Fla.: CRC Press, 1991.

Singer, Amy. *Constructing Ottoman Beneficence: An Imperial Soup Kitchen in Jerusalem*. Albany: State University of New York Press, 2002.

Siraisi, Nancy G. *Medieval and Early Renaissance Medicine: An Introduction to Knowledge and Practice*. University of Chicago Press, 1990.

Skinner, Gwen. *The Cuisine of the South Pacific*. Harper Collins, 1985.

Slicher van Bath, B. H. *The Agrarian History of Western Europe, A.D. 500–1850*. Translated by Olive Ordish. London: E. Arnold, 1963.

Smith, A. K. "Eating Out in Imperial Russia: Class, Nationality, and Dining before the Great Reforms." *Slavic Review* 65, no. 4 (2006): 747–768.

Smith, Andrew. *Pure Ketchup: A History of America's National Condiment, with Recipes*. Columbia: University of South Carolina Press, 1996.

Smith, Bruce D. *The Emergence of Agriculture.* New York: Scientific American Library, 1995.

Smith, David F., and Jim Phillips, eds. *Food, Science, Policy and Regulation in the Twentieth Century: International and Comparative Perspectives.* New York: Routledge, 2000.

Smith, Eliza. *The Compleat Housewife; or, Accomplished Gentlewoman's Companion.* 1728. 16th reprint. Kings Langley, UK: Arlon House, 1983.

Smith, J. M. "Dietary Decadence and Dynastic Decline in the Mongol Empire." *Journal of Asian History* 34, no. 1 (2000): 35–52.

———. "Mongol Campaign Rations: Milk, Marmots and Blood?" *Journal of Turkish Studies* 8 (1984): 223–28.

Smith, Pamela H. *The Business of Alchemy.* Princeton, N.J.: Princeton University Press, 1997.

Smith, Paul Jakov. *Taxing Heaven's Storehouse: Horses, Bureaucrats, and the Destruction of the Sichuan Tea Industry, 1074–1224.* Cambridge, Mass.: Harvard University Asia Center, 1991.

Smith, Robert. "Whence the Samovar." *Petits Propos Culinaires* 4 (1980): 57–72.

Smith, R. E. F., and David Christian. *Bread and Salt: A Social and Economic History of Food and Drink in Russia.* Cambridge: Cambridge University Press, 1984.

So, Yan-Kit. *Classic Food of China.* London: Macmillan, 1992.

Sokolov, Raymond A. *Why We Eat What We Eat: How the Encounter Between the New World and the Old Changed the Way Everyone on the Planet Eats.* New York: Summit Books, 1991.

Soler, Jean. "The Semiotics of Food in the Bible." In *Food and Drink in History,* edited by R. Forster and O. Ranum. Baltimore: Johns Hopkins University Press, 1979.

Solomon, Jon. "The Apician Sauce." In *Food in Antiquity,* edited by John Wilkins, David Harvey, and Mike Dobson, 115–31. Exeter, UK: University of Exeter Press, 1996.

Solt, George. "Ramen and US Occupation Policy." In *Japanese Foodways, Past, and Present,* edited by Stephanie Assmann and Eric C. Rath. Urbana: University of Illinois Press, 2010.

Song, Yingxing [Sung Ying-Hsing]. *T'ien kung k'ai wu: Chinese Technology in the Seventeenth Century.* Translated and annotated by E-tu Zen Sun and Shiou-chuan Sun. College Station: Pennsylvania State University Press, 1996.

Sorabji, Richard. *Animal Minds and Human Morals: The Origins of the Western Debate.* Ithaca, N.Y.: Cornell University Press, 1993.

Sorokin, Pitirim Aleksandrovich. *Hunger as a Factor in Human Affairs.* Gainesville: University Presses of Florida, 1975.

Spang, Rebecca L. *The Invention of the Restaurant: Paris and Modern Gastronomic Culture.* Cambridge, Mass.: Harvard University Press, 2000.

Spary, Emma C. "Making a Science of Taste: The Revolution, the Learned Life and the Invention of 'Gastronomie.'" In *Consumers and Luxury: Consumer Culture in Europe, 1750–1850,* edited by Maxine Berg and Helen Clifford. Manchester: Manchester University Press, 1999.

Speake, Jennifer, and J. A. Simpson, eds. *The Oxford Dictionary of Proverbs.* New York: Oxford University Press, 2003.

Spencer, Colin. *British Food: An Extraordinary Thousand Years of History.* New York: Columbia University Press, 2003.

———. *Vegetarianism: A History.* Da Capo Press, 2004.

Ssu-hsieh, C. "The Preparation of Ferments and Wines." Edited by T. L. Davis. Translated by Huang Tzu-ch'ing and Chao Yun-ts'ung. *Harvard Journal of Asiatic Studies* (1945): 24–44.

Stahl, Ann B. "Plant-Food Processing: Implications for Dietary Quality." In *Foraging and Farming: The Evolution of Plant Exploitation,* edited by David R. Harris and Gordon C. Hillman, 171–94. London: Unwin Hyman, 1989.

Standage, Tom. *An Edible History of Humanity.* New York: Walker, 2009.

Starks, Tricia. *The Body Soviet: Propaganda, Hygiene, and the Revolutionary State.* Madison: University of Wisconsin Press, 2008.

Stathakopoulos, Dionysios. "Between the Field and the Plate." In *Eat, Drink, and Be Merry (Luke 12:19): Food and Wine in Byzantium; Papers of the 37th Annual Spring Symposium of Byzantine Studies, in Honour of Professor A. A. M. Bryer,* ed. Leslie Brubaker and Kallirroe Linardou, 27–38. Burlington, Vt.: Ashgate, 2007.

Stavely, Keith W. F., and Kathleen Fitzgerald. *America's Founding Food: The Story of New England Cooking.* Chapel Hill: University of North Carolina Press, 2004.

Stead, Jennifer. "Navy Blues: The Sailor's Diet, 1530–1830." In *Food for the Community: Special Diets for Special Groups,* edited by C. Anne Wilson. Edinburgh: Edinburgh University Press, 1993.

———. "Quizzing Glasse; or, Hannah Scrutinized, Part I." *Petits Propos Culinaires* 13 (1983): 9–24.

Stearns, Peter N. *European Society in Upheaval: Social History Since 1750.* 3rd ed. New York: Macmillan, 1992.

Steel, Flora Annie Webster. *The Complete Indian Housekeeper and Cook.* Edited by G. Gardiner, Ralph J. Crane, and Anna Johnston. New York: Oxford University Press, 2010.

Sterckx, Roel, ed. *Of Tripod and Palate: Food, Politics and Religion in Traditional China.* New York: Palgrave Macmillan, 2004. Preview http://site.ebrary.com/lib/alltitles/docDetail.action?docID=10135368 (accessed 4 December 2012).

Stoopen, Maria. "Las simientes del mestizaje en el siglo XVI." *Artes de México,* no. 36 (1997): 20–29.

Storck, John, and Walter Dorwin Teague. *Flour for Man's Bread: A History of Milling.* Minneapolis: University of Minnesota Press, 1952.

Strickland, Joseph Wayne. "Beer, Barbarism, and the Church from Late Antiquity to the Early Middle Ages." University of Tennessee–Knoxville, 2007. http://historyofthe ancientworld.com/2012/03/beer-barbarism-and-the-church-from-late-antiquity-to-the-early-middle-ages (accessed 15 August 2012).

Strong, Roy C. *Feast: A History of Grand Eating.* London: Jonathan Cape, 2002.

Suárez y Farías, María Cristina. "De ámbitos y sabores virreinales." In *Los espacios de la cocina mexicana,* ed. id., Socorro Puig, and María Stoopen. México, D.F.: Artes de México, 1996.

Sugiura, Yoko, and Fernán González de la Vara. *México antiguo.* Vol. 1 of *La cocina mexicana a través de los siglos,* edited by Enrique Krauze and Fernán González de la Vara. México, D.F.: Clío; Fundación Herdez, 1996.

Super, John C. *Food, Conquest, and Colonization in Sixteenth-Century Spanish America.* Albuquerque: University of New Mexico Press, 1988.

Super, John C., and Thomas C. Wright, eds. *Food, Politics, and Society in Latin America.* Lincoln: University of Nebraska Press, 1985.

Sutton, David C. "The Language of the Food of the Poor: Studying Proverbs with Jean-Louis Flandrin." In *Food and Language: Proceedings of the Oxford Symposium on Food and Cookery, 2009,* 330–39. Totnes, Devon, UK: Prospect Books, 2010.

Swinburne, Layinka. "Nothing but the Best: Arrowroot—Today and Yesterday." In *Disappearing Foods: Studies in Foods and Dishes at Risk; Proceedings of the Oxford Symposium on Food and Cookery,* edited by Harland Walker, 198–203. Totnes, Devon, UK: Prospect Books, 1995.

Swislocki, Mark. *Culinary Nostalgia: Regional Food Culture and the Urban Experience in Shanghai.* Stanford, Calif.: Stanford University Press, 2008.

Symons, Michael. *One Continuous Picnic: A History of Eating in Australia.* Adelaide: Duck Press, 1982.

———. *The Pudding That Took a Thousand Cooks: The Story of Cooking in Civilisation and Daily Life.* New York: Penguin Putnam, 1998.

Tandon, Prakash. *Punjabi Century, 1857–1947.* Berkeley: University of California Press, 1968.

Tang, Charles. "Chinese Restaurants Abroad." *Flavor and Fortune* 3, no. 4 (1996).

Tann, Jennifer, and R. Glyn Jones. "Technology and Transformation: The Diffusion of the Roller Mill in the British Flour Milling Industry, 1870–1907." *Technology and Culture* 37, no. 1 (1996): 36–69.

Tannahill, Reay. *Food in History.* New York: Stein & Day, 1973.

Taylor, Alan. *American Colonies: The Settling of North America.* Vol. 1 of *The Penguin History of the United States.* New York: Penguin Books, 2001.

Taylor, William B. *Drinking, Homicide, and Rebellion in Colonial Mexican Villages.* Stanford, Calif.: Stanford University Press, 1979.

Teich, Mikulas. "Fermentation Theory and Practice: The Beginnings of Pure Yeast Cultivation and English Brewing, 1883–1913." *History of Technology* 8 (1983): 117–33.

Temkin, Oswei. *"On Second Thought" and Other Essays in the History of Medicine and Science.* Baltimore: Johns Hopkins University Press, 2002.

Thirsk, Joan. *Alternative Agriculture: A History from the Black Death to the Present Day.* New York: Oxford University Press, 2000.

———. *Food in Early Modern England: Phases, Fads, Fashions, 1500–1760.* New York: Hambledon Continuum, 2009.

Thomas, B. "Feeding England During the Industrial Revolution: A View from the Celtic Fringe." *Agricultural History* 56, no. 1 (1982): 328–42.

———. "Food Supply in the United Kingdom During the Industrial Revolution." In *The Economics of the Industrial Revolution,* edited by Joel Mokyr, 137–50. London: George Allen & Unwin, 1985.

Thomas, John Philip, and Angela Constantinides Hero, eds. *Byzantine Monastic Foundation Documents: A Complete Translation of the Surviving Founders' Typika and Testaments.* Washington, D.C.: Dumbarton Oaks Research Library and Collection, 2001.

Thompson, David. *Thai Food.* Berkeley, Calif.: Ten Speed Press, 2002.

Thompson, E. P. "The Moral Economy of the English Crowd in the Eighteenth Century." *Past & Present,* no. 50 (1971): 76–136.

Thorne, Stuart. *The History of Food Preservation*. Totowa, N.J.: Barnes & Noble Books, 1986.

Thurmond, David L. *A Handbook of Food Processing in Classical Rome: For Her Bounty No Winter*. Leiden: Brill, 2006.

Tibbles, William. *Foods: Their Origin, Composition and Manufacture*. London: Baillière, Tindall & Cox, 1912.

Titcomb, Margaret. *Dog and Man in the Ancient Pacific, with Special Attention to Hawaii*. Bernice P. Bishop Museum special publication 59. Honolulu: Printed by Star-Bulletin Print. Co., 1969.

Titley, Norah M., trans. *The Ni'matnama Manuscript of the Sultans of Mandu: The Sultan's Book of Delights*. London: Routledge, 2005.

Toomre, Joyce Stetson. *Classic Russian Cooking: Elena Molokhovets' "A Gift to Young Housewives."* Bloomington: Indiana University Press, 1992.

Torres, Marimar. *The Catalan Country Kitchen: Food and Wine from the Pyrenees to the Mediterranean Seacoast of Barcelona*. Reading, Mass.: Addison-Wesley, 1992.

Toussaint-Samat, Maguelonne. *Histoire naturelle et morale de la nourriture*. Paris: Bordas, 1987. Translated by Anthea Bell as *A History of Food* (1992; rev. ed., Malden, Mass.: Wiley-Blackwell, 2009).

Trentmann, F. "Civilization and Its Discontents: English Neo-Romanticism and the Transformation of Anti-Modernism in Twentieth-Century Western Culture." *Journal of Contemporary History* 29, no. 4 (1994): 583–625.

———. *Free Trade Nation: Commerce, Consumption, and Civil Society in Modern Britain*. Oxford University Press, 2008.

Trubek, Amy B. *Haute Cuisine: How the French Invented the Culinary Profession*. Philadelphia: University of Pennsylvania Press, 2000.

Tschiffely, A. F. *This Way Southward: A Journey through Patagonia and Tierra del Fuego*. New York: Norton, 1940.

Unschuld, Paul U. *Medicine in China: A History of Ideas*. Berkeley: University of California Press, 1985.

Unwin, Tim. *Wine and the Vine: An Historical Geography of Viticulture and the Wine Trade*. New ed. London: Routledge, 1996.

Vaduva, O. "Popular Rumanian Food." In *Food in Change: Eating Habits from the Middle Ages to the Present Day*, edited by Alexander Fenton and Eszter Kisbán, 99–103. Edinburgh: J. Donald, 1986.

Valenze, Deborah. *Milk: A Local and Global History*. New Haven, Conn.: Yale University Press, 2011.

Valeri, Renée. "Création et transmission due savoir culinaire en Scandinavie au 17e siècle." *Papilles*, nos. 10–11 (March 1996): 51–62. Reprinted in Association des Bibliothèques gourmandes, *Livres et recettes de cuisine en Europe, du 14e au milieu du 19e siècle: Actes du Congrès de Dijon, 28 et 29 octobre 1994*. Cognac, France: Le temps qu'il fait, 1996.

Veit, Helen Zoe. *Victory over Ourselves: American Food in the Era of the Great War*. Chapel Hill: University of North Carolina Press, forthcoming 2013.

Voth, Norma Jost. *Mennonite Food and Folkways from South Russia*. 2 vols. Intercourse, Pa.: Good Books, 1990.

Vries, Jan de. *The Dutch Rural Economy in the Golden Age, 1500–1700*. New Haven, Conn.: Yale University Press, 1974.

Vries, P. H. "Governing Growth: A Comparative Analysis of the Role of the State in the Rise of the West." *Journal of World History* 13, no. 1 (2002): 67–138.

Waldstreicher, David. *In the Midst of Perpetual Fetes: The Making of American Nationalism, 1776–1820.* Chapel Hill: University of North Carolina Press for the Omohundro Institute of Early American History and Culture, Williamsburg, Va., 1997.

Waley-Cohen, Joanna. *The Sextants of Beijing: Global Currents in Chinese History.* New York: Norton, 2000.

———. "Taste and Gastronomy in China." In *Food: The History of Taste,* edited by Paul Freedman, 99–134. Berkeley: University of California Press, 2007.

Walker, Harlan, ed. *Milk: Beyond the Dairy; Proceedings of the Oxford Symposium on Food and Cooking, 1999.* Totnes, Devon, UK: Prospect Books, 2000.

———. *Staple Foods: Proceedings of the Oxford Symposium on Food and Cookery, 1989.* London: Prospect Books, 1990.

Walton, John K. *Fish and Chips and the British Working Class, 1870–1940.* Leicester, UK: Leicester University Press, 1992.

Walvin, James. *Fruits of Empire: Exotic Produce and British Trade, 1660–1800.* London: Palgrave Macmillan, 1996.

Wandsnider, Luann A. "The Roasted and the Boiled: Food Composition and Heat Treatment with Special Emphasis on Pit-Hearth Cooking." *Journal of Anthropological Archaeology* 16 (1997): 1–48.

Wang, D. *The Teahouse: Small Business, Everyday Culture, and Public Politics in Chengdu, 1900–1950.* Stanford, Calif.: Stanford University Press, 2008.

Wang, Teresa, and E. N. Anderson. "Ni Tsan and His 'Cloud Forest Hall Collection of Rules for Drinking and Eating.'" *Petits Propos Culinaires* 60 (1998): 24–41.

Warde, Alan. *Consumption, Food and Taste: Culinary Antinomies and Commodity Culture.* Thousand Oaks, Calif.: Sage, 1997.

Warman, Arturo. *Corn and Capitalism: How a Botanical Bastard Grew to Global Dominance.* Chapel Hill: University of North Carolina Press, 2003.

Wasson, R. Gordon. *Soma: Divine Mushroom of Immortality.* New York: Harcourt, Brace & World, 1968.

Watson, Andrew M. *Agricultural Innovation in the Early Islamic World: The Diffusion of Crops and Farming Techniques, 700–1100.* New York: Cambridge University Press, 1983.

Watson, James L., ed. *Golden Arches East: McDonald's in East Asia.* Stanford, Calif.: Stanford University Press, 1997.

Watson, James L., and M. L. Caldwell. *The Cultural Politics of Food and Eating: A Reader.* Malden, Mass.: Wiley-Blackwell, 2005.

Watt, George. *The Commercial Products of India, Being an Abridgment of "The Dictionary of the Economic Products of India." Published Under the Authority of His Majesty's Secretary of State for India in Council.* Reprint ed. New Delhi: Today & Tomorrow's Printer & Publishers, 1966.

———. *A Dictionary of the Economic Products of India.* Delhi: Cosmo Publications, 1972.

"Waxworks: Like Life, Like Death." *The Economist,* 30 January 2003, 72.

Weaver, William Woys. *Sauerkraut Yankees: Pennsylvania-German Foods and Foodways.* Philadelphia: University of Pennsylvania Press, 1983.

Weber, Charles D. "Chinese Pictorial Bronzes of the Late Chou Period: Part II." *Artibus Asiae* 28, nos. 2–3 (1966): 271–311.

Weber, Eugen. *Peasants into Frenchmen: The Modernization of Rural France, 1870–1914.* Stanford, Calif.: Stanford University Press, 1976.

Weiner, M. "Consumer Culture and Participatory Democracy: The Story of Coca-Cola during World War II." *Food and Foodways* 6, no. 2 (1996): 109–29.

Westrip, Joyce. *Moghul Cooking: India's Courtly Cuisine.* London: Serif, 1997.

Wheaton, Barbara Ketcham. *Savoring the Past: The French Kitchen and Table from 1300 to 1789.* Philadelphia: University of Pennsylvania Press, 1983.

White, K. D. "Farming and Animal Husbandry." In *Civilization of the Ancient Mediterranean: Greece and Rome,* edited by Michael Grant and Rachel Kitzinger, vol. 1. New York: Scribner, 1988.

White, Lynn Townsend, Jr. *Medieval Technology and Social Change.* Oxford: Oxford University Press, 1966.

White, Merry. *Coffee Life in Japan.* Berkeley: University of California Press, 2012.

Wiley, A. S. "Transforming Milk in a Global Economy." *American Anthropologist* 109, no. 4 (2007): 666–77.

Wilk, Richard R. *Home Cooking in the Global Village: Caribbean Food from Buccaneers to Ecotourists.* New York: Berg, 2006.

Wilkins, John, F. D. Harvey, and Michael J. Dobson, eds. *Food in Antiquity.* Exeter, UK: University of Exeter Press, 1995.

Wilkins, John, and Shaun Hill. "The Sources and Sauces of Athanaeus." In *Food in Antiquity,* edited by John Wilkins, F. D. Harvey, and Michael J. Dobson, 429–38. Exeter, UK: University of Exeter Press, 1995.

Will, Pierre-Etienne, Roy Bin Wong, and James Z. Lee. *Nourish the People: The State Civilian Granary System in China, 1650–1850.* Ann Arbor: Center for Chinese Studies, University of Michigan, 1991.

Williams, Jacqueline B. *Wagon Wheel Kitchens: Food on the Oregon Trail.* Lawrence: University Press of Kansas, 1993.

Williams, Susan. *Savory Suppers and Fashionable Feasts: Dining in Victorian America.* New York: Pantheon Books in association with the Margaret Woodbury Strong Museum, 1985.

Wilson, C. Anne. *Food and Drink in Britain: From the Stone Age to the 19th Century.* London: Constable, 1973.

———. *Water of Life: A History of Wine-Distilling and Spirits; 500 BC–AD 2000.* Totnes, Devon, UK: Prospect Books, 2006.

Wilson, C. Anne, ed. *Food for the Community: Special Diets for Special Groups.* Edinburgh: Edinburgh University Press, 1993.

———. *Liquid Nourishment: Potable Foods and Stimulating Drinks.* Edinburgh: Edinburgh University Press, 1993.

Wind in the Pines: Classic Writings of the Way of Tea as a Buddhist Path. Fremont, Calif.: Asian Humanities Press, 1995.

Wolf, Eric R. *Europe and the People Without History.* Berkeley: University of California Press, 1982.

Woloson, Wendy A. *Refined Tastes: Sugar, Confectionery, and Consumers in Nineteenth-Century America.* Baltimore: Johns Hopkins University Press, 2002.

Wong, Roy Bin. *Political Economy of Food Supplies in Qing China.* Ann Arbor, Mich.: University Microfilms, 1987.

Wood, Gordon. *The Creation of the American Republic, 1776–1787.* Chapel Hill: University of North Carolina Press, 1969.

Woodforde, James. *The Diary of a Country Parson: The Reverend James Woodforde.* Edited by John Beresford. 5 vols. Oxford: Oxford University Press, 1924–31.

"A World of Thanks: World War I Belgian Embroidered Flour Sacks." http://hoover.archives .gov/exhibits/collections/flour%20sacks/index.html (accessed 15 August 2012).

Wrangham, Richard W. *Catching Fire: How Cooking Made Us Human.* New York: Basic Books, 2009.

Wriggins, Sally Hovey. *Xuanzang: A Buddhist Pilgrim on the Silk Road.* Boulder, Colo.: Westview Press, 1996.

Wright, Clifford A. *A Mediterranean Feast: The Story of the Birth of the Celebrated Cuisines of the Mediterranean from the Merchants of Venice to the Barbary Corsairs, with More than 500 Recipes.* New York: William Morrow, 1999.

Wu, David Y. H., and Tan Chee-Beng, eds. *Changing Chinese Foodways in Asia.* Hong Kong: Chinese University Press, 2001.

Wujastyk, Dominic. *The Roots of Ayurveda.* London: Penguin Books, 1998.

Wulff, Hans E. *The Traditional Crafts of Persia: Their Development, Technology, and Influence on Eastern and Western Civilizations.* Cambridge, Mass.: MIT Press, 1966.

Xenophon. *Cyropaedia.* Edited by Walter Miller. Cambridge, Mass.: Harvard University Press, 1914. www.perseus.tufts.edu/hopper/text?doc=Perseus:text:1999.01.0204 (accessed 4 December 2012).

Xinru, Liu. *Ancient India and Ancient China: Trade and Religious Exchanges, AD 1–600.* Delhi: Oxford University Press, 1988.

Yarshater, Ehsan, ed. *Encyclopædia Iranica.* London: Routledge & Kegan Paul, 1982.

Yates, Robin D. S. "War, Food Shortages, and Relief Measures in Early China." In *Hunger in History: Food Shortage, Poverty, and Deprivation,* edited by Lucile F. Newman, 146–77. New York: Blackwell, 1990.

Yoshida, Mitsukuni, and Tsune Sesoko. *Naorai: Communion of the Table.* Tokyo: Mazda Motor Corp., 1989.

Young, Carolin C. *Apples of Gold in Settings of Silver: Stories of Dinner as a Work of Art.* New York: Simon & Schuster, 2002.

Young, James Harvey. "Botulism and the Ripe Olive Scare of 1919–1920." *Bulletin of the History of Medicine* 56 (1976): 372–91.

Yue, Gang. *The Mouth That Begs: Hunger, Cannibalism, and the Politics of Eating in Modern China.* Durham, N.C.: Duke University Press, 1999.

Zaouali, Lilia. *Medieval Cuisine of the Islamic World: A Concise History with 174 Recipes.* Berkeley: University of California Press, 2009.

Zarrillo, S., D. M. Pearsall, J. S. Raymond, M. A. Tisdale, and D. J. Quon. "Directly Dated Starch Residues Document Early Formative Maize (*Zea mays* L.) in Tropical Ecuador." *Proceedings of the National Academy of Sciences* 105, no. 13 (2008): 5006–5011.

Zeder, Melinda A. *Feeding Cities: Specialized Animal Economy in the Ancient Near East.* Washington, D.C.: Smithsonian Institution Press, 1991.

Zeldin, Theodore. *France, 1848–1945.* Oxford: Clarendon Press, Oxford University Press, 1973.

————. *The French.* New York: Pantheon Books, 1982.

Zhou, Xun. *The Great Famine in China 1958–1962: A Documentary History.* New Haven, Conn.: Yale University Press, 2012.

Zimmermann, Francis. *The Jungle and the Aroma of Meat: An Ecological Theme in Hindu Medicine.* Berkeley: University of California Press, 1987.

Zizumbo-Villarreal, D., and P. Colunga-García Marín. "Early Coconut Distillation and the Origins of Mezcal and Tequila Spirits in West-Central Mexico." *Genetic Resources and Crop Evolution* 55, no. 4 (2008): 493–510.

Zubaida, Sami, and Richard Tapper, eds. *A Taste of Thyme: Culinary Cultures of the Middle East.* New York: Tauris Parke, 2000.

Zweiniger-Bargielowska, Ina, Rachel Duffett, and Alain Drouard, eds. *Food and War in Twentieth Century Europe.* Farnham, UK: Ashgate, 2011.

INDEX

CALIFORNIA STUDIES IN FOOD AND CULTURE

Darra Goldstein, Editor